P9-DTY-739

LAKE GENEVA PUBLIC LIBRARY
918 W. Main St.
Lake Geneva, WI 53147

Pie

Pie

300 Tried-and-True Recipes

for Delicious Homemade Pie

KEN HAEDRICH

The Harvard Common Press • Boston, Massachusetts

The Harvard Common Press
535 Albany Street
Boston, Massachusetts 02118
www.harvardcommonpress.com

© 2004 Ken Haedrich
All rights reserved. No part of this publication may be reproduced or
transmitted in any form or by any means, electronic or mechanical,
including photocopying, recording, or any information storage or
retrieval system, without permission in writing from the publisher.

Printed in the United States

LIBRARY OF CONGRESS CATALOGING-IN-PUBLICATION DATA

Haedrich, Ken
    Pie : 300 tried-and-true recipes for delicious homemade pie / Ken
Haedrich.
        p. cm.
    Includes index.
    ISBN 1-55832-253-1 (hc : alk. paper) — ISBN 1-55832-254-X pbk :
alk. paper)
    1. Pies. I. Title.
    TX773.H2195 2004
    641.8'652—dc22   2004003635

Special bulk-order discounts are available on this and other Harvard
Common Press books. Companies and organizations may purchase
books for premiums or resale, or may arrange a custom edition, by
contacting the Marketing Director at the address above.

10 9 8 7 6 5 4 3 2 1

Interior design by Richard Oriolo
Cover design by Night & Day Design
Photographs by Eric Roth Photography
Food preparation and styling by Mary Bandereck
Illustrations by Jackie Aher

This book is dedicated to my 15-year-old son, Sam, cursed with the father's too-large feet but blessed with a heart of gold. Thanks for all the cooking advice you've offered me, solicited or otherwise, over the years. Now it's my turn.

1. "Tons of snowboarding" may not look as good on the "other interests" section of your college application as you might hope.
2. Cars, gas, and insurance cost more than you make in a couple of weekends.
3. That shorthand u use in ur emails is fine 4 ur buds, but i like regulr english. so clean it up, bub. ☺
4. Unless you plan to become a plumber, I wish you'd reconsider the location of your waist.
5. I will start to look a little smarter as you start to look a little older. Promise.

With love,
Your father

CONTENTS

Here I go again, expressing my gratitude to those who have extended a helping hand in the writing of this book, as well as others—my supporting cast of characters—whose ongoing love, employment, and tolerance have helped make this possible. They include: • Cindy Littlefield, at *FamilyFun* magazine, with whom I've had the pleasure of working on a regular basis for quite a few

ACKNOWLEDGMENTS

years now. Also at *FamilyFun*, Jon Adolph, as well as David Sokol at *Disney Magazine*, *FamilyFun*'s sister publication. • I also wish to thank a number of other editors who, despite my regular whining about deadline extensions, have kept me in their good graces: Kristine Kidd, Barbara Fairchild, and Sarah Tenaglia at *Bon Appétit*; Georgia Orcutt, formerly of *Yankee*; Patsy Jamieson of *Eating Well*; Jenny Rosenstrach at *Real Simple*; and John Riha, Nancy Wall Hopkins, and Sandra Mosley at *Better Homes and Gardens*. • My agent, Meg Ruley, of the Jane Rotrosen Agency, has done a stellar job of hawking my writing wares for some fifteen years now. Thank you, Meg. Thanks, too, to Don Cleary of the Jane Rotrosen Agency.

To the hard-working crew of The Harvard Common Press, who do such a fine job of producing cookbooks: Bruce Shaw, Pam Hoenig, Valerie Cimino, Skye Stewart, Sunshine Erickson, Jodi Marchowsky, Abbey Phalen, Liza Beth, Betsy Young, Christine Alaimo, Dana Garczewski, Megan Weireter, Pat Jalbert-Levine, and Virginia Downes. And, of course, to Barbara Jatkola, my tireless copyeditor.

To all the rest whose recipes, tips, and input have enriched this volume in countless ways: Niel Koep, Rachel van Leer and Sarah Adolph, Friske Orchards, Mayor Barbara Skinner, Jeff and Jayne Rose, Joyce White, Van Eure, Tom Douglas and Shelley Lance, Alice Colombo, Maria Roman, Nancy Byal, Rose Calello, Jeanne Kelley, Dolores Kostelni, Vid and Annie Valdmanis, Betty Zaiger, Andrea Chesman, Robert Stehling, Jeff Paige, Diane Worthington, the late Richard Sax, Liz Reiter, Liz Smothers, Robert Rankin, Deborah Madison, Marion Cunningham, Jim and Linda Nolte, Michele Scicolone, Opal Lyons, Bill and Linda Biard, Marian Clark, Jerry Bechard, Patti's Restaurant, Robert Eichorn, and Joan and Thom Gorman.

To my children, Ben, Tess, Ali, and Sam; know that I'm tremendously proud to be your father; my parents, Warren and Muriel, who taught me what pie making is all about; and my siblings, Joe, Barb, Tom, Bill, Joanne, and Mary, and their wonderful families. A fellow could not have grown up with a better bunch. Many thanks, too, to my stepson, Bryan Moss, who sampled most everything in these pages, but wishes they had all be pumpkin.

Finally, to my wife, Bev Moss Haedrich, the hardest-working real-estate agent in Annapolis, Maryland. Only someone as faithful, loving, and loyal as she would have put up with almost two years' worth of pie buffet dinners, during which—horrors!—she claims to have gained nearly two full pounds.

Recently, I had the good fortune to give a talk at the Smithsonian Institution in Washington, D.C.—not far from my home in Annapolis, Maryland—to a group of young, aspiring food writers. Their hope—and my purpose for being there—was that I might pass on some useful nuggets of career wisdom based on my nearly quarter of a century as a food writer. Not far into my pres-

entation, one earnest young lady raised her hand and asked if I had any advice to offer on the sort of topics she should write about. My response was immediate, if not entirely original: Write about what you love. Convey some passion for your subject matter, and readers will naturally want to hear what you have to say. • The book you're holding should be ample evidence that I don't take my own advice lightly. Pie, in a word, is my passion. Since as far back as I can remember, watching my mom and dad make their apple pies together every fall as a young boy, I have simply loved pie. I can't really explain why. If one loves poetry, or growing orchids, or walking along the beach at sunset, the why isn't all that important. To me, pie is poetry that makes the world a better place.

Only it's better than actual poetry, some might say, because at the end of an hour or so, there emerges from your oven, or refrigerator, something really good to eat. That's where this book will come in handy, especially if you, like many home cooks I talk to, are a little less than confident when it comes to your pie-making skills. Being fully aware of this, one of my main objectives with this collection of recipes has been to build your confidence by first talking you through the process (starting on page 1) and giving you frequent pointers throughout on what to expect during the assembly and baking stages.

Note the phrase I just used—*build your confidence*. That's an important point, because pie-making mastery does not visit you overnight. It's put in place one piece at a time, like a cinder block wall, until you're left with a solid foundation. At least that's the way it was with me. Today, after decades of regular baking, I can make a good pie pretty much without fail. But I can tell you that the road here has been littered with some ugly ones, too. The great things about pie, however, are that even the ugly ones taste wonderful and, at least in my opinion, you can become about 85 percent proficient as a pie maker in short order. The other 15 percent you'll acquire over a lifetime.

A Pie for All Seasons and All Reasons

This is, to my knowledge, the single most comprehensive book that's ever been written on the subject of sweet pies. And if it pleases me to call that to your attention, I wouldn't be the least bit surprised if the breadth of this collection has left you wondering where you should begin. So perhaps a few words are in order to point you in the right direction.

I've always thought that the best pie making occurs within a context—that the context guides the cook, and the cook, in turn, rises to the challenge and does his or her best work. It's an organic process, predicated on circumstance.

The most obvious of contexts is the season, the logical starting point for many pie-making decisions. Let's say, for example, that it's getting to be late fall and your local farm stand shelves are sagging under the weight of crisp fresh apples. Well, it stands to reason that your baking plans are probably going to include an apple pie rather than a blueberry one, especially since blueberries are being flown in from afar and selling for $5 a half pint.

But season is by no means the only reliable context. How about expediency? Again, it's late fall, the middle of apple season. It's nine o'clock on a Monday evening and your

10-year-old son blithely hands you a flyer—one that's been crumpled up in his knapsack for a week—informing you that tomorrow is the class bake sale and you need to send in a pie. Sure, it may be apple season, but you're out of apples, and the only supermarket that's open is 20 miles away. The only fruit in sight is a bag of frozen blueberries in the freezer. Blueberry pie it is. Or maybe peanut butter pie, if that's what's in the cupboard. I think you get the point.

You don't have to search far to find a context for any pie: a special chocolate pie to honor a chocolate-loving guest; chess pie to take on a drive south to visit the family; custard pie, because you know it will look and taste gorgeous garnished with some berries from the garden. A simple craving will do. I've made more buttermilk pies than I can count, just because I was hungry for one.

Remember, Pie Making is Not Rocket Science, and You Don't Need a Lab to Bake One

It's just amazing how many cooking gizmos there are on the market today. Believe me, I like a clever kitchen tool as much as the next guy. But one of the things that has always appealed to me so much about pie making is the fact that you don't have to own a lot of fancy or expensive equipment to make one: a bowl, a paring knife, a rolling pin, a whisk, a pie pan. Remember, home cooks were making darn good pies long before gourmet shops were around. Same for ingredients: no matter how bare your cupboard, I can virtually guarantee that at this very moment, you have the necessary supplies on hand to make some sort of pie. Of course, when pie making becomes a regular part of your life, you'll stock your shelves accordingly—with flour, frozen fruit, cornstarch, chocolate, vanilla, sugar, and the like—so you can indulge your pie fancy whenever you please.

Although I've made every effort to consider the time constraints most of us are under these days, including taking a generous position toward refrigerated pie pastry and other convenience products, this is not a book of "instant" or "effortless" pies. I, for one, am a little wary of this widespread "instant-homemade" movement: you take a tub of whipped topping, stir in a can of this, and pour it into a pie shell. That's okay on occasion, but I believe most home cooks bake a pie because they want to engage their senses, do something that's tactilely rewarding. Pie making is a craft, after all, and one we can be proud of. Indeed, one of the most satisfying things about making a pie is showing it off just a little, then sharing what we've created. In the absence of effort and skill, there's little to feel particularly proud of. How much pride would you take in a dress you "made" if all you did was remove a premade front and premade back from a package, then stitch them together in two minutes? Very little, I imagine.

So go ahead, proceed fearlessly, and make some pie. Whether you're a beginner or a seasoned expert, I hope this book will serve as your trusted pie companion for years to come. May you discover recipes that delight, techniques that prove useful, and a word or two of wisdom that leads to a lifetime of happy pie baking for you and yours.

I'm one of those cookbook authors who has, for years, been admonishing

readers to *please* read the recipe through before starting it. It's no mystery

why: I find that if I take a comfortable seat, kick back, and let the visual steps

of the recipe start to develop in my mind while I read, I inevitably bring more

confidence and precision to the tasks at hand. It's sort of like looking at a

Required Reading: What It Takes to Make the Perfect Pie

map before beginning a journey to a place you've never been. • What follows

are some general guidelines for making a successful pie, from mixing the

pastry to getting it out of the oven. For the reasons I've just mentioned, I hope

you'll take a few minutes to read these important pages. If you're at home,

slide into a cozy chair. If you're at a bookstore, grab a latte and find a quiet

corner. Imagine doing each of the steps outlined, then gather your confi-

dence, get yourself into the kitchen, and start baking!

Of *Mise en Place* and Pies

ASK ANY CULINARY SCHOOL STUDENT about the meaning of the French term *mise en place*, and he or she will dive right into a thorough explanation. *Mise en place*—translated as "everything in its place"—is a core concept of the professional kitchen. It means, more or less, that before you so much as turn on a burner, you'd better gather all your ingredients, measure them out, and have the equipment you need ready to go. And while you're at it, sharpen your knife. *Mise en place* is the antithesis of—and antidote for—chaos and confusion in the kitchen.

The home cook would do well to borrow the concept and apply it to pie making. There's much to do before you actually turn on the oven, and the more organized you are, the more you'll enjoy making pies. I speak from experience: it's no fun to get halfway into the preparations for a crumb-topped apple pie, only to find you're out of butter. Or cinnamon.

Here, then, are some of my *mise en place* rules for baking a pie.

▶ Read the recipe first. Actually, read it twice. Not only will this familiarize you with the ingredients list, but it also will help you gauge the recipe's suitability. Do you have everything it calls for? Also, just as important, you'll start developing the mental photographs that will help you make the pie. In addition, reading the recipe will give you an idea when you'll be able to serve the pie. Does it need to be refrigerated overnight? Or can it be served more or less right away?

▶ Check your supplies of ingredients against the recipe's ingredients list. Procure the items you need.

▶ Measure and stage the necessary ingredients. If a recipe calls for cold shortening, put it on a plate in the freezer while you're making other preparations. Remember, your goal—once you start working on a recipe—is to be able to walk right through it without taking detours or making pit stops.

▶ Finally, make plans for your pie. Don't let it linger on the counter or in the fridge, slowly slipping past its prime. Once you've eaten your immediate share, determine how much of it to refrigerate (for short-term storage), freeze, or give away. Pies topped with whipped cream should be eaten the same day, if possible. If that means giving some to your neighbors, so be it.

Making the Perfect Pastry

If you already knew how to make a perfect pastry, chances are you wouldn't be reading this. So let's assume, for our purposes, that you have certain misgivings about making a respectable pie crust. Perhaps you've tried, only to fail miserably. Perhaps you've never even bothered to try, certain that you were born without the all-important "pie pastry gene." Maybe you *are* a real pro, but you're curious about what I have to say on the subject. Whatever the case may be, let's begin by taking a closer look at making good pie dough and see if you can gather the courage to dive right in and make your own perfect pastry. It is, I assure you, not a difficult thing to do.

Simply put, pie pastry is a blend of flour, sugar (sometimes), salt, fat—typically in the form of butter or solid vegetable shortening (such as Crisco)—and water. When these ingredients are properly mixed and handled, the result is a pie crust with a flaky texture and good flavor. For many of the pastries in this book, I have provided instructions for making the pastry three different ways: by hand, in a food processor, and with an electric mixer. Let's look at all three ways.

Making Pastry by Hand

For the beginner, making pastry by hand is the best way to learn. The process is very deliberate, and you won't get ahead of yourself the way you might with a machine. You'll also begin to develop the intuitive "touch" that all good pastry makers possess. You'll get a feel for how much to cut in the fat, the amount of water to add, and how much force to use when handling the dough.

To make pastry by hand, simply mix the dry ingredients in a bowl—something large enough to get your hands down into. Add the fat in pieces, then toss it with the flour. I talk more about the baking qualities of various fats in the headnote to each pastry recipe. But in a nutshell, vegetable shortening will give you great flakiness but little flavor. Butter will result in less flakiness and more flavor. And a blend of the two will give you both. Lard, which has fallen out of fashion and is no longer widely appreciated by home cooks, makes an excellent crust, yielding the ultimate in flakiness.

Before you start cutting in the fat with your pastry blender, break it up by hand so that the pieces aren't so large. Then start pushing down into the mixture with the pastry blender, literally cutting the fat into the flour. After every three or four pushes, stop and toss

Equipment Picks: Pastry Fork

Since I've discovered how handy this outsize fork is for so many aspects of pie making, I pay much less attention to my wire pastry blender than I used to. You can use the fork like a hand-held blender to cut fat into flour: just choke up on the handle and press down. But it does so many other things, too, and so well. Its grand size makes short work of blending the pastry when the water is added. When I'm partially prebaking a pastry, I use it to poke holes in the pie shell to keep it from puffing up. I whisk pecan and custard fillings with it, as well as melted chocolate. I mix fruit fillings with it and use it to "pull" meringue topping into short peaks. On off-pie days, I might use it when carving a roast or whipping up an omelet, pressing it into service in any of a dozen different ways. Everyone ought to have a fork like this. To view the one I own and like most, go to www.kingarthurflour.com.

the mixture up from the bottom of the bowl by hand. What you're doing with all of this cutting is creating little pockets of fat. When these pockets are flattened—when the dough is rolled—they create, essentially, fissures of fat. In the heat of the oven, the fat melts and the moisture in it causes the dough to expand, creating the flaky network that characterizes a good crust. Note that there are many fine home bakers who don't bother with a pastry blender at all. They simply rub the fat into the flour by hand, a method you might want to try if, indeed, you don't own a pastry blender.

When the fat is sufficiently cut in—leaving clumps the proverbial "size of small peas"—water is added to help bind the pastry. The mark of an experienced pastry maker is knowing just how much water to add, leaving the pastry neither too moist nor too dry. There are different schools of thought on how best to add the water. One of the most gifted pie makers I know, contrary to popular wisdom, stirs it in all at once with excellent results. Others add it a tablespoon at a time. I take the middle ground, usually adding half of it at first, then the rest about a tablespoon at a time. The risk of adding it too slowly is that you'll overmix the dough, activating the gluten in the flour—the stuff that makes dough elastic, which is fine in bread dough but an absolute no-no when making a pie crust. With my approach, you give the dough an overall dampening, then you incrementally bring it to the right consistency, but not too incrementally. Just a couple of stirring strokes with a big fork (see the box at left) after each bit of water should do it.

I hesitate to say this, but if you're a beginner and have to err when you're adding the water, err on the side of a bit too much rather than too little. Neither is ideal, but it's slightly easier and less frustrating to handle a dough that's too damp than one that's too dry and prone to cracking and crumbling. If your dough is dampish, make sure you use plenty of flour on your rolling pin and pastry to keep it from sticking.

Making Pastry in a Food Processor

Most cooks have no idea how simple it is to use a food processor to make pie pastry. I know this for a fact because, before every pie-making demonstration I give, I ask how many people in the crowd already do so. Maybe three or four out of a hundred will raise their hands. By the time the demonstration is over, most of the crowd has been converted to the food processor method.

Let me preface my comments by saying that unless you have a large-capacity food processor—the biggest (14-cup capacity) model Cuisinart makes—don't even bother. A smaller machine will not do a thorough, even job of mixing up a double-crust pastry. You can, however, make a single batch of pastry in a smaller machine.

The food processor does essentially the same thing you do by hand when you cut the fat into the flour. The difference is that the food processor is much more efficient. It works many times faster, and it cuts more sharply, with less of a rubbing action than you get by hand. You'll still get a flaky crust with a food processor, but the flakes tend to be smaller.

The key to making a good food processor pastry is the pulse button. The entire pastry is made with quick little pulses. Pulsing is crucial because that starting and stopping of the machine keeps tossing the mixture up from the bottom of the bowl, ensuring that the pastry is evenly mixed. All it takes is about five pulses to cut in the fat, after which I remove the lid and fluff the mixture with a fork. I do this because, even with the pulsing, the processor will start to compact some of the pastry under the blade. Fluffing frees it up.

As with pastry made by hand, the water is added in stages—first half of it, then the remainder. After all the water is added, continue to pulse the machine just until it forms large clumps that can be packed. If the pastry balls up around the blade, you've mixed it too much. Overprocessing often results in a pastry that's not as tender as it should be, so try not to do that next time.

Making Pastry with an Electric Mixer

Only in the past few years have I started making pastry with my electric mixer. I like this method, but since I came to it later in my pie-making career, I can't say I've become a real convert. There are, after all, only so many methods a fellow needs to make pastry. My preference, if I had to choose, would be one of the techniques I've just described. Still, perhaps you'd like to give it a try, and if you do, my observations may prove useful.

I use my KitchenAid stand mixer, which, unlike many cheaper hand mixers, has the slow speeds required for mixing the pastry sufficiently without overmixing it.

Begin by combining your dry ingredients in the mixer bowl. Toss them by hand or turn on the mixer to combine them. Add the fat in pieces. With the mixer on low speed, start mixing—or cutting—the fat and flour together. I've known cooks who use the flat beater attachment for this, but I think the wire whip better emulates the cutting action required. Blend the pastry on low speed for about 10 seconds, then stop the machine and fluff the mixture up from the bottom with a rubber spatula. As with the food processor, some of the pastry will settle and compact in the bottom of the bowl; your aim is to put it back into circulation.

Turn the machine back on low speed and continue to blend for a few more seconds. Sprinkle half of the water over the pastry and blend for a few seconds. Add the remaining water a tablespoon at a time, blending briefly after each addition. Stop the machine and gather up the pastry.

No matter the method you use, wrap and refrigerate your pastry as instructed in each recipe. As I often say, refrigerating a pastry is probably the single most important step you can take to achieve a dough that is easy to roll, is relatively easy to handle, and turns out good and flaky.

Convenience Pie Pastry

In a perfect world, we would all make our own pastry, all the time. And if that's the ideal, we sometimes fall a little short of the mark. We may have planned to make a pastry from scratch, only for life to intervene: A child falls ill. The dog gets sprayed by a skunk. A husband is rushed to the emergency room when the TV remote fuses to his hand and has to be surgically removed. This or, let's be honest, in spite of my rousing pep talk about how simple it is to make a good pastry from scratch, you just aren't buying it.

Okay, fine. I'm here to tell you that you can make a homemade pie on your own terms, without a homemade pastry. The answer is as close as the refrigerator case or frozen food section of your local supermarket.

Refrigerated Pie Pastry

Truth be told, I am a relative newcomer to refrigerated pie pastry. A dedicated pie maker since my late teens, I have always considered it a matter of pride that I made my own pastry from scratch, no matter the other demands on my time. I simply wasn't interested.

That changed one day when, working on an assignment for one of the magazines I write for, I was asked to make some pies with refrigerated pastry. And darned if I wasn't pretty impressed: The crusts came out flaky and tender. The flavor was good, if not quite homemade. And, well, you just couldn't beat the ease of it all: just unfold, line the pan, fill, and bake.

In the course of writing this book, I used a number of refrigerated pie pastries to test recipes. Here are some things I picked up along the way.

- Take the pastry out of the refrigerator about 15 minutes before you line your pan. The pastry will be more pliable and easier to handle when it isn't too cold. Refrigerate or freeze the pie shell while you make the filling.

- The pastry is meant to be used primarily in a 9-inch standard pie pan. There's not enough of it for most deep-dish pans. (See page 8 for the definitions and descriptions of various pie pans.) Used thus, there's just the right amount of pastry to sculpt an upstanding ridge on single-crust pies, which helps contain the filling.

- If the pastry cracks at one of the seams when you're unfolding it, don't worry. Just pinch it back together.

- Refrigerated pastry, I've noticed, has a tendency to brown faster than most homemade pastries I make. If you find that to be the case, simply place a piece of aluminum foil loosely over the pie during the last 10 to 15 minutes of baking to deflect the heat.

- You can, if you wish, use refrigerated pie pastry for virtually any pie in this book that specifies a 9-inch standard (not deep-dish) pie shell.

Frozen Pie Shells

In terms of convenience, frozen pie shells are even more cook-friendly than refrigerated pie pastry. But there are a few limitations and pet peeves worth mentioning.

The first is their size. Even frozen pie shells labeled "deep-dish" don't have the capacity of a 9-inch standard pie pan. Typically, they don't hold more than about 3 cups of fruit, maybe 4 if you're using apples or pears—fruit that isn't too juicy. Most pie recipes in general, including the ones in this book, will not fit very well into a frozen pie shell.

My second beef is the nature of the disposable aluminum pans they come in. Such pans not only deflect the heat, making a properly baked, well-browned crust difficult to achieve, but they also can be tricky to handle because they're so flimsy and tend to bend when they contain a hot pie. Indeed, rather than try to lift one of them out of the oven, I usually slide a rimless cookie sheet under the pan, using it like a giant spatula.

Finally, frozen pie shells tend to get pretty banged up en route to your supermarket. It's not unusual to find edges broken off or gaping holes, like puzzle pieces that have gone missing. The upshot? Choose carefully. And if you do take the frozen pie shell option, here are a few pointers to consider.

▶ I've tried a number of brands, and the one I like best is Marie Callender's. This company's pans are relatively sturdy and a little deeper than most, and the product tastes good, too. I also like Mrs. Smith's shells, perhaps the most sturdily packaged and therefore the least prone to damage.

▶ To get the best possible bottom crust, which is to say as browned as possible, bake the pie on a low oven rack. If you have a dark, heavy baking sheet, preheat it in the oven on a low rack and bake the pie directly on it.

▶ The filling for most 9½-inch deep-dish pies can be divided between two 9-inch frozen pie shells.

Choosing Your Pie Pan

As you might imagine, I own a number of pie pans. Not a ridiculous number—maybe a couple of dozen or so; heck, some guys own that many cars—but enough of them, in various materials and designs, to have formed some opinions about which ones I like and care to recommend.

First, let's look at the three pan sizes I recommend for the vast majority of the pies in this book: the *9-inch standard pan, the 9½-inch deep-dish pan, and the 9½- to 10-inch extra-deep-dish pie pan.*

Pie Equipment: Here's What's Selling

If anyone knows what pie bakers are buying these days, it's Cindy Fountain, retail director for the King Arthur Flour Baker's Store in Norwich, Vermont—possibly the biggest all-baking store in the country. Legions of dedicated bakers flock to it from all around the country every year. I sat down and talked to Cindy about what today's pie bakers want. Here's what she had to say.

"First of all, pies are back. There's a real resurgence of interest in baking a homemade pie nowadays. Presentation is more important to today's pie bakers than it was to past generations. We sell lots of the standard aluminum pans, but the gorgeous Polish pottery pie pans are really hot, too. For some reason, pie birds (see page 217) are all the rage now. People tell me they remind them of their grandmothers. Apparently, everyone's grandmother used to have one. The flour wands are big; this is something you fill with flour and shake over the dough to keep your pin from sticking (see page 319). As for rolling pins, we have a Vermont-made marble pin that's great for rolling. I have one myself, and I love the weight: three or four rolls, and I'm done. Our stainless steel pie chain is another steady seller. You use this as you would dried beans to weight down your pastry when you're prebaking a crust without a filling. Lots of people buy our mini pastry cutters so they can dress up their top crusts. And, of course, pie carriers: someone makes a beautiful pie, and they want a way to transport it so it doesn't get damaged en route."

To view some of these items, go to www.kingarthurflour.com.

The majority of pie recipes I see are written around the 9-inch standard pan. I say standard, but in fact there seem to be few standards when it comes to pie pans, a dilemma I wish Congress would remedy by enacting a new law. Anyway, a 9-inch standard pan is about 9 inches in diameter—measured across the opening—and 1 to $1^1/_4$ inches deep. Perhaps the best-selling pan of this design is the Pyrex 9-inch clear tempered-glass pan, which you see every time you walk down the baking aisle of your supermarket. Nearby, you'll also find the thin, shiny aluminum pans of roughly the same size. You can make a good pie in both of these pans, but given the choice, I would nearly always choose the Pyrex pan. It isn't sexy or particularly attractive, but for most everyday pies, you get excellent results— which is to say a nicely browned and evenly baked crust—with a glass pie pan. Glass tends to be a little slow in heating up, but once it does, it does a great job of browning.

The thin, shiny aluminum pan is less desirable. Thin aluminum tends to reflect a lot of heat without absorbing much of it—think of those aluminum shields we put in our car windshields. Believe me, I've upended many a pie, turning the whole thing out just to check a crust (oh, the things I do in the name of research), and time and again I've discovered an underdone crust baked in shiny aluminum. (I've also discovered that upended pie tastes just fine, thank you.)

Now if you shop at a fancier kitchenware store, you have a couple of more choices, including a heavier aluminum pan, still shiny, and a darker (usually nonstick) one. One big manufacturer of these pans is Chicago Metallic, which also makes stuff for the bakery trade, so you know its pans are sturdy. I've been a fan of this company's products for years.

When a shiny pan is heavier, you get better results because even if the pan reflects a certain amount of heat, it also absorbs it, thus the bottom crust browns better. The darker pan is better yet. Dark absorbs heat efficiently—the reason you don't wear a black top in the summer—and you wind up with a nicely browned crust, sometimes a little too browned, especially near the upper edge, but it usually isn't enough to quibble about.

Bottom line: if you're not satisfied with your current 9-inch pie pan, try a Pyrex pan or a heavier metal pan.

A 9-inch standard pan holds a certain amount of filling—about 4 cups give or take, a bit more if you're using firm, not-too-juicy fruit such as apples or pears. I think it makes a suitable pie for a small to medium-size family, with a few pieces left over for the next day. Sometimes you want a little extra pie, however—bigger slices, or a pie that's suitable for a larger family or a potluck supper. For those pies, I often use the next size up, a 9½-inch deep-dish pan.

For uniformity's sake, all of the pies in this book that call for such a pan were baked at least once in the one pan I know you can find no matter where you live: the Pyrex 9½-inch deep-dish pan. It measures 9½ inches across the opening and nearly 1¾ inches deep. That may not sound much bigger than a standard pan, but it will hold nearly half again as much filling, with a capacity of about 6 cups. The pan I'm describing has a sloping side and a very distinctive ruffled upper edge. If you can't find one at the supermarket, you can most certainly find one at a kitchenware store. This is my first choice for big, seasonal fruit pies, especially apple, pear, and peach. This pan also has something I wish more pie pans had: handles. They aren't particularly big, but they sure help when you're trying to take a hot pie out of the oven and place it on a cooling rack.

When I want to go really big, I turn to what I call my extra-deep-dish pie pans. This is not a standard term, but one I use to describe several oversize pans I've picked up along the way. These are just slightly larger than the regular deep-dish pans and can be used nearly interchangeably. (If you have too much filling for a pie pan, by the way, just put the little bit extra in a custard cup and bake it without a crust.)

Apart from these common and identifiable pans, there are many enameled pottery pans that not only do a fine job of browning the crust but also are very attractive and make for a lovely presentation. My favorites in this category are the Emile Henry pie plates you can find at Williams-Sonoma (see box) and other gourmet kitchen stores, as well as the lovely Polish pottery pie pans, with a capacity nearly equivalent to the deep-dish pan described above. These pans aren't cheap, put I think they're worth the outlay simply because everyone needs at least one pan that's a real looker. I buy mine from Twins Polish Pottery at www.twinspolishpottery.com.

Finally, there's one pan that I suggest you avoid: the disposable aluminum kind. This type of pan is okay in a pinch, but the flimsiness of the pan and the shininess of the material usually result in an underdone crust.

Rolling Your Pastry

Your pastry is made and chilled, your pan is standing by. Now what's the best way to roll your pastry and get it into the pan without the blessed thing falling apart?

There are, in fact, many ways to do just that. Whenever I give a pie-making demonstration and walk through the method I'm about to describe, several people will, inevitably, describe their own methods. Perhaps one likes to roll her dough on a marble counter, another likes a certain rolling pin, and a third has a favorite method for lifting the pastry into the pan. And I say bravo to that! If you have a way of doing this that already works just fine, stick with it. But if you're relatively new to rolling pastry or not satisfied with your method, this is the way I do it.

Emile Henry Pie Plates

In France, sweet pies as we know them don't exist. It's ironic, then, that a Frenchman named Jacques Henry was granted a U.S. patent for an American pie pan that's become something of a trendsetter.

The pans, with their graceful scalloped edges, are manufactured by Emile Henry, located in Marcigny, Burgundy, France. Burgundy clay is known for its superb heat diffusion and retention—qualities that help promote even browning and make these pans so superior for pies. Jacques Henry, a fifth-generation descendant of the founder, was inspired to create the pan from a turn-of-the-century baking dish he spotted in an old family photo.

Rugged, attractive, and roomy, the standard six-cup pie pan works for any deep-dish pie in this collection. I own several and use them often, especially when presentation counts. You can find Emile Henry pans in gourmet retail stores across the country.

Pins for Your Pies

Walk into any well-stocked kitchen store, and you're liable to find a half dozen or more rolling pins to choose from. How is a pie maker to choose? Here are some guidelines.

▶ Polished maple is the best hardwood for a rolling pin. It has a close, tight grain that won't absorb moisture or flavors from other foods you might use it on.

▶ Some bakers I know swear by their heavy marble pins. They like the weight because it does some of the work. Chill a marble pin before rolling out your pastry; the coolness will help.

▶ The handles are key. They shouldn't be stuck into the pin, or they're liable to break off when you bear down on a cold pastry. On better pins, a heavy metal rod extends through the barrel and well into each handle. Ball bearing construction is a must.

▶ It's nice to have more than one pin. Tapered French-style pins are good for starting cold pastry dough, but I prefer to finish rolling with a larger American-style pin. A 12- to 15-inch barrel is a good size for home pie makers.

▶ Avoid flea market pins. You don't know how or where they've been used. If you want to hang them on a wall, fine. A good rolling pin costs $25 to $30, and it's worth every penny.

Before you do anything else, butter or grease your pie pan. It isn't mandatory, and, in theory at least, there's plenty of fat in the pastry to prevent the crust from sticking. But some of my pans don't know this—especially the glass and pottery ones—so I do it anyway.

Now take a piece of waxed paper about 13 inches long and place it on your counter, with the curl down. Dust it *lightly* with flour. If you have a Formica-type counter, waxed paper has a tendency to skid around on it, so you can do one of two things. You can buy a Silpat baking mat (see page 14) and put it down first, under the waxed paper, or use it in place of the waxed paper. Or you can wipe the counter with a *slightly* damp dishrag, which will keep the waxed paper in place. I recommend the first option.

Put your cold but not too hard pastry in the center of the waxed paper and dust the top of it with flour. If you're making a double-crust pie, you've already been instructed to make one half of the pastry (for the shell) a little larger than the other. So make sure you have the correct disk of dough. Flour your rolling pin and roll it over the top of the pastry

From My "Overrated Techniques" File

I hate to break ranks on this, but I'm not a fan of rolling pastry between two pieces of plastic wrap, advice I see dispensed frequently. Why? Because the top piece inevitably sticks to the pastry, crimps, and buckles, requiring you to stop and straighten out the plastic after each pass of your rolling pin. It's not worth the hassle. It's far easier to use a single sheet of waxed paper underneath your pastry and a liberal-enough dusting of flour on top of the pastry—and on your pin—to prevent the dough from sticking. The pastry won't buckle if you use this method, and as long as it has been refrigerated, you shouldn't have any problem with it sticking to the pin. If you want to use two sheets of something (if you're a pastry novice, you may appreciate the added no-stick security), use a second sheet of waxed paper. I find it less troublesome than plastic wrap.

a couple of times, just to wake it up. At this point in the rolling, I sometimes use my tapered French-style pin, because the dough responds to it a little better than it does to my big pin, which is preferable once the dough starts to expand. The thin pin also gives me good directional control, so if I'm rolling along and my pastry starts to look like the state of Florida, I can use short passes to get it back in shape.

One of the key reasons for using waxed paper is that you can rotate the dough easily, just by turning the paper. You don't have to lift the dough itself off the counter, thereby risking a major tear or other catastrophe. Anyway, start pushing down on the dough, directly away from you, once or twice. When you've made a little progress, give the waxed paper a quarter turn and roll a couple of more times, always rolling more or less straight away from you. Keep in mind that you will need to adjust the degree of pressure you use depending on the type of pastry you've made: the higher the proportion of butter, the firmer the chilled pastry will be. A pastry made with all shortening will be relatively soft by comparison. As you roll, keep dusting the pastry and rolling pin with flour, as necessary, to keep them from sticking together. When the dough seems to be about halfway there, switch to your bigger rolling pin if you've started with a thin one—my big pin has a 3-inch-diameter by 12-inch-long roller—and finish rolling.

As you start to roll, don't be concerned if the dough cracks a little around the edge; it probably will. If it starts to get out of hand, however, just stop rolling and pinch the edge back together around the entire perimeter. That will make you feel better and limit the amount of future cracking. Also, always roll from the center out and ease up ever so slightly

The Silpat Solution

So there you are rolling along, 11 inches into a perfect 12-inch circle of pastry, when you discover that your dough is hopelessly stuck to the counter. What's a home baker to do? There's always waxed paper (see page 12), my favorite low-tech surface for rolling out pie pastry. But you might want to consider the Silpat, too. A relative newcomer to the market, the Silpat is a silicone-treated material that's both heat-resistant and virtually nonstick. Primarily intended as a reusable baking sheet liner, the Silpat's nonstick performance makes it a natural for rolling pastry. Simply roll your dough directly on the Silpat, invert it over your pie pan (just as you do with waxed paper), and peel off the Silpat. No need to flour it or apply oil.

Even if you still prefer waxed paper, you might consider the Silpat. Waxed paper has a tendency to slide around on Formica-type counters, and the Silpat can be used as a nonskid surface underneath the waxed paper. An 11 x 16-inch Silpat mat costs about $20 and can be found at housewares stores such as Bed Bath & Beyond and Sur La Table.

on the pressure as you approach the edge. One common error I've noticed with novice rollers is that they tend to press harder as they get near the edge, leaving the pastry too thin there and almost impossible to shape or sculpt. When you're done rolling, your entire circle of dough should be a uniform thickness.

Another reason I like waxed paper is because it has a built-in measure that let's you know when you're done rolling: it's 12 inches wide, the perfect size bottom pastry for a 9-inch standard pie pan. You know you've rolled enough when, provided your circle is actually round, you've reached the edges of the paper. To make a bottom pastry for a 9½-inch deep-dish pan, roll it 13 inches or even a tad wider, just a little off the paper on the factory edges.

Getting Your Pastry into the Pan

Now the challenge is to get the pastry safely into the pan without mishap. This could not be easier. With your pan nearby, put one hand over the pastry, fingers outstretched to better support it. Then in one fluid motion, invert the pastry and waxed paper directly over the pan. Using your fingers to check, center the pastry over the pan, then gently peel off the paper. Pull at a sharp angle, rather than in an upward motion, to keep the pastry from shifting position.

As you lift on the overhanging dough with one hand (to take the tension off the dough), gently tuck the pastry into the pan; your two hands will be directly opposite each other as you do this, working in concert. Don't blithely jam your fingers into the dough, or you'll stretch and perhaps tear it. Rather, nudge it into the bottom of the pan without stretching it. Continue in this fashion all around the pan. If you've rolled a pretty good circle and centered the dough nicely, you should have a relatively even overhang all around the pan. If the overhang is not quite even, don't worry. If it is extremely uneven and certain places have no overhang at all, snip some excess dough from another part of the pastry, moisten one side of it with a wet fingertip, and pinch it into place to fill in the gap. Finally, use a pastry brush to sweep any excess flour off the pastry edge.

If you're making a double crust pie, you'll want to keep that overhanging dough in place so that you can attach the top crust to it. Just put the pan directly in the refrigerator as is, taking care not to catch the edge of the pastry on anything. If I don't have room on a shelf, I usually put it on top of a bowl, above harm's way.

Forming the Pastry Edge

If you aren't attaching a top crust to your pie, you'll need to do something with that overhang before you go any further. You have several options.

In many if not most cases, in particular when you have a juicy fruit filling or another liquidy filling, you will want the added height of the pastry edge to help contain the filling. That extra one-half inch of height can mean the difference between a filling that stays where it should and one that spills over the edge, sending you looking for the oven cleaner.

To make what I call an *upstanding ridge*, fold the overhanging dough back, which is to say away from the inside of the pan. Pinch the dough against itself, sculpting it into a ridge. Mold it as you would clay. As you do this, you'll find that the edge will be thicker in some places, thinner in others. One thing you can do when you run into a thick spot is simply squeeze harder to push the excess farther out along the edge. Your goal in all this sculpting is a more or less uniform ridge about one-half inch high, perhaps a little less. You can leave the

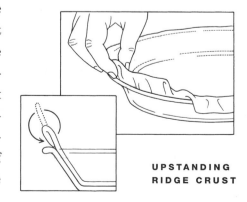

UPSTANDING RIDGE CRUST

Another One from My "Overrated Techniques" File

Ever see that trick, recommended in countless magazines and books, for rolling your pastry around your pin and then unrolling it over your pie pan? Well, I think it's a very cool idea, but it's not at all easy to execute. For starters, it requires you to hold a very heavy rolling pin in one hand while you somehow guide/roll the pastry around the pin with the other. Rolling or unrolling, the odds of your pastry tearing en route are much higher than you'd like. Instead, just roll your pastry out onto a sheet of waxed paper, invert it over your pie pan, and peel off the paper (see page 14).

edge just like that—your basic upstanding ridge—or you can make a scalloped edge, as shown in the picture at right.

In any event, place the pie shell in the refrigerator or freezer. Not only will this make the pastry more durable against the possibility that you'll knock the edge with your hand or a utensil and damage it while you're filling the pie, but it also will firm up the fat, which will help to keep the pastry flaky as it bakes.

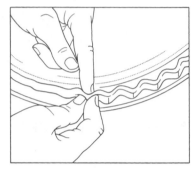

SCALLOPED EDGE CRUST

Prebaking the Pie Shell

For certain types of pies, you'll need to prebake the pastry, sometimes *partially*—as when the pie will be filled and then baked, such as with most custard pies—and other times *fully*—as when the pie will require no further baking, such as with cream pies.

I know it's not particularly convenient to prebake a pie shell. Even I get a little impatient with the process, especially if I'm in a hurry. But I think it's really worth the added time in the final analysis. Whenever I'm served a pie and the bottom crust is soggy or undercooked, I know the crust wasn't prebaked, and I consider the pie something of a failure. I'm not likely to say that—"Hey, lovely meal. Thanks for having us. But what gives with your bottom crust?"—but I can't help feeling that if you're going to take the time to bake a pie, you should do what you can to make sure it is properly baked.

You only need a couple of things to prebake a pie shell: aluminum foil and something to weight the foil and pastry down. The weight is necessary to hold the pastry in place so that it doesn't puff up, become misshapen, and not bake properly. Some bakers like special pie weights to hold the pastry down, but I just use dried beans. I have, I'm embarrassed to say, been using the same dried beans for about seven or eight years now. I keep them in an oatmeal box in my baking cupboard. They smell a little toasty—my wife, Bev, always asks me what's burning when I use them—but they're in fine shape otherwise, so I see no reason to throw them out.

Tear off a piece of aluminum foil about 16 inches long. That's more than you'll need to fit into your pan, but the excess makes the foil easy to lift when you're removing the beans. By the way, don't use heavy-duty foil; it's a little too rigid to shape easily. Center the foil over your pie shell and, just as you tucked the pastry into the pan, tuck the foil into the pie shell. (One of the reasons I like to freeze the pastry for 15 minutes is that you won't damage or change the shape of a pastry that's frozen firm when you're tucking and molding.) The bottom edge should be well defined, as should the sides. Basically, the foil should fit the pie shell like a second skin. Let the excess foil on the ends just flare out like wings. Don't bunch it around the pie pan, or you'll deflect heat away from the sides. Pour in enough dried beans to reach the top of the pan.

With your oven preheated to 400°F, bake the pie shell on the center rack for 15 minutes. This first stage of baking really sets the crust—not fully baking it, but allowing it to settle and take on the shape of the pan. You don't want to skimp on this part of the process, or the pastry will be more inclined to shrink when the weights are removed.

After 15 minutes, slide out the rack—you don't have to remove the pie from the oven—and slowly lift up on the sides of the foil to remove the weights. You may not even need oven mitts to do this because as soon as the aluminum foil hits the room-temperature air, it cools right off (this being a perfect illustration of why I don't like flimsy aluminum pans; they don't hold heat). Put the foil and weights on the counter, somewhere out of the way. Take a fork and prick the pastry all over the bottom, perhaps seven or eight times, covering as much area as possible. As you stick the fork in, give it a little twist to enlarge the holes slightly, because small holes have a way of closing up. I generally don't worry about pricking the side of the pastry unless I see it start to puff; then I open the oven door and stick a fork in to deflate it.

Lower the oven temperature to 375°F and continue to bake the pie shell for 10 to 12 minutes for a *partially prebaked* pie shell or 15 to 17 minutes for a *fully prebaked* pie shell. Check on the pie shell once or twice during this time to make sure it isn't puffing up; if it is, prick the problem spot with a fork. Look for visual clues that the pastry is properly baked. A *partially prebaked* pie shell will just be starting to brown, ever so lightly. A *fully prebaked* pie shell will be golden brown and look fully baked. Bear in mind that these times for the second phase of the baking (without the beans) are approximate. For instance, the type of pastry may affect the baking time. Just use your best judgment.

As soon as you remove the pie shell from the oven, use the back of a spoon to gently press the side crust back into position anywhere it might have sagged or slightly puffed. Take care not to push so hard that you break the crust, leaving a place where the filling can run out. Also, whisk an egg white until frothy, then paint it over the holes you've poked to prevent the filling from leaking. Put the pie shell back in the hot oven to bake the egg white to a hard finish, about 2 minutes. Remove the pie shell from the oven and put it on a wire rack to cool.

Filling and Sealing a Double-Crust Pie

Of course, with most fruit pies, you won't be prebaking anything; the filling goes right into the uncooked pie shell. Let's first look at how double-crust pies, typically fruit pies, are handled.

Earlier I said to refrigerate the pastry for a double-crust pie. That will firm it up and make the pastry less likely to turn soggy when juicy fruit filling is added. Unlike the procedure for a single-crust pie, however, you don't freeze the bottom pastry, because the overhang would get too firm to attach to the top crust.

So here's where you stand: Your pie shell is in the refrigerator. Your fruit filling awaits. The assembly can begin, but first you must roll your top pastry.

The top pastry is rolled just as the bottom one was, only you don't have to roll it so large—just large enough to cover the pie plus enough for the overhang. Each recipe tells you just how large this is. Roll the pastry on the waxed paper and have it standing by. If, by chance, the phone rings and you're delayed for any reason, slide the paper and pastry onto a baking sheet and stick it in the fridge until you're ready to proceed. And if you want to make decorative cutouts in the top pastry, put the rolled dough in the freezer for 10 minutes to firm it up, then cut as desired.

The pastry is easier to handle when cool, so without delay get the filling into the refrigerated pie shell. If your filling contains apples, pears, or anything with edges that jut up and might tear the crust, smooth it out with your hands, laying those slices down flat. Now take a pastry brush and moisten the entire rim of the pie shell with water; this acts as the glue to help seal the pastries together. While you're at it, brush excess flour off your top pastry.

Pastry Cutouts

One of the easiest ways to give your pies that decorative edge, figuratively and literally, is by using cookie cutters to make pastry cutouts. You can use large cutters to make a centerpiece on your pie—for example, a big apple in the center of your double-crust apple pie—or smaller cutters to make a leaf border or to spell out a message such as "Happy Halloween." Look for cutters at your local arts and crafts store. If this sounds like fun—and if you have kids, I can assure you it will be—here are some tips to keep in mind.

> For just a few cutouts, use your pastry scraps to cut from. Roll the dough onto a sheet of waxed paper, then slide the paper and dough onto a baking sheet and freeze for 15 minutes. Cold dough cuts much easier than room-temperature dough.

> With double-crust pies, simply place the cutouts right on the top crust after you've brushed it with milk.

> To make a decorative border on a single-crust pie, your outouts can't be much larger than the rim of the pie pan, or they won't have enough support. Leaves work well because they can drape down into the pie shell and still look quite natural.

> Alternatively, you can make a cutout garland by baking the cutouts separately. Start with enough pastry for a single crust and roll it as above. Make the cutouts and transfer them to a greased baking sheet. Brush with 1 egg white beaten with 1 tablespoon water; try not to get the glaze on the sheet. Keep in mind that you'll need quite a few cutouts to go around the entire pie. Bake the cutouts in a preheated 375°F oven until golden brown, 10 to 15 minutes. Brush the edge of the baked pie shell with corn syrup and press the cutouts into place.

DECORATIVE BORDER WITH CRUST CUTOUTS

A Nice Set of Mini Cutters

My favorite tin of mini cookie cutters is a collection of six autumn designs: pumpkin, apple, oak leaf, maple leaf, acorn, and some sort of generic leaf, none more than about an inch wide. They're great for dressing up fall fruit pies, pumpkin pies, and maple pies (see Maple Cream Pie on page 476). When I'm not using them for pies, they're great for sugar cookies or special cutouts for gingerbread houses.

Here's a little tip for keeping all your cutters in top form. Since they're often made from tin, cutters will develop rust spots if you let water droplets sit on them after washing. To prevent this, place the just-washed cutters on a baking sheet and put them in the oven while it's cooling down. They'll dry right off.

You can find plenty of sources for mini cookie cutters online. Just use those three words to search. One company that seems to have an extensive collection of mini cutters is www.foosecookiecutters.com.

Just as you did earlier when you inverted your pie shell into the pan, invert the top pastry over the pie, center it, and remove the waxed paper. Press where you've moistened to seal. If you plan to make an upstanding ridge (see page 15), take a pair of scissors and trim the overhang so that it is about one-half inch wider than the top of the pan. Then turn the excess pastry back and pinch it into an upstanding ridge. Make a scalloped edge, if desired. Your other choice is to simply trim the pastry flush with the outside edge of the pan. Using a paring

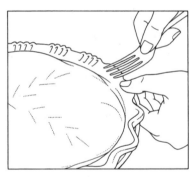

FORK-PRESSED FLUSH EDGE CRUST

knife, held perpendicular to the counter, run the blade around the edge of the pie; the excess pastry will fall right off. Press the tines of a fork around the edge to make an attractive seal. Both methods—upstanding edge and flush trim—have their pros and cons. An upstanding ridge is better insurance against the pie splitting at a seam and bubbling over, and it leaves quite a hefty edge of crust, which is fine if you like that. A flush-trimmed pastry is a little more likely to split at the seam, but you don't have that thick crust there. Either way, don't sweat it: in the grand scheme of things, these are minor concerns, and experience will dictate the choices you make.

Baking Your Pie

It might look like little more than a metal box, but your oven is a dynamic entity. You may think it just sits there, acting like a perfect gentleman. But it's fluctuating all the time: it heats up, gets real hot and then—after the temperature spikes—the heat levels off. When you open the oven to peak at a roast, the temperature in the oven falls, then rises, then levels off again. Some parts of your oven are hotter than others. Most ovens are hotter near the back, the top, and the bottom, and a little less so in the center and front.

So if you're going to bake a pie, you can't do it passively, just shoving the pie in and hoping for the best. You have to get to know your oven and its quirks, then take whatever steps are required to bake the perfect pie.

By and large, the ideal place to bake a pie is in the center of the oven. Nearly all of the recipes in this book instruct you to bake your pie on the center oven rack, and that's where you should start. In some ovens, the rack is slightly high or low of center. If that's the case, go with the slightly lower position. It's more important that the bottom of your pie get hot faster, to help set the crust, than the top of the pie.

Let's say, however, that after you've baked a few pies, you notice that the top keeps getting too brown too quickly. If so, your pie is telling you to bake it on the next lower rack. That should help. If problems persist with chronic overbrowning, your temperature gauge is not accurate and your oven needs to be recalibrated. Call in a pro and have it done. You can check this on your own by buying a good oven thermometer.

Now, when you're out on the beach on a hot summer day, you do your best to tan evenly: you turn over frequently, apply suntan lotion, angle yourself this way and that to get the job done. We don't fuss quite that much with our pies, but there is a little something you can do to facilitate even browning and baking. About halfway through the baking, rotate your pie 180 degrees, "so that the part of the pie that faced the back of the oven now faces forward." Those are the words I use in nearly all of my recipes. The reason you should do this is that most ovens are hotter in the back than they are in the front, and this little rotating exercise acts as an equalizer. You can check for yourself. Thirty minutes into the baking, peek at your pie. The edge of the crust will be several shades darker toward the back.

When I'm baking a fruit pie, I do something else midway through: I slide an aluminum foil–lined baking sheet onto the rack below the pie to catch any spills. I don't put it on the same rack for a couple of reasons. For one, it slows down the baking by temporarily cutting off the direct heat to the bottom of the pan. Second, if the pie does bubble over, the juice runs down the side and oozes under it, making a sticky mess on the bottom of the pan. When the foil-lined sheet is one rack below, the worst that can happen is that the juice will run onto part of the oven rack and harden there, and you can then rub it off with a stiff brush.

The time to start checking your pie is about 10 minutes before it's supposed to be done. Don't open the oven, if you can help it; just turn on the light and look in. With experience, you'll be able to tell if you're on schedule. A custard pie will be just slightly soupy; you will have to nudge it to check. A fruit pie will be showing the first evidence of bubbling juice along the edge. Pecan and pumpkin pie will be starting to swell. These are the little signs that I look for and have tried to clue you in on wherever possible.

Cooling Your Pie

When I was a boy and my mom and dad would bake their wonderful apple pies, I would loiter near the kitchen, ever hopeful for instant pie gratification. No, my dad would tell me, the pie has to cool down first. It was a hard lesson for a kid to swallow, but now I have a better understanding of just how right he was.

Very few pies are fit to be eaten straight out of the oven. A custard pie, for instance, will have little of the tight, creamy texture and mellow flavor it develops as it cools. Warm pecan pie is limp-gooey, not firm-gooey, the way it should be. Fruit pies lack body and flavor nuance if they're served too hot, and the juices are very likely to leak out everywhere if you cut into the pie too soon.

A trip to the cooling rack—followed by a stint in the fridge, if necessary—will take care of all that. A cooling rack is such an ordinary item, but it serves such an important function by allowing air to circulate under the bottom of the pie, which in turn keeps the pie crust from becoming soggy. If I can use the beach analogy again, it's the difference between lying directly on your towel in the sand—your back gets sweaty—and swinging on a rope hammock—your back stays dry. So never skip this step, even if you can put hot pots and pans right on your kitchen counter.

Cooling a fruit pie enables a couple of things to happen: it allows some of the juice to reabsorb into the fruit, and it allows the rest of it to thicken. The cooler the pie gets, the firmer it becomes. Thus, when to eat your fruit pie becomes something of a judgment call,

The Shelf Life of Pies

Fresh homemade pie has a life expectancy that's typically measured in hours, not days. Still, there are times when you'll want to bake a pie ahead or save a slice or two for an arriving visitor. That said, here are my recommendations for keeping pies.

- **Fresh fruit pies:** Best served the same day, fresh fruit pies made without dairy products (other than butter) in the filling will keep at average room temperature for 2 days. If you think you'll need to keep a pie longer, immediately refrigerate it. You'll buy an extra day.

- **Dried fruit pies:** If they contain no dairy products, they'll typically last 2 to 3 days at average room temperature and 5 or 6 days in the refrigerator.

- **Custard pies:** Immediately refrigerate them after cooling. Finish the last slice by day 3.

- **Cream pies:** The filling will be fine for up to 3 days, provided you immediately refrigerate them once they are cooled. The whipped cream toppings are far less stable. A topped pie should be eaten within 24 hours. One way to extend this time is to top only the served slices with freshly whipped cream.

- **Nut pies:** That pecan pie you love so much will keep in the fridge for 3 or 4 days.

- **Pumpkin pies:** Refrigerated, they will keep for 2 or 3 days.

since the ideal texture is somewhere between firm and juicy. You don't want the juice to run all over creation when you serve it, but you also don't want the filling to be overly taut. For most fruit pies, I find that the best filling consistency is reached after about two hours of cooling. At that point, the pie is still warmish. There is still a little free-floating juice, but the slice has just enough body to support itself. That's the ideal slice. Throughout this collection, I've advised how long to cool and/or refrigerate each pie. You may not always agree with me, but at least you'll have someplace to start.

It's Time to Bake

That's quite enough talking about pies. Now it's time to actually bake one. If this is your first time, proceed fearlessly, beginning with one of the traditional pastries, such as Basic Shortening Pie Pastry (page 30) or Basic Flaky Pie Pastry (page 31). Use the hand method for mixing the pastry, then graduate up to the food processor; it's good to learn by touch first. Start with a fruit pie—perhaps one of the apple pies or double-crust summer fruit pies. Don't worry too much about looks in the beginning. Your ability to make a pretty pie will evolve as you master the various skills involved. And be patient with yourself. Even if things don't work out perfectly the first time, it won't be long before you're the best pie baker in the neighborhood and every pie you bake is perfect.

If the following 11 chapters of pie recipes are the flesh of this book, this chapter is the backbone: the recipes here support and give shape to the good pies that follow. Although their role is more or less a supporting one, their importance is not to be underestimated. Simply note, if you will, the crucial role of a supporting cast in a successful film. One good starring performance

Pie Pastries and Crumb Crusts

is rarely enough to make a great film. The same goes for pie: a good filling is key, but without a decent crust, your pie isn't going to win top honors. • Now that I've set the bar rather high, let me put you at ease by telling you that making a good crust is well within your capabilities. For the life of me, I can't understand why pastry making is made out to be such a difficult task. When you consider how few ingredients are involved, how quickly the dough is mixed, how little it is handled, and how effortless it is to roll, there's simply nothing intimidating about it. It's like learning to tie your shoes: it took a few tries, but once you learned the technique, you never forgot it.

For the most part, the following recipes can be divided into two categories: those you roll, the pastry crusts, and those you pat into the pan, the crumb crusts. Although most rolled pie pastries are based on a more or less similar formula, the recipes here represent a range of textures and flavors, achieved by some simple adjustments of the basic ingredients. One of your goals as a pie maker should be a working familiarity with a variety of pastries, leaving you better equipped to decide which sort of pastry to use with a given pie. Looking back on my own pie-making history, I seem to have gone through phases where I preferred one sort of pastry over another. I might have spent the better part of a year making butter pastry, then another stretch when I preferred shortening pastry. There's no irrefutable way to proceed. Although each of the pies in this collection has one or more recommended pastries that I think work well, in time you may decide that you prefer something else. My recommendation will get you started, but it is by no means the last word on the matter.

Crumb crusts aren't really pastries per se. They're loose mixtures, generally made with graham cracker or cookie crumbs, mixed with butter, and patted into your pie pan. These crusts aren't as versatile as pastry crusts, but they are very easy to prepare and require no rolling. Although the crusts themselves are usually prebaked, they're generally used with pies that will require no further cooking—cream pies, for instance, or ice cream pies.

Finally, there is one other type of pastry here, something of a cross between the two I've just mentioned: a press-in pastry.

Whatever your level of expertise as a pastry maker, I suggest that you read the previous chapter before starting out. If you haven't made pastry before or it's been a while, I think you'll find some words of encouragement there to shore up your self-confidence. Even if you are an old pro, I think it's always a good idea to weigh your own experience against someone else's. Even now, with more than 30 years of pie making behind me, I pick up new ideas when I talk to other pie makers.

With that, let me wish you the best of luck with all your pastries and leave you with a few important tips to remember (see box on next page).

Pointers for Perfect Pastry

▶ When all-purpose flour is called for in a pastry, be sure to use just that: bleached all-purpose flour. Do not use unbleached flour, bread flour, or any other flour unless recommended. Other flours often contain too much gluten-forming proteins, which will make dough elastic and may contribute to a tough crust.

▶ When butter is called for, make sure it is fresh and of good quality. I like saving money as much as the next fellow, but I'm generally less than pleased with store brand or other generic butters. Almost exclusively, I used Land O Lakes unsalted butter for the pastries in this collection. I believe this is the gold standard for home cooks.

▶ When vegetable shortening is called for, I like Crisco, and I've become partial to the stick form because it's so easy to measure. If you're using the bulk canned variety, pack it firmly into dry measuring cups and level off the top. Note that I said *firmly*; you don't want any air gaps that may result in a short measure.

▶ Unless otherwise noted, refrigerate all pastries for at least 45 minutes before rolling. They'll be much more cooperative if they've had a chance to chill.

▶ Food processor pastries should not be overprocessed, or they will not be as flaky or as tender as you would like. Pay close attention to the processing instructions with each recipe.

▶ For ease of handling, always roll your pastry on floured waxed paper. The pastry will be a cinch to maneuver and will not stick to the counter and need to be pried off. Also don't forget to flour your rolling pin.

All-Butter Pie Pastry

I'm very fond of this all-butter pastry for a number of reasons. One, with all the butter you just can't argue with the flavor. The butter also gives it a nice gold color, even more so if you make the sturdy version with the egg yolk (see Recipe for Success). It's easy to roll and handle, too, which is why I often choose to use this pastry at my baking demonstrations. It isn't as flaky as some of the other crusts—all-butter pastries never are—but the advantages make this a good pastry to have in your repertoire. Of all the pastries in this collection, I think this is the easiest one to make in a food processor.

MAKES A SINGLE OR DOUBLE CRUST FOR A 9-INCH STANDARD PIE OR 9 1/2-INCH DEEP-DISH PIE

FOR A SINGLE CRUST	FOR A DOUBLE CRUST
1 1/2 cups all-purpose flour	2 3/4 cups all-purpose flour
1 1/2 teaspoons sugar	1 tablespoon sugar
1/2 teaspoon salt	1 teaspoon salt
1/2 cup (1 stick) cold unsalted butter, cut into 1/4-inch pieces	1 cup (2 sticks) cold unsalted butter, cut into 1/4-inch pieces
1/4 cup cold water	About 1/2 cup cold water

1. TO MAKE IN A FOOD PROCESSOR Put the flour, sugar, and salt in the food processor. Pulse several times to mix. Scatter the butter over the dry ingredients and pulse 7 or 8 times to cut the butter in well. Remove the lid and fluff the mixture with a fork, lifting it up from the bottom of the bowl. Drizzle half of the water over the dry ingredients. Pulse 5 or 6 times, until the mixture is crumbly. Fluff the pastry and sprinkle on the remaining water. Pulse 5 or 6 times more, until the pastry starts to form clumps. Overall, it will look like coarse crumbs. Dump the contents of the processor bowl into a large bowl.

TO MAKE BY HAND Combine the flour, sugar, and salt in a large bowl. Toss well, by hand, to mix. Scatter the butter over the dry ingredients and toss to mix. Using a pastry blender, 2 knives, or your fingertips, cut or rub the butter into the flour until it is broken into pieces the size of split peas. Sprinkle half of the water over the dry mixture. Toss well with a fork to dampen the mixture. Add the remaining water in 2 stages and continue to toss and mix, pulling the mixture up from the bottom of the bowl.

TO MAKE WITH AN ELECTRIC MIXER Combine the flour, sugar, and salt in a large bowl. Add the butter, tossing it with the flour. With the mixer on low speed, blend the butter into the flour until you have what looks like coarse, damp meal. Turning the mixer on and off, add half of the water. Mix briefly on low speed. Add the remaining water, mixing slowly until the dough starts to form large clumps. If you're using a stand mixer, stop periodically to stir the mixture up from the bottom of the bowl. Do not overmix.

2. Test the dough by squeezing some of it between your fingers; if it seems a little dry and not quite packable, drizzle a teaspoon or so of cold water over the dough and work it in with your fingertips. Using your hands, pack the dough into a ball (or 2 balls if you are making a double crust) as you would pack a snowball. If you're using this to make a double-crust pie, make one ball slightly larger than the other; this will be your bottom crust. Knead each ball once or twice, then flatten the balls into ¾-inch-thick disks on a floured work surface. Wrap the disks in plastic and refrigerate for at least an hour or overnight before rolling.

Recipe for Success

▶ **Make sure the butter is good and cold—right from the fridge—especially if you're making this in a food processor, because the friction created by the machine softens it fairly quickly.**

▶ **Remember not to let the pastry ball up around the food processor blade. You want to stop running the machine when the pastry is still in clumps.**

▶ **All-butter pastry turns pretty firm in the fridge. If it's refrigerated for more than an hour, give it 5 to 10 minutes at room temperature before rolling. Note that the dough can be frozen for up to a month.**

▶ **To make a sturdier pastry, one with slightly more durability—useful, say, when you're making a freeform pie—add 2 large egg yolks to the double-crust recipe and 1 large egg yolk to the single-crust recipe. Put them in a glass measuring cup and add enough water to equal the required amount of liquid for that recipe. Blend with a fork, then add to your pastry as usual.**

Butter Bits

▶ **The word "butter" comes from the Greek *bous*, meaning "cow," and *tyros*, meaning "cheese." As early as 1850, the expression "to butter" meant to flatter. It didn't become "butter up" until the late 1930s.**

▶ **By government edict, all butter must contain at least 80 percent milkfat.**

▶ **The remaining 20 percent of butter is made up of 18 to 18.5 percent water and 1 to 2 percent curd, or milk solids.**

▶ **"Sweet butter" is a term used for unsalted butter.**

Basic Shortening Pie Pastry

This is a fairly standard shortening pastry, the one that I grew up with and that my dad made so deftly. It produces a flaky, tender crust that's suitable for most of the pies you'll make. It's particularly wonderful with double-crust fruit pies. Unlike butter, solid vegetable shortening is soft and easy to combine with the dry ingredients. I don't even bother to give food processor directions for mixing the dough, since it is almost as fast to make it by hand. (I do, however, give electric mixer directions.) Once you've mastered this recipe, you'll feel a boost of confidence about your pie-making skills.

MAKES A SINGLE OR DOUBLE CRUST FOR A 9-INCH STANDARD PIE OR 9½-INCH DEEP-DISH PIE

FOR A SINGLE CRUST

1½ cups all-purpose flour

1 tablespoon sugar

½ teaspoon salt

½ cup cold vegetable shortening, cut into pieces

¼ cup cold water

FOR A DOUBLE-CRUST

2¾ cups all-purpose flour

1 tablespoon sugar

1 teaspoon salt

1 cup cold vegetable shortening, cut into pieces

6 to 8 tablespoons cold water

1. **TO MAKE BY HAND** Put the flour in a large, wide bowl that you'll have no trouble getting both hands into as you mix the dough. Add the sugar and salt. Mix well, tossing with your hands. Add the shortening here and there. Using your fingertips, a pastry blender, or 2 knives, rub or cut the shortening into the dry ingredients until the mixture resembles coarse, damp meal. You want to end up with both large and small clumps in the mixture. With a fork in one hand and your cold water in the other, add half of the water to the pastry. You needn't measure it; you can just pour. Mix the dough with the fork, pulling up the dry ingredients from the bottom of the bowl and pushing down to mix everything well. Add the remaining water in 2 stages, mixing until the dough coheres. The dough should feel dampish but not wet. Don't add more water than you need.

TO MAKE WITH AN ELECTRIC MIXER Combine the flour, sugar, and salt in a large bowl. Add the shortening, breaking it into smaller pieces and tossing it with the flour. With the mixer on low speed, blend the shortening into the flour until you have what looks like coarse, damp meal, with both large and small clumps. Sprinkle on half of the water. Turning the machine on and off, mix briefly on low speed. Add the remaining water in 2 stages, mixing slowly until the dough starts to form large clumps. If you're using a stand mixer, stop periodically to stir the mixture up from the bottom of the bowl. Do not overmix.

2. Dust your work surface with flour and turn the dough out onto it. If you're making a double crust, divide the dough into 2 pieces, one—the piece you'll use for the bottom pastry—somewhat larger than the other. Place each piece on a sheet of plastic wrap. Flatten the dough, with floured hands, into disks about ³/₄ inch thick. Wrap them in plastic and refrigerate for at least an hour or overnight before rolling.

FRIED PIE PASTRY The pastry we use to make fried pies is essentially this one, with a bit less fat and 1 egg added—both of which make the dough a little sturdier. Make the following changes to the double-crust recipe: Reduce the shortening to ³/₄ cup. Place 1 large egg in a 1-cup glass measure and beat, then add enough water to make ¹/₂ cup liquid. Use as much of the liquid as necessary to make the dough.

Recipe for Success

▶ To make the dough easy to handle, I like to cut my shortening (I use the easy-to-measure-and-cut sticks) and put it on a plate before I do anything else. This goes in the freezer for about 10 minutes while I'm preparing the rest of my ingredients.

▶ Shortening really sticks to your hands when you're rubbing it to make pastry. For the easiest cleanup, wipe off the excess with paper towels before running your hands under hot water.

▶ The dough may be frozen for up to a month.

Basic Flaky Pie Pastry

This pie pastry is used frequently throughout this collection because it yields such excellent results. I sometimes call it a half-and-half pastry, referring to the equal amounts of vegetable shortening and butter—the former for flakiness, the latter for flavor. It can be made in a food processor if you have a large-capacity machine. But I'll repeat my usual advice, which is to make it by hand or with an electric mixer if you don't. Both methods are quite easy. If you could have only one pastry to work with, this would probably be it.

MAKES A SINGLE OR DOUBLE CRUST FOR A 9-INCH STANDARD PIE OR 9¹/₂-INCH DEEP-DISH PIE

FOR A SINGLE CRUST

1 1/2 cups all-purpose flour

1 tablespoon sugar

1/2 teaspoon salt

1/4 cup (1/2 stick) cold unsalted butter, cut into 1/4-inch pieces

1/4 cup cold vegetable shortening, cut into pieces

1/4 cup cold water

FOR A DOUBLE CRUST

3 cups all-purpose flour

1 tablespoon sugar

1 teaspoon salt

1/2 cup (1 stick) cold unsalted butter, cut into 1/4-inch pieces

1/2 cup cold vegetable shortening, cut into pieces

1/2 cup cold water

1. TO MAKE IN A FOOD PROCESSOR Put the flour, sugar, and salt in the food processor. Pulse several times to mix. Scatter the butter over the dry ingredients and pulse the machine 5 or 6 times to cut it in. Fluff the mixture with a fork, lifting it up from the bottom of the bowl. Scatter the shortening over the flour and pulse 5 or 6 times. Fluff the mixture again. Drizzle half of the water over the flour mixture and pulse 5 or 6 times. Fluff the mixture and sprinkle on the remaining water. Pulse 5 or 6 times more, until the dough starts to form clumps. Overall, it will look like coarse crumbs. Dump the contents of the processor bowl into a large bowl. Test the pastry by squeezing some of it between your fingers. If it seems a little dry and not quite packable, drizzle a teaspoon or so of cold water over the pastry and work it in with your fingertips.

TO MAKE BY HAND Combine the flour, sugar, and salt in a large bowl. Toss well, by hand, to mix. Scatter the butter over the dry ingredients and toss to mix. Using a pastry blender, 2 knives, or your fingertips, cut or rub the butter into the flour until it is broken into pieces the size of small peas. Add the shortening and continue to cut until all of the fat is cut into small pieces. Sprinkle half of the water over the mixture. Toss well with a fork to dampen the mixture. Add the remaining water, 1 1/2 to 2 tablespoons at a time, and continue to toss and mix, pulling the mixture up from the bottom of the bowl on the upstroke and gently pressing down on the downstroke. Dough made by hand often needs a bit more water. If necessary, add water 1 or 2 teaspoons at a time until the pastry can be packed.

TO MAKE WITH AN ELECTRIC MIXER Combine the flour, sugar, and salt in a large bowl. Add the butter, tossing it with the flour. With the mixer on low speed, blend the butter into the flour until you have what looks like coarse, damp meal, with both large and small clumps. Add the shortening and repeat. Turning the mixer on and off, add half of the water. Mix briefly on low speed. Add the remaining water, mixing slowly until the dough starts to form large clumps. If you're using a stand mixer, stop periodically to stir the mixture up from the bottom of the bowl. Do not overmix.

2. Using your hands, pack the pastry into a ball (or 2 balls if you are making a double crust) as you would pack a snowball. If you're making a double crust, make one ball slightly larger than the other; this will be your bottom crust. Knead each ball once or twice, then flatten the balls into 3/4-inch-thick disks on a floured work surface. Wrap the disks in plastic and refrigerate for at least an hour or overnight before rolling.

> **WHOLE WHEAT PIE PASTRY** Follow the basic recipe above, substituting 1 cup whole wheat flour for 1 cup of the all-purpose flour for a double crust, 1/2 cup whole wheat flour for a single crust. Proceed as directed.

> **CHEDDAR CHEESE PIE PASTRY** Reduce the flour to 2 3/4 cups in the double-crust recipe. (Do not reduce the flour for a single crust.) When using a food processor, after you've added the shortening, pulse 3 or 4 times. Add 1 cup (1/2 cup for single crust) finely shredded sharp cheddar cheese and pulse 3 or 4 times more. Add the water and proceed as directed above. When making the dough by hand or with an electric mixer, add the cheese after you have cut or mixed in all of the fat. Toss with your hands to mix, then add the water as instructed for each method.

Recipe for Success

▶ **I use this pastry so often that I tend to make it in large batches. More than half of the time required to make pastry is spent getting out the ingredients, putting them away, and washing the utensils. That said, I may make a double batch of crust, 3 or 4 times over, then freeze it for up to a month. I wrap each disk in plastic, then in aluminum foil. I take the dough out of the freezer the day before I plan to use it and let it thaw in the fridge. It works like a charm.**

And You Thought You Had Pastry Problems

"I have had a number of small horrors . . . mostly involving pie crust, something I haven't quite gotten the knack of. One of my pies fell apart. One was so odd-looking my husband took a picture of it, and one had the texture and resilience of old parchment."

—Laurie Colwin, *Home Cooking* (Knopf, 1992)

Extra-Flaky Pie Pastry

This is perhaps the best behaving of all the pastries in this collection, thanks to the addition of cake flour. The benefit of cake flour is twofold: it makes the pastry more shrink-resistant when it is prebaked, and it makes the pastry extra tender and flaky, due to the soft nature of the wheat used in the flour. This pastry can be used for just about any pie, but it's a particularly good choice when the filling is somewhat refined or delicate. Make it by hand or with an electric mixer if you don't have a large-capacity food processor.

MAKES A SINGLE OR DOUBLE CRUST FOR A 9-INCH STANDARD PIE OR 9$^{1}/_{2}$-INCH DEEP-DISH PIE

FOR A SINGLE CRUST

1 cup all-purpose flour

$^{2}/_{3}$ cup cake flour

1 tablespoon sugar

$^{1}/_{2}$ teaspoon salt

$^{1}/_{4}$ cup ($^{1}/_{2}$ stick) cold unsalted butter, cut into $^{1}/_{4}$-inch pieces

5 tablespoons cold vegetable shortening, cut into pieces

$^{1}/_{4}$ cup cold water

FOR A DOUBLE CRUST

2 cups all-purpose flour

1 cup cake flour

1 tablespoon sugar

1 teaspoon salt

$^{1}/_{2}$ cup (1 stick) cold unsalted butter, cut into $^{1}/_{4}$-inch pieces

$^{1}/_{2}$ cup plus 2 tablespoons cold vegetable shortening, cut into pieces

$^{1}/_{2}$ cup cold water

1. **TO MAKE IN A FOOD PROCESSOR** Put the flours, sugar, and salt in the food processor. Pulse several times to mix. Scatter the butter over the dry ingredients and pulse 5 or 6 times to cut it in. Fluff the mixture with a fork, lifting it up from the bottom of the bowl. Scatter the shortening over the flour and pulse 5 or 6 times. Fluff the mixture again. Drizzle half of the water over the flour mixture and pulse 5 or 6 times. Fluff the mixture and sprinkle on the remaining the water. Pulse 5 or 6 more times, until the dough starts to form clumps. When it reaches this point, do not continue to process. Empty the crumbs into a large bowl.

TO MAKE BY HAND Combine the flours, sugar, and salt in a large bowl and mix well. Scatter the butter over the dry ingredients and cut or rub it in, using a pastry blender, 2 knives, or your fingertips until the butter is broken into fine pieces. Add the shortening and repeat. Sprinkle half of the water over the dry mixture. Toss well with a fork to dampen the mixture. Add the remaining water in 2 stages and continue to toss and mix.

Add more water if needed. Typically, hand-mixed pastry will require a little more water than machine-mixed.

TO MAKE WITH AN ELECTRIC MIXER Combine the flours, sugar, and salt in a large bowl. Add the butter and toss with the flour. With the mixer on low speed, blend the butter into the flour until you have what looks like coarse, damp meal, with both large and small clumps. Add the shortening and repeat. Turning the mixer on and off, add half of the water and mix briefly on low speed. Add the remaining water, mixing until the dough starts to form large clumps. If you're using a stand mixer, stop periodically to stir the mixture up from the bottom of the bowl. Do not overmix.

2. Using your hands, pack the dough as you would a snowball. If making a double crust, divide the dough in half, making one half—for your bottom crust—a little larger than the other. Knead each piece 2 or 3 times. Put each in the center of a piece of plastic wrap and flatten it into a disk about $3/4$ inch thick. Wrap in the plastic and refrigerate until firm enough to roll, about an hour or overnight.

Recipe for Success

‣ If you don't have cake flour, substitute $1/4$ cup cornstarch for $1/4$ cup of the all-purpose flour. Sift it into the flour, then proceed as directed.

‣ The dough may be frozen for up to a month.

Those Pastry Trimmings

Every time you trim the edge of a double-crust pie, you're left with a small handful of dough. What should you do with it? It's not enough to make another pie, and if you're not making decorative cutouts, it seems simpler just to toss it.

Here's a better idea. Flatten it into a $1/4$-inch-thick disk, wrap it in plastic, slide it into a zipper-topped plastic storage bag, and put it in the freezer. After you've done this 3 or 4 times, you'll have enough dough to make another pie shell. Just take the bag out of the freezer the day before you plan to use it and leave it in the fridge. Then unwrap and stack the disks, loosely cover with plastic wrap, and let sit at room temperature until they're soft enough to roll; they'll fuse together as you do. Don't worry if the pastries aren't all the same sort; nobody will notice the difference.

Lard Pie Pastry

Whoever said that lard makes the flakiest pie crust is absolutely right. If you've never had a lard crust—and there was a time in this country when it would have been nearly the only kind you would have had—you'll be amazed at just how much flake there is. For the uninitiated, one challenge you'll have to master is knowing how much water to add to the pastry. This can be a bit tricky at first, because lard has an oily, elastic texture like that of solid vegetable shortening (only more so) and it's less apparent when sufficient water has been added. The solution is to stick to one brand of lard and the same pastry recipe, then adjust the water each time you make it until you've got it down pat. This is an excellent pastry for any double-crust fruit pie.

MAKES A SINGLE OR DOUBLE CRUST FOR A 9-INCH STANDARD PIE OR 9¹/₂-INCH DEEP-DISH PIE

FOR A SINGLE CRUST

1¹/₄ cups all-purpose flour

¹/₂ teaspoon salt

¹/₂ cup cold lard, cut into pieces

3 to 4 tablespoons cold water, as needed

FOR A DOUBLE CRUST

2¹/₂ cups all-purpose flour

1 teaspoon salt

1 cup cold lard, cut into pieces

¹/₃ to ¹/₂ cup cold water, as needed

1. **TO MAKE IN A FOOD PROCESSOR** Put the flour and salt in the food processor. Pulse several times to mix. Scatter the lard over the dry ingredients and pulse 5 or 6 times to cut it in. Fluff the mixture with a fork, lifting it up from the bottom of the bowl. Drizzle 1¹/₂ tablespoons (3 tablespoons for double crust) of the water over the mixture and pulse 5 or 6 times. Fluff the mixture and sprinkle on another 1¹/₂ tablespoons (2¹/₂ tablespoons for double crust) water. Pulse 3 or 4 times more, until the dough starts to form clumps. Overall, it will look like coarse crumbs. Dump the contents of the processor bowl into a large bowl. Test the dough by squeezing it between your fingers. If it seems a little dry, drizzle more water over it, about ¹/₂ tablespoon at a time, working it in by hand.

TO MAKE BY HAND Combine the flour and salt in a large bowl. Toss well, by hand, to mix. Scatter the lard over the flour and toss to mix. Using a pastry blender, 2 knives, or your fingertips, cut or rub the lard into the flour until it is broken into small clumps. Drizzle 1¹/₂ tablespoons (3 tablespoons for double crust) of the water over the mixture and combine, then sprinkle on another 1¹/₂ tablespoons (2¹/₂ tablespoons for double crust) water and combine.

TO MAKE WITH AN ELECTRIC MIXER Combine the flour and salt in a large bowl. Blend briefly to mix. Add the lard. With the mixer on low speed, blend it into the flour until you have what looks like coarse, damp meal. Turning the mixer on and off, blend in 1½ tablespoons (3 tablespoons for double crust) of the water, mixing briefly on low speed. Sprinkle on another 1½ tablespoons (2½ tablespoons for double crust) water, mixing slowly until the dough forms large clumps. If you're using a stand mixer, stop periodically to stir the mixture up from the bottom of the bowl.

2. Using your hands, pack the pastry into a ball (2 if you're making a double crust) as you would pack a snowball. If you're making a double crust, make one ball slightly larger than the other; this will be your bottom crust. Knead each ball once or twice, then flatten the balls into ¾-inch-thick disks on a floured work surface. Wrap the disks in plastic and refrigerate for at least an hour or overnight before rolling.

Recipe for Success

▶ I think this is a good pastry for beginning pie makers. A chilled lard crust has more plasticity—moldability, essentially—than just about any other pastry. It's less likely to crack and holds its shape very nicely. So don't shy away from this one, thinking you need to possess some sort of old-fashioned wisdom to try it.

▶ Not all lard is created equal. The best is known as leaf lard, which comes from the fat around a pig's kidneys. There are discernible flavor differences among brands of lard, and the only way to find a lard you like is to bake with several. Bottom line: the pastry should have a rich, pleasant taste that's more or less neutral and not overpowering. Commonly sold in both tubs and bricks, lard has a shortening-like consistency and, like shortening, is best measured by firmly packing it into the appropriate dry measure and leveling the top.

▶ The dough may be frozen for up to a month.

Crisco Chronology	
1911	Crisco introduced.
1912	First Crisco ad and cookbook.
1923	Crisco available in hermetically sealed cans.
1930	First Crisco Jewish cookbook.
1949	First Crisco TV commercial.
1981	Butter Flavor Crisco introduced.
1991	Crisco available in sticks.

Maria's Shortbread Pie Pastry

Maria Roman's pastry, which I use for her wonderful walnut pie on page 343, is somewhat different from other shortbread pastries. The main difference is the proportion of butter to flour. There's less fat in this one, so the crust is a little drier and sturdier than some, particularly around the edge of the walnut pie, where it is almost biscotto-like in texture. Nonetheless, I think you'll agree that it's just the right pastry for this pie, and you may well end up using it for other enclosed pies. Note that this pastry is best made with a heavy-duty stand mixer. Lacking one, I suggest starting with a hand-held mixer, then working in the flour by hand (see Recipe for Success).

MAKES A DOUBLE CRUST FOR A 9-INCH STANDARD PIE OR 9^1/$_2$-INCH DEEP-DISH PIE

10 tablespoons (1^1/$_2$ sticks) unsalted butter, slightly softened

^{3}/$_4$ cup sugar

1 large egg

1^1/$_2$ teaspoons finely grated lemon zest

^{1}/$_4$ teaspoon salt

3 cups all-purpose flour

2 tablespoons cold water

1. Using an electric mixer, beat the butter, sugar, egg, lemon zest, and salt together in a large bowl until well blended. Gradually add the flour, about ^{1}/$_2$ cup at a time, until all of it has been added and the mixture comes together into a ball. Add the water and slowly beat it in or work it in by hand.

2. Put the dough on a lightly floured surface and divide it into 3 pieces, 2 of them just a little larger than the third. Wrap each of the 2 larger pieces in plastic and refrigerate for 30 minutes before rolling. Divide the smaller piece into 2 equal-size balls, wrap them in the same piece of plastic, and refrigerate.

Recipe for Success

▶ There's just too much dough here to make this from start to finish with a hand-held mixer; it will clump up between the beaters and stress the motor. If that's all you have, however, go ahead and beat the butter, sugar, egg, lemon zest, and salt in a large bowl as instructed. Then simply work in the flour by hand, adding about ^{1}/$_2$ cup at a time.

Yeasted Butter Pastry

Here is the pastry I use for Fresh Peach and Brown Sugar Pizza Pie (page 99). If you've ever eaten a French *galette*—an open-faced tart with a fruit or custard topping—you have some idea of what to expect: a slightly bready, rich dough that's sturdy yet tender. This dough is easily made in the food processor, followed by a quick hand-kneading.

MAKES ENOUGH PASTRY FOR 1 LARGE PIE

^{1}/2 cup lukewarm water

1 package (about 2 teaspoons) active dry yeast

2 cups all-purpose flour

1^1/2 tablespoons sugar

^{1}/2 teaspoon salt

5 tablespoons cold unsalted butter, cut into ^{1}/4-inch pieces

1 large egg yolk

1. Measure the water in a 1-cup glass measure. Sprinkle the yeast over the water, mixing briefly with a fork. Set aside for 5 minutes to dissolve.

2. Meanwhile, place the flour, sugar, and salt in a food processor and pulse several times to mix. Scatter the butter over the dry mixture and pulse 7 or 8 times, until the butter is broken into very small pieces.

3. Add the egg yolk to the yeast mixture and blend with a fork. Add the liquid to the food processor and pulse repeatedly, until the dough coheres, then run the machine nonstop for 8 to 10 seconds to knead the dough.

4. Place the dough in an oiled medium-size bowl, rotating the dough to coat the entire surface. Cover the bowl with plastic wrap and set aside to rise in a warmish spot for 1 hour. If for some reason you need to delay the rising, simply put the dough in the refrigerator.

Recipe for Success

▸ To end up with the best texture, make sure that your butter is good and cold and that you don't overprocess the dough while you're mixing it.

Cornmeal Pie Pastry

I often make this pastry during the holidays. It just seems to fit in with what I think of as early American pies, such as cranberry, pumpkin, and apple. It contains just enough butter to have a great flavor, but what I like best is the little bit of cornmeal crunch. Be aware that a crust made from this pastry may turn a deep golden brown around the edge. Cornmeal will toast up like that, but it's seldom serious, and the darkening is limited to a very small area. One thing you can do to mitigate the browning somewhat is to use an aluminum foil shield like the one described in Recipe for Success.

MAKES A SINGLE OR DOUBLE CRUST FOR A 9-INCH STANDARD PIE OR 9$^1/_2$-INCH DEEP-DISH PIE

FOR A SINGLE CRUST

1 cup plus 2 tablespoons all-purpose flour

$^1/_4$ cup fine yellow cornmeal

1 tablespoon sugar

$^1/_2$ teaspoon salt

2 tablespoons cold unsalted butter, cut into $^1/_4$-inch pieces

$^1/_4$ cup cold vegetable shortening, cut into pieces

$^1/_4$ cup cold buttermilk

FOR A DOUBLE CRUST

2$^1/_4$ cups all-purpose flour

$^1/_2$ cup fine yellow cornmeal

2 tablespoons sugar

1 teaspoon salt

$^1/_4$ cup ($^1/_2$ stick) cold unsalted butter, cut into $^1/_4$-inch pieces

$^1/_2$ cup cold vegetable shortening, cut into pieces

$^1/_2$ cup cold buttermilk

1. TO MAKE IN A FOOD PROCESSOR Put the flour, cornmeal, sugar, and salt in the food processor. Pulse several times to mix. Scatter the butter over the dry ingredients and pulse 5 or 6 times to cut it in. Fluff the mixture with a folk, lifting it up from the bottom of the bowl. Scatter the shortening over the flour and pulse 5 or 6 times. Fluff the mixture again. Drizzle half of the buttermilk over the flour mixture and pulse 4 or 5 times. Fluff the mixture and sprinkle with the remaining buttermilk. Pulse again, briefly, until the dough forms clumps. It will be damper than some crusts you've seen because of the buttermilk. Dump the contents of the processor into a large, shallow bowl.

TO MAKE BY HAND Combine the flour, cornmeal, sugar, and salt in a large bowl. Toss well, by hand, to mix. Scatter the butter over the dry ingredients and toss to mix. Using a pastry blender, 2 knives, or your fingertips, cut or rub the butter into the flour until it is broken into pieces the size of split peas. Add the shortening and continue to cut until all the fat is cut into small pieces. Sprinkle half of the buttermilk over the dry mixture. Toss well with a fork to dampen the mixture. Add the remaining buttermilk and continue to toss and mix, pulling the mixture up from the bottom of the bowl on the upstroke and gently pressing down on the downstroke. If it seems necessary, add a bit more buttermilk until the pastry can be packed.

TO MAKE WITH AN ELECTRIC MIXER Combine the flour, cornmeal, sugar, and salt in a large bowl. Add the butter, tossing it with the flour. With the mixer on low speed, blend the butter into the flour until you have what looks like coarse, damp meal, with both large and small clumps. Add the shortening and repeat. Turning the mixer on and off, add half of the buttermilk. Mix briefly on low speed. Add the remaining buttermilk, mixing slowly until the dough starts to form large clumps. If you're using a stand mixer, stop periodically to stir the mixture up from the bottom of the bowl. Do not overmix.

2. Using your hands, pack the pastry into a ball (or 2 if you're making a double crust) as you would pack a snowball. If you're making a double crust, make one ball slightly larger than the other; this will be your bottom crust. Knead each ball once or twice, then flatten the balls into ³/₄-inch-thick disks on a floured work surface. Wrap the disks in plastic and refrigerate for at least an hour or overnight before rolling.

Recipe for Success

▶ There are times when I like to use a coarse, stone-ground cornmeal in baking, but this is not one of them. The coarser the grind, the more likely it is you'll have trouble with this pastry cracking apart as you handle it. I suggest using Quaker brand cornmeal here.

▶ This pastry will keep in the freezer for up to a month.

▶ To prevent overbrowning of the crust, make a foil shield. Tear off a sheet of aluminum foil about 3 feet long. Fold it lengthwise into thirds and wrap it around the pan. It will stand up on its own. Simply overlap the ends; there's no reason to pinch them together. When the pie is done, remove the shield and save it for future use.

Nutty Pie Pastry

Nut pastries are suitable for all sorts of pies. The flavor teams up nicely with fruit, in particular pears, figs, and apples, as it does with chocolate and, of course, nuts. Nut pastries tend to be a little trickier to handle than others, given the added coarseness of the ground nuts. It is important that the nuts be very finely ground—here with the sugar to help keep them from turning oily—and then inspected by hand for larger bits that might impede rolling. Give the pastry time to chill so that the butter can firm up, but not too much time: the more solid a nut pastry becomes, the more likely it is that it will crack. About 45 minutes in the refrigerator is just right. If you need only half of this recipe, you can freeze the other half for up to 2 months.

MAKES 2 SINGLE CRUSTS OR 1 DOUBLE CRUST FOR A 9-INCH STANDARD PIE OR 9½-INCH DEEP-DISH PIE

$2/3$ cup pecan or walnut halves or whole blanched almonds

$1^1/2$ tablespoons sugar

$2^1/2$ cups all-purpose flour

1 teaspoon salt

$3/4$ cup ($1^1/2$ sticks) cold unsalted butter, cut into $1/4$-inch pieces

2 tablespoons cold vegetable shortening, cut into pieces

About 5 tablespoons cold water

1. Combine the nuts and sugar in a food processor, grinding the nuts in a succession of long bursts. They should not become flour-fine, but almost. (Almonds are likely to require more chopping than walnuts or pecans.) Carefully minding the blade, reach in and feel around for any large pieces of nuts, breaking them up by hand or removing them and chopping them with a knife. Add the flour and salt to the machine and pulse to mix. Scatter the butter over the dry ingredients and pulse 4 or 5 times. Fluff the mixture with a fork, lifting it up from the bottom. Scatter the shortening over the flour and pulse 4 or 5 times. Fluff again. Drizzle 3 tablespoons of the water over the flour mixture and pulse 5 or 6 times. Fluff the pastry and sprinkle on the rest of the water. Pulse 5 or 6 more times, until the dough starts to form clumps. Dump the contents of the processor bowl into a large bowl.

2. Using your hands, pack the pastry into 2 balls as you would pack a snowball. If you're making a double crust, make one ball slightly larger than the other; this will be your bottom crust. If you're making 2 single crusts, make the balls the same size. Knead each one once or twice, then flatten them into $3/4$-inch-thick disks on a floured work surface. Wrap the disks in plastic and refrigerate for about 45 minutes before rolling.

Recipe for Success

▶ Perhaps the most important aspect of making a nut crust is getting the consistency of the ground nuts just right. They should be finely ground but not to a powdery or flour-like consistency, or they'll start to turn into something like nut butter. Adding the sugar helps keep the texture granular. Keep an eye on the texture as you pulse the machine (don't keep it running), and stop to inspect the nuts often to monitor your progress.

▶ Thanks to the added fat in the form of nut oil, this pastry requires less water than other recipes of this size. Expect the dough to seem more buttery than some pastries as you near the end of the mixing cycle. It feels similar to a rich tart pastry, if you're familiar with that.

Jeffrey Steingarten on Making the Perfect Pastry

"Perfect American piecrust must be seven things at once—flaky, airy, light, tender, crisp, well browned, and good tasting. The tricky ones are flaky, tender, and crisp—because these are independent virtues. Getting flaky, tender, and crisp to happen at the same time in the same pie seems nearly impossible. Yet millions of American women and men in the early 1900s could do it in their sleep, and probably tens of thousands can today."

—*The Man Who Ate Everything* (Knopf, 1997)

Louise Piper's Oil Pastry

This recipe was given to me by Louise Piper, a perennial winning pie maker at the Iowa State Fair. She tells me she's been using this recipe for nearly 40 years. It's very simple to prepare and needs no refrigeration. Expect to roll it very thin, which will help you achieve a surprisingly flaky crust. This makes just enough dough for a double-crust 9-inch standard pie.

MAKES A DOUBLE CRUST FOR A 9-INCH STANDARD PIE

2 cups all-purpose flour

1 teaspoon salt

$1/2$ cup vegetable oil (Louise uses Wesson)

$1/4$ cup cold whole or reduced-fat (2%) milk

1. Combine the flour and salt in a large bowl. Measure the oil and milk into the same glass measuring cup, but do not stir. Add to the flour and mix briskly to combine. The dough will pull together into a ball.

2. Divide the dough in half, making one half—for the bottom pastry—a little larger than the other. Wrap the smaller half in plastic wrap and leave it at room temperature. Roll the larger half right away and line your pie pan with it. Roll the other half of the pastry as directed in your recipe.

Recipe for Success

▶ Because it is made with oil instead of solid fat, this pie pastry can be—and should be—rolled right away.

▶ Elizabeth's Pie (page 192) instructs you to roll the pastry between 2 sheets of waxed paper. Typically, I use only 1 sheet to roll on, but it works well to use the 2 with that recipe.

"Promises and piecrust are made to be broken."

—JONATHAN SWIFT

Louise Piper, Iowa Pie Maker

As pie makers go, Louise Piper is something of a legend in the modern-day annals of the Iowa State Fair. It takes a bit of prying, but when pressed, this modest registered nurse will tell you that she's won more than her share of ribbons at the fair, one of the largest in the country. In 1992 and 1997, she took home the pie sweepstakes, the prize awarded to the winner of the most blue ribbons in the division. She's won the best pie overall "two or three times" and a fistful of second- and third-place ribbons. Her recipe for Elizabeth's Pie (page 192) won a second-place red ribbon in 2003.

With that sort of resumé, I thought that Louise would be a good one to ask about what it takes to make a prize-winning pie. She was happy to share some advice.

- ▶ "Make your edges as attractive as possible." Louise has learned that appearance really counts and an attractive edge always scores with the judges. She makes a pretty straightforward scalloped edge, using essentially the same technique I do (see page 16).

- ▶ "Use pastry cutouts" (see page 19)—again, because they add to the overall good looks of the pie. She likes to arrange six leaf cutouts in a circle on top of a pie, about one inch in from the edge. She adds them to the top crust about halfway into the baking so that they don't get too dark.

- ▶ "Bake only one pie at a time." It takes longer that way, especially if you're entering more than one pie, "but the pie bakes and browns more evenly."

- ▶ "Use sugar and milk for the glaze." Nothing fancy, she says, but the combination does a good job of making a golden crust. She sprinkles the sugar first, then drizzles on the milk.

- ▶ "Do something a little different." You get points for originality. If she wins a prize for one of her pies, she won't enter the same recipe again in successive years.

- ▶ "Use the best fruit and ingredients you can. Most of us who enter pies agree that the closer to home you get your ingredients, the better the pie."

Tender Cream Cheese Pastry

When I have a very delicate filling or a pie that doesn't require the sturdiest of crusts, I often turn to this pastry. Rich, with a slightly tangy flavor, it's great for turnovers and other little pies. Be aware that cream cheese pastry has a tendency to soften up fairly quickly when you roll it. The warm summer months can wreak havoc on this dough in an un-air-conditioned kitchen. If the dough does start to get soft and sticks to your rolling pin, simply slide the pastry—waxed paper and all—onto a baking sheet and put it in the fridge for five minutes before proceeding. The best way to mix this is with a large stand mixer. If you don't have one, use the hand method.

MAKES A SINGLE OR DOUBLE CRUST FOR A 9-INCH STANDARD PIE OR 9¹/₂-INCH DEEP-DISH PIE

FOR A SINGLE CRUST

¹/₂ cup (1 stick) unsalted butter, softened

4 ounces (half an 8-ounce package) full-fat cream cheese, softened

¹/₄ teaspoon salt

1 tablespoon confectioners' sugar, sifted

1¹/₂ cups all-purpose flour

FOR A DOUBLE CRUST

1 cup (2 sticks) unsalted butter, softened

One 8-ounce package full-fat cream cheese (don't use lowfat or nonfat), softened

¹/₂ teaspoon salt

2 tablespoons sifted confectioners' sugar

2³/₄ cups all-purpose flour

1. TO MAKE WITH AN ELECTRIC MIXER Combine the butter, cream cheese, and salt in the bowl of a stand mixer fitted with the flat beater attachment. Blend for 30 to 45 seconds on medium-low speed. Stop once or twice, if necessary, to scrape the build-up from the beater. Stopping the machine before each addition, first add the confectioners' sugar and ¹/₂ cup (1 cup for double crust) of the flour. With the mixer on low, blend until the flour is incorporated. Add another ¹/₂ cup (1 cup for double crust) of the flour and blend. Add the remaining flour. When all of the flour has been added and the dough starts to ball up around the beater, stop the machine. Remove the bowl and scrape the dough onto a lightly floured work surface.

TO MAKE BY HAND Using a wooden spoon, cream the butter, cream cheese, and salt together in a large bowl. Stir in the confectioners' sugar, then add the flour about ¹/₂ cup at a time, stirring well after each addition. When the dough coheres, turn it out onto a floured surface.

2. Gently knead 2 or 3 times. Divide the dough into 2 pieces. If you're making a double crust, make one piece—the bottom pastry—a little larger than the other. If you're making a single crust, make the pieces the same size. Knead each piece into a ball, then flatten it into a disk about ³/₄ inch thick. Wrap the disks in plastic and refrigerate for at least an hour, preferably longer, until firm enough to roll but not too solid.

Recipe for Success

▸ The temperature of the butter and cream cheese will have an impact on how easily and successfully the dough is mixed. Be sure the butter is yielding but not squishy soft. The same goes for the cream cheese. If the ingredients are too cold, you run the risk of overmixing the dough, resulting in a tough crust. If they're too warm, the butter will start to melt into the dough, resulting in a less tender pastry.

▸ The dough may be frozen for up to a month.

Patsy's Cottage Cheese Pastry

This is the pastry that my friend Patsy Jamieson uses for her freeform pies (see pages 158 and 187). As she says, it's pretty much foolproof and it's a cinch to make in a food processor. I recommend it for just about any *crostata*-like pie, but do note that it contains a fair amount of sugar and browns easily. Keep a close eye on it during the last few minutes of baking, and cover the pie with aluminum foil if it starts to get too dark.

MAKES ENOUGH PASTRY FOR 1 LARGE FREEFORM PIE

2 cups all-purpose flour

2 teaspoons baking powder

¹/₂ teaspoon salt

4 teaspoons cold unsalted butter, cut into ¹/₄-inch pieces

³/₄ cup lowfat cottage cheese

¹/₂ cup sugar

¹/₄ cup canola oil or other vegetable oil

2 tablespoons lowfat milk

1¹/₂ teaspoons vanilla extract

1. In a medium-size bowl, combine the flour, baking powder, and salt. Whisk well to mix. Add the butter and blend with a pastry blender or rub between your fingers until the mixture is crumbly and the butter is broken into small bits.

2. Purée the cottage cheese in a food processor. Add the sugar, oil, milk, and vanilla. Process until smooth, stopping once or twice to scrape down the bowl. Add the dry mixture to the processor bowl and pulse several times, just until the dough clumps together. Do not overmix.

3. Turn the dough out onto a lightly floured work surface and knead several times. Shape the dough into a ball, then flatten it into a thick disk. Sprinkle the dough with flour, then wrap in plastic. Refrigerate for at least 30 minutes or up to 3 hours before rolling.

Recipe for Success

▶ Patsy is the food editor of *Eating Well* magazine, which specializes in healthy, lowfat cooking. Thus, she uses lowfat dairy products for this dough. I've also used full-fat products, which work equally well.

Dolores's Skillet Crust

Here is a simple, made-in-a-skillet pie crust that, as my friend Dolores Kostelni says, even skittish pie makers will find a dream to prepare. She uses it with her strawberry and rhubarb pie on page 144, but I see no reason why it wouldn't work for all kinds of fruit pies.

MAKES ENOUGH FOR A CRUMB-TOPPED 9¹/₂-INCH DEEP-DISH PIE

2¹/₄ cups all-purpose flour

1 cup sugar

¹/₄ teaspoon salt (Dolores doesn't call for it, but I suggest a little)

³/₄ cup (1¹/₂ sticks) unsalted butter

1 teaspoon vanilla extract

1. Combine the flour, sugar, and salt in a medium-size bowl. Set aside.

2. Melt the butter in a very large skillet over medium to low heat. Stir in the vanilla. Add the dry mixture and turn off the heat. Stir the flour and butter with a wooden spoon until the mixture is evenly mixed. Be patient: it will be a little clumpy, but just keep working it. Set the crumbs aside to cool for several minutes.

3. When the crumbs are cool enough to handle, transfer about two-thirds of them to a buttered 9¹/₂-inch deep-dish pie pan. Press them into the bottom and up the side of the pan.

Recipe for Success

▶ Make sure to use a large skillet, preferably one with tall, straight sides, so that the mixture doesn't spill over the edge when you stir.

▶ Do melt the butter gently. You're not trying to brown it.

Simple Press-In Pie Pastry

Press-in pastry, sometimes called pat-in pastry, can be made any number of ways. Some recipes start with soft butter, and some—such as this one—start with cold. This is fairly similar to the other pastries in this collection, with a couple of differences: it has more sugar and more butter, which makes the dough a little easier to handle and keeps it good and tender. The extra sweetener also allows you to use part of the pastry, if you like, for a crumb topping. A food processor makes short work of the preparation.

MAKES ENOUGH FOR ONE 9^1/$_2$-INCH DEEP-DISH PIE SHELL, ONE 9-INCH STANDARD PIE SHELL AND CRUMB TOPPING, OR SEVERAL INDIVIDUAL-SIZE PIES

1^3/$_4$ cups all-purpose flour

^{1}/$_4$ cup sugar

^{1}/$_2$ teaspoon salt

10 tablespoons (1^1/$_4$ sticks) cold unsalted butter, cut into ^{1}/$_4$-inch pieces

2^1/$_2$ tablespoons cold water

1. Combine the flour, sugar, and salt in a food processor. Pulse to mix. Scatter the butter over the dry ingredients and pulse until thoroughly combined. The butter should be nearly undetectable. Sprinkle the water over the mixture. Pulse 4 or 5 times, then fluff with a fork. Continue to pulse until the mixture forms fine crumbs that can be pressed together.

2. Transfer the crumbs to a pie pan and press them evenly into the bottom and up the side of the pan. For fruit pies, place in the freezer for 15 minutes before filling. For cream pies and other pies, place in the freezer for 15 minutes, then fully prebake and let cool according to the instructions on page 16.

Recipe for Success

▶ This isn't necessary, but when I'm saving half of this for a crumb topping, I like to mix the reserved portion with an additional 2 tablespoons sugar, rubbing it in gently. It makes for a slightly sweeter topping, more like the others in this collection.

▶ Note that the butter and dry mixture are blended more thoroughly here than in other pastry recipes. This makes for a crust that's a little more crumbly in texture and less likely to suffer the toughening consequences of overhandling.

Meringue Pie Crust

This meringue crust is the shell for my angel pies (see pages 188 and 419), so named because they're nearly light enough to float away. A meringue crust can be baked in a pie pan, but I've experimented with a variety of methods and this is by far the most successful, with a sheet of parchment paper placed between the meringue and the baking sheet. You have to shape the crust somewhat with your rubber spatula, and flare up the sides to help contain the filling, but that's child's play. Once you've mastered this recipe, you'll be looking for excuses to make it frequently.

MAKES 1 LARGE PIE SHELL

4 large egg whites, at room temperature

$1/4$ teaspoon cream of tartar

$1/2$ cup superfine sugar

1 teaspoon vanilla extract

1. Preheat the oven to 250°F. Get out a large baking sheet and line it with parchment paper. Grease the parchment very lightly. Set aside.

2. Using an electric mixer, beat the egg whites in a clean, dry large bowl on medium-high speed until they hold soft peaks. Beat in the cream of tartar. Gradually add the sugar, 1 tablespoon at a time, until the whites are thick and glossy but not dry. Add the vanilla and beat briefly.

3. Using a large rubber spatula, mound the meringue in the center of the parchment paper. Smooth it into a large, flat circle about 11 inches in diameter. Flare the edges upward, creating sidewalls. They needn't be too tall unless your filling is on the runny side. (The ones in this book are not.)

4. Place on the center oven rack and bake, without opening the oven, until the shell has a medium-golden color and a good crisp exterior, about $1^{1}/2$ hours. Let the pie shell cool in the closed oven for 1 hour.

5. Carefully transfer the shell, on the paper, to a cooling rack. Let cool thoroughly, then fill and serve. If you're not using it right away, wrap well in plastic and store at room temperature.

Recipe for Success

▶ Remember the rule for separating eggs: do it while they're cold, but beat the whites when they're at room temperature. To hasten the warming process, you can put your bowl of egg whites inside another bowl of very warm water. Stir them with a wooden spoon to warm them evenly. Use a metal bowl for the whites if you're doing this. It will warm the whites much more quickly than a glass or ceramic bowl.

▶ Even if you have a large nonstick baking sheet, I recommend using the parchment paper. It makes handling the meringue that much easier.

Graham Cracker Crumb Crust

Graham cracker crumb crusts are great for all kinds of pies, especially creamy pies and ice cream pies. If you find yourself making this kind of crust often, keep a box of graham cracker crumbs on hand rather than starting with crackers and grinding them yourself. It's just faster and a lot more convenient that way. By the way, to make $1^3/_4$ cups graham cracker crumbs, you'll need to use about 12 whole crackers. Grind them to a fine meal in a food processor, or stick them in a zipper-topped plastic storage bag and roll over them with a rolling pin.

MAKES ENOUGH FOR ONE 9-INCH STANDARD OR 9$^1/_2$-INCH DEEP-DISH PIE SHELL

$1^3/_4$ cups graham cracker crumbs

2 tablespoons firmly packed light brown sugar

$^1/_2$ teaspoon ground cinnamon

Big pinch of salt

6 tablespoons ($^3/_4$ stick) unsalted butter, melted

1. Preheat the oven to 350°F. Lightly butter your choice of pie pan and set aside.

2. Combine the graham cracker crumbs, brown sugar, cinnamon, and salt in a large bowl. Mix briefly with your fingers. Add the butter and incorporate well, mixing first with a fork, then with your hands, rubbing thoroughly to form evenly dampened crumbs.

3. Spread the crumbs evenly and loosely in the pan, pressing them into the bottom and up the side. Refrigerate for 5 to 10 minutes.

4. Place on the center oven rack and bake for 7 minutes. Let cool on a wire rack before filling. For ice cream pies and other icebox pies, refrigerate the thoroughly cooled pie shell for 10 minutes before filling.

VANILLA WAFER CRUMB CRUST Substitute 1¾ cups finely ground vanilla wafers for the graham cracker crumbs. (You'll need to start with about 4 cups crumbled cookies. I use Nabisco Nilla Wafers.) Add 2 tablespoons flour to the dry mixture and mix as above, adding 1 to 2 teaspoons water to help hold it together.

Recipe for Success

▶ I like brown sugar rather than granulated sugar in my graham cracker crusts, because brown sugar has a certain amount of stickiness that helps hold the crust together. Incidentally, a tiny bit of water will make a graham cracker crust easier to press into the pan. While you're mixing your crust and your hands are still covered with crumbs, dampen your fingertips under running water, then shake them into the crumb mixture. Continue to mix; you'll see the difference right away.

Those Crumbly Crumb Crusts

You know how graham cracker and other crumb crusts can sometimes be a little crumbly and resist your best efforts to press them into the pan? Well, here's a little tip. If that happens to you, mix 1 tablespoon flour into the dry ingredients, then add about 1 teaspoon water along with the butter. Mix well, using your hands to rub everything together thoroughly. Modest amounts of these 2 ingredients can make a once uncooperative crumb crust behave splendidly.

Nutty Graham Cracker Crust

This nut variation can be used wherever a plain graham cracker crust is specified. It tastes delicious and has, as you might expect, a distinct nutty flavor that complements many pie fillings. Try it using walnuts, pecans, dry-roasted peanuts, or natural (undyed) pistachios.

MAKES ENOUGH FOR ONE 9-INCH STANDARD OR 9^1/$_2$-INCH DEEP-DISH PIE SHELL

^{3}/$_4$ cup coarsely chopped nuts of your choice

2 tablespoons firmly packed light brown sugar

2 tablespoons all-purpose flour

1 cup plus 2 tablespoons graham cracker crumbs

^{1}/$_4$ teaspoon ground cinnamon

Big pinch of salt

^{1}/$_4$ cup (^{1}/$_2$ stick) unsalted butter, melted

1. Preheat the oven to 350°F. Lightly butter your choice of pie pan and set aside.

2. Combine the nuts, brown sugar, and flour in a food processor and process in a number of long bursts until the nuts are very finely chopped. Dump the mixture into a large bowl. Run your fingers through them, breaking up any bigger pieces the machine might have missed. Stir in the graham cracker crumbs, cinnamon, and salt. Add the butter and incorporate well. Mix first with a fork, then with your hands, and rub everything together thoroughly to form evenly dampened crumbs.

3. Spread the crumbs evenly and loosely in the pie pan, pressing them into the bottom and up the side. Refrigerate for 5 to 10 minutes.

4. Place on the center oven rack and bake for 7 minutes. Let cool on a wire rack before filling. For ice cream pies and other icebox pies, refrigerate the thoroughly cooled pie shell for 10 minutes before filling.

Recipe for Success

▶ If you happen to have a small amount of several different nuts on hand or you just want to mix things up, this crust tastes great made with more than one kind of nut. Simply use ^{3}/$_4$ cup total.

Chocolate Wafer Crumb Crust

Here is a good, basic recipe to use whenever you want an easy-to-make chocolate crust. I prefer Nabisco Famous Chocolate Wafers.

MAKES ENOUGH FOR ONE 9-INCH STANDARD OR 9¹/₂-INCH DEEP-DISH PIE SHELL

30 chocolate wafers

2 tablespoons firmly packed light brown sugar

1 tablespoon all-purpose flour

Big pinch of salt

1/4 cup (1/2 stick) unsalted butter, melted

1. Preheat the oven to 350°F. Lightly butter your pie pan.

2. Combine the wafers, brown sugar, flour, and salt in a food processor. Using long pulses, grind the wafers to a very fine texture. They should be both slightly gritty and floury. Dump the crumbs into a large bowl and add the butter. Mix, first with a fork, then with your hands, rubbing thoroughly to blend. If the mixture still seems a little crumbly, drizzle on 1/2 teaspoon water and rub again.

3. Spread the crumbs evenly in the pie pan, pressing them into the bottom and up the side. Refrigerate for 5 to 10 minutes.

4. Place on the center oven rack and bake for 6 minutes. Let cool on a wire rack before filling. For ice cream pies and other icebox pies, refrigerate the thoroughly cooled pie shell for 10 minutes before filling.

Recipe for Success

▸ I like to refrigerate all my crumb crusts for 5 to 10 minutes before I bake them. It helps firm up the crumbs and keep them in place while the crust bakes.

Julia Child's Rolling Pins

"When Julia declared (while tossing one over her shoulder) that the rolling pins found in most American kitchens were 'toys,' she proceeded to show her television viewers what real French rolling pins ('the sports car of the pin world') were all about. She pulled out a heavy wooden pin, a solid piece of smooth dense wood with no handles measuring over 19 inches long. Julia stored her rolling pins in a copper stock pot on top of a counter in the pastry pantry, just off the main kitchen. There are six rolling pins—each distinctive—in the collection."

—Julia Child's Kitchen at the Smithsonian, www.americanhistory.si.edu/juliachild

Oreo Crumb Crust

I like this simple crumb crust, using one of America's favorite cookies, for many of my icebox and ice cream pies. It's a snap to make in a food processor.

MAKES ENOUGH FOR ONE 9-INCH STANDARD OR 9¹/₂-INCH DEEP-DISH PIE SHELL

3 cups coarsely broken Oreo cookies (18 to 20 cookies)

Pinch of ground cinnamon

2 tablespoons unsalted butter, melted

2 to 3 teaspoons milk

1. Preheat the oven to 325°F.

2. Combine the Oreo cookies and cinnamon in a food processor. Pulse repeatedly in long bursts to make fine crumbs. Transfer the crumbs to a large bowl. Add the butter and mix well, first with a fork, then with your hands, rubbing the mixture until evenly combined. Add the milk and rub again until the crumbs clump together when pressed between your fingers.

3. Transfer the crumbs to a 9-inch standard or 9¹/₂-inch deep-dish pie pan, pressing them into the bottom and about halfway up the side—higher if using the smaller pan. Refrigerate for 5 to 10 minutes.

4. Place on the center oven rack and bake for 6 minutes. Transfer to a wire rack and let cool thoroughly. Refrigerate for 10 minutes before filling.

Recipe for Success

▶ If you're improvising an ice cream pie made with Oreo cookies, use more Oreos in the filling and on top. Just smooth a thick layer of ice cream in the shell, embed a thick layer of broken cookies, and add more ice cream. Sprinkle the top—especially if the top layer is whipped cream—with finely ground Oreos. You'll never hear any complaints about too many Oreos.

Amaretti Crumb Crust

Here's a clever idea for a pie crust from my friends at the Millbrook Inn in Waitsfield, Vermont. The pie they make with this crust (see page 565) has a delicious amaretto fudge filling—a perfect match with the dry little Italian cookies known as amaretti. If you can't find amaretti at your local supermarket, ask if the store will order them for you.

MAKES ENOUGH FOR ONE 9¹/₂-INCH DEEP-DISH PIE

6 tablespoons (³/₄ stick) unsalted butter, cut into pieces

1 ounce unsweetened chocolate, coarsely chopped

1¹/₄ cups amaretti crumbs (see Recipe for Success)

2 tablespoons sugar

1. Combine the butter and chocolate in a small saucepan over low heat, stirring until melted. Let cool to room temperature.

2. Meanwhile, combine the amaretti crumbs and sugar in a medium-size bowl. Add the chocolate mixture and stir well to combine. Transfer the crumbs to a pie pan, pressing them into the bottom and up the side. Refrigerate for 5 to 10 minutes.

Recipe for Success

▶ If you can't find the amaretti at your supermarket, try an Italian market. Some places carry them only around the holidays.

▶ To crush the amaretti, simply put them in a sturdy zipper-topped plastic storage bag and roll them thoroughly with a rolling pin.

▶ If you like, you can make this crust in a 9- or 9¹/₂-inch (3-inch-deep) springform pan. Simply press the crumbs into the pan as described above. During baking, put a large aluminum foil–lined baking sheet on the rack below to catch any butter that might leak out of the pan.

Choco-Nut Press-In Pie Crust

This recipe was given to me by the good folks at the Patchwork Quilt Country Inn in Middlebury, Indiana. They use it to make their wildly popular Coffee Toffee Pie, an exquisite dessert. As I explain in the pie recipe (see page 538), this is something of an unorthodox crust, but it works well. Although I haven't tried it, I think it would also work with many of the icebox and ice cream pies in this collection, especially those featuring chocolate.

MAKES ENOUGH FOR ONE 9-INCH STANDARD OR 9¹/₂-INCH DEEP-DISH PIE SHELL

2 ounces unsweetened chocolate, coarsely chopped

¹/₂ cup firmly packed light brown sugar

³/₄ cup coarsely chopped walnuts

1 box Jiffy pie crust mix

2 to 2¹/₂ tablespoons cold water, as needed

¹/₂ teaspoon vanilla extract

1. Preheat the oven to 350°F. Lightly butter the pie pan of your choice.

2. Put the chocolate in a food processor and pulse until well ground. Add the brown sugar and pulse again, grinding the chocolate more finely. Add the walnuts and pulse briefly to finely chop the nuts. Dump the mixture into a large bowl and add the pie crust mix. Toss well with your hands until evenly mixed. Blend 2 tablespoons of the water and the vanilla together in a cup. Drizzle the mixture over the dry ingredients and mix thoroughly until the crumbs can be easily packed. If necessary, add another ¹/₂ tablespoon water to make a packable mixture.

3. Spread the crumbs evenly in the prepared pan, pressing them evenly into the bottom and up the side. Refrigerate for 10 minutes.

4. Place on the center oven rack and bake until the crust turns a shade or two darker, about 12 minutes. Let cool on a wire rack before filling. For ice cream pies and other icebox pies, refrigerate the thoroughly cooled pie shell for 10 minutes before filling.

Recipe for Success

▶ As you work the mixture with your hands once you've added the water, it may still seem dry. If so, don't be shy about adding that last ¹/₂ tablespoon water. The real test is whether the mixture can be packed, since it needs to stay in place against the side of the pan. Pinch it to find out.

Pie in the Eye

According to reports by CNN and the British Broadcasting Corporation (BBC), an increasing number of world figures are being targeted by subversive bakers with a penchant for pie throwing. High-profile victims of pie attacks include Bill Gates, former Canadian prime minister Jean Chrétien, and Dutch finance minister Gerrit Zalm, who was beaned with an organic banana cream pie at the opening of the Amsterdam Stock Exchange in 1999. One observer, Rodney Barker of the London School of Economics, thinks it's the anarchist's way of knocking down the high and mighty a notch or two. "The whole thing about cream pies," he reportedly told CNN, "is that it allows you to make your point without actually hurting anybody."

Lest you believe these pie throwers are without scruples, activists abide by a "pie wielder's code." The pie must be "deposited lovingly" rather than simply thrown. The attacker should try to wear some sort of silly costume. And the attack should humiliate but not injure.

Of course, the pie can't be second-rate. "We use only the finest patisserie," one pie thrower told a reporter for Britain's *Observer* newspaper, "ordered at the last minute from small local bakeries. Quality is everything."

For home pie bakers like you and me, summer arrives bearing far more quandaries than answers—most of them, of course, arising from the embarrassment of possible pie choices. Strawberry or strawberry-rhubarb? Plain peach, white peach, or peach-cherry? Double crust or almond crumb topping? Should a home cook be inclined to devote an entire summer to little else than

A Profusion of Summer Fruit Pies

the baking of fruit pies—and I've come pretty darn close—it would still be nearly impossible to cover all the bases. • Nonetheless, we give it our best shot, because this window of opportunity doesn't last forever. Indeed, against summer's typically casual stride, keeping pace with the steady parade of glorious summer fruits is a challenge to even the most dedicated pie baker. Mini fruit seasons arrive in full glory, collide with one another, and then depart until next year. Experienced pie makers anticipate and seize these fleeting moments.

Given the rather generous section that follows, I'm afraid I've done little to help you narrow your summer pie-making choices (especially when you consider that I don't even include berry pies here; they have their own chapter). The aforementioned peach pies are covered quite thoroughly, as are cherry, plum, apricot, and rhubarb—alone and in combination with one another. Many sport crumb toppings, while others have full top crusts or lattice crusts—always a head-turning way to finish a fruit pie. So, you have some serious pie-baking decisions to make.

Let me leave you with this one piece of advice—and it's not the only time you'll hear me mention it—to help you narrow your choices: time your pies to the market. Get the best fruit you can at the peak of its season and only then pick a pie to bake. As any experienced pie baker will tell you, choosing good fruit is about 75 percent of the battle.

Tips for Baking Sensational Summer Fruit Pies

▶ If possible, buy fruit the same day you plan to make your pie. Scrutinize it carefully. If you're buying a quantity of fruit, inspect each piece for signs of spoilage or mold.

▶ Don't hesitate to take a bite out of a piece of fruit to check the flavor and texture. I do this frequently (and, of course, always offer to pay the cashier a dime for my sampling). I'd rather buy one lousy peach than eight, then have to return them.

▶ Store your fruit properly once you get it home. Fresh fruit is so expensive these days that few of us can afford to lose any of it due to our own neglect. Don't store peaches and other stone fruit in a bag in one big jumble on the counter. Separate the fruit so it doesn't touch and bruise.

▶ Summer fruit can be very juicy, so always put a large aluminum foil–lined baking sheet on the rack below the pie during the second half of the baking to catch any spills.

▶ Don't underbake juicy summer fruit pies. The thickener needs time to "take" so that the juice develops the proper body. Underbaked pies may also have a raw-thickener flavor.

▶ Don't forget the lemon juice in summer fruit pies. Rare is the fruit pie that doesn't benefit from the slight tang of lemon.

▶ As with other fruit pies, let summer fruit pies cool for at least one hour, preferably two or more, before slicing. Otherwise, the filling will be runny and the slices not nearly as neat.

All-Rhubarb Pie

Alaskan Eskimos and Afghans—Waverly Root tells us in *Food* (Simon and Schuster, 1980)—eat rhubarb raw. The rest of us, when we eat it at all, like it cooked in a pie. (Rhubarb is, after all, also known as pie plant.) Here's a pie recipe for those who like their rhubarb straight up, without infringement from other fruit such as strawberries or raspberries, two common pie companions. There's a fair amount of sugar in the pie, to counter rhubarb's tart flavor, and a little orange juice and zest for added zing. Rhubarb gives off a lot of juice, so do let the pie rest for several hours before serving to give the juices plenty of time to set.

MAKES 8 SERVINGS

1 recipe Basic Flaky Pie Pastry, Double Crust (page 32) or Tender Cream Cheese Pastry, Double Crust (page 46), refrigerated

FILLING

5 cups fresh rhubarb stalks sliced crosswise 1/2 inch thick

1 1/4 cups plus 2 tablespoons sugar

2 tablespoons orange juice

Grated zest of 1/2 orange

Big pinch of salt

1/4 teaspoon ground nutmeg

3 tablespoons cornstarch

2 tablespoons cold unsalted butter, cut into small pieces

GLAZE

Milk or light cream

Sugar

1. If you haven't already, prepare the pastry and refrigerate until firm enough to roll, 1 to 1 1/2 hours.

2. On a sheet of lightly floured waxed paper, roll the larger portion of the pastry into a 12-inch circle with a floured rolling pin. Invert the pastry over a 9-inch standard pie pan, center, and peel off the paper. Gently tuck the pastry into the pan, without stretching it, and let the overhang drape over the edge. Place in the refrigerator for 15 minutes.

3. Combine the rhubarb, 1 1/4 cups of the sugar, the orange juice, orange zest, salt, and nutmeg in a large bowl. Mix well, then set aside for 20 minutes. Preheat the oven to 400°F.

4. Combine the remaining 2 tablespoons sugar and the cornstarch in a small bowl, then stir the mixture into the rhubarb. Turn the filling into the chilled pie shell and smooth the top of the fruit with your hands. Dot the filling with the butter.

5. Roll the other half of the pastry into a 10-inch circle on a sheet of lightly floured waxed paper. Moisten the outer edge of the pie shell with a pastry brush. Invert the top pastry over the filling, center, and peel off the paper. Press the top and bottom pastries together along the dampened edge. Using a pair of scissors, trim the pastry to an even 1/2-inch overhang all around. Turn the pastry back and under, sculpting the edge into an upstanding ridge. Poke several steam vents in the top of the pie with a fork or paring knife, including a couple along the edge so you can check the juices there later. To glaze the pie, brush the top pastry with a little milk and sprinkle lightly with sugar.

6. Place the pie on the center oven rack and bake for 30 minutes. Reduce the oven temperature to 375°F and rotate the pie 180 degrees, so that the part that faced the back of the oven now faces forward. Just in case, slide a large aluminum foil–lined baking sheet onto the rack below to catch any spills. Continue to bake until the pie is golden brown,

about 25 minutes. When done, you should notice thick juices bubbling out of the steam vents along the edge.

7. Transfer the pie to a wire rack and let cool for at least 3 hours, preferably longer, before serving.

Recipe for Success

▶ Because of the red color, rhubarb makes an attractive lattice-top pie. Follow the lattice weaving instructions on page 71.

▶ Even though this is an all-rhubarb pie, feel free to substitute a cup or two of raspberries for an equal amount of sliced rhubarb.

▶ If your rhubarb comes with leaves attached, do not eat them. They contain something called oxalic acid, which can cause sickness or even death.

Sumner, Washington, Rhubarb Custard Pie

I had seen several references to Sumner, Washington, declaring the town to be the rhubarb pie capital of the country. I love that sort of boast, so I called the mayor, Barbara Skinner, and asked her if she'd care to comment. She told me, quite frankly, that she wasn't sure where the pie title came from. But she informed me that Sumner—a town of 8,800 in the southern Puget Sound area, where she was born and raised—is in the fertile Puyallup Valley, which produces 90 percent of the rhubarb grown in this country. Fair enough. As the town's mayor, would she be willing to share the best local recipe for rhubarb pie? Indeed, she would, and by the end of the day, she'd sent me this recipe from the local St. Andrew's Church cookbook, adding a note that "everyone in the church is a good cook." They must be, because the pie is quite excellent—a thick layer of rhubarb on top of a very light custard. I think you'll enjoy this quite a bit.

MAKES 8 SERVINGS

1 recipe Basic Flaky Pie Pastry, Single Crust (page 31), refrigerated

FILLING
3 cups diced fresh rhubarb stalks
1 1/2 cups sugar
3 tablespoons all-purpose flour
Big pinch of salt

1/2 teaspoon ground nutmeg
2 large eggs
2 tablespoons milk
1 tablespoon cold butter, cut into small pieces

GARNISH
Fresh Whipped Cream (page 605)

1.   If you haven't already, prepare the pastry and refrigerate until firm enough to roll, about 1 hour.

2.   On a sheet of lightly floured waxed paper, roll the pastry into a 12-inch circle with a floured rolling pin. Invert the pastry over a 9-inch standard pie pan, center, and peel off the paper. Tuck the pastry into the pan, without stretching it, and sculpt the edge into an upstanding ridge. Place in the freezer for 15 minutes. Preheat the oven to 375°F.

3.   Combine the rhubarb, sugar, flour, salt, and nutmeg in a large bowl. Toss well, then set aside for several minutes to juice. Whisk the eggs and milk together in a small bowl. Add to the fruit, stirring well to combine. Scrape the filling into the chilled pie shell, smoothing the top of the fruit with a spoon. Dot the filling with the butter.

4.   Place the pie on the center oven rack and bake until the top is crusted over and the filling is set, 50 to 55 minutes, rotating the pie 180 degrees halfway through the baking, so that the part that faced the back of the oven now faces forward.

5.   Transfer the pie to a wire rack and let cool. Serve barely warm, at room temperature, or chilled, with a dollop of whipped cream.

Recipe for Success

▶ I didn't try this, but Barbara mentioned that adding a couple of drops of red food coloring to the pie will give it a more rhubarb red color.

▶ Don't expect this to bake up like other custard pies. The "custard" here is more of a translucent jelly that settles on the bottom of the pie, not a traditional creamy custard surrounding the fruit.

▶ Be aware that the leaves of the rhubarb plant are toxic and should never be consumed.

Fresh Sweet Cherry Pie with Coconut-Almond Crunch Topping

For most of us, fresh cherry pie is serious business. First, the fruit is generally expensive. Then, even after we've plunked down our cash, there's the matter of the pits, which need to be removed one by one, an undertaking requiring an investment of time and one rather extensive apron to guard against errant juice (see Recipe for Success). With so much at stake, a fresh cherry pie is, justifiably, one of early summer's rare and enduring pleasures. This version incorporates some of my favorite tricks to bring out the best cherries have to offer. I think a shot of cherry liqueur or peach schnapps is a great flavor enhancement, as are a few drops of vanilla. All of it works great in a double crust, but I think a better choice is a classic coconut-almond crunch topping. Do serve this slightly warm, with a big scoop of vanilla ice cream.

MAKES 8 SERVINGS

1 recipe Basic Flaky Pie Pastry, Single Crust (page 31) or Basic Shortening Pie Pastry, Single Crust (page 30), refrigerated

FILLING

4¹/₂ cups fresh sweet cherries, stemmed and pitted

¹/₃ cup plus 3 tablespoons sugar

3 tablespoons cherry liqueur or peach schnapps

2 teaspoons fresh lemon juice

¹/₄ teaspoon vanilla extract

2 tablespoons cornstarch

COCONUT-ALMOND CRUNCH TOPPING

¹/₂ cup sugar

¹/₄ cup whole, slivered, or sliced almonds

³/₄ cup all-purpose flour

¹/₂ cup sweetened flaked coconut

¹/₄ teaspoon salt

5 tablespoons cold unsalted butter, cut into ¹/₄-inch pieces

GARNISH

Vanilla ice cream

1. If you haven't already, prepare the pastry and refrigerate until firm enough to roll, about 1 hour.

2. On a sheet of lightly floured waxed paper, roll the pastry into a 12-inch circle with a floured rolling pin. Invert the pastry over a 9-inch standard pie pan, center, and peel off the paper. Tuck the pastry into the pan, without stretching it, and sculpt the edge into an upstanding ridge. Place in the freezer for 15 minutes. Preheat the oven to 400°F.

3. Combine the cherries, ¹/₃ cup of the sugar, the cherry liqueur, lemon juice, and vanilla in a large bowl. Stir well, then set aside for 15 minutes to juice. In a small bowl, combine the remaining 3 tablespoons sugar and the cornstarch, then stir the mixture into the fruit. Turn the filling into the chilled pie shell, smoothing the top with a spoon. Place the pie on the center oven rack and bake for 30 minutes.

4. Meanwhile, make the topping. Combine the sugar and almonds in a food processor and pulse until the nuts are chopped. Add the flour, coconut, and salt. Pulse briefly to mix. Scatter the butter over the top and pulse until the mixture starts to form gravelly crumbs. Dump the crumbs into a large bowl and rub between your fingers until the mixture forms large, buttery crumbs. Refrigerate until ready to use.

5. Remove the pie from the oven and reduce the temperature to 375°F. Carefully dump the crumbs in the center of the pie, spreading them evenly over the surface with your hands. Tamp them down lightly. Return the pie to the oven, placing it so that the part that faced the back of the oven now faces forward. Just in case, slide a large aluminum foil–lined baking sheet onto the rack below to catch any spills. Bake until the juices bubble thickly around the edge, about 30 minutes. If the top starts to get too brown, cover loosely with aluminum foil for the last 15 minutes.

6. Transfer the pie to a wire rack and let cool. Serve while still barely warm with a scoop of ice cream.

Recipe for Success

> ▶ **To mitigate the juice spatter that always accompanies cherry pitting, I often do this outside on the picnic table. When that's not possible, I work inside a large plastic bag.**

Sing a Song of Sixpence

Sing a song of sixpence,
A pocket full of rye,
Four-and-twenty blackbirds
Baked in a pie.
When the pie was opened,
The birds began to sing,
Wasn't that a dainty dish
To set before the king?

Pitting Cherries

One of my good editor friends swears by the paper clip method for pitting cherries. You take a paper clip, bend it open, stick it into the cherry, and give a gentle push. The pit comes right out, she says. Or maybe you're supposed to pull, not push—I forget. What I do remember is that when she first told me about this trick several years ago, I tried it several times and never could get the knack of it.

When I'm pitting cherries, I like to do it outside at the picnic table, if I can, this being one of the most spatter-prone activities a cook can tackle. Inside or out, I think the best way to pit cherries is to work with your hands inside a plastic bag to help contain the juice. I simply pull off the stems, throw a few cherries in a large clear plastic bag, and give them a good squeeze—not hard enough to crush the cherries, just flatten them somewhat. If the cherries are ripe, this squeeze will free up the pits, although you may have to coax them out with a finger. If the cherries aren't ripe, the pits won't be quite as cooperative.

It's a bit tiresome putting the cherries inside the bag, then taking them out. But if you pick a nice sunny summer day, you'll lose track of time and enjoy yourself thoroughly.

Rainier Cherry Pie with a Grated Top Crust

How could you not like a cherry that tastes something like a peach? That, at least, was my thought when I tasted a Rainier cherry for the first time at my local supermarket. Unlike any other cherry you've ever seen, a Rainier cherry has a peachy yellow skin and flesh, with just a mottled blush of red. To my taste buds, the flavor of the cherry has a hint of vanilla, which I play up with a smidgen of vanilla extract in the filling. This exquisite pie is excellent with peach or vanilla ice cream. Incidentally, if you've never made a grated top crust before, I think you'll be pleasantly surprised. Instead of rolling, you simple grate—or shred—the block of pastry onto the fruit. It's quite easy and attractive.

MAKES 8 TO 10 SERVINGS

1 recipe All-Butter Pie Pastry, Double Crust (page 28) or Basic Flaky Pie Pastry, Double Crust (page 31), modified as instructed in step 1 and refrigerated

FILLING

5 cups fresh Rainier cherries, stemmed and pitted

1/3 cup plus 2 tablespoons granulated sugar

1 tablespoon fresh lemon juice

1/4 teaspoon vanilla extract

2 1/2 tablespoons cornstarch

GLAZE

About 1 tablespoon coarse sugar (see page 69) or granulated sugar

GARNISH

Vanilla or peach ice cream

1. If you haven't already, prepare the pastry. Shape the smaller half into a block rather than a disk. Refrigerate the larger half until firm enough to roll, about 1 hour, and place the other half—the block—in the freezer (see Recipe for Success).

2. On a sheet of lightly floured waxed paper, roll the larger half of the pastry into a 13-inch circle with a floured rolling pin. Invert the pastry over a 9 1/2-inch deep-dish pie pan, center, and peel off the paper. Tuck the pastry into the pan, without stretching it, and sculpt the edge into an upstanding ridge. Place in the freezer for 15 minutes. Preheat the oven to 400°F.

3. In a large bowl, combine the cherries, 1/3 cup of the granulated sugar, the lemon juice, and vanilla. Mix well, then set aside for 10 minutes to juice. Combine the remaining 2 tablespoons granulated sugar and the cornstarch in a small bowl, then stir the mixture into the fruit. Turn the filling into the chilled pie shell and smooth the top of the fruit with your hands or a spoon.

4. Using the large holes of a box grater, grate the other half of the pastry over the top of the fruit, as if it were a block of cheese, covering the filling more or less evenly. Sprinkle the coarse sugar evenly over the pastry.

5. Place the pie on the center oven rack and bake for 30 minutes. Reduce the oven temperature to 375°F and rotate the pie 180 degrees, so that the part that faced the back of the oven now faces forward. Just in case, slide a large aluminum foil–lined baking sheet onto the rack below to catch any spills. Continue to bake until the top is golden brown and the juices bubble thickly around the edge, 25 to 30 minutes.

6. Transfer the pie to a wire rack and let cool for at least 2 hours before serving. Garnish with ice cream.

Recipe for Success

▶ If you have kids who like to bake with you, one of the nice things about making a Rainier cherry pie is the absence of cherry red juices squirting all over creation as you pit the cherries. It's sort of a kid-proof cherry.

▶ Rainier cherries lack the tartness of some cherries, so consider adding an additional $1/2$ tablespoon fresh lemon juice for a little more pucker.

▶ The consistency of the pastry "block" should be firm but not frozen solid.

Coarse Sugar

Granulated sugar is fine for sprinkling on pie pastry. It gives your top crust a fetching golden finish and sandy-sugary texture. When you want a bit more crunch, however, try coarse sugar, also known as sanding sugar. The crunchy texture is especially nice when you have a soft fruit filling, as in the recipe opposite. Keep coarse sugar in a jar or other tightly covered container and store it in your pantry. It's available in several shades of white and golden brown at specialty food stores and from the King Arthur Flour Baker's Catalogue, available online at www.kingarthurflour.com. Try it on muffins, too.

Lattice-Top Deep-Dish Sour Cherry Pie

Sour cherries are prized for the wonderful pies they make. They have a special flavor and unique tartness not found in other types of cherries. In many parts of the country, the trickiest part of making a sour cherry pie is finding the cherries. Not only are they somewhat fragile, but their tartness isn't embraced by consumers who, for the most part, expect cherries to be sweet. If your local supermarket doesn't carry them, check farmers' markets. The key to making a good sour cherry pie, I believe, is to add just enough sugar to tame the tartness, not overwhelm it. The other trick is to use sufficient thickening to gel the prodigious amount of juice. Other than that, I keep the filling fairly simple, with a little lemon juice and zest, a dab of butter, and a pretty lattice top so the bright red cherries can peek through. Do use an extra-deep-dish pie pan, if you have one. This is a very juicy pie, and the added depth will help contain the juice.

MAKES 8 TO 10 SERVINGS

1 recipe Basic Flaky Pie Pastry, Double Crust (page 31) or All-Butter Pie Pastry, Double Crust (page 28), modified as instructed in step 1 and refrigerated

FILLING

6 cups fresh sour cherries, stemmed and pitted

1¼ cups plus 3 tablespoons sugar

¼ cup cornstarch

2 teaspoons fresh lemon juice

Grated zest of 1 lemon

2 tablespoons cold unsalted butter, cut into small pieces

GLAZE

Milk or light cream

Sugar

1. If you haven't already, prepare the pastry as directed, making one half of it just slightly larger than the other. Shape the larger half into a disk and the other half into a square, both about ³/₄ inch thick. Wrap the pastry as usual and refrigerate until firm enough to roll, about 1 hour.

2. On a sheet of lightly floured waxed paper, roll the disk of pastry into a 13½-inch circle with a floured rolling pin. Invert the pastry over a 9½-inch deep-dish pie pan (see Recipe for Success), center, and peel off the paper. Gently tuck the pastry into the pan, without stretching it, and sculpt the overhang into an upstanding ridge. Place in the refrigerator for 15 minutes.

3. Place the cherries in a large bowl. Mix the sugar and cornstarch together in a small bowl, then stir the mixture into the fruit. Stir in the lemon juice and zest. Set aside for 10 minutes to juice. Preheat the oven to 400°F.

4. On another sheet of lightly floured waxed paper, roll the remaining pastry into a 12 x 10-inch rectangle. With a pastry wheel or pizza cutter, cut the pastry into 8 lengthwise strips, each 1¼ inches wide. (In other words, you should have 8 strips measuring 12 inches long and 1¼ inches wide.) Set aside.

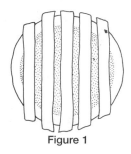

Figure 1

5. Turn the filling into the chilled pie shell, moistening the rim of the shell slightly. Smooth the top of the filling with your hands or a spoon. Dot the filling with the butter. Lay 5 pastry strips vertically across the pie, evenly spaced, as shown in figure 1. Fold back strips 2 and 4 and lay another strip directly across the center of the pie, as shown in figure 2. Unfold the folded strips, then fold back strips 1, 3, and 5. Lay another perpendicular strip across the pie, as shown in figure 3. Unfold the folded strips, then fold up strips 1, 3, and 5 on the other side of the pie. Place another perpendicular strip across the pie, as shown in figure 4, then unfold strips 1, 3, and 5. Trim the strips, then pinch the ends of the strips into the edge of the pastry. Lightly brush the pastry strips with milk and sprinkle the top of the pie with sugar.

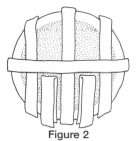

Figure 2

6. Place the pie on the center oven rack and bake for 30 minutes. Reduce the oven temperature to 375°F and rotate the pie 180 degrees, so that the part that faced the back of the oven now faces forward. Just in case, slide a large aluminum foil–lined baking sheet onto the rack below to catch any spills. Continue to bake until the top is golden brown and any visible juices bubble thickly, 35 to 40 minutes.

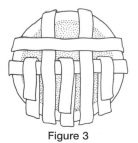

Figure 3

7. Transfer the pie to a wire rack and let cool for at least 2 hours before serving.

Recipe for Success

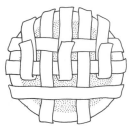

Figure 4

▶ **Ripe sour cherries are very easy to pit. After you pull off the stem, you can simply squeeze the pit out of the stem end.**

▶ **Don't omit the lemon juice and zest, thinking the cherries will be tart enough. The lemon flavor is very good with the cherries.**

About Lattice-Top Pies

Whenever I give a pie-baking demonstration, the part of the program that really brings the house down is when I make a lattice-top pie. The audience is there to learn the nuances of making flaky pastry and how to roll it out without a catastrophe—information they absorb with appreciation. But more often than not, they actually break into applause when they see me assemble a lattice-top pie.

No small part of their exuberance has to do with the fact that they can't believe how easy it is. Most cooks, I'm afraid, believe that nobody other than food stylists and culinary school graduates can actually make a lattice crust. But after they see me demonstrate just how simple it is, they realize this is something they, too, can do right in their own kitchens. (To see just how easy, turn to the diagrams on page 71.)

Here, then, are a few tips for making foolproof lattice-top pies.

> ▶ For clean, even cutting, make sure the dough has been well chilled after rolling. Dough that's room temperature won't have the same clean lines.

> ▶ Don't, however, try to weave the lattice until the chilled strips have warmed up slightly. Otherwise, they'll be stiff, not flexible enough to weave.

> ▶ You'll probably figure this out, but use the shorter strips on the edge of your pie and the longer ones in the center.

> ▶ Don't use whole-grain or nut pastries to make a lattice, if possible. The coarse particles tend to make these pastries prone to crumbling when handled too much.

> ▶ Colorful fruit tends to make the prettiest lattice-top pies, given the greater contrast between the lighter crust and the dark filling, but don't limit yourself in this way. Some of my favorite lattice pies are made with apples.

Dense Cherry-Almond Coffeecake Pie

I have in my files all manner of almond cakes, all of which I'm wild about, from chocolate tortes to moist sour cream coffeecakes. I also have this: a pie in the tradition of the latter, just moist and dense enough to require a pastry to contain it. We begin by putting a single layer of cherries in a partially prebaked pie shell. Then a rich sour cream filling, thickened with almond meal and eggs, is poured over the fruit. As it bakes, a delicious cake-like filling forms around the cherries, leaving a lovely golden almond crust on top. Rich and tasty as it is, I love this served just barely warm, with a bit of coffee or vanilla ice cream.

MAKES 10 SERVINGS

1 recipe Basic Flaky Pie Pastry, Single Crust (page 31) or Basic Shortening Pie Pastry, Single Crust (page 30), refrigerated

FILLING

2 cups pitted sweet cherries, fresh or individually frozen (not packed in syrup), partially thawed

1 cup whole almonds

1/3 cup all-purpose flour

1 1/3 cups granulated sugar

1/4 teaspoon salt

3 large eggs, at room temperature

2 large egg yolks, at room temperature

1 cup full-fat sour cream

2 tablespoons firmly packed light brown sugar

2 tablespoons unsalted butter, melted

1 teaspoon vanilla extract

1/4 teaspoon almond extract

1. If you haven't already, prepare the pastry and refrigerate until firm enough to roll, about 1 hour.

2. On a sheet of lightly floured waxed paper, roll the pastry into a 13-inch circle with a floured rolling pin. Invert the pastry over a 9½-inch deep-dish pie pan, center, and peel off the paper. Tuck the pastry into the pan, without stretching it, and sculpt the edge into an upstanding ridge. Place in the freezer for 15 minutes, then partially prebake and let cool according to the instructions on page 16. Reduce the oven temperature to 350°F.

3. Place the cherries on a double layer of paper towels and set them aside for 15 minutes. Meanwhile, combine the almonds, flour, 1/3 cup of the granulated sugar, and the salt in a food processor and pulse until the mixture resembles coarse meal. Set aside.

4. Using an electric mixer, lightly beat the eggs, egg yolks, sour cream, the remaining 1 cup granulated sugar, and the brown sugar until smooth. Blend in the butter and extracts. Stir the almond flour into the liquid, blending until smooth. Arrange the cherries in a single layer in the cooled pie shell. Ladle the filling over the cherries.

5. Place the pie on the center oven rack and bake for 30 minutes, then rotate the pie 180 degrees, so that the side that faced the back of the oven now faces forward. Continue to bake until the filling is set in the center and the surface of the pie is a rich, uniform golden brown, 25 to 30 minutes.

6. Transfer the pie to a wire rack and let cool. Serve just barely warm or at room temperature.

Recipe for Success

▶ Typically, you wouldn't want to drain or blot off any juice when you're making a cherry pie. Because of the cake-like texture of the filling, however, this one is a little different. If too much cherry juice bleeds into the filling, it loses some of its cake-like texture. That's why we drain the cherries first.

▶ Make sure to refrigerate leftovers, but gently rewarm the pie before serving, especially if you're planning to serve it with ice cream.

If You Happen to Get Bored
Waiting for Your Cherry Pie to Bake . . .

. . . try knotting cherry stems with your tongue. But you'll have to be fast to break the record, set in 1999 in Orlando, Florida. In three minutes, Al Gliniecki of Gulf Breeze, Florida, managed to do 39 of them, enough to twist, turn, and ultimately tongue-tie his way into the *Guinness Book of World Records*.

Friske Orchards' Michigan Balaton Cherry Pie

One of the new varieties of cherries available in this country is the Balaton, a European favorite named for a lake in its native Hungary. It has the tangy taste of a sour cherry, but the smooth, satisfying flavor of a sweet one, and a deep burgundy color that makes for a striking pie. After years of experimental plantings in the United States, Balaton cherries are now commercially grown in Michigan, Wisconsin, New York, and Utah. One Michigan farm that does a brisk business in Balaton cherries is Friske Orchards, run by Richard Friske and his family (see box, next page). In addition to selling spectacular homegrown fruit, Friske Orchards produces delicious pies to showcase that fruit. Here is the Balaton cherry pie the Friskes bake, and when you try it, you'll know why they sell as many as 100 of these on a busy fall weekend day. So do try to get your hands on some Balatons, but be advised: once you've tried these cherries, you may not be satisfied with any other kind. Note that the Friskes make this with both a top crust and the very cinnamony crumb topping used here.

MAKES 8 TO 10 SERVINGS

1 recipe Basic Shortening Pie Pastry, Single Crust (page 30) or All-Butter Pie Pastry, Single Crust (page 28), refrigerated

FILLING

4 cups fresh Balaton cherries, stemmed and pitted

1/2 cup granulated sugar

1 1/2 tablespoons cornstarch

1/4 teaspoon almond extract

CINNAMON CRUMB TOPPING

3/4 cup all-purpose flour

1/2 cup quick-cooking rolled oats

1/2 cup firmly packed light brown sugar

2 teaspoons ground cinnamon

1/2 cup (1 stick) cold unsalted butter, cut into 1/4-inch pieces

1. If you haven't already, prepare the pastry and refrigerate until firm enough to roll, about 1 hour.

2. On a sheet of lightly floured waxed paper, roll the pastry into a 12-inch circle with a floured rolling pin. Invert the pastry over a 9-inch standard pie pan, center, and peel off the paper. Tuck the pastry into the pan, without stretching it, and sculpt the overhang into an upstanding ridge. Place in the freezer for 15 minutes.

3. Place the cherries in a large bowl. Mix the granulated sugar and cornstarch together in a small bowl, then stir the mixture into the fruit. Stir in the almond extract. Set aside for 10 minutes. Preheat the oven to 400°F.

4. Scrape the filling into the chilled pie shell, smoothing the fruit with a spoon. Place the pie on the center oven rack and bake for 25 minutes.

5. Meanwhile, make the topping. Combine the flour, oats, brown sugar, and cinnamon in a food processor and pulse to mix. Scatter the butter over the dry ingredients and pulse until the mixture resembles fine crumbs. Transfer to a large bowl and rub the mixture between your fingers to make large, buttery crumbs. Refrigerate until ready to use.

6. After 25 minutes, remove the pie from the oven and reduce the temperature to 375°F. Carefully dump the crumbs in the center of the pie and spread evenly over the surface with your hands. Tamp them down lightly. Return the pie to the oven, placing it so that the part that faced the back of the oven now faces forward. Just in case, slide a large aluminum foil–lined baking sheet onto the rack below to catch any spills. Continue to bake until the juices bubble thickly around the edge, about 25 minutes.

7. Transfer the pie to a wire rack and let cool for at least 2 hours before serving.

Recipe for Success

▸ **At Friske Orchards, they use a shortening crust, but the European heritage of the Balaton suggests a buttery partnership as well. That's why I also recommend the all-butter crust.**

▸ **The flavor of the fruit really carries this pie, so little is needed by way of enhancements. The little bit of almond extract is the perfect, subtle touch. Even if you like the flavor of almond, don't be tempted to add more, or it may intrude.**

▸ **These are very juicy cherries, so do have your foil-lined baking sheet in place to catch any spills.**

Friske Orchards

Richard Friske knows good pie fruit. He should. His family-owned Friske Orchards grows more than 300 hundred acres' worth in northwestern Michigan's fruit country: red sour cherries, black sweet cherries, Red Haven peaches, and Northern Spy apples. Much of this fruit is sold fresh at Friske's farm stand, a lot goes into the hundreds of homemade pies the orchard sells, and the rest is frozen. Friske is something of a pioneer in the marketing of what's known as IQF—individually quick frozen—fruit. Properly handled and frozen, Richard says, IQF fruit is as close to using fresh fruit as possible.

"To make a superior pie, you have to start with superior fruit," he advises. That requires thoughtful stewardship of the land and intensive orchard management. Friske's cherry trees, for instance, are pruned aggressively to allow for as much sunlight as possible in order to yield fruit with a deeper color.

If you live in Michigan, you're in luck: Friske Orchards sells its frozen fruit, including sliced apples—which, Richard says, are indistinguishable from fresh in a baked pie—through a network of food markets in the state. The rest of us can have his frozen fruit shipped overnight. For price information and availability, call Friske Orchards at (231) 599-2604, or visit Friske's Web site, www.friske.com.

"Floating Top" Cherry–Vanilla Bean Pie

Here are a couple of neat tricks you can use on a lot of fruit pies. The first is including a vanilla bean in the filling. I usually keep a vanilla bean or two around the kitchen for one reason or another. Sometimes I'll have a slit section, or a section I've scraped the seeds from but haven't discarded, since there's still a lot of flavor to be gleaned from it. Baking a section of slit bean in a fruit filling releases the vanilla flavor nicely. I particularly like the flavor it adds to cherry, peach, and pear pies. The other thing I do here is use a "floating" top crust. A floating crust is not attached to the sides. Rather, a circle of dough—slightly smaller than the top of the pie—is simply placed over the filling; it just floats there, in other words. The juice bubbles up and makes a ring around the pie: the darker the fruit, such as blackberries or cherries, the more striking the effect.

MAKES 8 TO 10 SERVINGS

1 recipe Basic Flaky Pie Pastry, Double Crust (page 31) or Extra-Flaky Pie Pastry, Double Crust (page 34), refrigerated

FILLING

4 cups fresh sweet cherries, stemmed and pitted

1/3 cup plus 2 tablespoons sugar

2 teaspoons fresh lemon juice

2 tablespoons cornstarch

Pinch of ground nutmeg

One 3- to 4-inch section of vanilla bean, slit lengthwise

GLAZE

Milk or light cream

Sugar

1.   If you haven't already, prepare the pastry and refrigerate until firm enough to roll, about 1 hour.

2.   On a sheet of lightly floured waxed paper, roll half of the pastry into a 12-inch circle with a floured rolling pin. Invert the pastry over a 9-inch standard pie pan, center, and peel off the paper. Tuck the pastry into the pan, without stretching it, and sculpt the edge into an upstanding ridge. Place in the freezer for 15 minutes. When the 15 minutes are up, preheat the oven to 400 degrees.

3.   Combine the cherries, 1/3 cup of the sugar, and the lemon juice in a medium-size bowl. Mix well, then set aside for 10 minutes to juice. Mix together the remaining 2 tablespoons sugar and the cornstarch in a small bowl, then stir the mixture into the fruit along with the nutmeg. Set aside.

4.   On another sheet of floured waxed paper, roll the other half of the pastry into a 10-inch circle. If you're not particularly steady-handed, use a bowl or another template for the next step. Cut a 7-inch circle in the pastry using a paring knife or pastry wheel. Remove the outer pastry scraps and save for another use. Keep the circle of pastry nearby.

5.   Turn the filling into the chilled pie shell, smoothing the top with a spoon. Bury the vanilla bean in the fruit, right in the center of the pie (so you can find it easily later). Invert the top pastry over the filling, center, and peel off the paper. Brush the top pastry with milk and sprinkle with sugar.

6.   Place the pie on the center oven rack and bake for 30 minutes. Reduce the oven temperature to 375°F and rotate the pie 180 degrees, so that the part that faced the back of the oven now faces forward. Just in case, slide a large aluminum foil–lined baking sheet onto the rack below to catch any spills. Bake until the top of the pie is golden brown and the juices bubble thickly all around the edge, 25 to 30 minutes.

7. Transfer the pie to a wire rack and let cool for at least 2 hours. Remove the vanilla bean before serving.

Recipe for Success

▶ Another attractive way to do this is to use decorative pastry cutouts (see page 19), such as diamonds or circles, to "attach" the floating crust to the rim. Lay 6 or 8 cutouts evenly around the perimeter, placing them partly on the floating pastry and partly on the rim, spanning the fruit filling.

Poetic Pies

From the oven hot and steaming,
With the ruby bubbles gleaming,
As they boil up through the craters in little puffs and sighs,
There's restless invitation
To the palate's delectation
In the odor and the look of those "poetic" cherry pies.

Oh, their juice than wine is richer!
It is poured from out the pitcher
Where is stored the luscious nectar distilled at summer's prime.
Show these pies to Doctor Tanner,
He would forthwith strike his banner
And put off the fasting racket to a more convenient time.

—Ellen P. Allerton, *Walls of Corn and Other Poems*

Double-Cherry Pie

This delicious pie is from the **Cherry Marketing Institute**, whose job it is to promote the use of sour cherries, also known as pie cherries or tart cherries. (The most common variety, incidentally, is the Montmorency.) This recipe includes two kinds of sour cherries—fresh and dried—along with sugar and just a bit of butter, nutmeg, and almond extract to highlight the flavor of the cherries.

MAKES 8 TO 10 SERVINGS

1 recipe Basic Flaky Pie Pastry, Double Crust (page 31) or Tender Cream Cheese Pastry, Double Crust (page 46), refrigerated

FILLING

$4^1/_2$ cups pitted sour cherries, fresh, individually frozen (not packed in syrup; partially thawed), or canned (drained)

1 cup dried sour cherries

1 cup sugar

2 tablespoons quick-cooking tapioca

$^1/_2$ teaspoon almond extract

$^1/_4$ teaspoon ground nutmeg

1 tablespoon cold unsalted butter, cut into small pieces

GLAZE

Milk or light cream

Sugar

1. If you haven't already, prepare the pastry and refrigerate until firm enough to roll, about 1 hour.

2. On a sheet of lightly floured waxed paper, roll the larger portion of the pastry into a 13-inch circle with a floured rolling pin. Invert the pastry over a $9^1/_2$-inch deep-dish pie pan, center, and peel off the paper. Gently tuck the pastry into the pan, without stretching it, and let the overhang drape over the edge. Place in the refrigerator for 15 minutes.

3. Combine the pitted cherries, dried cherries, sugar, tapioca, and almond extract in a large bowl and mix well. Set aside for 10 minutes to juice. Preheat the oven to 375°F.

4. Roll the other half of the pastry into a 10-inch circle on a sheet of lightly floured waxed paper. Turn the filling into the chilled pie shell, smoothing the top of the fruit with a spoon. Sprinkle the nutmeg over the fruit and dot the filling with the butter. Moisten the edge of the pie shell with a pastry brush. Invert the top pastry over the filling, center, and peel off the paper. Press the top and bottom pastries together along the dampened edge. Using a knife, trim the pastry flush with the edge of the pan, then crimp the edge with a fork. Poke several steam vents in the top of the pie with a paring knife, twisting the knife to enlarge the holes slightly. Put a couple of the holes along the edge so you can check the juices there later. To glaze the pie, brush a little milk over the pastry and sprinkle lightly with sugar.

5.   Place the pie on the center oven rack and bake for 30 minutes, then rotate the pie 180 degrees, so that the part that faced the back of the oven now faces forward. Just in case, slide a large aluminum foil–lined baking sheet onto the rack below to catch any drips. Continue to bake until the juices bubble thickly up through the steam vents, 30 to 35 minutes. If the top starts to get too brown, loosely drape a piece of aluminum foil over the pie during the last 15 minutes.

6.   Transfer the pie to a wire rack and let cool for at least 2 hours. This is best eaten slightly warm or at room temperature.

Recipe for Success

▶   **Do try to find sour cherries to make this pie, but don't neglect it if all you can find are sweet cherries. When using sweet, reduce the sugar by about half and add 1 tablespoon fresh lemon juice to the filling.**

▶   **At the very least, you should be able to find the dried sour cherries, most likely at a gourmet or health food store. They're rather expensive, but they're worth the price of admission to make this great pie.**

The Ultimate Four-Cherry Pie

I can't resist a profusion of fresh cherries in the market, a situation that often finds me with several bags of my favorite pie cherries on hand simultaneously: sweet, sour, and the Rainier cherries I like so much for pies. Rummaging further in my pantry, I can nearly always find a partial bag of dried cherries. When all of these are combined in a pie, it makes what I consider the ultimate cherry pie, one in which no one cherry dominates but all contribute to a unique flavor. Add a top crust if you like, but my first choice is this brown sugar topping.

MAKES 8 TO 10 SERVINGS

1 recipe Extra-Flaky Pie Pastry, Single Crust (page 34) or Basic Flaky Pie Pastry, Single Crust (page 31), refrigerated

FILLING

2 cups fresh sour cherries, stemmed and pitted

2 cups fresh Rainier cherries, stemmed and pitted

1 cup fresh sweet cherries, stemmed and pitted

$1/2$ cup dried sour or sweet cherries

$1/2$ cup plus 2 tablespoons granulated sugar

1 tablespoon fresh lemon or orange juice

Grated zest of $1/2$ orange

1 teaspoon vanilla extract

3 tablespoons cornstarch

BROWN SUGAR TOPPING

$1/2$ cup firmly packed light brown sugar

$1/2$ cup all-purpose flour

Big pinch of salt

$1/4$ cup ($1/2$ stick) cold unsalted butter, cut into $1/4$-inch pieces

1. If you haven't already, prepare the pastry and refrigerate until firm enough to roll, about 1 hour.

2. On a sheet of lightly floured waxed paper, roll the pastry into a 13-inch circle with a floured rolling pin. Invert the pastry over a $9^1/2$-inch deep-dish pie pan, center, and peel off the paper. Gently tuck the pastry into the pan, without stretching it, and sculpt the overhang into an upstanding ridge. Place in the freezer for 15 minutes. Preheat the oven to 400°F.

3. In a large bowl, combine all the cherries, $1/2$ cup of the granulated sugar, the lemon juice, orange zest, and vanilla. Mix well and set aside for 10 to 15 minutes to juice. Mix the remaining 2 tablespoons granulated sugar and the cornstarch together in a small bowl, then stir the mixture into the fruit. Turn the filling into the chilled pie shell and smooth the top of the fruit with a spoon. Place the pie on the center oven rack and bake for 30 minutes.

4. Meanwhile, make the topping. Combine the brown sugar, flour, and salt in a food processor and pulse to mix. Scatter the butter over the dry ingredients and pulse until the mixture resembles fine crumbs. Empty the crumbs into a large bowl and rub them between your fingers to make large, buttery crumbs. Refrigerate until ready to use.

5. Remove the pie from the oven and reduce the temperature to 375°F. Carefully dump the crumbs in the center of the pie, spreading them over the surface with your hands. Tamp them down lightly. Return the pie to the oven, placing it so that the part that faced the back of the oven now faces forward. Just in case, slide a large aluminum

A Crash Course in Cherries

▶ The leading producer of sour cherries is Michigan, producing about 75 percent of the annual crop, or some 200 to 250 million pounds.

▶ The primary variety of sour cherry grown in the United States is the Montmorency, prized for preserves, jelly, juice, and—of course—pie.

▶ Most sweet cherries are grown in the Pacific Coast states, although Michigan does produce 20 percent of the annual crop.

▶ There are more than 1,000 varieties of sweet cherries. The most famous sweet cherry is the Bing.

▶ Pie makers take note: the third week of July is usually the peak of the harvest.

▶ The average cherry tree produces 7,000 cherries. It takes about 250 of them to make a pie.

foil–lined baking sheet onto the rack below to catch any spills. Bake until the top is dark golden brown and the juices bubble thickly around the edge, about 30 minutes.

6. Transfer the pie to a wire rack and let cool for at least 2 hours before serving.

Recipe for Success

▶ You'll diminish the subtle cherry notes if you oversweeten this pie, so resist the temptation (if you're so inclined) to add more sugar to the filling.

▶ Pitting cherries (see page 67) usually leaves them broken, somewhat crushed, or in several pieces. That's about as chopped as they need to be, so don't worry about cutting them further.

▶ For the purest, clearest cherry flavor, omit the vanilla extract in the filling and substitute granulated sugar for the brown sugar in the topping.

Double-Crust Cherry-Blackberry Pie

A pound each of frozen cherries and frozen blackberries go into this any-time-of-year fruit pie. The filling is berry-dark and juicy, and it tastes particularly delicious in the cream cheese pastry.

MAKES 8 TO 10 SERVINGS

1 recipe Tender Cream Cheese Pastry, Double Crust (page 46), refrigerated

FILLING

One 1-pound bag individually frozen pitted sweet cherries (not packed in syrup), partially thawed

One 1-pound bag individually frozen blackberries (not packed in syrup), partially thawed

1/2 cup plus 2 tablespoons granulated sugar

1 tablespoon fresh lemon juice

Grated zest of 1 lemon

3 tablespoons cornstarch

1/4 teaspoon ground nutmeg

1/4 teaspoon ground ginger

GARNISH

Confectioners' sugar

1. If you haven't already, prepare the pastry and refrigerate until firm enough to roll, about 1 1/2 hours.

2. On a sheet of lightly floured waxed paper, roll the larger portion of the pastry into a 12-inch circle with a floured rolling pin. Invert the pastry over a 9-inch standard pie pan, center, and peel off the paper. Gently tuck the pastry into the pan, without stretching it, and let the overhang drape over the edge. Place in the refrigerator for 15 minutes.

3. Combine the cherries, blackberries, 1/2 cup of the granulated sugar, the lemon juice, and lemon zest in a large bowl. Mix gently several times (see Recipe for Success) and set aside for 10 minutes. Preheat the oven to 400°F.

4. In a small bowl, combine the remaining 2 tablespoons granulated sugar, cornstarch, nutmeg, and ginger. Add to the fruit and mix briefly.

5. On another sheet of lightly floured waxed paper, roll the other half of the pastry into an 11-inch circle. Turn the filling into the chilled pie shell and smooth with a spoon. Lightly moisten the rim of the pie shell with a wet finger or pastry brush. Invert the top pastry over the filling, center, and peel off the paper. Press the top and bottom pastries together along the dampened edge. Trim the pastry with scissors or a paring knife, leaving

an even ½-inch overhang all around, then sculpt the overhang into an upstanding ridge. Poke several steam vents in the top of the pie with a fork or paring knife. Put a couple of the vents near the edge of the crust so you can check the juices there later.

6. Place the pie on the center oven rack and bake for 30 minutes. Reduce the oven temperature to 375°F and rotate the pie 180 degrees, so that the part that faced the back of the oven now faces forward. Just in case, slide a large aluminum foil–lined baking sheet onto the rack below to catch any spills. Continue to bake until the top is golden brown and any juices visible at the steam vents bubble thickly, 30 to 35 minutes.

7. Transfer the pie to a wire rack and let cool for 15 to 20 minutes. While it is still quite warm, dust the top lightly with confectioners' sugar. Once the pie has cooled completely, dust it again. Let the pie cool for at least 1 hour before serving.

Recipe for Success

▶ **Frozen blackberries, like fresh, tend to be quite juicy and fragile once they have partially thawed. That said, avoid the temptation to overmix the fruit. Too much mixing will cause the berries to break up, leaving the pie with fewer whole berries and less textural interest.**

All-Peach Pie with Coconut-Almond Crumb Topping

We all know that the season for truly good, ripe peaches is short—far shorter than the amount of time they occupy supermarket produce aisles during the summer months. When the quality of peaches is not what it should be, I like to use frozen fruit instead. Frozen peaches are a relative bargain, compared to fresh or canned, and the quality is very good. I'll repeat here what I say elsewhere: the quality of frozen produce in this country is quite often superior to that of fresh, in large part because there is very little time between harvesting and processing. That said, you can make an excellent peach pie with frozen fruit. I like to add a good amount of lemon juice and zest, both of which lend an aura of freshness, and a little nutmeg and vanilla to replace those subtle flavor notes that get lost in the processing.

MAKES 8 TO 10 SERVINGS

1 recipe Basic Flaky Pie Pastry, Single Crust (page 31), refrigerated

FILLING

Two 1-pound bags frozen sliced peaches, partially thawed

1^1/2 tablespoons fresh lemon juice

Finely grated zest of 1 lemon

1/3 cup plus 3 tablespoons sugar

2 tablespoons cornstarch

1/2 teaspoon vanilla extract

1/4 teaspoon ground nutmeg

COCONUT-ALMOND CRUMB TOPPING

1 cup all-purpose flour

2/3 cup sugar

1/4 teaspoon salt

1/2 cup sliced almonds

1/2 cup sweetened flaked coconut

6 tablespoons (3/4 stick) cold unsalted butter, cut into 1/4-inch pieces

1 tablespoon milk

1. If you haven't already, prepare the pastry and refrigerate until firm enough to roll, about 1 hour.

2. On a sheet of lightly floured waxed paper, roll the pastry into a 13-inch circle with a floured rolling pin. Invert the pastry over a 9^1/2-inch deep-dish pie pan, center, and peel off the paper. Gently tuck the pastry into the pan, without stretching it, and sculpt the overhang into an upstanding ridge. Place in the freezer for 15 minutes.

3. Combine the peaches, lemon juice, lemon zest, and 1/3 cup of the sugar in a large bowl and toss well to mix. Set aside for 10 minutes to juice. Preheat the oven to 400°F.

4. In a small bowl, mix the cornstarch with the remaining 3 tablespoons sugar. Sprinkle this mixture over the fruit and mix well. Stir in the vanilla and nutmeg. Turn the filling into the chilled pie shell and smooth the filling with your hands to even it out. Place the pie on the center oven rack and bake for 35 minutes.

5. Meanwhile, make the topping. Combine the flour, sugar, salt, almonds, and coconut in a food processor and pulse several times to mix. Scatter the butter over the top and pulse until the mixture resembles fine crumbs. Add the milk and process again until the crumbs are gravelly. Transfer to a large bowl and rub gently between your fingers to make the crumbs uniform in texture. Refrigerate until ready to use.

6. Remove the pie from the oven and reduce the temperature to 375°F. Carefully dump the crumbs in the center of the pie and spread them evenly with your hands. Press on the crumbs gently to compact them. Return the pie to the oven, placing it so that the part that faced the back of the oven now faces forward. Just in case, slide a large aluminum foil–lined baking sheet onto the rack below to catch any spills. Bake until the juices bubble thickly around the edge, about 30 minutes.

7.   Transfer the pie to a wire rack and let cool for at least 1 hour before serving.

Recipe for Success

▶   **The juiciest pies, such as this one, seem to need a very thick layer of crumb topping, the way we do it here. If you use too little topping, it tends to just soak into the juice, and you end up with a sludge-topped pie rather than a crumb-topped pie. Don't worry if you think there's too much topping. Use all of it, and the pie will be great.**

Peaches and Cream Pie

This open-faced pie tastes like peach ice cream—not surprising, since the three main ingredients are peaches, cream, and confectioners' sugar. In summer, try to use fresh peaches if you have them, but you'll get an excellent pie with frozen peaches as well. The finishing touch is a sprinkling of brown sugar that goes on for the last 15 minutes of baking, giving the pie a delicious caramel coating. Plan ahead, because you have to chill this pie before serving.

MAKES 8 TO 10 SERVINGS

1 recipe Basic Flaky Pie Pastry, Single Crust (page 31), All-Butter Pie Pastry, Single Crust (page 28), or Tender Cream Cheese Pastry, Single Crust (page 46), refrigerated

FILLING
2^1/$_2$ to 3 cups peeled, pitted, and sliced ripe peaches or one 1-pound bag frozen sliced peaches, partially thawed

1 cup heavy or whipping cream

^{1}/$_2$ cup confectioners' sugar, sifted

Big pinch of salt

^{1}/$_2$ teaspoon vanilla extract

^{1}/$_2$ cup firmly packed light brown sugar

1.   If you haven't already, prepare the pastry and refrigerate until firm enough to roll, about 1 hour.

2.   On a sheet of lightly floured waxed paper, roll the pastry into a 13-inch circle with a floured rolling pin. Invert the pastry over a 9^1/$_2$-inch deep-dish pie pan, center, and peel off the paper. Tuck the pastry into the pan, without stretching it, and sculpt the edge so

it is more or less flush with the top of the pan. Place in the freezer for 15 minutes. Preheat the oven to 400°F.

3. Distribute the peach slices evenly in the chilled shell. Combine the cream, confectioners' sugar, salt, and vanilla in a medium-size bowl and whisk to blend. Slowly pour the cream over the peaches. Use a fork, if necessary, to rearrange the peach slices evenly in the shell.

4. Place the pie on the center oven rack and bake for 30 minutes. Remove from the oven and reduce the temperature to 350°F. Sprinkle the brown sugar evenly over the pie, then return it to the oven, placing it so that the part that faced the back of the oven now faces forward. Bake until the filling is bubbly and the top is caramel-colored, 15 to 20 minutes. The filling will still be liquidy.

5. Transfer the pie to a wire rack and let cool thoroughly. Cover with loosely tented aluminum foil and refrigerate for at least 4 hours or overnight before serving.

Recipe for Success

▸ **Unlike other similar recipes, this is not a custard pie, because it contains no eggs. Thus, as I indicate in the recipe, the filling typically looks liquidy when the pie comes out of the oven. Don't bake the pie longer, though, in hopes that the filling will firm up. The thickening occurs as the pie cools.**

How to Blanch a Peach

One bite of a peach is all it takes to tell whether you'll want to peel your pie-bound fruit: If the skin is thick and chewy, peel it. If not, you probably don't have to bother.

If you're going to peel, you can, of course, use a sharp paring knife. If you're good, you won't remove much of the precious flesh underneath. If you're not, you may want to consider blanching.

To blanch your peaches, bring 2 to 3 quarts of water to a boil in a large saucepan. Using a slotted spoon, lower the peaches into the boiling water one at a time. Count to 15, then remove the peach. Let it cool briefly, then just slide off the skin. The first one is your test peach: if the skin doesn't slip right off, give the next one 30 seconds. The trick is to submerge the peach just long enough to loosen the skin, but not so long that the flesh underneath gets too soft, making it difficult to handle when you slice it.

Peach-Mascarpone Cream Pie

There are other peach custard pies in this collection, but this one is no doubt the richest, thanks to the mascarpone cheese, heavy cream, and unabashed number of egg yolks. That said, I think of it as a once-a-year proposition, made with only the softest and juiciest summer peaches. The tender peaches almost melt into the golden custard, obscuring the boundary between the two. The edge of the pie has a slightly dry texture, like New York–style cheesecake, while the center is creamy and moist. This is a decadent and caloric pie, but it's also delicious, light, and far from the ordinary.

MAKES 8 TO 10 SERVINGS

1 recipe Basic Flaky Pie Pastry, Single Crust (page 31), refrigerated

FILLING
3 cups peeled, pitted, and sliced ripe peaches
²/₃ cup plus 2 tablespoons sugar
3 tablespoons all-purpose flour

5 large egg yolks
³/₄ cup heavy or whipping cream
1 teaspoon vanilla extract
8 ounces (about 1 cup) mascarpone cheese

1. If you haven't already, prepare the pastry and refrigerate until firm enough to roll, about 1 hour.

2. On a sheet of lightly floured waxed paper, roll the pastry into a 13-inch circle with a floured rolling pin. Invert the pastry over a 9½-inch deep-dish pie pan, center, and peel off the paper. Gently tuck the pastry into the pan, without stretching it, and sculpt the overhang into an upstanding ridge. Place in the freezer for 15 minutes.

3. Combine the peaches, 2 tablespoons of the sugar, and the flour in a medium-size bowl. Mix well and set aside.

4. Combine the egg yolks and remaining ²/₃ cup sugar in the top of a double boiler set over, not in, barely simmering water. Whisk the yolks until they're thick and lemon-colored, 7 to 8 minutes. Remove from the heat and whisk in the cream and vanilla. Set aside for 10 minutes to cool. Preheat the oven to 375°F.

5. Put the mascarpone and ½ cup of the custard in a large bowl. Using an electric mixer, blend briefly until smooth. Blend in the remaining custard, ½ cup at a time, until all of the custard is added.

6. Transfer the peaches to the chilled pie shell, smoothing the fruit with a spoon. Slowly pour the mascarpone custard over the peaches. Using a fork, move the peaches around slightly so that the custard flows under and around them.

7. Place the pie on the center oven rack and bake for 10 minutes. Reduce the oven temperature to 350°F and continue to bake until the custard is set and the top is golden brown, though perhaps not uniformly so, about 35 minutes. Rotate the pie 180 degrees, so that the part that faced the back of the oven now faces forward, about 15 minutes before it is finished baking. To check for doneness, give the pie a little nudge. The filling shouldn't seem soupy at the center.

8. Transfer the pie to a wire rack and let cool. Serve barely warm or at room temperature. Or cover the cooled pie with loosely tented aluminum foil, refrigerate, and serve cold.

Recipe for Success

▶ It isn't really the same, by a long shot, but in a pinch you could substitute 1/2 cup each full-fat sour cream and cream cheese for the mascarpone cheese.

▶ If you don't have ripe peaches, try another peach pie, one that's not so dependent on perfect summer fruit. Consult the index for some ideas.

Lemonade-Peach Pie

Fresh peaches and lemonade concentrate give this pie an unmistakable summer flavor. The store-bought frozen pie shell lets you get this in the oven in a thrice. The crunchy streusel topping takes less than five minutes to prepare and adds a delicious finish.

MAKES 8 SERVINGS

1 store-bought frozen 9-inch deep-dish pie shell

FILLING

4 cups peeled, pitted, and thinly sliced ripe peaches

1/3 cup frozen lemonade concentrate, thawed

1/4 cup sugar

2 1/2 tablespoons quick-cooking tapioca

STREUSEL TOPPING

3/4 cup all-purpose flour

1/3 cup sugar

1/4 teaspoon ground cinnamon

1/8 teaspoon salt

5 tablespoons cold unsalted butter, cut into 1/4-inch pieces

1. Remove the pie shell from the package but leave it in the freezer. Preheat the oven to 400°F.

2. Combine all the filling ingredients in a medium-size bowl. Turn the filling into the frozen pie shell and smooth the top with a spoon. Place the pie on the center oven rack and bake for 25 minutes.

3. Meanwhile, make the topping. Put the flour, sugar, cinnamon, and salt in a food processor and pulse several times to mix. Scatter the butter over the top and pulse until the mixture resembles fine crumbs. Empty the crumbs into a medium-size bowl and rub between your fingers to make large, buttery crumbs. Refrigerate until ready to use.

4. Remove the pie from the oven and reduce the temperature to 375°F. Carefully dump the crumbs on the pie, spreading them evenly over the surface with your hands. Tamp them down lightly. Return the pie to the oven, placing it so that the part that faced the back of the oven now faces forward. Just in case, slide a large aluminum foil–lined baking sheet onto the rack below to catch any drips. Continue to bake until the topping is golden brown and the juices bubble thickly around the edge, about 25 minutes.

5. Transfer the pie to a wire rack and let cool for at least 2 hours before serving.

Recipe for Success

▶ **Remember to be careful when handling store-bought pie shells, because the edges tend to get brittle as they bake. The best way to get them in and out of the oven is by using a small rimless baking sheet as an oversize spatula, sliding it under the pan.**

▶ **Instead of peaches, substitute fresh nectarines, if you like.**

Peachy Peach Butter Pie with Sour Cream Topping

One of the best ways to make a really peachy peach pie is to add peach butter. If you've never tried it, peach butter is like apple butter—a thick fruit spread made primarily from the fruit itself, with some sugar, lemon juice, and spices added for good measure. I use Kauffman's peach butter, out of Bird-in-Hand, Pennsylvania. (Don't you love that name?) I get it at the Pennsylvania Dutch Market here in Annapolis, Maryland, although I've seen peach butters sold elsewhere as well. I combine it with juicy fresh peaches, sugar, spices, and flour and bake the pie until it's bubbly and thick. Once it cools down, I spread brown sugar–sweetened sour cream over the top, which makes a great creamy contrast to the chunky fruit filling.

MAKES 8 TO 10 SERVINGS

1 recipe All-Butter Pie Pastry, Single Crust (page 28) or Basic Flaky Pie Pastry, Single Crust (page 31), refrigerated

FILLING

4 cups peeled, pitted, and sliced ripe peaches

1 cup peach butter

1/2 cup granulated sugar

Grated zest of 1 lemon

2 tablespoons all-purpose flour

1/2 teaspoon ground cinnamon

1/4 teaspoon ground nutmeg

SOUR CREAM TOPPING

11/4 cups sour cream, preferably full-fat

1/4 cup firmly packed light brown sugar

1/2 teaspoon vanilla extract

1. If you haven't already, prepare the pastry and refrigerate until firm enough to roll, about 1 hour.

2. On a sheet of lightly floured waxed paper, roll the pastry into a 13-inch circle with a floured rolling pin. Invert the pastry over a 9½-inch deep-dish pie pan, center, and peel off the paper. Gently tuck the pastry into the pan, without stretching it, and sculpt the overhang into an upstanding ridge. Place in the freezer for 15 minutes.

3. In a large bowl, combine all the filling ingredients. Set aside for 10 minutes to juice. Preheat the oven to 400°F.

4. Pour the filling into the chilled pie shell, smoothing the top of the fruit with a spoon. Place on the center oven rack and bake for 30 minutes. Reduce the oven temperature to 375°F and rotate the pie 180 degrees, so that the part that faced the back of the oven now faces forward. Continue to bake until the filling bubbles thickly, 30 to 35 minutes.

5. Transfer the pie to a wire rack and let cool for 2 hours. Cover with loosely tented aluminum foil and refrigerate for at least 2 hours.

6. At least 30 minutes before serving, make the topping. Combine the sour cream and brown sugar in a small saucepan over low heat. Heat, stirring continuously, until the sour cream is runny, 2 to 3 minutes. Do not let the mixture boil. Remove from the heat and stir in the vanilla. Slowly pour the mixture over the center of the pie, gently shaking and tilting the pie so that the topping runs up to the edge. Refrigerate for 30 minutes before serving.

Recipe for Success

▶ **As I mentioned earlier, some brands of peach butter already contain spices. Taste yours to see how spicy it is. If the spices are bold, reduce the amount of cinnamon and nutmeg added to the filling here.**

▶ **This filling may appear to have thickened after 30 to 40 minutes, but don't be tempted to remove the pie from the oven before you see it bubble. It won't be as juicy as a traditional fruit pie, but it should be bubbly-thick in several locations.**

Triple Vanilla Bean–Scented All-Peach Pie

The sweet, delicate flavor of summer peaches pairs up beautifully with vanilla. So when I'm feeling extravagant and totally in the thrall of the summer peach harvest, I slit open a vanilla bean, scrape out the seeds, and grind them with a cup of sugar. Then I use this vanilla sugar three different ways: to sweeten the filling, to sprinkle over the pie crust when it comes out of the oven, and to flavor the whipped cream I serve with the pie. It's a little indulgent—vanilla beans costing what they do—but worth every penny for this best-of-summer peach pie.

MAKES 8 TO 10 SERVINGS

1 recipe Basic Flaky Pie Pastry, Double Crust (page 31) or Basic Shortening Pie Pastry, Double Crust (page 30), refrigerated

FILLING

1 plump vanilla bean

1 cup sugar

3 tablespoons cornstarch

5 cups peeled, pitted, and thickly sliced ripe peaches

2 teaspoons fresh lemon juice

2 tablespoons cold unsalted butter, cut into small pieces

GARNISH

1 cup cold heavy or whipping cream

1. If you haven't already, prepare the pastry and refrigerate until firm enough to roll, about 1 hour.

2. On a sheet of lightly floured waxed paper, roll the larger portion of the pastry into a 12-inch circle with a floured rolling pin. Invert the pastry over a 9-inch standard pie pan, center, and peel off the paper. Gently tuck the pastry into the pan, without stretching it, and let the overhang drape over the edge. Place in the refrigerator for 15 minutes.

3. Slit the vanilla bean lengthwise. With the blade of a paring knife, scrape the seeds out of the bean and into a food processor. Add the sugar and process for about 1 minute. (If the machine sends up a cloud of sugar dust through the feed tube, just cover the tube with your hand.) Transfer the vanilla sugar to a small bowl. Mix ½ cup of the vanilla sugar with the cornstarch in another bowl and keep it nearby.

4. Combine the peaches, sugar-cornstarch mixture, and lemon juice in a large bowl. Mix well and set aside. Preheat the oven to 400°F.

5. On another sheet of floured waxed paper, roll the other half of the pastry into a 10-inch circle with a floured rolling pin. Turn the filling into the chilled pie shell, smoothing the top with your hands or a spoon. Dot the top of the fruit with the butter. Lightly moisten the rim of the pie shell. Invert the top pastry over the filling, center, and peel off the paper. Press the top and bottom pastries together along the dampened edge. Using the back of a butter knife or pastry knife, trim the pastry flush with the edge of the pan. Poke several steam vents in the top of the pie with a fork or paring knife. Put a couple of the vents near the edge of the crust so you can check the juices there later.

6. Place the pie on the center oven rack and bake for 30 minutes. Reduce the oven temperature to 375°F and rotate the pie 180 degrees, so that the part that faced the back of the oven now faces forward. Just in case, slide a large aluminum foil–lined baking sheet onto the rack below to catch any spills. Continue to bake until the top is a deep golden brown and the juices visible at the side vents bubble thickly, about 30 minutes.

7. Transfer the pie to a wire rack and immediately sprinkle half the remaining vanilla sugar (about ¼ cup) over the top. Set aside on the wire rack to cool for at least 2 hours.

8. Shortly before serving, using a chilled medium-size bowl and chilled beaters, whip the cream with an electric mixer until it holds soft peaks. Add the remaining vanilla sugar and continue to beat until stiff but not grainy. Serve a large dollop of whipped cream with each slice of pie.

Picking and Handling Those Perfect Pie Peaches

The most important step in making the best peach pie—and this goes for nearly all fruit pies—is choosing good fruit. And that's not always as easy as you might think. Looks alone aren't necessarily an accurate indicator: the best-looking fruit can often disappoint. Here, then, are some things to keep in mind when selecting peaches.

▶ Use your nose. A good peach will have a sweet, peachy smell.

▶ Apply gentle finger pressure. Peaches should yield slightly. If they're rock hard—and they often are—just wait until better fruit comes along. Or use frozen.

▶ Stay away from greenish peaches. They were picked too early and won't make a good pie.

▶ Buy only enough ripe peaches for your immediate use. Ripe peaches are delicate and won't last more than a day or two once you get them home.

▶ Store fully ripe peaches in the refrigerator, in a single layer. Use within 1 to 2 days. Store slightly underripe fruit at room temperature, again in a single layer. Turn frequently to minimize bruising.

Recipe for Success

▶ Make sure to choose a fat, supple vanilla bean about 8 inches long, meaning it's fully mature. It should have a clear, lovely fragrance and should not smell of smoke, which could be an indication of improper curing.

▶ Do sprinkle the vanilla sugar on the pie as soon as it comes out of the oven so that some of it can "melt" into the top crust. Expect much of it to remain gritty, however.

Adolph Family Peach Swirl Pie

For our purposes, a pie is some sort of sweet filling with a pastry or crumb crust under, over, or around it. And with one or two exceptions, I've clung steadfastly to that definition. But not here, for two good reasons. Good Reason #1: this is delicious, and it does, after all, have what you'd call a *cake* crust and is baked in a pie pan. Good Reason #2: the recipe was given to me by Jon Adolph, the editor of *FamilyFun* magazine, where I am a contributing editor—a position I'd just as soon keep. All kidding aside, this really is a wonderful pie, a family favorite often baked by Jon's mother-in-law, Rachel van Leer, and his wife, Sarah. A layer of cream cheese custard bakes up in pockets within the coffeecake crust. That's topped with a layer of peaches and a sour cream and brown sugar glaze, which go on for the last five minutes of baking. Call it just plain scrumptious. Serve it for breakfast or dessert.

MAKES 8 TO 10 SERVINGS

CAKE CRUST

1 cup all-purpose flour, sifted

1 teaspoon baking powder

1/2 teaspoon salt

1/2 cup (1 stick) unsalted butter, softened

2/3 cup granulated sugar

2 large eggs, at room temperature

1 teaspoon vanilla extract

1 tablespoon reserved syrup from canned peaches (see topping)

CREAM CHEESE CUSTARD

One 3-ounce package full-fat cream cheese, softened

1/3 cup granulated sugar

1/4 cup full-fat sour cream

1 large egg

1/4 teaspoon salt

TOPPING

1 cup full-fat sour cream

2 tablespoons firmly packed light brown sugar

One 29-ounce can sliced peaches in syrup, drained but 1 tablespoon syrup reserved for crust

1. Butter a 9½-inch deep-dish pie pan. Preheat the oven to 325°F.

2. To make the cake crust, combine the flour, baking powder, and salt in a medium-size bowl. Set aside. Using an electric mixer, cream the butter in a large bowl, gradually adding the granulated sugar. Beat in the eggs, one at a time, beating well after each addition. Blend in the vanilla and peach syrup. Stir in the dry mixture until evenly blended. Scrape the batter into the prepared pie pan, smoothing it evenly over the bottom and about halfway up the side. Set aside.

3. To make the cream cheese custard, use an electric mixer to beat the cream cheese, granulated sugar, sour cream, egg, and salt together in a medium-size bowl. Slowly pour the mixture over the cake crust. Place on the center oven rack and bake for 30 minutes. Meanwhile, as the pie bakes, blend the sour cream and brown sugar for the topping in a small bowl.

4. Remove the pie from the oven and arrange the peaches on top. Put a few in the center and arrange the rest of them like the spokes of a wheel, radiating out from the center. Spoon the sour cream topping over and around the peaches, smoothing it with the back of the spoon. Put the pie back in the oven and bake for 5 minutes.

5. Transfer the pie to a wire rack and let cool to room temperature before serving.

Recipe for Success

▶ **The Adolph family recipe calls for canned peaches, but I don't see any reason you couldn't make this with peeled fresh peach slices. Use a tablespoon of their juice in place of the reserved syrup.**

▶ **For that matter, I think you could use many other fresh summer fruits here as well, from nectarines to fresh berries.**

▶ **Sarah says she sometimes substitutes up to half plain yogurt for an equal measure of sour cream in the cake. That's handy to know, especially if you don't have enough sour cream on hand.**

Colonial Rose Inn's Peach Custard Pie

This one really hits my personal bull's-eye, because it has everything I like in a pie: peaches, custard, and crumb topping. As the pie bakes, the various elements almost melt into one, forming a sort of peach custard. Use very ripe and juicy summer peaches. My thanks to Jeff and Jayne Rose, owners of the Colonial Rose Inn in Grand Detour, Illinois, for providing this recipe.

MAKES 8 TO 10 SERVINGS

1 recipe Basic Flaky Pie Pastry, Single Crust (page 31) or All-Butter Pie Pastry, Single Crust (page 28), refrigerated

FILLING

1 cup full-fat sour cream

1 cup sugar

3 large egg yolks

1/4 cup all-purpose flour

1 teaspoon vanilla extract

4 large ripe peaches, peeled, pitted, and thickly sliced

STREUSEL TOPPING

1/2 cup all-purpose flour

1/2 cup sugar

1/4 cup (1/2 stick) cold unsalted butter, cut into 1/4-inch pieces

1. If you haven't already, prepare the pastry and refrigerate until firm enough to roll, about 1 hour.

2. On a sheet of lightly floured waxed paper, roll the pastry into a 13-inch circle with a floured rolling pin. Invert the pastry over a 9½-inch deep-dish pie pan, center, and peel off the paper. Tuck the pastry into the pan, without stretching it, and sculpt the edge into an upstanding ridge. Place in the freezer for 15 minutes. Preheat the oven to 425°F.

3. In a large bowl, whisk together the sour cream, sugar, egg yolks, flour, and vanilla until smooth. Set aside. Arrange the peach slices in the chilled pie shell in tight, stacked concentric circles. You don't have to make it look perfect, just relatively neat. Slowly and evenly pour the sour cream mixture over the peaches. Gently shake the pan to help the mixture settle between the peaches. Place the pie on the center oven rack and bake for 30 minutes.

4. Meanwhile, make the streusel topping. Combine the flour, sugar, and butter in a large bowl, tossing to blend. Using your fingers, rub the butter into the dry ingredients until the mixture resembles coarse crumbs. Refrigerate until ready to use.

5. Remove the pie from the oven and reduce the temperature to 400°F. Dump the streusel in the center of the pie, spreading it evenly over the top with your hands. Tamp it down very gently. Return the pie to the oven, placing it so that the part that faced the back of the oven now faces forward. Continue to bake until the topping is golden brown, about 25 minutes. If the top starts to get too dark, cover with loosely tented aluminum foil during the last 10 minutes.

6. Transfer the pie to a wire rack and let cool for at least 2 hours. I prefer this pie cold, but it's also very good at room temperature or slightly warm. Once the pie has cooled to room temperature, cover with loosely tented aluminum foil and refrigerate before serving.

Recipe for Success

▶ Jeff Rose bakes this a little hotter than I typically bake custard pies, but the density of the sour cream filling seems to protect the custard from "breaking" and becoming watery.

▶ This same denseness of filling makes it a little difficult to judge when the pie is done. Jeff suggests sticking a knife in the center of the pie. If it comes out clean, the pie is done.

Fresh Peach and Brown Sugar Pizza Pie

This is probably closer to a pizza than it is to a pie, but you won't much care once you've tried it. The pastry bakes up bready and buttery and makes a good sturdy base for the sliced peach topping. A brown sugar and flour mixture is sprinkled over the crust to absorb the juice from the peaches. Then a little more of it is rubbed together with butter and spread over the peaches, creating a caramel-like streusel topping. It's different and delicious—a little too bready, perhaps, for dessert after a filling meal, but perfect following a light meal or as a summer baking project with the kids, who'll finish this off with their friends in no time flat.

MAKES 8 TO 10 SERVINGS

1 recipe Yeasted Butter Pastry (page 39)

Cornmeal

FILLING

4 cups peeled, pitted, and thickly sliced ripe peaches

3 tablespoons granulated sugar

$1/3$ cup firmly packed light brown sugar

$1/4$ cup all-purpose flour

$1/4$ teaspoon ground cinnamon

2 tablespoons cold unsalted butter, cut into small pieces

1. If you haven't already, prepare the pastry and let it rise for 1 hour according to the pastry directions. Meanwhile, lightly oil a large baking sheet and dust it with cornmeal.

2. After an hour of rising, punch the dough down gently once or twice, but not vigorously as you would a regular yeast dough. Put the dough on a floured work surface and dust it lightly with flour. Gently roll the pastry into a 13- to 14-inch circle, keeping it, as best you can, of even thickness. Transfer the pastry to the prepared baking sheet, pinching the edge of the dough into an upstanding ridge. Refrigerate for 15 minutes. Preheat the oven to 425°F.

3. Combine the sliced peaches and granulated sugar in a medium-size bowl and toss gently. Set aside for 10 minutes to juice. Meanwhile, mix the brown sugar, flour, and cinnamon together in a small bowl.

4. Remove the pastry from the refrigerator and sprinkle 2 tablespoons of the brown sugar mixture over it. By hand, lift the peaches out of their juice and arrange them in a single, random layer on the pastry. (Reserve the peach juice for another use, if you like; there won't be much of it.) Wash and dry your hands, then add the butter to the remaining brown sugar mixture and rub it in until you have coarse, buttery crumbs. Spread the crumbs evenly over the peaches.

5. Put the baking sheet on the center oven rack and bake for 15 minutes. Reduce the oven temperature to 375°F and rotate the baking sheet 180 degrees, so that the part that faced the back of the oven now faces forward. Continue to bake until the crust is golden brown and the juices bubble thickly on top, 10 to 12 minutes.

6. Slide the pizza onto a large wire rack. Let cool for 10 to 15 minutes, then slice and serve.

Recipe for Success

▶ **You could, if you like, make this with a combination of stone fruits: apricots, peaches, and nectarines.**

▶ **Given the bread-like texture of this pastry, it really is best eaten as soon as possible—preferably within 30 minutes, but up to a couple of hours, of coming out of the oven.**

Peach and Damson Plum Preserves Pie

You can, on occasion, get around the problem of inferior—or nonexistent—fresh fruit by using preserves in your pie filling. Such was the case here when I needed to make a plum pie but couldn't get my hands on any decent fresh plums. I substituted a jar of quality damson plum preserves, adding moisture and a fruit touch with some ripe peaches. I could have added a top crust, but since I was using the walnut pastry, I decided to go with a walnut crumb topping. The pie came out splendidly, as I trust you'll agree.

MAKES 8 TO 10 SERVINGS

1/2 recipe Nutty Pie Pastry (page 42) made with walnuts, refrigerated

FILLING

1 1/2 cups peeled, pitted, and diced ripe peaches

1 1/2 tablespoons granulated sugar

1 tablespoon all-purpose flour

1 1/4 cups damson plum preserves

WALNUT CRUMB TOPPING

3/4 cup all-purpose flour

3/4 cup finely chopped walnuts

1/3 cup rolled oats (old-fashioned or quick-cooking)

1/3 cup firmly packed light brown sugar

1/2 teaspoon ground cinnamon

1/4 teaspoon salt

5 tablespoons unsalted butter, melted

1. If you haven't already, prepare the pastry and refrigerate until firm enough to roll, about 45 minutes. It's best not to overchill nut pastries or they can be tricky to handle.

2. On a sheet of lightly floured waxed paper, roll the pastry into a 12-inch circle with a floured rolling pin. Invert the pastry over a 9-inch standard pie pan, center, and peel off the paper. Tuck the pastry into the pan, without stretching it, and sculpt the edge into a ridge that's just slightly higher than the edge of the pan. Place in the freezer for 15 minutes. Preheat the oven to 400°F.

3. Combine the peaches, granulated sugar, and flour in a small bowl. Toss to mix.

4. Spread half of the preserves evenly in the chilled pie shell. Spoon the peach mixture over the preserves, smoothing it with a spoon. Dab the remaining preserves here and there on top of the peaches, then smooth. Place the pie on the center oven rack and bake for 15 minutes.

5. Meanwhile, make the topping. Combine the flour, walnuts, oats, brown sugar, cinnamon, and salt in a large bowl. Toss with your hands to mix. Stir in the butter, mixing first with a fork, then with your hands. Rub the topping until you have evenly mixed, coarse crumbs. Refrigerate until ready to use.

6. Remove the pie from the oven and reduce the temperature to 375°F. Dump the crumbs in the center of the pie, spreading them over the top with your hands. Tamp them down slightly. Return the pie to the oven, placing it so that the part that faced the back of the oven now faces forward. Continue to bake until the fruit bubbles thickly around the edge and the topping is golden brown, 30 to 35 minutes.

7. Transfer the pie to a wire rack and let cool. Serve just barely warm or at room temperature.

Recipe for Success

▶ Using the same basic formula, consider your other filling options. Fig preserves are wonderful with diced pears, as are peach preserves with diced apples. Both are great with this nut pastry.

▶ If you'd like to alter the construction of the pie, assemble it as for Linzer Pie (page 577), adding strips of pastry across the top. You'll need the full pastry recipe. It looks very pretty with the dark red plum preserves peeking up through the lattice.

Pennsylvania Dutch Market Peach and Sour Cherry Pie

One of my favorite places to shop in Annapolis, Maryland, where I live, is the Pennsylvania Dutch Market. An impressive assemblage of food vendors under one roof, the market attracts shoppers from miles around and for good reason: the food and selection are always good, the portions large, and the prices what you would have expected to pay 10 or 15 years ago. Come summer, the market is one of the few in the area where I can find the sour cherries I love so much in pies—right when the Lancaster County, Pennsylvania, peaches come to market as well. I love combining the two in this pie—the tartness and color of the cherries providing a perfect contrast to the sweetness of the peaches. It's one of those classic summer pies I like to take along when we're invited for a cookout or patio party, always with a half gallon of good vanilla ice cream.

MAKES 8 TO 10 SERVINGS

1 recipe Basic Flaky Pie Pastry, Single Crust (page 31) or All-Butter Pie Pastry, Single Crust (page 28), refrigerated

FILLING

4 cups peeled, pitted, and sliced ripe peaches

2 cups ripe fresh sour cherries, stemmed and pitted

2/3 cup granulated sugar

1 tablespoon fresh lemon juice

1/4 cup firmly packed light brown sugar

3 tablespoons cornstarch

Big pinch of ground nutmeg

OATMEAL CRUMB TOPPING

1 cup all-purpose flour

1/2 cup rolled oats (old-fashioned or quick-cooking)

2/3 cup firmly packed light brown sugar

1/2 teaspoon ground cinnamon

1/4 teaspoon salt

1/2 cup (1 stick) cold unsalted butter, cut into 1/4-inch pieces

1. If you haven't already, prepare the pastry and refrigerate until firm enough to roll, about 1 hour.

2. On a sheet of lightly floured waxed paper, roll the pastry into a 13-inch circle with a floured rolling pin. Invert the pastry over a 9½-inch deep-dish pie pan, center, and peel off the paper. Gently tuck the pastry into the pan, without stretching it, and sculpt the overhang into an upstanding ridge. Place in the freezer for 15 minutes.

3. Combine the peaches, cherries, granulated sugar, and lemon juice in a large bowl. Mix well, then set aside for 10 minutes to juice. Preheat the oven to 400°F.

4. In a small bowl, combine the brown sugar and cornstarch. Stir the mixture into the fruit along with the nutmeg. Turn the filling into the chilled pie shell and smooth the top of the fruit with your hands. Place the pie on the center oven rack and bake for 30 minutes.

5. Meanwhile, make the crumb topping. Put the flour, oats, brown sugar, cinnamon, and salt in a food processor and pulse several times to mix. Scatter the butter over the top and pulse until the mixture resembles fine crumbs. Empty the crumbs into a large bowl and rub them between your fingers until you have large, buttery crumbs. Refrigerate until ready to use.

6. Remove the pie from the oven and reduce the temperature to 375°F. Carefully dump the crumbs in the center of the pie, spreading them over the surface with your hands. Tamp them down lightly. Return the pie to the oven, placing it so that the part that faced the back of the oven now faces forward. Just in case, slide a large aluminum foil–lined baking sheet onto the rack below to catch any spills. Continue to bake until the top is dark golden brown and the juices bubble thickly at the edge, 35 to 40 minutes. If the topping starts to get too dark, loosely cover the pie with tented aluminum foil during the last 15 minutes of baking.

7. Transfer the pie to a wire rack and let cool for at least 2 hours before serving.

Recipe for Success

▶ If you can't find fresh sour cherries, look for frozen. Drained canned sour cherries also will do in a pinch.

▶ Either peel the peaches by hand or use the blanching method described on page 88.

▶ Feel free to substitute another streusel-like topping if you don't have oats or simply prefer something else.

Peach-Blueberry Cobbler Pie

Those of you who own a copy of my previous pie book, *Apple Pie Perfect* (Harvard Common Press, 2002), will remember that the cobbler pie is an invention I credit to my wife, Bev. Long story short: When I was writing my last book, Bev insisted that I include a recipe for an apple cobbler. I reminded her that it was a book of pies and cobblers didn't fit the profile. She told me, in so many words, that if I just put a crust under it, it would still be a pie. So I did, and it was wonderful—wonderful enough to invent this peach and blueberry version. Adding a cobbler topping is not really that much of a stretch. The topping simply replaces the top crust, and if it's a little heavier than pastry, no one seems to mind. Indeed, the biscuit-like topping is right at home on the juicy peaches and blueberries, flavored with lemon and nutmeg. You'll think of this as a new summer classic.

MAKES 8 TO 10 SERVINGS

1 recipe Extra-Flaky Pie Pastry, Single Crust (page 34) or Basic Flaky Pie Pastry, Single Crust (page 31), refrigerated

FILLING

3 1/2 cups peeled, pitted, and thickly sliced ripe peaches

1 1/2 cups fresh blueberries, picked over for stems

1/3 cup plus 2 tablespoons sugar

1 tablespoon fresh lemon juice

2 teaspoons grated lemon zest

1/4 teaspoon ground nutmeg

1 1/2 teaspoons cornstarch

COBBLER TOPPING

1¹/₄ cups all-purpose flour

5 tablespoons sugar

¹/₂ teaspoon baking soda

¹/₂ teaspoon baking powder

¹/₄ teaspoon salt

¹/₄ cup (¹/₂ stick) cold unsalted butter, cut into ¹/₄-inch pieces

²/₃ cup buttermilk

1 large egg

¹/₂ teaspoon vanilla extract

GARNISH

Fresh Whipped Cream (page 605)

1. If you haven't already, prepare the pastry and refrigerate until firm enough to roll, about 1 hour.

2. On a sheet of lightly floured waxed paper, roll half the pastry into a 13- to 13¹/₂-inch circle with a floured rolling pin. Invert the pastry over a 9¹/₂- to 10-inch extra-deep-dish pie pan, center, and peel off the paper. Tuck the pastry into the pan, without stretching it, and sculpt the edge into an upstanding ridge. Place in the freezer for 15 minutes.

3. Combine the peaches, blueberries, ¹/₃ cup of the sugar, the lemon juice, lemon zest, and nutmeg in a large bowl. Toss to combine, then set aside for 10 minutes. Preheat the oven to 400°F.

4. In a small bowl, combine the remaining 2 tablespoons sugar and the cornstarch, then stir the mixture into the fruit. Turn the filling into the chilled pie shell, smoothing the fruit with your hands. Place on the center oven rack and bake for 30 minutes. Reduce the oven temperature to 375°F and rotate the pie 180 degrees, so that the part that faced the back of the oven now faces forward. Continue to bake for 10 minutes.

5. Meanwhile, make the topping. Sift the flour, 4 tablespoons of the sugar, the baking soda, baking powder, and salt together in a medium-size bowl. Add the butter and rub it into the flour with your fingers or cut it in with a pastry blender until the mixture resembles coarse crumbs. Blend the buttermilk, egg, and vanilla together in a small bowl. Make a well in the dry mixture and add the liquid. Stir the batter until evenly blended.

6. Remove the pie from the oven and spoon the cobbler topping evenly over the fruit. Sprinkle the topping with the remaining 1 tablespoon sugar. Return the pie to the oven, placing it so that the part that faced the back of the oven now faces forward. Just in case, slide a large aluminum foil–lined baking sheet onto the rack below to catch any spills. Bake until the top is golden brown, 23 to 25 minutes.

7. Transfer the pie to a wire rack and let cool for at least 20 minutes before serving. This is best served within an hour or so (see Recipe for Success). Garnish with a dollop of whipped cream.

Recipe for Success

❯ If you like, substitute nectarines for the peaches.

❯ This is best eaten within about an hour because after that, the porous cobbler topping tends to absorb the juices, almost like a sponge. The pie still tastes great after that happens, but it isn't as juicy.

Fresh Peach and Red Currant Pie

Here's a pie I generally make only once or twice a year, depending on the availability and quality of fresh currants. When I lived in New Hampshire, I had a secret spot where, if I was willing to patiently pick these fragile berries one by one, I could count on finding just enough for a pie or two. These days, when they're available, I buy them at the Whole Foods Market here in Annapolis, Maryland. (Generally speaking, their fragility is a problem for marketers, and thus few retailers carry them.) If you've never had a fresh currant, they're extremely tart, so much so that it's a puckery challenge to eat them right off the bush. That tartness makes them a good addition to this peach pie. Look for both of these fruits in the market at about the same time—July or August, when they're at their best.

MAKES 8 TO 10 SERVINGS

1 recipe Basic Flaky Pie Pastry, Double Crust (page 31) or Tender Cream Cheese Pastry, Double Crust (page 46), refrigerated

FILLING

5 cups peeled, pitted, and sliced ripe peaches

1 cup sugar

2 1/2 to 3 tablespoons cornstarch

1 tablespoon fresh lemon juice

1/4 teaspoon ground cinnamon

2 cups fresh red currants, picked over for stems

GLAZE

Milk or light cream

Sugar

1. If you haven't already, prepare the pastry and refrigerate until firm enough to roll, 1 to 1$\frac{1}{2}$ hours.

2. On a sheet of lightly floured waxed paper, roll the larger portion of the pastry into a 13-inch circle with a floured rolling pin. Invert the pastry over a 9$\frac{1}{2}$-inch deep-dish pie pan, center, and peel off the paper. Gently tuck the pastry into the pan, without stretching it, and let the overhang drape over the edge. Place in the refrigerator for 15 minutes. Preheat the oven to 400°F.

3. Put the peaches in a large bowl. In a small bowl, mix together the sugar and cornstarch, using the larger amount if the peaches seem very juicy. Add the mixture to the peaches and toss well to mix. Stir in the lemon juice and cinnamon. Add the currants and toss once or twice. Don't overdo it, because they're fragile, and you don't want them to fall apart.

4. On another sheet of lightly floured waxed paper, roll the top pastry into an 11-inch circle. Turn the filling into the chilled pie shell and smooth the top with your fingers. Dampen the edge of the pie shell with a wet fingertip or pastry brush, then invert the top pastry over the filling, center, and peel off the paper. Press the top and bottom pastries together along the dampened edge. Trim the pastry, leaving an even $\frac{1}{2}$-inch overhang all around, then sculpt the overhang into an upstanding ridge. Poke several steam vents in the top with a fork or paring knife. Put a couple of the vents near the edge of the crust so you can check the juices there later. Brush the top with a little milk and sprinkle lightly with sugar.

5. Place the pie on the center oven rack and bake for 30 minutes. Reduce the oven temperature to 375°F and rotate the pie 180 degrees, so that the part that faced the back of the oven now faces forward. Just in case, slide a large aluminum foil–lined baking sheet onto the rack below to catch any spills. Continue to bake until the juices visible at the steam vents bubble thickly, 30 to 35 minutes.

6. Transfer the pie to a wire rack and let cool for at least 1 hour. Serve warm or at room temperature.

Recipe for Success

▸ **If the asking price for 2 cups of currants seems exorbitant, simply buy fewer and add another cup of sliced peaches. Reduce the sugar by about $\frac{1}{4}$ cup if you do. The pie will still be wonderful.**

Deep-Dish Nectarine Pie with Almond Crumb Topping

Here's a little tip: all of the stone fruits—peaches, nectarines, apricots, and plums—have an affinity for almonds, a flavor that can be used to your advantage. This juicy, summer-fresh nectarine pie flavored with almond extract and topped with an almond streusel is one of the pies I most look forward to making come midsummer. Choose your nectarines carefully. If they have a green tinge, they will not ripen properly. Like peaches, they should yield to gentle finger pressure but not feel mushy, as they sometimes do, given their habit of overripening quickly. There's no need to peel the skins; they soften up nicely as the pie bakes.

MAKES 8 TO 10 SERVINGS

1 recipe Basic Flaky Pie Pastry, Single Crust (page 31) or Extra-Flaky Pie Pastry, Single Crust (page 34), refrigerated

FILLING

6 cups pitted and sliced ripe nectarines, unpeeled

Scant 1/2 cup plus 2 tablespoons sugar

1 1/2 tablespoons fresh lemon juice

2 teaspoons grated lemon zest

2 1/2 tablespoons cornstarch

1/4 teaspoon almond extract

ALMOND CRUMB TOPPING

3/4 cup whole or slivered almonds

1/2 cup sugar

1/2 cup all-purpose flour

1/4 teaspoon salt

6 tablespoons (3/4 stick) cold unsalted butter, cut into 1/4-inch pieces

1.   If you haven't already, prepare the pastry and refrigerate until firm enough to roll, about 1 hour.

2.   On a sheet of lightly floured waxed paper, roll half of the pastry into a 13-inch circle with a floured rolling pin. Invert the pastry over a 9 1/2-inch deep-dish pie pan, center, and peel off the paper. Tuck the pastry into the pan, without stretching it, and sculpt the edge into an upstanding ridge. Place in the freezer for 15 minutes. Preheat the oven to 400°F.

3.   In a large bowl, combine the nectarines, 1/2 cup of the sugar, the lemon juice, and lemon zest. Set aside for 10 minutes to juice. Combine the remaining 2 tablespoons sugar

and the cornstarch in a small bowl, then stir the mixture into the fruit. Stir in the almond extract. Scrape the filling into the chilled pie shell, smoothing the fruit with a spoon. Place the pie on the center oven rack and bake for 30 minutes.

4. Meanwhile, make the topping. Combine the almonds and sugar in a food processor, pulsing in short bursts to chop the almonds well. Add the flour and salt and pulse briefly to mix. Scatter the butter over the dry ingredients and pulse until the mixture looks like fine crumbs. Dump the crumbs into a large bowl and rub between your fingers to make large, buttery crumbs. Refrigerate until ready to use.

5. Remove the pie from the oven and reduce the temperature to 375°F. Carefully dump the crumbs in the center of the pie, spreading them evenly and tamping them lightly with your hands. Return the pie to the oven, placing it so that the part that faced the back of the oven now faces forward. Just in case, slide a large aluminum foil–lined baking sheet onto the rack below to catch any spills. Continue to bake until the juices bubble thickly around the edge, 30 to 40 minutes.

6. Transfer the pie to a wire rack and let cool for at least 2 hours before serving.

Recipe for Success

▶ **The same filling can be used in a double-crust pie or with a different crumb topping.**

▶ **If you'd like to try a nectarine-blueberry combination, reduce the nectarines by 2 cups and add 2 cups ripe fresh blueberries.**

No-Peel Nectarine-Lime Pie

By using a store-bought frozen pie shell and not peeling the nectarines, you can make a fresh summer pie that's as simple as it is delicious and crowd-pleasing. Another timesaving grace: I use a melted-butter streusel, about the easiest sort of topping there is. Lemon is wonderful in just about any fruit pie, but lime—I use both the juice and the zest here—has a little more pizzazz, and I like the sassy accent it gives to the nectarines.

MAKES 8 SERVINGS

1 store-bought frozen 9-inch deep-dish pie shell

FILLING

4 cups pitted and sliced ripe nectarines, unpeeled

1/3 cup plus 2 tablespoons sugar

1 tablespoon fresh lime juice

1/2 teaspoon grated lime zest

1 1/2 to 2 tablespoons cornstarch

Pinch of ground nutmeg

STREUSEL TOPPING

1 cup all-purpose flour

1/2 cup sugar

1/4 teaspoon salt

Pinch of ground cinnamon

1/2 teaspoon grated lemon zest (optional)

5 tablespoons unsalted butter, melted

1. Remove the pie shell from its package but leave it in the freezer until you're ready to fill it.

2. Combine the nectarines, 1/3 cup of the sugar, the lime juice, and lime zest in a large bowl and mix well. Set aside for 15 minutes to juice. Preheat the oven to 400°F.

3. After 15 minutes, check the accumulated juice. If the nectarines are pretty much covered with juice, use 2 tablespoons of the cornstarch. If not, use 1 1/2 tablespoons. In a small bowl, mix the cornstarch with the remaining 2 tablespoons sugar. Stir the mixture into the fruit along with the nutmeg. Turn the filling into the frozen pie shell, smoothing the top with a spoon. Place the pie on the center oven rack and bake for 30 minutes.

4. Meanwhile, make the topping. Combine the flour, sugar, salt, cinnamon, and lemon zest (if using) in a medium-size bowl. Pour the butter over them. Mix first with a fork to blend, then switch to your hands and rub gently until the mixture has the texture of gravelly crumbs. Refrigerate until ready to use.

5. Remove the pie from the oven and reduce the temperature to 375°F. Carefully dump the topping in the center of the pie and spread evenly over the surface with your hands. Tamp the crumbs down lightly. Return the pie to the oven, placing it so that the part that faced the back of the oven now faces forward. To catch any spills, slide a large aluminum foil–lined baking sheet onto the rack below. Bake until you see the juices bubbling thickly at the edge, 25 to 35 minutes. If the top starts to get too brown, cover loosely with aluminum foil for the last 10 minutes.

6. Transfer the pie to a wire rack and let cool for at least 1 hour before serving.

Recipe for Success

▶ Use only ripe fresh nectarines, and be selective about the ones you choose. Like peaches, they should yield to gentle finger pressure. Each nectarine should have a light but distinct fruity fragrance and feel weighty—which is to say juicy—in proportion to its size.

Easy Apricot Pie with Simple Press-In Pastry

Come summer, sometimes it's just less trouble to forget about a rolled pastry and opt for the press-in kind. That's what I do here, filling the shell with ripe fresh apricots. This shell is not prebaked—just refrigerated, to help firm it up before the fruit goes in. As for the filling, I keep that simple, too: apricots, sugar, lemon juice, and cornstarch. I add an oatmeal crumb topping during the last part of the baking, then brown it lightly. Feel free to use peaches in place of some of the apricots.

MAKES 8 TO 10 SERVINGS

1 recipe Simple Press-In Pie Pastry (page 49), refrigerated

FILLING
5 cups pitted and sliced fresh apricots (see Recipe for Success), unpeeled

1/2 cup plus 2 tablespoons sugar

1 tablespoon fresh lemon juice

2 tablespoons cornstarch

OATMEAL CRUMB TOPPING
2/3 cup all-purpose flour

1/2 cup rolled oats (old-fashioned or quick-cooking)

1/2 cup sugar

1/4 teaspoon salt

5 tablespoons cold unsalted butter, cut into 1/4-inch pieces

1. Prepare the pastry and press it into the bottom and most of the way up the side of a 9½-inch deep-dish pie pan. Place in the freezer for 15 minutes.

2. Combine the apricots, ½ cup of the sugar, and the lemon juice in a large bowl. Set aside for 10 minutes to juice. Preheat the oven to 375°F.

3. In a small bowl, combine the remaining 2 tablespoons sugar and the cornstarch, then stir the mixture into the fruit. Scrape the filling into the chilled pie shell, smoothing the top with a spoon. Place the pie on the center oven rack and bake for 30 minutes.

4. Meanwhile, make the topping. Combine the flour, oats, sugar, and salt in a food processor and pulse to chop the oats well. Scatter the butter over the top and pulse until the mixture resembles fine crumbs. Transfer the mixture to a medium-size bowl and rub between your fingers to make large, buttery crumbs. Refrigerate until ready to use.

5. Remove the pie from the oven and carefully dump the crumbs in the center of the pie, spreading them evenly over the surface with your hands. Tamp them down lightly. Return the pie to the oven, placing it so that the part that faced the back of the oven now faces forward. Just in case, slide a large aluminum foil–lined baking sheet onto the rack below to catch any drips. Continue to bake until the top is golden brown and any juices visible near the edge bubble thickly, 20 to 25 minutes.

6. Transfer the pie to a wire rack and let cool for at least 2 hours before serving.

Recipe for Success

▶ **Fresh apricots can sometimes be a little dry. If you find that even after 20 minutes, your apricots aren't all that juicy, add a tablespoon or so of orange juice or lemonade.**

▶ **Some people find the flavor of an all-apricot pie a little too forward. You can soften the flavor with peaches, sliced apples, or even raspberries or blueberries, for a mixed-fruit pie.**

Apricot-Strawberry Pie

This may seem like an unlikely combination for a fruit pie, but it actually works quite nicely, with the soft and sweet strawberry flavor gently subduing the more pronounced taste of the apricots. I like to serve this with vanilla or a fruit-flavored ice cream.

MAKES 8 TO 10 SERVINGS

1 recipe Extra-Flaky Pie Pastry, Double Crust (page 34) or Tender Cream Cheese Pastry, Double Crust (page 46), refrigerated

FILLING

3 cups pitted and sliced fresh apricots, unpeeled

1/3 cup plus 3 tablespoons sugar

1 tablespoon fresh lemon juice

2 tablespoons cornstarch

1 1/2 cups hulled and sliced fresh strawberries

GLAZE

Milk or light cream

Sugar

GARNISH

Vanilla, peach, or strawberry ice cream

1. If you haven't already, prepare the pastry and refrigerate until firm enough to roll, about 1 hour.

2. On a sheet of lightly floured waxed paper, roll the larger portion of the pastry into a 12-inch circle with a floured rolling pin. Invert the pastry over a 9-inch standard pie pan, center, and peel off the paper. Gently tuck the pastry into the pan, without stretching it, and let the overhang drape over the edge. Place in the refrigerator for 15 minutes.

3. Combine the apricots, 1/3 cup of the sugar, and the lemon juice in a large bowl. Mix well and set aside to juice for 30 minutes. In a small bowl, combine the remaining 3 tablespoons sugar and the cornstarch, then stir the mixture into the apricots. Add the strawberries and mix gently. Preheat the oven to 400°F.

4. Roll the other half of the pastry into a 10-inch circle on a sheet of lightly floured waxed paper. Turn the filling into the chilled pie shell, smoothing the top with your hands or a spoon. Lightly moisten the rim of the pie shell. Invert the top pastry over the filling, center, and peel off the paper. Press the top and bottom pastries together along the dampened edge. Using the back of a butter knife or pastry knife, trim the pastry flush with the edge of the pan and crimp the edge with a fork. Poke several steam vents in the top of the pie with a fork or paring knife. Put a couple of the vents near the edge of the crust so you can check the juices there later. To glaze the pie, lightly brush the pastry with milk and sprinkle with sugar.

5. Place the pie on the center oven rack and bake for 30 minutes. Reduce the oven temperature to 375°F and rotate the pie 180 degrees, so that the part that faced the back of the oven now faces forward. Just in case, slide a large aluminum foil–lined baking sheet onto the rack below to catch any spills. Continue to bake until the top is golden brown and any visible juices bubble thickly through the steam vents, about 30 minutes.

6. Transfer the pie to a wire rack and let cool for at least 2 hours. Serve with ice cream.

Recipe for Success

▸ **If you're fonder of strawberries than you are of apricots, adjust the balance of fruit accordingly, up to equal portions of both.**

▸ **This is more of a spring than a summer combination, but you could reduce the amount of apricots and include a thinly sliced stalk of rhubarb in their place.**

▸ **The reason for the longer than usual juicing of the fruit here has to do with the typical dryness of apricots. Thirty minutes allows more time for the sugar to draw out a good amount of juice from the apricots and thus yield a juicy pie.**

Catoctin Mountain Apricot-Blueberry Pie

When you think of Maryland, you probably think of blue crab, which is, of course, our more or less official state comestible. But out in the western part of the state, and a distance from the Chesapeake Bay, Maryland has some great farm country and orchards, where the determined traveler and pie maker can find excellent fruit for pies. My wife, Bev, and I stumbled upon several of these farm stands and orchards on a trip to an area known as Catoctin Mountain Park, where we hiked and swam in a lovely mountain lake. At a tidy operation called Catoctin Mountain Orchard, run by the Black family, we found excellent fresh apricots, blueberries, plums, and sour cherries—alongside the family's own orchard-baked pies. One pie that caught our eye was the apricot-blueberry, which was the inspiration for this pie. We made it with the orchard's fruit, and it was one of the best pies of the summer.

MAKES 8 TO 10 SERVINGS

1 recipe Basic Shortening Pie Pastry, Single Crust (page 30) or Basic Flaky Pie Pastry, Single Crust (page 31), refrigerated

FILLING

3 cups pitted and sliced fresh apricots, unpeeled

2 cups fresh blueberries, picked over for stems

2/3 cup plus 2 tablespoons granulated sugar

1 tablespoon fresh lemon juice

3 tablespoons cornstarch

1/4 teaspoon ground nutmeg

BROWN SUGAR TOPPING

1/2 cup firmly packed light brown sugar

1/2 cup all-purpose flour

1/4 teaspoon ground cinnamon

Big pinch of salt

1/4 cup (1/2 stick) cold unsalted butter, cut into 1/4-inch pieces

1. If you haven't already, prepare the pastry and refrigerate until firm enough to roll, about 1 hour.

2. On a sheet of lightly floured waxed paper, roll the pastry into a 13-inch circle with a floured rolling pin. Invert the pastry over a 9½-inch deep-dish pie pan, center, and peel off the paper. Gently tuck the pastry into the pan, without stretching it, and sculpt the overhang into an upstanding ridge. Place in the freezer for 15 minutes.

3. In a large bowl, combine the apricots, blueberries, ²/₃ cup of the granulated sugar, and the lemon juice. Mix well and set aside for 30 minutes to juice. Near the end of the 30 minutes, preheat the oven to 400°F.

4. In a small bowl, combine the cornstarch and remaining 2 tablespoons granulated sugar. Stir the mixture into the fruit along with the nutmeg. Turn the filling into the chilled pie shell, leveling the top of the fruit with a spoon. Place the pie on the center oven rack and bake for 30 minutes.

5. Meanwhile, make the topping. Combine the brown sugar, flour, cinnamon, and salt in a food processor and pulse several times to mix. Scatter the butter over the dry ingredients and pulse until the mixture resembles fine crumbs. Empty the crumbs into a large bowl and rub them between your fingers to make large, buttery crumbs. Refrigerate until ready to use.

6. Remove the pie from the oven and reduce the temperature to 375°F. Carefully dump the crumbs in the center of the pie, spreading them over the surface with your hands. Tamp them down lightly. Return the pie to the oven, placing it so that the part that faced the back of the oven now faces forward. Just in case, slide a large aluminum foil–lined baking sheet onto the rack below to catch any spills. Bake until the top is dark golden brown and the juices bubble thickly at the edge, 35 to 40 minutes. If the topping starts to get too dark, cover the pie with loosely tented aluminum foil during the last 15 minutes of baking.

7. Transfer the pie to a wire rack and let cool for at least 2 hours before serving.

Recipe for Success

▶ **This makes a gorgeous double-crust pie. Indeed, the one we saw at the orchard had a top crust. I've also made it with a lattice crust, which is perhaps the best-looking option of all.**

▶ **The reason for the longer than usual juicing of the fruit here has to do with the typical dryness of apricots. Thirty minutes allows more time for the sugar to draw out a good amount of juice from the apricots and thus yield a juicy pie.**

Apricot-Mango Pie with Coconut Crumb Topping

If you're looking for a pie with distinctly tropical overtones, this is it. Given the unreliability of out-of-season fresh apricots, I consider this a summer pie—although I have had pretty good results with drained canned apricots. For the mango, you can use fresh fruit, of course (see Recipe for Success), but for convenience you can't beat those jars of long mango slices found in the produce section of the grocery store. Just drain and cut into chunks.

MAKES 8 TO 10 SERVINGS

1 recipe Basic Flaky Pie Pastry, Single Crust (page 31), refrigerated

FILLING

4 cups pitted and sliced fresh apricots, unpeeled

2 cups peeled mango chunks

1/3 cup plus 1 tablespoon sugar

1 tablespoon fresh lemon juice

1 teaspoon grated lemon zest

1 tablespoon cornstarch

COCONUT CRUMB TOPPING

2/3 cup all-purpose flour

1/2 cup sugar

1/2 cup sweetened flaked coconut

1/4 teaspoon salt

5 tablespoons cold unsalted butter, cut into 1/4-inch pieces

1.   If you haven't already, prepare the pastry and refrigerate until firm enough to roll, about 1 hour.

2.   On a sheet of lightly floured waxed paper, roll the pastry into a 12-inch circle with a floured rolling pin. Invert the pastry over a 9-inch standard pie pan, center, and peel off the paper. Tuck the pastry into the pan, without stretching it, and sculpt the edge into an upstanding ridge. Place in the freezer for 15 minutes.

3.   Combine the apricots, mango, 1/3 cup of the sugar, the lemon juice, and lemon zest in a large bowl. Toss well, then set aside for 15 minutes. Preheat the oven to 400°F.

4.   Combine the remaining 1 tablespoon sugar and the cornstarch in a small bowl, then stir the mixture into the fruit. Turn the filling into the chilled pie shell and smooth the top with your hands. Place the pie on the center oven rack and bake for 30 minutes.

5. Meanwhile, make the topping. Combine the flour, sugar, coconut, and salt in a food processor, pulsing to mix. Scatter the butter over the top and pulse until the mixture resembles fine crumbs. Empty the crumbs into a large bowl and rub gently between your fingers to make buttery, gravelly crumbs. Refrigerate until ready to use.

6. Remove the pie from the oven and reduce the temperature to 375°F. Carefully dump the crumbs in the center of the pie and spread them evenly over the surface with your hands. Press down gently to compact them. Return the pie to the oven, placing it so that the part that faced the back of the oven now faces forward. Just in case, slide a large aluminum foil–lined baking sheet onto the rack below to catch any spills. Continue to bake until the top is golden brown and the juices bubble thickly at the edge, about 30 minutes. If necessary, cover with loosely tented aluminum foil during the last 15 minutes to prevent the pie from browning too much.

7. Transfer the pie to a wire rack and let cool for at least 2 hours before serving.

Recipe for Success

▶ **To peel a fresh mango, slice the skin lengthwise and remove the peel. Cutting lengthwise and avoiding the large pit in the center, cut off a large slab of flesh on either side. Cut the remaining flesh off the pit in chunks.**

Fresh Plum and Port Pie

Juicy, ripe plums are one of the best summer fruits to eat out of hand: the flavor is sweet-tart, refreshing, and wonderfully subtle. But a lot of people don't realize that in addition to being a fine uncooked fruit, plums make a swell pie. Indeed, the French adore their fresh plum tarts. Here's a plum pie made with reduced port, which adds a fruity accent to the sweet fruit and provides an ample amount of juice for the plums to cook in and become melt-in-your-mouth soft. To finish things off, the crumb topping gives the pie an irresistible flavor and crunch.

`MAKES 8 TO 10 SERVINGS`

1 recipe Basic Flaky Pie Pastry, Single Crust (page 31) or All-Butter Pie Pastry, Single Crust (page 28), refrigerated

FILLING

1/2 cup ruby port

7 cups pitted and sliced plums, unpeeled

1/2 cup sugar

1/4 cup quick-cooking tapioca

2 tablespoons raspberry preserves (optional)

1 tablespoon fresh lemon juice

1/2 teaspoon grated lemon zest

COCONUT-ALMOND CRUMB TOPPING

3/4 cup all-purpose flour

1/2 cup sugar

1/4 teaspoon salt

1/3 cup sliced almonds

1/3 cup sweetened flaked coconut

6 tablespoons (3/4 stick) cold unsalted butter, cut into 1/4-inch pieces

1 tablespoon milk

1.   If you haven't already, prepare the pastry and refrigerate until firm enough to roll, about 1 hour.

2.   On a sheet of lightly floured waxed paper, roll the pastry into a 13-inch circle with a floured rolling pin. Invert the pastry over a 9½-inch deep-dish pie pan, center, and peel off the paper. Gently tuck the pastry into the pan, without stretching it, and sculpt the overhang into an upstanding ridge. Place in the freezer for 15 minutes.

3.   Bring the port to a boil in a medium-size nonreactive saucepan. Continue to boil until reduced by roughly one-half; check by pouring it into a heatproof measuring cup. Combine the plums, sugar, and reduced port in a large bowl. Set aside for 10 minutes. Preheat the oven to 400°F.

4.   Stir the tapioca, raspberry preserves (if using), lemon juice, and lemon zest into the fruit. Turn the filling into the chilled pie shell and smooth the top with your hands. Place the pie on the center oven rack and bake for 30 minutes.

5.   Meanwhile, make the topping. Put the flour, sugar, salt, almonds, and coconut in a food processor and pulse several times to mix. Scatter the butter over the top and pulse until the mixture resembles fine crumbs. Add the milk and process again until the crumbs are gravelly. Transfer the crumbs to a medium-size bowl and rub gently between your fingers to make them uniform in texture. Refrigerate until ready to use.

6.   Remove the pie from the oven and reduce the temperature to 375°F. Carefully dump the crumbs in the center of the pie, spreading them over the surface with your hands. Tamp down gently to compact them. Return the pie to the oven, placing it so that the part that faced the back of the oven now faces forward. Just in case, slide a large alu-

minum foil–lined baking sheet onto the rack below to catch any drips. Continue to bake until the juices bubble thickly at the edge, 30 to 35 minutes. If necessary, cover with loosely tented aluminum foil during the last 20 minutes to prevent the pie from browning too much.

7. Transfer the pie to a wire rack and let cool for at least 1 hour before serving.

Recipe for Success

▶ The best advice I can give you for making plum pie is pretty straightforward: wait for the best-of-summer plums. I know I've said that about other fruit, but it bears repeating here. Plums are perhaps the trickiest of fruits to buy because even though the skins may look dark, ripe, and inviting, the flesh may be disappointing. Even the finger pressure test will often fail, because yielding flesh is not necessarily an indicator of peak ripeness. Instead, the plum might just be old and mushy.

Italian Prune Plum Pie

Little Italian prune plums aren't only good for turning into prunes. They're good fresh—compact, tasty, easy to handle—and even better baked in a pie. With a couple of pounds of plums and some refrigerated pie pastry, you can have this pie in the oven in minutes. If you need a pie on the fly for a pool party or an early fall tailgate party, this is a great choice.

MAKES 8 SERVINGS

2 store-bought refrigerated pie pastries

FILLING

4 cups halved (lengthwise) and pitted prune plums

^{1}/$_3$ cup plus 2 tablespoons sugar

1 tablespoon fresh lemon juice

1^1/$_2$ tablespoons cornstarch

1. Line a 9-inch standard pie pan with 1 round of the pastry. Tuck the pastry into the pan, without stretching it, and let the overhang drape over the edge. Place in the refrigerator for 15 minutes. Preheat the oven to 400°F.

2. Combine the plums, ^{1}/$_3$ cup of the sugar, and the lemon juice in a large bowl. Set aside for 5 minutes to juice. Combine the remaining 2 tablespoons sugar and the cornstarch in a small bowl, then stir the mixture into the fruit. Turn the filling into the chilled pie shell, smoothing the top of the fruit with a spoon. Moisten the edge of the pie shell with a pastry brush. Place the other round of pastry over the filling, pressing along the edge to seal. Trim the pastry with scissors, leaving an even ½-inch overhang. Sculpt the pastry into an upstanding ridge. Using a fork or paring knife, poke several steam vents in the top pastry. Put a few of the vents near the edge so you can check the juices there later.

3. Place the pie on the center oven rack and bake for 30 minutes. Reduce the oven temperature to 375°F and rotate the pie 180 degrees, so that the part that faced the back of the oven now faces forward. Just in case, slide a large aluminum foil–lined baking sheet onto the rack below to catch any spills. Continue to bake until the juices bubble thickly at the edge and the top is golden brown, about 25 minutes.

4. Transfer the pie to a wire rack and let cool. Serve just barely warm or at room temperature.

Recipe for Success

‣ Choose prune plums that are uniformly dark and yielding without being overly so. Avoid fruit with soft, mushy spots. Incidentally, if you have young children, buy extra plums for eating out of hand. Children really like the kid-friendly size.

‣ If you're looking for a fast way to turn this into a crumb pie, use a store-bought frozen 9-inch deep-dish pie shell. Bake for 30 minutes with the fruit, then reduce the oven temperature to 375°F and bake with any of the crumb toppings in this book. One that works particularly well is the topping for The Easiest Apple Pie on page 197.

Deep-Dish Pluot Pie with Oatmeal-Walnut Crumb Topping

I was shopping at my local Whole Foods Market one early-summer day and happened upon a display of Pluots, also sold as plumcots, which, though I had never tasted one, I knew to be a cross between a plum and an apricot. The produce manager was kind enough to offer me a taste, and I was immediately smitten. It was sweeter than any plum I'd ever had and juicier than an apricot, but with the delicate flavor of both. Back home, I called Leith Zaiger, whose family owns the trademarked name of Pluot. They've developed about 30 commercially viable varieties, with many more still under development. Leith told me that Pluots are quickly catching up with plums in terms of sales. Consumers like the same things about Pluots that I did when I first tasted them: sweet flavor, nice texture. After our discussion and a little lesson on using Pluots in pies, I took to the kitchen and baked this pie. Leith's mother, Betty, the resident pie maker in the Zaiger family, also gave me her favorite Pluot pie recipe (see page 122). Do try it, too.

MAKES 8 TO 10 SERVINGS

1 recipe Basic Flaky Pie Pastry, Single Crust (page 31) or Basic Shortening Pie Pastry, Single Crust (page 30), refrigerated

FILLING

5¹/₂ to 6 cups pitted and sliced Pluots (see Recipe for Success)

¹/₂ cup plus 2 tablespoons sugar

1 tablespoon fresh lemon juice

1 teaspoon grated lemon zest

Big pinch of ground nutmeg

3 tablespoons cornstarch

OATMEAL-WALNUT CRUMB TOPPING

³/₄ cup all-purpose flour

³/₄ cup finely chopped walnuts

¹/₃ cup rolled oats (old-fashioned or quick-cooking)

¹/₂ teaspoon ground cinnamon

¹/₄ teaspoon salt

6 tablespoons (³/₄ stick) unsalted butter, melted

1. If you haven't already, prepare the pastry and refrigerate until firm enough to roll, about 1 hour.

2. On a sheet of lightly floured waxed paper, roll the larger portion of the pastry into a 13¹/₂-inch circle with a floured rolling pin. Invert the pastry over a 9¹/₂- to 10-inch extra-deep-dish pie pan, center, and peel off the paper. Gently tuck the pastry into the pan, without stretching it, and sculpt the overhang into an upstanding ridge. Place in the freezer for 15 minutes.

3. Combine the Pluots, ¹/₂ cup of the sugar, lemon juice, lemon zest, and nutmeg in a large bowl. Mix well, then set aside for 15 minutes to juice. Preheat the oven to 400°F.

4. Combine the remaining 2 tablespoons sugar and the cornstarch in a small bowl, then stir the mixture into the fruit. Turn the filling into the chilled pie shell and smooth the top with a spoon. Place the pie on the center oven rack and bake for 30 minutes.

5. Meanwhile, make the topping. Combine the flour, walnuts, oats, cinnamon, and salt in a large bowl. Toss with your hands to mix. Pour the butter over the top and stir with a fork to combine. Then switch to your hands and rub the mixture gently to make uniform gravelly crumbs. Refrigerate until ready to use.

6. Remove the pie from the oven and reduce the temperature to 375°F. Carefully dump the crumb topping in the center of the pie and spread evenly over the surface with your hands. Tamp the crumbs down lightly. Return the pie to the oven, placing it so that the part that faced the back of the oven now faces forward. To catch any spills, slide a large aluminum foil–lined baking sheet onto the rack below. Bake until you see the juices bubbling thickly at the edge, 25 to 35 minutes. If the top starts to get too brown, cover loosely with aluminum foil for the last 10 minutes.

7. Transfer the pie to a wire rack and let cool for at least 2 hours before serving.

Recipe for Success

> ▶ Pluots tend to be very juicy, which is why I recommend the extra-deep-dish pan. If you only have a standard deep-dish pan, you may want to limit the fruit to 5 to 5^1/$_2$ cups.

> ▶ You can blanch Pluots, like peaches (see page 88), to remove the skins, but they tend to bake up fairly soft, and I don't think it's necessary. Also, a lot of the deep burgundy color is in the skin, so you will lose some of that color if you peel them. Still, if you'd rather, blanch them for about 15 seconds, and the skins will slide right off.

Betty Zaiger's Pluot Pie

Betty Zaiger is the matriarch of the family that has bred more than 30 commercial varieties of the Pluot, a cross between a plum and an apricot. (Read more about Pluots, pages 120–121.) Betty's pie is a little different from my own crumb-topped Pluot pie (see page 120). For one, she uses no top crust or crumb crust. Rather, she cooks the filling on top of the stove, thickens it with cornstarch, and pours it directly into a fully prebaked crust. To boost the flavor of the fruit, she swears by peach schnapps, so a healthy dose is added along with the cornstarch. Betty says she often serves this pie at her family's Wednesday meeting with fruit growers, and she says it creates quite a stir when word gets out that her Pluot pie is on the menu. For a simple garnish, do what Betty does: serve it with a dollop of whipped cream.

MAKES 8 TO 10 SERVINGS

1 recipe Basic Flaky Pie Pastry, Single Crust (page 31) or Basic Shortening Pie Pastry, Single Crust (page 30), refrigerated

FILLING

4 cups pitted and sliced Pluots

2/3 cup water

1/2 to 3/4 cup sugar, to your taste

1/3 to 1/2 cup peach schnapps, to your taste

2 tablespoons cornstarch

Big pinch of ground nutmeg

1. If you haven't already, prepare the pastry and refrigerate until firm enough to roll, about 1 hour.

2. On a sheet of lightly floured waxed paper, roll the pastry into a 13-inch circle with a floured rolling pin. Invert the pastry over a 9½-inch deep-dish pie pan, center, and peel off the paper. Tuck the pastry into the pan, without stretching it, and sculpt the edge into an upstanding ridge. Place in the freezer for 15 minutes, then fully prebake and let cool according to the instructions on page 16.

3. Combine the Pluots, water, and sugar in a medium-size nonreactive saucepan. Bring to a boil, then cook at a low boil until the fruit is soft, about 10 minutes. Meanwhile, combine the peach schnapps and cornstarch in a small bowl, blending well. When the fruit is soft, stir in the cornstarch mixture. Continue to cook at a low boil for 1 minute, then remove from the heat and stir in the nutmeg. Let the filling cool for several minutes, then turn it into the cooled pie shell, smoothing the top with a spoon.

4. Transfer the pie to a wire rack and let cool thoroughly. Cover with loosely tented aluminum foil and refrigerate until quite firm, at least 2 hours. Serve chilled.

Recipe for Success

▶ Review the tips for fully prebaking a pie shell on page 16. One pointer that bears repeating is the importance of baking the crust until it is golden brown on the bottom. If you don't, the pastry may taste a little raw.

▶ In my Pluot pie recipe (see page 120), I speak briefly about peeling the Pluots. Betty says she never bothers, because once the fruit is simmered for 10 minutes, the skins are very soft and unobtrusive.

Champagne Grape Pie

Those pearl-size champagne grapes that you see in the produce department are actually a variety known as Black Corinth. Dried, they're called currants, and you've probably used them to bake into muffins, buns, or scones. They've become quite popular in recent years, in part because of their petite size and sweet flavor and in part because those of us who entertain think they look so attractive on a cheese and fruit platter. Not surprisingly, they make a very good fresh pie, and—sweet as they are—they require little added sugar. A bit of lemon juice and a delicate pastry, and you have a delicious, pure-grape pie you'd be proud to serve your family or guests. Look for champagne grapes starting in late July or early August.

MAKES 8 TO 10 SERVINGS

1 recipe Extra-Flaky Pie Pastry, Double Crust (page 34), refrigerated

FILLING

4 cups champagne grapes, stemmed (see Recipe for Success)

1/4 cup plus 1 1/2 tablespoons sugar

1 tablespoon fresh lemon juice

2 1/2 tablespoons cornstarch

GLAZE

Milk or light cream

Sugar

1. If you haven't already, prepare the pastry and refrigerate until firm enough to roll, about 1 hour.

2. On a sheet of lightly floured waxed paper, roll the larger portion of the pastry into a 12-inch circle with a floured rolling pin. Invert the pastry over a 9-inch standard pie pan, center, and peel off the paper. Gently tuck the pastry into the pan, without stretching it, and let the overhang drape over the edge. Place in the refrigerator for 15 minutes.

3. In a medium-size bowl, combine the grapes, 1/4 cup of the sugar, and the lemon juice. Mix well and set aside to juice for 10 minutes. Preheat the oven to 400°F.

4. On another sheet of floured waxed paper, roll the other half of the pastry into a 10-inch circle. Combine the remaining 1 1/2 tablespoons sugar and the cornstarch in small bowl, then stir the mixture into the fruit. Turn the filling into the chilled pie shell, smoothing the top with a spoon. Lightly moisten the rim of the pie shell. Invert the top pastry over the filling, center, and peel off the paper. Press the top and bottom pastries together along the dampened edge. Using the back of a butter knife or pastry knife, trim the pastry flush with the edge of the pan, then pinch the edges together to seal. Poke several steam vents in the top of the pie with a fork or paring knife. Put a couple of the vents near the edge of the crust so you can check the juices there later. To glaze the pie, lightly brush the pastry with milk and sprinkle with sugar.

5. Place the pie on the center oven rack and bake for 30 minutes. Reduce the oven temperature to 375°F and rotate the pie 180 degrees, so that the part that faced the back of the oven now faces forward. Just in case, slide a large aluminum foil–lined baking sheet onto the rack below to catch any spills. Continue to bake until the top is golden brown and any visible juices bubble thickly through the steam vents, 25 to 30 minutes.

6. Transfer the pie to a wire rack and let cool for at least 2 hours before serving.

Recipe for Success

▶ Champagne grapes sometimes have a white "bloom" on them, which could be mistaken for mold. The bloom, however, is an indication of ripeness and need not be avoided.

▶ The easiest way to remove the grapes from the stems is to "rake" them off with a wide-set fork or, lacking one of those, your hands.

▶ Although you set the fruit aside to juice, you may not actually get all that much juice until the pie is baked.

Seedless Black Grape Pie

It's not easy in most parts of the country to find the sort of grapes needed to make a flavorful pie. Most are firm and less than ripe. If you keep your eyes open, however, you will occasionally find some that are softer, sweeter, and juicer than usual. When you do, consider turning them into a pie. I've added a few tablespoons of reduced red wine to the filling to provide some of that winy flavor your taste buds might expect to find in a pie such as this.

MAKES 8 TO 10 SERVINGS

1 recipe Basic Flaky Pie Pastry, Double Crust (page 31), refrigerated

FILLING

1/2 cup Merlot, Cabernet Sauvignon, or other dry red wine

51/2 cups halved seedless black grapes

1/3 cup plus 2 tablespoons sugar

2 teaspoons fresh lemon juice

21/2 tablespoons cornstarch

2 tablespoons cold unsalted butter, cut into small pieces

1. If you haven't already, prepare the pastry and refrigerate until firm enough to roll, about 1 hour.

2. On a sheet of lightly floured waxed paper, roll the larger portion of the pastry into a 12-inch circle with a floured rolling pin. Invert the pastry over a 9-inch standard pie pan, center, and peel off the paper. Gently tuck the pastry into the pan, without stretching it, and let the overhang drape over the edge. Place in the refrigerator for 15 minutes.

3. Bring the wine to a boil in a medium-size nonreactive saucepan. Boil rapidly for several minutes, until reduced to 2 to 3 tablespoons. Keep a heatproof measuring cup nearby to check. Combine the grapes, reduced wine, $1/3$ cup of the sugar, and the lemon juice in a medium-size bowl. Mix well, then set aside for 10 minutes to juice. Preheat the oven to 400°F.

4. Combine the cornstarch and remaining 2 tablespoons sugar in a small bowl. Stir the mixture into the fruit. Turn the filling into the chilled pie shell and smooth the top with a spoon. Dot the filling with the butter.

5. Roll the other half of the pastry into a 10-inch circle on a sheet of lightly floured waxed paper. Moisten the outer edge of the pie shell with a pastry brush. Invert the top pastry over the filling, center, and peel off the paper. Press the top and bottom pastries together along the dampened edge. Using the back of a butter knife, trim the pastry flush with the edge of the pan. With the back of a fork, press the tines all along the edge to seal. Using the fork, poke several steam vents in the top of the pie, including a couple along the edge so you can check the juices there later.

6. Place the pie on the center oven rack and bake for 30 minutes. Reduce the oven temperature to 375°F and rotate the pie 180 degrees, so that the part of the pie that faced the back of the oven now faces forward. Just in case, slide a large aluminum foil–lined baking sheet onto the rack below to catch any spills. Continue to bake until golden brown, about 25 minutes. When done, you may notice thick juices bubbling out of the steam vents along the edge.

7. Transfer the pie to a wire rack and let cool for at least 2 hours before serving.

Recipe for Success

▶ **Grapes can be deceiving when it comes to juiciness. They might not look all that juicy even after they've been sugared and set aside for 10 minutes. But don't let that fool you into using less cornstarch. My experience is that grape pies are very juicy—remember, most grapes are grown for their juice—and you'll need every bit of the cornstarch recommended here to achieve the proper texture.**

Grape and Fig Pie

I think the best fruit to mix with fresh black grapes is dried figs. You end up with a gorgeous deep purple filling and juice, aromatically suggestive of the Mediterranean. Instead of poaching the figs, as I sometimes do when I'm using them in pies, I simply steam them for a few minutes. That softens them but leaves them sufficiently absorbent to soak up the copious juice that bakes out of the grapes. Garnished with sweetened mascarpone, this is a wonderful pie to follow a light Mediterranean meal.

MAKES 8 TO 10 SERVINGS

1 recipe Basic Flaky Pie Pastry, Double Crust (page 31), refrigerated

FILLING

1 1/2 cups stemmed and diced dried Black Mission figs (see Recipe for Success)

4 cups halved seedless black grapes

1/2 cup sugar

2 teaspoons fresh lemon juice

1 teaspoon grated lemon zest

1 1/2 tablespoons Frangelico or 1/2 teaspoon vanilla extract (optional)

1 1/2 tablespoons cornstarch

1 tablespoon cold unsalted butter, cut into small pieces

GARNISH

Sweetened Mascarpone Cheese (page 606)

1. If you haven't already, prepare the pastry and refrigerate until firm enough to roll, about 1 hour.

2. On a sheet of lightly floured waxed paper, roll the larger portion of the pastry into a 12-inch circle with a floured rolling pin. Invert the pastry over a 9-inch standard pie pan, center, and peel off the paper. Gently tuck the pastry into the pan, without stretching it, and let the overhang drape over the edge. Place in the refrigerator for 15 minutes.

3. Place the figs in a steamer basket set in a saucepan (or directly in the saucepan) and add about 1/2 inch of water to the pan. Cover tightly and bring the water to a boil. Reduce the heat slightly and simmer-steam the figs for 5 minutes. Drain in a colander or sieve.

4. In a large bowl, combine the grapes, figs, all but about 2 tablespoons of the sugar, the lemon juice, lemon zest, and Frangelico (if using). Mix well, then set aside for 15 minutes. Preheat the oven to 400°F.

5. Mix the cornstarch and remaining 2 tablespoons sugar together in a small bowl. Sprinkle the mixture over the fruit and stir to combine. Turn the filling into the chilled pie shell and smooth the top. Dot the filling with the butter.

6. Roll the other half of the pastry into a 10-inch circle on a sheet of lightly floured waxed paper. Moisten the outer edge of the pie shell with a pastry brush. Invert the top pastry over the filling, center, and peel off the paper. Press the top and bottom pastries together along the dampened edge. Using the back of a butter knife, trim the pastry flush with the edge of the pan. With the back of a fork, press the tines all along the edge to seal. Using the fork, poke several steam vents in the top of the pie, including a couple along the edge so you can check the juices there later.

7. Place the pie on the center oven rack and bake for 30 minutes. Reduce the oven temperature to 375°F and rotate the pie 180 degrees, so that the part of the pie that faced the back of the oven now faces forward. Just in case, slide a large aluminum foil–lined baking sheet onto the rack below to catch any spills. Continue to bake until the pie is golden brown, about 25 minutes. When done, you may notice thick juices bubbling out of the steam vents along the edge.

8. Transfer the pie to a wire rack and let cool for at least 2 hours before serving. Garnish each slice with sweetened mascarpone.

Recipe for Success

‣ **Other types of dried figs will work, too, including Turkish figs, but I prefer the Black Mission variety. Lacking figs altogether, you can substitute pitted prunes.**

‣ **If your figs are pleasantly moist—that is, it doesn't feel like a workout to eat them—you can actually skip the steaming.**

Watermelon Rind Pie

When you eat a piece of watermelon, you take the last juicy bite and toss out the rind, right? Well, not if you want to bake one of the more unusual pies in this collection. A holdover from the days when thrifty farm wives were reluctant to waste a scrap of food, this pie gets its primary ingredient not from the flesh of the watermelon—like Watermelon Chiffon Pie (page 485)—but from the peeled rind. First you cook the diced rind in lightly sugared water until tender. Then you combine it with raisins, nuts, brown sugar, vinegar, and spices. Does it taste anything like watermelon? Not really. It's actually something like mock mincemeat, making this more of a fall pie than a summer one. Serve this to your family and friends and see if they can guess what's in it.

MAKES 8 TO 10 SERVINGS

1 recipe Basic Flaky Pie Pastry, Double Crust (page 31) or Basic Shortening Pie Pastry, Double Crust (page 30), refrigerated

FILLING

3 cups peeled and diced watermelon rind

3/4 cup granulated sugar

1/2 cup dark raisins

1/2 cup chopped walnuts or pecans

3 tablespoons cider vinegar

2 tablespoons firmly packed light brown sugar

1 tablespoon all-purpose flour

1/2 teaspoon ground cinnamon

1/4 teaspoon ground cloves

1/4 teaspoon ground nutmeg

1/4 teaspoon salt

GLAZE

1 large egg white, lightly beaten

Granulated sugar

1. If you haven't already, prepare the pastry and refrigerate until firm enough to roll, about 1 hour.

2. Combine the watermelon rind and 1/4 cup of the granulated sugar in a large saucepan. Add water just to cover. Bring to a boil, partially cover, and continue to boil until the rind is tender and translucent, 20 to 25 minutes. Drain well, then transfer the rind to a large bowl and let cool.

3. On a sheet of lightly floured waxed paper, roll the larger portion of the pastry into a 12-inch circle with a floured rolling pin. Invert the pastry over a 9-inch standard pie pan, center, and peel off the paper. Gently tuck the pastry into the pan, without stretching it, and let the overhang drape over the edge. Place in the refrigerator for 15 minutes. Preheat the oven to 400°F.

4. Stir the remaining 1/2 cup granulated sugar into the cooled rind. Stir in the raisins, nuts, vinegar, and brown sugar, then stir in the flour, spices, and salt.

5. On another sheet of floured waxed paper, roll the other half of dough into a 10-inch circle. Turn the filling into the chilled pie shell, smoothing the top with your hands or a spoon. Lightly moisten the rim of the pie shell. Invert the top pastry over the filling, center, and peel off the paper. Press the top and bottom pastries together along the dampened edge. Trim the pastry with scissors or a paring knife, leaving an even 1/2-inch overhang all around, then sculpt the overhang into an upstanding ridge. Poke several steam vents in the top of the pie with a fork or paring knife; put a couple of the vents near the edge of the crust so you can check the juices there later. To glaze the pie, lightly brush the pastry with the beaten egg white and sprinkle lightly with granulated sugar.

6. Place the pie on the center oven rack and bake for 30 minutes. Reduce the oven temperature to 375°F and rotate the pie 180 degrees, so that the part that faced the back of the oven now faces forward. Just in case, slide a large aluminum foil–lined baking sheet onto the rack below to catch any spills. Continue to bake until the top is dark golden brown, 25 to 30 minutes. This is not a particularly juicy pie, so you may or may not see juices bubbling up through the steam vents.

7. Transfer the pie to a wire rack and let cool for at least 1 hour. Serve slightly warm or at room temperature.

Recipe for Success

▶ **When you peel the rind, be sure to remove all of the outermost skin with a sharp peeler, since it's the toughest part of the skin. Don't undercook the rind, thinking it will soften further as it bakes. Because of the vinegar in the filling, this isn't likely to happen.**

Crumb-Topped Zapple Pie

Here's an idea I borrowed from *The Classic Zucchini Cookbook*, published by my friends at Storey Books (2002). Zapple pie, if you're wondering, is the name of a sweet zucchini pie that tastes like an apple pie—or reasonably close to it. Zucchini doesn't taste like anything, and if you add enough cinnamon, nutmeg, and lemon juice to something that tastes like nothing, then throw on a crumb topping, you'll have an approximation of a real apple pie—kind of like a vegetable version of mock apple pie (see page 246). Anyway, I was intrigued by the whole idea of a sweet zucchini pie, so with the authors' recipe as my blueprint, I started playing around with variations of my own. I added apple juice concentrate to increase its apple credibility, as well as apple cider vinegar for tang. I also added some raisins, because I thought they belonged. In the end, you may not think it's real apple pie, but I think you'll enjoy it nonetheless, especially if you—like many gardeners—have more zucchini in the summer than you know what to do with.

MAKES 8 TO 10 SERVINGS

1 recipe Basic Shortening Pie Pastry, Single Crust (page 30), refrigerated

FILLING

6 cups peeled, halved lengthwise, and thinly sliced zucchini

2/3 cup granulated sugar

2 tablespoons frozen apple juice concentrate, thawed

1 teaspoon ground cinnamon

1/4 teaspoon ground nutmeg

1/4 teaspoon salt

2 tablespoons cornstarch

1/3 cup fresh lemon juice

1 tablespoon cider vinegar

CRUMB TOPPING

1/2 cup all-purpose flour

1/2 cup firmly packed light brown sugar

1/2 cup pecan halves

1/4 teaspoon salt

1/4 cup (1/2 stick) cold unsalted butter, cut into 1/4-inch pieces

1. If you haven't already, prepare the pastry and refrigerate until firm enough to roll, about 1 hour.

2. On a sheet of lightly floured waxed paper, roll the pastry into a 13-inch circle with a floured rolling pin. Invert the pastry over a 9½-inch deep-dish pie pan, center, and peel off the paper. Tuck the pastry into the pan, without stretching it, and sculpt the edge into an upstanding ridge. Place in the freezer for 15 minutes. Preheat the oven to 400°F.

3. Meanwhile, in a large, heavy soup pot, combine the zucchini, sugar, apple juice concentrate, cinnamon, nutmeg, and salt over medium-high heat and gradually heat, stirring occasionally, until the liquid starts to boil. Reduce the heat slightly and simmer until the zucchini is tender but not mushy, about 10 minutes.

4. Blend the cornstarch and lemon juice together in a small bowl, stirring until smooth. When the zucchini is tender, stir the cornstarch slurry into the pot and cook, stirring nonstop to prevent sticking, for 1 to 1½ minutes. The juice will thicken noticeably. Remove the pan from the heat and stir in the vinegar.

5. To make the crumb topping, combine the flour, brown sugar, pecans, and salt in a food processor and pulse several times to chop the nuts. Scatter the butter over the dry ingredients and pulse until the mixture resembles fine crumbs. Transfer to a bowl and rub between your fingers to make large, buttery crumbs.

6. Spoon the filling into the chilled pie shell, smoothing the top with a spoon. Dump the crumbs in the center of the pie, spreading them evenly over the top. Tamp them down gently with your hands. Place the pie on the center oven rack, reduce the temperature to 350°F, and bake for about 40 minutes, rotating the pie 180 degrees halfway through the baking, so that the part that faced the back of the oven now faces forward. When done, you may or may not see thick juice bubbling around the edge. The best indication of doneness is total elapsed time.

7. Transfer the pie to a wire rack and let cool. Serve slightly warm, at room temperature, or chilled. This is best served the same day it is made.

Recipe for Success

▶ **Choose small to medium-size zucchini for the filling. The flesh will be firmer, more apple-like, and better able to hold its shape.**

▶ **Do watch the amount of time you cook the zucchini. This pie is charming when there's a little texture to it and slightly less so if the zucchini is overcooked.**

▶ **The pie can be made with a top crust instead of the crumb topping.**

Fruits of the Forest Pie (Fruit Version) with Coarse Sugar Glaze

I'd been hearing about various "fruits of the forest" pies for some time before I actually started researching recipes. When I finally did, I found that they fall into two distinct categories—nut fillings (see page 356) and fruit fillings. My guess is that the nut versions came first, since one might well consider them fruits of the forest. Then, I imagine, someone appropriated the fanciful name and applied it to a delicious mixed-fruit pie, and the idea caught on in spite of the geographic misrepresentation. This, obviously, falls into the latter category. And if the blueberries are, perhaps, the closest this pie gets to the forest, we'll overlook that because it's so delicious. For the glaze, I use coarse sugar, which offers some good crunchy contrast to the soft filling. The best time to make this pie is mid- to late summer.

MAKES 8 TO 10 SERVINGS

1 recipe Basic Shortening Pie Pastry, Double Crust (page 30), refrigerated

FILLING

2 medium-size ripe peaches, peeled, pitted, and sliced

1 large ripe pear, peeled, cored, and sliced

1 large Granny Smith or other tart apple, peeled, cored, and sliced

1 cup fresh blueberries, picked over for stems

1 cup hulled and sliced fresh strawberries

1/2 cup chopped pineapple, fresh or canned (drained)

1/2 cup plus 3 tablespoons granulated sugar

1/2 teaspoon ground ginger

1/4 teaspoon ground nutmeg

1 tablespoon fresh lemon juice

3 tablespoons cornstarch

GLAZE

Milk or light cream

Coarse sugar (see page 69)

1. If you haven't already, prepare the pastry and refrigerate until firm enough to roll, about 1 hour.

2. On a sheet of lightly floured waxed paper, roll the larger portion of the pastry into a 13-inch circle with a floured rolling pin. Invert the pastry over a 9 1/2-inch deep-dish pie pan, center, and peel off the paper. Gently tuck the pastry into the pan, without stretching it, and let the overhang drape over the edge. Place in the refrigerator for 15 minutes.

3. In a large bowl, combine the fruit, 1/2 cup of the granulated sugar, the ginger, nutmeg, and lemon juice. Toss well to mix, then set aside for 10 minutes to juice. Mix the remaining 3 tablespoons granulated sugar and the cornstarch together in a small bowl, then stir the mixture into the fruit. Preheat the oven to 400°F.

4. On another sheet of lightly floured waxed paper, roll the other half of the pastry into an 11-inch circle. Turn the filling into the chilled pie shell, smoothing the fruit with a spoon. Lightly moisten the rim of the pie shell. Invert the top pastry over the filling, center, and peel off the paper. Press the top and bottom pastries together along the dampened edge. Trim the pastry with scissors or a paring knife, leaving an even 1/2-inch overhang all around, then sculpt the overhang into an upstanding ridge. Poke several steam vents in the top of the pie with a fork or paring knife. Put a couple of the vents near the edge of the crust so you can check the juices there later. To glaze the pie, lightly brush the pastry with milk and sprinkle with coarse sugar.

5. Place the pie on the center oven rack and bake for 30 minutes. Reduce the oven temperature to 375°F and rotate the pie 180 degrees, so that the part that faced the back

of the oven now faces forward. Just in case, slide a large aluminum foil–lined baking sheet onto the rack below to catch any drips. Bake until the juices bubble thickly at the steam vents and the top is golden brown, 35 to 45 minutes. If the top of the pie starts to get too dark, cover with loosely tented aluminum foil during the last 10 to 15 minutes.

6. Transfer the pie to a wire rack and let cool for at least 2 hours before serving.

Recipe for Success

▶   This is the combination of fruits I like best in this pie, but there is a lot of room for flexibility here. You can use blackberries or raspberries in place of the strawberries, nectarines in place of the peaches, and 2 apples instead of a pear and an apple.

▶   If you happen to have fruit cookie cutters, especially small ones, an arrangement of fruit pastry cutouts (see page 19) on top is very pretty and hints at what's to come.

Robin Hood: Prize Pie Baker?

"Pies, contrary to popular belief, were not invented in North America. Probably every bread-making people of the Old World used dough as a container in which to bake fruit or other food and so make their bread more interesting. Those venison pasties (turnovers) that Robin Hood fed to his merry men were pies of a sort, and the prologue to the Cook's tale in Chaucer's *The Canterbury Tales* tells of an unethical pie dealer who was notorious for selling pasties 'That hath been twies hoot and twies coold.'"

—Jonathan Norton Leonard, *American Cooking: New England* (Time-Life Books, 1970)

"White" Summer Fruit Pie

I love the so-called white summer fruits—white peaches, white nectarines, and the blushing orange-white Rainier cherries—for their unusual shades and unique flavors. (Rainier cherries taste peachy to me, and white peaches have a floral fragrance and flavor I don't find with other peaches.) Bring these fruits together in one crust, and you have a pie with a rather distinct flavor and hue. Here I combine either white peaches or nectarines and Rainier cherries in a streusel-topped pie with an unexpected flavor. The trick to doing this right is simply waiting, patiently, for the two crops to come to market at the same time, in late June and July, before making this pie. But, as you'll discover, it is well worth the wait.

MAKES 8 TO 10 SERVINGS

1 recipe Basic Flaky Pie Pastry, Single Crust (page 31) or All-Butter Pie Pastry, Single Crust (page 28), refrigerated

FILLING

4 cups peeled, pitted, and sliced ripe white peaches or nectarines

2 cups fresh Rainier cherries, stemmed, halved, and pitted

1/3 cup plus 3 tablespoons sugar

1 tablespoon fresh orange or lemon juice

1 teaspoon grated orange or lemon zest

2 1/2 tablespoons cornstarch

Pinch of ground nutmeg

STREUSEL TOPPING

1/2 cup all-purpose flour

1/2 cup sugar

Big pinch of salt

Big pinch of ground cinnamon

1/4 cup (1/2 stick) cold unsalted butter, cut into 1/4-inch pieces

1. If you haven't already, prepare the pastry and refrigerate until firm enough to roll, about 1 hour.

2. On a sheet of lightly floured waxed paper, roll the pastry into a 13-inch circle with a floured rolling pin. Invert the pastry over a 9 1/2-inch deep-dish pie pan, center, and peel off the paper. Tuck the pastry into the pan, without stretching it, and sculpt the edge into an upstanding ridge. Place in the freezer for 15 minutes.

3. In a large bowl, combine the fruit, 1/3 cup of the sugar, the orange juice, and orange zest. Toss gently to combine, then set aside for 10 minutes to juice. Preheat the oven to 400°F.

4. Combine the remaining 3 tablespoons sugar and the cornstarch in a small bowl. Stir the mixture into the fruit along with nutmeg. Turn the filling into the chilled pie shell and smooth the top of the fruit with your hands or a spoon. Place the pie on the center oven rack and bake for 30 minutes.

5. Meanwhile, make the topping. In a large bowl, combine the flour, sugar, salt, and cinnamon. Toss gently to mix. Rub the butter into the dry ingredients until the mixture resembles coarse crumbs. Refrigerate until ready to use.

6. Remove the pie from the oven and reduce the temperature to 375°F. Dump the topping in the center of the pie and spread it evenly over the fruit with your hands. Tamp it down gently. Return the pie to the oven, placing it so that the part that faced the back of the oven now faces forward. Just in case, slide a large aluminum foil–lined baking sheet onto the rack below to catch any spills. Continue to bake until the topping is golden brown and the juices bubble thickly around the edge, 25 to 30 minutes.

7. Transfer the pie to a wire rack and let cool for at least 2 hours before serving.

Recipe for Success

▶ **With some of my peach and nectarine pies, I don't bother to peel the fruit, because the skins are very soft. But with this pie and filling, which I consider somewhat refined, I do.**

▶ **You may be wondering whether you can make this pie with another type of cherry. Of course you can, and it will be delicious, but the flavor will be very different from the one intended.**

▶ **Remember, there are 2 ways to peel a peach: with a sharp paring knife and by blanching method (see page 88). Either works fine here.**

Fresh summer berries are so irresistible in homemade pies that it seemed

only right to give them their own showcase. This chapter is precisely that, and

if you occasionally stumble upon an errant fig, peach, or slice of rhubarb here

and there, remember that the more than two dozen recipes that follow are

connected by a single purpose: to celebrate those black, red, and blue

Berry Good Pies

summer jewels that steal the show in some of our most memorable pies. •

Not that we don't all sometimes rely on not-fresh fruit to tide us over or aug-

ment the berries we have on hand. There are times, after all, when you just

have to have a berry pie and the only reasonably priced fruit to be had is

found in a can or the freezer case. For that reason, a few of these recipes

specify alternatives to fresh. But most of them more or less take for granted

that you're going to be baking with fresh picked. • My intention was to make

this chapter as inclusive as possible, but I make no apologies for that fact that my own bias in berry pies is readily transparent: blueberry pies outnumber all others. I used to grow blueberries at my former home in New Hampshire. What the bears and birds didn't get first, I would turn into pies. And delectable pies they were. This supports my belief that the best pies I've ever eaten have been those made by cooks with local ingredients. That's something to keep in mind as you peruse this chapter. And if blueberry isn't your favorite, you're sure to find a berry pie that's just right for you.

The $900 Pie

The Darby, Montana, Public Library has a friend in Emma Lee Nicholson—81 years old and a lifetime resident of Darby. According to a report in a July 2003 issue of the *Missoulian* newspaper, Emma Lee's sour cream and raisin pie sold for $900 at a pie auction to benefit the construction of a new town library. It was the last pie of the evening to be auctioned, and Emma Lee, who is something of a local pie-baking celebrity, thought it would fetch much less. "I guessed $40," she reportedly told her granddaughter.

The winning bidders, Sharon and Ron Wilkerson of Missoula, took the pie home after the auction, ate a couple of pieces, and served the rest to several guests the following day. The pie auction raised $3,267.50 for the new library, including $300 for one of Emma Lee's strawberry pies.

Tips for Baking Beautiful Berry Pies

▶ Don't jump on the berry pie bandwagon too early. The best berries come to market in mid- to late season. For the best price, shop at farmers' markets, where competing vendors will try to undersell one another.

▶ Inspect baskets of berries carefully. Find out when the berries were picked. The same day or the day before is best. Fresh berries are the most fragile of fruits and are easily damaged by their own weight and by one or more spoiled berries. I always take a whiff of a berry basket. If I detect a moldy smell, I don't buy it. One or two moldy berries can taint the flavor of an entire pie.

▶ If you must rinse berries, don't do it until you're ready to use them. Because raspberries have a cavity, they need to be inverted on paper towels after rinsing to drain the excess water.

▶ Use berries in pies right away, preferably the same day you buy them. If you're keeping them overnight, pour them into a wide container so that they don't continue to sit under their own weight.

▶ Mix all berry fillings very carefully, or you'll crush the fruit. A few crushed berries are fine, but for the most part you want to maintain their shape and texture.

▶ Don't overfill a berry pie. Fresh berries produce a lot of juice, and you'll minimize bubbling over if the pan isn't full.

▶ As with other fruit pies, don't underbake a berry pie, or the filling will not thicken properly. The visible juices should be bubbling thickly before you remove the pie from the oven.

▶ Let your berry pie cool for at least one hour, preferably two or more, before slicing, to keep the filling from oozing everywhere.

All-Strawberry Pie

As I've said elsewhere, there are those who think that strawberries are, for the most part, unsuitable for pies because they bake up so soft. I say nonsense. Sure, they cook up soft, but so do many other fruits. Just because strawberries don't stay firm doesn't mean you should eliminate them from your pie repertoire. Like so many other fresh fruit pies, I tend to make this one only during local fresh berry season. I like to add some form of mint to the mix, since the two share harvest times and taste so good together. Minced fresh mint is fine, although it tends to turn a little dark in the baking, which may be somewhat unappealing if you're serving the pie to guests. Instead, you might consider a drop or two of mint oil, or, as I use here, white crème de menthe. Along with the nutmeg, it adds a soft flavor to the fruit that everyone seems to like.

MAKES 8 TO 10 SERVINGS

1 recipe Basic Flaky Pie Pastry, Double Crust (page 31), refrigerated

FILLING

4 cups hulled and thickly sliced fresh strawberries

1/2 cup sugar

2 tablespoons cornstarch

1 tablespoon white crème de menthe (optional; see headnote)

1 tablespoon fresh lemon juice

1/4 teaspoon ground nutmeg

1 tablespoon cold unsalted butter, cut into small pieces

GLAZE

Sugar

Milk or light cream

1. If you haven't already, prepare the pastry and refrigerate until firm enough to roll, about 1 hour.

2. On a sheet of lightly floured waxed paper, roll the larger portion of the pastry into a 12-inch circle with a floured rolling pin. Invert over a 9-inch standard pie pan, center, and peel off the paper. Gently tuck the pastry into the pan, without stretching it, and let the overhang drape over the edge. Place in the refrigerator for 15 minutes.

3. Put the strawberries in a large bowl. Mix the sugar and cornstarch together in a small bowl, then add the mixture to the fruit and toss well. Add the crème de menthe (if using), lemon juice, and nutmeg and toss again. Set aside for 10 minutes. Preheat the oven to 400°F.

4. On another sheet of lightly floured waxed paper, roll the other half of the pastry into an 11-inch circle. Turn the filling into the chilled pie shell and smooth the fruit with a spoon. Dot the top with the butter. Lightly moisten the rim of the pie shell. Invert the top pastry over the filling, center, and peel off the paper. Press the top and bottom pastries together along the dampened edge. Trim the pastry with scissors or a paring knife, leaving an even 1/2-inch overhang all around, then sculpt the overhang into an upstanding ridge. Poke several steam vents in the top of the pie with a fork or paring knife. Put a couple of the vents near the edge of the crust so you can check the juices there later. Sprinkle the top crust evenly with sugar, then with milk.

5. Place the pie on the center oven rack and bake for 30 minutes. Reduce the oven temperature to 375°F and rotate the pie 180 degrees, so that the part that faced the back of the oven now faces forward. Just in case, slide a large aluminum foil–lined baking sheet onto the rack below to catch any drips. Bake until the juices bubble thickly at the steam vents and the top is golden brown, 35 to 45 minutes. If the top of the pie starts to get too dark, cover it with loosely tented aluminum foil during the last 10 to 15 minutes.

6. Transfer the pie to a wire rack and let cool for at least 2 hours to let the juices settle and firm up before serving.

Recipe for Success

▶ **This really is meant to be an all-strawberry pie, with the purity of flavor you hope for from such a pie. But if you just can't resist adding that handful of left-over raspberries or cherries you have hanging around, I'll understand.**

▶ **This also will work as a crumb-topped pie. Simply choose one of the crumb toppings in this collection, adding it halfway through the baking. (If you're uncertain how this is done, read a crumb-topped pie recipe before proceeding.)**

▶ **If your strawberries are a little lackluster, add 2 tablespoons strawberry preserves to the filling to enhance the flavor.**

Strawberry-Rhubarb Crumb Pie

Spring should never pass without at least one or two rhubarb pies issuing from your oven. Rhubarb pie is a rite of spring, and a little later in the season, when the strawberries come along, the two make great partners. Their flavors are so bright and agreeable that you need little more than sugar and lemon to accent them. This makes an excellent lattice-top pie, so try it that way, too. But I really love the way it tastes with the cornmeal crumb topping.

MAKES 8 TO 10 SERVINGS

1 recipe Basic Flaky Pie Pastry, Single Crust (page 31), refrigerated

FILLING

3 cups fresh rhubarb stalks sliced crosswise $1/2$ inch thick

$3/4$ cup granulated sugar

$1 1/2$ tablespoons fresh lemon juice

Grated zest of 1 lemon

4 cups hulled and halved (quartered if large) fresh strawberries

$1/4$ cup quick-cooking tapioca

CORNMEAL CRUMB TOPPING

$3/4$ cup all-purpose flour

$1/4$ cup fine yellow cornmeal

$2/3$ cup firmly packed light brown sugar

$1/2$ teaspoon ground cinnamon

$1/4$ teaspoon salt

$1/2$ cup (1 stick) cold unsalted butter, cut into $1/4$-inch pieces

1.   If you haven't already, prepare the pastry and refrigerate until firm enough to roll, about 1 hour.

2.   On a sheet of lightly floured waxed paper, roll the pastry into a 13-inch circle with a floured rolling pin. Invert the pastry over a $9 1/2$-inch deep-dish pie pan, center, and peel off the paper. Tuck the pastry into the pan, without stretching it, and sculpt the edge into an upstanding ridge. Place in the freezer for 15 minutes. Preheat the oven to 400°F.

3.   Combine the rhubarb, granulated sugar, lemon juice, and lemon zest in a large bowl. Toss well to mix, then set aside for 10 minutes.

4.   Add the strawberries and tapioca to the bowl and toss well. Scrape the filling into the chilled pie shell and smooth the top with your hands. Place the pie on the center oven rack and bake for 30 minutes.

5. Meanwhile, make the topping. Combine the flour, cornmeal, brown sugar, cinnamon, and salt in a food processor and pulse several times to mix. Scatter the butter over the top and pulse until the mixture resembles fine crumbs. Empty the crumbs into a medium-size bowl and rub between your fingers to make large, buttery crumbs. Refrigerate until ready to use.

6. Remove the pie from the oven and reduce the temperature to 375°F. Carefully dump the crumbs in the center of the pie, spreading them evenly over the surface with your hands. Tamp them down gently. Return the pie to the oven, placing it so that the part that faced the back of the oven now faces forward. Just in case, slide a large aluminum foil–lined baking sheet onto the rack below to catch any spills. Continue to bake until the juices bubble thickly around the edge, 30 to 40 minutes. If necessary, cover with loosely tented aluminum foil during the last 10 minutes to prevent the top from getting too dark.

7. Transfer the pie to a wire rack and let cool for at least 1 hour before serving.

Recipe for Success

▶ **When you're shopping for rhubarb, buy solid, crisp, bright red stalks. If the stalks seem too wide, halve them lengthwise before slicing them crosswise to make the filling. Toss the leaves, if they happen to be attached. They'll make you sick if you eat them.**

Dolores's Strawberry and Rhubarb Crumb Pie in a Skillet Crust

I first "met" Dolores Kostelni when she interviewed me about apple pie for her radio show, *The Happy Cook*, on WREL-AM radio out of Lexington, Virginia. Turns out that Dolores also loves to make pies and is a self-described "intrepid lover of desserts." When Dolores found out I was working on a new pie book, she kindly agreed to send me this, one of her favorite pie recipes. I was immediately intrigued: what did she mean by a "skillet crust"? Turns out that her ingenious crust is mixed in, well, a big skillet: you melt butter, add your dry ingredients, and stir it all up. Some of it gets pressed into a large pie pan; the rest is used for a crumb topping. As for the filling, it's a spring classic. Cardamom and ginger, she reminds us, are in the same family, and their flavors are wonderful together, as well as with the strawberries and rhubarb. This is fine pie indeed. (P.S.—Check out Dolores's great cookbook, *Cookies by the Dozen*, published by Warner Books, 1995.)

MAKES 8 TO 10 SERVINGS

1 recipe Dolores's Skillet Crust (page 48)

FILLING

1 1/2 pounds fresh rhubarb stalks, trimmed of any leaves and sliced crosswise 1/4 inch thick (about 4 cups)

2 cups hulled and sliced fresh strawberries

3/4 cup sugar

Juice of 1 lemon

1/4 to 1/3 cup all-purpose flour (see Recipe for Success)

1/2 teaspoon ground cardamom

1/4 teaspoon ground ginger

1. Prepare the crust and press nearly 2 cups of it into the bottom and up the side of a 9 1/2- to 10-inch extra-deep-dish pie pan as directed. Set aside. Reserve the rest of the crust mixture for the topping.

2. In a large bowl, combine the rhubarb, strawberries, sugar, lemon juice, flour, cardamom, and ginger. Set aside for 10 minutes. Preheat the oven to 350°F.

3. Turn the filling into the pie shell, smoothing the top with your hand or a spoon. Crumble the reserved crust mixture evenly over the pie, pressing down on it gently.

4. Place the pie on the center oven rack and bake for 30 minutes, then reduce the oven temperature to 325°F and rotate the pie 180 degrees, so that the part that faced the back of the oven now faces forward. Just in case, slide a large aluminum foil–lined baking sheet onto the rack below to catch any spills. Continue to bake until the top is golden brown and the juices bubble thickly around the edges, 40 to 50 minutes. If the top starts to get too dark, cover with loosely tented aluminum foil during the last 15 minutes of baking.

5. Transfer the pie to a wire rack and let cool for at least 2 hours before serving.

Recipe for Success

▶ Dolores says, "Older, thicker stalks of rhubarb, like big strawberries, tend to be dry, so use the lesser amount of flour to absorb their juice if this is the case."

▶ Note that because of the large amount of sugar in the crust, Dolores bakes the pie at a relatively low temperature for a fruit pie. Don't increase the oven temperature in an effort to hurry the pie along; you'll just scorch the crust.

Strawberry-Raspberry Mint Pie

I've never bought the conventional wisdom that strawberries don't make a good pie because their texture is too soft and won't hold up to baking. Sure, strawberry pies do have a very soft texture, but I don't really consider that a problem. With enough cornstarch, the filling will indeed firm up as the pie cools, leaving you with the texture of thick preserves. Unless the strawberries are fresh, local, and in season, I often prefer frozen strawberries to fresh, which can be lacking in flavor much of the time. Here we use a bag of frozen strawberries and mix it with a bag of raspberries, and the result is a delicious pie in a tender cream cheese crust. I like to include a little mint, which gives the pie a summery sparkle even in the dead of winter.

MAKES 8 TO 10 SERVINGS

1 recipe Tender Cream Cheese Pastry, Double Crust (page 46), refrigerated

FILLING

One 1-pound bag individually frozen strawberries (not packed in syrup), partially thawed

One 1-pound bag individually frozen raspberries (not packed in syrup), partially thawed

2/3 cup granulated sugar

1/4 cup cornstarch

1 1/2 tablespoons orange liqueur or 1/2 teaspoon orange extract

1 tablespoon fresh lemon juice

1/4 teaspoon ground cinnamon

1/4 teaspoon ground nutmeg

Small handful of fresh mint leaves or 1/2 teaspoon crumbled dried mint

2 tablespoons cold unsalted butter, cut into small pieces

GARNISH

Confectioners' sugar

1. If you haven't already, prepare the pastry and refrigerate until firm enough to roll, 1 to 1½ hours.

2. On a sheet of lightly floured waxed paper, roll the larger portion of the pastry into a 12-inch circle with a floured rolling pin. Invert the pastry over a 9-inch standard pie pan, center, and peel off the paper. Gently tuck the pastry into the pan, without stretching it, and let the overhang drape over the edge. Place in the refrigerator for 15 minutes.

3. If the strawberries are whole or in large pieces, use a sharp knife to cut them in half or into large bite-size pieces. Combine the strawberries and raspberries in a large bowl. Mix the granulated sugar and cornstarch together in a small bowl. Add the mixture to the fruit and mix briefly. Add the orange liqueur, lemon juice, cinnamon, nutmeg, and mint and toss to mix. Set the fruit mixture aside for 15 minutes. Preheat the oven to 400°F.

4. On another sheet of lightly floured waxed paper, roll the other half of the pastry into an 11-inch circle. Turn the filling into the chilled pie shell and smooth the top with a spoon. Dot the top with the butter. Lightly moisten the rim of the pie shell with a wet finger or pastry brush. Invert the top pastry over the filling, center, and peel off the paper. Press the top and bottom pastries together along the dampened edge. Trim the pastry with scissors or a paring knife, leaving an even ½-inch overhang all around, then sculpt the overhang into an upstanding ridge. Poke several steam vents in the top of the pie with a fork or paring knife. Put a couple of the vents near the edge of the crust so you can check the juices there later.

5. Place the pie on the center oven rack and bake for 30 minutes. Reduce the oven temperature to 375°F and rotate the pie 180 degrees, so that the part that faced the back of the oven now faces forward. Just in case, slide a large aluminum foil–lined baking sheet onto the rack below to catch any spills. Bake until the top of the pie is golden brown and any juices visible at the steam vents bubble thickly, 30 to 35 minutes.

6. Transfer the pie to a wire rack and let cool for 15 to 20 minutes. While it is still quite warm, dust the top lightly with confectioners' sugar. Once the pie has cooled, dust it again. Let the pie cool for at least 1 hour before serving.

Recipe for Success

▶ **This filling is quite soft and therefore settles low in the pan. By contrast, the top crust is likely to remain somewhat domed. This is not an unfamiliar situation to pie makers. There is something you can do, however, to shrink the distance between crust and filling so the pastry snuggles up to the fruit. As soon as the** pie comes out of the oven, drape a clean tea towel over it. Let it sit there for 1 minute, steam-softening the crust, then very gently press down on the towel and pastry to collapse it a little. There's no guarantee that the pastry won't shatter or break slightly, but it's usually not a disaster. Note that the more pronounced the pastry dome is, the more difficult it is to do this without serious breakage. The tender cream cheese pastry is probably the best dough to try this little trick on.

Vid and Annie's Fresh Raspberry Crumb Pie

Here's a pie I like to make two or three times a summer. When my New Hampshire friends Vid and Annie Valdmanis would give me boxes of fresh raspberries from their garden, I would quickly turn around and bake those fragile fruits into pies like this, lest they slide past their prime. So I dedicate this pie to Vid and Annie, for all the great berries they generously bestowed on me.

MAKES 8 TO 10 SERVINGS

1 recipe Basic Shortening Pie Pastry, Single Crust (page 30) or Basic Flaky Pie Pastry, Single Crust (page 31), refrigerated

FILLING

4 cups fresh raspberries

1/2 cup plus 3 tablespoons sugar

2 teaspoons fresh lemon juice

1 1/2 tablespoons cornstarch

1/4 teaspoon ground nutmeg

2 to 3 tablespoons seedless raspberry jam (optional)

CRUMB TOPPING

1/2 cup all-purpose flour

1/2 cup sugar

1/2 teaspoon ground cinnamon

1/4 teaspoon salt

1/4 cup (1/2 stick) cold unsalted butter, cut into 1/4-inch pieces

GARNISH

Vanilla, peach, or strawberry ice cream

1. If you haven't already, prepare the pastry and refrigerate until firm enough to roll, about 1 hour.

2. On a sheet of lightly floured waxed paper, roll the pastry into a 12-inch circle with a floured rolling pin. Invert the pastry over a 9-inch standard pie pan, center, and peel off the paper. Tuck the pastry into the pan, without stretching it, and sculpt the edge into an upstanding ridge. Place in the freezer for 15 minutes. Preheat the oven to 400°F.

3. Combine the raspberries, $\frac{1}{2}$ cup of the sugar, and the lemon juice in a large bowl. Toss gently to mix, then set aside for 10 minutes to juice. Meanwhile, combine the remaining 3 tablespoons sugar and the cornstarch and nutmeg in a small bowl. Stir the mixture into the fruit.

4. Spread the raspberry jam, if using, inside the chilled pie shell. Scrape the filling into the shell, smoothing the fruit with a spoon. Place the pie on the center oven rack and bake for 25 minutes.

5. Meanwhile, make the topping. Combine the flour, sugar, cinnamon, and salt in a food processor. Scatter the butter over the dry mixture and pulse until the mixture resembles fine crumbs. Dump the crumbs into a large bowl and gently rub between your fingers to make large, buttery crumbs. Refrigerate until ready to use.

6. Remove the pie from the oven and reduce the oven temperature to 375°F. Carefully dump the crumbs in the center of the pie and spread them evenly over the top with your hands. Return the pie to the oven, placing it so that the part that faced the back of the oven now faces forward. Just in case, slide a large aluminum foil–lined baking sheet onto the rack below to catch any spills. Continue to bake until the juices bubble thickly around the edge of the pie, about 25 minutes.

7. Transfer the pie to a wire rack and let cool. Serve barely warm or at room temperature, accompanied by ice cream.

Recipe for Success

▸ Due to their fragile nature, raspberries are quite prone to mold. For that reason, I always give them the sniff test before purchasing. If I detect any trace of mold, which is often very difficult to see, I pass. Even the smallest amount of mold will taint the flavor of a pie.

▸ Juicy berry pies like this one are sometimes tricky to team up with a crumb topping, as the topping has a tendency to absorb excess juice. If I see a lot of juice in a filling when I'm ready to add the topping, I sprinkle several tablespoons of rolled oats (quick-cooking work best) over the pie and return it to the oven for about 5 minutes. The oats absorb the juice and form something of a barrier. I then add the topping and proceed as usual. It works pretty well.

Breitbach's Raspberry Pie

I had heard that the raspberry pie at Breitbach's Country Dining in Balltown, Iowa—the state's oldest bar and restaurant—had a stellar reputation. So I called Cindy Breitbach, the resident pie maker, to find out what makes her raspberry pie such a hit. I should mention that Cindy, who learned to make pies from her grandmothers—"both fine pie makers"—has been making pies since the age of 10, so one suspects she has that pie maker's touch. The way she tells it, the raspberry pie that everyone raves about could not be easier: it's just raspberries, black-berries, sugar, and tapioca. Lemon juice? No, she thinks there is enough acidity in the fruit itself. And in yet another vote of confidence for frozen fruit, she says that's what she uses. As for the crust, hers is a shortening double crust—"nothing fancy about that either." Maybe not, but the pie is wonderful.

MAKES 8 TO 10 SERVINGS

1 recipe Basic Shortening Pie Pastry, Double Crust (page 30), refrigerated

FILLING

3 cups individually frozen raspberries (not packed in syrup), partially thawed

1 cup individually frozen blackberries (not packed in syrup), partially thawed

1¹/4 cups sugar

3 tablespoons quick-cooking tapioca

GLAZE

Sugar

1. If you haven't already, prepare the pastry and refrigerate until firm enough to roll, about 1 hour.

2. On a sheet of lightly floured waxed paper, roll the larger portion of the pastry into a 13-inch circle with a floured rolling pin. Invert the pastry over a 9¹/2-inch deep-dish pie pan, center, and peel off the paper. Gently tuck the pastry into the pan, without stretching it, and let the overhang drape over the edge. Place in the refrigerator for 15 minutes.

3. In a large bowl, combine the berries, sugar, and tapioca. Toss gently to combine, then set aside for several minutes. Preheat the oven to 350°F.

4. Roll the other half of the pastry into an 11-inch circle on a sheet of lightly floured waxed paper. Turn the filling into the chilled pie shell, smoothing the fruit with a spoon. Lightly moisten the rim of the pie shell. Invert the top pastry over the filling, center, and

peel off the paper. Press the top and bottom pastries together along the dampened edge. Using the back of a butter knife or paring knife, trim the pastry flush with the edge of the pan. Poke several steam vents in the top of the pie with a fork or paring knife. Put a couple of the vents near the edge of the crust so you can check the juices there later. Sprinkle the top of the pie lightly with sugar.

5. Place the pie on the center oven rack and bake for 30 minutes, then rotate the pie 180 degrees, so that the part that faced the back of the oven now faces forward. Just in case, slide a large aluminum foil–lined baking sheet onto the rack below to catch any spills. Continue to bake until the juices bubble thickly at the steam vents, about 45 minutes. Cindy says it is important to give the pie a thorough baking, "so the beads of tapioca disappear."

6. Transfer the pie to a wire rack and let cool. Serve just slightly warm or at room temperature.

Recipe for Success

▶ **Cindy uses the same trick I do to prepare frozen fruit for baking. She puts it in a bowl in the microwave and heats it just until the fruit is nearly thawed. Remember that using hard-frozen fruit increases the baking time and often results in an overbaked crust.**

New Hampshire Raspberry and Red Currant Pie

This pie always reminds me of my days in New Hampshire, when I would make it a few times each summer. The timing was pretty much preordained: right about the time my secret red currant picking spot would bear fruit, my friends Vid and Annie Valdmanis would start delivering the first of the raspberries from their home garden. Thus blessed, I would always make a double-crust pie of roughly equal amounts of fruit so they could share the limelight. Nowadays, I usually buy my red currants from the local Whole Foods Market here in Annapolis, Maryland. These tart, translucent red jewels team up wonderfully with the raspberries—sweet-tart, brilliant red, and absolutely delicious.

MAKES 8 TO 10 SERVINGS

1 recipe Tender Cream Cheese Pastry, Double Crust (page 46), refrigerated

FILLING

2 1/2 cups fresh raspberries

2 cups fresh red currants, picked over for stems

1/2 cup plus 3 tablespoons sugar

2 tablespoons red currant jelly (optional)

1 teaspoon fresh lemon juice

3 tablespoons cornstarch

1 tablespoon cold unsalted butter, cut into small pieces

GLAZE

Milk or light cream

Sugar

1. If you haven't already, prepare the pastry and refrigerate until firm enough to roll, about 1 hour.

2. On a sheet of lightly floured waxed paper, roll the larger portion of the pastry into a 12-inch circle with a floured rolling pin. Invert the pastry over a 9-inch standard pie pan, center, and peel off the paper. Gently tuck the pastry into the pan, without stretching it, and let the overhang drape over the edge. Place in the refrigerator for 15 minutes.

3. In a large bowl, combine the raspberries, currants, 1/2 cup of the sugar, the jelly (if using), and lemon juice. Toss gently to mix, then set aside for 10 minutes to juice. Preheat the oven to 400°F.

4. Roll the other half of the pastry into a 10-inch circle on a sheet of lightly floured waxed paper. Combine the remaining 3 tablespoons sugar and the cornstarch in a small bowl. Stir the mixture gently into the fruit. Turn the filling into the chilled pie shell, smoothing the top with your hands or a spoon. Dot the filling with the butter. Lightly moisten the rim of the pie shell. Invert the top pastry over the filling, center, and peel off the paper. Press the top and bottom pastries together along the dampened edge. Using the back of a butter knife or pastry knife, trim the pastry flush with the edge of the pan, reserving the scraps for decoration, if desired. Poke several steam vents in the top of the pie with a fork or paring knife. Put a couple of the vents near the edge of the crust so you can check the juices there later. To glaze the pie, lightly brush the pastry with milk and sprinkle with sugar. If you want to add a decorative flourish to the pie, shape a very thin "stem" of a currant branch, 3 or 4 inches long, and lay it in the center of the pie, arching the top gracefully to one side. Make little balls of dough—the currants—about 1/4 inch in diameter and place them in clusters on either side of the stem.

5. Place the pie on the center oven rack and bake for 30 minutes. Reduce the oven temperature to 375°F and rotate the pie 180 degrees, so that the part that faced the back

of the oven now faces forward. Just in case, slide a large aluminum foil–lined baking sheet onto the rack below to catch any spills. Continue to bake until the top is dark golden brown and the juices bubble thickly at the steam vents, about 30 minutes.

6. Transfer the pie to a wire rack and let cool for at least 2 hours before serving.

Recipe for Success

▶ Do toss the fruit gently when you mix it, because both the raspberries and the currants are fragile. Rough handling will turn them into a texture-less mush. By the same token, gently "rake" the currants off the stems with your fingers to avoid mashing them.

▶ If you happen to taste the filling and find the currants quite tart (they are), don't be tempted to add more sugar. Hiding their tartness behind too much sugar detracts from their unique flavor.

Raspberry and Fresh Fig Freeform Pie

Jeanne Thiel Kelley is one of the best home bakers I know. A freelance food writer and contributing editor at *Bon Appétit*, Jeanne lives in California. When I told her I was working on a book of pies and asked her if she had any neat California-style pies in her files, she immediately thought of this one. I'm glad she did, because the combination of fresh figs and raspberries is one I've never considered. Now I'm here to tell you that they work beautifully together. Jeanne likes to add an egg yolk to her pastry, to keep it on the sturdy side, so note that I've modified my All-Butter Pie Pastry to satisfy her requirements. Jeanne tops off this delicious pie with an unusual honey-anise whipped cream that's out of this world.

MAKES 8 SERVINGS

1 recipe All-Butter Pie Pastry, Single Crust (page 28), modified as instructed in step 1 and refrigerated

FILLING

1/4 cup granulated sugar

1/4 cup firmly packed light brown sugar

1 tablespoon all-purpose flour

Two 6-ounce baskets fresh raspberries

2 cups (about 10 ounces) small, fresh black figs, stemmed and quartered

2 tablespoons honey

HONEY-ANISE WHIPPED CREAM

1 cup cold heavy or whipping cream

2 tablespoons honey

2 tablespoons anisette or other anise-flavored liqueur

Words of Pastry Wisdom from a Test Kitchen Pro

Jeanne Thiel Kelley knows about the challenges facing home pie bakers. A contributing editor at *Bon Appétit* and a former staff member of the *Bon Appétit* test kitchen, Jeanne attended La Varenne cooking school in France and has worked on a variety of cookbooks. Her experience, she says, has taught her that the key to mastering pies is a great crust. Here are her tips for building what she calls "crust confidence."

▶ Use a good recipe for classic pie crust, obtained from a reliable resource—a friend or family member with a tried-and-true formula, or one of the recipes here, of course.

▶ Experiment with making the crust by hand and in a food processor. Find the technique that works best for you. There is no right or wrong way.

▶ Practice makes perfect. With time, you'll be able to gauge when the fat is correctly blended into the dry ingredients and just how much liquid to add for a crust that is neither dry and crumbly nor wet and sticky.

▶ A freeform pie is a great choice for the beginning baker. The simple technique allows the novice to focus on the crust and get it right.

Look for Jeanne's *Holiday Baking*, a Williams-Sonoma book (Time-Life, 1999).

1. Prepare the pastry as directed, substituting 1 egg yolk for 1 tablespoon of the water; simply blend the yolk with the water. Refrigerate until firm enough to roll, about 1 hour. Position an oven rack in the upper third of the oven and preheat the oven to 400°F.

2. Mix the sugars and flour together in a large bowl. Add three-quarters of the raspberries and all of the figs. Toss gently to combine, then set aside.

3. To make the freeform crust, on a sheet of lightly floured waxed paper, roll the pastry into a 12-inch circle with a floured rolling pin. Invert the pastry onto a rimless baking sheet and peel off the paper, letting the pastry drape over the edge of the sheet, if necessary. Imagine an 8-inch circle in the center of the pastry and spoon the fruit into it. Using a metal spatula or dough scraper to help you lift the pastry, fold the overhanging dough over the filling.

FREEFORM CRUST

4. Place the baking sheet on the upper oven rack and bake until the crust is golden brown and the juice bubbles thickly in the center of the pie, about 35 minutes.

5. Transfer the baking sheet pie to a wire rack and drizzle the honey over the pie. Let cool on the sheet. If the pie has leaked juice, loosen it in those areas with a spatula while the pie is still quite warm.

6. While the pie is still warm, make the whipped cream. Using a chilled medium-size bowl and chilled beaters, beat the cream, honey, and anisette until soft peaks form. Scatter the remaining raspberries over the pie and serve garnished with whipped cream.

Recipe for Success

▸ Jeanne has some good ideas to share about making this pie. She likes to roll the pastry between 2 sheets of parchment paper, then slide it onto the baking sheet. She removes the top sheet of paper but leaves the bottom one in place for the pie to bake on. The parchment, she explains, is also useful for folding the pastry over the filling: just lift up on the parchment and fold it over the fruit.

▸ Keep in mind that the season for making this pie is limited, especially if you live in a place where fresh figs are hard to find. Look for them in late summer.

Blackberry Silk Pie

When I lived in New Hampshire, I spent more time than I should have engaged in one of the most enjoyable, least profitable hobbies a fellow could have: picking wild blackberries. I used to say I did it for the kids—all four of mine loved to come along—but in fact I liked trudging through the thorny bushes as much as they did, always emerging with at least enough berries to make one of my favorite blackberry pies. What I do here is make a blackberry puree, strain it, and then blend it with the usual custard ingredients: cream, eggs, and sugar. The color of the filling is a beautiful dark-berry red, with an ultra-smooth texture that reminds me of silk—thus the name. The best thing about it? You don't need a patch of wild berries down the road to try this. It works equally well with fresh blackberries—ripe and in season—or frozen ones.

MAKES 8 TO 10 SERVINGS

1 recipe Basic Flaky Pie Pastry, Single Crust (page 31), refrigerated

FILLING

1 pint fresh blackberries or one 1-pound bag individually frozen blackberries (not packed in syrup), partially thawed

1 cup sugar

3 large eggs, at room temperature

1 tablespoon cornstarch

1½ cups heavy or whipping cream, at room temperature

½ cup light cream, at room temperature

1 teaspoon vanilla extract

GARNISH

Ripe fresh blackberries (optional)

1. If you haven't already, prepare the pastry and refrigerate until firm enough to roll, about 1 hour.

2. On a sheet of lightly floured waxed paper, roll the pastry into a 13-inch circle with a floured rolling pin. Invert the pastry over a 9½-inch deep-dish pie pan, center, and peel off the paper. Tuck the pastry into the pan, without stretching it, and sculpt the edge so it is slightly higher than the rim. Place in the freezer for 15 minutes, then partially prebake and let cool according to the instructions on page 16. Reduce the oven temperature to 300°F.

3. Combine the berries and ¼ cup of the sugar in a food processor and process for about 30 seconds, long enough to make a smooth puree. Put a mesh sieve over a large bowl and pour the puree into the sieve. Using a rubber spatula, force the puree through the mesh, leaving just the seeds. Discard the seeds.

4. In a large bowl, whisk the eggs until frothy. Add the remaining ¾ cup sugar and the cornstarch and whisk until well blended. Blend in the heavy cream, light cream, vanilla, and 1 cup of the puree, mixing until evenly blended. (Save the extra puree for another use. It's great on pancakes, with fresh berries, or with cheesecake or crepes.) Ladle the filling into the cooled pie shell.

5. Place the pie on the center oven rack and bake for 50 to 60 minutes, rotating the pie 180 degrees halfway through the baking, so that the part that faced the back of the oven now faces forward. When done, the filling will likely have puffed somewhat. The center may seem a little jiggly; that's fine. If after the allotted time, the pie seems overly puffy and the center a little underdone, turn the oven off and leave the pie in the hot oven for 10 to 15 minutes.

6. Transfer the pie to a wire rack and let cool to room temperature. Cover the pie with loosely tented aluminum foil and refrigerate for at least 2 hours. To serve, spoon some of the leftover puree onto each plate and over each slice and garnish with blackberries, if desired.

Recipe for Success

▶ Since this is essentially a custard pie, you should observe the "low and slow" rule of baking. If you try to rush this pie by raising the oven temperature, the custard will "break" and result in a watery filling.

Sour Cream–Blackberry Pie

Like Marionberry Pie (page 162), this recipe comes courtesy of the Oregon Raspberry and Blackberry Commission. The idea couldn't be more deliciously simple: Just put some berries in the bottom of a pie shell and pour a sweetened sour cream mixture over the top. Dust with streusel and bake. The creamy part of the filling bakes up something like a moist, spongy cake, covering the fruit below. I've tinkered with the commission's original recipe just a little, adding a couple of eggs (for a firmer filling), a pinch of salt, and some orange zest. In addition to blackberries, I've also made this with raspberries. It works beautifully either way, and I can't see any reason why the same basic formula couldn't be adapted to any other berry as well.

MAKES 8 TO 10 SERVINGS

1 recipe Basic Flaky Pie Pastry, Single Crust (page 31) or Tender Cream Cheese Pastry, Single Crust (page 46), refrigerated

FILLING

2 large eggs, at room temperature

2 cups full-fat sour cream, at room temperature

3/4 cup granulated sugar

1/3 cup all-purpose flour

1/2 teaspoon vanilla extract

1/2 teaspoon grated orange zest

Big pinch of salt

3 cups fresh blackberries, raspberries, or other berries

STREUSEL TOPPING

3 tablespoons all-purpose flour

2 tablespoons firmly packed light brown sugar

1 tablespoon unsalted butter, melted

1. If you haven't already, prepare the pastry and refrigerate until firm enough to roll, about 1 hour.

2. On a sheet of lightly floured waxed paper, roll the pastry into a 13-inch circle with a floured rolling pin. Invert the pastry over a 9½-inch deep-dish pie pan, center, and peel off the paper. Tuck the pastry into the pan, without stretching it, and sculpt the edge into an upstanding ridge. Place in the freezer for 15 minutes, then partially prebake and let cool according to the instructions on page 16. Reduce the oven temperature to 350°F.

3. Whisk the eggs in a large bowl just until frothy. Add the sour cream, granulated sugar, flour, vanilla, orange zest, and salt, whisking again until evenly blended. Spread the berries evenly in the cooled pie shell, then ladle the sour cream mixture over them.

4. To make the streusel, combine the flour and brown sugar in a small bowl and mix with your fingers. Add the butter, stirring with a fork. Switch to your fingers and gently rub the topping until it is crumbly. Add a bit more brown sugar or granulated sugar if the mixture is too clumpy. Sprinkle the topping evenly over the sour cream filling.

5. Place the pie on the center oven rack and bake until the filling is set, about 35 minutes. When done, the filling will likely have puffed slightly and will no longer seem liquid-loose. Don't expect the top of the pie to brown much, if at all, because it isn't in the oven quite long enough.

6. Transfer the pie to a wire rack and let cool thoroughly. Serve at room temperature, or cover with loosely tented aluminum foil and refrigerate before serving.

Recipe for Success

▶ **If you rinse your berries in a colander before using them (I suspect you do, unless you grow them or are certain of the source), be sure to drain them well on paper towels to keep the pie filling from getting watery. I start by lining a baking sheet with a double layer of paper towels. I give the berries a quick rinse with cold water, then a shake or two to knock off any excess water. Then I upend them onto the paper towels and gently spread them out to (at least partially) air-dry. If I'm using raspberries, I turn them stem end down so that any water that's trapped in the berries drains out.**

Patsy's Blackberry-Rhubarb Freeform Pie

My friend and colleague Patsy Jamieson, food editor of *Eating Well* magazine, knows her way around pies, as you'll discover when you try this blackberry rhubarb version baked *crostata-*style. She calls this pie a celebration of spring—spring indeed being something to celebrate when you live and work where she does, in northern Vermont. In addition to fresh rhubarb, Patsy uses frozen blackberries, a great complementary flavor and color enhancer. (You can, of course, use fresh blackberries when they're in season.) Since Patsy's specialty is reduced-fat recipes, you'll be delighted how much great flavor there is in this pie with a relatively small amount of butter. Her crumb topping, made with orange juice concentrate, is delicious.

MAKES 10 SERVINGS

1 recipe Patsy's Cottage Cheese Pastry (page 47), refrigerated

FILLING AND TOPPING

2/3 cup all-purpose flour

1/4 cup firmly packed light brown sugar

1/2 teaspoon ground cinnamon

2 teaspoons cold salted or unsalted butter, cut into 1/4-inch pieces

1 tablespoon canola oil or other vegetable oil

1 tablespoon frozen orange juice concentrate, thawed

1/4 cup sliced almonds

3 cups fresh rhubarb stalks sliced crosswise 1/2 inch thick

1 cup individually frozen blackberries (not packed in syrup), partially thawed

3/4 cup plus 1 teaspoon granulated sugar

1 large egg white

1 tablespoon water

1. If you haven't already, prepare the pastry and refrigerate until firm enough to roll, about 1 hour.

2. Combine the flour, brown sugar, and cinnamon in a medium-size bowl. Reserve 2 tablespoons of this mixture in a small bowl. Add the butter to the larger portion and rub it into the dry mixture with your fingers until crumbly. Add the oil and orange juice concentrate, tossing lightly with a fork to blend. Add the almonds, then rub the mixture gently between your fingers to form evenly mixed crumbs. Refrigerate until ready to use.

3. Combine the rhubarb, blackberries, and 3/4 cup of the granulated sugar in a medium-size bowl and place in the refrigerator. Preheat the oven to 425°F. Line a large

baking sheet with lightly oiled parchment paper or aluminum foil. (Juicy fillings like this often spring a leak, and lining the sheet will make the cleanup much easier.)

4. On a sheet of lightly floured waxed paper, roll the pastry into a 13½-inch circle with a floured rolling pin. Invert the pastry over the baking sheet, center, and peel off the paper. Without upsetting the overhanging dough, put the entire baking sheet in the refrigerator for 5 minutes to refirm the pastry. Imagine an 8-inch circle in the center of the pastry. Sprinkle the 2 tablespoons reserved flour–sugar mixture over this area. Pour the fruit filling over the same area, then even it out with your hands or a fork. Sprinkle the topping evenly over the fruit.

5. Using a spatula to help you lift the pastry, fold the uncovered portion over the filling. The pastry will sort of self-pleat as you do so. (See the illustration of a freeform crust on page 153 for what this should look like.) Whisk the egg white and water together in a small bowl and brush the mixture over the exposed pastry. Sprinkle with the remaining 1 teaspoon sugar.

6. Place the pie on the center oven rack and bake for 15 minutes. Reduce the oven temperature to 350°F and continue to bake until the crust is golden brown and the fruit bubbly, 25 to 35 minutes. Rotate the baking sheet 180 degrees, so that the side that faced the back of the oven now faces forward, about 15 minutes before it is done. If the pie starts to get a little too dark, cover with loosely tented aluminum foil.

7. Transfer the pie, on the sheet, to a wire rack. Let cool for 10 minutes, then slide the pie, with the foil or parchment, onto the rack to finish cooling. Serve warm.

Recipe for Success

> ▸ It's always best to line your baking sheet with aluminum foil or parchment when you're baking a juicy freeform pie such as this one. Invariably, hot juice will seep through a thin spot in the pastry. There's really no way to stop the leak, and the best thing to do is nothing, because the leaking juice will harden and plug the hole. If you do spring a leak, it helps to run a spatula between the pie and the parchment or foil as soon as the pie comes out of the oven to keep the pie from sticking.

Deep-Dish Blackberry-Peach Double-Crust Pie

This is a favorite pie from my New Hampshire days, when I used to make it with handpicked blackberries and, when I could get my hands on them, Reliance peaches, a delicious cold-hardy peach developed by Dr. Elwyn Meader of Rochester, New Hampshire. It's a very thick summer pie with so much fruit that I bake it in one of my extra-deep-dish pie pans. (You can bake it in a 9½-inch deep-dish pan, but you'll have to reduce the amount of fruit to about 6½ cups.)

Peaches can be peeled by hand, with a sharp paring knife, but here we use another method: blanching them. Blanching really takes no longer than peeling by hand and the upside is you don't lose any of the precious sweet flesh that you're bound to cut off when using a knife. The combination of peaches and blackberries in a flaky double crust is hard to beat.

MAKES 8 TO 10 SERVINGS

1 recipe Basic Flaky Pie Pastry, Double Crust (page 31), refrigerated

FILLING

6 to 8 small to medium-size ripe peaches

4 cups fresh or individually frozen blackberries (not packed in syrup), partially thawed

½ cup plus 3 tablespoons sugar

3½ tablespoons cornstarch

¼ teaspoon ground nutmeg

1 tablespoon fresh lemon juice

1 teaspoon grated lemon zest

2 tablespoons cold unsalted butter, cut into small pieces

GLAZE

Milk or light cream

Sugar

1. If you haven't already, prepare the pastry and refrigerate until firm enough to roll, about 1 hour.

2. While the pastry chills, blanch the peaches as described on page 88. After you slip off the skins, slice the peaches into a large measuring cup; you'll need 4 cups. (Reserve any remaining peaches for another use.) Combine the sliced peaches, blackberries, and ½ cup of the sugar in a large bowl. Toss well to combine and set aside for 15 minutes.

3. On a sheet of lightly floured waxed paper, roll the larger portion of the pastry into a 13½-inch circle with a floured rolling pin. Invert the pastry over a 9½- to 10-inch extra-deep-dish pie pan, center, and peel off the paper. Gently tuck the pastry into the pan, without stretching it, and let the overhang drape over the edge. Place in the refrigerator for 15 minutes.

4. In a small bowl, mix the remaining 3 tablespoons sugar with the cornstarch. Stir the mixture into the fruit along with the nutmeg, lemon juice, and lemon zest. Preheat the oven to 400°F.

5. On another sheet of lightly floured waxed paper, roll the other half of the pastry into an 11½-inch circle. Turn the filling into the chilled pie shell. Smooth the fruit with a spoon and dot with the butter. Lightly moisten the rim of the pie shell. Invert the top pastry over the filling, center, and peel off the paper. Press the top and bottom pastries together along the dampened edge. Trim the pastry with scissors or a paring knife, leaving an even ½-inch overhang all around, then sculpt the overhang into an upstanding ridge. Poke several steam vents in the top of the pie with a fork or paring knife. Put a couple of the vents near the edge of the crust so you can check the juices there later. To glaze the pie, lightly brush the pastry with milk and sprinkle with sugar.

6. Place the pie on the center oven rack and bake for 30 minutes. Reduce the oven temperature to 375°F and rotate the pie 180 degrees, so that the part that faced the back of the oven now faces forward. Just in case, slide a large aluminum foil–lined baking sheet onto the rack below to catch any drips. Continue to bake until the juices bubble thickly at the steam vents and the top is golden brown, 35 to 45 minutes. If the top starts to get too dark, cover it with loosely tented aluminum foil during the last 15 minutes.

7. Transfer the pie to a wire rack and let cool for at least 2 hours before serving.

Recipe for Success

> Whatever pie pan you use, there should be at least ¹/₂ to ³/₄ inch of headroom between the top of the filling and the rim of the pan to minimize spillover.

A Guardian Angel for Pie Bakers

Besides being irresistibly delicious, fruit pies have something else in common: they like to bubble over late in the baking and leave a mess all over the oven floor. You, of course, know this and take precautions, sliding a large aluminum foil–lined baking sheet onto the rack below the pie to catch the spills.

I've recently run across another clever product that doubles nicely for a foil-lined baking sheet. It's called an oven guard, and it looks a little like a dark metal donut with flared edges to contain any spills. You bake your pie right on top of the oven guard; the hole in the center allows direct heat penetration to the center of the pie, so your pie shell browns nicely. I like to use it for the second half of the baking, just as I do my foil-lined sheet. If the pie does spill over, the finish is nonstick and the drips can be easily washed off. Look for an oven guard at kitchenware stores and at www.kingarthurflour.com.

Marionberry Pie

Marionberries, fans say, are a more complex- and delicious-tasting blackberry—"the Cabernet of blackberries," as they're called. Named for Marion County, Oregon, fresh Marionberries are a rarity outside the Northwest. So for advice on making the best Marionberry pie, I went to the Oregon Raspberry and Blackberry Commission and found this great recipe on its Web site, www.oregon-berries.com. (I know it's great because I made it with regular, everyday blackberries and it was wonderful.) This isn't a baked pie; the filling is cooked in a saucepan and poured into a prebaked crust. Half of the berries are cooked and thickened with cornstarch. The other half are folded into the cooked berries, so the filling has a nice blend of cooked and fresh flavors and textures. Since nearly all Marionberries are sold frozen, that's what this pie is made with. If you can't find frozen Marionberries, use blackberries, fresh or frozen. This pie is great served with whipped cream or vanilla ice cream.

MAKES 8 TO 10 SERVINGS

1 recipe Basic Flaky Pie Pastry, Single Crust (page 31), refrigerated

FILLING

5 cups individually frozen Marionberries or blackberries (not packed in syrup)

2 tablespoons fresh lemon juice

1 cup sugar

1/4 cup cornstarch

1. If you haven't already, prepare the pastry and refrigerate until firm enough to roll, about 1 hour.

2. On a sheet of lightly floured waxed paper, roll the pastry into a 12-inch circle with a floured rolling pin. Invert the pastry over a 9-inch standard pie pan, center, and peel off the paper. Tuck the pastry into the pan, without stretching it, and sculpt the edge into an upstanding ridge. Place in the freezer for 15 minutes, then fully prebake and let cool according to the instructions on page 16.

3. Place half of the frozen berries and the lemon juice in a medium-size, preferably nonstick nonreactive saucepan. Using a pastry blender or potato masher, mash the berries well. Place over low heat and start heating the berries gently. Meanwhile, mix the sugar and cornstarch together in a small bowl. When the berries have put off a fair amount of juice, stir in this mixture. Increase the heat slightly and bring the berry mixture to a boil, stirring often. Boil for 1 minute, stirring virtually nonstop to keep the fruit from spattering. Remove from the heat and scrape the fruit into a shallow bowl. Let cool, then refrigerate for about 1 hour.

4. Gently fold the remaining berries into the chilled fruit. Scrape the filling into the cooled pie shell and smooth the top with a spoon. Cover with loosely tented aluminum foil and refrigerate for at least 1 hour before serving.

Recipe for Success

▶ **As the pie shell gets no further baking, make sure it is fully prebaked to a rich golden brown.**

▶ **This pie is best served the same day. The filling will trap and absorb a certain amount of juice released by the whole frozen berries, but eventually It will start to puddle in the filling.**

Marionberry Pie with Hazelnut Crumb Topping

This pie features two of Oregon's premier agricultural products, Marionberries, considered by some to be the best-tasting type of blackberries, and hazelnuts, the latter toasted and scattered over the fruit in the form of a crumb topping. The hazelnuts—whose flavor components are sometimes compared to those in some wines and Brie cheese—add a sharp toasted flavor to the sweet fruit. It's really a wonderful combination.

MAKES 8 TO 10 SERVINGS

1 recipe Basic Flaky Pie Pastry, Single Crust (page 31), refrigerated

FILLING

4^1/$_2$ cups Marionberries or blackberries, fresh or individually frozen (not packed in syrup), partially thawed

^{2}/$_3$ cup sugar

1^1/$_2$ tablespoons cornstarch

1 tablespoon fresh lemon juice

Pinch of salt

HAZELNUT CRUMB TOPPING

^{3}/$_4$ cup hazelnuts, toasted (see box)

^{1}/$_2$ cup sugar

^{1}/$_4$ teaspoon salt

6 tablespoons (^{3}/$_4$ stick) cold unsalted butter, cut into ^{1}/$_4$-inch pieces

1 tablespoon milk or light cream

1.   If you haven't already, prepare the pastry and refrigerate until firm enough to roll, about 1 hour.

2.   On a sheet of lightly floured waxed paper, roll the pastry into a 12-inch circle with a floured rolling pin. Invert the pastry over a 9-inch standard pie pan, center, and peel off the paper. Tuck the pastry into the pan, without stretching it, and sculpt the edge into an upstanding ridge. Place in the freezer for 15 minutes. Preheat the oven to 400°F.

3.   Put the Marionberries in a large bowl. Mix the sugar and cornstarch together in a small bowl, then stir the mixture into the fruit along with the lemon juice and salt. Set aside for 10 minutes to juice. Scrape the filling into the chilled pie shell and smooth the top with a spoon. Place the pie on the center oven rack and bake for 30 minutes.

4.   Meanwhile, make the topping. Combine the hazelnuts, sugar, and salt in a food processor and pulse until the nuts are fairly well chopped. Scatter the butter over the top and pulse again until the mixture resembles fine crumbs. Sprinkle the milk over the mixture and pulse again briefly. Transfer the topping to a medium-size bowl and rub it between your fingers to make damp, gravelly crumbs. Refrigerate until ready to use.

5.   Remove the pie from the oven and reduce the temperature to 375°F. Carefully dump the crumbs in the center of the pie, spreading them evenly over the surface with your hands. Tamp them down lightly. Return the pie to the oven, placing it so that the part that faced the back of the oven now faces forward. Just in case, slide a large aluminum foil–lined baking sheet onto the rack below to catch any drips. Continue to bake until the juices bubble thickly around the edge, 30 to 40 minutes. If necessary, cover with loosely tented aluminum foil for the last 15 minutes to keep the top from turning too dark.

6.   Transfer the pie to a wire rack and let cool for at least 2 hours before serving.

Recipe for Success

▸ **Much as I love the hazelnut's distinctive flavor here, if you'd rather not bother with them and you have other nuts on hand that don't require peeling, such as pecans or walnuts, those will work fine, too.**

▸ **This recipe works wonderfully as a mixed-fruit pie. If you like, substitute half raspberries or blueberries, or even 2 cups thinly sliced pears, for an equal amount of the Marionberries.**

Toasting Hazelnuts

To toast hazelnuts, preheat the oven to 350°F. Spread the hazelnuts on a large baking sheet and place in the oven, toasting until the skins blister and the nuts look richly golden brown, 10 to 12 minutes. Immediately tilt the nuts onto a clean tea towel, fold the towel over, and let sit for 1 minute. Then vigorously rub the nuts—right in the towel—to remove the skins. Don't worry if you don't get all the skins off. Transfer the nuts to a plate and let cool thoroughly.

Loganberry Pie with Sour Cream Topping

My favorite book on American Northwest cooking is Janie Hibler's *Dungeness Crabs and Blackberry Cobblers* (Knopf, 1991). I'm sorry to say I've not spent much time in the northwestern states, but with Hibler's book, I have been an enthusiastic armchair traveler there, tasting my way through wild mushroom pizzas, delicious salmon and caper spreads, and wonderful berry pies and tarts. Loganberries, Hibler writes, are a variety of blackberry grown commercially in the Pacific Northwest. Their intense berry flavor and slight tartness, she says, make them perfect candidates for pies and preserves. Although loganberries can add an irresistible splash of color and flavor to mixed-fruit pies, it is a real treat to use them alone in a pie. Here, adapted from a recipe in Hibler's book, is a pie in which I do just that. The pie is first baked open-faced, then cooled briefly and draped with a sweet-tart sour cream coating. It's a great taste of the Northwest and a fine way to enjoy these delicious berries.

MAKES 8 TO 10 SERVINGS

1 recipe Basic Shortening Pie Pastry, Single Crust (page 30) or Basic Flaky Pie Pastry, Single Crust (page 31), refrigerated

FILLING

4 cups loganberries, fresh or individually frozen (not packed in syrup), partially thawed

1 cup sugar

1 tablespoon fresh lemon juice

2 tablespoons cornstarch

SOUR CREAM TOPPING

1 1/4 cups full-fat sour cream

3 tablespoons sugar

1 teaspoon vanilla extract

1.   If you haven't already, prepare the pastry and refrigerate until firm enough to roll, about 1 hour.

2.   On a sheet of lightly floured waxed paper, roll the pastry into a 12-inch circle with a floured rolling pin. Invert the pastry over a 9-inch standard pie pan, center, and peel off the paper. Tuck the pastry into the pan, without stretching it, and sculpt the edge into an upstanding ridge. Place in the freezer for 15 minutes.

3.   Combine the loganberries, 3/4 cup of the sugar, and the lemon juice in a large bowl. Mix well and set aside for 10 minutes. Preheat the oven to 400°F.

4.   Mix the remaining 1/4 cup sugar and the cornstarch together in a small bowl, then stir the mixture into the fruit. Turn the filling into the chilled pie shell and smooth the top of the fruit with a spoon.

5.   Place the pie on the center oven rack and bake for 25 minutes. Reduce the oven temperature to 375°F and rotate the pie 180 degrees, so that the part that faced the back of the oven now faces forward. Just in case, slide a large aluminum foil–lined baking sheet onto the rack below to catch any drips. Continue to bake until the juices bubble thickly around the edge and in the center of the pie, 20 to 25 minutes.

6.   Transfer the pie to a wire rack and let cool for 30 minutes.

7.   To make the topping, combine the sour cream and sugar in a small, heavy saucepan over low heat. Stirring virtually nonstop, gently heat the mixture until it is warm and thin enough to pour, about 3 minutes. Stir in the vanilla. Slowly pour the sour cream over the center of the pie or simply smooth it out with a spoon. Gently jiggle the pie to spread the topping.

8.   Put the pie back on the rack and let cool thoroughly. Serve at room temperature or cover with loosely tented aluminum foil and refrigerate until serving. I prefer it slightly chilled.

Recipe for Success

‣ Be careful not to overheat the sour cream mixture or it will curdle in the pan and become unusable.

‣ For a slight caramel flavor, use brown sugar in place of the granulated sugar in the topping.

‣ Don't worry too much if the sour cream and pie juices bleed together when you add the topping. It's bound to happen a bit, and a little berry color in the white sour cream will only whet the appetite.

Blueberry–Sour Cream Pie

This is one of the easiest pies you can make, even more so if you cheat a little and use a store-bought graham cracker crust. A layer of frozen blueberries cooked on the stovetop and thickened with cornstarch goes on top of the crust. Once that has cooled, a layer of blended, sweetened cream cheese and sour cream is spooned on top. And that's all there is to it. It looks, and tastes, almost like an upside-down blueberry cheesecake, but with a lot less effort. If fresh blueberries are in season, you can press a handful of them into the cooked berries when you spoon them into the pie shell. The combination of uncooked and cooked berries is very good.

MAKES 8 TO 10 SERVINGS

1 recipe Graham Cracker Crumb Crust (page 51) or 1 large store-bought graham cracker crust

FILLING

One 1-pound bag individually frozen blueberries (not packed in syrup)

1 1/2 tablespoons fresh lemon juice

1/3 cup granulated sugar

2 tablespoons cornstarch

1/2 teaspoon vanilla extract

Handful of fresh blueberries (optional)

CREAM CHEESE–SOUR CREAM TOPPING

One 8-ounce package full-fat cream cheese, softened

1/3 cup confectioners' sugar, sifted

2 tablespoons granulated sugar

1 teaspoon finely grated lemon zest

1/2 cup full-fat sour cream

1/4 teaspoon vanilla extract

GARNISH

Handful of fresh blueberries or threads of lemon zest (optional)

1. Prepare the crust and press it into the bottom and up the side of a 9½-inch deep-dish pie pan. Refrigerate, prebake, and let cool as directed. If you're using a store-bought crust, prebake as directed on the package and let cool.

2. Combine the frozen blueberries and lemon juice in a medium-size nonreactive saucepan. Cover, and cook over medium to low heat until the blueberries are almost simmering in their own liquid. Mix the granulated sugar and cornstarch together in a small bowl, then stir the mixture into the blueberries. Bring the fruit to a boil, stirring. Once the fruit starts to boil, reduce the heat a little and cook, stirring nonstop, for 1½ minutes. Remove from the heat and stir in the vanilla. Scrape the fruit into a shallow bowl and let cool for 15 minutes.

3. Spoon the partially cooled filling into the cooled pie shell and smooth with a spoon. If you're using fresh berries, scatter them over the fruit and press them into the cooked berries. Refrigerate for 30 to 60 minutes.

4. Meanwhile, make the topping. Using an electric mixer, beat the cream cheese, sugars, and lemon zest together in a medium-size bowl until smooth. Add the sour cream and vanilla and blend briefly until smooth. Spoon the filling over the chilled pie and smooth the top with a spoon. Cover with loosely tented aluminum foil and refrigerate for at least 2 hours.

5. Just before serving, garnish with the blueberries or lemon zest, if desired.

Recipe for Success

▶ When you're spooning the creamy topping over the fruit, take care that all of the topping is in place before you start to smooth it out. That way, you're more likely to avoid dipping the back of your spoon into the fruit filling and smearing blue streaks across the otherwise perfectly white surface. If that does happen and you're bothered by the streaks, you can always crush some vanilla wafers in a food processor or by hand and sprinkle them over the top to hide your boo-boo. Or you can garnish the pie with fresh berries.

Blueberry–Yogurt Cheese Pie

When you drain yogurt of all its whey, or extra liquid, you end up with what's known as yogurt cheese. It's not really cheese, but it does have a soft cream cheese–like consistency that's firm enough to support a layer of cooked blueberries and thus make a fine pie. You'll need to start this pie the day before you plan to serve it, because the yogurt needs plenty of time to drain and get relatively firm. Once this pie is assembled, give it a couple of hours in the fridge to firm up before serving. Instead of making this in a standard 9-inch pie pan, you can also use a large store-bought graham cracker crust.

MAKES 8 TO 10 SERVINGS

1 recipe Graham Cracker Crumb Crust (page 51) or 1 large store-bought graham cracker crust

FILLING

One 1-pound bag individually frozen blueberries (not packed in syrup)

1/4 cup orange juice

1/3 cup plus 2 tablespoons granulated sugar

1 1/2 tablespoons cornstarch

2 teaspoons fresh lemon juice

1 teaspoon minced candied (crystallized) ginger (optional)

One 32-ounce container plain yogurt (see Recipe for Success), drained for at least 12 hours (see box)

1/3 cup confectioners' sugar, sifted

1/4 teaspoon vanilla extract

GARNISH

Long threads of lemon zest (optional)

1. Prepare the crust and press it into the bottom and up the side of a 9-inch standard pie pan. Refrigerate, prebake, and let cool as directed. Or simply prebake a store-bought crust as directed on the package and let cool.

2. About an hour or so before you plan to assemble the pie, combine the frozen blueberries, orange juice, and 1/3 cup of the granulated sugar in a medium-size nonreactive saucepan over medium heat. Cook, stirring occasionally, until hot and the berries have put off a lot of their juice, about 5 minutes. Mix together the remaining 2 tablespoons granulated sugar and the cornstarch in a small bowl. Stir the mixture into the blueberries. Bring the berries to a boil, stirring, and gently boil for about 1 1/2 minutes, until thickened. Remove from the heat and stir in the lemon juice and ginger (if using). Scrape the berries into a wide bowl and let cool to room temperature. Once cooled, refrigerate for at least 30 minutes.

3. To assemble the pie, transfer the drained yogurt to a medium-size bowl. Stir in the confectioners' sugar until smooth, then stir in the vanilla. Spoon the yogurt into the cooled pie shell, smoothing it over the bottom and up the sides. Spoon the cooled blueberries over the yogurt and smooth with a spoon. Garnish, if desired, with long threads of lemon zest. Cover with loosely tented aluminum foil and refrigerate for at least 1 hour or overnight before serving.

Recipe for Success

▶ I've made this pie with full-fat, lowfat, and nonfat yogurt, and they all work. I think you get better results, however, with full-fat yogurt. I'm not sure why, but it seems to drain better—perhaps because of the greater amount of starch in the lowfat and nonfat versions—and yield a firmer yogurt cheese, thus a firmer pie. I prefer Stonyfield Farm yogurt, made in New Hampshire.

Making Yogurt Cheese

The day before you plan to serve this pie, line a colander with cheesecloth or a clean, damp, very thin cotton tea towel. Place the colander in a bowl. Empty the yogurt into the cloth, pull up the sides of the cloth, and gather them on top of the yogurt. Put the bowl in the refrigerator and let the yogurt drain for at least 12 hours.

Wild Blueberry–Maple Pie with a Cornmeal Crust

The fun of writing your own pie cookbook is that you don't have to justify weighting the material toward your personal favorites. So without apology, I present yet another blueberry pie that I simply love. I think of this as a sort of "Best of New England" blueberry pie: small, sweet-tart wild blueberries sweetened with real maple syrup. The earthy cornmeal crust is a nod to earlier times, when cornmeal was much more commonly used in American kitchens. It's crunchy yet tender, the perfect crust when you want a rustic pie for your family or a casual gathering. I like to serve it with vanilla ice cream.

MAKES 8 TO 10 SERVINGS

1 recipe Cornmeal Pie Pastry, Double Crust (page 40), refrigerated (see Recipe for Success)

FILLING

3 cups wild blueberries, canned (drained), frozen (partially thawed), or fresh (picked over for stems)

1/4 cup pure maple syrup, preferably light or medium amber

2 tablespoons sugar

1 1/2 tablespoons cornstarch

1 tablespoon fresh lemon juice

1/8 teaspoon ground cinnamon

1.   If you haven't already, prepare the pastry and refrigerate until firm enough to roll, about 1 hour.

2.   On a sheet of lightly floured waxed paper, roll the larger portion of the pastry into a 12-inch circle with a floured rolling pin. Please note that this pastry is a little softer than some and the graininess from the cornmeal makes it slightly more fragile, so proceed delicately and with a well-floured pin. Invert the pastry over a 9-inch standard pie pan, center, and peel off the paper. Gently tuck the pastry into the pan, without stretching it, and let the overhang drape over the edge. Place in the refrigerator for 15 minutes.

3.   Combine the blueberries and maple syrup in a medium-size bowl. Combine the sugar and cornstarch in a small bowl, then stir the mixture into the blueberries along with the lemon juice and cinnamon. Turn the filling into the chilled pie shell, smoothing the fruit with a spoon. Preheat the oven to 400°F.

4.   Roll the other half of the pastry into a 10-inch circle on a sheet of lightly floured waxed paper. Moisten the outer edge of the pie shell with a pastry brush. Invert the top

pastry over the filling, center, and peel off the paper. Press the top and bottom pastries together along the dampened edge. Using a knife, trim the pastry flush with the edge of the pan. Pinch and push the pastry slightly down inside the pan so that it sits just below the edge. Doing so will protect the pastry, which has a tendency to overbrown along the edge. Poke several steam vents in the top of the pie with a paring knife, twisting the knife to enlarge the holes slightly. Put a couple of the vents along the edge so you can check the juices there later.

5. Place the pie on the center oven rack and bake for 25 minutes. Reduce the oven temperature to 350°F and rotate the pie 180 degrees, so that the part that faced the back of the oven now faces forward. Just in case, slide a large aluminum foil–lined baking sheet onto the rack below to catch any spills. Continue to bake until the juices bubble thickly along the edge, 25 to 30 minutes. If the top pastry starts to get too brown, cover the pie with loosely tented aluminum foil during the last 10 to 15 minutes.

6. Transfer the pie to a wire rack and let cool for at least 1 hour before serving.

Recipe for Success

▶ **If you've never rolled a pie pastry before, it might be better to use another pastry to make this pie—perhaps Basic Flaky Pie Pastry (page 31) or All-Butter Pie Pastry (page 28). Cornmeal pastry is a little temperamental and is better made by someone with a little rolling experience.**

▶ **Don't worry if the crust develops large cracks as it bakes. It is somewhat brittle because of the cornmeal, and occasionally the buildup of steam in the filling can cause enough pressure to break the crust, usually along the edge.**

Spoken Like a True-Blue Yankee

"Cherry pie was never as important in New England as in other parts of the United States. Yankees prefer blueberry pie, which, when properly baked, is a glorious thing. Unfortunately, it is often made badly. Restaurant and store-bought blueberry pies usually have more flour or cornstarch in them than blueberries, and many home-baked blueberry pies are too runny."

—Jonathan Norton Leonard, *American Cooking: New England* (Time-Life Books, 1970)

Wyman's Wild Blueberry Lattice-Top Pie

Wyman's, founded in 1874 in Milbridge, Maine, is a big name in wild blueberry production. If you don't have a local source for wild blueberries, you'll probably end up with canned or frozen Wyman's berries. How are wild blueberries different from cultivated ones? They're smaller, with a more distinctive, sweeter flavor, and they're a little chewier as well. If you've never tried them, you really should. This lattice-top pie, Wyman's house recipe, is a great showcase for their flavor and deep blue color.

MAKES 8 TO 10 SERVINGS

1 recipe Basic Flaky Pie Pastry, Double Crust (page 31) or All-Butter Pie Pastry, Double Crust (page 28), modified as instructed in step 1 and refrigerated

FILLING

5 cups wild blueberries, fresh (picked over for stems), canned (drained), or frozen (partially thawed)

$1/2$ oup sugar

2 tablespoons cornstarch

1 tablespoon all-purpose flour

$1/8$ teaspoon ground cinnamon

$1/8$ teaspoon salt

$1/2$ teaspoon grated lemon zest

GLAZE

Milk or light cream

Sugar

1. Prepare the pastry as directed, shaping half of it into a disk and the other half into a square; both should be about $3/4$ inch thick. Wrap the pastry as usual and refrigerate until firm enough to roll, about 1 hour.

2. On a sheet of lightly floured waxed paper, roll the round portion of pastry into a 12-inch circle with a floured rolling pin. Invert the pastry over a 9-inch standard pie pan, center, and peel off the paper. Gently tuck the pastry into the pan, without stretching it, and sculpt the overhang into an upstanding ridge. Place in the refrigerator for 15 minutes.

3. Place the berries in a large bowl. In a small bowl, combine the sugar, cornstarch, flour, cinnamon, and salt. Stir the mixture into the fruit, then stir in the lemon zest. Preheat the oven to 425°F.

4. On another sheet of lightly floured waxed paper, roll the square portion of dough into a rectangle about 10 inches square. Using a pastry wheel or pizza cutter and a ruler, cut the pastry into 8 lengthwise strips about 1 inch wide. Turn the filling into the chilled pie shell, smoothing the top with a spoon. Lay 5 strips vertically across the pie, evenly

spaced, as shown in figure 1. Fold back strips 2 and 4, then lay another strip directly across the center of the pie, as shown in figure 2. Unfold the folded dough strips, then fold back strips 1, 3, and 5. Lay another perpendicular strip across the pie, as shown in figure 3. Unfold the folded strips, then fold up strips 1, 3, and 5 on the other side of the pie. Place another perpendicular strip across the pie, as shown in figure 4, then unfold strips 1, 3, and 5. Trim the strips, then pinch the ends into the edge of the pastry. Lightly brush the pastry strips with milk and sprinkle the top of the pie with sugar.

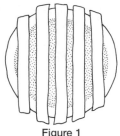

Figure 1

5. Place the pie on the center oven rack and bake for 25 minutes. Reduce the oven temperature to 350°F and rotate the pie 180 degrees, so that the part that faced the back of the oven now faces forward. Just in case, put a large aluminum foil–lined baking sheet onto the rack below to catch any spills. Continue to bake until the top pastry is golden brown and any visible juices bubble thickly near the center, 35 to 40 minutes.

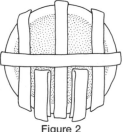

Figure 2

6. Transfer the pie to a wire rack and let cool for at least 2 hours before serving.

Recipe for Success

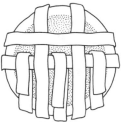

Figure 3

▶ **Read about lattice-top pies on page 72 before making this pie.**

▶ **The Wyman's recipe doesn't call for it, but I like to add 1 tablespoon fresh lemon juice to the filling.**

▶ **If you're using Wyman's canned blueberries packed in water, you can boil down 1 cup of the drained juice from the cans to about one-quarter of its volume and add this to the filling for extra flavor. If you do, also add 1 teaspoon cornstarch.**

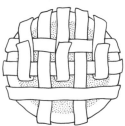

Figure 4

Blueberry-Lime Pie

If you want a simple, low-stress, but delicious blueberry pie that can be made with frozen berries, here it is. To give the pie an unmistakable lime flavor, I use both grated lime zest and frozen limeade concentrate, a convenient product that allows you to use less sugar in the filling. Let this cool well before slicing, or it will be rather runny.

MAKES 8 TO 10 SERVINGS

1 recipe Basic Flaky Pie Pastry, Double Crust (page 31), refrigerated

FILLING

One 1-pound bag individually frozen blueberries (not packed in syrup), partially thawed (see Recipe for Success)

1/3 cup thawed frozen limeade concentrate

3 tablespoons sugar

3 tablespoons quick-cooking tapioca

1 teaspoon grated lime zest

GLAZE

Milk or light cream

Sugar

1. If you haven't already, prepare the pastry and refrigerate until firm enough to roll, about 1 hour.

2. On a sheet of lightly floured waxed paper, roll the larger portion of the pastry into a 12-inch circle with a floured rolling pin. Invert the pastry over a 9-inch standard pie pan, center, and peel off the paper. Gently tuck the pastry into the pan, without stretching it, and let the overhang drape over the edge. Place in the refrigerator for 15 minutes. Preheat the oven to 400°F.

3. Combine the blueberries, limeade concentrate, sugar, tapioca, and lime zest in a large bowl. Mix well, but try not to crush the blueberries. Set aside.

4. On another sheet of lightly floured waxed paper, roll the other half of the pastry into an 11-inch circle. Turn the filling into the chilled pie shell and smooth the top with a spoon. Lightly moisten the rim of the pie shell with a wet finger or pastry brush. Invert the top pastry over the filling, center, and peel off the paper. Press the top and bottom pastries together along the dampened edge. Trim the pastry with scissors or a paring knife, leaving an even 1/2-inch overhang all around, then sculpt the overhang into an upstanding ridge. Poke several steam vents in the top of the pie with a fork or paring knife. Put a couple of the vents near the edge of the crust so you can check the juices there later. Brush the top of the pie lightly with milk and sprinkle with sugar.

5. Place the pie on the center oven rack and bake for 30 minutes. Reduce the oven temperature to 375°F and rotate the pie 180 degrees, so that the part that faced the back of the oven now faces forward. Just in case, slide a large aluminum foil–lined baking sheet onto the rack below to catch any drips. Continue to bake until the top of the pie is golden brown and any juices visible at the steam vents bubble thickly, 20 to 25 minutes.

6. Transfer the pie to a wire rack and let cool for at least 2 hours before serving.

Recipe for Success

▸ It's not necessary to completely thaw the berries before you mix the filling. In fact, slightly cold and firm is okay, because it keeps the berries from turning to mush when you mix them. If you haven't taken them out of the freezer ahead, spread the frozen berries in a glass pie pan or other wide microwave-safe dish and heat them on medium power for about 30 seconds. Check and continue heating, if necessary, until they are partially thawed.

Blueberry-Peach Pie with Pecan Crumb Topping

For as long as I can remember, my favorite two fruits have been blueberries and peaches. And they are, to my pie maker's mind, infallible partners in a mixed-fruit pie. If for some reason I had to choose but one kind of mixed-fruit pie to eat for the rest of my life, this would be it: blueberries and peaches, topped with a pecan crumb topping. I readily admit to making this pie with frozen blueberries and, from time to time, frozen peaches. It's still great but, like most fruit pies, not what it can be with all fresh fruit, in season. My idea of a perfect summer afternoon would be some breezy conversation with friends or family on my deck, all of us nibbling on slices of this pie, with the hum of my ice cream maker in the background churning up a batch of fresh peach or vanilla ice cream.

MAKES 8 TO 10 SERVINGS

1 recipe Basic Flaky Pie Pastry, Single Crust (page 31), refrigerated

FILLING

3 cups wild or regular blueberries, fresh (picked over for stems) or frozen (partially thawed)

3 cups peeled, pitted, and sliced ripe peaches or frozen sliced peaches, partially thawed

1/2 cup plus 2 tablespoons sugar

1 tablespoon fresh lime juice

Grated zest of 1 lime

3 tablespoons cornstarch

PECAN CRUMB TOPPING

3/4 cup all-purpose flour

3/4 cup pecan halves

1/2 cup sugar

1/4 teaspoon salt

6 tablespoons (3/4 stick) cold unsalted butter, cut into 1/4-inch pieces

1 tablespoon milk or light cream

1. If you haven't already, prepare the pastry and refrigerate until firm enough to roll, about 1 hour.

2. On a sheet of lightly floured waxed paper, roll the pastry into a 13-inch circle with a floured rolling pin. Invert the pastry over a 9½-inch deep-dish pie pan, center, and peel off the paper. Tuck the pastry into the pan, without stretching it, and sculpt the edge into an upstanding ridge. Place in the freezer for 15 minutes. Preheat the oven to 400°F.

3. In a large bowl, combine the blueberries, peaches, ½ cup of the sugar, the lime juice, and lime zest. Mix well, then set aside for 10 minutes. Mix together the cornstarch and remaining 2 tablespoons sugar in a small bowl, then stir the mixture into the fruit.

4. Turn the filling into the chilled pie shell, smoothing the top with a spoon or your hands. Place the pie on the center oven rack and bake for 30 minutes.

5. Meanwhile, make the topping. Combine the flour, pecans, sugar, and salt in a food processor. Pulse several times to chop the nuts coarsely. Scatter the butter over the top and pulse again until the mixture resembles fine crumbs. Sprinkle the milk over the mixture and pulse again briefly. Transfer the topping to a medium-size bowl and rub it between your fingers to make damp, gravelly crumbs. Refrigerate until ready to use.

6. Remove the pie from the oven and reduce the temperature to 375°F. Carefully dump the crumbs in the center of the pie, spreading them evenly over the surface with your hands. Tamp them down lightly. Return the pie to the oven, placing it so that the part that faced the back of the oven now faces forward. Just in case, slide a large aluminum foil–lined baking sheet onto the rack below to catch any drips. Continue to bake until the juices bubble thickly around the edge, 30 to 40 minutes. If necessary, cover the pie with loosely tented aluminum foil for the last 15 minutes to keep the top from getting too dark.

7. Transfer the pie to a wire rack and let cool for at least 2 hours before serving.

Recipe for Success

▶ Although you can use either kind of blueberries, I like the small wild ones here. Given the choice, I think I'd choose frozen or canned (drained) wild blueberries over fresh regular ones.

▶ Canned peaches will work fine, too. My first choice would be sliced peaches in syrup, drained of all but a little of the juice.

Blueberries for Sale, 20 Cents a Quart

"Wild blueberries are best for pie. Picking them is still a considerable industry in Maine, where great areas of barren land are covered with low bushes that in season are covered with small, somewhat acid berries. In the rest of New England the bushes do best on burned-over forestland. This was the ravaged condition of much of Cape Cod's interior when I was a boy. Sometimes I picked as many as 20 quarts a day, which I divided between my family, gratis, and the grocery store across Main Street from our house, at 20 cents a quart. . . . The large cultivated berries that grow on big bushes in marshy areas are apt to be too sweet to make perfect pies. Yet even the sweetest can be remedied with a touch of lemon juice."

—Jonathan Norton Leonard, *American Cooking: New England* (Time-Life Books, 1970)

Blueberry-Pineapple Piña Colada Pie

This pie is absolutely delicious, with a tropical island flavor that makes it the perfect dessert for an islands theme party. But don't wait until then to try it! The secret ingredient? Frozen piña colada concentrate. It's great made with frozen or canned blueberries, but do use the little wild ones for the best flavor. This would be the perfect tailgate party pie, even more so at a Jimmy Buffet concert.

MAKES 8 TO 10 SERVINGS

1 recipe Basic Flaky Pie Pastry, Single Crust (page 31), refrigerated

FILLING

3 cups wild blueberries, canned (drained), frozen (partially thawed), or fresh (picked over for stems)

1 cup canned crushed pineapple, drained

1/3 cup thawed frozen piña colada concentrate

1/4 cup sugar

1 1/2 tablespoons cornstarch

1 tablespoon light or dark rum (optional)

1/2 teaspoon coconut or vanilla extract

Pinch of salt

COCONUT CRUMB TOPPING

3/4 cup all-purpose flour

3/4 cup sweetened flaked coconut

1/2 cup sugar

1/4 teaspoon salt

5 tablespoons cold unsalted butter, cut into 1/4-inch pieces

1. If you haven't already, prepare the pastry and refrigerate until firm enough to roll, about 1 hour.

2. On a sheet of lightly floured waxed paper, roll the pastry into a 12-inch circle with a floured rolling pin. Invert the pastry over a 9-inch standard pie pan, center, and peel off the paper. Tuck the pastry into the pan, without stretching it, and sculpt the edge into an upstanding ridge. Place in the freezer for 15 minutes. Preheat the oven to 400°F.

3. Combine the blueberries, pineapple, and piña colada concentrate in a large bowl. Mix the sugar and cornstarch together in a small bowl, then stir the mixture into the fruit. Stir in the rum (if using), coconut extract, and salt. Scrape the filling into the chilled pie shell and smooth the top with a spoon. Place the pie on the center oven rack and bake for 30 minutes.

4. Meanwhile, make the coconut crumb topping. Put the flour, coconut, sugar, and salt in a food processor and pulse briefly to mix. Scatter the butter over the top and pulse until the mixture starts to form gravelly crumbs. Dump the crumbs into a large bowl and rub between your fingers to form large, buttery crumbs. Refrigerate until ready to use.

5. Remove the pie from the oven and reduce the temperature to 375°F. Carefully dump the crumbs in the center of the pie, spreading them evenly over the surface with your hands. Tamp them down lightly. Return the pie to the oven, placing it so that the part that faced the back of the oven now faces forward. Just in case, slide a large aluminum foil–lined baking sheet onto the rack below to catch any spills. Continue to bake until the juices bubble thickly around the edge, about 30 minutes. If the top starts to get too brown, cover loosely with aluminum foil for the last 15 minutes.

6. Transfer the pie to a wire rack and let cool for at least 1 hour before serving.

Recipe for Success

▶ Remember that a pie made with frozen fruit can take as much as 20 to 30 minutes more to bake than one made with fresh. This is enough time to overbake the crust, especially the exposed areas. That why it's important that your fruit not be fully frozen when it goes into the pie shell. Once you've mixed the filling, it won't do any harm to let it sit in the bowl for an extra 15 to 20 minutes at room temperature to let the fruit thaw even longer before you turn it into the shell.

▶ Watch the pie closely during the last 20 minutes. Coconut tends to brown quickly, and the pie may have to be covered with aluminum foil near the end of the baking.

Jumble Berry Pie

Perhaps you've seen jumble berries around your home. Typically, they arrive in the summer when fresh berries are irresistibly in season: first a few leftover pancake blueberries, then some strawberries or a pint of raspberries dropped off by a friend. Before you know it, you have a jumble of berries. When that happens to me, I like to make this five-berry pie, throwing in some frozen cranberries for tartness and taste. (I always keep a few bags in the freezer.) It makes a wonderful finale for any summer meal and a fitting salute to berry season, served with vanilla ice cream. You'll need 5½ to 6 cups berries, in roughly the proportions given below, but feel free to tilt the balance one way or another as you like. If you enjoy this pie, also try one of the bumble berry pies on pages 184 and 185.

MAKES 8 TO 10 SERVINGS

1 recipe Basic Flaky Pie Pastry, Double Crust (page 31) or Tender Cream Cheese Pastry, Double Crust (page 46), refrigerated

FILLING

1¹⁄₄ cups fresh blueberries, picked over for stems

1¹⁄₄ cups hulled and sliced fresh strawberries

1 cup fresh raspberries

1 cup fresh blackberries

1 cup cranberries, fresh (picked over for stems) or frozen (partially thawed), coarsely chopped

¹⁄₂ cup sugar

1¹⁄₂ tablespoons cornstarch

¹⁄₄ teaspoon ground nutmeg

Pinch of salt

1 tablespoon fresh lemon juice

1 teaspoon grated lemon zest

GLAZE

Heavy cream (see Recipe for Success)

Sugar

1. If you haven't already, prepare the pastry and refrigerate until firm enough to roll, about 1 hour.

2. On a sheet of lightly floured waxed paper, roll the larger portion of the pastry into a 12-inch circle with a floured rolling pin. Invert the pastry over a 9-inch standard pie pan, center, and peel off the paper. Gently tuck the pastry into the pan, without stretching it, and let the overhang drape over the edge. Place in the refrigerator for 15 minutes.

3. Combine the berries in a large bowl. Mix the sugar and cornstarch together in a small bowl, then stir the mixture into the fruit. Stir in the nutmeg, salt, lemon juice, and lemon zest. Set aside for 10 minutes. Preheat the oven to 400°F.

4. Roll the other half of the pastry into a 10-inch circle on a sheet of lightly floured waxed paper. Turn the filling into the chilled pie shell, smoothing the fruit with a spoon. Moisten the outer edge of the pie shell with a pastry brush. Invert the top pastry over the filling, center, and peel off the paper. Press the top and bottom pastries together along the dampened edge. Trim the edge to an even ¹⁄₂ inch all around, then sculpt the overhang into an upstanding ridge. Poke several steam vents in the top of the pie with a fork or paring knife. Put a couple of the vents near the edge so you can check the juices there later. Brush the top of the pie generously with heavy cream and sprinkle with sugar.

5. Place the pie on the center oven rack and bake for 30 minutes. Reduce the oven temperature to 375°F and rotate the pie 180 degrees, so that the part that faced the back of the oven now faces forward. Just in case, slide a large aluminum foil–lined baking sheet onto the rack below to catch any spills. Continue to bake until the juices, most likely visible at the steam vents, bubble thickly, 25 to 30 minutes. If the top pastry starts to get too brown, cover with loosely tented aluminum foil during the last 10 minutes.

6. Transfer the pie to a wire rack and let cool for at least 1 hour before serving.

Recipe for Success

▶ **As much as possible, use fresh berries here. When they're not available, frozen is fine, but do let the berries thaw partially first. Some drained canned berries are okay, too.**

▶ **Using heavy cream, rather than milk or light cream, for the glaze yields a different result. It forms a second skin on top of the pastry—a brittle, blistered layer something like phyllo dough. It's quite delicious and adds another dimension of flavor and interest to any double-crust pie.**

Orange-Berry Pie

Another fast pie made with frozen convenience products, this can be in the oven in about 5 minutes if you have a bag of mixed berries on hand. The orange flavor goes particularly well with vanilla ice cream, just the flourish this pie needs.

MAKES 8 TO 10 SERVINGS

1 store-bought frozen 9-inch deep-dish pie shell

FILLING

One 1-pound bag individually frozen mixed berries (not packed in syrup), partially thawed

2 tablespoons thawed frozen orange juice concentrate

$1/3$ cup sugar

$1^1/_2$ tablespoons cornstarch

Pinch of salt

STREUSEL TOPPING

$1/2$ cup all-purpose flour

$1/2$ cup sugar

$1/4$ teaspoon ground cinnamon

$1/8$ teaspoon salt

4 tablespoons cold unsalted butter, cut into $1/4$-inch pieces

1. Remove the pie shell from the package but leave it in the freezer for now. Preheat the oven to 400°F.

2. Combine the berries and orange juice concentrate in a large bowl. In a small bowl, mix together the sugar, cornstarch, and salt, then stir the mixture into the fruit. Turn the filling into the frozen pie shell. Place the pie on the center oven rack and bake for 25 minutes.

3. Meanwhile, make the topping. Place the flour, sugar, cinnamon, and salt in a food processor and pulse several times to mix. Scatter the butter over the top and pulse until the mixture resembles fine crumbs. Empty the crumbs into a medium-size bowl and rub between your fingers to make large, buttery crumbs. Refrigerate until ready to use.

4. Remove the pie from the oven and reduce the temperature to 375°F. Carefully dump the crumbs over the pie, spreading them evenly over the surface with your hands. Tamp them down lightly. Return the pie to the oven, placing it so that the part that faced the back of the oven now faces forward. Just in case, slide a large aluminum foil–lined baking sheet onto the rack below to catch any drips. Continue to bake until the topping is golden brown and the juices bubble thickly around the edge, about 25 minutes.

5. Transfer the pie to a wire rack and let cool for at least 2 hours before serving.

Recipe for Success

▶ **Typically, bags of frozen mixed berries contain large strawberries. If that's indeed the case, be sure to cut each of them into several smaller pieces for better distribution before mixing the filling.**

▶ **If your berries are frozen solid, you can get them to the partially thawed state by putting them in the microwave on defrost for 2 to 3 minutes.**

The Dean of American Cooking Weighs In on Pies

"If winters were cold, pies were made in quantity and put out to freeze. The varieties were limited to the supplies at hand, but dried fruit was always available to the thrifty housekeeper. Sometimes the pies were layered. For instance, fresh or dried and simmered apple slices might be topped with custard or a cottage cheese custard; and mince might be topped with apple, cranberries, pumpkin, or sometimes apple and custard. Such recipes do not appear in cookbooks, but have come down to us in old diaries or literature of the time."

—James Beard, *James Beard's American Cookery* (Little, Brown and Company, 1972)

Dundee Arms Inn Bumble Berry Pie

The Dundee Arms Inn on Prince Edward Island is a Victorian-era home built in 1903 by a prosperous local businessman. Today owner and innkeeper Pat Sands presides over this lovingly restored Charlottetown guest house, well-known for its delicious cuisine. One of the guests' favorite desserts is this version of bumble berry pie. Bumble berry (it's often spelled as one word) refers generally to a mixed-berry pie that often includes rhubarb and apple. In this rather unusual version, the top crust is not rolled. Instead, the pastry is formed into a ball, frozen, and then grated over the filling as if it were a block of cheese. I thought this rather odd at first, but then I was taken by how clever it is—so much so that I've used this trick for several other pies in this collection.

MAKES 8 TO 10 SERVINGS

1 recipe Basic Flaky Pie Pastry, Double Crust (page 31), refrigerated

FILLING

1 cup fresh raspberries

1 cup fresh blueberries, picked over for stems

1 cup hulled and sliced fresh strawberries

1 cup fresh rhubarb stalks sliced crosswise 1/2 inch thick

1 cup granulated sugar

2 tablespoons fresh lemon juice

1/3 cup all-purpose flour

2 tablespoons cold unsalted butter, cut into small pieces

GLAZE

About 1 tablespoon coarse sugar (see page 69) or granulated sugar

1. If you haven't already, prepare the pastry and refrigerate until firm enough to roll, about 1 hour.

2. On a sheet of lightly floured waxed paper, roll the larger half of the pastry into a 13-inch circle with a floured rolling pin. Invert the pastry over a 9½-inch deep-dish pie pan, center, and peel off the paper. Tuck the pastry into the pan, without stretching it, and sculpt the edge into an upstanding ridge. Place in the freezer for 15 minutes. Also place the unrolled pastry in the freezer. Preheat the oven to 400°F.

3. Combine the berries, rhubarb, sugar, and lemon juice in a large bowl. Toss gently to mix. Add the flour and toss again gently. Turn the filling into the chilled pie shell, smoothing the top of the fruit with a spoon. Dot the top of the filling with the butter.

4. Using the large holes of a box grater, grate the other half of the pastry directly over the fruit, as if it were a block of cheese. Using a fork, gently move the gratings here and there for an even covering. Sprinkle the coarse sugar over the top.

5. Place the pie on the center oven rack and bake for 30 minutes. Reduce the oven temperature to 375°F and rotate the pie 180 degrees, so that the part that faced the back of the oven now faces forward. Just in case, slide a large aluminum foil–lined baking pan onto the rack below to catch any spills. Continue to bake until the top is golden brown and the juices bubble thickly around the edge, 25 to 30 minutes.

6. Transfer the pie to a wire rack and let cool for at least 2 hours before serving.

Recipe for Success

▶ The pastry chef at the Dundee Arms Inn likes to use fresh fruit here, but feel free to substitute some frozen fruit, if necessary. When using fresh fruit, toss gently to maintain the shape of the fruit.

▶ Don't be too concerned about making the top of the pastry nice and even. If it's a little clumpy, that's fine. The pastry tends to settle in the heat of the oven, leaving a cobbler-like finish.

Bumble Berry Pie II

So enamored was I of both the name bumble berry and the Dundee Arms version of this great pie (see page 184) that I decided to create another version that could be made simply, with store-bought pie pastry. In addition to the blackberries and blueberries, this one has a shredded apple, a plum, and cherries. The apple and plum are a little hard to identify once the pie has baked, but they give it a wonderfully complex flavor that I think you'll enjoy.

MAKES 8 TO 10 SERVINGS

2 store-bought refrigerated pie pastries

FILLING

1 cup fresh blueberries, picked over for stems

1 cup fresh blackberries or raspberries

1 cup pitted sweet or sour cherries, canned (drained) or fresh

1 plum or Pluot (see page 120), unpeeled, pitted, and thinly sliced

1 large Granny Smith or other tart apple, peeled, cored, and shredded

1 teaspoon fresh lemon juice

$1/3$ cup plus 3 tablespoons sugar

$2^{1}/_2$ tablespoons cornstarch

$1/8$ teaspoon ground nutmeg

2 tablespoons cold unsalted butter, cut into small pieces

1. If you haven't already, remove the pie pastries from the refrigerator and let sit at room temperature for 15 to 20 minutes. Remove one of pastries from the package and line a 9-inch standard pie pan with it. Refrigerate.

2. Combine the fruit and lemon juice in a large bowl. Add $1/3$ cup of the sugar and toss well to mix. Set aside for 10 minutes. Preheat the oven to 400°F.

3. Combine the remaining 3 tablespoons sugar, the cornstarch, and nutmeg in a small bowl, then stir the mixture into the fruit. Turn the filling into the chilled pie shell, smooth the top, and dot with the butter. Using a wet finger or pastry brush, moisten the rim of the pie shell. Remove the other pastry from the package. Unfold, draping it over the top of the pie. Press the top and bottom pastries together at the dampened edge. Trim the pastry to an even $1/2$ inch all around, then sculpt the overhang into a upstanding ridge. Poke several steam vents in the top of the pie with a fork or paring knife. Put a couple of the vents near the edge so you can check the juices there later.

4. Place the pie on the center oven rack and bake for 30 minutes Reduce the oven temperature to 375°F and rotate the pie 180 degrees, so that the part that faced the back of the oven now faces forward. Just in case, slide a large aluminum foil–lined baking sheet on the rack below to catch any spills. Bake until the top is dark golden brown and the juices visible at the steam vents bubble thickly, 25 to 30 minutes.

5. Transfer the pie to a wire rack and let cool for at least 2 hours before serving.

Recipe for Success

▶ **This pie tastes delicious with almost any combination of fresh, frozen, or canned fruit. Try to use at least some fresh fruit, for best flavor and texture. And remember that frozen fruit should be partially thawed prior to mixing the filling.**

▶ **If you prefer a more textured pie, dice the apple rather than grating it.**

Patsy's Mixed-Berry Freeform Pie

Like my friend Patsy Jamieson, food editor of *Eating Well* magazine, I love to mix berries in summer pies. Here she does just that in a freeform pie with a base of cheesecake-like custard, which Patsy says makes a creamy contrast to the berries. Instead of a traditional butter pastry, this one uses Patsy's excellent cottage cheese pastry. In addition to the cottage cheese, it contains oil and baking powder, so the baked texture is more cake-like than crumbly, the way pastry typically is. It tastes delicious and makes a wonderful container for this special summer pie.

MAKES 8 TO 10 SERVINGS

1 recipe Patsy's Cottage Cheese Pastry (page 47), refrigerated

FILLING

4 ounces (half of an 8-ounce package) reduced-fat cream cheese (Neufchâtel cheese), softened

1/4 oup sugar

1 teaspoon cornstarch

1 large egg yolk

2 teaspoons grated lemon zest

1 teaspoon vanilla extract

4 cups fresh mixed berries, such as blackberries, raspberries, and blueberries (picked over for stems)

GLAZE

1 large egg white

1 tablespoon water

2 tablespoons sugar

1.   If you haven't already, prepare the pastry and refrigerate for 1 hour, as directed.

2.   Line a large baking sheet with lightly oiled parchment paper or aluminum foil. Preheat the oven to 400°F.

3.   Using an electric mixer, beat the cream cheese, sugar, and cornstarch together in a medium-size bowl until smooth. Blend in the egg yolk, lemon zest, and vanilla until smooth. Set aside.

4.   On a sheet of lightly floured waxed paper, roll the pastry into a 14-inch circle. Invert the pastry over the lined baking sheet, center, and peel off the paper, letting the pastry drape slightly over the edges, if necessary. Without upsetting the overhanging dough, put the entire baking sheet in the refrigerator for 5 minutes to refirm the pastry (see Recipe for Success).

5.   Remove the baking sheet and pastry from the refrigerator. Imagine a circle about 8 inches in diameter in the center of the pastry. Spread the cream cheese mixture over that area, leaving a wide border all around. Pile the berries evenly over the mixture. Using

a metal spatula to help you lift it, fold the uncovered perimeter of pastry up and over the filling, enclosing it. The pastry will sort of self-pleat as you do this. (See the illustration of a freeform crust on page 153.)

6. To make the glaze, whisk the egg white with the water in a small bowl. Brush glaze lightly over the exposed portion of the pastry. Sprinkle the berries and pastry with the sugar.

7. Place the pie on the center oven rack and bake until the crust is deep golden brown, about 30 minutes. Transfer the baking sheet and pie to a wire rack and let cool for 10 minutes, then slide the pie, with the lining, onto the rack. Serve slightly warm or at room temperature.

Recipe for Success

▸ Because of the baking powder, Patsy's pastry is a little more delicate than some, which is why I give it an intermediate rest in the fridge to help firm it up for more handling. If you have a small fridge or a rather full one and putting the pastry—on a large baking sheet—in it is impractical, you can use an alternative method. Start rolling the pastry on the waxed paper as directed, until it is 10 or 11 inches in diameter. Slide the dough and paper onto a small baking sheet or tray, cover with plastic wrap, and refrigerate for 10 minutes. Then proceed with the rolling and filling.

Angel Pie with Berries, Cream, and Custard

You don't hear much about angel pie anymore. I think it's quite old-fashioned, and since it's really a dish of the moment—to be enjoyed soon after it's topped—you will rarely find anything like it in restaurants or bakeries. An angel pie is always made with a meringue crust—a good choice when you've just made a dish with lots of yolks and have the whites on hand. You can bake it in a pie pan, but after much trial and error, I've decided the best way to make the crust is freeform, on a parchment-lined baking sheet, to avoid any problems with sticking. The fun part comes after the crisp-cooked meringue is baked and you get to decide how to top it. Here we take a very elegant approach, mounding whipped cream, fresh raspberries and blueberries, and then custard sauce over everything. It's sliced and served right away, so the meringue stays crunchy and delicious. It's good for any occasion, but it's especially fitting for those traditionally female gatherings like tea parties and showers.

MAKES 8 SERVINGS

1 recipe Meringue Pie Crust (page 50)

Fresh Whipped Cream (page 605)

1/2 to 3/4 cup fresh raspberries

1/2 to 3/4 cup fresh blueberries, picked over for stems

Crème Anglaise (page 606)

1. If you haven't already, prepare the meringue crust and set it aside to cool. Note that this is about a 2 1/2-hour proposition from start to finish, because of the extended baking and cooling.

2. When you are ready to serve the pie, carefully place the crust on a large, flat serving platter. Smooth the whipped cream over the crust, then scatter the berries over the cream. Drizzle the top with the crème anglaise, just enough for decorative purposes. Slice and serve the pie in wedges, drizzling each piece with additional crème anglaise.

Recipe for Success

▶ Handle the meringue carefully when you're moving it, or it may shatter; it's somewhat fragile. If the worst happens, don't worry: just put the pieces back together, and when the other ingredients are added, no one will be the wiser.

▶ Use other berries on top, if you like. Small strawberries are great.

▶ If you shape the meringue into a rectangle, you'll have a great flag shape for a patriotic pie. Use white whipped cream and red and blue berries to create your own Fourth of July flag. Kids love this project.

It Must Be the Pie Diet

"When you look at the tremendous quantities of desserts they cook and eat, it's amazing that any Midwesterners are able to fit through a normal size doorway. Strangely enough, the majority of people in the Midwest are quite thin. . . . Many Midwestern community and church cookbooks, instead of starting out conventionally with chapters on appetizers and soups and proceeding through the rest of the meal to dessert and beverages, plunge right in and start off with the sweets. First things first."

—Glenn Andrews, *Food from the Heartland* (Prentice Hall, 1991)

Three-Berry Shortcake Pie

This is similar to Peach-Blueberry Cobbler Pie (page 104), though perhaps even truer to the shortcake theme because it uses all berries. Unlike the other version, the filling here is partially cooked on top of the stove. It's poured into a partially baked pie shell, the topping is spooned on right away, and the pie is baked for about 25 minutes. The shorter baking time helps preserve some of the berries' texture. As for the topping, this one has a little cornmeal for added texture, and it's made with milk instead of buttermilk. This makes a great breakfast, brunch, or dessert pie.

MAKES 8 TO 10 SERVINGS

1 recipe Basic Flaky Pie Pastry, Single Crust (page 31), refrigerated

FILLING

$1^1/2$ cups fresh blueberries, picked over for stems

$1^1/2$ cups fresh raspberries or blackberries

$1^1/2$ cups hulled and thickly sliced fresh strawberries

$1/3$ cup sugar

1 tablespoon fresh lemon juice

$1/4$ cup orange juice

1 tablespoon plus 1 teaspoon cornstarch

SHORTCAKE TOPPING

1 cup all-purpose flour

$1/4$ cup fine yellow cornmeal

$1/4$ cup sugar

$1^1/2$ teaspoons baking powder

$1/2$ teaspoon salt

$1/4$ cup ($1/2$ stick) cold unsalted butter, cut into $1/4$-inch pieces

$1/2$ cup milk

1 large egg

$1/2$ teaspoon vanilla extract

GARNISH

Fresh Whipped Cream (page 605)

1. If you haven't already, prepare the pastry and refrigerate until firm enough to roll, about 1 hour.

2. On a sheet of lightly floured waxed paper, roll half of the pastry into a 13- to $13^1/2$-inch circle with a floured rolling pin. Invert the pastry over a $9^1/2$- to 10-inch extra-deep-dish pie pan, center, and peel off the paper. Tuck the pastry into the pan, without stretching it, and sculpt the edge into an upstanding ridge. Place in the freezer for 15 minutes. Partially prebake and let cool according to the directions on page 16.

3. In a large saucepan, combine the berries, sugar, and lemon juice over medium heat. Slowly heat, stirring occasionally, until the berries put off a good deal of juice, 5 to 7 minutes. In a small bowl, combine the orange juice and cornstarch. Stir the mixture into the fruit. Bring the fruit to a low boil and cook, stirring, for about $1\frac{1}{2}$ minutes, until slightly thickened. Remove from the heat. Preheat the oven to 400°F.

4. To make the topping, sift the flour, cornmeal, sugar, baking powder, and salt together in a medium-size bowl. Add the butter and cut it into the dry ingredients until the mixture resembles coarse crumbs. Beat the milk, egg, and vanilla together in a small bowl. Make a well in the dry ingredients, add the liquid, and stir until evenly mixed. Set aside.

5. Reheat the fruit, bringing it to a boil. Pour the filling into the cooled pie shell. Spoon the topping evenly over the fruit.

6. Place the pie on the center oven rack. Just in case, slide a large aluminum foil–lined baking sheet onto the rack below to catch any spills. Bake until the topping is golden brown and cooked through, 22 to 25 minutes.

7. Transfer the pie to a wire rack and let cool for 20 to 30 minutes before serving. This is best served within 2 hours.

Recipe for Success

▶ **If you have an extra-deep-dish pie pan, now is the time to use it. The combination of the juicy fruit and the cobbler topping raises the level of the liquid considerably. A typical $9\frac{1}{2}$-inch deep-dish pan is barely adequate.**

▶ **Nearly any combination of fresh berries will work fine here. Use $4\frac{1}{2}$ to 5 cups fruit.**

▶ **If you like whole-grain flours, feel free to substitute up to $\frac{1}{2}$ cup whole wheat flour for an equal amount of the all-purpose flour.**

▶ **The shortcake topping for this pie and the cobbler topping on pages 104–105 are interchangeable.**

Elizabeth's Pie

Elizabeth is the granddaughter of Louise Piper (see page 45), one of the stellar pie bakers and consistent winners at the Iowa State Fair. This particular pie, a mixed-fruit affair, earned Louise a ribbon at the 2003 fair. The combination of fruit and other filling ingredients was first suggested years earlier by her six-year-old granddaughter. Since then, the pie has become a family tradition. Louise bakes the pie in an oil crust that she's been using for years. It's a little trickier to handle than pastry made with solid fat, but I was very impressed with the flaky, delicate result. For thickening, she uses both quick-cooking tapioca and flour, because, as Louise says, the pie is very juicy. It does, however, set up fairly firm. My personal favorite way to eat this pie is barely warm, when it's still juicy but not runny.

MAKES 8 SERVINGS

1 recipe Louise Piper's Oil Pastry (page 44)

FILLING

1 cup sugar

¹/₄ cup all-purpose flour

2 tablespoons quick-cooking tapioca

¹/₂ teaspoon ground cinnamon

¹/₄ cup honey

1 cup peeled, cored, and diced tart apple (Louise likes Jonathan or Red Rome; Granny Smith is good, too)

1 cup fresh red raspberries

1 cup hulled and sliced fresh strawberries

1 cup diced fresh rhubarb stalks

2 tablespoons cold unsalted butter, cut into small pieces

GLAZE

Sugar

Milk or light cream

1. If you haven't already, prepare the pastry. Wrap in plastic but do not refrigerate. Set aside.

2. Combine the sugar, flour, tapioca, and cinnamon in a large bowl. Toss well to mix. Add the honey, apple, berries, and rhubarb and mix gently but thoroughly. Set aside. Preheat the oven to 375°F.

3. Put the larger half of the pastry between 2 sheets of *unfloured* waxed paper. Using your rolling pin, roll the pastry into a 12-inch circle. Peel off the top sheet of paper. Invert the pastry over a 9-inch standard pie pan, center, and peel off the paper. Gently tuck the pastry into the pan, without stretching or tearing it, and let the overhang drape over

the edge. Using the same sheets of waxed paper, roll the other half of the dough into a 10-inch circle. Remove the top sheet of paper.

4. Scrape the filling into the pie shell, smoothing the fruit with a spoon. Dot the fruit with the butter. Dampen the edge of the pie shell with a pastry brush. Invert the top pastry over the filling, center, and slowly peel off the paper, pressing down along the edge to seal. Sculpt the overhanging dough into an upstanding ridge. Sprinkle the top of the pie generously with sugar, then drizzle with milk. Using a fork or paring knife, poke several steam vents in the top of the pie. Put at least one of them along the edge so you can check the juices there later.

5. Place the pie on the center oven rack and bake for 30 minutes, then rotate the pie 180 degrees, so that the part that faced the back of the oven now faces forward. Just in case, slide a large aluminum foil–lined baking sheet onto the rack below to catch any spills. Continue to bake until the top is a rich golden brown and any juices visible at the steam vents bubble thickly, 20 to 25 minutes.

6. Transfer the pie to a wire rack and let cool. Serve just barely warm or at room temperature.

Recipe for Success

> I find that Louise's pastry works best if rolled shortly after making it. That's why I don't refrigerate it the way I typically do other pastries.

> The dough will need to be rolled very thin to make a 12-inch circle. Don't be surprised if it is a little crumbly at the edge. Just handle it delicately.

> I usually glaze my pies with milk first, then with sugar, but Louise does it just the opposite. It makes a slight difference in the texture—the sugar sort of gathers into crunchy waves rather than being uniformly crunchy. I like it. Try it yourself and see.

Piecing Together a Pie Chronology

No one knows for certain who baked the first pie. Some historians believe that it was the Romans. The first written recipe for a pie, they tell us, came from Cato the Censor (234–139 B.C.), who printed a recipe for a goat cheese and honey pie in a rye crust. Here are a few more things we know about the evolution of pie.

- *The Oxford English Dictionary* notes that the word "pie" was "evidently a well-known popular word in 1362," although it most likely referred to meat and fowl pies, not dessert pies.

- In 1475, the Italian writer Platina offered a recipe for a squash pie sprinkled with sugar and rose water. Could this have been an early ancestor of our pumpkin pie?

- Fruit pies likely did not exist much before the 1500s. In Tudor and Stuart times, English pies were made with pears, apples, and quinces.

- Pie came to America with the English settlers, who baked their pies in pans known as "coffyns." Pastry crust was not their forte. It was typically meant only to contain the pie, not to be eaten.

- Pies have long been a large part of the New England diet. Apple pie for breakfast is a New England tradition. The 1877 diary of a Vermont housewife counts her annual output of pies at 427—and this without refrigerated pie pastry!

- Pie is still America's favorite dessert, with apple leading the pack.

Apple is America's signature pie—not just something we love to eat, but one of those rare, universal symbols of things we hold dear. It's no wonder, then, that making an apple pie is one of fall's enduring rites. To a large extent, whether it tastes delicious or is store-bought or homemade is irrelevant: apple pie enjoys iconic stature in this country, and we cherish it all the same.

Make Mine Apple

You may have a single, irrefutable memory of what constitutes a true apple pie—perhaps it was the one your grandmother or mother made—but the most surprising thing about apple pie is just how varied it can be. Nobody knows this better than me. My book *Apple Pie Perfect* (Harvard Common Press, 2002) is a collection of 100 recipes for apple pie. That I was able to add considerably to that total here speaks volumes about apple pie's adaptable nature. • One of the things I love most about apple pie is that it marks the unofficial start of the fall baking season. Relief from the oppressive summer heat arrives, bringing with it a renewed interest in dusting off favorite recipes and baking almost every weekend. Outings are planned to secure the best local apples. Warm, fresh pies are delivered to friends and family, strengthening ties that have been loosened by months of vacations and far-flung endeavors. Apple pie brings us home, in a very real sense, and envelops us in the warmth of domestic well-being.

Here's hoping all your apple pies are memorable.

"If you want to make an apple pie from scratch, you must first create the universe."

—CARL SAGAN

Tips for Baking Delicious Apple Pies

▶ Start with the best fruit you can find. The box on page 233 will point you in the right direction. If you have access to local orchards, talk to the people who grow the apples. They can give you guidance on regional apple varieties that may be perfect for pies.

▶ You can improve the flavor of lackluster fruit with the addition of lemon juice, apple butter, or boiled cider.

▶ To make a more compact pie with a dense filling, cut some of the fruit into slices and some into small chunks. You'll get more fruit into the filling that way.

▶ Avoid using too much sugar in apple pies. Sweetness is fine, but you don't want to obscure the pleasant tart flavor tones of good apples.

▶ Don't underbake your apple pies, or the thickening will not "take," leaving you with a runny mess. In most cases, you want to see thick—not thin—juices bubbling up in the pie filling.

▶ Always cool your pie for at least one hour, preferably two, before slicing it, or the filling will not have ample time to set.

The Easiest Apple Pie

This is an even easier version of a shortcut apple pie that appears in my book *Apple Pie Perfect* (Harvard Common Press, 2002). The idea of a very easy quasi-homemade apple pie appeals to quite a few people, apparently. One of them is interviewer Robin Young at WBUR, a National Public Radio station in Boston. Robin invited me to be on her show, where I actually made a pie live, on the radio, while she interviewed me about apple pie—a first for me. During the interview, she brought out her version of my Easiest Apple Pie of All, which she had baked at the studio shortly before my arrival. It was duly impressive, and I was delighted and flattered that she had tried one of the recipes from my book. Anyway, this is an apple pie for those with neither the time nor the inclination to make a pie from scratch. It makes unabashed use of convenience products, adding just enough homemade touches—including a fresh apple and a scratch crumb topping—to leave your family wondering how much trouble you've actually gone to. If you have a need for speed, or just convenience, this is the pie for you.

MAKES 8 TO 10 SERVINGS

1 store-bought refrigerated pie pastry

FILLING

One and a half 21-ounce cans apple pie filling

1 large Granny Smith or other tart, juicy apple, peeled, cored, and finely chopped

1 tablespoon fresh lemon juice

1/2 cup dark raisins, dried currants, or sweetened dried cranberries (sold as Craisins)

1/4 teaspoon ground cinnamon

CRUMB TOPPING

1/2 cup all-purpose flour

1/2 cup sugar

1/4 teaspoon ground cinnamon

Big pinch of salt

1/4 cup (1/2 stick) cold unsalted butter, cut into 1/4-inch pieces

1.   Line a 9-inch standard pie pan with the pastry. Fold the excess pastry back and pinch the edge into an upstanding ridge. Place in the freezer for 15 minutes. Preheat the oven to 400°F.

2.   Combine the apple pie filling, apple, lemon juice, raisins, and cinnamon in a medium-size bowl. Turn the filling into the chilled pie shell and smooth the top with your hands or a spoon. Place the pie on the center oven rack and bake for 30 minutes.

3.   Meanwhile, make the topping. Put the flour, sugar, cinnamon, and salt in a food processor and pulse several times to mix. Scatter the butter over the dry mixture and pulse until the mixture resembles fine crumbs. Empty the crumbs into a large bowl and rub the mixture between your fingers to make large, buttery crumbs. Refrigerate until ready to use.

4.   Remove the pie from the oven and reduce the temperature to 375°F. Carefully dump the crumbs in the center of the pie, spreading them evenly over the surface with your hands. Tamp them down lightly. Return the pie to the oven, placing it so that the part that faced the back of the oven now faces forward. Just in case, slide a large aluminum foil–lined baking sheet onto the rack below to catch any drips. Continue to bake until the juices bubble thickly around the edge, about 25 minutes.

5.   Transfer the pie to a wire rack and let cool for at least 1 hour before serving.

Recipe for Success

▶   **The purpose of the apple here is to give the canned pie filling a little contrasting texture and fresh flavor. Even with a juicy apple, however, it isn't necessary to add more thickener, because there is already plenty in the canned filling.**

My Dad, Warren Haedrich, on Making Apple Pie

"I always started with flour, butter, and Crisco, plus a tin cup filled with cold water and a few ice cubes to keep it cold. I liked working on a large maple board, which I floured so all was ready when I mixed the butter—cut into little squares with several tablespoons of Crisco—into the flour with a wire pastry blender. I would mix this combination with enough cold water to easily handle everything, then make up two balls for chilling in the refrigerator.

"After that, I would help your mother core, peel, and slice the apples. We decided New York State McIntosh were our favorites. I don't remember how many we would cut up. I do remember that there were a lot of sliced apples and we never thought we could get that many in a 9-inch pie plate. We used a glass pie plate at one time, but at some point shifted to a shiny metal one. Those who ate the pie never seemed to mind.

"The apples got a coating of nutmeg (just a small amount) and some cinnamon (a larger amount), a heavy dusting of brown sugar, and the rest of the stick of butter I didn't use for the crust. Then I got busy rolling out the dough using waxed paper until it looked right but was thick enough to handle. I lined the pie plate with the dough, with an extra inch hanging over the edge, then we poured the apples onto the dough. We would put the top layer on, slit the top dough, brush it with milk, dust it with a small amount of sugar, and put it in the oven until it was done. We learned to put foil under the pie rack, to catch the drippings. Altogether, it smelled wonderful and tasted even better."

- By the same token, the thickener in canned filling reduces the amount of time needed for cooling. I recommend 1 hour, but you could get by with 30 minutes.

- If you prefer a top crust instead of a crumb topping, that will work fine. Simply moisten the edge of the pie shell, drape the top crust over the pie, and seal. Trim and crimp the edge as usual.

Golden Delicious Apple Pie with Oatmeal Crumb Topping

Since my book *Apple Pie Perfect* (Harvard Common Press) was published in 2002, I've traveled quite some distance giving perhaps 50 or more apple pie–baking demonstrations. Many of the questions asked during these demos have to do with pie apples—namely, which ones are best for pies. I spend several minutes discussing a wide variety, but knowing that many cooks feel limited to the 10 or 15 common supermarket varieties, I often put in a word for the good old Golden Delicious apple. Detractors call it insipid, and it can be at its worst. But then again, any apple can be insipid, especially one past its prime. It's been my experience that fresh Golden Delicious apples have a good apple flavor, are reasonably juicy, and hold their shape fairly well in a pie, softening up nicely in the oven. Here's a great basic apple pie built on the Golden Delicious, with the oatmeal crumb topping that's earned this pie its distinction as the "best apple pie I've ever eaten" by more than a few of my friends and neighbors.

MAKES 8 TO 10 SERVINGS

1 recipe Basic Flaky Pie Pastry, Single Crust (page 31), refrigerated

FILLING

7 cups peeled, cored, and thinly sliced Golden Delicious apples

1/3 cup plus 1 tablespoon granulated sugar

Juice and grated zest of 1 lemon

1/4 teaspoon ground nutmeg

1 1/2 tablespoons cornstarch

OATMEAL CRUMB TOPPING

1 cup all-purpose flour

1/2 cup rolled oats (old-fashioned or quick-cooking)

2/3 cup firmly packed light brown sugar

1/2 teaspoon ground cinnamon

1/4 teaspoon salt

1/2 cup (1 stick) cold unsalted butter, cut into 1/4-inch pieces

1. If you haven't already, prepare the pastry and refrigerate until firm enough to roll, about 1 hour.

2. On a sheet of lightly floured waxed paper, roll the pastry into a 13-inch circle with a floured rolling pin. Invert the pastry over a 9 1/2-inch deep-dish pie pan, center, and peel off the paper. Gently tuck the pastry into the pan, without stretching it, and sculpt the edge into an upstanding ridge. Place in the freezer for 15 minutes.

3. Combine the apples, 1/3 cup of the granulated sugar, and the lemon juice and zest in a large bowl. Mix well, then set aside for 10 minutes. Preheat the oven to 400°F.

4. In a small bowl, mix the remaining 1 tablespoon sugar with the nutmeg and cornstarch. Add the mixture to the apples and stir the fruit well. Turn the filling into the chilled pie shell and smooth with your hands to even it out. Place the pie on the center oven rack and bake for 30 minutes.

5. Meanwhile, make the crumb topping. Put the flour, oats, brown sugar, cinnamon, and salt in a food processor and pulse several times to mix. Scatter the butter over the top.

Pulse repeatedly until the mixture resembles fine crumbs. Empty the crumbs into a large bowl and rub them between your fingers until you have large, buttery crumbs. Refrigerate until ready to use.

6. Remove the pie from the oven and reduce the temperature to 375°F. Carefully dump the crumbs in the center of the pie, spreading them over the surface with your hands. Tamp them down lightly. Return the pie to the oven, placing it so that the part that faced the back of the oven now faces forward. Just in case, slide a large aluminum foil–lined baking sheet onto the rack below to catch any spills. Bake until the top is dark golden brown and the juices bubble thickly at the edge, 30 to 35 minutes. If necessary, cover the pie with loosely tented aluminum foil during the last 15 minutes of baking to keep the top from browning too much.

7. Transfer the pie to a wire rack and let cool for at least 1 hour before serving.

Recipe for Success

▶ **My crumb pies tend to have a lot of crumb topping**—perhaps a little too much for some people. I think, at the very least, the crumbs should cover the pie in a compact, thickish layer. You can always use fewer crumbs if you prefer, bagging the extra and freezing them for another pie or muffin recipe.

An Apple Peeler You'll Really Like

If you're in the market for a new apple peeler—and you certainly should be if yours is dull, slips around in your grip, or is otherwise frustrating to wield—check out the selection of OXO brand peelers at your local kitchenware shop. I own several of them, and I say it's about time someone made a peeler that performs like a tool and not a toy. Most notably, OXO peelers have a substantial slip-proof, rubberized grip that you can really get your hand around. That alone makes these far superior to other peelers. The swivel blade is blessedly sharp and makes for a smooth, shallow cut, perfect for peeling those pie apples without gouging the precious flesh.

Brown Sugar Apple Pie

This pie differs from the previous one in that it is the blueprint for an apple pie you'd make in a 9-inch standard pie pan, as opposed to a 9½-inch deep-dish pan. As such, most of the ingredients are scaled down and the baking time is slightly less, although the techniques involved are virtually identical. One change I've made is using brown sugar instead of granulated, the way my mom and dad used to make their apples pies. Brown sugar adds a caramel note to the pie, which purists disparage for masking the true flavor of the apples and the rest of us simply enjoy. Another obvious difference: you don't get as many slices—six big pieces or eight smaller ones.

MAKES 6 TO 8 SERVINGS

1 recipe Basic Flaky Pie Pastry, Double Crust (page 31), refrigerated

FILLING

6 cups peeled, cored, and thinly sliced Golden Delicious, Gala, Northern Spy, or other apples (see pages 232–233 for recommendations)

½ cup firmly packed light brown sugar

1 tablespoon fresh lemon juice

Big pinch of salt

1 tablespoon granulated sugar

1 tablespoon cornstarch

¼ teaspoon ground cinnamon (optional)

GLAZE

Milk or light cream

Granulated sugar

1.   If you haven't already, prepare the pastry and refrigerate until firm enough to roll, about 1 hour.

2.   On a sheet of lightly floured waxed paper, roll the larger portion of the pastry into a 12-inch circle with a floured rolling pin. Invert the pastry over a 9-inch standard pie pan, center, and peel off the paper. Gently tuck the pastry into the pan, without stretching it, and let the overhang drape over the edge. Place in the refrigerator for 15 minutes.

3.   Combine the apples, brown sugar, lemon juice, and salt in a large bowl. Toss well, then set aside for 15 minutes. Preheat the oven to 400°F. Mix the granulated sugar and cornstarch together in a small bowl. Stir the mixture into the apples along with the cinnamon, if using. Scrape the filling into the chilled pie shell and smooth the top with your hands.

4.   Roll the other half of the pastry into a 10-inch circle on a sheet of lightly floured waxed paper. Moisten the outer edge of the pie shell with a pastry brush. Invert the top

pastry over the filling, center, and peel off the paper. Press the top and bottom pastries together along the dampened edge. Using the back of a butter knife, trim the pastry flush with the edge of the pan. With the back of a fork, press the tines all along the edge to seal. Using the fork, poke several steam vents in the top, including a couple along the edge so you can check the juices there later. Brush the top with a little milk and sprinkle with granulated sugar.

5.   Place the pie on the center oven rack and bake for 30 minutes. Reduce the oven temperature to 375°F and rotate the pie 180 degrees, so that the part of the pie that faced the back of the oven now faces forward. Just in case, slide a large aluminum foil–lined baking sheet onto the rack below to catch any drips. Bake until golden brown, about 25 minutes. When done, you should notice thick juices bubbling out of the steam vents along the edge.

6.   Transfer the pie to a wire rack and let cool for at least 2 hours, preferably longer, before serving.

Recipe for Success

▶   **When I'm baking an apple pie and I'm not sure if the apples are done, I often use a long, thin bamboo skewer to check the apples, much the way you would use a toothpick to check a cake. I keep a supply on hand just for this purpose. When I suspect the pie is done, I stick the skewer down into one of the steam vents I've made near the center of the pie (the center always takes the longest to cook). As the skewer enters the apples, there should be almost no resistance. If there is, the pie probably needs at least 10 more minutes of baking.**

Apple Pie with Cheddar Cracker Topping

Combining cheddar cheese and apples is an old New England tradition. (Also see the recipe on page 206.) The filling is pretty standard—apples, a little sugar, some lemon—but the crumb topping, made from cheddar cheese crackers, butter, and cheese, is probably unlike any you've ever had. The topping goes on during the last 20 minutes and bakes up golden and crunchy, in perfect contrast to the soft apple filling.

MAKES 8 TO 10 SERVINGS

1 recipe Basic Flaky Pie Pastry, Single Crust (page 31) or All-Butter Pie Pastry, Single Crust (page 28), refrigerated

FILLING

6 cups peeled, cored, and thinly sliced apples (see pages 232–233 for recommendations)

1/4 cup plus 2 tablespoons sugar

Big pinch of salt

2 teaspoons fresh lemon juice

1/2 teaspoon grated lemon zest

11/2 tablespoons cornstarch

CHEDDAR CRACKER TOPPING

21/2 cups Cheez-It cheddar cheese crackers, preferably the white cheddar variety

1/4 cup (1/2 stick) cold unsalted butter, cut into 1/4-inch pieces

3/4 cup finely shredded sharp white cheddar cheese

1. If you haven't already, prepare the pastry and refrigerate until firm enough to roll, about 1 hour.

2. On a sheet of lightly floured waxed paper, roll the pastry into a 12-inch circle with a floured rolling pin. Invert the pastry over a 9-inch standard pie pan, center, and peel off the paper. Tuck the pastry into the pan, without stretching it, and sculpt the edge into an upstanding ridge. Place in the freezer for 15 minutes. Preheat the oven to 400°F.

3. Combine the apples, 1/4 cup of the sugar, the salt, lemon juice, and lemon zest in a large bowl. Set aside for 10 minutes to juice.

4. Combine the remaining 2 tablespoons sugar and cornstarch in a small bowl, then stir the mixture into the apples. Turn the filling into the chilled pie shell and smooth the top with your hands. Place the pie on the center oven rack and bake for 30 minutes. Reduce the heat to 375°F and bake for 10 minutes more.

5. Meanwhile, make the cracker topping. Place the crackers in a food processor and pulse until you have fairly fine—but not too fine—crumbs. Scatter the butter over the crumbs and pulse again to make a mixture that looks gravelly and buttery. Add the cheese and pulse 2 or 3 times to mix.

6. When the pie has baked for a total of 40 minutes, remove it from the oven. Carefully dump the crumbs over the top, spreading them evenly with your hands. Press gently to compact them. Return the pie to the oven, placing it so that the part that faced the back of the oven now faces forward. Just in case, slide a large aluminum foil–lined baking sheet onto the rack below to catch any drips. Bake until the top is a rich toasted brown and the juices visible at the edge bubble thickly, about 20 minutes. If the topping starts to get too brown, loosely drape a piece of aluminum foil over the top during the last 5 to 10 minutes of baking.

The Search for Granny Smith

Granny Smith is a fine pie apple. But would your real granny make the best Granny Smith? Here's a way to find out. Every year, the Washington Apple Commission launches a search for Granny Smith—a nationwide hunt to find the perfect grandmother to promote the state's famous green fruit. According to the commission's press materials, it's looking for someone who personifies the healthful attributes of Washington's apples. In addition, the candidate should:

- Be sweet to the core and have good moral fiber.

- Be handpicked by children, grandchildren, spouse, or friends.

- Have beauty that's more than skin-deep and just the right amount of maturity.

- Have "a-peel."

If you think your own granny qualifies, go to the Washington Apple Commission's Web site, www.bestapples.com, for more details.

7. Transfer the pie to a wire rack and let cool for 30 minutes to 1 hour. This pie is best served warm.

Recipe for Success

- Try to find juicy apples to use in this recipe, because the topping is dry and crumbly and the pie can use the juice. Adding 1 or 2 Granny Smith apples will help, since they're generally pretty juicy.

- One nice trick to get the most from the cheddar topping is to rewarm the pie in the oven for 5 to 8 minutes before serving. Two to 3 minutes before taking it out of the oven, sprinkle the top with an additional 1/2 to 1 cup shredded sharp white cheddar cheese. As soon as the cheese melts, take the pie out of the oven and serve right away.

Cheddar-Crusted Apple-Pear Pie

Traditionally, a thick slab of cheddar cheese is placed on top of a hot slice of apple pie, and then, after a brief pause to let the cheese soften, pie and cheese are eaten together. You can still do that with this pie, but for an extra cheddar kick, I bake some cheese right into the crust. It smells great as it bakes, mingling with the fragrance of the apples, and tastes wonderful, too, something like cheese straws, if you're familiar with them. This can be made with all apples if you like, but I like to combine the apples with some sliced pears.

MAKES 8 SERVINGS

1 recipe Cheddar Cheese Pie Pastry, Double Crust (page 33), refrigerated

FILLING

4 cups peeled, cored, and sliced Golden Delicious, Granny Smith, Northern Spy, or other apples (see pages 232–233 for recommendations)

3 cups cored and sliced ripe fresh pears, peeled or unpeeled

$1/3$ cup sugar

$1^1/2$ tablespoons cornstarch

Pinch of salt

2 teaspoons fresh lemon juice

2 tablespoons cold unsalted butter, cut into small pieces

1.   If you haven't already, prepare the pastry and refrigerate until firm enough to roll, about 1 hour.

2.   On a sheet of lightly floured waxed paper, roll the larger portion of the pastry into a 13-inch circle with a floured rolling pin. Invert the pastry over a $9^1/2$-inch deep-dish pie pan, center, and peel off the paper. Gently tuck the pastry into the pan, without stretching it, and let the overhang drape over the edge. Place in the refrigerator for 15 minutes.

3.   Combine the apples, pears, and $1/4$ cup of the sugar in a large bowl. Toss to mix, then set aside to juice for 10 minutes. Preheat the oven to 400°F.

4.   Mix the remaining sugar, the cornstarch, and salt in a small bowl. Add the mixture to the fruit and toss well. Stir in the lemon juice.

5.   On another sheet of lightly floured waxed paper, roll the other half of the pastry into an $11^1/2$-inch circle. Turn the filling into the chilled pie shell and smooth the top with your hands. Dot the filling with the butter. Lightly moisten the rim of the pie shell. Invert the top pastry over the filling, center, and peel off the paper. Press the top and bottom

pastries together along the dampened edge. Trim the pastry with scissors or a paring knife, leaving an even ½-inch overhang all around, then sculpt the overhang into an upstanding ridge. Poke several steam vents in the top crust with a fork or paring knife. Put a couple of the vents near the edge of the crust so you can check the juices there later.

6. Place the pie on the center oven rack and bake for 30 minutes. Reduce the oven temperature to 375°F and rotate the pie 180 degrees, so that the part that faced the back of the oven now faces forward. Just in case, slide a large aluminum foil–lined baking sheet onto the rack below to catch any drips. Bake until the top is dark golden brown and any juices visible at the steam vents bubble thickly, 35 to 40 minutes.

7. Transfer the pie to a wire rack and let cool briefly before serving.

Recipe for Success

▶ Use a good sharp or extra-sharp cheddar in the pastry because it makes a world of difference in the flavor of the finished pie. There are many fine cheddars on the market, but I think Cracker Barrel is consistently the best.

▶ Because of the cheese, this is one of those pies I prefer to eat while it's still very warm. The more the pie cools, the more muted the flavor of the cheddar becomes. Cool slices can easily be warmed in the microwave or, wrapped in aluminum foil, in a hot oven.

Throw in a Few Dump Trucks of Ben & Jerry's, and That's One Heck of a Pie à la Mode

The world's largest apple pie was baked on August 16, 1997, by 300 volunteers for the North Central Washington Museum in Wenatchee, Washington. The prodigious pie required 32,000 pounds of apples, 7,000 pounds of sugar and flour, and, in the words of one observer, one really strange-looking oven—a 10,000-pound insulated lid that "baked" the pie for 5 hours. Much to the delight of the pastry crew, we suspect, the pie had no top crust. Yield: about 70,000 slices.

Honey Apple-Currant Pie in a Whole Wheat Crust

A lot of good bakers like to incorporate a whole-grain pastry into their fruit pies. There's something entirely apropos about enclosing fresh-picked fall apples, pears, or cranberries in a wholesome pie pastry. Here we take the earthy profile one step further by using honey as the primary sweetener. Honey is sweeter than sugar, so we use a little less sweetener than usual for a pie of this size. I like this with a top crust but another option would be to use this pastry—or perhaps the Nutty Pie Pastry (page 42)—for the bottom crust, then add any of the crumb toppings in this collection about midway through the baking.

MAKES 8 TO 10 SERVINGS

1 recipe Whole Wheat Pie Pastry, Double Crust (page 33), refrigerated

FILLING

7 cups peeled, cored, and sliced apples (see pages 232–233 for recommendations)

3/4 cup dark dried currants

1/3 cup honey

2 tablespoons sugar (optional)

1 1/2 tablespoons fresh lemon juice

Grated zest of 1/2 lemon

2 1/2 tablespoons all-purpose flour

1/2 teaspoon ground cinnamon

2 tablespoons cold unsalted butter, cut into small pieces

GLAZE

Milk or light cream

Sugar

1. If you haven't already, prepare the pastry and refrigerate until firm enough to roll, about 1 hour.

2. On a sheet of lightly floured waxed paper, roll the larger portion of the pastry into a 13-inch circle with a floured rolling pin. Invert the pastry over a 9 1/2-inch deep-dish pie pan, center, and peel off the paper. Gently tuck the pastry into the pan, without stretching it, and let the overhang drape over the edge. Place in the refrigerator for 15 minutes.

3. Combine the apples, currants, honey, sugar (if using), lemon juice, and lemon zest in a large bowl. Toss well, then set aside for 10 minutes. Preheat the oven to 375°F.

4. On another sheet of lightly floured waxed paper, roll the other half of the pastry into an 11 1/2-inch circle. Add the flour and cinnamon to the fruit and mix well. Turn the filling into the chilled pie shell. Dot the top of the filling with the butter. Moisten the edge of the pie shell with a wet fingertip or pastry brush. Invert the top pastry over the filling, center, and peel off the paper. Press the pastries together along the dampened edge, then trim the excess dough with scissors or a paring knife to an even ½ inch all around. Sculpt the edge into an upstanding ridge. Using a fork or paring knife, poke several steam vents near the edge of the pie so you can check the juices there later. Lightly brush the pie with milk and sprinkle with sugar.

5. Place the pie on the center oven rack and bake for 30 minutes. Rotate the baking sheet 180 degrees, so that the part of the pie that faced the back of the oven now faces forward. Just in case, slide a large aluminum foil–lined baking sheet onto the rack below to catch any spills. Continue to bake until the juices bubble thickly at the edge, 30 to 40 minutes.

6. Transfer the pie to a wire rack and let cool for at least 1 hour before serving.

Recipe for Success

▶ Whole wheat flour contains flecks of oil-rich wheat germ, so whole wheat pie pastry has a tendency to brown faster than pastries made with white flour. When you're making a fruit pie with whole wheat pastry, it's a good idea to bake the pie a little slower. That's why I bake this pie at 375°F for the entire time rather than the usual 400°F for the first 30 minutes.

Apple and Dried Apricot Pie

Dried fruit is a good way to add an element of surprise and complementary flavor to fresh fruit pies. You can use it right from the box or bag, as is, or you can get a little fancier, as I do here, and poach the fruit first. (Another good example of using dried fruit this way is Very Fig and Walnut Pie on page 316.) Not only does poaching soften the fruit—and some fruits, such as figs, can often use a serious softening—but it also leaves you with a sweet, flavorful poaching liquid, which I like to boil down to a syrup and add to the filling. With apples, dried fruit, and walnuts, this is a good choice for a winter pie, when the supply of good fresh fruit is limited.

MAKES 8 TO 10 SERVINGS

1 recipe Tender Cream Cheese Pastry, Double Crust (page 46), refrigerated

FILLING

1 1/2 cups diced dried apricots

2 cups apple or apricot juice (see Recipe for Success)

2 or 3 lemon slices

5 cups peeled, cored, and sliced Granny Smith or other tart apples

1/3 cup granulated sugar

1/2 cup coarsely chopped walnuts

3 tablespoons all-purpose flour

1 tablespoon fresh lemon juice

1/4 teaspoon ground cinnamon

1 1/2 tablespoons cold unsalted butter, cut into small pieces

GARNISH

Confectioners' sugar

1. If you haven't already, prepare the pastry and refrigerate until firm enough to roll, for 1 to 1 1/2 hours.

2. While the pastry is chilling, poach the apricots. Combine the apricots, apple juice, and lemon slices in a medium-size nonreactive saucepan. Bring to a boil, reduce the heat to medium-low, cover, and gently simmer for 20 minutes. Remove from the heat and drain the apricots, reserving the liquid. Return the liquid to the saucepan. Remove the lemon slices from the apricots and discard.

3. In a large bowl, combine the apples, granulated sugar, walnuts, flour, lemon juice, and cinnamon and toss well. Stir in the apricots. Let stand at room temperature for 15 minutes.

4. While the fruit sits, bring the poaching liquid to a boil. Continue to boil rapidly until the liquid in the pan is reduced to between 1/4 and 1/3 cup, just enough syrupy liquid to cover the bottom of the pan. Pour the liquid over the fruit and toss well. Set the filling aside. Preheat the oven to 400°F.

5. On a sheet of lightly floured waxed paper, roll half of the pastry into a 12-inch circle with a floured rolling pin. Invert the pastry over a 9-inch standard pie pan, center, and peel off the paper. Gently tuck the pastry down into the pan, without stretching it, and let the overhang drape over the edge. Place in the refrigerator for 5 minutes.

6. Roll the other half of the pastry into an 11-inch circle on a sheet of lightly floured waxed paper. Turn the filling into the chilled pie shell and smooth the top with your hands. Dot the filling with the butter. Dampen the edge of the pie shell with a wet fingertip or pastry brush. Invert the top pastry over the filling, center, and peel off the paper. Press the top and bottom pastries together along the dampened edge. Trim the pastry, leaving an

Baking Your Way into the CIA

If you or someone you know is thinking about pursuing a career in the culinary arts, your way with apple pie could earn you a hefty scholarship.

The Culinary Institute of America, thought by many to be the nation's top school of its kind, sponsors what it calls the All-American Apple Pie Recipe Contest. This contest, the institute says, "challenges prospective students to demonstrate their understanding of cooking basics."

Interested applicants, who must be in their junior year of high school or older, are asked to submit a recipe for an original apple pie, a photo of the pie, and a personal statement of up to 100 words describing who they are and what is special about the recipe. The top 20 entrants each receive $4,000 toward their freshman year tuition at the CIA and a free trip to the institute, in Hyde Park, New York, for a VIP visit. In addition, 10 runners-up each receive a $1,500 honorable mention scholarship.

For more information or to receive an official contest packet, call the institute at (800) 285-4627.

even ½-inch overhang all around, then sculpt this into an upstanding ridge. Poke several steam vents in the top of the pie with a fork or paring knife. Put a couple of the vents near the edge of the crust so you can check the juices there later.

7. Place the pie on the center oven rack and bake for 25 minutes. Reduce the oven temperature to 375°F and rotate the pie 180 degrees, so that the part that faced the back of the oven now faces forward. Just in case, slide a large aluminum foil–lined baking sheet onto the rack below to catch any drips. Continue to bake until the top is golden brown and the juices visible at the steam vents bubble thickly, 25 to 30 minutes.

8. Transfer the pie to a wire rack. While the pie is still hot, dust the top with confectioners' sugar. Let cool for at least 1 hour before serving.

Recipe for Success

▶ **Dried apricots have a pretty strong, concentrated flavor—strong enough to dominate the flavor of the apples. If that appeals to you, poach the apricots in apricot juice. Otherwise, use apple juice. You'll still get plenty of apricot flavor, but it won't be quite so forward. In either case, I recommend using unfiltered juice, available at health food stores.**

Cinnamon Applesauce Pie

Cooks of another era would often make applesauce pies as their supplies of storage apples dwindled and then ran dry. It's easy to understand why they would have embraced the idea, what with all the other chores to be done, because a jar of applesauce relieves a busy home-maker of the peeling and slicing required for a fresh apple pie. I think you'll like this pie for the same reason. If you have a jar of your own homemade applesauce, by all means use it. Otherwise, just use Mott's or another good-quality brand. You'll need some sugar to sweeten things up, a bit of lemon to kick up the flavor, and some cinnamon to add a little spice. Unless you like hot applesauce, you'll probably (like me) prefer this pie cold.

MAKES 8 SERVINGS

1 recipe Basic Flaky Pie Pastry, Single Crust (page 31), refrigerated

FILLING

2 large eggs, at room temperature

1 large egg yolk, at room temperature

1/3 cup granulated sugar

1/3 cup firmly packed light brown sugar

2 cups sweetened applesauce

1/4 cup (1/2 stick) unsalted butter, melted

1 tablespoon fresh lemon juice

1 teaspoon grated lemon zest

1/2 teaspoon ground cinnamon

1/4 teaspoon salt

1. If you haven't already, prepare the pastry and refrigerate until firm enough to roll, about 1 hour.

2. On a sheet of lightly floured waxed paper, roll the pastry into a 12-inch circle with a floured rolling pin. Invert the pastry over a 9-inch standard pie pan, center, and peel off the paper. Tuck the pastry into the pan, without stretching it, and sculpt the edge into an upstanding ridge. Place in the freezer for 15 minutes. Preheat the oven to 400°F.

3. Combine the eggs, egg yolk, and sugars in a large bowl. Using an electric mixer, blend the ingredients on medium speed until well mixed, about 30 seconds. Add all the remaining ingredients and beat again until evenly blended. Carefully pour the filling into the chilled pie shell.

4. Place the pie on the center oven rack and bake for 15 minutes. Reduce the oven temperature to 350°F. and continue to bake until the filling is set, about 30 minutes more. Rotate the pie 180 degrees, so that the part that faced the back of the oven now faces forward, about 15 minutes before it is done. The pie's surface should have a flat finish, although the center will still be glossy.

5. Transfer the pie to a wire rack and let cool thoroughly. Cover with loosely tented aluminum foil and refrigerate for at least 2 hours before serving.

Recipe for Success

▶ You may be wondering why you need additional sugar to sweeten this pie when you're already using sweetened applesauce. The reason is that the amount of sugar used to make the sauce isn't likely to be enough to deliver a decidedly sweet flavor to the pie. That said, not all applesauces are sweetened equally. You may use less sugar than I've called for, then taste the filling and see if you want to add more. If so, just beat it right into the filling before it goes in the pie shell.

Aunt Marge's Apple Butter Pie

I have a soft spot for my wife Bev's aunt Marge. The first time I met her, she waited a respectable five minutes or so and then, in the direct manner I supposed was common to West Virginia women, said, "And just when are you going to make my niece an honest woman?" If I harbored any uncertainty up to that point, I quickly assured her it wouldn't be long. (And it wasn't.) Since I've known her, and well before that, Aunt Marge has been sending Bev large jars of homemade apple butter every fall, made by the ladies of her church, Fairview Methodist Church in Charleston, West Virginia. So large are the jars that I've always had enough extra to make a couple of these pies with each batch. The texture is something like a rich pumpkin pie, smooth and well spiced. Extra spice is seldom needed, because most apple butters have lots of it. Like pumpkin pie, this would be a great choice for Thanksgiving dinner. Serve it cold, with whipped cream.

MAKES 8 TO 10 SERVINGS

1 recipe Basic Flaky Pie Pastry, Single Crust (page 31), refrigerated

FILLING
3 large eggs, at room temperature

1/2 cup sugar

1 3/4 cups spiced apple butter (see Recipe for Success)

1/3 cup light cream or half-and-half

1/4 teaspoon salt

1 tablespoon fresh lemon juice

1 teaspoon grated lemon zest

1/2 teaspoon vanilla extract

1/4 cup (1/2 stick) unsalted butter, melted

GARNISH
Fresh Whipped Cream (page 605)

1. If you haven't already, prepare the pastry and refrigerate until firm enough to roll, about 1 hour.

2. On a sheet of lightly floured waxed paper, roll the pastry into a 12-inch circle with a floured rolling pin. Invert the pastry over a 9-inch standard pie pan, center, and peel off the paper. Tuck the pastry into the pan, without stretching it, and sculpt the edge so it is just slightly higher than the rim. Place in the freezer for 15 minutes, then partially prebake and let cool according to the instructions on page 16.

3. Combine the eggs and sugar in a large bowl. Using an electric mixer, beat on medium-high speed until thoroughly blended, about 30 seconds. Add the apple butter, cream, salt, lemon juice, and lemon zest. Beat again until smooth. Blend in the vanilla and butter. Carefully pour the filling into the cooled pie shell.

4. Place the pie on the center oven rack and bake for 15 minutes. Reduce the oven temperature to 350°F and continue to bake until the sides just start to puff and the filling is set, about 30 minutes. Rotate the pie 180 degrees, so that the part that faced the back of the oven now faces forward, about 15 minutes before it is done. The very center of the pie will probably look a little glossy compared to most of the perimeter.

5. Transfer the pie to a wire rack and let cool completely. Cover with loosely tented aluminum foil and refrigerate for at least 2 hours. Serve with a dollop of whipped cream.

Recipe for Success

▶ Since there are no uniform standards for making apple butter, taste the brand you choose to determine both how sweet it is and how well spiced. Then taste the filling, too, before it goes into the pan. You may decide that it needs more or less sugar than specified. As for the spices, if the apple butter doesn't have a distinctly spicy edge, you'll probably want to add a little ground cinnamon and cloves to the filling as well.

We Couldn't Agree More

"When you can make a good pie, you will have a special gift to give others that money can't buy."

—Marion Cunningham, *Cooking with Children* (Knopf, 1995)

Apple-Pear White Wine Pie

The soft, fruity flavor of a Chardonnay or Chenin Blanc is a wonderful enhancement for a pie made with apples and pears. I stir the sugar into the fruit, saturate the mixture with white wine, and let it sit for an hour to really juice well. Then I drain off the accumulated juice and boil it to concentrate the flavors of the fruit and wine. This is a classy fruit pie that's best served with— what else?—a glass of the same wine you used in the pie. (It's fun to see if anyone is able to taste the connection between the two.)

MAKES 8 TO 10 SERVINGS

1 recipe Basic Flaky Pie Pastry, Double Crust (page 31) or Tender Cream Cheese Pastry, Double Crust (page 46), refrigerated

FILLING

4 cups peeled, cored, and sliced apples (see pages 232–233 for recommendations)

3 cups peeled, cored, and sliced ripe fresh pears

1/3 cup plus 2 tablespoons sugar

1 cup Chardonnay, Chenin Blanc, or other fruity white wine

2 1/2 tablespoons cornstarch

1/2 teaspoon grated lemon zest

1/8 teaspoon vanilla extract

Big pinch of salt

2 tablespoons cold unsalted butter, cut into small pieces

1. If you haven't already, prepare the pastry and refrigerate until firm enough to roll, 1 to 1½ hours.

2. On a sheet of lightly floured waxed paper, roll the larger portion of the pastry into a 12-inch circle with a floured rolling pin. Invert the pastry over a 9-inch standard pie pan, center, and peel off the paper. Gently tuck the pastry into the pan, without stretching it, and let the overhang drape over the edge. Place in the refrigerator for 15 minutes.

3. Combine the apples, pears, and ⅓ cup of the sugar in a large bowl. Mix well, add the wine, and mix again. Set aside for 1 hour, stirring occasionally.

4. Drain off all the juice and transfer it to a medium-size nonreactive saucepan. Bring to a boil, then continue to boil gently until reduced to ½ to ⅔ cup. Have a heatproof measuring cup nearby to check. Pour the reduced juice back over the fruit and mix well.

5. In a small bowl, combine the remaining 2 tablespoons sugar and the cornstarch, then stir the mixture into the fruit. Stir in the lemon zest, vanilla, and salt. Turn the filling into the chilled pie shell and dot the top with the butter.

6.   Roll the other half of the pastry into a 10-inch circle on a sheet of lightly floured waxed paper. Moisten the outer edge of the pie shell with a pastry brush. Invert the top pastry over the filling, center, and peel off the paper. Press the top and bottom pastries together along the dampened edge. Using the back of a butter knife, trim the pastry flush with the edge of the pan. With the back of a fork, press the tines all along the edge to seal. Poke several steam vents in the top of the pie with the fork or a paring knife, including a couple along the edge so you can check the juices there later.

7.   Place the pie on the center oven rack and bake for 30 minutes. Reduce the oven temperature to 375°F and rotate the pie 180 degrees, so that the side that faced the back of the oven now faces forward. Just in case, slip a large aluminum foil–lined baking sheet onto the rack below to catch any spills. Bake until the pie is golden brown, 25 to 30 minutes. When done, you may notice thick juices bubbling out of the steam vents along the edge.

8.   Transfer the pie to a wire rack and let cool for at least 2 hours before serving.

Recipe for Success

▶ **This is one pie where it pays to find a superior-tasting apple, best done in the fall and from a local grower. Some apples actually have a complex, winy flavor—not surprisingly, the Winesap variety stands out—that would be delicious in this pie. It's worth inquiring to see if someone in your area grows Winesap or other notable antique apples.**

▶ **I prefer not to serve this pie with whipped cream or ice cream. The richness can overwhelm the subtle flavors of the pie.**

Sounds Like It's Worth the Detour

Every August, the little town of Braham, Minnesota, holds its annual pie festival. This isn't just any pie festival, but one befitting the "Homemade Pie Capital of Minnesota"—so declared by Governor Rudy Perpich back in 1990. The one-day affair draws more than 5,000 hungry visitors, to whom some 150 volunteers serve up more than 500 homemade baked fruit pies. If you can drag yourself away from the pie table long enough, you might be lucky enough to catch some tunes by the Apple Chords Barbershop Quartet or hear the Pie-Alluia Chorus performing at the south end of the town park.

Pie Birds

Pie birds—or pie funnels, as they're called in England—have been used by home cooks since Victorian times. Placed in the center of a pie, with the top pastry draped over the bird through a slit in the crust, this hollow ceramic figure helps support the crust and allow steam to escape through a vent in the bird's beak.

Not all pie birds are birds, incidentally. Some of them are chefs, bakers, pigs, elephants, frogs, golfers, witches, and Santas, to name just a few. Blackbirds, as you might imagine, are a perennial hot seller.

In recent years, pie birds have become highly collectible in the United States. A 97-cent "Benny the Baker" pie bird, produced in the 1950s by New Jersey's Cardinal China Company, is worth about $60 today. A 1950 "Black Chef" wearing a white chef's hat is worth about $150.

To use a pie bird, line your pie pan with pastry, place the bird in the center, and add the filling. Make a small slit in the center of the top pastry, then lower the pastry onto the pie, sliding the bird's head through the slit. With the head sticking through, pinch the pastry around the bird's shoulders. The vent will release steam as the pie bakes.

Nancy Byal's Cider-Infused Apple Pie

Smart pie bakers like Nancy Byal know that you can cram the most apples in your apple pie by partially precooking them first. Nancy, the former food editor of *Better Homes and Gardens* magazine, knows her way around her Iowa kitchen. And she knows apples, too. Her husband, Wayne, used to run an apple orchard that was started by his father and uncle in the 1930s. Back then, says Nancy, Iowa was a significant apple-producing state—something that changed virtually overnight in 1940 when the devastating Armistice Day blizzard killed many of the state's fruit trees. During that storm, the temperature dropped from 70°F to 0°F in a matter of hours.

As you might imagine, Nancy made many apple pies during her husband's tenure at the orchard. This was a family favorite—a thick apple pie made with cider-cooked apples, a little sugar and spice, and not much else. The cider is boiled down and added back to the pie, so it has a pure, clean apple flavor. Nancy likes to use Jonathan apples, a variety that she says is very traditional in Iowa.

MAKES 8 TO 10 SERVINGS

1 recipe Basic Flaky Pie Pastry, Double Crust (page 31), refrigerated

FILLING

12 cups peeled, cored, and sliced Jonathan, Golden Delicious, Rome, or other apples (see pages 232–233 for recommendations)

3/4 cup apple cider

3/4 cup sugar

1/3 cup all-purpose flour

1/2 teaspoon ground cinnamon

1/2 teaspoon ground nutmeg

Pinch of salt

1 tablespoon cold salted or unsalted butter, cut into small pieces

GLAZE

Milk or light cream

Sugar

1. If you haven't already, prepare the pastry and refrigerate until firm enough to roll, about 1 hour.

2. On a sheet of lightly floured waxed paper, roll the larger portion of the pastry into a 13-inch circle with a floured rolling pin. Invert the pastry over a 9 1/2-inch deep-dish pie pan, center, and peel off the paper. Gently tuck the pastry into the pan, without stretching it, and let the overhang drape over the edge. Place in the refrigerator for 15 minutes.

3. Combine the apples and cider in a large nonreactive pot. Bring to a boil, cover, and cook over relatively high heat for 5 minutes, stirring once or twice. Drain the apples, reserving the juice. Transfer the juice to a small nonreactive saucepan and reduce over medium-high heat to 1/4 cup. Combine with the apples in a large bowl and let cool.

4. Preheat the oven to 375°F. In a small bowl, combine the sugar, flour, cinnamon, nutmeg, and salt. Stir into the cooled apples and set aside.

5. On another sheet of lightly floured waxed paper, roll the other half of the pastry into an 11 1/2-inch circle. Turn the filling into the chilled pie shell and smooth the top with your hands. Dot the filling with the butter. Lightly moisten the rim of the pie shell. Invert the top pastry over the filling, center it, and peel off the paper. Press the top and bottom pastries together along the dampened edge. Trim the pastry with scissors or a paring knife, leaving an even 1/2-inch overhang all around, then sculpt the overhang into an upstanding ridge. Poke several steam vents in the top of the pie with a fork or paring knife. Put a couple of the vents near the edge of the crust so you can check the juices there later. Using a pastry brush, brush the pie lightly with milk, then sprinkle with sugar.

6. Place the pie on the center oven rack and bake for 30 minutes, then rotate the pie 180 degrees, so that the part that faced the back of the oven now faces forward. Just in case, slide a large aluminum foil–lined baking sheet onto the rack below to catch any drips. Continue to bake until the top of the pie is golden brown and any juices visible at the steam vents bubble thickly, 35 to 40 minutes. If the pie starts to get too dark, cover with loosely tented aluminum foil during the last 15 minutes.

7. Transfer the pie to a wire rack and let cool for at least 2 hours before serving.

Recipe for Success

▶ Nancy likes to use more than one type of apple in this pie, including those listed in the ingredients. Each, she says, has something to offer, and together they yield a pie with a well-rounded flavor and texture.

▶ Use more spices, if you like, but Nancy keeps it to a minimum so that the flavor of the apples shines through.

From My "Dubious Pie" File

This is a group of pie recipes I've seen or collected but somehow haven't gotten around to testing.

▶ PICKLE PIE: One Utah newspaper thought the recipe was good enough to print.

▶ SAUERKRAUT PIE: Vaguely intriguing, until I saw the crème de cacao, brandy, and Oreo crust.

▶ JICAMA PIE: So *that's* what you're supposed to do with the stuff!

▶ HORSERADISH APPLE PIE: Still under development, last I heard. I can hardly wait.

Love Apple Pie

Given the fact that I myself make a very delicious apple pie with fresh tomatoes, I should not have been surprised to learn of the existence of a pie made with ketchup. From what I can piece together of the story, sometime in the mid-1970s, the Heinz test kitchen developed a recipe for Love Apple Pie—love apples being another name for tomatoes. The idea seems not to have caught on, but Heinz gamely reintroduced the recipe in the late 1990s, hoping it would strike a chord among a new generation of American pie makers. Once I got over my misgivings, I made the pie and thought it was very good. It has the spicy sweetness of the ketchup, which doesn't seem at all out of place and is, in fact, virtually undetectable. The recipe here is a little different from the original. I sweetened it up a bit, using a little brown sugar in addition to the granulated sugar, and found it more to my taste.

MAKES 8 TO 10 SERVINGS

1 recipe Basic Shortening Pie Pastry, Single Crust (page 30) or Basic Flaky Pie Pastry, Single Crust (page 31), refrigerated

FILLING

1/3 cup Heinz ketchup

2 teaspoons fresh lemon juice

6 cups peeled, cored, and sliced tart apples

1/3 cup sugar

1 tablespoon firmly packed light brown sugar

CRUMB TOPPING

2/3 cup all-purpose flour

1/3 cup sugar

1 teaspoon ground cinnamon

1/3 cup unsalted butter or margarine, softened

1.   If you haven't already, prepare the pastry and refrigerate until firm enough to roll, about 1 hour.

2.   On a sheet of lightly floured waxed paper, roll the pastry into a 12-inch circle with a floured rolling pin. Invert the pastry over a 9-inch standard pie pan, center, and peel off the paper. Tuck the pastry into the pan, without stretching it, and sculpt the edge into an upstanding ridge. Place in the freezer for 15 minutes. Preheat the oven to 425°F.

3.   Combine the ketchup and lemon juice in a large bowl. Add the apples and sugar and stir well. Scrape the filling into the chilled pie shell, smoothing the top with your hands.

4. To make the topping, combine the flour, sugar, and cinnamon in a large bowl, tossing it with your hands. Add the butter, rubbing it gently into the flour mixture until well mixed. Carefully dump the crumbs in the center of the pie, spreading them evenly over the surface with your hands. Tamp them down lightly.

5. Place the pie on the center oven rack and bake until the juices bubble thickly around the edge, 40 to 45 minutes. Rotate the pie 180 degrees halfway through the baking, so that the part that faced the back of the oven now faces forward. Slide a large aluminum foil–lined baking sheet onto the rack below to catch any drips. If the top of the pie starts to get a little too dark, cover loosely with aluminum foil during the final 10 minutes of baking.

6. Transfer the pie to a wire rack to cool. Serve barely warm or at room temperature.

Recipe for Success

▶ Good as this is, I wouldn't go announcing the secret ingredient until dessert is over. I think you run into less resistance that way.

Washington State Granny Smith Apple Pie

I called LaVerne Bergstrom of the Washington Apple Commission, whose job it is to promote Washington State apples, to ask if there's anything cooks in her state do to make a particularly delicious or notable pie with Granny Smith apples. As you might expect, she was quick to point out that many home bakers like Grannies for their tartness, juiciness, and complex flavor. That said, she told me that bakers in the know often use less than the usual amount of sugar to make a Granny Smith pie. The flavor of the apples is so good, she said, less sugar is required. She went on to describe a technique she likes for making a Granny Smith pie—one she once saw Martha Stewart demonstrate. You just layer Granny Smith apples in a pie shell and sprinkle a little sugar and thickener over them. I thought this sounded like an interesting approach, so I tried doing it myself, with excellent results. I added an easy crumb topping made with melted butter, but a top pastry crust would be an excellent choice, too.

MAKES 8 TO 10 SERVINGS

1 recipe Basic Flaky Pie Pastry, Single Crust (page 31), refrigerated

FILLING

1/3 cup sugar

1 1/2 tablespoons cornstarch

1/8 teaspoon salt

7 cups peeled, cored, and sliced Granny Smith apples (see Recipe for Success)

1 tablespoon fresh lemon juice

CRUMB TOPPING

6 tablespoons (3/4 stick) unsalted butter

1 1/4 cups all-purpose flour

1/2 cup sugar

1/4 teaspoon salt

1/2 teaspoon ground cinnamon

1. If you haven't already, prepare the pastry and refrigerate until firm enough to roll, about 1 hour.

2. On a sheet of lightly floured waxed paper, roll the pastry into a 13-inch circle with a floured rolling pin. Invert the pastry over a 9 1/2-inch deep-dish pie pan, center, and peel off the paper. Tuck the pastry into the pan, without stretching it, and sculpt the edge into an upstanding ridge. Place in the freezer for 15 minutes. Preheat the oven to 400°F.

3. Mix the sugar, cornstarch, and salt together in a small bowl. Set aside. Combine the apples and lemon juice in a large bowl. Sprinkle about 1 tablespoon of the sugar mixture evenly over the chilled pie shell. Arrange a single, compact layer of apples, flat side down, in the shell. Sprinkle with 1 tablespoon of the sugar mixture. Arrange a second layer of apples over the first and sprinkle with another tablespoon of the sugar mixture. Continue until all the apples and sugar mixture have been used. Place the pie on the center oven rack and bake for 30 minutes.

4. Meanwhile, make the crumb topping. In a medium-size saucepan, melt the butter over very low heat. As it melts, combine the flour, sugar, salt, and cinnamon in a medium-size bowl. Pour the melted butter over the flour mixture and mix well with a fork. Using your fingertips, rub the mixture gently until it forms more or less even, damp crumbs. Set aside.

5. Remove the pie from the oven and reduce the temperature to 375°F. Carefully dump the crumb topping in the center of the pie and spread evenly over the surface with your hands. Tamp the crumbs down lightly. Return the pie to the oven, placing it so that the part that faced the back of the oven now faces forward. To catch any spills, slide a large aluminum foil–lined baking sheet onto the rack below. Bake until you see the juices bubbling thickly at the edge, about 35 minutes. If the top starts to get too brown, cover loosely with aluminum foil for the last 15 minutes.

6. Transfer the pie to a wire rack and let cool for at least 1 hour before serving.

Recipe for Success

▶ Not everyone likes Granny Smith apples for a pie, because they bake up soft. Although I've found that to be the case much of the time, I don't think soft apples are a bad thing. Indeed, I've spoken with many people over the years who much prefer a softer, saucy apple filling to a more textured one. You can always use a couple of Golden Delicious apples along with the Grannies to add a little texture to the pie.

Liz Reiter's All-Granny Slug-O-Bourbon Spiced Apple Pie

Liz Reiter is my pie-making editor pal from Kentucky and my expert on the pies in that neck of the woods. (Do read her fun sidebar on page 225.) Earlier in her career, Liz made pies for some restaurants in and around the Louisville area, including this apple pie, about which she has strong opinions (see Recipe for Success). Anyway, I know a thing or two about apple pie myself, and one thing I can tell you is that I was delighted to add this pie to my collection. It's spicy, bold, and has attitude; bourbon will do that. You'll want to give this one a try.

MAKES 8 TO 10 SERVINGS

1 recipe Basic Flaky Pie Pastry, Double Crust (page 31), refrigerated

FILLING

4 large or 3 extra-large Granny Smith apples, peeled, cored, and cut into chunks

3/4 cup sugar

2 tablespoons all-purpose flour

1/2 teaspoon ground cinnamon

1/4 teaspoon ground nutmeg

1/4 teaspoon ground cloves

Pinch of salt

Slug of bourbon (Liz calls it a "one-two count slug")

3 tablespoons cold unsalted butter, cut into small pieces

GARNISH

Sugar

1. If you haven't already, prepare the pastry and refrigerate until firm enough to roll, about 1 hour.

2. On a sheet of lightly floured waxed paper, roll the larger portion of the pastry into a 13-inch circle with a floured rolling pin. Invert the pastry over a 9½-inch deep-dish pie pan, center, and peel off the paper. Gently tuck the pastry into the pan, without stretching it, and let the overhang drape over the edge. Place in the refrigerator for 15 minutes.

3. In a large bowl, combine the apples, sugar, flour, spices, and salt. Mix well, then set aside for 15 minutes. Stir in the bourbon. Preheat the oven to 400°F.

4. Roll the other half of the pastry into an 11-inch circle on a sheet of lightly floured waxed paper. Turn the filling into the chilled pie shell, smoothing the fruit with your hands. Dot the filling with the butter. Lightly moisten the rim of the pie shell. Invert the top pastry over the filling, center, and peel off the paper. Press the top and bottom pastries together along the dampened edge. Using the back of a butter knife or pastry knife, trim the pastry flush with the edge of the pan and crimp the edge with a fork. Poke several steam vents in the top of the pie with a fork or paring knife. Put a couple of the vents near the edge of the crust so you can check the juices there later. To glaze the pie, sprinkle the top lightly with sugar.

5. Place the pie on the center oven rack and bake for 30 minutes. Reduce the oven temperature to 350°F and rotate the pie 180 degrees, so that the part that faced the back of the oven now faces forward. Just in case, slide a large aluminum foil–lined baking sheet onto the rack below to catch any spills. Continue to bake until the top is golden brown and any visible juices bubble thickly through the steam vents, about 30 minutes.

6. Transfer the pie to a wire rack and let cool for at least 2 hours before serving.

Recipe for Success

▶ Liz's pastry is a little different from my own, but similar enough that she said it would be fine to recommend the Basic Flaky Pie Pastry.

▶ Liz says, "I hate pastry blenders; they smoosh everything together." She prefers making her pastry with 2 knives or a food processor.

▶ And this: "I hate it when the apple slices are so thin that it makes applesauce. That's why I specify chunks."

A Slice of Kentucky (Pie) Culture

"In Kentucky, change comes slowly. Even young people may use the phrase 'a while back,' meaning not months or even years, but decades.

"At the *Courier-Journal*, people still call and ask for Cissy Gregg, a former food editor who retired in 1962. Told she's no longer there, they may laugh and say, 'Honey, it just doesn't seem like it's been that long.'

"And it really doesn't, once you're away from the highway, with chain restaurants clustered at every exit. In almost every small town, you can still walk into an unair-conditioned family restaurant with gray-haired wait staff and customers who seem like family.

"In this restaurant, there are usually some living room knickknacks or family pictures hanging on the walls to dress up the place. The aged floor will be freshly washed, and the air may smell faintly of bleach. And there's liable to be a counter lined with glass cake keepers.

"In at least one of these keepers, if you're lucky and the regular customers haven't already eaten it all, you'll see one of our real Kentucky pies.

"Maybe it's buttermilk, with soft filling oozing thickly. Maybe it's a so-sweet-only-a-southerner-could-stand-it coconut cream; a creamy, tart lemon meringue; or a gooey chocolate-nut. Whatever the case, it's sure to be as full of sugar as a Kentucky conversation.

"And after you've had a bit, you want more. You want to be able to make this anytime you please.

"'Our cook makes these every day,' the restaurant owner may say. 'She doesn't usually like to give people the recipes—they all came from her mama—but you can ask her.'

"You and the cook may drawl compliments at each other for a little while. Like any good southerner, she'll avoid a definite yes or no answer at first. But if you're lucky, and polite as can be, she'll take you into her confidence eventually.

"When you leave, the recipe scrawled onto a bit of notepaper or napkin, you'll never know if she shared everything. Maybe she kept just one ingredient secret.

"Even if you suspect such a sweet deception, however, you'll happily keep trying to re-create that glue-your-teeth-together sugary treat that is a real Kentucky pie."

—Liz Reiter, Assistant Food Editor, *Louisville Courier-Journal*

Cooked-Fruit Apple Pie

Frequently during my cooking classes and demonstrations, someone asks what they can do about eliminating the space that remains between the crust and the apples after they've baked an apple pie. Frankly, I say, there's not a whole lot you can do about it after the fact—although you might want to try the little trick I mention in the Recipe for Success on pages 146–147. But there is something you can do to eliminate that gap altogether: cook the apples ahead of time. Cooking the apples shrinks their mass by nearly one-half, so there is no gap when the pie is baked. The pastry just snuggles up to the apples and stays there. The key to preparing this pie is to cook the apples just enough but not too much. You want them to shrink but not lose their crunch and texture altogether. So pay careful attention to the precooking step here. I think you'll like this approach to apple pie. You may not care to do this all the time, but it's worth trying to see how the flavor and texture differ from the traditional approach.

MAKES 8 TO 10 SERVINGS

1 recipe Basic Flaky Pie Pastry, Double Crust (page 31), refrigerated

FILLING

2 tablespoons unsalted butter

8 cups peeled, cored, and thickly sliced (about 1/3 inch thick) Golden Delicious apples (see Recipe for Success)

1/2 cup sugar

1 tablespoon cornstarch

2 teaspoons fresh lemon juice

1/2 cup dark raisins

1/4 teaspoon ground cinnamon

1. If you haven't already, prepare the pastry and refrigerate until firm enough to roll, about 1 hour.

2. On a sheet of lightly floured waxed paper, roll the larger portion of the pastry into a 12-inch circle with a floured rolling pin. Invert the pastry over a 9-inch standard pie pan, center, and peel off the paper. Gently tuck the pastry into the pan, without stretching it, and let the overhang drape over the edge. Place in the refrigerator for 15 minutes.

3. Melt the butter in a very large skillet over medium-high heat. Add the apples and cook, stirring very often, for 3 to 4 minutes. Add most of the sugar, reserving a tablespoon or two, and continue to cook, still stirring often, for 2 to 3 minutes. As the apples cook, mix the remaining sugar with the cornstarch. Stir this mixture into the apples and cook for another minute. The apples should have shrunk by now, but they should still have some of their crunch. Transfer the apples to a large, shallow casserole. Stir in the lemon juice, raisins, and cinnamon. Spread the filling evenly in the casserole and let cool thoroughly. Preheat the oven to 400°F when it's almost there.

4. Turn the cooled filling into the chilled pie shell and smooth the top with your hands. Roll the other half of the pastry into a 10-inch circle on a sheet of lightly floured waxed paper. Moisten the outer edge of the pie shell with a pastry brush. Invert the top pastry over the filling, center, and peel off the paper. Press the top and bottom pastries together along the dampened edge. Using the back of a butter knife, trim the pastry flush with the edge of the pan. With the back of a fork, press the tines all along the edge to seal. Poke several steam vents in the top of the pie with the fork.

5. Place the pie on the center oven rack and bake until nicely browned, 40 to 45 minutes. Rotate the pie 180 degrees halfway through the baking, so that the part that faced the back of the oven now faces forward. You should not experience any trouble with the pie bubbling over, but just in case, slide a large aluminum foil–lined baking sheet onto the rack below.

6. Transfer the pie to a wire rack and let cool for at least 30 minutes before serving.

Recipe for Success

▸ **Don't substitute another variety of apple unless you're certain it will hold up well in the cooking. Most apples will likely get too soft in the intense heat of the skillet. Northern Spy may work well, although I haven't actually tried it. Do spread the apples out, as directed. If you pile them up, they'll continue to cook from the surrounding heat, resulting in overly soft apples.**

Sugar-Dusted Apple Strudel Pie

I've noticed that a number of apple pie recipes, including some previous winners from the American Pie Council's National Pie Championships (see page 387), call for the entire filling to be mixed ahead and then left in the fridge overnight. I wondered what this was all about—how leaving the filling to sit would affect the pie—so I tried it and liked the results. For one thing, the apples get very moist and soft, because they sit in their own juices for hours. They also settle, reducing in volume by as much as one-third. This makes for a compact, full-flavored pie that I quite like. The filling suggests a very light, flaky, and tender dough, so I use my favorite cream cheese pastry. Dusted with confectioners' sugar, this pie reminds me very much of a traditional apple strudel.

MAKES 8 TO 10 SERVINGS

FILLING

5 cups peeled, cored, and thinly sliced Granny Smith apples

$1/4$ cup granulated sugar

2 tablespoons all-purpose flour

$1/4$ teaspoon ground cinnamon

1 tablespoon fresh lemon juice

Pinch of salt

CRUST

1 recipe Tender Cream Cheese Pastry, Double Crust (page 46), divided as instructed in step 2 and refrigerated

GARNISH

Confectioners' sugar

1. Prepare the filling at least 4 hours or up to 12 hours before assembling the pie. Place the apples in a large bowl. In a small bowl, combine the granulated sugar, flour, and cinnamon, then stir the mixture into the apples. Stir in the lemon juice and salt and toss well. Cover the bowl with plastic wrap and refrigerate, stirring every hour or so, when you think of it. Remove the filling from the refrigerator about 1 hour before you plan to use it.

2. If you haven't already, prepare the pastry, dividing it into equal halves. Refrigerate for 1 to $1^1/2$ hours.

3. When you're ready to assemble and bake the pie, preheat the oven to 400°F. On a sheet of lightly floured waxed paper, roll half of the pastry into a 12-inch circle with a floured rolling pin. Invert the pastry over a 9-inch standard pie pan, center, and peel off the paper. Gently tuck the pastry down into the pan, without stretching it, and let the overhang drape over the edge. Place in the refrigerator for 15 minutes.

4. Roll the other half of the pastry into a 12-inch circle on a sheet of lightly floured waxed paper. Turn the filling into the chilled pie shell and smooth the top with your hands. Dampen the edge of the pie shell with a wet fingertip or pastry brush. Invert the top pastry over the filling, center, and peel off the paper. Press the top and bottom pastries together along the dampened edge. Trim the pastry, leaving an even $1/2$-inch overhang all around, then sculpt the overhang into an upstanding ridge. Poke several steam vents in the top of the pie with a fork or paring knife. Put a couple of the vents near the edge of the crust so you can check the juices there later.

5. Place the pie on the center oven rack and bake for 25 minutes. Reduce the oven temperature to 375°F and rotate the pie 180 degrees, so that the part that faced the back of the oven now faces forward. Continue to bake until the top of the pie is golden and the juices visible at the steam vents bubble thickly, 25 to 30 minutes. Since this pie is not prone to bubbling over, you probably won't need a baking sheet under it to catch drips.

6. Transfer the pie to a wire rack. While the pie is still hot, dust the top with confectioners' sugar. Let cool for at least 1 hour before serving.

Recipe for Success

▶ **Full-flavored Granny Smith apples are excellent here, but there are any number of other good choices. If apples are in season and the selection is wide, you might consider Northern Spy, Gravenstein, or Winesap, all of which have great flavor and a nice balance of tartness and sweetness.**

▶ **Dusting the pie with confectioners' sugar while it is still hot gives you 2 sugar layers. The part closest to the pie more or less melts in place, while the sugar on top remains powdery. It's a nice touch that you'll miss if you wait until the pie is cool before dusting it.**

Caramel Apple-Pecan Pie

A reporter from a large Illinois newspaper asked me if I thought the current caramel apple pie craze had anything to do with the resurgence of pie making in this country. I was clueless about the caramel apple pie craze, but I launched into a dazzling answer, as if I had been personally responsible for starting it. Then I hung up the phone and quickly started inventing my own recipe, basing it on one the reporter had recently tried and fallen in love with. So here is my version, which has a pecan crumb topping covered with a layer of caramel and pecans. It has great eye appeal—just like a caramel apple—and the pecan, apple, and caramel flavors couldn't be more delicious together. So have at it—and just remember, you read about it here first.

MAKES 8 TO 10 SERVINGS

1 recipe Basic Flaky Pie Pastry, Single Crust (page 31), modified as instructed in step 1 and refrigerated

10 caramels, each cut into 4 pieces

FILLING

7 cups peeled, cored, and sliced Golden Delicious apples (see Recipe for Success)

1/2 cup firmly packed light brown sugar

1 tablespoon fresh lemon juice

2 tablespoons granulated sugar

1 tablespoon cornstarch

1/2 teaspoon ground cinnamon

1 teaspoon vanilla extract

PECAN CRUMB TOPPING

3/4 cup all-purpose flour

3/4 cup pecan halves

1/2 cup granulated sugar

1/4 teaspoon salt

6 tablespoons (3/4 stick) cold unsalted butter, cut into 1/4-inch pieces

CARAMEL AND GARNISH

3 tablespoons unsalted butter, cut into pieces

1 tablespoon water

30 caramels

Large handful of pecan halves

1/2 cup chopped pecans

1. Prepare the pastry according to the recipe, using a total of 3 tablespoons sugar. Refrigerate until firm enough to roll, about 1 hour.

2. On a sheet of lightly floured waxed paper, roll the pastry into a 13-inch circle with a floured rolling pin. Invert the pastry over a 9 1/2-inch deep-dish pie pan, center, and peel off the paper. Tuck the pastry into the pan, without stretching it, and sculpt the edge into an upstanding ridge. Scatter the caramel pieces in the pie shell and place in the freezer while you make the filling. Preheat the oven to 400°F.

3. Combine the apples, brown sugar, and lemon juice in a large bowl. Mix well, then set aside for 5 to 10 minutes to juice. Mix the granulated sugar and cornstarch together in a small bowl. Stir the mixture into the fruit along with the cinnamon and vanilla. Scrape the filling into the chilled pie shell, smoothing the fruit with your hands. Put the pie on the center oven rack and bake for 30 minutes.

4. Meanwhile, make the crumb topping. Combine the flour, pecan halves, granulated sugar, and salt in a food processor. Pulse several times, chopping the nuts coarsely. Scatter the butter over the dry mixture and pulse the machine again until the mixture resembles fine crumbs. Transfer the crumbs to a medium-size bowl and rub the mixture between your fingers to make damp, gravelly crumbs. Refrigerate until ready to use.

5. Remove the pie from the oven and reduce the temperature to 375°F. Carefully dump the crumbs in the center of the pie, spreading them evenly over the surface with your hands. Tamp them down lightly. Return the pie to the oven, placing it so that the part that faced the back of the oven now faces forward. Just in case, slide a large aluminum foil–lined baking sheet onto the rack below to catch any drips. Bake until the juices bubble thickly around the edge, 30 to 40 minutes. If necessary, cover the pie with loosely tented aluminum foil for the last 15 minutes to keep the top from getting too dark.

6. Transfer the pie to a wire rack and let cool for about 1 hour.

7. While the pie is still warm—approaching the 1-hour mark—prepare the caramel. Combine the butter, water, and caramels in the top of a double boiler. Melt the caramels over, not in, barely simmering water. This may take 10 minutes or more. To facilitate the melting, press down on them as they start to soften and melt. When melted, whisk the mixture until it is smooth, then drizzle the caramel over the entire surface of the pie. Immediately press the pecan halves into the caramel in a random fashion, then sprinkle the chopped pecans over the top as well. Let cool for another hour before serving.

Recipe for Success

▶ Golden Delicious isn't the only variety of apple you can use here, but since it holds its shape well, I consider it a good candidate. Feel free to substitute 1 or 2 Granny Smith or other tart apples for contrast. See pages 232–233 for other recommendations.

▶ You can make this pie with walnuts, but I think the pecan halves give it a very attractive and classy look.

▶ Work quickly after you pour the caramel over the pie so that it doesn't firm up before you add the pecans.

Another One for the Record Books

In 1976, 16-year-old Kathy Wafler Madison of Wolcott, New York, pared her way into the history books by peeling the longest apple peel on record. According to the *Guinness Book of World Records*, the peel measured 2,068 inches, or roughly 172 feet, long—more than half the length of a football field. Using a special horticultural knife adapted by her father, Kathy spent 11 hours creating the record strand, which measured on average one-thirty-second inch wide. Asked if she had any advice for those who would care to break her record, she replied, "Get a big apple. And have a lot of patience."

Pie Apples at a Glance

I give quite a few apple pie–baking demonstrations each year, and many more interviews on the subject, and the question that always comes up is, Which kind of apples make the best pie? The fact is, most of them do—as long as they're fresh and juicy. A certain amount of tartness helps, too, as well as complexity of flavor. I delve into the subject of pie apples in detail in my book *Apple Pie Perfect* (Harvard Common Press, 2002), which includes a section on antique apples by my friend Mike Berst, one of the smartest apple experts in the country. It's worth consulting if, like me, you're an apple pie aficionado. Meanwhile, here are some observations to lead you in the right direction.

- ▶ BALDWIN An all-purpose red-skinned apple with a mild, sweet-tart flavor and crisp texture. Aromatic, it stores well and makes a commendable pie.

- ▶ BRAEBURN Varies in color from greenish gold to red with yellow markings. The flesh is smooth, juicy, and crisp, with a good flavor. Thumbs up.

- ▶ CORTLAND Common in the Northeast and one of Vermont's leading apples. For pies, the early ones are tarter and generally better than the later ones, which tend to be fairly sweet.

- ▶ FUJI One of the best-selling apples in Japan, it's a cross between a Red Delicious and a Ralls Janet. More prized as a dessert apple—one that's eaten out of hand—than a baking apple, it has a spicy flavor and juiciness that I quite like in pies.

- ▶ GOLDEN DELICIOUS A reliable, all-purpose apple with legions of both fans and detractors, the latter who don't care for the apple's sometimes bland flavor. The skin is soft enough to leave on, and the slices hold their shape well. When fresh and juicy, this is a fine pie apple.

- ▶ GRAVENSTEIN Thought to be one of the best early apples for pie makers, ripening in late August. It has a creamy, sweet-tart flesh and makes a delicious pie.

- **JONAGOLD** A cross between a Jonathan and a Golden Delicious, it doesn't store well but has a sweet, creamy, juicy flesh that tastes great in a pie.

- **JONATHAN** Some think it ranks as one of the best pie apples; others are less effusive. It has a soft, fine-textured flesh with a spicy flavor that I believe translates well into pies.

- **MACOUN** Developed in New York State, the Macoun is a cross between a McIntosh and a Jersey Black. Generally considered to be a dessert apple, some say it makes a much better pie apple than the McIntosh.

- **McINTOSH** Some love, others despise the McIntosh's fine-textured flesh, which tends to turn very soft when baked. I prefer the early Macs more than the later ones, as they're generally sweeter, firmer, and more distinctive.

- **NORTHERN SPY** Spies are for pies, the saying goes, and this is perhaps the quintessential pie apple—tart, tangy, juicy, and firm. Sometimes hard to find outside of farm stands, the Northern Spy is an excellent storage apple.

- **RED DELICIOUS** This is the one apple that, unequivocally, does *not* make a decent pie. Bred more for good looks than flavor or texture, it lacks the personality needed for a successful apple pie.

- **WINESAP** A superior, late-ripening apple with sweet-tart, winy, juicy flesh. The complex flavor has made it a favorite of cider makers for hundreds of years. Though hard to find, it's worth the look.

Mile-Deep Apple Ring Pie

You've heard of mile-high pies, of course, but here's a mile-deep one—a little stunt I accomplish by using a chicken fryer–like pan or deep cast-iron skillet to bake this top crust–only pie. The ideal pan should stand 3¼ to 3½ inches tall, with a diameter of about 10 inches. Any deep-dish casserole or pan of those approximate dimensions will probably do nicely. One of the things I like best about this pie is its straightforward rusticity: it's just apple rings, sugar, thickener, and maple syrup. I top it with a butter pastry and bake. The pie slowly sinks as the apples cook down and settle. It reminds me of a simple country pie that a farm family might make in the fall, when fresh apples are plentiful. Kids like to help with this one because they get to core the whole apples to make the rings.

MAKES 8 TO 10 SERVINGS

1 recipe All-Butter Pie Pastry, Single Crust (page 28), refrigerated

FILLING

⅓ cup sugar

¼ cup all-purpose flour

1 teaspoon ground cinnamon

7 or 8 good-size apples (see Recipe for Success; half of them should be Golden Delicious), peeled

¼ cup pure maple syrup

2 tablespoons cold unsalted butter, cut into small pieces

GLAZE

Milk or light cream

Sugar

1. If you haven't already, prepare the pastry and refrigerate it until firm enough to roll, about 1 hour. Preheat the oven to 400°F. Get out your baking pan (see headnote) and butter it well.

2. Combine the sugar, flour, and cinnamon in a small bowl. Set aside.

3. Using an apple corer, core the apples, then slice them into rings about ¼ inch thick. Layer the apple rings in the pan, overlapping them slightly. Sprinkle each layer generously with the sugar mixture. Continue layering and sprinkling until you're within ½ inch of the rim. Drizzle the maple syrup over the apples, then dot with the butter.

4. On a sheet of lightly floured waxed paper, roll the pastry into an 11- to 12-inch circle with a floured rolling pin; you want it slightly larger than the pan's diameter. Invert the pastry over the pan, center, and peel off the paper. Tuck the pastry down into the pan.

Using a fork or paring knife, make a few steam vents in the top. Brush the pastry with milk and sprinkle with sugar.

5. Place the pie on one of the lower oven racks and bake for 40 minutes. Reduce the oven temperature to 375°F and rotate the pie 180 degrees, so that the part that faced the back of the oven now faces forward. Continue to bake until the top is golden brown and the apples are tender, 30 to 40 minutes. Use a skewer or paring knife poked through the top crust to make sure the apples are done. Because of the depth of the pie, don't expect to see juices bubbling up along the edge.

6. Transfer the pie to a wire rack and let cool for at least 20 minutes before serving. Rather than cut this pie into slices, you may want to spoon it out, because it may be difficult to make neat cuts. That's part of the pie's rustic charm.

Recipe for Success

▶ This is a good pie to use more than one type of apple—Golden Delicious for firmness, maybe a Granny Smith or two for tartness and juiciness. Don't be afraid to experiment. You'll likely end up with the best features of each apple in your pie.

▶ If you're not using a cast-iron pan, add 1 tablespoon fresh lemon juice to the apples. Don't use the lemon juice with cast iron because the juice may react with the iron and cause an off flavor.

Calvados-Apple Custard Pie

The Normandy region of France is known for its fine dairy products, including smooth, rich cheese, butter, and crème fraîche. It's also a center of French apple production and thus cider, the basic ingredient in the twice-distilled apple brandy known as Calvados. This pie is a nod to Normandy, where Calvados-spiked apple tarts are common. In the French tradition, one would search high and low for the best fresh, crisp apples, whose complex flavor would dignify such a fine dessert. If you have access to antique apples, I suggest that you do the same. Otherwise, I recommend Northern Spy, Greening, or even Golden Delicious—the last not the equal of the others in terms of flavor, but it will hold up nicely in the pie. Serve this as the finale to a French-inspired menu—barely warm, if you prefer, or, the way I like it, chilled for several hours.

MAKES 8 TO 10 SERVINGS

1 recipe All-Butter Pie Pastry, Single Crust (page 28) or Basic Flaky Pie Pastry, Single Crust (page 31), refrigerated

FILLING

2 tablespoons unsalted butter

3 large apples (see headnote), peeled, cored, and thickly sliced (about 1/3 inch thick)

2 tablespoons plus 1/2 cup sugar

1/4 cup plus 2 tablespoons Calvados

1 1/4 cups heavy or whipping cream

3 large eggs

1/2 teaspoon vanilla extract

Big pinch of salt

1. If you haven't already, prepare the pastry and refrigerate until firm enough to roll, about 1 hour.

2. On a sheet of lightly floured waxed paper, roll the pastry into a 13-inch circle with a floured rolling pin. Invert the pastry over a 9½-inch deep-dish pie pan, center, and peel off the paper. Tuck the pastry into the pan, without stretching it, and sculpt the edge into an upstanding ridge. Place in the freezer for 15 minutes, then partially prebake and let cool according to the instructions on page 16. Reduce the oven temperature to 350°F.

3. Melt the butter in a large, preferably nonstick nonreactive skillet. Stir in the apples and cook over medium-high heat, stirring often, for 2 minutes. Stir in 2 tablespoons of the sugar and cook for 1 minute. Add ¼ cup of the Calvados and continue to cook, stirring, until the liquid boils off, 1 to 2 minutes. Remove from the heat and scrape the apples onto a large plate to cool.

4. Meanwhile, heat the heavy cream and remaining ½ cup sugar in a small saucepan over medium heat, stirring, until fairly warm, 2 to 3 minutes. Remove from the heat. Beat the eggs until frothy in a medium-size bowl, then stir in about ½ cup of the warm cream. Gradually stir in the rest of the cream along with the vanilla, salt, and remaining 2 tablespoons Calvados.

5. Turn the cooled apples into the cooled pie shell, spreading them evenly. Ladle the custard over the apples. After the first couple of ladlefuls, move the apples around slightly to make sure the custard is flowing underneath them. Ladle on the rest of the custard, taking care that you don't overfill the pie shell.

6. Place the pie on the center oven rack and bake for 25 minutes. Rotate the pie 180 degrees, so that the part that faced the back of the oven now faces forward. Continue to bake until the custard is set in the center, 20 to 25 minutes.

7. Transfer the pie to a wire rack and let cool. Serve barely warm or at room temperature, or cover loosely with aluminum foil, refrigerate, and serve cold.

Recipe for Success

▶ When you're precooking the apples, make sure they don't get too soft. If that starts to happen, pick up the pace and get them off the heat and onto the plate as soon as possible.

▶ To check the pie for doneness, you may have to stick a paring knife down into the center of the custard. Simply find a gap between the apples and probe gently. It's fine if the custard looks barely set, but it should not be runny.

Pennsylvania Dutch Sour Cream–Apple Pie

Custard pies such as this often show up in places like Wisconsin and Vermont, or just about anywhere apples and dairy farms coexist, sometimes side by side. The custard part of the equation is more typically made with heavy or light cream, but here we use sour cream, resulting in a tangy, more full-bodied custard. (You could, if you like, substitute a full-fat yogurt such as Stonyfield Farm.) It's all very rich and delicious, and even more so with the crunchy-sweet walnut topping.

MAKES 8 TO 10 SERVINGS

1 recipe Basic Flaky Pie Pastry, Single Crust (page 31) or All-Butter Pie Pastry, Single Crust (page 28), refrigerated

FILLING

1 1/4 cups full-fat sour cream

3/4 cup granulated sugar

1 large egg

1/4 cup all-purpose flour

1/4 teaspoon salt

2 teaspoons vanilla extract

7 to 8 cups peeled, cored, and thinly sliced Granny Smith, Northern Spy, or Golden Delicious apples

WALNUT STREUSEL TOPPING

1 cup all-purpose flour

1/2 cup granulated sugar

1/2 cup firmly packed light brown sugar

1 teaspoon ground cinnamon

Big pinch of salt

3/4 cup chopped walnuts

6 tablespoons (3/4 stick) unsalted butter, melted

1. If you haven't already, prepare the pastry and refrigerate until firm enough to roll, about 1 hour.

2. On a sheet of lightly floured waxed paper, roll the pastry into a 13-inch circle with a floured rolling pin. Invert the pastry over a 9½-inch deep-dish pie pan, center, and peel off the paper. Tuck the pastry into the pan, without stretching it, and sculpt the edge into an upstanding ridge. Place in the freezer for 15 minutes. Preheat the oven to 400°F.

3. In a large bowl, whisk together the sour cream, granulated sugar, egg, flour, salt, and vanilla until evenly blended. Add the apples and mix well. Turn the filling into the chilled pie shell and smooth the top with your hands, laying the apple slices down flat.

4. Place the pie on the center oven rack and bake for 15 minutes. Reduce the oven temperature to 350°F and bake for 30 minutes more.

5. Meanwhile, make the topping. Combine the flour, sugars, cinnamon, salt, and walnuts in a large bowl. Add the butter and stir with a fork, then switch to your hands, rubbing the mixture gently between your fingers until it forms uniform crumbs. Refrigerate until ready to use.

6. Remove the pie from the oven and carefully dump the streusel topping in the center, spreading it evenly over the surface with your hands. Tamp the topping down lightly. Return the pie to the oven, placing it so that the part that faced the back of the oven now faces forward. Just in case, slide a large aluminum foil–lined baking sheet onto the rack below to catch any spills. Continue to bake until the topping is golden brown, about 20 minutes.

7. Transfer the pie to a wire rack and let cool for at least 2 hours before serving. I prefer to serve this pie chilled. If you do, too, when the pie is thoroughly cooled, cover with loosely tented aluminum foil and refrigerate for at least 2 hours.

Recipe for Success

▶ When an apple pie is cooked in a thick custard such as this, expect the apples to stay a little on the firm side. They never seem to get quite as soft as they do in an apple pie made without the custard.

▶ You'll notice that this streusel topping, made with melted butter, is crunchier than streusel made with solid butter. You can, if you like, substitute one of the many other crumb toppings in this collection.

The Mother of All Apple Pies

A couple of times each fall, I pull out my really big Emile Henry pie plate—I call it my Hummer of pie plates—and bake a mondo apple pie. I like doing it for the shock value, because pies this size seldom make public appearances. But I also do it out of need: I don't know what it's like around your house, but come autumn, we have apples multiplying like rabbits. The best way I know to use them is by making a pie. This pie will also answer a question I've heard frequently since writing my book *Apple Pie Perfect* (Harvard Common Press, 2002): can I mix different kinds of apples when I make an apple pie? My response is a resounding yes! Like kids who wind up with the best traits of both parents, a mixed-apple pie has the best qualities of all the apples used. I like a couple of Grannies for tartness, Golden Delicious for texture, Gala for flavor, and McIntosh for a bit of sauciness. But don't feel limited to those. By the way, the pan I use for this measures almost 12 inches across, is 2 inches deep, and holds a good 12 to 13 cups of sliced apples.

MAKE 12 TO 14 SERVINGS

1 recipe Basic Flaky Pie Pastry, Double Crust (page 31), modified as instructed in step 1 and refrigerated

FILLING

12 to 13 cups peeled, cored, and sliced apples (see headnote)

3/4 cup sugar

Juice of 2 lemons

1/3 cup all-purpose flour

1/2 teaspoon ground nutmeg

1/4 cup (1/2 stick) cold unsalted butter, cut into small pieces

PECAN CRUMB TOPPING

1 1/4 cups pecan halves

1 cup all-purpose flour

3/4 cup sugar

1/2 teaspoon salt

1 teaspoon ground cinnamon

1/2 cup (1 stick) cold unsalted butter, cut into 1/4-inch pieces

1. If you haven't already, prepare the pastry but don't divide it in half. Leave it whole and flatten the entire thing into a disk about 3/4 inch thick. Refrigerate until firm enough to roll, about 1 hour. Meanwhile, get out a pan like the one I describe in the headnote or a similar one. You may have a casserole dish that will work. Set aside.

2. Place two overlapping sheets of waxed paper on your counter to roll the pastry on. Dust with flour. Put the pastry on the seam and, using a floured rolling pin, roll it into a 17-inch circle (or thereabouts). Invert the pastry over the pan, center, and peel off the paper. Gently tuck the pastry into the pan, without stretching it, and sculpt the edge into an upstanding ridge. Place in the freezer or refrigerator while you make the filling. Preheat the oven to 400°F.

3.   In your largest bowl, combine the apples, sugar, and lemon juice. Set aside for 10 minutes. Stir in the flour and nutmeg. Turn the filling into the chilled pie shell, smoothing it with your hands so that the apple slices lie flat. Dot the top of the pie with the butter. Put the pie on the center oven rack and bake for 30 minutes.

4.   Meanwhile, make the crumb topping. Combine the pecans, flour, sugar, and salt in a food processor and pulse several times to chop the nuts coarsely. Scatter the butter over the dry mixture and pulse again until the mixture resembles fine crumbs. Transfer the topping to a large bowl and rub the mixture between your fingers to make damp, gravelly crumbs. Refrigerate until ready to use.

5.   Remove the pie from the oven and reduce the temperature to 375°F. Carefully dump the crumbs in the center of the pie, spreading them evenly over the surface with your hands. Tamp them down lightly. Return the pie to the oven, placing it so that the part that faced the back of the oven now faces forward. Just in case, slide a large aluminum foil–lined baking sheet onto the rack below to catch any spills. Bake until the juices bubble thickly around the edge, 35 to 45 minutes. If the top of the pie starts to get too brown, drape a piece of aluminum foil over it for the last 10 minutes of baking.

6.   Transfer the pie to a rack and cool. Serve barely warm or at room temperature.

Recipe for Success

▶   Don't be intimidated by the size of this pie or the outsize rolling job required for the pastry. It's no more difficult to roll a 17-inch circle than it is to roll a 12-inch one. Just take it nice and easy, and keep your pastry and pin floured.

▶   Especially when you bake a pie for an extended period, like this one, there's a chance the edge will get well browned. Either just forget about it—it affects very little of the pie crust—or make a customized aluminum foil shield to cover the edge of the crust.

We Think We'll Pass, Too, Thank You

"There's a truck stop along Interstate 80 in Western Pennsylvania that has a billboard claiming it serves the world's worst pie. I've been meaning to stop in for years, but . . . I haven't yet made it."

—Posting at www.roadfood.com

Rose Calello's Salem Cross Inn Apple Pie

For the past several years, the Salem Cross Inn in West Brookfield, Massachusetts, has sponsored the Best Apple Pie in New England Contest. All the contestants must bake their pies in the inn's old-fashioned wood-fired beehive oven, which presents challenges that few of us face with our modern ovens (see box, page 242). The following recipe is from Rose Calello, winner of the contest in 2000 and 2001.

MAKES 8 TO 10 SERVINGS

1 recipe Basic Shortening Pie Pastry, Double Crust (page 30), refrigerated (see Recipe for Success)

FILLING

8 cups peeled, cored, and thinly sliced Golden Delicious apples

1 tablespoon fresh lemon juice

2/3 cup sugar

2 1/2 tablespoons all-purpose flour

3/4 teaspoon ground cinnamon

1/4 teaspoon ground nutmeg

Pinch of salt

1 tablespoon cold unsalted butter, cut into small pieces

GLAZE

1 large egg white, lightly beaten

1. If you haven't already, prepare the pastry and refrigerate until firm enough to roll, about 1 hour.

2. On a sheet of lightly floured waxed paper, roll the larger portion of the pastry into a 12-inch circle with a floured rolling pin. Invert the pastry over a 9-inch standard pie pan, center, and peel off the paper. Gently tuck the pastry into the pan, without stretching it, and let the overhang drape over the edge. Place in the refrigerator for 15 minutes.

3. Combine the apples and lemon juice in a large bowl, tossing to blend. Stir in the sugar, flour, cinnamon, nutmeg, and salt. Set aside. Preheat the oven to 375°F.

4. On another sheet of lightly floured waxed paper, roll the other half of the pastry into an 11 1/2-inch circle. Turn the filling into the chilled pie shell; it will mound quite high in the shell. Smooth the filling with your hands, laying the apples slices down so they don't poke through the crust. Dot the top of the fruit with the butter. Lightly moisten the rim of the pie shell. Invert the top pastry over the filling, center, and peel off the paper. Press the top and bottom pastries together along the dampened edge. Trim the pastry with scissors or a paring knife, leaving an even 1/2-inch overhang all around, then sculpt the overhang

Salem Cross Inn Apple Pie Contest

The 300-year-old beehive brick oven used for the Salem Cross Inn's apple pie contest measures about 4 feet by 5 feet and consists of such a large thermal mass that it must be fired the day before the baking takes place. According to Martha Salem, the inn's owner, the oven is first loaded with pieces of hardwood, then the fire is set and left to burn for many hours. The remaining ash and coals are scraped into a built-in ash pit.

Martha and her brother, Robert, who presides over the oven, know that it is ready when a little flour tossed on the oven's floor turns just the right shade of toasted brown, and when an arm extended into the oven can be held there for precisely 8 seconds without singing a hair. This is admittedly a bit imprecise by modern standards, but the whole point of the contest, says Martha, is to celebrate the sort of intuitive baking our ancestors did so well on a regular basis.

The apple pies are hustled into the oven, then quickly removed and scrutinized by their creators, one from each New England state. Back into the oven they go—some for just a few minutes, others for much longer, according to individual design. Finally, the judges announce the winner, and everyone shares in the satisfaction of helping to re-create a slice of American culinary history.

(*Note:* Martha Salem has put the apple pie contest on hold for 2004 but plans to sponsor it again in the future. For the latest information, consult the inn's Web site, www.salemcrossinn.com.)

into an upstanding ridge. Poke several steam vents in the top of the pie with a fork or paring knife. Put a couple of the vents near the edge of the crust so you can check the juices there later. To glaze the pie, lightly brush the pastry with the beaten egg white.

5. Place the pie on the center oven rack and bake for 30 minutes, then rotate the pie 180 degrees, so that the part that faced the back of the oven now faces forward. Just in case, slide a large aluminum foil–lined baking sheet onto the rack below to catch any spills. Continue to bake until the juices bubble thickly through the side steam vents, another 30 to 35 minutes. If the top of the pie starts to get too dark, cover loosely with aluminum foil during the last 15 minutes.

6. Transfer the pie to a wire rack and let cool for at least 2 hours before serving.

Recipe for Success

▶ Rose uses part regular and part Butter Flavor Crisco to make the pastry for this pie. To make a pastry that's similar to Rose's, follow the directions for Basic Shortening Pie Pastry, but use ²/₃ cup Butter Flavor Crisco and ¹/₃ cup regular Crisco. In addition, substitute firmly packed light brown sugar for the granulated sugar.

Liz Smothers's Sugarless Apple-Berry Pie

Liz Smothers is the matriarch of the Julian Pie Company, with stores in Julian and Santa Ysabel, near San Diego, California. Liz, who inherited her mother's love for pie making, and her husband, Keith, opened their first small pie shop in Julian at the base of Volcan Mountain in 1986. Two years later, they bought an apple farm so they could grow the apples for their pies, and by 1992 they had opened a second, larger bakery to accommodate the great demand for their pies. You get the picture: Liz knows how to bake a fine pie. Those whose diets are sugar restricted will find this pie incredibly satisfying. Heck, I find it scrumptious, and, as you might have noticed, I'm not shy about using sugar. The apple juice concentrate Liz uses adds a certain sweetness to the pie, as do the fresh berries and apples. All told, this is a great recipe for just about any pie lover.

MAKES 8 TO 10 SERVINGS

1 recipe Basic Shortening Pie Pastry, Double Crust (page 30), modified as instructed in step 1 and refrigerated

FILLING

6 cups peeled, cored, and sliced Golden Delicious apples

1/3 cup frozen apple juice concentrate, thawed, or 3/4 cup apple juice

2 to 3 tablespoons all-purpose flour

1 teaspoon ground cinnamon

1 to 1 1/2 cups fresh blueberries (picked over for stems), raspberries, or hulled and sliced strawberries, to your taste

2 tablespoons cold unsalted butter, cut into small pieces

GLAZE

1 large egg white whisked with 1 tablespoon water

1.   If you haven't already, prepare the pastry, omitting the sugar. Refrigerate until firm enough to roll, about 1 hour.

2.   On a sheet of lightly floured waxed paper, roll the larger portion of the pastry into a 13-inch circle with a floured rolling pin. Invert the pastry over a 9 1/2-inch deep-dish pie pan, center, and peel off the paper. Tuck the pastry into the pan, without stretching it, and let the overhang drape over the edge. Place in the refrigerator for 15 minutes.

3.   Combine the apples, apple juice concentrate, 2 tablespoons of the flour (3 tablespoons if using apple juice), and cinnamon in a large bowl. Set aside for 10 minutes. Preheat the oven to 350°F.

4.   On another sheet of lightly floured waxed paper, roll the other half of the pastry into an 11-inch circle. Pour the berries into the chilled pie shell, making one thick layer.

Turn the apples into the shell and smooth the top with your hands. Dot the filling with the butter. Lightly moisten the rim of the pie shell. Invert the top pastry over the filling, center, and peel off the paper. Press the top and bottom pastries together along the dampened edge. Trim the pastry with scissors or a paring knife, leaving an even ½-inch overhang all around, then sculpt the overhang into an upstanding ridge. Poke several steam vents in the top of the pie with a fork or paring knife. Put a couple of the vents near the edge of the crust so you can check the juices there later. Brush the top of the pie with the egg white mixture.

5. Place the pie on the center oven rack and bake for 45 minutes, then rotate the pie 180 degrees, so that the part that faced the back of the oven now faces forward. Slide a large aluminum foil–lined baking sheet onto the rack below to catch any drips. Continue to bake until the top is golden brown, the apples are tender (check with a skewer), and the juices bubble through the vents at the edge, about 30 minutes.

6. Transfer the pie to a wire rack and let cool for at least 2 hours before serving.

Recipe for Success

▶ **Liz is equally enthusiastic about all of the berries you might use for this pie. Your choice should depend on what's fresh, available, and tempting. A combination of berries would work well, too, if you have some of each on hand.**

▶ **Liz likes to bake her fruit pies longer and slower than I do. I generally start them at a higher temperature, then turn down the heat. Try both methods and see which you prefer.**

Ozark Pie

This recipe and others like it are variously called Ozark Mountain pie, Ozark pie cake, and Ozark apple pie, but they're all very similar: an apple (and often nut) filling in a sweet batter that manages to form both a crusty top and a defined bottom crust. It's one of just a handful of pies I've included in this collection that make their own crusts. Notice the absence of butter. A few of the recipes I've seen do use butter, but that makes the pie more cake-like and less crusty, so I've left it out. If you have only one apple and a desire to make a simple pie, this one is for you.

MAKES 8 SERVINGS

1 large egg

1 large egg yolk

1/2 cup granulated sugar

1/4 cup firmly packed light brown sugar

1/2 teaspoon vanilla extract

1/2 cup plus 1 tablespoon all-purpose flour

1 1/2 tablespoons baking powder

1/2 teaspoon ground cinnamon

1/4 teaspoon ground nutmeg

1 large apple (any type), peeled, cored, and cut into chunks

1/2 cup chopped pecans or walnuts

GARNISH

Fresh Whipped Cream (page 605)

1. Butter a 9 1/2-inch deep-dish pie pan (see Recipe for Success). Set aside. Preheat the oven to 350°F.

2. Combine the egg, egg yolk, granulated sugar, and brown sugar in a large bowl. Using an electric mixer, beat until light and airy, about 2 minutes. Blend in the vanilla.

3. Sift the flour, baking powder, cinnamon, and nutmeg into a separate bowl. Stir into the batter along with the apple and nuts. Scrape the mixture into the prepared pan, smoothing the top with your hands.

4. Place the pie on the center oven rack and bake until the top is dark golden brown and crusted over, about 30 minutes. The apples will most likely be visible through the crust.

5. Transfer the pie to a wire rack and let cool. Serve barely warm or at room temperature, garnished with whipped cream.

Recipe for Success

▶ **This is a fairly shallow pie, no more than about 1 inch tall. To make a higher pie, use a 9-inch standard pie pan and increase the baking time 5 to 8 minutes.**

▶ **Any apple will do here. Just use what you have on hand.**

▶ **This makes a very nice breakfast dish. To shorten the morning preparations, combine the dry ingredients the night before and also chop the apple. Toss the apple with a little lemon juice, cover, and refrigerate overnight.**

The Original Ritz Mock Apple Pie

The original mock apple pie made with Ritz crackers is still, after all these years, the gold standard of the mock cracker pie genre and by far Nabisco's most requested recipe. Cool, I thought, but how does the pie taste? Like a throwback to another era? Or can it stand on its own merits? I started out with a serious skeptical streak—how could wet crackers double as apples?—but ended up a believer. Even my wife, Bev, guessed "apples" when I gave her a bite of this. It tastes most appley while it's still warm, so serve it thus, with a scoop of vanilla ice cream.

MAKES 8 TO 10 SERVINGS

1 recipe Basic Shortening Pie Pastry, Double Crust (page 30), refrigerated, or 2 store-bought refrigerated pie pastries

FILLING

36 Ritz crackers, coarsely broken (scant 2 cups)

1 3/4 cups water

2 cups sugar

2 teaspoons cream of tartar

2 tablespoons fresh lemon juice

Grated zest of 1 lemon

2 tablespoons cold unsalted butter or margarine, cut into small pieces

1/2 teaspoon ground cinnamon

GARNISH

Vanilla ice cream

1. If you haven't already, prepare the pastry and refrigerate until firm enough to roll, about 1 hour.

2. On a sheet of lightly floured waxed paper, roll the larger portion of the pastry into a 12-inch circle with a floured rolling pin. Invert the pastry over a 9-inch standard pie pan, center, and peel off the paper. Gently tuck the pastry into the pan, without stretching it, and let the overhang drape over the edge. If you're using a store-bought pastry, simply line the pie pan with it. Put the cracker crumbs in the prepared crust. Place in the refrigerator for 15 minutes.

3. Bring the water, sugar, and cream of tartar to a boil in a medium-size saucepan over high heat. Reduce the heat to medium and simmer for 15 minutes. Remove from the heat and stir in the lemon juice and zest. Let cool to lukewarm.

4. Slowly pour the cooled syrup over the cracker crumbs in the chilled pie shell. Dot the filling with the butter and sprinkle with the cinnamon. On a separate sheet of floured waxed paper, roll the other half of the pastry into a 10-inch circle. Lightly moisten the rim of the pie shell. Invert the top pastry over the filling, center, and peel off the paper. Or drape the other store-bought pastry over the filling. Press the top and bottom pastries together along the dampened edge. Using the back of a butter knife or pastry knife, trim the pastry flush with the edge of the pan. Make several steam vents in the top of the pie with the tip of a paring knife.

5. Place the pie on the center oven rack and bake until the top crust is crisp and dark golden brown, 30 to 35 minutes.

6. Transfer the pie to a wire rack and let cool. Serve slightly warm with scoops of vanilla ice cream.

Recipe for Success

▶ I consider this a very casual pie and wouldn't hesitate to use store-bought pastry when preparing it.

▶ This is deviating from tradition, and I admit I haven't tried it, but if you substituted a little apple cider for the water, you'd probably have an even more authentic-tasting mock apple pie.

Iowa Pie Politics

Apparently, Congressman Dick Gephardt believes that presidential aspirations and a love for homemade pie go hand in hand. Gearing up for his 2004 presidential bid and the Iowa caucuses, the Missouri congressman launched the Great Gephardt Iowa Pie Challenge, calling on Iowans to help him find the "tastiest, flakiest, fruitiest, creamiest, most scrumptious slices of pie in Iowa." The candidate enjoyed "deep-dish" support from all Iowans, but especially those who made and loved Iowa pies. Voters were invited to visit his official Web site, where they could recommend a stop on his statewide pie tour and follow his progress on the site's "pie chart." Among the pies recommended were the mile-high pie at Stone's Restaurant in Marshalltown and the apple pies at Cronk's Café in Denison and the Chrome Diner in Algona.

Mrs. Smith's Pies

To the millions of Americans with neither the time nor the inclination to make their own pies, the name that means the next best thing to homemade is Mrs. Smith's. One of the nation's top bakeries, Mrs. Smith's enjoys an impressive 90 percent brand awareness in the United States. Indeed, we've all eaten a slice of Mrs. Smith's pie and, considering the millions the company turns out each year, you can't help but admire the way a mass-produced food product can maintain such a generous amount of homemade charm.

According to a company spokesperson, that's because the principles of quality that governed the real Mrs. Smith are still in practice today. In the early 1900s, a homemaker named Amanda Smith of Pottstown, Pennsylvania, started baking pies in her home kitchen. She enjoyed a reputation as a serious baker, with exacting standards, so the townsfolk would bring her their fruit. She, in turn, would bake it into pies, a service she provided in exchange for her customers' excess fruit. One day, on a whim, her son Robert thought he'd try selling some of her pies at the local YMCA. He quickly sold out, and before long he was delivering pies all over the area in his old Dodge coupe. A bakery icon had been born.

Today Mrs. Smith's pies are baked in facilities across the country and are available just about anywhere you look. If she were alive today, Amanda Smith would no doubt be tickled to learn that her fruit pies are still the company's biggest sellers, with good old apple accounting for 60 to 65 percent of the pies sold, followed by pumpkin, cherry, and berry. This all adds up to a great American success story and a delicious slice of our pie heritage.

To a lot of people, fall is more or less defined by two pies: apple and then, for a day, pumpkin. Which is a fine start. But limiting your fall pie making to apple and pumpkin is like narrowing your choices to vanilla and chocolate at the ice cream parlor. There's a whole lot else going on here, and you neglect the possibilities at your pie-making peril. • Pears are near the top of my favorite fall

Cranberry, Pear, Pumpkin, and Other Classic Fall Pies

pie fruits, in some ways the equal of apples. Pears tend to be very juicy, always an asset to fruit pies. Ripe pears have a soft, buttery flesh that makes for a meltingly tender slice of pie. I find their aroma intoxicating, and they match up well with other fruits, such as cranberries—one of fall's other pie treasures. • An all-cranberry pie is a real treat, but more typically I like to use cranberries as an accent, not the prevailing theme. Used judiciously, cranberries will not steal the show, but instead will highlight the flavors of other fruit. They add the tartness that's often lacking in store-bought fruit, and a splash of color that fits right in with both early fall and the holiday season.

Pumpkin and sweet potato pies are other fall standards I've included here. Perhaps more so than any other pies in this collection, these have had to pass the most rigid scrutiny: having tasted too many bland versions of both, I have pretty high standards in this category. You can rest assured that the pumpkin and sweet potato pies in the following pages are either rich, exotic, or otherwise jazzed up to capture my fancy—like Triple-Layer Pumpkin-Chocolate Pie on page 282.

So take a minute to thumb through this section and see what looks good. Once you've baked a few of these pies, I doubt that you'll ever again think of fall pie baking as just apple and pumpkin.

Tips for Baking Fabulous Fall Pies

▶ Choose pears that are weighty in proportion to their size, an indication of freshness and juici-ness. Ripe pears will yield to moderate finger pressure. Pears often require further ripening at home, on the kitchen counter in a closed paper bag.

▶ If your pears seem unusually juicy, increase the amount of thickener slightly.

▶ Like apple pies and nearly all fruit pies, be sure not to underbake your pear pie, or the thickener won't have time to "set" the juices. Bake until any visible juices bubble thickly.

▶ Purchase cranberries that are bright red. Early in the season, you may notice berries that are half white and half red. They'll not have as much flavor as bright red ones.

▶ If you freeze your cranberries, bring them to room temperature before adding them to a pie fill-ing. Frozen berries will make for sluggish baking and, likely, an overbaked crust.

▶ In most cases, pumpkin pies should be baked in a partially prebaked pie shell. If they are not, the bottom crust may not have a fully baked flavor.

▶ Don't freeze pumpkin pies. The filling and crust tend to separate when you do.

▶ Keep in mind that pumpkin is, more or less, a custard-type pie and therefore requires moderate heat. Never raise the temperature in an effort to accelerate the baking. One indication that you've overbaked a pumpkin pie is a watery filling when you cut into the pie.

All-Pear Pie with Maple and Candied Ginger

Pears have always been one of my favorite fruits. When I was a kid, my mom would often open up several cans of pears after dinner—dessert for me and my six siblings—and I'd quickly be in gourmet heaven. I still love pear desserts, especially this double-crust pie featuring maple syrup and candied ginger. As with the canned pears of my youth, I can't get enough of it. I like to make this in the fall, when pears are abundant and juicy, and I'll often bring it to a potluck or other special event. The all-pear filling never ceases to delight: it's just not a filling that many cooks consider. Note that I don't usually bother to peel pears, as the skins of most varieties are very soft and not chewy, unlike apple skins.

MAKES 8 TO 10 SERVINGS

1 recipe Basic Flaky Pie Pastry, Double Crust (page 31), refrigerated

FILLING

7 cups cored and sliced ripe pears, unpeeled

1/3 cup sugar

1/4 cup pure maple syrup (see Recipe for Success)

2 tablespoons quick-cooking tapioca

1/2 teaspoon vanilla extract

1 1/2 tablespoons fresh lemon juice

Grated zest of 1 lemon (optional)

1 tablespoon minced candied (crystallized) ginger or 1/2 teaspoon ground ginger

2 tablespoons cold unsalted butter, cut into small pieces

GLAZE

Milk or light cream

Sugar

1. If you haven't already, prepare the pastry and refrigerate until firm enough to roll, about 1 hour.

2. On a sheet of lightly floured waxed paper, roll the larger portion of the pastry into a 13-inch circle with a floured rolling pin. Invert the pastry over a 9 1/2-inch deep-dish pie pan, center, and peel off the paper. Gently tuck the pastry into the pan, without stretching it, and let the overhang drape over the edge. Place in the refrigerator for 15 minutes.

3. Combine the pears, sugar, maple syrup, tapioca, vanilla, lemon juice, lemon zest (if using), and ginger in a large bowl. Toss well and set aside. Preheat the oven to 400°F.

4. On another sheet of lightly floured waxed paper, roll the other half of the pastry into an 11 1/2-inch circle. Turn the filling into the chilled pie shell and smooth the fruit with your hands. Dot the top of the fruit with the butter. Lightly moisten the edge of the pie shell with a wet fingertip or pastry brush. Invert the top pastry over the filling, center, and peel off the paper. Press the top and bottom pastries together along the dampened edge. Trim the pastry with scissors or a paring knife, leaving an even 1/2-inch overhang all around, then sculpt the overhang into an upstanding ridge. Poke several steam vents in the top of the pie with a fork or paring knife. Put a couple of the vents near the edge of the crust so you can check the juices there later. Brush the top of the pie with a little milk and sprinkle with sugar.

5. Place the pie on the center oven rack and bake for 30 minutes. Reduce the oven temperature to 375°F and rotate the pie 180 degrees, so that the part that faced the back of the oven now faces forward. Just in case, slide a large aluminum foil–lined baking sheet onto the rack below to catch any spills. Continue to bake until the juices bubble thickly at the edge, 30 to 35 minutes.

6. Transfer the pie to a wire rack and let cool for at least 2 hours—preferably longer, since this is a juicy pie—before serving.

Recipe for Success

▶ This also makes a very good-looking lattice-top pie. (See page 71 for directions.)

▶ If you don't have any pure maple syrup on hand, substitute an equal amount of firmly packed light brown sugar.

Streusel-Topped Pear Pie with Walnut Crust

I'm a big fan of pear pies, as you might have guessed from the number of them scattered throughout this collection. Here's one that has a sturdy walnut pastry and is topped with what I call blond streusel—blond because it only has white or light ingredients, as opposed to the more typical cinnamon and brown sugar. Any good, juicy pear will do here. If you want to play up the pear flavor, add a tablespoon or two of pear brandy. Even better, keep the bottle out and serve some with the pie.

MAKES 8 TO 10 SERVINGS

1/2 recipe Nutty Pie Pastry (page 42) made with walnuts, refrigerated

FILLING

5 1/2 cups peeled, cored, and sliced ripe pears

1/2 cup sugar

2 tablespoons cornstarch

1 tablespoon fresh lemon juice

1 to 2 tablespoons pear brandy (optional), to your taste

1/4 teaspoon ground cinnamon

Pinch of ground nutmeg

Pinch of salt

BLOND STREUSEL TOPPING

1 cup all-purpose flour

2/3 cup sugar

1/4 teaspoon salt

6 tablespoons (3/4 stick) cold unsalted butter, cut into 1/4-inch pieces

1 tablespoon milk or light cream

1. If you haven't already, prepare the pastry and refrigerate until firm enough to roll, about 1 hour. It's best not to overchill nut pastries, or they can be difficult to handle.

2. On a sheet of lightly floured waxed paper, roll the pastry into a 13-inch circle with a floured rolling pin. Invert the pastry over a 9½-inch deep-dish pie pan, center, and peel off the paper. Gently tuck the pastry into the pan, without stretching it. Note that because of the walnuts, this pastry is a little more delicate than some and should be eased into the pan as carefully as possible. Sculpt the overhang into an upstanding ridge. Place in the freezer for 15 minutes. Preheat the oven to 400°F.

3. Place the pears in a large bowl. Mix the sugar and cornstarch together in a small bowl. Add the mixture to the fruit and stir well. Stir in the lemon juice, pear brandy (if using), cinnamon, nutmeg, and salt. Turn the filling into the chilled pie shell, smoothing the top with your hands. Place the pie on the center oven rack and bake for 35 minutes.

4. Meanwhile, make the streusel topping. Combine the flour, sugar, and salt in a food processor. Scatter the butter over the dry ingredients. Pulse until the mixture resembles fine crumbs. Add the milk and pulse again. Dump the mixture into a medium-size bowl and gently rub between your fingers to make large, buttery crumbs. Refrigerate until ready to use. (See Recipe for Success.)

5. Remove the pie from the oven and reduce the temperature to 375°F. Carefully dump the crumbs in the center of the pie, spreading them evenly over the surface with your hands. Press down gently to compact them. Return the pie to the oven, placing it so that the part that faced the back of the oven now faces forward. Just in case, slide a large aluminum foil–lined baking sheet onto the rack below to catch any spills. Continue to bake until the juices bubble thickly around the edge, 30 to 35 minutes. If necessary, cover the pie with loosely tented aluminum foil during the last 15 minutes, to prevent the streusel from getting too brown.

6. Transfer the pie to a wire rack and let cool for at least 1 hour before serving.

Recipe for Success

▶ **Juicy pears can be very, well, juicy. That juice can sometimes present a problem when you're making a streusel-topped pie. The juice can saturate the topping, turning some of it to sludge. To prevent that from happening, about 5 minutes before I add the topping to the pie, I sprinkle a small handful of quick-cooking rolled oats over the juiciest parts. The oatmeal absorbs some of the excess juice and forms a sort of barrier between the filling and the topping. The result? Less streusel sludge and more streusel.**

Pears for Your Pies

Provided they're fresh, juicy, and ripe, nearly all pears are excellent in pies. But their ripeness is sometimes difficult to judge, especially with the variety of skin colors available. Like peaches, pears are ripe when they yield to finger pressure, without feeling overly soft. Keep in mind that pears do not ripen well on trees. Pears are harvested mature but unripe—which is often how you'll find them in the market—and must be ripened after harvest. The easiest way to do this when you get them home is to place them in a paper bag and ripen them right on the counter. Check them daily to see how they're progressing. Store ripe pears in the fridge for two to three days.

Here are some pear varieties you'll want to try in your pies.

▶ BOSC Highly aromatic. Its dense flesh makes for great pies.

▶ COMICE Perhaps the sweetest, juiciest variety.

▶ RED BARTLETT Skin is bright red when fully ripe. Very sweet and juicy, excellent in pies.

▶ YELLOW BARTLETT Same flavor, texture, and qualities as Red Bartlett. Ripens to bright yellow.

Pear Pie with Almond Cake Topping

This is one of my favorite pies of all time—a medium-thick filling of soft pears topped with something like a delicate almond torte. (For a wonderful variation, you can replace the almonds with pecan halves.) It's no more difficult to make than a streusel-topped pie, since the almond cake topping is mixed right in the food processor. The topping makes this pie somewhat more refined, so consider serving it if you're entertaining. Top it with vanilla, butter pecan, or coffee ice cream.

MAKES 8 TO 10 SERVINGS

1 recipe All-Butter Pie Pastry, Single Crust (page 28) or Basic Flaky Pie Pastry, Single Crust (page 31), refrigerated

FILLING

5 1/2 cups peeled, cored, and thinly sliced ripe pears (see Recipe for Success)

1/3 cup plus 2 tablespoons sugar

1 tablespoon fresh lemon juice

1 teaspoon grated lemon zest

1 1/2 tablespoons cornstarch

Big pinch of ground nutmeg or cardamom

ALMOND CAKE TOPPING

1 cup whole almonds

1/3 cup sugar

3 tablespoons all-purpose flour

1/4 cup sweetened flaked coconut

1 teaspoon baking powder

1/4 teaspoon salt

1/4 cup (1/2 stick) unsalted butter, at room temperature but not soft, cut into 1/4-inch pieces

1 large egg

1/2 teaspoon vanilla extract

1/4 teaspoon almond extract (optional)

1. If you haven't already, prepare the pastry and refrigerate until firm enough to roll, about 1 hour.

2. On a sheet of lightly floured waxed paper, roll the pastry into a 13-inch circle with a floured rolling pin. Invert the pastry over a 9 1/2-inch deep-dish pie pan, center, and peel off the paper. Tuck the pastry into the pan, without stretching it, and sculpt the edge into an upstanding ridge. Place in the freezer for 15 minutes.

3. Combine the pears, 1/3 cup of the sugar, the lemon juice, and lemon zest in a large bowl. Set aside for 10 minutes. Preheat the oven to 400°F.

4. Combine the remaining 2 tablespoons sugar, the cornstarch, and nutmeg in a small bowl, then stir the mixture into the fruit. Scrape the filling into the chilled pie shell. Place the pie on the center oven rack and bake for 30 minutes, then reduce the oven temperature to 375°F and bake for 10 minutes more.

5. Meanwhile, prepare the cake topping. Put the almonds, sugar, flour, coconut, baking powder, and salt in a food processor and pulse until the nuts are very finely chopped. Scatter the butter over the top and pulse until it is well incorporated and the mixture is crumbly. Whisk the egg, vanilla, and almond extract (if using) together in a small bowl. Add to the processor and pulse again, just until the mixture starts to gather around the blade. Scrape the cake batter into a bowl.

6. Remove the pie from the oven. Using a soup spoon, dollop the cake batter more or less evenly over the fruit. Don't worry if it is lumpy or otherwise imperfect because it

will settle during baking. Return the pie to the oven, placing it so that the part that faced the back of the oven now faces forward. Continue to bake until the top is a rich golden brown and the batter is cooked through, 20 to 22 minutes. You most likely will not need to worry about the pie bubbling over, but if it starts to, slide a large aluminum foil–lined baking sheet onto the rack below.

7. Transfer the pie to a wire rack and let cool for at least 2 hours. This pie is best served barely warm or at room temperature

Recipe for Success

▶ You don't have to peel the pears, because their skins are so soft. I recommend it here, however, because this pie is a little more "formal" than some, and I prefer the refined look of no skins.

▶ If you plan to serve this pie for a party, make it the same day. This will help preserve the wonderful texture of the cake topping, because it won't have a chance to absorb any moisture from below. You want it to be a little on the dry side.

Pear and Jalapeño Jelly Pie

If you read a lot of recipes like I do, you've probably seen pears and black pepper teamed up on more than one occasion. I used to think this was a bit strange, but once I tried it—grinding black pepper onto sliced ripe pears and serving them with a bit of cheese—I realized just how good the combination is. My own forays into pear-pepper partnering led to this spicy pear pie, sweetened with jalapeño jelly and jazzed up with a little five-spice powder. The spices and jelly envelop the pears, leaving a warm and subtly exotic aftertaste. I think you'll be surprised at how good this is.

MAKES 8 TO 10 SERVINGS

1 recipe Basic Flaky Pie Pastry, Double Crust (page 31) or Basic Shortening Pie Pastry, Double Crust (page 30), refrigerated

FILLING

4¹/₂ to 5 cups peeled, cored, and sliced ripe pears

¹/₂ cup jalapeño jelly

2 tablespoons unsalted butter

¹/₄ cup sugar

2 tablespoons cornstarch

¹/₄ teaspoon Chinese five-spice powder

Big pinch of salt

GLAZE

Milk or light cream

Sugar

GARNISH

Vanilla or butter pecan ice cream

1. If you haven't already, prepare the pastry and refrigerate until firm enough to roll, about 1 hour.

2. On a sheet of lightly floured waxed paper, roll the larger portion of the pastry into a 12-inch circle with a floured rolling pin. Invert the pastry over a 9-inch standard pie pan, center, and peel off the paper. Gently tuck the pastry into the pan, without stretching it, and let the overhang drape over the edge. Place in the refrigerator for 15 minutes. Preheat the oven to 400°F.

3. Put the pears in a large bowl. Combine the jelly and butter in a small saucepan over medium heat. Heat until the butter melts, then whisk to smooth the mixture and pour it over the pears. Combine the sugar, cornstarch, five-spice powder, and salt in a small bowl. Stir the mixture into the fruit and set aside.

4. On another sheet of floured waxed paper, roll the other half of the pastry into a 10-inch circle. Turn the filling into the chilled pie shell, smoothing the top with your hands. Lightly moisten the rim of the shell. Invert the top pastry over the filling, center, and peel off the paper. Press the top and bottom pastries together along the dampened edge. Using the back of a paring knife, trim the pastry flush with the edge of the pan, then pinch the pastries together to seal. Poke several steam vents in the top of the pie with a fork or paring knife. Put a couple of the vents near the edge of the crust so you can check the juices there later. To glaze the pie, lightly brush the pastry with milk and sprinkle with sugar.

5. Place the pie on the center oven rack and bake for 30 minutes. Reduce the oven temperature to 375°F and rotate the pie 180 degrees, so that the part that faced the back of the oven now faces forward. Just in case, slide a large aluminum foil–lined baking sheet onto the rack below to catch any spills. Continue to bake until the top is golden brown and any visible juices bubble thickly through the side steam vents, 25 to 30 minutes.

6. Transfer the pie to a wire rack and let cool for at least 1 hour. Serve with scoops of ice cream.

Recipe for Success

- I imagine that there are any number of good jalapeño jellies on the market, but I use Knott's Berry Farm, available—I believe—at most supermarkets.

- If you like, you can substitute up to half sliced apples for an equal amount of sliced pears.

Five-Spice Pear-Apple Pie

In the winter, I love to make poached pears flavored with star anise, a flavor scheme I thought would adapt nicely to a pie. Anise is one of the more exotic spices in five-spice powder, and it really stands out in this mixed-fruit pie, lending a heady fragrance and warming flavor. I have made the same pie with a top and bottom crust, but I prefer the cornmeal streusel. It covers the pie with a light crunch and is the perfect complement to the spicy filling.

MAKES 8 TO 10 SERVINGS

1 recipe Whole Wheat Pie Pastry, Single Crust (page 33) or Basic Flaky Pie Pastry, Single Crust (page 31), refrigerated

FILLING

3 1/2 cups peeled, cored, and sliced Granny Smith, Cortland, Northern Spy, or other apples (see pages 232–233 for recommendations)

3 1/2 cups cored and sliced ripe pears, peeled or unpeeled

Grated zest of 1 lemon

1 tablespoon fresh lemon juice

2 tablespoons orange juice

3/4 cup granulated sugar

1 1/2 tablespoons cornstarch

2 teaspoons Chinese five-spice powder

CORNMEAL STREUSEL TOPPING

3/4 cup all-purpose flour

1/4 cup fine yellow cornmeal

2/3 cup firmly packed light brown sugar

1/4 teaspoon salt

1/2 cup (1 stick) cold unsalted butter, cut into 1/4-inch pieces

1. If you haven't already, prepare the pastry and refrigerate until firm enough to roll, about 1 hour.

2. On a sheet of lightly floured waxed paper, roll the pastry into a 13-inch circle with a floured rolling pin. Invert the pastry over a 9 1/2-inch deep-dish pie pan, center, and peel off the paper. Tuck the pastry into the pan, without stretching it, and sculpt the edge into an upstanding ridge. Place in the freezer for 15 minutes.

3. Combine the apples, pears, lemon zest, lemon juice, orange juice, and 1/2 cup of the granulated sugar in a large bowl. Set aside for 10 minutes. Preheat the oven to 400°F.

4. Mix together the remaining 1/4 cup sugar, the cornstarch, and five-spice powder in a small bowl. Stir the mixture into the fruit. Turn the filling into the chilled pie shell and smooth the filling with your hands to even it out. Place the pie on the center oven rack and bake for 30 minutes.

5. Meanwhile, make the topping. Put the flour, cornmeal, brown sugar, and salt in a

Keep Those Pie Spices Fresh

If you like to make pies, you probably spend a lot of money on spices. So you've probably noticed that they aren't as cheap as they used to be. Add up the cost of a few jars, and you might have been able to purchase a package tour to the exotic places they came from instead.

Under the circumstances, it pays to keep your spices in good shape after you get them home. Here are some guidelines for doing just that.

▶ Give your old spices the sniff test. If they don't tantalize your senses, throw them away and get fresh ones.

▶ Keep them away from the heat. The biggest mistake cooks make is keeping spices too near the stove. Heat destroys the volatile oils that give spices their distinctive flavor.

▶ Don't store them in the sunlight. Direct sunlight will also wreak havoc on their flavor. Find a dark, low-humidity cabinet to store them in.

▶ Rule of thumb: Don't buy any more of a given spice than you'll use in six to nine months.

▶ If you really want your pies to sparkle, get a spice grinder and use whole spices. Whole spices will last for years.

food processor and pulse several times to mix. Scatter the butter over the mixture and pulse until it resembles fine crumbs. Empty the crumbs into a medium-size bowl and rub them between your fingers to make large, buttery crumbs. Refrigerate until ready to use.

6. Remove the pie from the oven and reduce the oven temperature to 375°F. Carefully dump the crumbs in the center of the pie, spreading them evenly over the surface with your hands. Tamp them down lightly. Return the pie to the oven, placing it so that the part that faced the back of the oven now faces forward. Just in case, slide a large aluminum foil–lined baking sheet onto the rack below to catch any spills. Continue to bake until the juices bubble thickly around the edge, another 30 minutes.

7. Transfer the pie to a wire rack and let cool for at least 1 hour before serving.

Recipe for Success

▶ I recommend keeping a jar of five-spice powder on your spice shelf. In a pinch, if you'd like to approximate it with spices on hand, you can mix cinnamon, ground fennel seed, ground cloves, and ground white pepper—more of the first two, less of the cloves, and much less of the pepper. Use 1½ teaspoons of your homemade powder in this pie. Bury 2 whole star anise in the center of the pie (so that you can find and remove them when you cut the first slices).

Pear-Raspberry Lattice-Top Pie

My favorite pies for lattice tops are the ones with red fillings, like this one. Here we mix juicy sliced pears with fresh or frozen raspberries, which give the filling a deep, rosy blush. I've always loved the softness of pear fillings, and it's one of the things I like most about this pie. If you make this in early fall, you may be able to use all fresh fruit. When the local raspberries are no longer in season, use frozen.

MAKES 8 TO 10 SERVINGS

1 recipe Basic Flaky Pie Pastry, Double Crust (page 31), or All-Butter Pie Pastry, Double Crust (page 28), modified as instructed in step 1 and refrigerated

FILLING

5 1/2 cups cored and sliced ripe pears, peeled or unpeeled

2 cups raspberries, fresh or individually frozen (not packed in syrup), partially thawed

3/4 cup sugar

1 tablespoon fresh lemon juice

1 teaspoon grated lemon zest

1/4 teaspoon ground cardamom or ginger

2 1/2 tablespoons cornstarch

2 tablespoons cold unsalted butter, cut into small pieces

GLAZE

Milk or light cream

Sugar

1. Prepare the pastry as directed, shaping half of it into a disk and the other half into a square; both should be about 3/4 inch thick. Wrap the pastry as usual and refrigerate until firm enough to roll, about 1 hour.

2. On a sheet of lightly floured waxed paper, roll the disk of pastry into a 13-inch circle with a floured rolling pin. Invert the pastry over a 9 1/2-inch deep-dish pie pan, center, and peel off the paper. Gently tuck the pastry into the pan, without stretching it, and sculpt the overhang into an upstanding ridge. Place in the refrigerator for 15 minutes.

3. Combine the pears, raspberries, 1/2 cup of the sugar, the lemon juice, lemon zest, and cardamom in a large bowl. Mix well and set aside for 10 minutes. Mix the remaining 1/4 cup sugar and the cornstarch together in a small bowl, then stir the mixture into the fruit. Preheat the oven to 400°F.

4. On another sheet of lightly floured waxed paper, roll the other piece of dough into a rectangle about 12 inches long and 10 inches wide. Using a pastry wheel or pizza cutter, cut the pastry into 8 lengthwise strips, each about 1 1/4 inches wide and 12 inches long. Set aside.

5. Turn the filling into the chilled pie shell, taking care to smooth the top so that no pear slices jut up, which could tear the lattice. Dot the top of the pie with the butter. Lay 5 pastry strips vertically across the pie, evenly spaced, as shown in figure 1. Fold back strips 2 and 4, then lay another strip directly across the center of the pie, as shown in figure 2. Unfold the folded dough strips, then fold back strips 1, 3, and 5. Lay another perpendicular strip across the pie as shown in figure 3. Unfold the folded strips, then fold up strips 1, 3, and 5 on the other side of the pie. Place another perpendicular strip across the pie, as shown in figure 4, then unfold strips 1, 3, and 5. Trim the strips, then pinch the ends into the edge of the pastry. Lightly brush the pastry strips with milk and sprinkle the pie with sugar.

6. Place the pie on the center oven rack and bake for 25 minutes, then reduce the oven temperature to 375°F and rotate the pie 180 degrees, so that the part that faced the back of the oven now faces forward. Just in case, place a large aluminum foil–lined baking sheet on the rack below to catch any spills. Continue to bake until the top of the pie is golden brown and any visible juices bubble thickly, 35 to 40 minutes.

7. Transfer the pie to a wire rack and let cool for at least 2 hours before serving.

Recipe for Success

- **Read about lattice-top pies (see page 72) before making this.**

- **If you're unfamiliar with cardamom, pick up a jar at the market. It tastes particularly good with pear baked goods. Don't overdo it, though; a little goes a long way.**

- **Blackberries are excellent in place of the raspberries in this pie.**

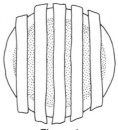

Figure 1

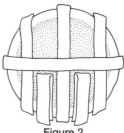

Figure 2

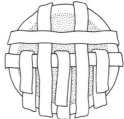

Figure 3

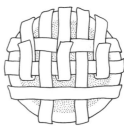

Figure 4

National Pie Day

You knew there had to be one, right? So mark your calendars accordingly: January 23. Created by the American Pie Council, National Pie Day is dedicated to the celebration of pie, plain and simple. The council says it's the perfect opportunity to pass on the love and enjoyment of pie eating and making to future generations. How best to do this? Here are a few of the council's suggestions.

▶ Make pie. Bake your favorite, and share it with a friend.

▶ Teach pie making. Go to a local school, senior center, or civic club and show the people there how it's done.

▶ Hold a pie night. Invite a number of your friends to bring their favorite pies for an irresistible pie buffet.

▶ Throw a pie-making contest. Invite everyone in your community to participate. Ask local chefs and cooking teachers to be judges and award fanciful prizes.

▶ Hold a pie auction. Donate the proceeds to a worthy cause.

And in general, do as much fun pie stuff as possible on this special day.

Pear and Fig Pie with a Pine Nut Crust

Anytime I see a recipe with pears and figs—a combination I just adore—I pay attention. So when I came across Mary Ann Esposito's recipe for a dried fig, pear, and pine nut pie in her book *Celebrations Italian Style* (William Morrow, 1995), I had to make it. That delicious pie turned out to be the inspiration for this one. The filling is what might loosely be called a Mediterranean mincemeat, with a little tangerine zest and juice added to brighten the dried and fresh fruits. Pine nuts are used twice, in the filling and embedded in the crust. It's a handsome touch for a tasty pie.

MAKES 8 TO 10 SERVINGS

1 recipe Basic Flaky Pie Pastry, Double Crust (page 31), refrigerated

FILLING

3 large ripe pears, peeled, cored, and sliced crosswise

1 cup stemmed and diced dried figs

1/4 cup sugar

1/2 cup fresh tangerine or orange juice (see Recipe for Success)

1 teaspoon grated tangerine or orange zest

2 tablespoons honey

1 tablespoon fresh lemon juice

3/4 cup pine nuts

GLAZE

Milk or light cream

Sugar

1. If you haven't already, prepare the pastry and refrigerate until firm enough to roll, about 1 hour.

2. On a sheet of lightly floured waxed paper, roll the larger portion of the pastry into a 13-inch circle with a floured rolling pin. Invert the pastry over a 9¹/₂-inch deep-dish pie pan, center, and peel off the paper. Gently tuck the pastry into the pan, without stretching it, and let the overhang drape over the edge. Place in the refrigerator for 15 minutes.

3. Combine one-third of the pears, the figs, sugar, tangerine juice, and tangerine zest in a medium-size nonreactive saucepan. Bring to a boil over medium heat, then reduce the heat slightly, cover, and simmer for about 10 minutes, until the fruit has absorbed most of the liquid. Remove from the heat and stir in the remaining pears, the honey, lemon juice, and ¹/₂ cup of the pine nuts. Set aside. Preheat the oven to 400°F.

4. On a fresh sheet of lightly floured waxed paper, roll the other half of the pastry into an 11-inch circle. Strew the remaining ¹/₄ cup pine nuts over the pastry. Using your rolling pin, gently roll the nuts into the pastry, embedding them deeply.

5. Turn the filling into the chilled pie shell, moistening the edge of the shell with a pastry brush or finger. Invert the top pastry onto your outstretched hand or another sheet of waxed paper, then invert it over the filling, nut side up. Press the top and bottom pastries together along the edge to seal. Trim the pastry with scissors or a paring knife, leaving an even ¹/₂-inch overhang all around, and sculpt it into an upstanding ridge. Poke several steam vents in the top of the pie with a fork or paring knife. Put a couple of the vents near the edge of the crust so you can check the juices there later. To glaze the pie, brush lightly with milk and sprinkle with sugar.

6. Place the pie on the center oven rack and bake for 20 minutes. Reduce the oven temperature to 375°F and rotate the pie 180 degrees, so that the part that faced the back

A Slice of Sara Lee

Sara Lee is one of the nation's top producers of quality baked goods. Many of us grew up eating Sara Lee cheesecake or pound cake for dessert and hearing the company's catchy jingle—"Nobody doesn't like Sara Lee!"—on TV. And did you know that the company's founder, Charles Lubin, named his bakery business after his daughter? How sweet!

Pies are no small part of Sara Lee's business. During the holiday season, Sara Lee bakes more than 20 million pumpkin pies to keep up with the demand. In late 2002, Sara Lee's Traverse City, Michigan, bakery produced its 3 billionth pie. Here are some other interesting tidbits:

▶ Sara Lee's facility in Traverse City bakes more than 420,000 pies each day. If you placed one year's worth of Sara Lee pies side by side, the line would stretch nearly around the world.

▶ Sara Lee's pie shopping list for a year includes 60 million apples; more than 20 million pounds of cherries, blueberries, strawberries, peaches, pumpkins, and rhubarb; more than 40 million pounds of flour; and 75 million eggs.

To learn more about Sara Lee and find some pie preparation tips, go to www.saralee.com.

---

of the oven now faces forward. Just in case, slide a large aluminum foil–lined baking sheet onto the rack below to catch any drips. Continue to bake until the juices bubble thickly at the steam vents and the top is golden brown, 35 to 45 minutes. If the top starts to get too dark, cover it with loosely tented aluminum foil during the last 10 to 15 minutes.

7. Transfer the pie to a wire rack and let cool for at least 2 hours before serving.

Recipe for Success

▶ Dried figs can vary greatly in their degree of dryness. If yours seem quite dry— maybe after sitting for months in your cupboard—increase the tangerine or orange juice to $3/4$ cup.

Pear and Fig Pie with Hazelnut Crumb Topping

As much as any pie in this book, this one has several distinctive elements—figs, pears, and hazelnuts—that add up to more than the sum of its parts. It's classy, too. I often serve it if I'm looking for a pie that's a little more sophisticated and refined than most. Since good fresh figs can be difficult to procure, I always use dried and poach them to add flavor, tenderness, and juiciness. The poaching liquid—pear juice, which you may have to buy at a health food store— is then reduced and used to sweeten and flavor the pie. The figs are mixed with ripe pear slices and baked with a toasted hazelnut topping. It's all so delicious together, I think you'll agree that these flavors were made for one another.

MAKES 8 TO 10 SERVINGS

1 recipe Basic Flaky Pie Pastry, Single Crust (page 31), refrigerated

FILLING

2 cups dried Black Mission figs, stemmed

About 2 cups pear juice

4 large ripe pears, peeled, cored, and sliced

$1/3$ cup plus 3 tablespoons sugar

$2^{1}/_{2}$ tablespoons cornstarch

1 tablespoon fresh lemon juice

Grated zest of 1 orange

HAZELNUT CRUMB TOPPING

1 cup hazelnuts, toasted (see page 163)

$2/3$ cup sugar

$3/4$ cup all-purpose flour

$1/4$ teaspoon ground cinnamon

$1/4$ teaspoon salt

$1/2$ cup (1 stick) cold unsalted butter, cut into $1/4$-inch pieces

1. If you haven't already, prepare the pastry and refrigerate until firm enough to roll, about 1 hour.

2. On a sheet of lightly floured waxed paper, roll the pastry into a 13-inch circle with a floured rolling pin. Invert the pastry over a $9^{1}/_{2}$-inch deep-dish pie pan, center, and peel off the paper. Gently tuck the pastry down into the pan, without stretching it, and sculpt the edge into an upstanding ridge. Place in the freezer for 15 minutes.

3. Halve the figs or cut them into quarters if they're very large. Place them in a medium-size nonreactive saucepan and add enough pear juice to cover by about $1/2$ inch.

Bring to a boil, reduce the heat to low, cover, and gently simmer for 30 minutes. Preheat the oven to 400°F.

4. Using a slotted spoon, transfer the figs to a large bowl. Increase the heat and boil any remaining liquid until it becomes syrupy and just covers the bottom of the pan. You should have ¼ to ⅓ cup. Pour this over the figs and mix. Add the pears and ⅓ cup of the sugar and toss well. In a small bowl, mix the remaining 3 tablespoons sugar with the cornstarch. Add the mixture to the fruit and mix again. Stir in the lemon juice and orange zest. Turn the filling into the chilled pie shell and smooth the top with your hands to even it out. Place the pie on the center oven rack and bake for 35 minutes.

5. Meanwhile, make the hazelnut crumb topping. Place the toasted hazelnuts and sugar in a food processor and pulse until the nuts are well chopped but not overly so. Add the flour, cinnamon, and salt and pulse again to mix. Scatter the butter over the dry ingredients and pulse until the mixture resembles medium-fine crumbs. Empty the crumbs into a medium-size bowl and rub between your fingers to make large, buttery crumbs. Refrigerate until ready to use.

6. Remove the pie from the oven and reduce the temperature to 375°F. Carefully dump the crumbs in the center of the pie, spreading them evenly over the surface with your hands. There will be a lot of crumbs, but use them all. Tamp them down lightly. Return the pie to the oven, placing it so that the part that faced the back of the oven now faces forward. Just in case, place a large aluminum foil–lined baking sheet on the rack below to catch any spills. Continue to bake until the juices bubble thickly around the edge, 35 to 40 minutes. If necessary, cover the pie loosely with aluminum foil during the last 10 to 15 minutes of baking to keep the top from browning too much.

7. Transfer the pie to a wire rack and let cool for at least 1 hour before serving.

Recipe for Success

▶ **Often when I'm baking a pie such as this that involves an extra step or two—in this case, poaching the figs—I'll try to get those steps done the day before. Here the figs can be poached up to 2 days ahead and kept in the refrigerator. Don't be concerned if they soak up much of the liquid as they sit; that won't affect the outcome of the pie. If you think of it, bring the figs to room temperature before you proceed with making the filling. Don't forget, too, that the pastry can always be made—or made, rolled, and put in the pie pan—the day before as well.**

Very Cranberry-Pear Pie

I think cranberries are one of the most underused pie fruits, perhaps because of their reputation as being quite tart. In fact, that tartness is easily balanced with the correct amount of sugar and contributes to the delicious, full flavor of this brightly colored pie. Finely chopping the cranberries, as I do here, makes for a compact pie. And letting them sit in the sugar for a while allows them to start juicing and accelerates the cooking process. A top crust could be used, but I prefer a thick nut crumb topping; either walnuts or pecans work beautifully. This is an excellent pie for the holidays.

MAKES 8 TO 10 SERVINGS

1 recipe Basic Flaky Pie Pastry, Single Crust (page 31), refrigerated

FILLING

3 cups fresh cranberries, picked over for stems

$1/2$ cup plus 1 tablespoon granulated sugar

2 large ripe pears, unpeeled, cored, and coarsely chopped

1 tablespoon fresh lemon juice

Finely grated zest of 1 orange

$1^1/2$ tablespoons cornstarch

$1/4$ teaspoon ground cinnamon

$1/4$ teaspoon ground cardamom

NUT CRUMB TOPPING

1 cup walnut or pecan halves

$1/3$ cup granulated sugar

$1/3$ cup firmly packed light brown sugar

$3/4$ cup all-purpose flour

$1/4$ teaspoon salt

$1/2$ cup (1 stick) cold unsalted butter, cut into $1/4$-inch pieces

1. If you haven't already, prepare the pastry and refrigerate until firm enough to roll, about 1 hour.

2. On a sheet of lightly floured waxed paper, roll the pastry into a 13-inch circle with a floured rolling pin. Invert the pastry over a $9^1/2$-inch deep-dish pie pan, center, and peel off the paper. Gently tuck the pastry into the pan, without stretching it, and sculpt the edge into a short upstanding ridge. Place in the freezer for 15 minutes.

3. Combine the cranberries and $1/2$ cup of the sugar in a food processor and pulse 5 or 6 times, until the cranberries are well chopped. Transfer to a large bowl and mix in the pears, lemon juice, and orange zest. Mix well and set aside for 20 minutes to juice. Preheat the oven to 400°F.

4. In a small bowl, mix the remaining 1 tablespoon sugar with the cornstarch, cin-

Just Put It There in the Corner, Next to the Flour

Is the thought of all that rolling, mixing, and crimping just too much to handle sometimes? Maybe you ought to consider buying a Colborne Straight Line Pie System, like the big boys use.

Colborne is the largest manufacturer of commercial pie-making equipment in the country. The company's first pie machines were invented by founder Oliver Colborne in the early 1900s. Even he would be impressed by the 9D Colborne sells today. Basically an all-in-one pie maker, the fully automated unit does everything a human pie maker does—shape the dough, roll it, and get it into the pan. It also deposits the filling, crimps the edges, puts on a lattice top (that and the streusel depositor will cost you extra), and delivers the pie to the oven. This to the tune of some 120 to 200 pies *per minute*. All you need is about 50 feet of floor space in your kitchen and about $1.6 million to pay for the machine. Save your pennies, because you also need a 100-foot-long tunnel oven to handle the output.

namon, and cardamom. Add to the fruit and mix well. Turn the filling into the chilled pie shell. Smooth the top with your hands to even it out. Place the pie on the center oven rack and bake for 35 minutes.

5. Meanwhile, make the crumb topping. Put the nuts, sugars, flour, and salt in a food processor and pulse several times to mix. Scatter the butter over the top and pulse until the mixture resembles medium-fine crumbs. Transfer to a large bowl, then rub the crumbs between your fingers to make large, buttery crumbs. Refrigerate until ready to use.

6. Remove the pie from the oven and reduce the temperature to 375°F. Carefully dump the topping in the center of the pie, spreading the crumbs evenly over the surface with your hands. Tamp them down lightly. Return the pie to the oven, placing it so that the part that faced the back of the oven now faces front. Just in case, slide a large aluminum foil–lined baking sheet onto the rack below to catch any spills. Continue to bake until the juices bubble thickly around the edge, 30 to 35 minutes. If necessary, cover with loosely tented aluminum foil during the last 10 to 15 minutes to keep the crumbs from browning too much.

7. Transfer the pie to a wire rack and let cool for at least 1 hour before serving.

Recipe for Success

▶ If you like cranberry pie, do what I do and buy a case of cranberries in the fall, when they're on sale, and freeze them. That way, you can make this and other cranberry pies throughout the year.

Cranberry-Cherry Peekaboo Pie

Here's a fun way to make a see-through pie—by cutting a number of holes in the top crust. If you don't have one, you'll need to pick up a small round cutter between 1 and 1½ inches in diameter. If you're using the larger size, it looks better if you cut in some sort of a regular pattern—perhaps eight holes around the edge, to fall in the center of each slice, with another grouping in the middle. With the smaller cutter, the holes can be more random. In any case, the holes make great little windows to view the deep red filling and give the pie a special folk art feel. Did I mention that this cranberry-cherry filling tastes great? If holes aren't your thing, just use the top crust without the holes.

MAKES 8 TO 10 SERVINGS

1 recipe Basic Flaky Pie Pastry, Double Crust (page 31), Tender Cream Cheese Pastry, Double Crust (page 46), or All-Butter Pie Pastry, Double Crust (page 28), refrigerated

FILLING

3 cups fresh cranberries, picked over for stems

3 cups pitted fresh sweet cherries, fresh or individually frozen (not packed in syrup), partially thawed

1 cup sugar

1 tablespoon fresh lemon or orange juice

Grated zest of 1 orange

2½ tablespoons cornstarch

GLAZE

Milk or light cream

Sugar

1. If you haven't already, prepare the pastry and refrigerate until firm enough to roll, about 1 hour.

2. On a sheet of lightly floured waxed paper, roll the larger portion of the pastry into a 13-inch circle with a floured rolling pin. Invert the pastry over a 9½-inch deep-dish pie pan, center, and peel off the paper. Gently tuck the pastry into the pan, without stretching it, and let the overhang drape over the edge. Place in the refrigerator for 15 minutes.

3. On a separate sheet of floured waxed paper, roll the other half of the pastry into an 11-inch circle. Lift the paper and slide the paper and pastry onto a small baking sheet. Place in the freezer for 15 minutes.

4. In a large bowl, combine the cranberries, cherries, ¾ cup of the sugar, the lemon juice, and orange zest. Mix well and set aside for 15 minutes. Mix the cornstarch and re-

maining ¼ cup sugar together in a small bowl, then stir the mixture into the fruit. Preheat the oven to 400°F.

5.   Remove the top pastry from the freezer. Using a round 1- to 1½-inch cutter, cut a number of holes in the pastry (see headnote), none of them within 1 inch of the edge. Remove the holes (see Recipe for Success), keeping the pastry nearby. Scrape the filling into the chilled pie shell and smooth the top with your hands to even it out. Using a pastry brush, lightly moisten the edge of the pie shell. Invert the top pastry over the filling, center, and slowly and carefully peel off the paper. Press the top and bottom pastries together along the dampened edge. Trim the pastry with scissors or a paring knife, leaving an even ½-inch overhang all around, then sculpt the overhang into an upstanding ridge. Brush the top with a little milk and sprinkle lightly with sugar. Take care not to drag your brush over the exposed fruit, or you'll streak the top pastry.

6.   Place the pie on the center oven rack and bake for 30 minutes. Reduce the oven temperature to 375°F and rotate the pie 180 degrees, so that the part that faced the back of the oven now faces forward. To catch any spills, slide a large aluminum foil–lined baking sheet onto the rack below. Continue to bake until the top crust is dark golden brown and the juices bubble thickly, 30 to 35 minutes.

7.   Transfer the pie to a wire rack and let cool for at least 2 hours before serving.

Recipe for Success

▸   **There are several things you can do with the circles you cut out of the top pastry. You can pack them together, refrigerate, and save for making a small pie (a good option if you have kids who like to bake). Or you can offset them over the holes, so that the holes are partially covered. Put them in place after you've brushed the pastry with milk but before you sprinkle it with sugar. Or you can cut them in half and decorate the edge of the pie with them. If you do this, press the edges of the top and bottom pastries together to seal, then trim flush to the edge without making an upstanding ridge. Crimp the pastries together with a fork, then arrange the half circles, evenly spaced or in any pattern that pleases you, around the edge.**

The Simplest Cranberry-Apple Crumb Pie

One of the magazines I write for frequently is *FamilyFun*, for which I am a contributing editor. (If you have youngsters in the 8- to 12-year-old range, it's a must read.) A while back, one of the editors there asked me to come up with the easiest cranberry-apple pie I could, one that used a store-bought pastry, for the sake of convenience. And it had to have one of those crumb toppings, because, as she put it, "those are so yummy." This is the pie. She loved it, and I hope you will, too.

MAKES 8 TO 10 SERVINGS

1 store-bought refrigerated pie pastry

FILLING

2 cups fresh cranberries, fresh (picked over for stems) or frozen (partially thawed)

2 large apples (any type), peeled, quartered, cored, and thinly sliced crosswise

$2/3$ cup sugar

1 tablespoon fresh lemon juice

$1 1/2$ cups all-purpose flour

CRUMB TOPPING

$1/2$ cup all-purpose flour

$1/2$ cup sugar

$1/4$ teaspoon ground cinnamon

$1/4$ cup ($1/2$ stick) cold unsalted butter, cut into $1/4$-inch pieces

1. Line a 9-inch standard pie pan with the pastry, turning the top edge back and sculpting it into an upstanding ridge. Place in the freezer for 15 minutes. Preheat the oven to 400°F.

2. Put the cranberries in a large bowl and add the apples, stirring to combine. Stir in the sugar, lemon juice, and flour. Set aside for 10 minutes.

3. Scrape the filling into the chilled pie shell and smooth the top with your hands. Bake on the center oven rack for 30 minutes.

4. Meanwhile, make the topping. Combine the flour, sugar, and cinnamon in a medium-size bowl. Add the butter and rub it into the dry ingredients until the mixture resembles coarse crumbs. Refrigerate until ready to use.

5. Remove the pie from the oven and reduce the temperature to 375°F. Sprinkle the topping over the filling and press gently to compact. Return the pie to the oven, placing it so that the part that faced the back of the oven now faces forward. Just in case, slide a large aluminum foil–lined baking sheet onto the rack below to catch any spills. Continue to bake until the topping is golden brown and the juices bubble thickly around the edge, 25 to 30 minutes.

6. Transfer the pie to a wire rack and let cool for at least 1 hour before serving.

Recipe for Success

▶ **For a refresher on pie apples, see pages 232–233.**

▶ **To make this even simpler, use a store-bought frozen pie shell, but keep in mind that it won't hold as much filling. Reduce each filling ingredient by roughly one-quarter.**

Cranberry-Apple-Orange Freeform Pie

Sometimes I get the urge to make a simple pie like this one—no top crust or crumb topping, just a large bottom crust that gets folded up to partially enclose the filling. You can apply this technique to just about any fruit pie with great results. Here's one fall version I'm particularly fond of.

MAKES 8 TO 10 SERVINGS

1 recipe Basic Flaky Pie Pastry, Single Crust (page 31), refrigerated

FILLING

2 cups fresh cranberries, picked over for stems

2/3 cup sugar

3 large Golden Delicious, Northern Spy, Granny Smith, or other firm apples (see pages 232–233 for recommendations), peeled, quartered, cored, and sliced crosswise

1/3 cup orange juice

Grated zest of 1 orange

1/2 teaspoon vanilla extract

3 tablespoons all-purpose flour

1/4 teaspoon ground cinnamon

1. If you haven't already, prepare the pastry and refrigerate until firm enough to roll, about 1 hour.

2. Combine the cranberries and sugar in a food processor and pulse until the cranberries are coarsely chopped. Transfer to a large bowl and add all the remaining filling ingredients, tossing well to combine. Set the mixture aside for 30 minutes. Preheat the oven to 400°F a few minutes before you start to assemble the pie.

3.   On a sheet of lightly floured waxed paper, roll the pastry into a 14-inch circle with a floured rolling pin. The pastry will extend about 1 inch beyond the edge of the paper. Invert the pastry over a 9½-inch deep-dish pie pan, center, and peel off the paper. Gently ease the pastry into the pan, simultaneously lifting up on the edge of the pastry as you tuck it into the pan. Let the pastry drape over the edge. Turn the filling into the pie shell and smooth the top. Fold the overhanging dough up over the filling. The dough will self-pleat as you do this, and you'll have a 3- or 4-inch "window" of exposed filling in the center.

4.   Place the pie on the center oven rack and bake for 30 minutes. Reduce the oven temperature to 375°F and rotate the pie 180 degrees, so that the part that was facing the back of the oven now faces forward. Continue to bake until the juices bubble thickly up through the center of the pie, 30 to 35 minutes.

5.   Transfer the pie to a wire rack and let cool for at least 1 hour before serving.

Recipe for Success

▸ **You can do a couple of fun things with the gap in the center of the pie, where the pastry doesn't cover the filling. The simplest is a mini mountain of Fresh Whipped Cream (page 605), spooned right into the hole. The other is a serious pool of Crème Anglaise (page 606) poured into the hole; this will ooze over the fruit and seep throughout the pie. In either case, let the pie cool considerably, until barely warm, before adding the garnish, so that the heat doesn't destabilize it.**

Jellied Cranberry-Pecan Pie

Fresh cranberries go into a lot of my fall and winter pies. I buy bags of them on sale and store them in the freezer. Dried cranberries are wonderful in pies, too. But did you know that you can also use canned cranberry sauce in pies? It makes a delicious alternative. I call this a jellied pie because the filling—flavored with lemon zest, vanilla, and a splash of maple syrup—has a jelly-like consistency and color, contributed to in part by the cranberry sauce. The pecans give it an additional autumn emphasis and a bit of crunch to boot. Consider this one for your Thanksgiving holiday lineup.

MAKES 8 TO 10 SERVINGS

1 recipe Whole Wheat Pie Pastry, Single Crust (page 33), Lard Pie Pastry, Single Crust (page 36), or Basic Flaky Pie Pastry, Single Crust (page 31), refrigerated

FILLING

1/2 cup firmly packed light brown sugar

3 tablespoons all-purpose flour

1/8 teaspoon ground cinnamon

1/8 teaspoon salt

3 large eggs

1/4 cup (1/2 stick) unsalted butter, melted

1/2 cup light corn syrup

2 tablespoons pure maple syrup or honey

1/2 teaspoon vanilla extract

1 teaspoon grated lemon zest

1 cup chopped pecans

1 cup whole-berry cranberry sauce (see Recipe for Success)

1. If you haven't already, prepare the pastry and refrigerate until firm enough to roll, about 1 hour.

2. On a sheet of lightly floured waxed paper, roll the pastry into a 12-inch circle with a floured rolling pin. Invert the pastry over a 9-inch standard pie pan, center, and peel off the paper. Tuck the pastry into the pan, without stretching it, and sculpt the edge so it is just slightly higher than the rim of the pan. Place in the freezer for 15 minutes, then partially prebake and let cool according to the instructions on page 16. Reduce the oven temperature to 350°F.

3. In a large bowl, combine the brown sugar, flour, cinnamon, and salt. Rub them together well, breaking up any clumps of sugar. Whisk in the eggs, followed by the butter, corn syrup, maple syrup, vanilla, and lemon zest. Stir in the pecans and cranberry sauce. Carefully pour the filling into the cooled pie shell.

4. Place the pie on the center oven rack and bake until the filling is set, 40 to 45 minutes, rotating the pie 180 degrees halfway through the baking, so that the part that faced the back of the oven now faces forward. When done, the filling should not be soupy in the center. Give the pie a little nudge to check.

5. Transfer the pie to a wire rack and let cool to room temperature. Serve immediately, or cover with loosely tented aluminum foil and refrigerate for several hours before serving.

Recipe for Success

▶ Don't measure the cranberry sauce directly from the can because the jellied part tends to settle to the bottom. Empty the entire can into a small bowl, stir well, and then measure it.

Libby's Famous Pumpkin Pie

When I write cookbooks, I don't normally lift recipes right off the box top or can. But when the recipe is as reliable and famous as this one—by rights, the most frequently made pie in America—it's worth adding to a collection as inclusive as this. There are no real tricks or secrets here, just a straightforward approach to making a very pumpkiny pumpkin pie, with a familiar taste and creamy texture. The liquid is evaporated milk, which—because it contains less water than fresh milk—contributes to the smooth texture. It's just a fine recipe all around, and it's reprinted here with the permission of Nestle. Don't use a store-bought frozen pie shell; it's not large enough to hold all of the filling. However, you can use a 9-inch standard pie pan lined with store-bought refrigerated pastry.

MAKES 8 SERVINGS

1 recipe Basic Flaky Pie Pastry, Single Crust (page 31), refrigerated

FILLING

3/4 cup sugar

1/2 teaspoon salt

1 teaspoon ground cinnamon

1/2 teaspoon ground ginger

1/4 teaspoon ground cloves

2 large eggs

One 15-ounce can Libby's 100% Pure Pumpkin

One 12-ounce can Nestlé Carnation evaporated milk

GARNISH

Fresh Whipped Cream (page 605; optional)

1.   If you haven't already, prepare the pastry and refrigerate until firm enough to roll, about 1 hour.

2.   On a sheet of lightly floured waxed paper, roll the pastry into a 12-inch circle with a floured rolling pin. Invert the pastry over a 9-inch standard pie pan, center, and peel off the paper. Tuck the pastry into the pan, without stretching it, and sculpt the edge into an upstanding ridge. Place in the freezer for 15 minutes. Preheat the oven to 425°F.

3.   Combine the sugar, salt, and spices in a small bowl. Beat the eggs in a large bowl. Stir in the pumpkin and sugar-spice mixture. Gradually stir in the evaporated milk. Pour into the chilled pie shell.

4.   Place the pie on the center oven rack and bake for 15 minutes. Reduce the oven temperature to 350°F and rotate the pie 180 degrees, so that the part that was facing the back of the oven now faces forward. Continue to bake until a knife inserted near the center comes out clean, 40 to 50 minutes.

Cranking Out Those Holiday Pies

If you're like me, what comes to the table *after* the Thanksgiving meal is as important as what comes to the table *during* the meal. What comes after, of course, is pie, and no doubt you've experienced times when the demand has put a strain on both your and your kitchen's ability to keep up with the meal and juggle the pies. Here are some suggestions to keep those pies coming.

▶ Remember that nearly all pie pastries freeze well and can be made at least a month ahead of when you'll need them. Take them out of the freezer the day before and thaw in the refrigerator.

▶ Decide on your pie menu a week ahead and check your supply of staples. Buy plenty, knowing that you'll need extra flour, sugar, vanilla, butter, and the like in the weeks to come. Overlooked ingredients will try your patience and tax your time with extra trips to the grocery store.

▶ To save time, compartmentalize your movements. Don't make one pastry, then the filling, then the pastry for the next pie. Make all the pastry you need, plus an extra portion for good measure.

▶ To avoid oven congestion on Thanksgiving Day, bake your pies the day before. Unless your oven is very large, avoid baking them more than one at a time, if possible, so that they bake as evenly as possible. Fruit and pumpkin pies—the ones you'll most likely be making—will hold up fine for 24 hours. Pumpkin pies should be refrigerated overnight, but fruit pies will be fine if you simply keep them cool. Protect them well and store them in the cellar, mudroom, or pantry.

▶ Cool or cold fruit pies can be warmed in a low oven for about 20 minutes before serving. This will loosen the juices and take off the cold edge.

5. Transfer the pie to a wire rack and let cool for 2 hours. Serve immediately, or cover with loosely tented aluminum foil and refrigerate before serving. Garnish with whipped cream, if desired.

Recipe for Success

▶ I mentioned above that there is too much filling here for a store-bought frozen pie shell. However, as it mentions on the Libby's label, you can bake 2 shallow pies by dividing the filling between 2 such shells. Bake at 425°F for 15 minutes, then reduce the oven temperature to 350°F and bake for 20 to 30 minutes.

▶ Also from the Libby's can: (1) Do not freeze the pie, as this will cause the crust to separate from the filling. (2) You can substitute $1^3/_4$ teaspoons pumpkin pie spice for the other spices, but the taste will be a little different.

Maple Pumpkin Pie

I've always had to work at loving pumpkin pie. I mean, I like it, but to really love it, I've had to make some special provisions over the years—such as sweetening them with maple syrup, as I do here. The two flavors—pumpkin and maple—seem to have a certain affinity for each other. When I lived in New England, I often made a side dish of mashed pumpkin with a touch of maple syrup for sweetener. It's delicious alongside baked ham and roast chicken. I recommend dark, cooking-grade maple syrup here, because the deep, caramel flavor comes through and flatters the pumpkin. I also use dark brown sugar, as a frugal cook such as myself has a hard time adding a full cup of expensive maple syrup to anything.

MAKES 8 TO 10 SERVINGS

1 recipe Basic Flaky Pie Pastry, Single Crust (page 31), refrigerated

FILLING

3 large eggs

1 cup light cream or half-and-half

$1/2$ cup pure maple syrup, preferably dark

1 teaspoon vanilla extract

$1/2$ cup firmly packed dark brown sugar

$1^1/2$ tablespoons all-purpose flour

1 teaspoon ground ginger

$1/2$ teaspoon ground cinnamon

$1/4$ teaspoon ground cloves

$1/4$ teaspoon ground nutmeg

$3/4$ teaspoon salt

One 15-ounce can or $1^3/4$ cups fresh (see page 286) pumpkin puree

GARNISH

Fresh Whipped Cream (page 605)

1. If you haven't already, prepare the pastry and refrigerate until firm enough to roll, about 1 hour.

2. On a sheet of lightly floured waxed paper, roll the pastry into a 13-inch circle with a floured rolling pin. Invert the pastry over a $9^1/2$-inch deep-dish pie pan, center, and peel off the paper. Tuck the pastry into the pan, without stretching it, and sculpt the edge until it is even with the rim. Place in the freezer for 15 minutes, then partially prebake and let cool according to the instructions on page 16. Reduce the oven temperature to 350°F.

3. Beat the eggs lightly in a medium-size bowl. Whisk in the cream, maple syrup, and vanilla. Combine the brown sugar, flour, spices, and salt in a small bowl. Add the mixture to the wet ingredients and stir well to combine. Add the pumpkin and blend well with a whisk. Carefully pour the filling into the cooled pie shell.

4. Place the pie on the center oven rack and bake for 25 minutes, then rotate the pie 180 degrees, so that the part that was facing the back of the oven now faces forward. Continue to bake until the filling is set, about 25 minutes. When the pie is done, the center will not be soupy. The outer area will have puffed a little, and the edges of the pie will have a slight sheen, although the center portion may not.

5. Transfer the pie to a wire rack and let cool. Serve warm or at room temperature. Or cover with loosely tented aluminum foil and refrigerate until well chilled. Serve garnished with whipped cream.

Recipe for Success

▶ **Do look for the subtle sheen differences on the surface of the pie, as described in step 4. If you can get the pie out of the oven while the center still has a shiny surface, it should be perfectly baked.**

Spiced Pumpkin Indian Pudding Pie

A cross between Indian pudding and pumpkin pie, this has a cornmeal-thickened base that's cooked on the stovetop before being blended with eggs, sugar, pumpkin, and spices. Served warm, it has a pudding-soft consistency. Served cold, it's more like pumpkin pie, with a firmer, custard-like filling. This makes a large pie that will be greeted warmly at any Thanksgiving or holiday dinner.

`MAKES 8 TO 10 SERVINGS`

1 recipe Basic Flaky Pie Pastry, Single Crust (page 31), refrigerated

FILLING

2 cups whole or reduced-fat (2%) milk

1/3 cup fine yellow cornmeal (see Recipe for Success)

1/4 teaspoon salt

2 tablespoons unsalted butter, cut into 1/2-inch pieces

1/2 cup granulated sugar

1/2 cup firmly packed light brown sugar

1 cup pumpkin puree, canned or fresh (see page 286)

1 teaspoon vanilla extract

1/2 teaspoon ground cinnamon

1/2 teaspoon ground ginger

1/2 teaspoon ground nutmeg

1/4 teaspoon ground cloves

3 large eggs, lightly beaten

GARNISH

Fresh Whipped Cream (page 605) or vanilla ice cream

1. If you haven't already, prepare the pastry and refrigerate until firm enough to roll, about 1 hour.

2. On a sheet of lightly floured waxed paper, roll the pastry into a 13-inch circle with a floured rolling pin. Invert the pastry over a $9^1/_2$-inch deep-dish pie pan, center, and peel off the paper. Tuck the pastry into the pan, without stretching it, and sculpt the edge so it is just slightly higher than the rim. Place in the freezer for 15 minutes, then partially pre-bake and let cool according to the instructions on page 16. Increase the oven temperature to 400°F.

3. Combine the milk and cornmeal in a medium-size saucepan and bring to a simmer over medium heat, whisking frequently. Don't let the liquid reach a rapid boil. As the mixture starts to thicken, continue to whisk virtually nonstop until it reaches the consistency of thin hot cereal, 1 to 2 minutes. Transfer to a medium-size bowl and whisk in the salt, butter, and sugars. Let cool for 10 minutes, then whisk in the pumpkin, vanilla, and spices. Add the eggs, whisking to blend. Slowly pour the filling into the cooled pie shell.

4. Place the pie on the center oven rack and bake for 15 minutes, then reduce the oven temperature to 350°F and rotate the pie 180 degrees, so that the part that faced the back of the oven now faces forward. Continue to bake until the filling is set in the center, about 30 minutes. To check the pie, give it a quick little nudge. It should wobble but not seem soupy in the center.

5. Transfer the pie to a wire rack and let cool. Serve barely warm, or let cool to room temperature, cover with loosely tented aluminum foil, and refrigerate before serving. Garnish with a dollop of whipped cream or a scoop of ice cream.

Recipe for Success

- ▶ Be sure to use fine cornmeal here. Coarse-ground cornmeal will not give the pie the same sort of smooth, uniform texture.

- ▶ If you substitute $1/_4$ cup each unsulfured molasses and pure maple syrup for the brown sugar, this will taste even more like Indian pudding.

Ben's Pumpkin Cheesecake Pie

The sort of pumpkin pie I like best tastes more like cheesecake than traditional pumpkin pie. Years ago, finding the texture of pumpkin pie a little too dry for my taste, I started adding cream cheese to my recipes and found the result much to my liking. You can bake this in any pastry, but I like the earthiness of the cornmeal crust here; it's a good match for the pumpkin. If you're pressed for time, you don't have to prebake the pastry, but you'll get a better result if you do, possibly avoiding that slightly underbaked taste. The recipe is named for my oldest son, Ben, whose taste in pumpkin pie runs close to my own.

MAKES 8 TO 10 SERVINGS

1 recipe Cornmeal Pie Pastry, Single Crust (page 40), refrigerated

FILLING

One 8-ounce package full-fat cream cheese, softened

1/2 cup granulated sugar

1/2 cup firmly packed light brown sugar

2 large eggs, at room temperature

1 large egg yolk, at room temperature

1/2 teaspoon vanilla extract

Finely grated zest of 1 lemon

1/2 teaspoon ground cinnamon

1/2 teaspoon ground nutmeg

1/4 teaspoon ground ginger

1/4 teaspoon salt

1 cup pumpkin puree, canned or fresh (see page 286)

2/3 cup light cream or half-and-half

1. If you haven't already, prepare the pastry and refrigerate until firm enough to roll, about 1 hour.

2. On a sheet of lightly floured waxed paper, roll the pastry into a 13-inch circle with a floured rolling pin. Invert the pastry over a 9 1/2-inch deep-dish pie pan, center, and peel off the paper. Tuck the pastry into the pan, without stretching it, and sculpt the edge so it is slightly higher than the rim. Place in the freezer for 15 minutes, then partially prebake and let cool according to the instructions on page 16. Reduce the oven temperature to 350°F.

3. Using an electric mixer, cream the cream cheese, gradually beating in the sugars. Blend in the eggs and egg yolk, one at a time, on medium speed. Blend in the vanilla, lemon zest, spices, and salt. Add the pumpkin and cream and blend until smooth and evenly mixed. Pour the filling into the cooled pie shell and smooth the top.

4.   Place the pie on the center oven rack and bake for 20 minutes. Rotate the pie 180 degrees, so that the part that faced the back of the oven now faces forward. Bake for about 20 minutes more, until the top has puffed slightly and perhaps cracked around the perimeter. The center may seem a little wobbly, but it should not be soupy.

5.   Transfer the pie to a wire rack and let cool to room temperature. Cover with loosely tented aluminum foil and refrigerate for at least 4 hours or overnight before serving.

Recipe for Success

▶   Occasionally, I add a thick chocolate glaze to the top of this pie. It's a delicious touch. Prepare a batch of Warm Mocha Sauce (page 607), then let it cool until thick but still pourable. It will still be slightly warm. Pour most or all of the sauce over the pie, tilting it to spread the sauce evenly. Refrigerate for at least 30 minutes before serving.

Triple-Layer Pumpkin-Chocolate Pie

Now here's a pumpkin pie that will get you rave reviews, at least in part because the slices have such a handsome profile. We begin with a cheesecake-like pumpkin filling, half of which is blended with a good amount of semisweet chocolate. The chocolate portion goes into the shell first, then is briefly baked to stabilize it. The "plain" pumpkin filling goes on top, and the pie is baked some more. The topping is a thin layer of sweetened sour cream. Once cooled, the pie has three colorfully distinct layers and tastes delicious, much to the surprise of those—and there have been a few—whom I've had to assure that chocolate and pumpkin are perfect partners on the dessert plate. Try this; I think you'll like it.

MAKES 10 TO 12 SERVINGS

1 recipe Basic Flaky Pie Pastry, Single Crust (page 31), refrigerated, or Graham Cracker Crumb Crust (page 51), or 1 large store-bought graham cracker crust

FILLING

2 tablespoons unsalted butter

4 ounces semisweet chocolate, coarsely chopped

Four 3-ounce packages full-fat cream cheese, softened

1 1/2 cups sugar

2 large eggs, at room temperature

1 cup pumpkin puree, canned or fresh (see page 286)

1/2 teaspoon vanilla extract

1/4 teaspoon ground cinnamon

1/4 teaspoon ground nutmeg

1/4 teaspoon ground cloves

1/4 teaspoon salt

1 cup full-fat sour cream

1. If you are using the pastry and haven't already prepared it, prepare it now and refrigerate until firm enough to roll, about 1 hour. If you are using the graham cracker crust, prepare the crust and press it into the bottom and up the side of a 9½-inch deep-dish pie pan. Refrigerate, prebake, and let cool as directed. Or simply prebake a store-bought crust as directed on the package and let cool.

2. On a sheet of lightly floured waxed paper, roll the pastry, if using, into a 13-inch circle with a floured rolling pin. Invert the pastry over a 9½-inch deep-dish pie pan, center, and peel off the paper. Tuck the pastry into the pan, without stretching it, and sculpt the edge into an upstanding ridge. Place in the freezer for 15 minutes, then partially prebake and let cool according to the instructions on page 16.

3. Reduce the oven temperature to 350°F. Place the butter in the top of a double boiler set over, not in, barely simmering water. When the butter is partially melted, add the chocolate. Heat for 5 to 7 minutes, until melted, then whisk until smooth. Remove the top of the double boiler and set it aside to partially cool the chocolate.

4. Using an electric mixer, cream the cream cheese on medium speed in a large bowl, gradually adding 1¼ cups of the sugar. Beat in the eggs, one at a time, then blend in the pumpkin, vanilla, spices, and salt until evenly combined. Pour slightly less than half of the filling into a separate bowl and stir in the melted chocolate until evenly blended. Pour the chocolate filling into the cooled pie shell and gently shake the pan to settle the filling.

5. Place the pie on the center oven rack and bake for 20 minutes. Transfer to a wire rack and let cool for 15 minutes.

6. Carefully ladle the remaining plain pumpkin filling over the cooled chocolate layer. Shake the pan gently to settle the filling. Return to the oven, placing the pie so that the part that faced the back of the oven now faces forward. Bake until the pumpkin layer is set, 35 to 40 minutes. When done, the perimeter of the filling will have puffed somewhat but not so much that it develops large cracks.

7. Transfer the pie to a wire rack and let cool until the filling settles down and flattens out, 30 to 45 minutes.

8. Combine the sour cream and remaining ¼ cup sugar in a small saucepan over very low heat and warm, stirring often, for 2 to 4 minutes. When the sour cream is fairly thin—and slightly warmer than body temperature, carefully pour it over the top of the pie. Immediately shake and tilt the pie to cover it with the topping. Return the pie to the rack and let cool thoroughly, then cover with loosely tented aluminum foil and refrigerate for at least 3 hours before serving.

Recipe for Success

▶ The chocolate layer is partially prebaked to maintain its integrity when the plain pumpkin layer is added. The prebaking firms up the chocolate, and the short cooldown allows a slight skin to form, which helps keep the pumpkin layer from sinking into the chocolate. Keep all of this in mind as you're handling the pie. To emphasize the break between layers, you also might sprinkle a fairly dense layer of chopped walnuts or pecans over the chocolate as soon as the pie comes out of the oven, pressing them ever so gently to embed them in the chocolate.

Diane's Pumpkin-Praline Pie

There are pumpkin pies for purists, bereft of fanfare and flourishes. And then there are over-the-top pumpkin pies, for when you want to wow the crowd. This falls into the second category. Indeed, I would say it crowns the category. When I asked Diane Rossen Worthington, a celebrated California cook and cookbook author, if she'd be kind enough to let me include her "most requested" holiday pie in this collection, she quickly gave me the go-ahead. The thick, creamy pumpkin layer would make a great pie on its own, but Diane goes one better— first cooling the pie, then topping it with a brown sugar–pecan praline mixture, which she caramelizes under the broiler. The pie is gorgeous to slice—first carving into the crunchy praline, then the soft pumpkin. Once you've tried it, plain pumpkin pie won't taste the same. Please note that I've made one small change to Diane's spices: I use a little cinnamon and cloves in place of the allspice she prefers.

MAKES 8 TO 10 SERVINGS

1 recipe Basic Flaky Pie Pastry, Single Crust (page 31), refrigerated

FILLING

3 large eggs, at room temperature

$2/3$ cup sugar

One 15-ounce can or $1 3/4$ cups fresh (see page 286) pumpkin puree

$1/4$ cup light cream or half-and-half

$1/2$ teaspoon salt

$1/2$ teaspoon ground ginger

$1/2$ teaspoon ground nutmeg

$1/4$ teaspoon ground cinnamon

$1/4$ teaspoon ground cloves

3 tablespoons bourbon or 1 teaspoon vanilla extract

PRALINE TOPPING

$1 1/4$ cups chopped pecans

$3/4$ cup firmly packed light brown sugar

$1/4$ cup ($1/2$ stick) unsalted butter, melted

2 tablespoons heavy or whipping cream

$1/4$ teaspoon ground cinnamon

GARNISH

Fresh Whipped Cream (page 605)

1. If you haven't already, prepare the pastry and refrigerate until firm enough to roll, about 1 hour.

2. On a sheet of lightly floured waxed paper, roll the pastry into a 13-inch circle with a floured rolling pin. Invert the pastry over a $9 1/2$-inch deep-dish pie pan, center, and peel off the paper. Tuck the pastry into the pan, without stretching it, and sculpt the edge into an upstanding ridge. Place in the freezer for 15 minutes, then partially prebake and let cool according to the instructions on page 16. Reduce the oven temperature to 350°F.

3. Combine the eggs and sugar in a large bowl. Using an electric mixer, beat on high speed until light and lemon-colored, about 3 minutes. Add the pumpkin, light cream, salt, spices, and bourbon and blend on low speed until evenly mixed. Pour the filling into the cooled pie shell.

4. Place the pie on the center oven rack and bake for 20 minutes, then rotate the pie 180 degrees, so that the part that faced the back of the oven now faces forward. Continue to bake until the filling is set, 40 to 45 minutes. When done, the perimeter of the pie will have puffed very slightly. Also, the very center will look a little glossy compared to the perimeter, which will have a flatter finish.

Homemade Pumpkin Puree

Most of the time, I reach for canned pumpkin when I want to make a pumpkin pie. Canned gets high grades for both flavor and convenience; it would take one sophisticated palate to tell the difference between canned and fresh pumpkin puree.

Come October, however, many of us get the urge to bake a real pumpkin and make a genuine pumpkin pie from scratch. Here's a simple way to do just that.

Select a small pumpkin of the sort generally referred to as a sugar pie pumpkin. These are smaller than carving pumpkins and have a denser, sweeter flesh. Preheat the oven to 375°F. Wash off the pumpkin, then cut it in half crosswise and scoop out the seeds. (The seeds can be roasted separately, by the way. They make a great snack.) Put about 1/2 cup water in a large roasting pan, then add the pumpkin cut side up or down—it doesn't much matter. Bake until the flesh is very tender when pierced with a paring knife, 45 to 60 minutes. Let the pumpkin cool, then scoop out the flesh and discard the skin. Puree the flesh in a food processor before adding it to your recipe. That's all there is to it.

5. Transfer the pie to a wire rack and let cool completely. The praline can be added once the pie has cooled, or the pie can be covered and refrigerated until you're ready to add the praline. The praline will need to stabilize for at least 10 minutes before serving.

6. When you're ready to add the praline, preheat the broiler. Adjust one of the oven racks so that it is 6 to 8 inches away from the broiler. Combine all the topping ingredients in a medium-size bowl and stir well. Scrape the praline evenly over the pie and smooth with a spoon. Place the pie on a baking sheet and set it under the broiler (see Recipe for Success) until the topping is melted and bubbly. As it bubbles, move the baking sheet a couple of times, changing the position of the pie slightly so that it browns evenly. This entire process may take less than 1 minute—do not walk away from the oven!

7. Transfer to a wire rack and let cool at least 10 minutes. Or let cool thoroughly, cover with loosely tented aluminum foil, and refrigerate. Serve with whipped cream.

Recipe for Success

▸ **Diane says to watch the pie like a hawk when you put it under the broiler, because it can bubble and brown very quickly and take you by surprise. Don't leave the stove area, and do consider leaving the oven door open so that you can both hear what is going on and moderate the intense broiler heat just a little.**

▸ **Diane likes to press some additional pecan halves right into the warm praline as soon as the pie comes out of the oven for a pretty garnish.**

Muirhead Pumpkin Butter and Pecan Pie

I seldom write a recipe around a product that isn't widely available in most supermarkets, but I'm going to make an exception for something called Pecan Pumpkin Butter made by a New Jersey company named Muirhead. (You can find Muirhead online at www.muirheadfoods.com.) Muirhead's pumpkin butter is pureed pumpkin cooked to a thick, delicious paste, then combined with finely chopped pecans, sugar, lemon juice, and spices. It's mainly a spread for biscuits, toast, and English muffins, but after one taste, you'll know why I love it as the base for this creamy, perfectly spiced pie. This is one of my favorite fall desserts.

MAKES 8 TO 10 SERVINGS

1 recipe Basic Flaky Pie Pastry, Single Crust (page 31), refrigerated

FILLING

3 large eggs, at room temperature

One 13.5-ounce jar (about 1 1/3 cups) Muirhead Pecan Pumpkin Butter

1/2 cup heavy or whipping cream

1/4 cup light cream or half-and-half

3 tablespoons sugar

1/4 teaspoon salt

1 1/2 cups coarsely chopped pecans

1. If you haven't already, prepare the pastry and refrigerate until firm enough to roll, about 1 hour.

2. On a sheet of lightly floured waxed paper, roll the pastry into a 12-inch circle with a floured rolling pin. Invert the pastry over a 9-inch standard pie pan, center, and peel off the paper. Tuck the pastry into the pan, without stretching it, and sculpt the edge into an upstanding ridge. Place in the freezer for 15 minutes, then partially prebake and let cool according to the instructions on page 16. Reduce the oven temperature to 350°F.

3. Whisk the eggs in a large bowl just until frothy. Add the pumpkin butter, heavy cream, light cream, sugar, and salt and whisk well to combine. Stir in the pecans, then turn the filling into the cooled pie shell. Using a fork, gently rake through the filling to distribute the nuts evenly.

4. Place the pie on the center oven rack and bake for 25 minutes, then rotate the pie 180 degrees, so that the part that faced the back of the oven now faces forward. Continue to bake until the filling is barely set in the center, 15 to 20 minutes. When done, the edge of the pie may have puffed slightly.

5. Transfer the pie to a wire rack and let cool. The pie can be served slightly warm or at room temperature. Or it can be thoroughly cooled, covered with loosely tented aluminum foil, and refrigerated before serving.

Recipe for Success

▶ **For an even nuttier flavor, toast the pecans in a preheated 350°F oven until fragrant, 7 to 8 minutes, before adding them to the pie.**

▶ **Do not substitute canned pumpkin puree for the pumpkin butter—it will not work.**

Honey Pumpkin-Date Pie with Golden Marshmallow Topping

Here's an over-the-top pumpkin pie that's as fetching as it is delicious. The creamy filling is sweetened with honey and speckled with soft dates. The real treat, though, is the golden marshmallow topping. Just before serving, spread mini marshmallows over the pie, then quickly brown them under the broiler. This is best served chilled, with the warm marshmallows on top, so plan on making the pie the day before you plan to serve it, or very early the same day, then finish it right before serving.

MAKES 10 TO 12 SERVINGS

1 recipe Graham Cracker Crumb Crust (page 51)

FILLING

1¹/4 cups pumpkin puree, canned or fresh (see page 286)

3 large eggs, at room temperature

³/4 cup heavy or whipping cream

¹/2 cup full-fat sour cream

¹/2 cup honey

2 tablespoons unsulfured molasses

1 teaspoon ground ginger

1 teaspoon ground cinnamon

¹/2 teaspoon ground cloves

¹/2 teaspoon ground nutmeg

1 cup soft dates, pitted and cut into bite-size pieces

GOLDEN MARSHMALLOW TOPPING

2 to 2¹/2 cups mini marshmallows

1. Prepare the crust and press it into the bottom and up the side of a 9¹/2-inch deep-dish pie pan. Refrigerate, prebake, and let cool as directed. Increase the oven temperature to 400°F.

Those First Pumpkin Pies

From a multitude of sources, we know that the earliest settlers learned to make pumpkin "pie" from the Native Americans. It wasn't pumpkin pie as we know it today. The filling would have likely been a primitive medley of bread pieces, nuts, honey, and, in time, milk and spices, tucked in a hollowed-out pumpkin and baked over ashes. If all this sounds austere, it must have tasted heavenly to families struggling for survival.

According to Waverly Root and Richard de Rochemont in their book *Eating in America* (William Morrow, 1976), the first American cookbook to contain a recipe for "pumpkin" pie was Amelia Simmons's *American Cookery*, published in 1796. Credited as being the first true American cookbook, it became something of a bestseller in its day, gaining wide popularity through a number of editions.

2. In a large bowl, combine the pumpkin, eggs, heavy cream, sour cream, honey, and molasses. Using an electric mixer, blend briefly on medium-low speed until evenly mixed. Blend in the spices, then stir in the dates. Slowly pour the filling into the cooled pie shell, raking the dates with a fork to distribute them evenly.

3. Place the pie on the center oven rack and bake for 20 minutes. Reduce the oven temperature to 325°F and rotate the pie 180 degrees, so that the part that faced the back of the oven now faces forward. Continue to bake until the filling is set but still somewhat jiggly in the center, 25 to 30 minutes.

4. Transfer the pie to a wire rack and let cool thoroughly, then cover with loosely tented aluminum foil and refrigerate for at least 3 hours or overnight.

5. When you're ready to serve the pie, preheat the broiler. Spread the marshmallows evenly over the top of the pie in a single, tightly packed layer. Slide the pie onto a rack under the broiler and lightly brown the marshmallows. Keep a close eye on the pie; the marshmallows will brown quickly (see Recipe for Success). Slice and serve right away.

Recipe for Success

▶ Given the richness of this pie, the dramatic topping, and the near imperative that it be eaten right out of the oven, think of it as one you'd prepare for a crowd. Obviously, Thanksgiving is a good occasion. This does, incidentally, reheat nicely. Just put the pie in a hot oven for 3 to 4 minutes, and the marshmallows will be crisp on the outside and soft on the inside.

▶ The marshmallows will go from golden to gone in seconds. Don't even close the oven door when you're browning them, and position the oven rack at a comfortable distance from the broiler.

Five-Spice Winter Squash Pie

For the most part, winter squash and pumpkin can be used interchangeably in pies. That said, there are a few differences. I find most cooked winter squash to be a little drier than pumpkin. The color is a paler orange, and the flavor is milder, too. One advantage of squash over pumpkin is that a squash is a little smaller and easier to cut and handle, and therefore easier to bake. Of course, none of this makes much difference if you're using canned squash. But given the quality and availability of winter squash in the fall, it's fun—once in a while—to bake your own and turn it into a pie. My favorite version of squash pie contains a good amount of Chinese five-spice powder, which is a little like pumpkin pie spice with ground star anise added. It lends the pie a warming and festive flavor and makes this a good candidate for a Thanksgiving dessert.

MAKES 8 TO 10 SERVINGS

1 recipe Basic Flaky Pie Pastry, Single Crust (page 31) or Whole Wheat Pie Pastry, Single Crust (page 33), refrigerated

FILLING

1 large butternut squash, 2 large delicata squash, or one 15-ounce can squash puree

1 cup firmly packed light brown sugar

3 large eggs, at room temperature

3/4 cup light cream or half-and-half, at room temperature

2 teaspoons Chinese five-spice powder

1/4 teaspoon salt

1 tablespoon all-purpose flour

1 teaspoon vanilla extract

GARNISH

Fresh Whipped Cream (page 605)

1. Before you prepare the pastry, if you're using fresh squash, preheat the oven to 400°F. Cut off a little of the stem end of the squash and halve it lengthwise. Scoop the seeds out of the cavity. Place the squash flat side down in a large, shallow oiled casserole and add just enough water to cover the bottom. Cover loosely with aluminum foil and bake for about 50 minutes. Remove the foil and continue to bake until the squash is very tender (test it with a paring knife), about 10 minutes. Transfer the squash to a plate and let cool.

2. If you haven't already, prepare the pastry and refrigerate until firm enough to roll, about 1 hour.

3. On a sheet of lightly floured waxed paper, roll the pastry into a 13-inch circle with a floured rolling pin. Invert the pastry over a 9 1/2-inch deep-dish pie pan, center, and peel off the paper. Gently tuck the pastry into the pan, without stretching it, and sculpt the edge so it is just slightly higher than the rim. Place in the freezer for 15 minutes, then partially prebake and let cool according to the instructions on page 16. Reduce the oven temperature to 350°F.

4. When the squash is cool enough to handle, spoon $1^3/_4$ cups firmly packed flesh out of the skin and put it (or the canned puree) in a food processor with the brown sugar. Process briefly, until smooth. Add the eggs, light cream, five-spice powder, salt, flour, and vanilla and process briefly. Slowly pour the filling into the cooled pie shell.

5. Place the pie on the center oven rack and bake for about 50 minutes, rotating the pie 180 degrees halfway through the baking, so that the part that faced the back of the oven now faces forward. When done, the perimeter of the pie will be somewhat risen and puffy, though not so much that it develops large cracks. The filling will be set and generally have a flat finish, although the center may be shiny.

6. Transfer the pie to a wire rack and let cool. Serve slightly warm or at room temperature. Or cover with loosely tented aluminum foil, refrigerate, and serve cold. Garnish with a dollop of whipped cream.

Recipe for Success

▶ **You'll end up with a creamier pie if you don't bake the squash in too much water. That's why I recommend using just a little water in the pan, then removing the foil when the squash is almost done, so that any excess water evaporates. If you use more water, the squash will soak it up, and your pie will be watery and not as creamy.**

Traditional Sweet Potato Pie

Sweet potato pie may not be the national icon that pumpkin pie is, but it has much to recommend it. Like pumpkins, the meaty texture of sweet potatoes makes for a wonderfully dense filling with a creamy consistency. The flavor is unique and sweet, and the color is similarly lovely. To help keep this recipe distinct from those for pumpkin pie, I don't repeat all the traditional pumpkin pie spices, but rather limit the spices here to cinnamon and nutmeg.

MAKES 8 TO 10 SERVINGS

1 recipe Basic Flaky Pie Pastry, Single Crust (page 31), refrigerated

FILLING

2 large sweet potatoes

1/3 cup granulated sugar

1/3 cup firmly packed light brown sugar

2 large eggs

1 large egg yolk

1 cup light cream or half-and-half

1 teaspoon vanilla extract

1 teaspoon fresh lemon juice

1/2 teaspoon ground cinnamon

1/2 teaspoon ground nutmeg

Scant 1/2 teaspoon salt

1. If you haven't already, prepare the pastry and refrigerate until firm enough to roll, about 1 hour.

2. Meanwhile, bake the sweet potatoes. Preheat the oven to 400°F. Put the sweet potatoes on a large baking sheet. Pierce them deeply with a paring knife several times. Bake until tender throughout (check with a paring knife), about 1 hour. Set aside to cool. When cool enough to handle, scoop the flesh into a food processor and process until smooth. Dump the puree into a medium-size bowl. Return 1½ cups of the puree to the food processor. Don't worry if you come up a little short. If you have extra, save it for another use.

3. On a sheet of lightly floured waxed paper, roll the pastry into a 12-inch circle with a floured rolling pin. Invert the pastry over a 9-inch standard pie pan, center, and peel off the paper. Tuck the pastry into the pan, without stretching it, and sculpt the edge into an upstanding ridge. Place in the freezer for 15 minutes, then partially prebake and let cool according to the directions on page 16. Reduce the oven temperature to 350°F.

4. Add the sugars, eggs, and egg yolk to the food processor and process with the sweet potato puree until smooth. Add the cream, vanilla, lemon juice, cinnamon, nutmeg, and salt and process again until smooth. Carefully pour the filling into the cooled pie shell.

5. Place the pie on the center oven rack and bake for 30 minutes, then rotate the pie 180 degrees, so that the part that faced the back of the oven now faces forward. Continue to bake until the center is set and the edge has risen slightly, 15 to 20 minutes.

6. Transfer the pie to a wire rack and let cool. Serve barely warm or at room temperature. Or cover with loosely tented aluminum foil, refrigerate, and serve cold.

Recipe for Success

▸ Since you're baking sweet potatoes anyway, why not bake a couple of extras and use them to thicken soups or stews or for making muffins or quick breads. Or simply serve them mashed, as a side dish. Consult a general cookbook such as *Joy of Cooking* for recipes and serving ideas.

▸ To keep the color of the pie as bright as possible, use $^2/_3$ cup granulated sugar and leave out the brown sugar.

▸ Remember that this is essentially a custard pie, and, like other custard pies, it will turn watery if overbaked. Keep a close eye on it during the last 15 minutes of baking and remove it from the oven as soon as it is done.

Pass a Slice of That Sweet Potato Pie, Lover Boy

"In the case of the sweet potato, it is probable that its honeyed taste helped it to achieve quick popularity in Europe and America. When it first reached Europe, imported at the beginning of the sixteenth century by the Spaniards, who named it *batata*, it was endowed, quite gratuitously, with the reputation of being an aphrodisiac. For this or other reasons, it appealed to Henry VIII, who imported sweet potatoes from Spain and ate them in the form of pies, very sweet and heavily spiced; by the end of the sixteenth century many of his subjects were following suit."

—Waverly Root and Richard de Rochemont, *Eating in America* (William Morrow, 1976)

Fancy Sweet Potato Pie

Sweet potato pie, a southern specialty, has been an American tradition for more than 100 years. Like pumpkin pie, sweet potato pie tends to have a meaty, firm-bodied texture, although the flavor is somewhat more delicate and elusive than pumpkin, and it has a lighter orange hue. Pie makers reach into their pumpkin pie bag of tricks to nudge a sweet potato pie toward greatness. The same pumpkin pie spices make the rounds in sweet potato pies, as well as eggs, milk or cream, and a good measure of sweetener in the form of molasses, brown sugar, or even maple syrup. Our fancy version is a little light on the spices, but we include orange zest—a festive touch—and an optional splash of hazelnut or almond liqueur, to give this earthy pie an appropriately nutty flavor. I think it's best served cold, but it's also very good warm.

MAKES 8 TO 10 SERVINGS

1 recipe Basic Flaky Pie Pastry, Single Crust (page 31), refrigerated

FILLING

2 medium-large sweet potatoes

1/2 cup granulated sugar

1/2 cup firmly packed light brown sugar

3 tablespoons unsalted butter, melted

1/4 teaspoon ground nutmeg

1/4 teaspoon ground cloves

1/4 teaspoon ground cinnamon

Scant 1/2 teaspoon salt

2 large eggs

1 large egg yolk

Grated zest of 1 orange

2 tablespoons hazelnut or almond liqueur (optional)

1 cup light cream or half-and-half

GARNISH

Fresh Whipped Cream (page 605)

1.   If you haven't already, prepare the pastry and refrigerate until firm enough to roll, about 1 hour.

2.   On a sheet of lightly floured waxed paper, roll the pastry into a 13-inch circle with a floured rolling pin. Invert the pastry over a 9½-inch deep-dish pie pan, center, and peel off the paper. Tuck the pastry into the pan, without stretching it, and let the overhang drape over the edge. Trim the pastry flush with the outside edge of the pan, then crimp the edge with the tines of a fork. Place in the freezer for 15 minutes, then partially pre-bake and let cool according to the instructions on page 16. Leave the oven on.

3. Put the sweet potatoes on a large baking sheet. Pierce them deeply with a paring knife several times. Bake until tender to the center (check with a paring knife), about 1 hour. Set aside for 10 to 15 minutes to cool. Reduce the oven temperature to 350°F.

4. Spoon the sweet potato flesh into a liquid measuring cup, measuring out 2½ cups. (Don't worry if you're a little over or under.) Place in a food processor, add the sugars and butter, and process until smooth. Add the spices, salt, eggs, egg yolk, and orange zest. Process until combined. Add the liqueur, if using, and light cream. Process until smooth. Pour the filling into the cooled pie shell and smooth the top with a spoon.

5. Place the pie on the center oven rack and bake for 45 to 50 minutes, rotating the pie 180 degrees halfway through the baking, so that the part that faced the back of the oven now faces forward. When done, the filling should have puffed and cracked slightly around the perimeter. The center may wobble slightly, but it should still seem set. The center may look shiny, but the edge will have a flat finish.

6. Transfer the pie to a wire rack and let cool. Serve barely warm or at room temperature. Or cover with loosely tented aluminum foil, refrigerate, and serve cold. Garnish with whipped cream.

Recipe for Success

▶ **In my sweet potato pie trials, I both boiled and baked the potatoes and found that I prefer the results when baked. Baking takes longer, but it seems to concentrate the flavor without adding excess moisture to the pie. You get a creamier, fuller-bodied pie when the moisture comes from the cream and eggs. If you like, you can accelerate the pie-making process by baking the sweet potatoes the day before—perhaps when you have something else in the oven. Refrigerate them after they have cooled.**

Carrot Custard Pie

If you think carrot pie sounds like a gimmick, not so fast: sweet carrots are every bit as delicious as pumpkin in a pie. I take the light approach here, using enough carrots to give the pie an unmistakable flavor, but not so many that it tastes like a contest to include as much of the vegetable as possible. This lighter hand, I find, makes this much more inviting as a dessert pie. Serve this delicious, creamy pie for Thanksgiving or anytime you can get your hands on good fresh carrots.

MAKES 8 TO 10 SERVINGS

1 recipe Basic Flaky Pie Pastry, Single Crust (page 31), refrigerated

FILLING

1 1/2 cups peeled and thinly sliced carrots

1/2 cup granulated sugar

1/2 cup firmly packed light brown sugar

2 large eggs

1 large egg yolk

3/4 cup light cream or half-and-half

1/2 cup heavy or whipping cream

1/2 teaspoon vanilla extract

1/2 teaspoon ground ginger

1/8 teaspoon ground nutmeg

1/8 teaspoon salt

1. If you haven't already, prepare the pastry and refrigerate until firm enough to roll, about 1 hour.

2. On a sheet of lightly floured waxed paper, roll the pastry into a 12-inch circle with a floured rolling pin. Invert the pastry over a 9-inch standard pie pan, center, and peel off the paper. Tuck the pastry into the pan, without stretching it, and sculpt the edge so it is just slightly higher than the rim. Place in the freezer for 15 minutes, then partially prebake and let cool according to the instructions on page 16. Reduce the oven temperature to 350°F.

3. Put the carrots in a saucepan with enough lightly salted water to cover generously. Bring to a boil, then continue to boil until the carrots are very soft, 10 to 15 minutes. Drain and then let cool for 10 minutes.

4. Combine the carrots and sugars in a food processor and process until smooth. Add the eggs and egg yolk and process again until smooth. Scrape the mixture into a large bowl and whisk in the light cream, heavy cream, vanilla, ginger, nutmeg, and salt. Carefully pour the filling into the cooled pie shell.

5. Place the pie on the center oven rack and bake for 30 minutes, then rotate the pie 180 degrees, so that the part that faced the back of the oven now faces forward. Continue to bake until the filling is set and the edge has risen slightly, 20 to 25 minutes. When done, the center of the pie should not be soupy; a little wobbly is fine. Give the pie a little nudge to check. The filling should shake, not move in waves.

6. Transfer the pie to a wire rack and let cool to room temperature. Cover with loosely tented aluminum foil and refrigerate for several hours before serving.

Recipe for Success

▶ Buy the sweetest, freshest carrots you can get. Late-summer, freshly dug carrots are the best and will make the sweetest, most flavorful pie.

▶ This pie tastes very nice with a honey or maple syrup accent. Substitute either for the brown sugar in equal measure.

▶ As with any custard pie, take special care not to overbake the pie or the filling will become watery. At the very first indication that the center is set, remove the pie from the oven.

Spiced Parsnip Pie

This will not be everyone's idea of a dream pie, but some people—including gardeners and hearty country folk—may find it very appealing. To give the idea a context, think of pumpkin pie, but replace the pumpkin flavor with the sweetness of parsnips. To be sure, parsnips have a very dense, meaty texture, so it takes a bit of finesse to elevate them to sweet pie status. In plain English, that means plenty of sugar, spices, and light cream. These are blended with the pureed parsnips and a dash of vanilla, then poured into a large pie shell and baked to a turn. Think of this pie around the holidays, but don't rule it out in the spring either. Gardeners know that spring-dug parsnips are always the sweetest and best-tasting.

MAKES 10 TO 12 SERVINGS

1 recipe Extra-Flaky Pie Pastry, Single Crust (page 34) or Basic Shortening Pie Pastry, Single Crust (page 30), refrigerated

FILLING

4 cups trimmed, peeled, and coarsely chopped parsnips (about 1³/₄ pounds)

1¹/₄ cups light cream or half-and-half

3 large eggs

1 cup firmly packed light brown sugar

¹/₃ cup granulated sugar

¹/₄ cup (¹/₂ stick) unsalted butter, melted

1 tablespoon fresh lemon juice

2 teaspoons grated lemon zest

1 teaspoon ground cinnamon

¹/₂ teaspoon ground cloves

¹/₂ teaspoon ground nutmeg

¹/₂ teaspoon ground ginger

³/₄ teaspoon salt

1 teaspoon vanilla extract

GARNISH

Fresh Whipped Cream (page 605)

1. If you haven't already, prepare the pastry and refrigerate until firm enough to roll, about 1 hour.

2. On a sheet of lightly floured waxed paper, roll the pastry into a 13-inch circle with a floured rolling pin. Invert the pastry over a 9¹/₂-inch deep-dish pie pan, center, and peel off the paper. Gently tuck the pastry into the pan, without stretching it, and sculpt the overhang into an upstanding ridge. Place in the freezer for 15 minutes, then partially pre-bake and let cool according to the directions on page 16.

3. Put the parsnips in a large saucepan with just enough lightly salted water to cover. Bring to a boil, then continue to boil gently until tender, 12 to 18 minutes. Test a large chunk with a paring knife to be sure they are done. Drain in a colander and let cool for 10 minutes.

4. Combine the parsnips and light cream in a food processor and process until smooth. Add the eggs, sugars, butter, lemon juice, and lemon zest and process until smooth. Add the spices, salt, and vanilla and process again until smooth. Set aside, leaving the filling in the processor bowl. Preheat the oven to 375°F.

5. Process the filling for several seconds to mix, then pour into the cooled pie shell, smoothing the top with a spoon. Place on the center oven rack and bake for 30 minutes. Reduce the oven temperature to 350°F and rotate the pie 180 degrees, so that the part that faced the back of the oven now faces forward. Continue to bake until the edges have puffed and started to crack, 20 to 25 minutes. When done, the center of the pie will be firmly set.

Hold a Pie Auction

In these days of downsizing and slashed budgets, you have to be creative to fund a new school library, much-needed fire truck, or other worthy cause. In towns from Maine to California, citizens are turning to old-fashioned pie auctions as a source of income. Lest you think we're talking chump change here, think again: a pie auction can raise hundreds or even thousands of dollars for your pet project.

The idea is pretty simple. Participating bakers are asked to donate one or more of their best home-made pies. There's usually an entry fee, and often the pies are judged for appearance by a special panel and prizes are awarded. That same day, the pies are auctioned off at a special event. Looks are important: the best-looking pies often garner the biggest bucks. Pies baked by local celebrities, such as the mayor, usually do well, too.

Those in the know have some advice for would-be pie auctioneers. First, find a good auctioneer—a fast talker who has a sense of humor and can cajole the crowd into parting with their hard-earned dollars.

Second, encourage contestants to think beyond apple. A variety of attractive pies yields the best results.

And third, get the word out. Send out press releases and pie recipes, put up posters—anything to ensure a successful event.

6. Transfer the pie to a wire rack and let cool. Serve slightly warm, at room temperature, or—my favorite way—slightly chilled. Garnish with whipped cream.

Recipe for Success

▶ Judith and Evan Jones, in their informative *The L.L. Bean Book of* New *New England Cooking* (Random House, 1987), have a wonderful recipe for a parsnip pie sweetened with maple syrup, which would work well in this version. If you'd like to try it, substitute up to $1/2$ cup pure maple syrup for an equal amount of the brown sugar.

▶ This may look done—and appear set in the center—after just 30 minutes. Nonetheless, continue to bake the pie as directed for an additional 20 to 25 minutes.

Green Tomato–Mincemeat Pie

As a former New Englander, I know that green tomatoes aren't only a bittersweet harbinger of fall; they're also prime pie pickings. Indeed, no New Englander, or frugal home gardener anywhere, for that matter, would let a handful of not-gonna-ripen green tomatoes rot on the vine—not when there are delicious pies like this to be made. If you have doubts about cooking with green tomatoes, one bite of this pie will banish them forever. This is sweet-tart and spicy and tastes nothing like raw green tomatoes. In fact, about the only thing I can compare it to is mincemeat—thus the pie's name. It's perfect for all your fall get-togethers, including tailgate parties, and goes great with hot or cold apple cider.

MAKES 8 TO 10 SERVINGS

1 recipe Cornmeal Pie Pastry, Double Crust (page 40) or other double-crust pie pastry, refrigerated

FILLING

4 cups quartered, cored, seeded, and very thinly sliced green tomatoes

1/2 cup dark raisins

1/2 cup chopped walnuts or pecans

1/2 cup chopped pitted dates

1/3 cup granulated sugar

1/3 cup firmly packed light brown sugar

1/4 cup cider vinegar

3 tablespoons all-purpose flour

1/2 teaspoon ground cinnamon

1/2 teaspoon ground ginger

1/2 teaspoon ground cloves

Scant 1/2 teaspoon salt

1 teaspoon grated lemon zest

2 tablespoons cold unsalted butter, cut into small pieces

GLAZE

Milk or light cream

Sugar

1. If you haven't already, prepare the pastry and refrigerate until firm enough to roll, about 1 hour.

2. On a sheet of lightly floured waxed paper, roll the larger half of the pastry into a 13-inch circle with a floured rolling pin. Invert over a 9 1/2-inch deep-dish pie pan, center, and peel off the paper. Tuck the pastry into the pan, without stretching it, and let the overhang drape over the edge. Place in the refrigerator for 15 minutes.

3. In a large bowl, combine the tomatoes, raisins, nuts, dates, and sugars and mix well. Add the vinegar, flour, spices, salt, and lemon zest and mix again. Set aside for 10 minutes. Preheat the oven to 400°F.

4. Roll the other half of the pastry into an 11-inch circle on a sheet of lightly floured waxed paper. Turn the filling into the chilled pie shell, smoothing the top with your hands or a spoon. Dot the filling with the butter. Lightly moisten the rim of the shell. Invert the top pastry over the filling, center, and peel off the paper. Press the top and bottom pastries together along the dampened edge. Using the back of a paring knife, trim the pastry flush with the edge of the pan and crimp the edge with a fork. (Or don't trim the pastry and sculpt the edge into an upstanding ridge.) Poke several steam vents in the top of the pie with a fork or paring knife. Put a couple of the vents near the edge of the crust so you can check the juices there later. To glaze the pie, lightly brush the pastry with milk and sprinkle with sugar.

5. Place the pie on the center oven rack and bake for 30 minutes. Reduce the oven temperature to 375°F and rotate the pie 180 degrees, so that the part that faced the back of the oven now faces forward. Just in case, slide a large aluminum foil–lined baking sheet onto the rack below to catch any spills. Continue to bake until the top is golden brown and any visible juices bubble thickly through the steam vents, no more than 25 to 30 minutes.

6. Transfer the pie to a wire rack and let cool for at least 1 hour. Serve warm or at room temperature.

Recipe for Success

▸ **Green tomatoes can seem so rock hard that you may wonder if they'll ever soften as they bake. They will. Just slice them as thinly as possible, and they'll be fine.**

▸ **Some green tomatoes will have a few red spots on them, indicating the first signs of ripening. That's fine.**

▸ **Another test worth mentioning is to insert a sharp paring knife through the top crust in several places and down into the tomatoes to check for tenderness. When the pie is done, the tomatoes will offer little or no resistance.**

Green Tomato–Cranberry Pie with Cornmeal Crumb Topping

Given the prevalence of green tomatoes and maple syrup in New England, pies like this aren't really all that unusual in the region, although this one, with its cornmeal crumb topping, is perhaps more unusual than most. The dried cranberries are a pleasant surprise, as is the Chinese five-spice powder.

MAKES 8 TO 10 SERVINGS

1 recipe Basic Shortening Pie Pastry, Single Crust (page 30) or Basic Flaky Pie Pastry, Single Crust (page 31), refrigerated

FILLING

4 1/2 cups quartered, cored, seeded, and very thinly sliced green tomatoes

1/2 cup sweetened dried cranberries (sold as Craisins)

1/3 cup firmly packed light brown sugar

1/3 cup pure maple syrup

2 tablespoons fresh lemon juice

1 tablespoon cider vinegar

1 teaspoon Chinese five-spice powder

Scant 1/2 teaspoon salt

3 tablespoons all-purpose flour

CORNMEAL CRUMB TOPPING

1/3 cup all-purpose flour

1/4 cup fine yellow cornmeal

1/2 cup sugar

1/4 teaspoon ground cinnamon

1/4 teaspoon salt

1/4 cup (1/2 stick) cold unsalted butter, cut into 1/4-inch pieces

1.   If you haven't already, prepare the pastry and refrigerate until firm enough to roll, about 1 hour.

2.   On a sheet of lightly floured waxed paper, roll the pastry into a 12-inch circle with a floured rolling pin. Invert over a 9-inch standard pie pan, center, and peel off the paper. Gently tuck the pastry into the pan, without stretching it, and sculpt the overhang into an upstanding ridge. Place in the freezer for 15 minutes. Preheat the oven to 400°F

3.   In a large bowl, combine the green tomatoes, cranberries, brown sugar, maple syrup, lemon juice, and vinegar and mix well. Stir in the five-spice powder, salt, and flour. Turn the filling into the chilled pie shell, smoothing the top with your hands. Bake on the center oven rack for 30 minutes.

4.   Meanwhile, make the topping. In a food processor, combine the flour, cornmeal, sugar, cinnamon, and salt and pulse several times to mix. Scatter the butter over the top and

pulse until the mixture resembles fine crumbs. Empty the crumbs into a large bowl and rub them between your fingers to make large, buttery crumbs. Refrigerate until ready to use.

5. Reduce the oven temperature to 375°F, loosely drape a piece of aluminum foil over the pie, and bake for 10 minutes.

6. Remove the pie from the oven and spread the crumb topping over the pie. Tamp down lightly to compact the crumbs. Return the pie to the oven, placing it so that the part that faced the back of the oven now faces forward. Just in case, slide a large aluminum foil–lined baking sheet onto the rack below to catch any spills. Continue to bake until the topping is golden brown and the juices bubble thickly around the edge, 23 to 25 minutes.

7. Transfer the pie to a wire rack and let cool. Serve just slightly warm or at room temperature.

Recipe for Success

▶ For a filling with a more mincemeat-like texture, you can chop the tomatoes coarsely after you slice them.

▶ If you don't have any Chinese five-spice powder but you'd like to make the pie with ingredients on hand, substitute the spices used in Green Tomato–Mincemeat Pie (page 300).

▶ Another way you can do this is to use Cornmeal Pie Pastry (page 40) and make a double-crust pie.

Crock-Pot Fall Fruit Pie

Like a lot of cooks I know, I like my slow cooker. I may not use it as often as some, but once or twice a month, I unload all the odd utensils I store in it and make a mean stew or brisket. A while ago, I ran across an unlikely recipe for a Crock-Pot apple pie. I was, of course, a little incredulous: how could you make a pie, which requires dry heat, in a slow cooker, which is essentially a steamer? Turns out the result is pretty darn good—not really a pie in the traditional sense, with a crisp-dry crust and separate filling, but more of an apple pudding, with a moist top and bottom "crust." Indeed, it was good enough, and certainly interesting enough, to adapt and turn into a fall fruit pie, made with apples, pears, and cranberries. I think you'll like it very much. You have two options: prepare it late the night before for breakfast or make it in the morning for dinner.

MAKES 8 TO 10 SERVINGS

4 cups peeled, cored, and sliced Golden Delicious, Granny Smith, Northern Spy, Jonagold, or Gravenstein apples

3 cups peeled, cored, and sliced ripe pears

1 cup fresh cranberries, picked over for stems

1 teaspoon ground cinnamon

1/4 teaspoon ground cardamom

1/4 teaspoon ground nutmeg

1/8 teaspoon salt

1 1/2 cups baking mix (such as Bisquick)

3/4 cup whole or reduced-fat (2%) milk

3/4 cup granulated sugar

2 large eggs

3 tablespoons unsalted butter, softened

1/2 teaspoon vanilla extract

1/3 cup firmly packed light brown sugar

3 tablespoons cold unsalted butter, cut into 1/4-inch pieces

GARNISH

Fresh Whipped Cream (page 605) or cold light cream or half-and-half (optional)

1. Lightly butter or grease a 5- to 6-quart slow cooker. Add the apples, pears, and cranberries. Sprinkle the spices and salt over the fruit. Toss well to combine.

2. In a large bowl, combine 1/2 cup of the baking mix, the milk, granulated sugar, eggs, softened butter, and vanilla. Mix well, then pour over the apples.

3. In another bowl, combine the remaining 1 cup baking mix and the brown sugar. Add the cold butter and rub the mixture between your fingers until crumbly. Sprinkle evenly over the fruit.

4. Cover and cook on the low setting for 7 hours. When done, the fruit will be quite soft.

5. Unplug the pot and let cool for about 30 minutes. If you can't wait that long, cool briefly in individual bowls. Serve with whipped cream or light cream, if desired.

Recipe for Success

▸ A few options to consider: (1) Use equal amounts of apples and pears and leave out the cranberries. (2) Add a handful of raisins, chopped dried figs, apricots, or other dried fruit. (3) Use sweetened dried cranberries (sold as Craisins) instead of fresh.

▸ With such prolonged cooking, don't expect the apples and pears to hold their shape all that well, no matter what kind you use. They'll likely be quite soft, maybe even mushy, when the pie is finished cooking.

Splenda Fall Fruit and Cherry Pie

Quite often when I'm giving a pie-baking demonstration, someone will ask me about sugar-free pies and pies that diabetics can eat. Diabetic cooking isn't, frankly, something I'm well versed in, but I've learned—usually from diabetics in the crowd—what sweetener they like. Splenda comes up frequently. It tastes like sugar, because it's made from sugar, but it is then converted into a sweet, granular, sugar-like product that's fine to use in a diabetic diet. In pie fillings and other baking, you can substitute Splenda measure for measure for sugar, and the results are impressive. I've made a number of pies with it, and all have been delicious. Here's one I particularly like. Use fresh pears and apples but frozen cherries.

MAKES 8 TO 10 SERVINGS

1 recipe Basic Flaky Pie Pastry, Double Crust (page 31), modified as instructed in step 1 and refrigerated

FILLING

4 cups peeled, cored, and sliced Granny Smith, Northern Spy, or other tart apples

3 cups peeled, cored, and sliced ripe fresh pears

1 cup individually frozen pitted sweet cherries (not packed in syrup), partially thawed

1/2 cup Splenda sugar substitute

1 tablespoon fresh lemon juice

1 1/2 tablespoons cornstarch

1/4 teaspoon ground cinnamon

1/4 teaspoon ground nutmeg

1.   If you haven't already, prepare the pastry, omitting the sugar. Refrigerate until firm enough to roll, about 1 hour.

2.   On a sheet of lightly floured waxed paper, roll the larger portion of the pastry into a 13-inch circle with a floured rolling pin. Invert over a 9 1/2-inch deep-dish pie pan, center, and peel off the paper. Gently tuck the pastry into the pan, without stretching it, and let the overhang drape over the edge. Place in the refrigerator for 15 minutes.

3.   Combine the fruit, Splenda, and lemon juice in a large bowl and toss well to combine. Set aside for 10 minutes to juice. Stir in the cornstarch, cinnamon, and nutmeg (see Recipe for Success). Preheat the oven to 400°F.

4.   On another sheet of lightly floured waxed paper, roll the other half of the pastry into an 11-inch circle. Turn the filling into the chilled pie shell and smooth the fruit with a spoon. Lightly moisten the rim of the shell. Invert the top pastry over the filling, center, and peel off the paper. Press the top and bottom pastries together along the dampened

edge. Trim the pastry with scissors or a paring knife, leaving an even ½-inch overhang all around, then sculpt the overhang into an upstanding ridge. Poke several steam vents in the top of the pie with a fork or paring knife. Put a couple of the vents near the edge of the crust so you can check the juices there later.

5. Place the pie on the center oven rack and bake for 30 minutes. Reduce the oven temperature to 375°F and rotate the pie 180 degrees, so that the part that faced the back of the oven now faces forward. Just in case, slide a large aluminum foil–lined baking sheet onto the rack below to catch any drips. Bake until the juices bubble thickly at the steam vents and the top is golden brown, 35 to 45 minutes. If the top starts to get too dark, cover it with loosely tented aluminum foil during the last 10 to 15 minutes.

6. Transfer the pie to a wire rack and let cool for at least 2 hours before serving.

Recipe for Success

> ▸ **You've probably noticed that I typically mix the sugar and cornstarch together before adding it to fruit fillings, to get any lumps out of the cornstarch. Here the cornstarch is added separately, so make sure you mix the filling well to eliminate any lumps.**

> ▸ **In large measure, the quality of the fruit you use will determine the flavor score for this pie. If you make it with the best fall apples and pears, it will be as good as any fruit pie you could possibly bake—sugar or not.**

Grape and Fig Pie
page 127

**Watermelon
Chiffon Pie**
page 485

Like Virginia Diner's Peanut Pie
page 346

**Honey Pumpkin-Date Pie
with Golden Marshmallow Topping**
page 288

Classic Lemon Meringue Pie
page 482

**Creamsicle
Ice Cream Pie**
page 549

**Chocolate Brownie
Pecan Pie**
page 333

**All-Peach Pie
with Coconut-Almond
Crumb Topping**
page 85

Pick-Your-Own Triple-Strawberry Cream Pie
page 513

Sugar Pie
(Tarte au Sucre)
page 377

**Lattice-Top
Deep-Dish Sour
Cherry Pie**
page 70

**Sweet Summer
Corn Pie**

page 396

Caramel Apple-Pecan Pie
page 229

**Black Bottom
Chiffon Pie**
page 459

**Dahlia Bakery
Butterscotch Pies**
page 65

**Wild Blueberry–Maple
Pie with a Cornmeal Crust**
page 171

Georgia Orcutt's Thanksgiving Dried Fruit Pie

My friend and occasional editor Georgia Orcutt is into serious pie, so much so that she, her family, and lucky friends spend the Thanksgiving weekend helping themselves to a pie buffet she sets up in the dining room. In her words: "Several days before Thanksgiving, I start making pies with my dear friend Louise. We make 8 to 10, to feed as many people, and have plenty of leftovers for weekend visitors. We set up a pie buffet table with candles and fancy plates and a gorgeous flower arrangement, and eat pie throughout the entire holiday weekend, starting at breakfast."

This pie is a perennial on her table. It's nicknamed "Sally Darr"—a cook, apparently, whose name appeared on the original recipe that inspired Georgia's version. The pie has a thick, solid filling of mixed dried fruit. It's cooked on the stovetop first, with apple cider. Then it's mixed with a little sugar and lemon juice, turned into the pastry, and dotted with butter before being sealed in with the top crust. You'll have no problem getting a good 14 servings out of this one.

MAKES 12 TO 14 SERVINGS

1 recipe Basic Flaky Pie Pastry, Double Crust (page 31), refrigerated

FILLING

2 cups pitted prunes, coarsely chopped

2 cups dried apricots, coarsely chopped

1 cup dried Bing cherries

1/2 cup coarsely chopped dried apple rings

1 1/2 cups apple cider

1 cup chopped walnuts

1/3 cup sugar

1 tablespoon fresh lemon juice

2 to 3 tablespoons cold unsalted butter, cut into small pieces

1. If you haven't already, prepare the pastry and refrigerate until firm enough to roll, about 1 hour.

2. On a sheet of lightly floured waxed paper, roll the larger portion of the pastry into a 13-inch circle with a floured rolling pin. Invert the pastry over a 9 1/2-inch deep-dish pie pan, center, and peel off the paper. Gently tuck the pastry into the pan, without stretching it, and let the overhang drape over the edge. Place in the refrigerator for 15 minutes.

3. Combine the fruit in a large nonreactive saucepan and add the cider. Cover the pan, place over medium heat, and cook, stirring often, until the liquid is absorbed into the fruit, about 10 minutes. Remove from the heat and scrape the mixture into a shallow bowl to cool. When the mixture is nearly cooled, preheat the oven to 375°F.

4. Stir the walnuts, sugar, and lemon juice into the fruit. On another sheet of floured waxed paper, roll the other half of the pastry into an 11-inch circle. Scrape the filling into the chilled pie shell and dot with the butter. Lightly moisten the rim of the pie shell. Invert the top pastry over the filling, center, and peel off the paper. Press the top and bottom pastries together along the dampened edge. Using a pair of scissors, cut the pastry, leaving an even ½-inch overhang all around. Sculpt the edge into an upstanding ridge. Poke several steam vents in the top of the pie with a fork or paring knife.

5. Place on the center oven rack and bake until the top is a rich golden brown, 40 to 45 minutes, rotating the pie 180 degrees halfway through the baking, so that the part that faced the back of the oven now faces forward.

6. Transfer the pie to a wire rack and let cool to room temperature before serving.

Recipe for Success

▸ Georgia says, "The recipe is quite flexible. I've substituted some dried blueberries with success and also have tossed in the remnants of a bag of currants. Just remember to keep the total dried fruit at about 5½ cups."

▸ If your pie filling seems devoid of all liquid after it has cooled, stir an additional 3 to 4 tablespoons cider into it when you add the sugar.

▸ Since there are no eggs to be concerned with or thickener that needs to "take," the best indication of doneness is total elapsed time.

Funeral Pie

Invariably, the name of this pie turns most people off, but I can tell you that the pie itself is no disappointment. Funeral pie, a cornstarch-thickened raisin pie, is traditionally served at the wakes of Old Order Mennonites and Amish. According to most accounts, the tradition of serving raisin pie at wakes evolved because raisins have no season and could always be found in the pantry on short notice. If you've never tried this pie, I hope you won't wait for a funeral. It's excellent, a little like mincemeat, and good for any occasion.

MAKES 8 TO 10 SERVINGS

1 recipe Basic Flaky Pie Pastry, Double Crust (page 31), refrigerated

FILLING

2 cups dark raisins

2 cups water

1/2 cup granulated sugar

1/2 cup firmly packed light brown sugar

3 tablespoons cornstarch

1/2 teaspoon ground cinnamon

1/4 teaspoon salt

11/2 tablespoons fresh lemon juice

1 teaspoon grated lemon zest

2 tablespoons unsalted butter, cut into 1/2-inch pieces

GLAZE

Milk or light cream

Granulated sugar

1. If you haven't already, prepare the pastry and refrigerate until firm enough to roll, about 1 hour.

2. On a sheet of lightly floured waxed paper, roll the larger portion of the pastry into a 12-inch circle with a floured rolling pin. Invert the pastry over a 9-inch standard pie pan, center, and peel off the paper. Gently tuck the pastry into the pan, without stretching it, and let the overhang drape over the edge. Place in the refrigerator for 15 minutes.

3. Combine the raisins and 1 cup of the water in a large saucepan over low heat. Meanwhile, combine the sugars, cornstarch, cinnamon, and salt in a medium-size bowl. Whisk in the remaining 1 cup water, then pour the mixture into the saucepan. Increase the heat to medium-high and bring the mixture to a boil, stirring virtually nonstop. When it starts to boil, let it continue to boil for 1 minute, stirring nonstop to keep the mixture from spattering. Remove from the heat and stir in the lemon juice, lemon zest, and butter until the butter melts. Transfer to a large bowl and let cool partially before pouring it into the chilled pie shell. Preheat the oven to 400°F.

4. Roll the other half of the pastry into a 10-inch circle on a sheet of lightly floured waxed paper. Moisten the outer edge of the pie shell with a pastry brush. Invert the top pastry over the filling, center, and peel off the paper. Press the top and bottom pastries together along the dampened edge. Using a knife, trim the pastry flush with the edge of the pan. Using the back of a fork, press the tines along the edge to seal the pastry. Poke several steam vents in the top of the pie with the fork or a paring knife. To glaze the pie, brush the top with a little milk and sprinkle lightly with granulated sugar.

5. Place the pie on the center oven rack and bake until the crust is golden brown, about 40 minutes, rotating the pie 180 degrees halfway through the baking, so that the part that faced the back of the oven now faces forward. The color of the pastry and total elapsed time are the best indicators of doneness.

6. Transfer the pie to a wire rack and let cool thoroughly. Serve at room temperature.

Recipe for Success

▶ The filling for this pie is precooked and prethickened. The only thing you're really cooking here is the pastry, which is why the total elapsed time and color of the pastry are the best indicators of doneness.

▶ Since there are no dairy products in this pie, it will keep at room temperature for a couple of days. This room-temperature longevity, according to some accounts, partly explains the pie's popularity during times of grieving, when people's attention is elsewhere.

Dried Cranberry and Walnut Funeral Pie

So smitten was I with the previous funeral pie that I decided to take a similar approach with dried cranberries. Since I was only out to reshape the wheel and not reinvent it, I stuck to the same basic formula, plugging in what I thought would be some festive replacements suitable for holiday dining: dried cranberries instead of raisins, along with orange juice, ground cloves, and walnuts. My idea adapted quite nicely, if I do say so myself. Like the original funeral pie, this will remind you of a mock mincemeat pie, but don't let that deter you if you're not a mincemeat fan. This is delectable.

MAKES 8 TO 10 SERVINGS

1 recipe Basic Flaky Pie Pastry, Double Crust (page 31) or Tender Cream Cheese Pastry, Double Crust (page 46), refrigerated

FILLING

2 cups sweetened dried cranberries (sold as Craisins)

1 cup orange juice or cranberry juice cocktail

1 teaspoon grated orange zest

$2/3$ cup sugar

3 tablespoons cornstarch

$1/4$ teaspoon ground cloves

$1/4$ teaspoon salt

1 cup water

1 tablespoon unsalted butter, cut into $1/2$-inch pieces

1 tablespoon fresh lemon juice

$3/4$ cup chopped walnuts

GLAZE

Milk or light cream

Sugar

1.   If you haven't already, prepare the pastry and refrigerate until firm enough to roll, about 1 hour.

2.   On a sheet of lightly floured waxed paper, roll the larger portion of the pastry into a 12-inch circle with a floured rolling pin. Invert the pastry over a 9-inch standard pie pan, center, and peel off the paper. Gently tuck the pastry into the pan, without stretching it, and let the overhang drape over the edge. Place in the refrigerator for 15 minutes.

3.   Combine the cranberries, orange juice, and orange zest in a medium-size non-reactive saucepan. Place over low heat. As the cranberries start to heat, mix the sugar, cornstarch, cloves, and salt together in a small bowl. Stir in the water. Add the mixture to the saucepan, increasing the heat to medium. Bring to a boil, stirring, and let boil for 1 minute, stirring nonstop to prevent it from spattering. Remove from the heat and stir in the butter until melted. Then stir in the lemon juice and walnuts. Transfer to a bowl and let cool slightly. Preheat the oven to 400°F.

4.   Roll the other half of the pastry into a 10-inch circle on a sheet of lightly floured waxed paper. Turn the filling into the chilled pie shell, then moisten the outer edge of the shell with a pastry brush. Invert the top pastry over the filling, center, and peel off the paper. Press the top and bottom pastries together along the dampened edge. Using a knife, trim the pastry flush with the edge of the pan. Using the back of a fork, press the tines along the edge to seal. Poke several steam vents in the top of the pie with the fork or a paring knife. To glaze the pie, brush the top with a little milk and sprinkle lightly with sugar.

5.   Place the pie on the center oven rack and bake until the crust is golden brown, about 40 minutes, rotating the pie 180 degrees halfway through the baking, so that the part that faced the back of the oven now faces forward. The color of the pastry and total elapsed time are the best indicators of doneness.

6.   Transfer the pie to a wire rack and let cool thoroughly. Serve at room temperature.

Recipe for Success

▶   **You can, without drastically changing the outcome, substitute a bit of other dried fruit for the cranberries. If I have a couple of prunes or dried figs languishing in a bag in my pantry, I may well dice them and heat them with the cranberries. Even very dry, hard fruit can be salvaged in this pie.**

Thanksgiving Pie One-Upmanship

Let's face it, your Thanksgiving brood already knows who is bringing what pie for dessert. Hey, there's nothing wrong with tradition on Turkey Day. That's what the celebration is all about, isn't it? But if you don't mind taking a chance and stepping on tradition's toes for the sake of great eating, why not surprise them with one of these:

- **ALL-PEAR PIE WITH MAPLE AND CANDIED GINGER** (page 251): A nice departure from apple.

- **DRIED CRANBERRY AND WALNUT FUNERAL PIE** (page 310): A little like mock mincemeat, if that appeals.

- **FRUITS OF THE FOREST PIE (NUT VERSION)** (page 356): Not just pecan; this is the whole forest.

- **CHOCOLATE MOUSSE CHIFFON PIE** (page 495): Because there's always someone who'd rather eat chocolate.

- **MAPLE-PECAN-PUMPKIN CHIFFON PIE** (page 497): The familiar flavor in a lighter package.

Dried Pear and Date Pie with Glazed Nut Topping

When you simmer dried fruit in juice, then puree it in a food processor, you end up with a thick fruit sauce that can then be used to make a different sort of pie filling—much thicker and with a more concentrated flavor than a fresh fruit pie. That's what we do here with pears, spreading the sauce in the shell, then topping it with buttery-sweet mixed nuts. It makes for a dense, delicious pie—probably more suited to adults than kids—that should be served in thin slices and enjoyed with a glass of wine.

MAKES 10 TO 12 SERVINGS

1 recipe Basic Flaky Pie Pastry, Single Crust (page 31), refrigerated

FILLING

1 1/2 cups coarsely chopped dried pears

1/2 cup halved and pitted dates

2/3 cup pear juice, plus more for pureeing

1/4 cup granulated sugar

1 tablespoon fresh lemon juice

NUT TOPPING

1/4 cup (1/2 stick) unsalted butter, cut into pieces

1/4 cup firmly packed light brown sugar

3 tablespoons light corn syrup

1 1/4 cups roasted mixed nuts (cashews, pecans, hazelnuts, and almonds, but not peanuts)

GARNISH

Fresh Whipped Cream (page 605)

1. If you haven't already, prepare the pastry and refrigerate until firm enough to roll, about 1 hour.

2. On a sheet of lightly floured waxed paper, roll the pastry into a 12-inch circle with a floured rolling pin. Invert the pastry over a 9-inch standard pie pan, center, and peel off the paper. Tuck the pastry into the pan, without stretching it, and sculpt the edge into an upstanding ridge. Place in the freezer for 15 minutes.

3. Combine the pears, dates, pear juice, and granulated sugar in a medium-size nonreactive saucepan. Bring to a boil, then reduce the heat slightly, cover, and simmer until most of the liquid is absorbed, about 15 minutes. Remove from the heat and let cool briefly. Preheat the oven to 375°F.

4. Transfer the cooked fruit to a food processor. Add the lemon juice and about 1/4 cup pear juice. Process the fruit to a smooth, pasty puree, adding more pear juice as needed to make a puree with a consistency like that of very thick applesauce. This may take 1/2 cup or more of juice. Spread the puree evenly in the chilled pie shell.

5. To make the nut topping, combine the butter, brown sugar, and corn syrup in a medium-size heavy saucepan. Bring to a boil, stirring, and let boil for 1 minute. Stir in the nuts until evenly coated. Spoon the nut mixture over the filling, smoothing it with a spoon.

6. Place the pie on the center oven rack and bake until the nut topping is a deep golden brown and is bubbling vigorously, 35 to 40 minutes. Rotate the pie 180 degrees halfway through the baking, so that the part that faces the back of the oven now faces forward.

7. Transfer the pie to a wire rack and let cool to room temperature. Cut thin slices and serve with a dollop of whipped cream.

Recipe for Success

▶ The pear flavor really rules here, even with the dates. If you'd like to tone it down slightly, use equal amounts of the 2 fruits.

▶ The easiest way to buy the nuts for this pie is to purchase a bag of mixed nuts at a place like Trader Joe's. Find one without peanuts, because their flavor may crowd out that of the other nuts.

▶ This pie bakes just long enough to brown the bottom crust if you're using a glass or dark metal pan. If you want to be assured of a well-browned bottom crust, you might want to partially prebake the pastry first (see page 16).

▶ You can find pear juice at any health food store.

Chewy Medjool Date–Nut Pie

I love dates, and I'm always looking for new ways to eat them. When I'm in California, where you find the best dates, I often order a date milk shake. Years ago, I saw a date pie recipe in *Maida Heatter's Book of Great American Desserts* (Knopf, 1985), and I instantly knew she was onto something. The pie is wonderful—"gooey, very chewy, crunchy and yummy," as she describes it—and not unlike a pecan pie in texture. Maida Heatter says that this is the way they make pie in Indio, California, the prime date-growing area in the United States. Using her recipe as my model, I've made a few changes over the years and come up with my own version— gooey and chewy like hers and wonderful to eat. I'll repeat her advice that to make a proper date pie, you have to start with the softest dates you can find, not the hard dried ones that come in a box. Typically, I buy Medjool dates at the market; they're fairly easy to find and the quality is generally excellent. This should be served cold, with whipped cream.

MAKES 8 TO 10 SERVINGS

1 recipe Basic Flaky Pie Pastry, Single Crust (page 31), refrigerated

FILLING

4 large eggs

1/2 cup firmly packed light brown sugar

1/4 cup (1/2 stick) unsalted butter, melted

1 cup light corn syrup

1/2 teaspoon vanilla extract

Pinch of salt

11/2 cups soft Medjool dates, pitted and coarsely chopped

1 cup coarsely chopped walnuts or pecans

GARNISH

Fresh Whipped Cream (page 605)

1. If you haven't already, prepare the pastry and refrigerate until firm enough to roll, about 1 hour.

2. On a sheet of lightly floured waxed paper, roll the pastry into a 13-inch circle with a floured rolling pin. Invert the pastry over a 9½-inch deep-dish pie pan, center, and peel off the paper. Tuck the pastry into the pan, without stretching it, and sculpt the edge so it is just a little higher than the rim. Place in the freezer for 15 minutes, then partially pre-bake and let cool according to the instructions on page 16. Reduce the oven temperature to 350°F.

3. Combine the eggs and brown sugar in a large bowl. Using an electric mixer, beat on medium-high speed for 2 minutes. Add the butter and beat again briefly. Add the corn syrup, vanilla, and salt and beat for 30 seconds. Scatter the dates and nuts evenly in the cooled pie shell. Slowly pour the filling over them. If you think you've displaced some of the nuts and dates, slowly drag a fork around in the filling to even them out.

4. Place the pie on the center oven rack and bake until the perimeter has puffed up perhaps as much as 1 inch and the center seems set but perhaps a little jiggly, about 45 minutes. Rotate the pie 180 degrees halfway through the baking, so that the part that faced the back of the oven now faces forward. Try not to overbake.

5. Transfer the pie to a wire rack and let cool thoroughly, then cover with loosely tented aluminum foil and refrigerate for several hours before serving. Garnish with whipped cream.

Recipe for Success

▶ **If you shake a little flour over the dates, they'll be less likely to stick to your knife and clump up when you cut them. Some cooks prefer to cut them with scissors, which does a nice neat job.**

Very Fig and Walnut Pie

If you don't care for figs, this pie won't be of much interest to you. But if you love figs the way I do, you'll find it heavenly. The filling is made primarily from dried Turkish figs that have been poached in pear juice (available at health food stores). They're cooled, pureed with some of the poaching liquid, and blended with brown sugar, eggs, corn syrup, and a few flavorings—including lemon juice and zest, which help to lift the rather dense flavor of the figs and give it a slight zing. As for the walnuts, they add a bit of crunch to an otherwise thick, soft filling. Serve this with a dollop of unsweetened whipped cream.

MAKES 8 TO 10 SERVINGS

1 recipe Basic Flaky Pie Pastry, Single Crust (page 31), refrigerated

FILLING

1¹/₂ cups stemmed and halved dried Turkish figs

About 2 cups pear juice

¹/₂ cup firmly packed light brown sugar

3 large eggs

³/₄ cup light corn syrup

2 tablespoons fresh lemon juice

Grated zest of 1 lemon

1¹/₂ teaspoons vanilla extract

1 cup coarsely chopped walnuts

GARNISH

Fresh Whipped Cream (page 605), unsweetened

1. If you haven't already, prepare the pastry and refrigerate until firm enough to roll, about 1 hour.

2. Meanwhile, combine the figs and pear juice in a medium-size nonreactive saucepan and bring to a boil. Reduce the heat, cover, and gently simmer until the figs are very soft, 30 to 35 minutes. Remove from the heat. Using a slotted spoon, transfer the figs to a small bowl. Pour the cooking liquid into a glass measuring cup. Set aside.

3. On a sheet of lightly floured waxed paper, roll the pastry into a 13-inch circle with a floured rolling pin. Invert the pastry over a 9¹/₂-inch deep-dish pie pan, center, and peel off the paper. Tuck the pastry into the pan, without stretching it, and sculpt the edge so it is just slightly higher than the rim. Place in the freezer for 15 minutes, then partially prebake and let cool according to the instructions on page 16. Reduce the oven temperature to 350°F.

4. Combine the poached figs, brown sugar, and ½ cup of the poaching liquid in a food processor and process into a smooth puree. In a large bowl, whisk the eggs until frothy. Add the corn syrup, lemon juice, lemon zest, vanilla, and fig puree. Whisk again until evenly blended. Stir in the walnuts. Slowly pour the filling into the cooled pie shell.

5. Place the pie on the center oven rack and bake until the filling is set and has puffed slightly, about 45 minutes (see Recipe for Success). Rotate the pie 180 degrees halfway through the baking, so that the part that faced the back of the oven now faces forward.

6. Transfer the pie to a wire rack and let cool thoroughly. Cover with loosely tented aluminum foil and refrigerate for at least several hours. Serve with unsweetened whipped cream.

Recipe for Success

▶ Because this filling is very dense and thick, It's not as jiggly as some, so it's a little trickier to know when the pie is done. Don't be surprised if all indications point to the pie being done after 30 to 35 minutes. Nonetheless, give it a full 45 minutes in the oven before you remove it, just to be sure the eggs are fully cooked within the dense filling.

Date-Walnut Freeform Pie

Unabashedly rich and sweet, this freeform pie has a single thick layer of dates and walnuts baked in a delectable walnut crust. The moisture comes from heavy cream, most of which is warmed and poured over the dates to soften them; the rest gets mixed in when the nuts are added to the filling. These are spread over the crust, the sides are folded over the filling, and the pie is then baked to a turn. Be sure to use soft Medjool dates, the kind sold in most health food stores, and not the drier sugared kind that come in a box. This is excellent warm or at room temperature.

MAKES 8 TO 10 SERVINGS

¹/₂ recipe Nutty Pie Pastry (page 42) made with walnuts, refrigerated

FILLING

1 cup heavy or whipping cream

¹/₄ cup sugar

¹/₂ teaspoon vanilla extract

1¹/₂ cups soft Medjool dates, pitted and coarsely chopped

1¹/₂ cups coarsely chopped walnuts

¹/₄ teaspoon ground cinnamon

1.   If you haven't already, prepare the pastry and refrigerate until firm enough to roll, about 1 hour.

2.   While the pastry is chilling, combine ³/₄ cup of the cream and the sugar in a small saucepan over medium heat. Bring the mixture to a simmer, then reduce the heat to low and simmer gently for 2 minutes, stirring once or twice. Remove from the heat and stir in the vanilla.

3.   Put the dates in a large bowl and pour the hot cream over them. Let stand for 10 minutes, then add the walnuts and cinnamon and mix well. Set aside for 20 minutes. Preheat the oven to 375°F. Lightly butter a large baking sheet.

4.   On a sheet of lightly floured waxed paper, roll the pastry into a 14-inch circle with a floured rolling pin. (When the pastry extends about 1 inch off the sides of the paper, you're there.) Invert the pastry onto the center of the baking sheet.

5.   Moisten the filling with the remaining ¹/₄ cup cream (see Recipe for Success); mix well. Scrape the filling into the center of the pastry and carefully spread it into an even 9-inch circle—carefully, because it is a rather coarse filling and you don't want to rip the pastry. Fold the edge of the pastry over the filling, enclosing it. The pastry will sort of self-pleat as you do this.

6.   Place the baking sheet on the center oven rack and bake until the pastry is golden brown, about 35 minutes.

7.   Transfer the baking sheet to a wire rack and let cool. The pie can be cooled entirely on the sheet, but if you feel confident doing so, you can slide a metal spatula under it after about 30 minutes, then slide the pie onto the rack to finish cooling. Serve warm or at room temperature.

Flour Dusters

Throughout this pie collection, you're instructed to dust your rolling surface and rolling pin with flour. This keeps the pastry from sticking to your counter, pin, waxed paper, or whatever. There are a number of ways to do this. It's easy enough to grab a handful of flour and toss it in the proper direction, the way professional bakers do. But unless you want your kitchen to look like a professional bakery—which is to say, flour everywhere—you might try another approach. For years, I had one of those tin cups with a perforated lid that you can buy at any dime store. You just shake the flour where you want it. Nowadays, I use a clever gadget called a flour wand, which looks something like a wand with a wire spinning top on one end. When you squeeze the handle, the wires on the "top" separate, allowing you to dredge it through flour to fill it. When you want to dust your pastry or pin with flour, you gently squeeze the handles, again separating the wires and allowing the flour to come out. It's a little tricky to explain, but when you see one, you'll understand right away. You can find one of these sifters at www.kingarthurflour.com and other kitchen suppliers.

Recipe for Success

▶ With these freeform pies, it can be a little tricky to get your fingers under the pastry to fold it over the filling. If you need help, slide a thin-bladed metal spatula under the edge to lift it.

▶ The precise amount of cream you need to moisten the filling is hard to predict, although you'll most likely need all of it. You definitely want the filling well moistened, but not so much that cream is running all over the place when you spread the filling over the pastry. Use your judgment.

I know several people who are more or less indifferent to pie in general. They can't be bothered to make one, and they'll almost never order a slice when eating out. But offer one of these dear souls a slice of pecan pie, and everything immediately changes, indifference giving way to a sort of singular pie reverence. The very sight of a tawny pecan pie has been known to make

The Notable Nut: Pecan Pie and Beyond

such grown men emote and otherwise composed women gasp with surprised pleasure. • In a perhaps less dramatic fashion, pecan pie seems to have that effect on almost everyone. No matter how we feel about other kinds of pies, most of us have an undeniable soft spot for pecan. I don't know if it's the pecan's pleasing buttery crunch, its toasted-rich flavor, or the luscious, candy-like filling. Probably all of the above. But pecan pie holds a place of eminence in the pie world that's nearly unparalleled. • This chapter celebrates not just pecan but other nut pies as well—those made with walnuts, pine nuts, hazelnuts, and peanuts, too. Many are made in the traditional pecan fashion—the nuts surrounded by that gooey filling we so adore. But others are less so, leaning toward a brownie or fudge-like filling. Some feature a single nut; others, such as Fruits of the Forest Pie on page 356, share the spotlight. In every case, however, the nuts are there to make a bold statement, not just tossed in as an afterthought.

Even if you've already found the world's best pecan pie recipe, I hope that you'll give this chapter its due. You just might pick up a new trick or two, such as using browned butter in your pecan pie, as I do in Louisiana Browned-Butter Pecan Pie (page 323), to add a second layer of toasted flavor. Have fun!

Tips for Baking Noteworthy Nut Pies

▶ Shop around for nuts. You'll often find the best price by buying them in bulk. To be sure you're getting a fresh product and not one that's been sitting around for a while, shop where there is rapid inventory turnover.

▶ Store nuts in a cool, dark place, tightly sealed in plastic. This is especially important in the summer. Nuts can turn rancid quickly if left at room temperature during the warmer months. Buy only enough nuts to last for a month, or freeze them for up to two years.

▶ Taste the nuts from your pantry before using them to make sure they have a fresh flavor.

▶ In most cases, it's not necessary to toast nuts before using them in a pie. They'll usually rise to the surface anyway, toasting as the pie bakes.

▶ Pecan halves look most attractive on top of a pie, but they can present a problem when you cut into the pie. As you slice, the filling will get squished out under the large nuts. I find that it's better to chop nuts coarsely before adding them to the filling. Or leave the nuts in large pieces, place the pie in the freezer until it is partially frozen, and then slice it.

▶ Most nut pies contain eggs and therefore should not be overbaked—or baked too fast—lest the filling turn weepy. If your pie rises too quickly and develops lots of cracks, your oven is probably too hot and may need to be adjusted.

▶ With few exceptions, don't slice nut pies until they are thoroughly cooled or the filling will not have the proper candy-like texture.

Louisiana Browned-Butter Pecan Pie

If you've ever eaten a piece of genuine Louisiana pecan pie and wondered what that elusive nutty flavor is, pay attention: it might *not* have been the pecans. According to John Folse, a well-known Louisiana chef, it may have been browned butter. Ordinarily, we cooks try *not* to brown butter, to preserve the fresh flavor. But there are times when browning butter gives it a nutty flavor that's just right for our purposes—here, for instance. Folse and other good Louisiana chefs know that the browned butter adds an unexpected layer of flavor to pecan pie, elevating it above more ordinary versions. I think you'll agree that this recipe, inspired by one of his and the recipes of other southern chefs, is anything but ordinary.

MAKES 8 TO 10 SERVINGS

1 recipe Basic Flaky Pie Pastry, Single Crust (page 31), refrigerated

FILLING

1/2 cup (1 stick) unsalted butter

3 large eggs

1 cup firmly packed light brown sugar

1/2 cup dark corn syrup

2 tablespoons honey

2 teaspoons vanilla extract

1/8 teaspoon ground cinnamon

11/2 cups coarsely chopped pecans

GARNISH

Vanilla ice cream

1. If you haven't already, prepare the pastry and refrigerate until firm enough to roll, about 1 hour.

2. On a sheet of lightly floured waxed paper, roll the pastry into a 13-inch circle with a floured rolling pin. Invert the pastry over a 9 1/2-inch deep-dish pie pan, center, and peel off the paper. Tuck the pastry into the pan, without stretching it, and sculpt the edge into an upstanding ridge. Place in the freezer for 15 minutes, then partially prebake and let cool according to the directions on page 16.

3. Using a shiny skillet, so you can easily see what's happening in the pan, melt the butter over medium to medium-high heat. With wooden spoon in hand, stir the butter as you keep a close eye on it, waiting for it to brown. Once that starts to happen, it will go very quickly. The trick is to catch the butter while it is dark golden brown and before the little solids get too dark and burn. As soon as the butter reaches this point, in 2 to 4 minutes, pour it into a bowl and let cool slightly. Preheat the oven to 400°F.

4. Combine the eggs, brown sugar, corn syrup, honey, vanilla, and cinnamon in a large bowl. Whisk well to blend. Add the browned butter and whisk again until evenly combined. Stir in the pecans. Pour the filling into the cooled pie shell. Using a fork, gently rake the nuts to distribute them evenly.

5. Place the pie on the center oven rack and bake for 10 minutes. Reduce the oven temperature to 350°F and bake until the filling, including the very center, is set, 25 to 30 minutes. Rotate the pie 180 degrees about halfway through, so that the side that faced the back of the oven now faces forward. When done, the pie will have puffed slightly and developed cracks around the perimeter.

6. Transfer the pie to a wire rack and let cool thoroughly. Serve at room temperature, or cover loosely with aluminum foil, refrigerate, and serve slightly chilled with a scoop of vanilla ice cream.

Recipe for Success

▶ To repeat what I said above, a shiny skillet is the best background for monitoring the butter as it darkens. It's much more difficult to watch the progress if you're using, say, a black cast-iron pan or dark anodized aluminum one.

▶ Plan on not leaving the stove when you're browning the butter. Once the milk solids start to color, the browning can be complete within seconds.

▶ Don't hide the browned-butter flavor by serving this with anything but a fairly unobtrusive accompaniment, such as vanilla ice cream or whipped cream.

Butterscotch Pecan Pie

I think this is the quintessential pecan pie. There's no big secret to it—just a large handful of butterscotch chips. But when you taste it, you'll think butterscotch chips were invented to fulfill this purpose, adding yet another layer of caramel flavor to the already gooey, candy-like filling. This one is heavy on the pecans, incorporating a full two cups. You can use slightly less, if you like. Time was I toasted the pecans before making a pie with them. I don't do that anymore, because I've found that since they float to the surface anyway, they essentially toast as they bake. It is mandatory, as far as I'm concerned, to serve this with vanilla ice cream.

MAKES 8 TO 10 SERVINGS

1 recipe Basic Flaky Pie Pastry, Single Crust (page 31), refrigerated

FILLING

1 cup light corn syrup

$1/2$ cup firmly packed dark brown sugar

$1/4$ cup ($1/2$ stick) unsalted butter, cut into pieces

$3/4$ cup butterscotch chips

Generous pinch of salt

3 large eggs

1 large egg yolk

$1 1/2$ teaspoons vanilla extract

2 cups coarsely chopped pecans

1. If you haven't already, prepare the pastry and refrigerate until firm enough to roll, about 1 hour.

2. On a sheet of lightly floured waxed paper, roll the pastry into a 13-inch circle with a floured rolling pin. Invert the pastry over a $9 1/2$-inch deep-dish pie pan, center, and peel off the paper. Tuck the pastry into the pan, without stretching it, and sculpt the edge until it is even with the rim. Place in the freezer for 15 minutes, then partially prebake and let cool according to the instructions on page 16. Reduce the oven temperature to 350°F.

3. Gently warm the corn syrup, brown sugar, and butter together in a medium-size saucepan until the butter melts. Turn off the heat and add the butterscotch chips. Scatter them around rather than dumping them in one spot. Set the pan aside for 5 minutes, shaking it once or twice to move hot liquid over the chips. After 5 minutes, add the salt and whisk to smooth. Pour the mixture into a large bowl and let cool for 5 minutes.

4. In a medium-size bowl, whisk the eggs and egg yolk together just until frothy. Whisk in the vanilla. Whisk a little less than half of the hot liquid into the eggs until smooth. Add the rest of the hot liquid and whisk until smooth. Add the pecans and stir well. Turn the filling into the cooled pie shell. Using a fork, gently rake the filling to distribute the pecans evenly.

5. Place the pie on the center oven rack and bake until the perimeter of the filling has puffed up and perhaps cracked slightly, 40 to 45 minutes. Rotate the pie 180 degrees halfway through the baking, so that the part that faced the back of the oven now faces forward. When done, the center may wobble a little, but it shouldn't seem soupy.

6. Transfer the pie to a wire rack and let cool. Serve slightly warm or at room temperature. Or let cool thoroughly, cover with loosely tented aluminum foil, and refrigerate for several hours before serving.

Recipe for Success

▶ **Pecan pies look very attractive when made with pecan halves, but they present something of a problem when you cut them. When your knife hits a pecan, it tends to push down on the filling, rather than cut cleanly, leaving you with something of a botched job. Chopping the pecans coarsely results in neater cuts.**

▶ **Don't worry if the top of this pie bakes up a little darker than the tops of other pecan pies. The dark brown sugar and butterscotch chips make it so.**

What's in a Name?

Archaeologists have found evidence to suggest that Native Americans in what is now Texas used pecans more than 8,000 years ago. The word "pecan" comes from the North American French word *pacane*, meaning, more or less, "not so hard as to require a stone to crack."

Jack Daniel's Chocolate Chip Pecan Pie

If you like a little kick in your pecan pie, try this one made with Jack Daniel's—just enough to flavor the pie, but not so much as to overwhelm it with alcohol. This spirited pie is right at home on the holiday table.

MAKES 8 TO 10 SERVINGS

1 recipe Basic Flaky Pie Pastry, Single Crust (page 31), refrigerated

FILLING
4 large eggs, at room temperature
1 cup sugar
3/4 cup dark corn syrup

2 tablespoons Jack Daniel's whiskey
2 tablespoons unsalted butter, melted
1 teaspoon vanilla extract
1 cup pecan halves
1/2 cup semisweet chocolate chips

1. If you haven't already, prepare the pastry and refrigerate until firm enough to roll, about 1 hour.

2. On a sheet of lightly floured waxed paper, roll the pastry into a 13-inch circle with a floured rolling pin. Invert the pastry over a 9½-inch deep-dish pie pan, center, and peel off the paper. Tuck the pastry into the pan, without stretching it, and sculpt the edge into an upstanding ridge. Place in the freezer for 15 minutes, then partially prebake and let cool according to the instructions on page 16. Reduce the oven temperature to 350°F.

3. Combine the eggs, sugar, and corn syrup in a large bowl. Whisk well to combine. Add the whiskey, butter, and vanilla. Whisk again until evenly combined. Scatter the pecans and chocolate chips evenly over the cooled pie shell. Whisk the filling once more, then slowly pour it over the nuts and chips.

4. Place the pie on the center oven rack and bake until the filling is set, about 45 minutes, rotating the pie 180 degrees halfway through the baking, so that the side that faced the back of the oven now faces forward. When done, the top of the filling will be toasted brown and the perimeter slightly puffed.

5. Transfer the pie to a wire rack and let cool thoroughly. Serve at room temperature, or cover with loosely tented aluminum foil, refrigerate, and serve cold. Either way, it is wonderful.

Recipe for Success

- Not all recipes of this genre call for the pie shell to be partially prebaked, but I find that prebaking virtually guarantees a fully cooked, nicely browned crust.

- This pie freezes well. Thaw at room temperature 4 to 5 hours before serving.

- To get a good clean slice, partially freeze the pie before cutting. Use a sturdy knife, as the chocolate chips are very hard when frozen.

Alice Colombo's Race Day Chocolate Pecan Pie

Alice Colombo is a former assistant food editor with the *Louisville Courier-Journal*, in Kentucky. This recipe of hers, which first appeared in that paper, is for the pie that is traditionally served to mark the running of the Kentucky Derby. This version has a crusty cookie-like topping, and a very tender one at that, thanks to the cornstarch. Please note that Alice's original recipe does not specify a prebaked crust, as I do here. If you prefer to use an unbaked crust, feel free to do so.

MAKES 8 TO 10 SERVINGS

1 recipe Basic Flaky Pie Pastry, Single Crust (page 31) or Basic Shortening Pie Pastry, Single Crust (page 30), refrigerated

FILLING

2 large eggs

1 cup sugar

1/2 cup cornstarch

1/2 cup (1 stick) unsalted butter, melted and slightly cooled

2 tablespoons bourbon

1 cup chopped pecans

1 cup semisweet chocolate chips

GARNISH

1 cup cold heavy or whipping cream

2 to 3 teaspoons bourbon, to your taste

1. If you haven't already, prepare the pastry and refrigerate until firm enough to roll, about 1 hour.

2. On a sheet of lightly floured waxed paper, roll the pastry into a 12-inch circle with a floured rolling pin. Invert the pastry over a 9-inch standard pie pan, center, and peel off

the paper. Tuck the pastry into the pan, without stretching it, and sculpt the edge into an upstanding ridge. Place in the freezer for 15 minutes, then partially prebake and let cool according to the instructions on page 16. Reduce the oven temperature to 350°F.

3. In a large bowl, whisk the eggs. In a small bowl, mix the sugar and cornstarch together, then whisk the mixture into the eggs in 3 stages. Whisk in the butter and bourbon. Stir in the pecans and chocolate chips. Scrape the filling into the cooled pie shell.

4. Place the pie on the center oven rack and bake, until the top is crusty and golden brown, 45 to 50 minutes. Rotate the pie 180 degrees halfway through the baking, so that the part that faced the back of the oven now faces forward. Transfer the pie to a wire rack and let cool for at least 1 hour.

5. Meanwhile, make the garnish. Using a chilled medium-size bowl and chilled beaters, whip the cream with an electric mixer until it holds soft peaks. Add the bourbon and continue to beat until stiff but not grainy.

6. Serve the cooled pie with a dollop of the whipped cream.

Recipe for Success

▸ Alice says, "Everyone likes to prepare foods ahead for Kentucky Derby day. In that regard, this pie is a very good keeper. Here's how I freeze it: After baking, allow the pie to cool completely. Slip it into a zippered-top plastic bag and zip almost closed. Insert a drinking straw into the opening and suck out the air. Slip the straw out of the bag and immediately zip up the opening. There should be no air remaining in the bag. Freeze. Remove the pie from freezer several hours before serving. Rewarm it in the oven. Make the bourbon whipped cream the same day you plan to serve the pie."

Snowbird Mountain Lodge's Mocha Pecan Pie

I can always tell when I've stumbled upon a great pie if I can't stop eating it—before the pie is even baked. Such was the case with this delicious mocha pecan pie, courtesy of the Snowbird Mountain Lodge in the southern Appalachian Mountains of western North Carolina. Owner Robert Rankin says that his guests just can't get enough of this pie, which he has served at his beautiful country inn for nine years. He sells out whenever it's on the menu, especially during the Thanksgiving season. There's just a hint of coffee here underneath the more dominant chocolate flavor and the perfect amount of requisite pecan pie gooey-ness.

MAKES 8 TO 10 SERVINGS

1 recipe Basic Flaky Pie Pastry, Single Crust (page 31), refrigerated

FILLING

3 tablespoons unsweetened cocoa powder

2 teaspoons instant espresso or coffee granules

3 tablespoons unsalted butter, melted

1 tablespoon heavy or whipping cream

1 cup sugar

1 cup light corn syrup

3 large eggs, at room temperature

2 teaspoons vanilla extract

1/4 teaspoon salt

1 1/2 cups coarsely chopped pecans

1. If you haven't already, prepare the pastry and refrigerate until firm enough to roll, about 1 hour.

2. On a sheet of lightly floured waxed paper, roll the pastry into a 12-inch circle with a floured rolling pin. Invert the pastry over a 9-inch standard pie pan, center, and peel off the paper. Tuck the pastry into the pan, without stretching it, and sculpt the edge into an upstanding ridge. Place in the freezer for 15 minutes, then partially prebake and let cool according to the instructions on page 16. Reduce the oven temperature to 350°F.

3. Combine the cocoa, coffee, butter, and cream in a large bowl. Whisk to blend. Add the sugar, corn syrup, eggs, vanilla, and salt. Whisk again to smooth. Stir in the pecans, then pour into the cooled pie shell. Gently rake a fork through the filling to distribute the nuts evenly.

4. Place the pie on the center oven rack and bake for 30 minutes. Rotate the pie 180 degrees, so that the part that faced the back of the oven now faces forward. Continue to bake until the filling has puffed around the edge and the middle is set. To check, give the pie a quick little nudge. The filling should not move in waves below the crusty surface.

5. Transfer the pie to a wire rack and let cool thoroughly. The pie can be served at room temperature, but I think it has a better texture if it is covered with loosely tented aluminum foil and refrigerated for at least 1 hour before serving.

Recipe for Success

▶ Like all pecan pies, this one forms a crunchy crust on top of the filling. When you test the pie to determine whether it is done, watch what happens below the crusty surface. If it moves, wave-like, bake the pie for 7 to 10 minutes more.

▶ Robert says that a little orange flavor in the pastry is a wonderful complement to the mocha filling. He adds some grated orange zest to the pastry's dry ingredients and substitutes 1 tablespoon orange juice for an equal amount of corn syrup.

Pecan Particulars

▶ When buying pecans, look for plump nuts that are uniform in color and size. Shelled pecans can be kept in the refrigerator for about 9 months and in the freezer for up to 2 years.

▶ Pecans can be thawed and refrozen repeatedly during the 2-year freezing period without loss of flavor or texture.

▶ Airtight containers, such as jars with lids, are best for storing pecans in the refrigerator.

▶ Zipper-topped plastic storage bags are best for storing pecans in the freezer.

▶ After removal from cold storage, pecans will stay good at room temperature for an additional 2 months.

▶ In-shell pecans can be stored in a cool, dry place for 6 to 12 months.

Maple Pecan Pie

I'm a former Yankee with a wife from Charleston, South Carolina, so this pie is right up my alley. I think it's a truly elegant pie, an arranged marriage of northern sweetness and southern charm that never fails to make pie lovers weak in the knees. Maybe it's my imagination, but I swear this pie tastes best when I make it with pecans I pick up in South Carolina on a trip down there. This is a big pie—a fat layer of sticky-sweet filling beneath the crunch of pecans. I like to add a little bit of almond extract to the filling—I think it melts into the pecan flavor without seeming out of place—but you can leave it out if you wish. I serve this pie with a big scoop of vanilla or butter pecan ice cream.

MAKES 10 SERVINGS

1 recipe Basic Flaky Pie Pastry, Single Crust (page 31), refrigerated

FILLING

1/2 cup sugar

1/4 cup (1/2 stick) unsalted butter, melted and slightly cooled

3 large eggs

1 large egg yolk

3/4 cup pure maple syrup, preferably medium or dark amber

3/4 cup light corn syrup

1 1/2 teaspoons vanilla extract

1/2 teaspoon almond extract (optional)

2 teaspoons fresh lemon juice

1/4 teaspoon salt

1 1/2 cups coarsely chopped pecan halves

1. If you haven't already, prepare the pastry and refrigerate until firm enough to roll, about 1 hour.

2. On a sheet of lightly floured waxed paper, roll the pastry into a 13-inch circle with a floured rolling pin. Invert the pastry over a 9½-inch deep-dish pie pan, center, and peel off the paper. Tuck the pastry into the pan, without stretching it, and sculpt the edge into an upstanding ridge. Place in the freezer for 15 minutes, then partially prebake and let cool according to the instructions on page 16. Reduce the oven temperature to 350°F.

3. Combine the sugar, butter, eggs, and egg yolk in a large bowl. Using an electric mixer or whisk, beat the mixture briefly until blended. Add the maple syrup, corn syrup, vanilla, almond extract (if using), lemon juice, and salt. Beat for several seconds, until evenly blended. Stir in the pecans. Carefully pour the filling into the cooled pie shell. Using a fork, gently rake the nuts to distribute them evenly.

4. Place the pie on the center oven rack and bake for 30 minutes, then rotate the

pie 180 degrees, so that the part that faced the back of the oven now faces forward. Continue to bake until the filling has set, 20 to 25 minutes. When the pie is done, the perimeter will have puffed slightly and the center will not move in waves. Give the pie a quick little nudge to check it.

5. Transfer the pie to a wire rack and let cool thoroughly. Serve at room temperature, or cover with loosely tented aluminum foil and refrigerate for a couple of hours before serving. It has a better consistency for slicing when cold, but let the cold slices sit at room temperature for 15 minutes to enhance the flavor before serving.

Recipe for Success

▶ Rich and sweet pecan pie freezes very well and will stay in great shape for 4 to 6 weeks, so you might want to think about baking one of these and stashing it in the freezer for Thanksgiving or some other special occasion. Just wrap the pie in plastic, then cover snugly with aluminum foil. Thaw the pie at room temperature, then unwrap and heat in a 300°F oven for about 20 minutes to give it a freshly baked taste.

Chocolate Brownie Pecan Pie

Pecan pie is always a special treat—the cost of pecans being what it is—so I like to make a real splash when I serve one. Enter this pie. As with other pecan pies, the nuts float to the top, and a layer with a consistency somewhere between chocolate pudding and a fudge brownie forms underneath. As for serving, this pie is good warm but better, I think, at room temperature or chilled, when the texture of the chocolate has a firmer texture. This is excellent with whipped cream or vanilla ice cream.

`MAKES 8 TO 10 SERVINGS`

1 recipe Basic Flaky Pie Pastry, Single Crust (page 31), refrigerated

FILLING

2/3 cup light corn syrup

2/3 cup firmly packed light brown sugar

1/4 cup (1/2 stick) unsalted butter, cut into pieces

4 ounces semisweet chocolate, coarsely chopped

Generous pinch of salt

3 large eggs

1 large egg yolk

11/2 teaspoons vanilla extract

11/2 cups coarsely chopped pecan halves

1. If you haven't already, prepare the pastry and refrigerate until firm enough to roll, about 1 hour.

2. On a sheet of lightly floured waxed paper, roll the pastry into a 13-inch circle with a floured rolling pin. Invert the pastry over a $9\frac{1}{2}$-inch deep-dish pie pan, center, and peel off the paper. Tuck the pastry into the pan, without stretching it, and sculpt the edge so it is even with the rim. Place in the freezer for 15 minutes, then partially prebake and let cool according to the instructions on page 16. Reduce the oven temperature to 350°F.

3. Gently heat the corn syrup, brown sugar, and butter together in a medium-size saucepan until the butter melts. Turn off the heat and add the chocolate and salt. Let stand for 5 to 7 minutes, occasionally tilting and shaking the pan so the liquid runs over the chocolate. Whisk the mixture until smooth, then pour into a medium-size bowl and let cool for 10 minutes.

4. Whisk the eggs and egg yolk together in another medium-size bowl until frothy. Blend in the vanilla. Add about half of the slightly cooled chocolate mixture and whisk until smooth. Blend in the remaining chocolate mixture. Add the pecans and stir well. Pour the filling into the cooled pie shell. Using a fork, gently rake the nuts to distribute them evenly.

5. Place the pie on the center oven rack and bake until the filling has puffed and cracked slightly, especially around the edge, about 40 minutes. Rotate the pie 180 degrees halfway through the baking, so that the part that faced the back of the oven now faces forward. When done, it may be slightly wobbly at the center. Don't worry; the residual heat will continue to cook the pie.

6. Transfer the pie to a wire rack and let cool. Serve slightly warm or at room temperature. Or let cool thoroughly, cover with loosely tented aluminum foil, and refrigerate for several hours before serving.

Recipe for Success

▶ **Don't be tempted to use an unbaked pie shell to save a little time. The filling is fairly wet and may make for a pastry that tastes slightly raw.**

▶ **But don't be afraid to underbake the pie just slightly either. The worst that can happen is that it will turn out a little moist. If that's the case, you can simply refrigerate the pie to firm it up a bit before serving.**

Cream of Coconut Pecan Pie

It should come as no surprise that I did a good deal of the research for this pie collection online. Here's an example of a pie that was inspired by one I found at the Coco Lopez Web site. I thought adding cream of coconut to a pecan pie was quite a novel idea. It gives it a beautifully dense and creamy texture, as well as a smooth coconuty flavor. As is typical, the pecans float to the top, with a layer of something like coconut custard underneath. Served cold, this pie is scrumptious.

MAKES 8 TO 10 SERVINGS

1 store-bought frozen 9-inch deep-dish pie shell

FILLING
3 large eggs
1/2 cup firmly packed light brown sugar
1 cup canned cream of coconut, well stirred
2 tablespoons unsalted butter, melted

1/4 cup heavy or whipping cream
1 1/2 teaspoons vanilla extract
1 teaspoon distilled white vinegar or fresh lemon juice
1 cup coarsely chopped pecan halves

GARNISH
Fresh Whipped Cream (page 605; optional)

1. Remove the pie shell from its package but leave it in the freezer until you're ready to fill it. Preheat the oven to 350°F.

2. Whisk the eggs and brown sugar together in a large bowl until smooth. Whisk in the cream of coconut, butter, heavy cream, vanilla, and lemon juice. Stir in the pecans. Carefully pour into the chilled pie shell. Using a fork, gently rake to distribute the nuts evenly.

3. Place the pie on the center oven rack and bake for 20 minutes, then rotate the pie 180 degrees, so that the part that faced the back of the oven now faces forward. Continue to bake until the filling has puffed slightly around the edge and the center is set. To check, give the pie a quick little nudge. The filling should jiggle, not move in waves below the nut-crusted top.

4. Transfer the pie to a wire rack and let cool thoroughly. Cover with loosely tented aluminum foil and refrigerate for at least 2 hours. Serve garnished with whipped cream, if desired.

Recipe for Success

▶ Note that I do not specifically recommend prebaking the crust, since the original recipe does not, but I nearly always partially prebake the pie shell for a nut, custard, or other nonfruit pie.

Sawdust Pie

This sweet signature pie is one of the reasons Patti's 1880's Restaurant in Grand Rivers, Kentucky, has been winning awards and customers since it opened back in 1977. When you mix up the crumbly filling—made with coconut, graham cracker crumbs, and pecans—you'll have a better idea where the name comes from.

MAKES 10 SERVINGS

1 recipe Basic Flaky Pie Pastry, Single Crust (page 31) or Basic Shortening Pie Pastry, Single Crust (page 30), refrigerated

FILLING

7 large egg whites

1¹/2 cups sugar

1¹/2 cups graham cracker crumbs

1¹/2 cups sweetened flaked coconut

1¹/2 cups finely chopped (by hand) pecans

GARNISH

Fresh Whipped Cream (page 605)

Sliced ripe banana

1. If you haven't already, prepare the pastry and refrigerate until firm enough to roll, about 1 hour.

2. On a sheet of lightly floured waxed paper, roll the pastry into a 12-inch circle with a floured rolling pin. Invert the pastry over a 9-inch standard pie pan, center, and peel off the paper. Tuck the pastry into the pan, without stretching it, and sculpt the edge into an upstanding ridge. Place in the freezer for 15 minutes. Preheat the oven to 350°F.

3. Combine the egg whites and sugar in a large bowl, stirring well with a wooden spoon. Add the graham cracker crumbs, coconut, and pecans and stir until evenly combined. Scrape the filling into the chilled pie shell and smooth with a spoon.

4. Place the pie on the center oven rack and bake for 25 minutes, then rotate the pie 180 degrees, so that the part that faced the back of the oven now faces forward. Continue to bake until the surface is a rich golden brown and quite crusty, 10 to 15 minutes.

5. Transfer the pie to a wire rack and let cool. Serve warm or at room temperature, garnished with whipped cream and banana slices.

Take That, Texas!

It probably irks our longhorn brethren to tears, but Georgia—not Texas—is the nation's leader in pecan production, to the tune of some 88 million pounds a year. In case you were wondering, that's enough pecans to make roughly 176 million pecan pies—or so say our friends at the Georgia Pecan Commission. Here's what else they have to say.

▶ Assuming that a pie is 9 inches in diameter, it would take 97,812,000 pecan pies to circle the earth. (And yes, it would take more than a few of them to cross Texas.)

▶ Your average pecan pie uses $1/2$ to $3/4$ pound of pecans. It takes about 310 pecan halves to fill a 1-pound bag, so there are about 78 pecans in every pecan pie.

▶ The pecan is the only tree nut that is truly native to the United States.

▶ One irrigated, managed acre of pecan trees will produce about 1,000 pounds of pecans.

▶ Thomas Jefferson was so taken with the flavor of pecans that he had trees imported from Louisiana for his orchards at Monticello.

Recipe for Success

▶ This pie is very sturdy and will ship well to college students and other perpetually ravenous children. Bake it in a disposable aluminum pie pan or an inexpensive metal pan of the sort you buy at the supermarket. Slice the pie, then wrap it in aluminum foil. Freeze overnight. Put it in a box with lots cushioning, then ship it the fastest way possible—some sort of second-day service is fine.

▶ Don't overmix the filling. The more you work it, the stiffer and less spreadable it becomes.

▶ To make a chocolate sawdust pie, melt some semisweet chocolate chips in a zipper-topped plastic storage bag in the microwave. Press the melted chocolate into one corner of the bag, then snip off the corner and pipe the chocolate over the pie after the pie has cooled a bit.

▶ Note that I bake the pie a little longer than they do at Patti's. They recommend 25 to 30 minutes total.

Molasses Walnut Pie

Molasses pies date back quite far in U.S. history, given the fact that molasses played an important role in colonial America. Refined sugar was available in the 1700s, but it was far too expensive for widespread use. Molasses was much cheaper. In fact, it was the abundance of cheap molasses that fueled the profitable New England rum industry in the early years of this country. One imagines that pies such as this one were common among early cooks. Colonial cooks may have used maple syrup, another common sweetener of the time, to tone down the up-front flavor of the molasses. I use granulated sugar and light brown sugar to achieve the same effect here. I also use walnuts, which our forebears would have gathered and painstakingly shelled. This pie reminds me of Indian pudding, perhaps because of the inclusion of cornmeal. The texture is more akin to that of pecan pie—dense, with just the right amount of molasses flavor.

MAKES 8 TO 10 SERVINGS

1 recipe Basic Flaky Pie Pastry, Single Crust (page 31), refrigerated

FILLING

1/3 cup unsulfured molasses

1/4 cup light corn syrup

1/4 cup (1/2 stick) unsalted butter, cut into pieces

1/2 cup granulated sugar

1/2 cup firmly packed light brown sugar

3 large eggs

1 large egg yolk

1 teaspoon vanilla extract

2 tablespoons fine yellow cornmeal

1 1/2 cups coarsely chopped walnuts

1. If you haven't already, prepare the pastry and refrigerate until firm enough to roll, about 1 hour.

2. On a sheet of lightly floured waxed paper, roll the pastry into a 13-inch circle with a floured rolling pie. Invert the pastry over a 9 1/2-inch deep-dish pie pan, center, and peel off the paper. Tuck the pastry into the pan, without stretching it, and sculpt the edge so it is even with the rim. Place in the freezer for 15 minutes, then partially prebake and let cool according to the instructions on page 16. Reduce the oven temperature to 350°F.

3. Combine the molasses, corn syrup, and butter in a small saucepan and warm gently, stirring occasionally, just until the butter melts. Remove from the heat. Combine the sugars, eggs, and egg yolk in a large bowl, then whisk in about one-third of the molasses mixture. Add the rest of the molasses mixture, the vanilla, and cornmeal and whisk again.

Pie Judging, Iowa Style

It's doubtful that anyone has a better view of Iowa's pie landscape than Arlette Hollister. For the past 18 years, Arlette has held the post of food superintendent for the Iowa State Fair, overseeing the judging of more than 180 food divisions every year. It's no small task: the pie division alone has 30 classes, ranging from custard (one crust) to cottage cheese and chocolate-pecan.

The pie judging, Arlette says, takes place on a single day, in about a three-hour stretch. There are nine judges—including food editors, extension agents, and home economists among them—who "really know their pies," although they might not always agree. One might not care for a filling that's spilled over, but to another that's no big deal. They do have guidelines, though. The final score includes 25 percent for appearance, 30 percent for quality of the crust, 30 percent for the filling, and 15 percent for originality.

According to Arlette, the apple and cherry divisions are always crowded with entries. Less so is the eggnog division, not surprising for a fair that's held at the height of the summer. One of her personal favorite participants is a woman who bakes peanut butter pie. "She's just as sweet as can be, and every Father's Day she bakes a peanut butter pie for all the fathers in the small town where she lives," Arlette says. Now that's the true spirit of pie making.

Stir in the walnuts. Pour the filling into the cooled pie shell. Using a fork, gently rake the nuts to distribute them evenly.

4. Place the pie on the center oven rack and bake for 45 minutes, rotating the pie 180 degrees halfway through the baking, so that the part that faced the back of the oven now faces forward. When done, the edge will have puffed slightly, and the filling will jiggle when you give the pie a nudge. The center should not seem soupy.

5. Transfer the pie to a wire rack and let cool. Serve warm or at room temperature. Or let the pie cool thoroughly, cover with loosely tented aluminum foil, and refrigerate for several hours before serving.

Recipe for Success

▶ I mention elsewhere that this type of pie cuts most cleanly if you avoid leaving the nuts in large pieces. Also, you'll get the cleanest slice when the pie is partially frozen. So even if you plan to serve the pie at room temperature, you might want to partially freeze it before slicing it with a sharp serrated knife. Let the slices come to room temperature before serving. That's the way I like to do it, and I always end up with great slices.

Jeff's Chocolate Walnut Pie

This recipe is from my friend Jeff Paige, formerly the chef at Canterbury Shaker Village in New Hampshire, from his book *The Shaker Kitchen* (Clarkson Potter, 1994). Because it contains cocoa, it isn't as rich, creamy, or complex as some of the other pies in this book that call for semisweet or bittersweet chocolate. The upside is that you can make a chocolate-nut pie when the only chocolate you have on hand is cocoa. The result? Something like a very nutty brownie in a pastry crust. And like a brownie, it's excellent with vanilla ice cream.

MAKES 8 TO 10 SERVINGS

1 recipe Basic Flaky Pie Pastry, Single Crust (page 31), refrigerated

FILLING

2/3 cup dark corn syrup

1/4 cup (1/2 stick) unsalted butter, cut into pieces

1/2 cup sugar

1/3 cup unsweetened cocoa powder

1/4 teaspoon salt

3 large eggs, at room temperature

1 teaspoon vanilla extract

11/2 cups coarsely chopped walnuts

1. If you haven't already, prepare the pastry and refrigerate it until firm enough to roll, about 1 hour.

2. On a sheet of lightly floured waxed paper, roll the pastry into a 13-inch circle with a floured rolling pin. Invert the pastry over a 9½-inch deep-dish pie pan, center, and peel off the paper. Tuck the pastry into the pan, without stretching it, and sculpt the edge so it is just above the rim. Place in the freezer for 15 minutes, then partially prebake and let cool according to the instructions on page 16. Reduce the oven temperature to 350°F.

3. Gently warm the corn syrup and butter together in a small saucepan over medium heat until the butter melts. Set aside briefly to cool.

4. In a large bowl, sift together the sugar, cocoa, and salt. Whisk in the eggs and vanilla until well blended, then whisk in the warm corn syrup mixture. Stir in the nuts. Carefully pour the filling into the cooled pie shell. Using a fork, gently rake the nuts to distribute them evenly.

5. Place the pie on the center oven rack and bake until the filling is set, about 40 minutes, rotating the pie 180 degrees about halfway through the baking, so that the part

that faced the back of the oven now faces forward. When the pie is done, the filling may have puffed very slightly around the perimeter.

6. Transfer the pie to a wire rack and let cool thoroughly. Both the texture and the flavor of the pie will improve as it cools. I think it's best served slightly chilled, but not too cold. (Cover loosely with aluminum foil and refrigerate for at least 2 hours before serving.)

Recipe for Success

▶ Note that I say this pie may puff slightly around the edge. If you find that your custard, brownie, pecan, or other egg-based pies are puffing up considerably at the edge before the center is done, that's a sure sign your oven is too hot. Check the temperature with a reliable oven thermometer and adjust the setting as needed, or call in a professional to have the oven recalibrated.

Chocolate–Crème de Cacao Walnut Pie

Chocolate, crème de cacao, and molasses turn what at first appears to be a quasi-pecan pie into something quite different—a nut pie, yes, but one with a complex flavor scheme that let's you know with just one bite that the walnuts are a team player here, not the only taste in town. I line the pan with a walnut pastry, for a nutty emphasis, and serve with plain vanilla ice cream, so the deep, intriguing flavors shine through.

MAKES 8 TO 10 SERVINGS

1/2 recipe Nutty Pie Pastry (page 42) made with walnuts, refrigerated

FILLING

1 cup light corn syrup

1 tablespoon unsulfured molasses

1/4 cup (1/2 stick) unsalted butter, cut into pieces

1/4 cup semisweet chocolate chips

3 tablespoons crème de cacao

2 teaspoons vanilla extract

1/2 cup sugar

2 tablespoons all-purpose flour

1/4 teaspoon ground cinnamon

Big pinch of salt

3 large eggs, at room temperature

2 cups coarsely chopped walnuts

GARNISH

Vanilla ice cream

1. If you haven't already, prepare the pastry and refrigerate until firm enough to roll, about 45 minutes. It's best not to overchill nut pastries or they can be tricky to handle.

2. On a sheet of lightly floured waxed paper, roll the pastry into a 13-inch circle with a floured rolling pin. Invert the pastry over a 9½-inch deep-dish pie pan, center, and peel off the paper. Tuck the pastry into the pan, without stretching it, and sculpt the edge into a ridge that's just slightly higher than the edge of the pan. Place in the freezer for 15 minutes, then partially prebake and let cool according to the directions on page 16. Reduce the oven temperature to 350°F.

3. Gently heat the corn syrup, molasses, and butter in a small saucepan until the butter melts. Add the chocolate chips and remove from the heat. Wait 5 minutes, then whisk to smooth the chocolate. Whisk in the crème de cacao and vanilla. Set aside.

4. Combine the sugar, flour, cinnamon, and salt in a large bowl. Add the eggs and whisk well to blend. Scrape the chocolate mixture into the eggs, whisking to blend. Stir in the walnuts. Carefully pour the filling into the cooled pie shell. Using a fork, gently rake the nuts to distribute them evenly.

5. Place the pie on the center oven rack and bake until the center is set and the edge of the pie puffs and cracks slightly, 35 to 40 minutes. Rotate the pie 180 degrees halfway through the baking, so that the side that faced the back of the oven now faces forward. When done, the center should not be soupy. Give the pie a little nudge to check.

6. Transfer the pie to a wire rack and let cool thoroughly. Serve at room temperature, or cover loosely with aluminum foil, refrigerate, and serve cold. Garnish with ice cream.

Recipe for Success

> The walnut pastry is very good here, but you can use any pastry that will fit a 9½-inch deep-dish pie pan.

> To emphasize what I've mentioned elsewhere, you *could* get away with not prebaking the pie shell, but I don't recommend it. This type of pie doesn't bake as long as some, and so there's a good chance you'll end up with an undercooked pastry.

> If you don't have crème de cacao, you can substitute a coffee liqueur, such as Kahlúa. You'll wind up with a mocha taste instead of chocolate, but is that a bad thing? I don't think so.

Maria's Double-Crust Walnut Pie

My editor, Pam Hoenig, mentioned in passing one day that she had tasted a wonderful, and rather different, version of a walnut pie. Would I be interested in trying the recipe? Naturally I was, and within a few days I had a copy of her friend Maria Roman's recipe in my hands. Unlike other pies, this one is baked in a 9-inch springform pan. The pan is lined with a shortbread pie pastry, made with softened butter that's blended, not cut, into the dry ingredients. The filling is a rich, homemade caramel mixture with lots of chopped walnuts added. This pie is a little too runny if you cut into it while it's hot, but it has just the right slightly thickened texture after it has cooled somewhat. If you are or know a walnut lover, dessert doesn't get much better than this. Note that Maria—a stay-at-home mom who loves to cook, entertain, and try new recipes—says that this tastes wonderful with butter pecan ice cream.

MAKES 10 SERVINGS

1 recipe Maria's Shortbread Pie Pastry (page 38), refrigerated

FILLING

1 1/4 cups sugar

1/3 cup water

1 cup heavy or whipping cream

1 1/2 tablespoons honey

2 3/4 cups walnut halves, toasted (see Recipe for Success) and coarsely chopped

GLAZE

1 large egg yolk, lightly beaten

1. If you haven't already, prepare the pastry and refrigerate until firm enough to roll, about 1 hour. Coat a 9 1/2- to 10-inch round (3-inch-deep) springform pan with nonstick cooking spray or rub lightly with vegetable oil. Set aside.

2. On a sheet of lightly floured waxed paper, roll one of the larger pieces of dough into a 10- or 11-inch circle (depending on the size of your pan) with a floured rolling pin. Invert the pastry over the prepared pan, center, and peel off the paper. Tuck the pastry into the pan, pressing it gently into the bottom and lower part of the side. Take the smaller pieces of dough and roll them into 14-inch-long ropes. Place one rope in the bottom of the pan, up against the side. Repeat with the other rope, placing it against the opposite side. They'll be like overlapping snakes in the bottom of the pan. Press the coiled dough evenly and flatly against the side of the pan, about halfway up. Place in the refrigerator for 15 minutes.

3. Combine the sugar and water in a medium-size saucepan, preferably nonstick. Stir gently over medium-low heat until the sugar dissolves. Stop stirring and increase the heat to medium. Boil the sugar syrup, swirling the pan occasionally, until the mixture turns a medium to dark amber shade, 7 to 8 minutes. Remove from the heat and, with your arm outstretched in case the mixture spatters, add the cream, then the honey, stirring well to dissolve any bits of caramel that have formed. Stir in the walnuts. Set aside on a rack and let cool to room temperature.

4. Shortly before the mixture has finished cooling, remove the pan from the refrigerator. Preheat the oven to 350°F.

5. Roll the remaining piece of dough into a 9½- to 10-inch circle (depending on the size of your pan) on a sheet of lightly floured waxed paper. Spoon the caramel mixture into the chilled crust, smoothing the top. Using a pastry brush or finger, lightly moisten the upper ¼ inch of the pastry. Invert the top pastry onto your outstretched hand and peel off the paper. Carefully lower the pastry over the pie. Press the pastries together at the edge to seal. Brush the beaten egg yolk evenly over the top. Make 2 small steam vents in the top pastry with a sharp knife.

6. Place the pie on the center oven rack and bake for 20 minutes, then rotate the pie 180 degrees, so that the part that faced the back of the oven now faces forward. Continue to bake until the top is well browned, about 20 minutes.

7. Transfer the pie to a cooling rack and let cool. Serve slightly warm or at room temperature. (Remove the sides of the pan before slicing.)

Recipe for Success

▶ If you don't have much experience making caramel, you may wonder when it is done. The first thing, already mentioned, is the total elapsed time. So use a timer. Another thing is the color. If the caramel looks like it's getting too dark, quickly pull it off the heat and add the cream. A third indication that it's done is a very light plume of smoke—not steam—rising from the pan. Again, if you see that, pull it off the heat immediately.

▶ This may or may not happen, but when the pie is done, you may see the steam inside pushing the top pastry up. You also may notice a crack in the top crust where the filling is gently bubbling. But don't count on either. For this pie, time is the best overall indicator of doneness.

▶ To toast the walnuts, preheat the oven to 350°F. Spread the nuts evenly on a large baking sheet and toast until lightly browned, 7 to 8 minutes.

Oregon Caramel-Coffee Hazelnut Pie

Along with the many entities you'll find represented at www.oregonhazelnuts.org—including the Hazelnut Marketing Board, Oregon Hazelnut Commission, Nut Growers Society, and Oregon Association of Hazelnut Industries—you'll find a handful of great recipes for some of the dishes people in Oregon like to make with hazelnuts. Here's one that caught my eye: a hazelnut pie in the pecan pie mold—which is to say, a thick layer of candy-like goo under a topping of crunchy hazelnuts. I added the coffee, which I think is the perfect assertive match for the strong flavor of toasted hazelnuts. This is great with—what else?—coffee ice cream or Coffee Mascarpone (page 607).

MAKES 8 TO 10 SERVINGS

1 recipe Basic Flaky Pie Pastry, Single Crust (page 31) or All-Butter Pie Pastry, Single Crust (page 28), refrigerated

FILLING

1/2 cup firmly packed dark brown sugar

1 tablespoon instant espresso or coffee granules

1/2 cup (1 stick) unsalted butter, melted

3 large eggs, at room temperature

1 cup light corn syrup

1 teaspoon vanilla extract

1/4 teaspoon salt

1 1/2 cups hazelnuts, toasted (see page 163) and chopped by hand (see Recipe for Success)

1. If you haven't already, prepare the pastry and refrigerate until firm enough to roll, about 1 hour.

2. On a sheet of lightly floured waxed paper, roll the pastry into a 12-inch circle with a floured rolling pin. Invert the pastry over a 9-inch standard pie pan, center, and peel off the paper. Tuck the pastry into the pan, without stretching it, and sculpt the edge into an upstanding ridge. Place in the freezer for 15 minutes, then partially prebake and let cool according to the instructions on page 16. Reduce the oven temperature to 350°F.

3. Combine the brown sugar, coffee, and butter in a large bowl. Whisk well to combine. Whisk in the eggs, corn syrup, vanilla, and salt. Stir in the hazelnuts. Pour the filling into the cooled pie shell. Using a fork, gently rake the filling to distribute the hazelnuts evenly.

4. Place the pie on the center oven rack and bake for 25 minutes, then rotate the pie 180 degrees, so that the part that faced the back of the oven now faces forward.

Continue to bake until the center is set, 20 to 25 minutes. When done, the surface should not move in waves. To check, give the pie a quick nudge.

5. Transfer the pie to a wire rack and let cool thoroughly. Serve at room temperature, or cover with loosely tented aluminum foil, refrigerate, and serve cold.

Recipe for Success

▶ Hazelnuts are fairly firm, so chop them into relatively small pieces or the pie may present a textural challenge for some.

▶ While we're on the subject, whenever you're chopping nuts for this or any other nut pie, do it by hand unless otherwise instructed. Using a food processor will reduce some of the nuts to a fine, floury consistency, not typically the desired texture.

Like Virginia Diner's Peanut Pie

I had been hearing that a restaurant called the Virginia Diner, in Wakefield, Virginia, made the best peanut pie around, so I contacted one of the owners, who was quick to point out that the diner's peanut pie is indeed deliciously world famous. She described it as "like a pecan pie, only better," and, of course, she said, it is always made with great homegrown Virginia peanuts. Having learned that there's an inverse relationship between the level of self-hoopla and one's chances of securing a recipe, I held my breath when I finally got around to asking her whether she would be willing to share the recipe with me and my readers. Alas, she would not, but she was kind enough to direct me to a Web site, www.aboutpeanuts.com, which has a recipe for peanut pie that is "pretty similar." Would she care to enumerate the differences? "Sorry." Turns out the recipe at that Web site, reprinted here with permission, is so good that I've forgiven the Virginia Diner for not sharing theirs. This pie is superlative: a golden layer of roasted peanuts on top of a soft and yummy filling. I always serve it with a scoop of vanilla ice cream and Warm Mocha Sauce (page 607).

MAKES 8 TO 10 SERVINGS

1 recipe Basic Flaky Pie Pastry, Single Crust (page 31), refrigerated

FILLING

3 large eggs

1/2 cup sugar

11/2 cups dark corn syrup

1/4 cup (1/2 stick) unsalted butter, melted

1/4 teaspoon salt

1/2 teaspoon vanilla extract

11/2 cups chopped salted dry-roasted peanuts

1. If you haven't already, prepare the pastry and refrigerate until firm enough to roll, about 1 hour.

2. On a sheet of lightly floured waxed paper, roll the pastry into a 13-inch circle with a floured rolling pin. Invert the pastry over a 9½-inch deep-dish pie pan, center, and peel off the paper. Tuck the pastry into the pan, without stretching it, and sculpt the edge so it is even with the rim. Place in the freezer for 15 minutes, then partially prebake and let cool according to the instructions on page 16. Reduce the oven temperature to 350°F.

3. In a large bowl, whisk the eggs and sugar together just until frothy. Whisk in the corn syrup, butter, salt, and vanilla until well blended. Stir in the peanuts. Slowly pour the filling into the cooled pie shell. Using a fork, gently rake the peanuts to distribute them evenly.

4. Place the pie on the center oven rack and bake for 30 minutes, then rotate the pie 180 degrees, so that the part that faced the back of the oven now faces forward. Continue to bake until the filling is set and does not move in waves, about 20 minutes. To check, give the pie a quick nudge.

5. Transfer the pie to a wire rack and let cool thoroughly. Serve at room temperature, or cover with loosely tented aluminum foil and refrigerate for 1 to 2 hours before serving.

Recipe for Success

▶ **Be sure *not* to use unroasted peanuts here. The roasting really brings out the nut flavor. By the same token, do *not* use honey-roasted or other sweetened nuts or the pie may be too sweet.**

Trail Mix Peanut Butter Pie

This is something like a pecan pie, only made with peanuts, peanut butter, raisins, and chocolate chips—all the things most of us like in a trail mix. Consider taking a slice of this pie along on your next hike, bike ride, or cross-country ski. Sweet and rich, this pie packs an energy wallop and tastes extraordinary. And it's only slightly more difficult to prepare than your favorite trail mix. Since this pie freezes well, you can slice it into skinny wedges, wrap them in aluminum foil or freezer bags, and stash them in the freezer until you need them. Just throw a couple of slices in your fanny pack, and they'll be perfectly thawed by the time you need them.

MAKES 10 TO 12 SERVINGS

1 recipe Basic Flaky Pie Pastry, Single Crust (page 31), refrigerated

FILLING

3 large eggs, at room temperature

1 large egg yolk

1/2 cup granulated sugar

2 tablespoons firmly packed light brown sugar

1/3 cup smooth peanut butter

1 cup light corn syrup

1/4 cup (1/2 stick) unsalted butter, melted

1 teaspoon vanilla extract

1/2 cup salted dry-roasted peanuts

1/2 cup dark raisins

1/2 cup semisweet chocolate chips

1.   If you haven't already, prepare the pastry and refrigerate until firm enough to roll, about 1 hour.

2.   On a sheet of lightly floured waxed paper, roll the pastry into a 13-inch circle with a floured rolling pin. Invert the pastry over a 9½-inch deep-dish pie pan, center, and peel off the paper. Tuck the pastry into the pan, without stretching it, and sculpt the edge so it is just slightly above the rim. Place in the freezer for 15 minutes, then partially bake and let cool according to the instructions on page 16. Reduce the oven temperature to 350°F.

3.   Combine the eggs, egg yolk, and sugars in a large bowl and beat for 15 seconds with an electric mixer. Add the peanut butter, corn syrup, and butter and beat again until smooth. Blend in the vanilla. Stir in the peanuts and raisins. Scatter the chocolate chips evenly over the bottom of the cooled pie shell and slowly pour in the filling.

4.   Place the pie on the center oven rack and bake until the perimeter puffs slightly and the filling is set, about 40 minutes. Rotate the pie 180 degrees about halfway through the baking, so that the part that faced the back of the oven now faces forward.

5. Transfer the pie to a wire rack and let cool thoroughly. Serve at room temperature, or cover loosely with aluminum foil, refrigerate, and serve slightly chilled.

Recipe for Success

▶ **Another fun way to do this trail mix pie is in small, individual metal pie pans. The small size is the perfect hiking companion, and everyone gets a whole little pie—a morale-lifting touch during a long hike or outing. To keep it simple, make the pastry very thin, use it to line small pie pans, and don't bother to prebake the crusts—just freeze them before filling. Place the pans on a baking sheet, fill to the top, and bake at 350°F for 20 to 25 minutes, until puffy. Transfer to a wire rack and let cool thoroughly. Cover loosely with aluminum foil and refrigerate until cold. Remove from the pans—or loosen and put back in the pans, if you like, to keep them protected—then wrap and freeze until needed.**

Five Reasons You'll Probably Like My Peanut and Peanut Butter Pies

▶ **Of the 10 top-selling candy bars in the United States, 4 contain peanuts or peanut butter.**

▶ **Americans eat more than 600 million pounds of peanuts each year.**

▶ **Peanuts are a good source of folate, and that's good for you.**

▶ **Peanut butter is consumed in 89 percent of U.S. households. Yours is likely one of them.**

▶ **Peanuts account for more than two-thirds of all the snack nuts consumed.**

Peanut Butter Cheesecake Pie with Brown Sugar–Sour Cream Topping

This is essentially a cheesecake baked in a pie pan. The filling has a creamy, peanut buttery texture, with the occasional soft crunch of peanut butter chips. It's topped with a sour cream and brown sugar layer that's added once the cake has cooled a bit. This is a good one for the kids, but I've also brought it to a grown-up dinner party, where it was a big hit as a follow-up to the host's "comfort food" main course.

MAKES 10 SERVINGS

1 recipe Graham Cracker Crumb Crust (page 51) or Nutty Graham Cracker Crust (page 53) made with peanuts

FILLING
Four 3-ounce packages full-fat cream cheese, softened

1 cup smooth peanut butter

1 1/4 cups granulated sugar

3 large eggs

1 large egg yolk

1/2 cup full-fat sour cream

1 1/2 teaspoons vanilla extract

1 cup peanut butter chips

BROWN SUGAR–SOUR CREAM TOPPING

1 cup full-fat sour cream

1/4 cup firmly packed light brown sugar

A few drops of vanilla extract

1. Prepare the crust and press it into the bottom and up the side of a 9 1/2-inch deep-dish pie pan. Refrigerate, prebake, and let cool as directed. Reduce the oven temperature to 325°F. Adjust one of the oven racks to the lowest position. Fill a shallow baking pan about halfway with water and put it on the bottom rack to start steaming up the oven. Keep one rack in the center of the oven for baking the pie.

2. Combine the cream cheese and peanut butter in a large bowl. Using an electric mixer, cream the ingredients on low speed. Gradually add the granulated sugar, beating until evenly blended and scraping down the bowl as needed. Blend in the eggs and egg yolk, one at a time, until combined. Blend in the sour cream and vanilla. Fold in the peanut butter chips. Scrape the filling into the pan, smoothing it with a spoon or rubber spatula.

3. Place the pie on the center oven rack and bake for about 50 minutes, rotating the pie 180 degrees about halfway through the baking, so that the part that faced the back of the oven now faces forward. When the pie is done, the filling may be puffed slightly, though not too much, and the center will be wobbly but set. Additionally, the very center may have a shiny finish, whereas the rest of the pie will have a flat appearance.

4. Transfer the pie to a wire rack and let cool slightly.

5. While the pie is still slightly warm, make the topping. Combine the sour cream and brown sugar in a small saucepan over low heat, stirring well to smooth. Remove from the heat and stir in the vanilla. When the mixture is lukewarm, pour it over the center of the pie, immediately tilting the pie so that the topping runs up to the edge. Return to the rack and let cool thoroughly. Cover with loosely tented aluminum foil and refrigerate for at least 6 hours, preferably overnight, before serving.

Recipe for Success

▶ Take care not to overbeat the filling. You don't want to beat too much air into it, causing it to puff dramatically during baking and then fall, perhaps cracking. A stand mixer with a flat beater is best.

▶ The steaming water on the rack below the pie is not absolutely necessary, but it's a good trick to know. Cheesecakes are often baked with some sort of steam in the oven, as the moisture helps to keep the surface from drying out. Feel free to borrow this trick for any of the other cheesecake-type pies in this collection.

Macadamia–Chocolate Chunk Pie

On a recent trip to Hawaii, my wife, Bev, and I ran into a number of pies like this: macadamia nuts, chunks of chocolate, and a lingering whisper of coconut flavor. Back home, I put together our own version of this Hawaiian favorite using, of course, genuine island macadamia nuts. Throw a luau and serve this for dessert. Or make it to celebrate a friend's impending departure for the islands. Either way, it's fabulous with a big scoop of vanilla ice cream.

MAKES 8 TO 10 SERVINGS

1 recipe Basic Flaky Pie Pastry, Single Crust (page 31) or Basic Shortening Pie Pastry, Single Crust (page 30), refrigerated

FILLING

3 large eggs

3/4 cup firmly packed light brown sugar

1/2 cup dark corn syrup

1/4 cup (1/2 stick) unsalted butter, melted

1 teaspoon vanilla extract

1 1/4 cups chopped salted dry-roasted macadamia nuts (see Recipe for Success)

1/3 cup sweetened flaked coconut

1 cup semisweet chocolate chunks

1. If you haven't already, prepare the pastry and refrigerate until firm enough to roll, about 1 hour.

2. On a sheet of lightly floured waxed paper, roll the pastry into a 12-inch circle with a floured rolling pin. Invert the pastry over a 9-inch standard pie pan, center, and peel off the paper. Tuck the pastry into the pan, without stretching it, and sculpt the edge into an upstanding ridge. Place in the freezer for 15 minutes, then partially prebake and let cool according to the instructions on page 16. Reduce the oven temperature to 350°F.

3. In a large bowl, whisk the eggs until frothy. Whisk in the brown sugar and corn syrup. Add the butter and vanilla and whisk again. Stir in the macadamia nuts and coconut. Scatter the chocolate chunks evenly over the bottom of the cooled pie shell. Slowly pour the filling into the shell. Using a fork, gently rake the filling to distribute the solid pieces more or less evenly.

4. Place on the center oven rack and bake 30 minutes, then rotate the pie 180 degrees, so the part that faced the back of the oven now faces forward. Continue to bake until the filling is set and the top a rich golden brown, 25 to 30 minutes. To check for doneness, give the pie a quick nudge. The filling should be stable and show no signs of movement. Also, it will likely have puffed slightly, but not so much that there are large cracks.

5. Transfer the pie to a wire rack and let cool thoroughly. Cover with loosely tented aluminum foil and refrigerate for at least 2 hours or overnight before serving. If the pie is very cold, slice and let sit at room temperature for 15 to 20 minutes before serving.

Recipe for Success

▶ Don't leave the macadamia nuts in large pieces, or they'll squeeze the filling out of the pie when you cut it. Chop them small, by hand, though not overly fine.

▶ I like salted macadamias for this pie because a little saltiness makes for a good contrast in a sweet pie. If you find only unsalted nuts, by all means use them.

Pine Nut Pie

Mild and buttery-tasting, pine nuts give this sweet pie a soft crunch, a delicious flavor, and a golden mosaic surface pattern. There's just a touch of cinnamon, to complement the nuts without overpowering them, and a brown sugar caramel-like filling to show everything off. This is a real treat served with butter pecan ice cream.

MAKES 8 TO 10 SERVINGS

1 recipe Basic Flaky Pie Pastry, Single Crust (page 31), refrigerated

FILLING
1/2 cup firmly packed light brown sugar
2 tablespoons all-purpose flour
1/4 teaspoon ground cinnamon
Big pinch of salt
5 tablespoons unsalted butter, melted

3 large eggs
3/4 cup light corn syrup
1/2 teaspoon vanilla extract
1 cup pine nuts

GARNISH
Butter pecan, coffee, or vanilla ice cream

1. If you haven't already, prepare the pastry and refrigerate until firm enough to roll, about 1 hour.

2. On a sheet of lightly floured waxed paper, roll the pastry into a 12-inch circle with a floured rolling pin. Invert the pastry over a 9-inch standard pie pan, center, and peel off the paper. Tuck the pastry into the pan, without stretching it, and sculpt the edge into an upstanding ridge. Place in the freezer for 15 minutes. Preheat the oven to 350°F.

3. Combine the brown sugar, flour, cinnamon, and salt in a large bowl and rub well to combine. Whisk in the butter, then the eggs, adding them one at a time. Whisk in the corn syrup and vanilla. Stir in the pine nuts. Scrape the filling into the chilled pie shell. Using a fork, gently rake the nuts to distribute them evenly.

4. Place the pie on the center oven rack and bake for 40 to 45 minutes, rotating the pie 180 degrees halfway through the baking, so that the part that faced the back of the oven now faces forward. When done, the top will be a deep golden brown, and the filling will be set. Give the pie a little nudge to check. The filling should be wobbly but not soupy in the center.

5. Transfer the pie to a wire rack and let cool thoroughly. Serve at room temperature, or cover loosely with aluminum foil and refrigerate briefly before serving. Either way, don't forget the ice cream.

Recipe for Success

▸ Don't bother to toast the pine nuts before adding them to the pie. They will rise to the surface during baking and toast up very nicely.

▸ For a familiar touch, substitute $1/3$ cup chopped pecans for an equal amount of the pine nuts.

Almond-Coconut Pie

Here's a delicious pie with a half-cakey texture but just enough moisture to pass as a pie. One of the more appealing things about it is that the entire filling is made in a food processor; you won't leave a pile of bowls, beaters, and dirty utensils in your wake. To keep it really easy, you start with sliced almonds, which are chopped somewhat (see Recipe for Success) in the processor, saving you time and giving the pie the sort of fine texture it needs. I love this with fresh coffee for either dessert or breakfast.

MAKES 8 TO 10 SERVINGS

1 recipe All-Butter Pie Pastry, Single Crust (page 28) or $1/2$ recipe Nutty Pie Pastry (page 42) made with almonds, refrigerated

FILLING

$1^1/2$ cups sliced almonds

$2/3$ cup sugar

$1/4$ cup all-purpose flour

$1/4$ cup sweetened flaked coconut

$1^1/2$ teaspoons baking powder

$1/4$ teaspoon salt

$1/2$ cup (1 stick) unsalted butter, at room temperature but not too soft

2 large eggs

$1/2$ cup heavy or whipping cream

$1/2$ teaspoon vanilla extract

1. If you haven't already, prepare the pastry and refrigerate until firm enough to roll, about 1 hour.

2. On a sheet of lightly floured waxed paper, roll the larger portion of the pastry into a 12-inch circle with a floured rolling pin. Invert over a 9-inch standard pie pan, center,

and peel off the paper. Gently tuck the pastry into the pan, without stretching it, and sculpt the overhang into an upstanding ridge. Place in the freezer for 15 minutes. Preheat the oven to 400°F.

3. Combine the almonds and sugar in a food processor and pulse 5 or 6 times to partially chop the nuts. Add the flour, coconut, baking powder, and salt and pulse until the mixture is well combined and the nuts more finely chopped, though not pulverized. Add the butter in 3 or 4 large pieces and pulse until well incorporated. Add the eggs, cream, and vanilla and process until well blended, 6 to 8 seconds. Scrape the filling into the pie shell, smoothing the top with a spoon.

4. Place the pie on the center oven rack and bake for 15 minutes. Reduce the oven temperature to 350°F and rotate the pie 180 degrees, so that the part that faced the back of the oven now faces forward. Continue to bake until the filling rises somewhat and is set (not wobbly), 25 to 30 minutes.

5. Transfer the pie to a wire rack and let cool. Serve just barely warm or at room temperature.

Recipe for Success

▶ Make sure you don't overprocess the sliced almonds or they'll lose their pleasant, slight crunch.

▶ One thing I like to do with this pie, to retain a little extra moisture, is to cover it with plastic wrap while it is still just a tad warm. Whether you do this or not, you'll notice that the pie is a little moister on the second day than on the first. Both ways are delicious.

Fruits of the Forest Pie (Nut Version)

As I explained in the headnote to the fruit version of the same title (see page 132), fruits of the forest pies are more often made with fruit, but nuts seem to me the more authentic way to do it. Here's my favorite interpretation of the nut version, made with mixed nuts and nut liqueurs. I recommend simply buying a bag of roasted mixed nuts at a place like Trader Joe's. It's so much easier than buying the separate nuts and toasting them first. I leave most of them whole, to really show them off and whet the appetite. This crunchy, delicious pie may well be the granddaddy of nut pies—big, bold, and with a rich, nutty flavor accented by the liqueurs.

MAKES 8 TO 10 SERVINGS

1 recipe Basic Flaky Pie Pastry, Single Crust (page 31), refrigerated

FILLING

4 large eggs

1 cup light corn syrup

2/3 cup firmly packed light brown sugar

5 tablespoons unsalted butter, melted

1 tablespoon hazelnut liqueur

1 tablespoon almond liqueur

1 teaspoon vanilla extract

1/4 teaspoon almond extract

1/4 to 1/2 teaspoon salt

2 1/2 cups roasted mixed nuts (see Recipe for Success)

GARNISH

Fresh Whipped Cream (page 605)

1.   If you haven't already, prepare the pastry and refrigerate until firm enough to roll, about 1 hour.

2.   On a sheet of lightly floured waxed paper, roll the pastry into a 13-inch circle with a floured rolling pin. Invert the pastry over a 9½-inch deep-dish pie pan, center, and peel off the paper. Tuck the pastry into the pan, without stretching it, and sculpt the edge into an upstanding ridge. Place in the freezer for 15 minutes, then partially prebake and let cool according to the directions on page 16. Reduce the oven temperature to 350°F.

3.   Gently whisk the eggs in a large bowl until blended. Whisk in the corn syrup, brown sugar, butter, liqueurs, and extracts. Add the salt, using the lesser amount if the nuts are already salted. Set aside.

4.   Spread the nuts in the cooled pie shell. Remove any that seem too large for your taste—such as Brazil nuts—and chop them coarsely. Scatter them back in the shell. Ladle

the filling over the nuts. With the back of a spoon, push the nuts down into the filling to coat them; they'll pop back up right away.

5. Put the pie on the center oven rack and bake for 30 minutes, then rotate the pie 180 degrees, so that the part that faced the back of the oven now faces forward. Bake until the filling is set, 10 to 15 minutes. To check, give the pie a little nudge. It shouldn't be soupy in the center.

6. Transfer the pie to a wire rack and let cool thoroughly. Serve at room temperature, with a dollop of whipped cream.

Recipe for Success

▶ Look for a nut mixture without peanuts, as they tend to overwhelm other nuts. My ideal combination would include Brazil nuts, hazelnuts, cashews, pecans, and maybe almonds. I like having a little of the rain forest in my fruits of the forest pie.

▶ If 2¹/₂ cups of nuts seems like a bit much once they're in the pie shell, take out a few. But just remember, this is a pie for nut lovers. You wouldn't want to make it otherwise, right?

▶ Unlike for some of my nut pies, I don't chop the nuts here (for the most part) because I love the way the pie looks with whole nuts and large pieces. The big nuts may squeeze out some of the filling as you cut the pie, but you can make cleaner cuts by slicing it when it is very cold.

Chess, buttermilk, and custard pies are close relatives, enough so that I've

clustered them here in a single chapter. And although each category has its

distinguishing characteristics, all share a common ingredient that you, the

home pie baker, should find noteworthy: eggs. When a pie is made with eggs,

the rules change considerably. Unlike the chapters on fruit pies, where you

Rich, Sweet, and Simple:
Chess, Buttermilk, and Other Custard Pies

have heard me harp relentlessly about not underbaking them—lest the thick-

ener not "take"—I will now implore you to go slow and easy, taking care not

to *overbake* your pies. Bottom line: you can do little damage to an egg-based

pie if it is baked too slowly, but plenty if it is overbaked. Rather than acting as

a thickener, the eggs "break," or lose their ability to hold moisture, when

overbaked. If you've ever cooked cup custard too long, you have some idea

what awaits: a weepy pie and a weepy cook. • Cautionary notes aside, the thing I love most about these pies in general is their accessibility. These are, for the most part, pies that have long been the stock-in-trade of the everyday cook. Their history dates back to a day when the main concern of busy, thrifty homemakers and farm wives was to get a good meal on the table and to do it without contrivance or flourish. So they did what came naturally: whipped up some pie shells, sent Junior to the barn for some eggs and buttermilk or cream, and then beat everything together with some sugar and threw it in the oven. If it was August and they had more cherries on hand than they knew what to do with, they might toss some of those in, too. That's the carefree spirit of nearly all these pies, and you should keep that in mind if you, like so many modern cooks, have a preference for simple but homemade.

What makes these pies most interesting and delicious, however, is not their similarity but their differences. As great composers know, the theme can remain constant without diminishing the variations. Maple syrup adds of a tinge of color and the subtle flavor of New England to a custard pie. The combination of coffee and hazelnuts gives it an exotic Mediterranean flair. A spoonful of cornmeal provides body and texture to a chess pie, making it distinct from one made without. Such is the beauty of these pies, and my hope is that you'll have a chance to try them all.

Tips for Baking Celestial Chess, Buttermilk, and Custard Pies

▶ Even if you're using just-purchased cream, milk, or buttermilk, taste it before adding it to your filling. You never know when something may be "off" and you don't want to find that out when you're serving your future mother-in-law a slice of pie.

▶ As much as possible, use pure (not imitation) extracts in these pies. Custard fillings have a way of amplifying flavors, so you always want to start with the best.

▶ Take care not to overbake these pies, and do not bake them at too high a temperature. If your egg-based pies have a tendency to puff quickly and considerably, your oven is too hot. Set it 25°F to 35°F lower, and call in a professional to recalibrate the oven.

▶ When using eggs in a pie, make sure they're well blended, with the yolks and whites fully integrated, but don't overbeat. Beating air into the eggs may cause your fillings to be grainy.

▶ With few exceptions, these pies are best baked in a partially prebaked shell. If not, the crust of the finished pie has a tendency to taste somewhat raw.

▶ Consult each recipe for other clues, but in general the best indicator of doneness in nearly all these pies is the texture of the filling. It should be just barely set at the center, not soupy. The rest of the filling should be quivery or wobbly.

Classic Chess Pie

The thing I find so interesting about chess pie is not just the diversity of recipes but also the various mixing methods for them. In many of the recipes, the butter—and no shy amount of it— is melted and stirred or whisked into the filling. Here, however, it is creamed with the other ingredients, resulting in what looks like a creamy cake batter, at least up to the point when the lemon juice is added; then it becomes a bit curdled. The pie bakes up with a dark brown crust, which some say is a sign of a genuine chess pie. This is one excellent pie.

MAKES 10 TO 12 SERVINGS

1 recipe Basic Flaky Pie Pastry, Single Crust (page 31), refrigerated

FILLING

1/2 cup (1 stick) unsalted butter, softened

1 1/2 cups sugar

3 tablespoons all-purpose flour

Big pinch of salt

4 large eggs, at room temperature

1/3 cup fresh lemon juice

Grated zest of 1 lemon

1. If you haven't already, prepare the pastry and refrigerate until firm enough to roll, about 1 hour.

2. On a sheet of lightly floured waxed paper, roll the pastry into a 13-inch circle with a floured rolling pin. Invert over a 9 1/2-inch deep-dish pie pan, center, and peel off the paper. Tuck the pastry into the pan, without stretching it, and sculpt the edge so it is just slightly above the rim. Place in the freezer for 15 minutes, then partially prebake and let cool according to the instructions on page 16. Reduce the oven temperature to 350°F.

3. In a large bowl, cream the butter with an electric mixer, gradually adding the sugar about 1/4 cup at a time. Beat in the flour and salt; the mixture will be quite grainy. Beat in the eggs one at a time, beating well on medium-high speed after each addition. Blend in the lemon juice and zest on low speed. Scrape the filling into the cooled pie shell, smoothing the top with a spoon.

4. Place the pie on the center oven rack and bake until the top is very dark brown, about 45 minutes, rotating the pie 180 degrees about halfway through the baking, so that the part that faced the back of the oven now faces forward. When done, the filling will be set and not soupy at the center. Give the pie a little nudge to check.

5. Transfer the pie to a wire rack and let cool to room temperature. Cover with loosely tented aluminum foil and refrigerate for at least 2 hours before serving.

Recipe for Success

▸ Don't worry about the curdled look of the filling after you blend in the lemon juice. It has no correlation to the finished consistency, which is smooth, dense, and creamy.

▸ The very top of the pie will be a little spongy when the pie is almost done, so it can be hard to check for doneness. Look carefully at the center of the pie as you nudge it. If the center moves in waves, give it more time.

▸ When you finally cover the pie in the fridge, be sure to use tented aluminum foil, because the spongy top may stick to plastic wrap.

Homestead Chess Pie

This recipe, from the famed Homestead Restaurant in Lexington, Kentucky, first appeared in the *Louisville Courier-Journal*. According to my friend Liz Reiter, assistant food editor at the paper, then food editor Cissy Gregg published the recipe on September 24, 1954 (just a few days after I was born), and it has remained a classic of the genre ever since. The pie embodies the genius I so appreciate about chess pies: that so few simple ingredients can make such a wonderful pie. Typical of other chess pies, this one has a tablespoon of cornmeal, for added thickening, and a dash of vinegar, to cut the sweetness and lift the flavor. I really am crazy about this pie, which can be served warm, at room temperature, or slightly chilled.

MAKES 8 TO 10 SERVINGS

1 recipe Basic Flaky Pie Pastry, Single Crust (page 31) or Basic Shortening Pie Pastry, Single Crust (page 30), refrigerated

FILLING

3 large eggs

1 1/2 cups sugar

7 tablespoons salted or unsalted butter, softened

1 tablespoon fine yellow cornmeal

1 tablespoon vinegar (see Recipe for Success)

1 teaspoon vanilla extract

1. If you haven't already, prepare the pastry and refrigerate until firm enough to roll, about 1 hour.

2. On a sheet of lightly floured waxed paper, roll the pastry into a 12-inch circle with a floured rolling pin. Invert the pastry over a 9-inch standard pie pan, center, and peel off the paper. Tuck the pastry into the pan, without stretching it, and sculpt the edge so it is even with the rim. Place in the freezer for 15 minutes. Preheat the oven to 350°F.

3. In a large bowl, combine all the filling ingredients. Whisk well to mix thoroughly, then pour into the chilled pie shell.

4. Place the pie on the center oven rack and bake until a knife inserted in the center comes out clean, 30 to 35 minutes. Rotate the pie 180 degrees about halfway through the baking, so that the part that faced the back of the oven now faces forward. When done, the top of the pie will be a rich golden brown.

5. Transfer the pie to a wire rack and let cool for at least 30 minutes. Serve at any temperature you care to.

Recipe for Success

▶ The original recipe calls for an unbaked pie shell, as written here, but with many chess pies, I prefer to partially prebake the pie shell first (see page 16).

▶ The original recipe does not specify the kind of vinegar to be used. I use cider vinegar, but I imagine distilled white vinegar would work equally well.

Angus Barn Chocolate Chess Pie

The Angus Barn has been an institution in Raleigh, North Carolina, for more than 40 years. One of the most successful restaurants in the country, it is best known for its steaks—the restaurant serves some 600 to 700 a night—and consistently high standard of service. More than a few guests at the Angus Barn save room for the chocolate chess pie, which owner Van Eure says comes from an old church cookbook and was "doctored" by the original owners, Van's parents, Thad and Alice Eure. Van says, "This is best served at room temperature with whipped cream or vanilla ice cream."

MAKES 8 TO 10 SERVINGS

1 recipe Basic Flaky Pie Pastry, Single Crust (page 31), refrigerated

FILLING

1/2 cup (1 stick) unsalted butter

2 ounces semisweet chocolate, coarsely chopped

1 cup sugar

2 large eggs

1 teaspoon vanilla extract

Pinch of salt

1. If you haven't already, prepare the pastry and refrigerate until firm enough to roll, about 1 hour.

2. On a sheet of lightly floured waxed paper, roll the pastry into a 12-inch circle with a floured rolling pin. Invert the pastry over a 9-inch standard pie pan, center, and peel off the paper. Tuck the pastry into the pan, without stretching it, and sculpt the edge into an upstanding ridge. Place in the freezer for 15 minutes, then partially prebake and let cool according to the instructions on page 16. Reduce the oven temperature to 350°F.

3. In a medium-size saucepan, preferably nonstick, melt the butter over low heat. Turn off the heat and add the chocolate. Let the mixture stand until the chocolate has

Chess Pie: One Southerner's Thoughts

"Here is a mystery: Where did this thoroughly Southern pie get its name? The British had a cheese pie that was somewhat similar, but not the same. Chess pie by that name doesn't show up in American cookbooks until the twentieth century, at least not with any regularity, not even in the South. . . . As for its name, there are two stories among the many that seem to ring true. The first has to do with an old piece of Southern furniture called a pie safe or pie chest. It's a cupboard with perforated tin panels, and its name is derived from the fact that pies and other confections were put there for storage and safekeeping. Chess pie may have been called a chest pie at first, meaning that it held up well in the pie chest.

"The other story is even simpler and more appealing. It is that a creative Southern housewife came up with this concoction and tried it out on her husband. He loved it. 'What kind of pie is this?' he is said to have exclaimed. His wife shrugged and smiled. 'I don't know,' she said; 'it's ches' pie.'"

—John Egerton, *Southern Food* (Knopf, 1987)

melted, about 5 minutes, occasionally tilting the pan so the hot butter runs over the chocolate. Whisk the mixture until smooth and evenly blended. Let cool briefly.

4. In a medium-size bowl, whisk together the sugar, eggs, vanilla, and salt. Add the chocolate mixture and whisk until evenly blended. Slowly pour the filling into the cooled pie shell.

5. Place the pie on the center oven rack and bake until set, 30 to 40 minutes, rotating the pie 180 degrees halfway through the baking, so that the part that faced the back of the oven now faces forward. When done, the top will have crusted over. The filling may puff slightly, but don't expect it to rise much.

6. Transfer the pie to a wire rack and let cool completely. The pie can be served at room temperature, but I think it has a better texture if it's covered with loosely tented aluminum foil and refrigerated for a couple of hours first.

Recipe for Success

▶ Note that the original Angus Barn recipe does not specify prebaking the pie shell. That's my own personal preference.

Fancy Chocolate Chess Pie

Most recipes for chocolate chess pie use unsweetened cocoa powder or unsweetened chocolate, but here's a fancier one made with bittersweet chocolate. Like the following Lemon Chess
Pie, this one also incorporates cornmeal to help thicken it, but the viscosity of the rich, chocolaty filling makes the presence of the cornmeal less apparent. The filling bakes up into two distinct layers—a very thin, crispy top crust and a fat, oozing, pudding-like layer of chocolate
underneath. Slightly warm, the pie is runny and sensuous. Cold, it has the delectable texture of
gooey caramel. Either way, it's delicious.

MAKES 8 TO 10 SERVINGS

1 recipe Basic Flaky Pie Pastry, Single Crust
(page 31), refrigerated

FILLING

1/2 cup (1 stick) unsalted butter, cut into
pieces

4 ounces bittersweet chocolate, coarsely
chopped

1 1/4 cups sugar

2 tablespoons fine yellow cornmeal

1/4 teaspoon salt

3 large eggs, at room temperature

1 large egg yolk, at room temperature

1/4 cup whole milk or light cream

1 teaspoon vanilla extract

1.   If you haven't already, prepare the pastry and refrigerate until firm enough to roll,
about 1 hour.

2.   On a sheet of lightly floured waxed paper, roll the pastry into a 12-inch circle with
a floured rolling pin. Invert the pastry over a 9-inch standard pie pan, center, and peel off
the paper. Tuck the pastry into the pan, without stretching it, and sculpt the edge so it is
just slightly above the rim. Place in the freezer for 15 minutes, then partially prebake and
let cool according to the instructions on page 16. Reduce the oven temperature to 325°F.

3.   Put the butter in the top of a double boiler placed over, not in, barely simmering
water. Scatter the chocolate around the butter. Let the butter and chocolate stand for
about 5 minutes, until melted, stirring once or twice once the melting is well under way.
Remove the top insert, whisk the mixture to smooth, and set aside to cool briefly. Whisk
the mixture again until smooth.

4.   Combine the sugar, cornmeal, and salt in a large bowl, tossing with your hands to
mix. Add the eggs, egg yolk, milk, and vanilla and whisk until evenly mixed. Pour the

chocolate mixture into the bowl and whisk briefly until smooth. Pour the filling into the cooled pie shell.

5. Place the pie on the center oven rack and bake for 35 to 40 minutes, then rotate the pie 180 degrees, so that the part that faced the back of the oven now faces forward. Continue to bake until the pie develops a uniformly thin upper crust, 20 to 25 minutes. The entire top of the pie may puff up as a single piece, unlike many other egg-based pies, where just the edge alone will rise up.

6. Transfer the pie to a wire rack and let cool for at least 1½ hours. Serve slightly warm or at room temperature. Or cover loosely with aluminum foil, refrigerate, and serve cold.

Recipe for Success

▶ You may notice that, among the chocolate pies in this collection, the chocolate and butter are sometimes melted in a saucepan over direct heat, other times in a double boiler. Given chocolate's temperamental behavior, the double boiler method is safer and generally preferred; you're much less likely to scorch it if you take this less direct route. That said, it's sometimes simpler to just start melting the butter in a saucepan over low heat, drop in the chopped chocolate, and turn off the heat. The residual heat in the pan and from the cooktop is usually sufficient to melt the chocolate. If necessary, you can always turn the heat back on, very low, for 30 seconds to reheat the pan. Swirling the pan, so that the warm butter runs over the top of the chocolate, also facilitates melting. Don't use this direct stovetop method when you're melting chocolate alone, however. In that case, always use a double boiler or microwave oven.

Lemon Chess Pie

As I said elsewhere, one of the common threads you'll find running through many recipes for chess pie is a tablespoon or two of cornmeal, rather than flour, to assist with the thickening. The more chess pies I've made, the more I've come to appreciate this small gesture—not only because it's a uniquely southern way of cooking, but also for the extra bit of texture the cornmeal adds. It's a particularly nice touch in this lemon version, as it gives the filling a pleasantly faint coarseness. The yellow cornmeal also fits right in with the lemon profile. All told, this is a simple, delicious pie you'll want to make often.

MAKES 8 TO 10 SERVINGS

1 recipe Basic Flaky Pie Pastry, Single Crust (page 31), refrigerated

FILLING

1 1/2 cups sugar

2 tablespoons fine yellow cornmeal

1/4 teaspoon salt

3 large eggs, at room temperature

1 large egg yolk, at room temperature

1/2 cup whole milk or light cream

1/4 cup (1/2 stick) unsalted butter, melted

3 tablespoons fresh lemon juice

Grated zest of 1 lemon

1/2 teaspoon vanilla extract

1. If you haven't already, prepare the pastry and refrigerate until firm enough to roll, about 1 hour.

2. On a sheet of lightly floured waxed paper, roll the pastry into a 13-inch circle with a floured rolling pin. Invert the pastry over a 9 1/2-inch deep-dish pie pan, center, and peel off the paper. Tuck the pastry into the pan, without stretching it, and sculpt the edge so it is just slightly above the rim. Place in the freezer for 15 minutes, then partially prebake and let cool according to the instructions on page 16. Reduce the oven temperature to 350°F.

3. Combine the sugar, cornmeal, and salt in a large bowl. Toss with your hands to combine. Add the eggs and egg yolk, whisking well to blend. Whisk in the milk, butter, lemon juice, lemon zest, and vanilla. Slowly pour the filling into the cooled pie shell.

4. Place the pie on the center oven rack and bake for 30 minutes, then rotate the pie 180 degrees, so that the part that was facing the back of the oven now faces forward. Continue to bake until the top is dark golden brown and the filling is set, 15 to 20 minutes. The filling may still be a little jiggly in the center, but it shouldn't move in waves.

5. Transfer the pie to a wire rack and let cool to room temperature. Serve at room temperature or cover with loosely tented aluminum foil and refrigerate until ready to serve.

Recipe for Success

‣ **This is, by some standards, a fairly mild-tasting lemon chess pie. Among the many recipes I've seen, some contain as much as 1/3 cup lemon juice and the zest of a couple of lemons. It's a matter of taste; I tend to keep mine toned down because that's the way my wife, Bev, likes it best. You can add more lemon, if you like. Also, instead of extra lemon juice, you might simply add 1/2 teaspoon lemon extract.**

Indiana Buttermilk Pie

Here is a recipe that comes from my handwritten recipe files. The original source is lost in the mists of time, but it is not unlike many other simple recipes for buttermilk pie with roots in farm country: the ingredients are pared down to the basics, the technique is straightforward, and the pie itself is just plain delicious.

MAKES 8 TO 10 SERVINGS

1 recipe Basic Flaky Pie Pastry, Single Crust (page 31), refrigerated

FILLING

1/2 cup firmly packed light brown sugar

1/2 cup granulated sugar

3 tablespoons all-purpose flour

Pinch of salt

3 large eggs

1 large egg yolk

1 teaspoon vanilla extract

1 1/2 cups buttermilk

3 tablespoons unsalted butter, melted

1. If you haven't already, prepare the pastry and refrigerate until firm enough to roll, about 1 hour.

2. On a sheet of lightly floured waxed paper, roll the pastry into a 13-inch circle with a floured rolling pin. Invert the pastry over a 9 1/2-inch deep-dish pie pan, center, and peel off the paper. Tuck the pastry into the pan, without stretching it, and sculpt the edge so it is even with the rim. Place in the freezer for 15 minutes, then partially prebake and let cool according to the instructions on page 16. Reduce the oven temperature to 350°F.

3. Combine the sugars, flour, and salt in a food processor and pulse to combine. Add the eggs, egg yolk, and vanilla and pulse again. Add the buttermilk and butter and process for 5 to 7 seconds, until well blended. Slowly pour the filling into the cooled pie shell. (You may want to pour it into a large pitcher first, then pour it into the shell.)

4. Place the pie on the center oven rack and bake until the top is golden brown and the custard is set, about 40 minutes. Rotate the pie 180 degrees halfway through the baking, so that the part that faced the back of the oven now faces forward. When done, the center may move very slightly when the pan is shaken.

5. Transfer the pie to a wire rack and let cool thoroughly. Serve at room temperature, or cover with loosely tented aluminum foil and refrigerate before serving.

Recipe for Success

▶ No recipe with deep roots in farm country would call for a food processor. That's my own update, and indeed this filling could be blended with nothing more than a whisk.

Hominy Grill Buttermilk Pie

Charleston, South Carolina, locals know that some of the best food in town is a bit off the well-worn path most tourists travel. The Hominy Grill is one fine example. Chef-owner Robert Stehling, a seasoned veteran of restaurants in New York and other cities, has been dishing up his version of Southern food since settling here in 1996. The Hominy Grill is known for this great buttermilk pie, whose filling, I think, tastes something like lemon pudding cake. Unlike my own version of buttermilk pie on page 369, Chef Stehling's incorporates lemon juice, for extra tang, and beaten egg whites. And rather than melting the butter, he creams it with the sugar, as if you were making a cake. These steps give the pie a unique texture—creamy and custard-like underneath and soufflé-like on top. I think you'll love it. Note that this can be made in a 9-inch standard or 9½-inch deep-dish pie pan.

MAKES 8 TO 10 SERVINGS

1 recipe Basic Flaky Pie Pastry, Single Crust (page 31), refrigerated

FILLING

6 tablespoons (¾ stick) unsalted butter, softened

1 cup sugar

2 large eggs, separated

3 tablespoons all-purpose flour

1 tablespoon fresh lemon juice

½ teaspoon ground nutmeg

¼ teaspoon salt

1 cup buttermilk

1. If you haven't already, prepare the pastry and refrigerate until firm enough to roll, about 1 hour.

2. On a sheet of lightly floured waxed paper, roll the pastry into a 13-inch circle with a floured rolling pin. Invert the pastry over a 9-inch standard or 9½-inch deep-dish pie pan, center, and peel off the paper. Tuck the pastry into the pan, without stretching it, and let the overhang drape over the edge. Trim the pastry flush with the outside edge of the pan, then crimp the edge with the tines of a fork. Place in the freezer for 15 minutes, then

Buttermilk 101

If buttermilk pie seems like a throwback to bygone days, in fact it is. Perhaps that's because buttermilk itself is one of those items that American farm families traditionally had on hand, in copious amounts, year in and year out.

Indeed, once upon a time, when butter was made on the farm, families churned every two or three days. By the time they got around to the task, the cream they churned had often soured naturally. When this soured cream was churned and the butter floated to the top, what remained was a clean, sour, great-tasting liquid: buttermilk. With only so many ways to use it, buttermilk often found its way into the family's pies.

Buttermilk today is not the same product our farming ancestors knew. Generally speaking, there are two kinds: cultured and acidified. Cultured buttermilk is made much like yogurt is: milk is inoculated with a bacterial culture and fermented. Acidified buttermilk is soured with tartaric or citric acid. The cultured variety, which some say has a smoother flavor, is thought to be better for pies and most other baked goods.

And by the way, there is no butter in buttermilk. In fact, it has only about 90 to 120 calories per cup, since most of it is made with nonfat or 1 percent milk. So go right ahead and have that second piece of buttermilk pie!

partially prebake and let cool according to the instructions on page 16. Reduce the oven temperature to 350°F.

3. Using an electric mixer, cream the butter in a large bowl, gradually adding the sugar until it is completely incorporated. Don't worry if the mixture is somewhat clumpy. Add the egg yolks and blend again. Add the flour, lemon juice, nutmeg, and salt. Blend until thoroughly combined. With the mixer running on low speed, gradually blend in the buttermilk. The mixture may look a little curdled; that's okay.

4. In a medium-size bowl, using clean, dry beaters, whip the egg whites until they hold soft peaks. Pour a little of the buttermilk mixture into the whites, folding gently to combine. Gently fold the egg white mixture into the remaining buttermilk mixture until just combined; don't overdo it. Pour the custard into the cooled pie shell.

5. Place the pie on the center oven rack and bake until the top is a rich golden brown and the sides have puffed slightly, 35 to 45 minutes. Rotate the pie 180 degrees halfway through the baking, so that the part that faced the back of the oven now faces forward. The filling will jiggle as a whole, but the center will not seem soupy.

6. Transfer the pie to a wire rack and let cool. Serve warm or at room temperature. Or cool thoroughly, cover with loosely tented aluminum foil, and refrigerate before serving.

Recipe for Success

▶ Robert Stehling says, "Separate the eggs when they're cold, but whisk them at room temperature. When an egg is cold, the white will separate more readily from the yolk, and the yolk is less likely to rupture during the process. But if egg whites separate better just out of the fridge, they whip to their maximum volume at room temperature, in part because the surface tension of the white is lower at room temperature, making it easier for small air pockets to form."

Three Sisters Coconut Buttermilk Pie

This wonderful pie, from Joyce White's book *Brown Sugar* (HarperCollins, 2003) is one of the best buttermilk pies I've ever tasted. The way she tells it, the pie is a composite of three recipes sent to her by dear friends, just at the time she was experimenting with recipes for buttermilk pie. Once you try it, I think you'll agree that she's integrated the best qualities of her friends' recipes.

MAKES 8 TO 10 SERVINGS

1 recipe Basic Flaky Pie Pastry, Single Crust (page 31) or Basic Shortening Pie Pastry, Single Crust (page 30), refrigerated

FILLING
3 large eggs, at room temperature
2/3 cup sugar
3 tablespoons all-purpose flour

1/4 cup canned cream of coconut, well stirred

2 cups buttermilk

1 teaspoon vanilla extract

Pinch of salt

1 cup sweetened flaked coconut

1/4 to 1/2 teaspoon ground nutmeg, to your taste

1. If you haven't already, prepare the pastry and refrigerate until firm enough to roll, about 1 hour.

2. On a sheet of lightly floured waxed paper, roll the pastry into a 13-inch circle with a floured rolling pin. Invert the pastry over a 9½-inch deep-dish pie pan, center, and peel

off the paper. Tuck the pastry into the pan, without stretching it, and sculpt the edge into an upstanding ridge. Place in the freezer for 15 minutes, then partially prebake and let cool according to the instructions on page 16. Reduce the oven temperature to 350°F.

3. Whisk the eggs, sugar, and flour together in a large bowl. Whisk in the cream of coconut, buttermilk, vanilla, and salt. Stir in the flaked coconut and nutmeg until evenly combined. Slowly pour the filling into the cooled pie shell.

4. Place the pie on the center oven rack and bake for 20 minutes, then turn the pie 180 degrees, so that the part that faced the back of the oven now faces forward. Continue to bake until the center of the custard is set, about 20 minutes. To check, give the pie a little nudge. If it's ready, the filling will not move in waves. The edges of the filling may have puffed very slightly, though perhaps not. Expect to see minimal, if any, browning on top of the filling.

5. Transfer the pie to a wire rack and let cool thoroughly. The pie may be served at room temperature, but I prefer the flavor when it is slightly chilled. (Cover with loosely tented aluminum foil before refrigerating.)

Recipe for Success

▶ I like a very coconuty pie and have used as much as ¹/₃ cup cream of coconut with great results.

▶ To make this a sort of piña colada–flavored pie, you may add up to 2 tablespoons light or dark rum to the filling.

Amish Milk Pie

Milk pie is an Amish specialty, the simplest sort of pie you're likely to run across. The unusual thing about milk pie is that it is not thickened with eggs, like a custard pie, so the result is endearingly runny, meant to be eaten with a spoon. Not all milk pies are alike. Some call for molasses, others for brown or granulated sugar. Many specify evaporated milk, which has half the water content of regular milk, while others use light cream or sour milk. This version is a composite of the best ones I tested.

MAKES 8 TO 10 SERVINGS

1 recipe Basic Flaky Pie Pastry, Single Crust (page 31) or any other single-crust pastry, refrigerated

FILLING

1/2 cup granulated sugar

1/2 cup firmly packed light brown sugar

1/4 cup all-purpose flour

Big pinch of salt

1 1/4 cups evaporated milk or light cream

2 tablespoons cold unsalted butter, cut into small pieces

1/4 teaspoon ground cinnamon

1. If you haven't already, prepare the pastry and refrigerate until firm enough to roll, about 1 hour.

2. On a sheet of lightly floured waxed paper, roll the pastry into a 12-inch circle with a floured rolling pin. Invert the pastry over a 9-inch standard pie pan, center, and peel off the paper. Tuck the pastry into the pan, without stretching it. Sculpt the edge of the pastry into an even band, pushing the upper edge down so it is just below the rim of the pan. (That way, it will be somewhat protected from the oven's heat and less likely to get too browned.) Place in the freezer for 15 minutes. Preheat the oven to 375°F.

3. Put the sugars, flour, and salt in a pile in the chilled pie shell. Rub the mixture together with your fingers to combine, then spread evenly in the shell. Drizzle the evaporated milk over the dry ingredients, but don't mix it in. Dot the surface of the pie with the butter and sprinkle with the cinnamon.

4. Place the pie on the center oven rack and bake until the filling has turned golden brown and is bubbly, 45 to 50 minutes. Rotate the pie 180 degrees about halfway through the baking, so that the part that faced the back of the oven now faces forward. Note that the filling will still seem soupy even when the pie is fully baked.

5. Transfer the pie to a wire rack and let cool for at least 30 minutes before serving. The pie can be served at any temperature. If not serving right away, cover the thoroughly cooled pie with loosely tented aluminum foil and refrigerate until you're ready to serve.

Recipe for Success

▶ **If you do refrigerate this pie, the melted butter is likely to harden on the surface, a less-than-delectable situation. To remelt the butter and take the chill off the pie, warm it in a hot oven for about 5 minutes before serving.**

▶ **Milk pies are great for kids. This pie can be made in 4 small, individual pie pans. Simply give each child a portion of the dough to roll and divide the ingredients evenly among the little pie shells. For another similar kid-friendly recipe, see Little Cream Pies on page 424.**

Shoofly Pie

An all-molasses shoofly pie can be very good indeed, but I've learned from experience that my own shoofly pies are generally better liked when made with a blend of brown sugar and molasses. Sweet as it is, molasses can have a pretty forward flavor; the brown sugar seems to mellow it a bit. In any event, I think you'll agree that this pie is good—whether you make it with all molasses or both sweeteners, the way I recommend. Note that blackstrap molasses is both darker and somewhat more tart-bitter than unsulfured molasses.

MAKES 8 TO 10 SERVINGS

1 recipe Basic Flaky Pie Pastry, Single Crust (page 31), refrigerated

FILLING

1 cup all-purpose flour

1 cup firmly packed light brown sugar

1/4 teaspoon salt

1/4 teaspoon ground cinnamon

6 tablespoons (3/4 stick) cold unsalted butter, cut into 1/4-inch pieces

1/2 cup unsulfured or blackstrap molasses

3/4 cup boiling water

1/2 teaspoon baking soda

1/2 teaspoon vanilla extract

1 large egg, lightly beaten

1.   If you haven't already, prepare the pastry and refrigerate until firm enough to roll, about 1 hour.

2.   On a sheet of lightly floured waxed paper, roll the larger portion of the pastry into a 12-inch circle with a floured rolling pin. Invert over a 9-inch standard pie pan, center, and peel off the paper. Gently tuck the pastry into the pan, without stretching it, sculpting the overhang into an upstanding ridge. Place in the freezer for 15 minutes. Preheat the oven to 425°F.

3.   Combine the flour, 1/2 cup of the brown sugar, the salt, and cinnamon in a large bowl. Add the butter and rub or cut it into the dry ingredients with your fingers or a pastry blender, mixing until the mixture resembles fine meal that forms small clumps when you pinch it together. Set aside.

4.   In a medium-size bowl, combine the remaining 1/2 cup brown sugar and the molasses. Add the boiling water and stir to dissolve the sugar. Whisk in the baking soda, vanilla, and egg. Pour the mixture into the chilled pie shell. Scatter the crumbs evenly over the filling. Do not tamp them down.

5. Place the pie on the center oven rack and bake for 10 minutes. Reduce the oven temperature to 350°F and rotate the pie 180 degrees, so that the part that faced the back of the oven now faces forward. Continue to bake until the filling is set, about 25 minutes. When done, the filling should wobble as a whole, and the center should not be soupy.

6. Transfer the pie to a wire rack and let cool thoroughly before serving.

Recipe for Success

▶ **To make what's sometimes called a dry-bottom shoofly pie, spread half of the crumbs over the bottom of the pie, add the molasses filling, and spread the remaining crumbs on top.**

▶ **Incidentally, I've seen shoofly pie recipes that call for everything from molasses to honey, brown sugar, granulated sugar, and dark corn syrup, used in various proportions. I mention that just in case you don't have $1/2$ cup molasses on hand and would like to make up the difference with another sweetener.**

The Origin of Shoofly Pie

"There are many versions of shoofly pie, which can be loosely defined as a liquid filling of molasses, boiling water and baking soda in an unbaked pie shell, topped with a crumb mixture and baked. Each version has passionate advocates among the (Pennsylvania) Dutch. There's a rather dry one that is dunked in coffee, a wet-bottom one that is much moister and spicier, and a cakelike kind in which the filling and crumbs are mixed together. No one seems to know, incidentally, how the pie got its name. Logical thinkers tend to the theory that the sweet stickiness attracted flies, but there are various other theories, including one rather unlikely claim that the name came from the French *chou-fleur*, since the crumbs on the surface look like cauliflower."

—Jose Wilson, *American Cooking: The Eastern Heartland* (Time-Life Books, 1971)

Sugar Pie (Tarte au Sucre)

Sugar pie, a French Canadian specialty, is a relative of our shoofly pie (see page 375)—at least this version is. What the two have in common is a large quantity of streusel-like crumbs, which are scattered in the pie shell and over the top to help thicken the filling. As the pie bakes, the crumbs more or less float to the surface and form a thick layer on top—at least as thick as the sweet maple syrup layer below. This recipe is an adaptation of one I found in a book of food editors' favorite desserts and is credited to the late Madame Jehane Benoit, a cookbook author and leading authority on French Canadian cooking.

MAKES 8 TO 10 SERVINGS

1 recipe Basic Flaky Pie Pastry, Single Crust (page 31), refrigerated

FILLING

1 cup all-purpose flour

3/4 cup firmly packed light brown sugar

1/4 teaspoon salt

1/4 teaspoon ground cinnamon

6 tablespoons (3/4 stick) cold unsalted butter, cut into 1/4-inch pieces

1 cup pure maple syrup

1/2 teaspoon baking soda

1 large egg

1 large egg yolk

1/2 teaspoon vanilla extract

1. If you haven't already, prepare the pastry and refrigerate until firm enough to roll, about 1 hour.

2. On a sheet of lightly floured waxed paper, roll the pastry into a 13-inch circle with a floured rolling pin. Invert the pastry over a 9½-inch deep-dish pie pan, center, and peel off the paper. Tuck the pastry into the pan, without stretching it, and sculpt the edge so it is just slightly above the rim. Place in the freezer for 15 minutes, then partially prebake and let cool according to the instructions on page 16. Reduce the oven temperature to 350°F.

3. Combine the flour, brown sugar, salt, and cinnamon in a large bowl. Add the butter and cut it into the dry mixture with a pastry blender until it is broken into very small pieces. At that point, using your fingertips, continue to rub the mixture until you form crumbs that clump together when firmly pressed. Set aside.

4. In a small saucepan, gently heat the maple syrup until it is slightly warmer than body temperature. Transfer to a large bowl and whisk in the baking soda. Whisk the egg and egg yolk together in a small bowl just until frothy, then whisk into the warmed maple syrup. Stir in the vanilla.

5. Spread about half of the crumbs in the cooled pie shell. Slowly pour the maple filling over the crumbs. Scatter the remaining crumbs evenly over the filling, then set the pie on a large aluminum foil–lined baking sheet. Place on the center oven rack and bake until the filling has puffed considerably and turned dark golden brown, about 30 minutes. Rotate the pie 180 degrees about halfway through the baking, so that the part that faced the back of the oven now faces forward.

6. Transfer the pie to a wire rack and let cool thoroughly. It may be sliced and served while it is still slightly warm, but I think it's best served a little on the cool side.

Recipe for Success

▶ Don't be tempted to bake the pie much more than 30 minutes, even if the filling seems loose. Remember that those crumbs spread throughout the pie will absorb a good deal of moisture and will help to thicken the pie as it cools.

Maple Myth

"Though it is widely believed that the Native Americans were experienced sugar makers long before the white man arrived in North America, when and how they learned to make maple syrup is a mystery. A Native American legend has it that there was once a time when sap issued from the maple tree in near-pure syrup form, something that a formidable god by the name of Ne-naw-Bozhoo decided to bring to a halt. Anticipating, no doubt correctly, that syrup thus had would be too easily taken for granted, he diluted it with water. Sugar makers have been boiling the water out of sap ever since, in the pursuit of pure maple syrup."

—Ken Haedrich, *Maple Syrup Cookbook* (Storey Books, 1989)

French Canadian Walnut–Maple Syrup Vinegar Pie

The first recipe I ever saw for a vinegar pie came from my late friend Richard Sax, the well-known and much-beloved food writer. The recipe I'm referring to appears in my *Maple Syrup Cookbook* (Storey Books, 1989) and is attributed to a Quebec cousin of one of Richard's friends. Other than a few examples I've run across in books on New England cooking, I've not been able to uncover much background information regarding the use of vinegar in a sweet pie. Instinct tells me that the practice must have developed, as a matter of course, in places like New England and Canada, where the indigenous pies were very sweet—perhaps the result of a heavy hand with maple syrup. The vinegar, I reason, was simply a way to take the edge off the sweetness. As you'll see, there really is no vinegar flavor to this pie, which will remind you of a classic pecan pie. There's just a very pleasant hint of tartness. Richard's original recipe calls for some brewed tea, but I always thought that was a bit too subtle and have replaced it with orange juice. Once you've tried this, I think you'll make it a regular on your table.

MAKES 8 TO 10 SERVINGS

1 recipe Basic Flaky Pie Pastry, Single Crust (page 31), refrigerated

FILLING

3 large eggs

1 large egg yolk

3/4 cup sugar

1/4 cup orange juice

2 tablespoons cider vinegar

3/4 cup pure maple syrup

1/4 cup (1/2 stick) unsalted butter, cut into pieces

Generous pinch of salt

1 1/4 cups coarsely chopped walnuts

1. If you haven't already, prepare the pastry and refrigerate until firm enough to roll, about 1 hour.

2. On a sheet of lightly floured waxed paper, roll the pastry into a 13-inch circle with a floured rolling pin. Invert the pastry over a 9 1/2-inch deep-dish pie pan, center, and peel off the paper. Tuck the pastry into the pan, without stretching it, and sculpt the edge so it is even with the rim. Place in the freezer for at least 30 minutes, then partially prebake and let cool according to the instructions on page 16. Reduce the oven temperature to 350°F.

3. Combine the eggs, egg yolk, sugar, orange juice, and vinegar in a medium-size bowl and whisk to blend. Gently warm the maple syrup and butter together in a small saucepan just until the butter melts. Slowly whisk the mixture into the egg mixture along with the salt. Stir in the walnuts. Carefully pour the filling into the cooled pie shell. Using a fork, gently rake the nuts to distribute them evenly.

4. Place the pie on the center oven rack and bake until the surface is golden brown and the filling puffed up slightly but noticeably, 40 to 45 minutes. Rotate the pie 180 degrees halfway through the baking, so that the part that faced the back of the oven now faces forward. When done, the pie will seem set when shaken. It won't, in other words, move in waves, although the center may seem slightly wobbly.

5. Transfer the pie to a wire rack and let cool before serving. I like this best, by far, after it has been refrigerated. (Cover with loosely tented aluminum foil before refrigerating.)

Recipe for Success

▶ **When you're filling a pie such as this, with a very liquid filling, always position yourself right near the oven. That way, you'll avoid having to walk across the kitchen, balancing the pie and, perhaps, watching the filling spill all over the floor. Better, too, not to pull out the oven rack before the pie goes on. These racks are notoriously jerky, and the pie may spill when you're moving the rack. Just put the pie on the rack and slide the pie pan back by hand.**

Red Currant Jelly Pie

Jelly pie is a relative of transparent pie, which is, in turn—from what I've read, anyway—best known in Ohio and Kentucky (and perhaps beyond, since I did discover one recipe called Tennessee jelly pie). Jelly pie recipes have certain things in common—including copious amounts of butter, sugar, and eggs—but they have their points of departure as well. Red currant jelly is often called for, but sometimes it's spread in the pie shell, and other times it's added to the filling. Some recipes call for the egg whites to be beaten separately, and others call for the whole eggs to be beaten into the filling. I prefer the latter method and use it here. It gives the pie a custardy, more jelly-like texture: light, moist, and not too airy. Relatively sweet, this old-fashioned style pie tastes best with unsweetened whipped cream.

MAKES 8 TO 10 SERVINGS

1 recipe Basic Flaky Pie Pastry, Single Crust (page 31), refrigerated

FILLING

3/4 cup red currant jelly

1/2 cup (1 stick) unsalted butter, softened

1 cup sugar

2 teaspoons fine yellow cornmeal

1 tablespoon fresh lemon juice

2 large eggs, at room temperature

1 large egg yolk, at room temperature

1. If you haven't already, prepare the pastry and refrigerate until firm enough to roll, about 1 hour.

2. On a sheet of lightly floured waxed paper, roll the pastry into a 12-inch circle with a floured rolling pin. Invert the pastry over a 9-inch standard pie pan, center, and peel off the paper. Tuck the pastry into the pan, without stretching it, and sculpt the edge into an upstanding ridge. Place in the freezer for 15 minutes, then partially prebake and let cool according to the instructions on page 16. Reduce the oven temperature to 350°F.

3. Heat the jelly in a small saucepan over medium heat, whisking until smooth. Set aside to cool. With an electric mixer, beat the butter in a medium-size bowl, gradually adding the sugar. Blend in the cornmeal and lemon juice. When the jelly has cooled to room temperature, beat it into the butter mixture until evenly blended. Blend in the eggs, one at a time, and the egg yolk, beating just until smooth after each addition. Scrape the filling into the cooled pie shell and smooth it out.

4. Place the pie on the center oven rack and bake for 30 minutes, then rotate the pie 180 degrees, so that the part that faced the back of the oven now faces forward. Bake for 10 minutes, then reduce the oven temperature to 325°F. Bake until the filling has puffed considerably and set and the surface has browned quite a bit, about 10 minutes.

5. Transfer the pie to a wire rack and let cool to room temperature. Cover with loosely tented aluminum foil and refrigerate for at least 2 hours before serving.

Recipe for Success

▸ **Beating butter with sugar and eggs is not the usual way of making a pie filling, and it yields at least one result you may not be accustomed to: the filling tends to rise much more than with other pies. If that happens, don't feel the urge to get the pie out of the oven because of it. Continue to bake until the center is set. The usual little nudge will let you know if it's still soupy or done.**

▸ **This pie may emit a slight burning odor during the last few minutes of baking. It's just the surface caramelizing and it won't detract from the flavor.**

Osgood Pie

This pie has been described by one Texas writer as a "chess-like pie with a glistening, tangy custard studded with walnut pieces and fat, juicy raisins." Its origin is both unclear and, as far as I can tell, unsubstantiated. Both southern and midwestern cooks lay claim to it, but there's no solid evidence to suggest one over the other. It stands to reason, some stories maintain, that the pie was invented by a cook named Osgood, although who he or she was has not been determined. Most other accounts say that Osgood is simply an abbreviated form of "oh so good." Sounds sensible to me, but I'm just a Yankee with a sweet tooth, not a food historian. Incidentally, I prefer pecans here instead of walnuts. Both turn up frequently in the recipes I've seen, so use whichever you prefer.

MAKES 8 TO 10 SERVINGS

1 recipe Basic Shortening Pie Pastry, Single Crust (page 30), refrigerated

FILLING

1 cup dark raisins

4 large eggs, separated

1 1/2 cups sugar

1/4 cup (1/2 stick) unsalted butter, melted and slightly cooled

3 tablespoons cider vinegar

3/4 cup chopped pecans

1/2 teaspoon vanilla extract

1/2 teaspoon ground cinnamon

1/2 teaspoon ground nutmeg

1/4 teaspoon ground cloves

1.   If you haven't already, prepare the pastry and refrigerate until firm enough to roll, about 1 hour.

2.   On a sheet of lightly floured waxed paper, roll the pastry into a 13-inch circle with a floured rolling pin. Invert the pastry over 9½-inch deep-dish pie pan, center, and peel off the paper. Tuck the pastry into the pan, without stretching it, and sculpt the edge into an upstanding ridge. Place in the freezer for 15 minutes, then partially prebake and let cool according to the instructions on page 16. Increase the oven temperature to 400°F.

3.   Put the raisins in a small bowl and cover with hot water. Set aside for about 10 minutes.

4.   Combine the egg yolks, sugar, butter, and vinegar in a large bowl. Using an electric mixer, beat on medium-high speed for about 2 minutes. Drain the raisins and stir them into the egg mixture along with the pecans, vanilla, and spices.

5. In a medium-size bowl using clean, dry beaters, beat the egg whites until stiff peaks form. Add to the filling, folding them in gently but thoroughly with a large rubber spatula. Slowly pour the filling into the cooled pie shell. Using a fork, gently rake through the filling to distribute the raisins and nuts more or less evenly in the shell.

6. Place the pie on the center oven rack and bake for 10 minutes. Reduce the oven temperature to 350°F and bake until the filling is set, about 35 minutes. Rotate the pie 180 degrees, so that the part that faced the back of the oven now faces forward, about 15 minutes before it is done. Give the pie a little nudge and watch the surface carefully. The filling should not move in waves, not even slight waves. If in doubt, bake for 5 minutes more.

7. Transfer the pie to a wire rack and let cool thoroughly. Serve at room temperature, or cover with loosely tented aluminum foil and refrigerate before serving. I prefer it cold.

Recipe for Success

▶ The beaten egg whites do double duty here, first by lightening the filling and second by forming a sort of crunchy self-crust on top of the pie. While we're on the subject of egg whites, remember that it's best to separate eggs while they're cold. But for greater and faster volume, beat the whites once they're at room temperature or slightly warmer. You can help matters along by putting the bowl of egg whites into another bowl of very warm water for a few minutes before beating. Fold the beaten whites into the filling gently, sweeping a rubber spatula across the bottom of the bowl and up, then pushing down through the center of the filling. It's easier to demonstrate than to describe, but you get the idea.

Extra-Rich Lemon Custard Pie

Now here's a pie I would make if I had company coming and wanted a dessert that I could get into the oven quickly and would then have my guests begging for the recipe. It's not a fancy pie, just rich and delicious in the manner of solid, old-fashioned home cooking. The filling is based on a favorite custard recipe of mine from one of my earlier books, *Country Breakfasts* (Galahad Books, 2000). There's nothing to peel, core, or mess with, just a few liquids to blend. (I do suggest taking the time to partially prebake the pie shell.) There's a little lemon zest to grate, but that takes just a few seconds. Plan to leave enough time for the pie to cool and then chill. If you start it in the early afternoon, it will be ready for dinner.

MAKES 6 TO 8 SERVINGS

1 store-bought frozen 9-inch deep-dish pie shell

FILLING

1/2 cup light cream or half-and-half

1/3 cup sugar

5 large egg yolks

1 cup heavy or whipping cream

3/4 teaspoon lemon extract

1/2 teaspoon vanilla extract

1 to 2 teaspoons finely grated lemon zest, to your taste

GARNISH

Ripe fresh raspberries (optional)

1. Partially prebake the pie shell according to the directions on the package. Transfer to a wire rack and let cool thoroughly. Reduce the oven temperature to 325°F.

2. Gently whisk the light cream, sugar, and egg yolks together in a medium-size bowl. Add the heavy cream, extracts, and lemon zest. Whisk again, briefly, just until evenly blended. Carefully pour the filling into the cooled pie shell.

3. Place the pie on the center oven rack and bake for 30 minutes. Reduce the oven temperature to 275°F and rotate the pie 180 degrees, so that the part that faced the back of the oven now faces forward. Continue to bake until the center is just barely set, 20 to 25 minutes. To check, give the pie a quick nudge. The filling shouldn't seem soupy in the center.

4. Transfer the pie to a wire rack and let cool to room temperature. Cover with loosely tented aluminum foil and refrigerate for at least 2 hours before serving. Garnish with raspberries, if desired.

Recipe for Success

▶ Better restaurants often strain custards before baking them to remove unblended bits of egg. This is a little fussy, perhaps, for a homemade pie, but it does make the custard a little more refined. If you want to do this, strain the custard through a fine-mesh sieve into a bowl before adding the lemon zest. Stir in the zest, then pour the filling into the pie shell.

▶ Especially with a liquidy filling such as this, it's important to use caution with the flexible pans frozen pie shells come in. I suggest putting the pie shell on a rimless baking sheet before filling it, then carefully sliding it off the sheet and onto the oven rack.

Cherry Custard Pie

If you take rich custard and add fruit, either fresh or canned, you have the makings of a sensational open-faced pie. Here I do just that, and the result is a delectably smooth custard pie interrupted only by lovely, colorful sweet cherries. In appearance, it looks something like the French dessert *clafouti*—a sort of baked cherry pancake—but I think this has a lot more appeal. Canned sweet cherries are perfectly acceptable here. Of course, you could make this with halved fresh cherries, but the pie is very attractive indeed when they're whole. Prepare this pie well ahead of time so it has plenty of time to chill.

MAKES 8 TO 10 SERVINGS

1 recipe Basic Flaky Pie Pastry, Single Crust (page 31) or Basic Shortening Pie Pastry, Single Crust (page 30), refrigerated

FILLING

2 large eggs

1 large egg yolk

2/3 cup sugar

1 cup light cream or half-and-half

1/2 cup heavy or whipping cream

1/2 teaspoon vanilla extract

1 1/2 tablespoons kirsch, Grand Marnier, or triple sec (optional)

Pinch of salt

One 15-ounce can pitted sweet cherries, drained, or 1 1/2 cups fresh sweet cherries, stemmed and pitted

1. If you haven't already, prepare the pastry and refrigerate until firm enough to roll, about 1 hour.

2. On a sheet of lightly floured waxed paper, roll the pastry into a 12-inch circle with a floured rolling pin. Invert the pastry over a 9-inch standard pie pan, center, and peel off the paper. Tuck the pastry into the pan, without stretching it, and sculpt the edge so it is just slightly higher than the rim. Place in the freezer for 15 minutes, then partially prebake and let cool according to the instructions on page 16. Reduce the oven temperature to 350°F.

3. Combine the eggs, egg yolk, and sugar in a large bowl. Using an electric mixer, blend briefly on medium speed. Add the light cream, heavy cream, vanilla, kirsch (if using), and salt and blend briefly. Slowly pour the filling into the cooled pie shell. One by one, gently drop the cherries into the filling, spacing them more or less evenly.

4. Place the pie on the center oven rack and bake until the custard is set, about 45 minutes. Rotate the pie 180 degrees halfway through the baking, so that the part that faced the back of the oven now faces forward. When done, the filling will jiggle—not move in waves—when you give the pie a little nudge.

5. Transfer the pie to a wire rack and let cool thoroughly. Cover with loosely tented aluminum foil and refrigerate for at least 3 hours or overnight before serving.

Recipe for Success

▶ **If you like this idea of a fruity custard pie, consider substituting blackberries for all or some of the cherries.**

▶ **Don't be concerned if some of the color bleeds out of the fruit and tinges the custard. It's supposed to and there's really nothing you can do to prevent it.**

Maple Custard Pie

This is an uncomplicated pie with few ingredients and a wonderful flavor. The secret is really no secret: rich heavy cream and pure maple syrup, which, when combined with egg yolks, make for a thick custard. This recipe is based on one of my all-time favorite desserts, maple crème brûlée, from my *Maple Syrup Cookbook* (Storey Books, 1989). Can you substitute imitation syrup? No, not in this case; the pie just won't be the same. Serve this pie well chilled, preferably after a light meal. A nice time to serve it is in the spring, when the sap starts to run and the new maple syrup comes to market.

MAKES 8 TO 10 SERVINGS

1 recipe Basic Flaky Pie Pastry, Single Crust (page 31), refrigerated

FILLING

1¼ cups heavy or whipping cream

½ cup pure maple syrup (see Recipe for Success)

⅓ cup sugar

½ teaspoon vanilla extract

Pinch of salt

4 large egg yolks

1. If you haven't already, prepare the pastry and refrigerate until firm enough to roll, about 1 hour.

2. On a sheet of lightly floured waxed paper, roll the pastry into a 12- or 13-inch circle with a floured rolling pin. Invert the pastry over a 9-inch standard or 9½-inch deep-

The American Pie Council

America's clearinghouse for anything related to pies is the American Pie Council. Headquartered in Lake Forest, Illinois, this nonprofit organization is "committed to preserving America's pie heritage and promoting Americans' love affair with pies." Based on its Web site and the activities it sponsors, however, one would guess that our pie heritage is anything but fading.

The council's big shindig for pie bakers is the annual National Pie Championships. Crisco, as you might have guessed, is the main sponsor. At a weekend of pie seminars, games, and demonstrations, highlighted by the gut-busting Never-Ending Pie Buffet, commercial and amateur bakers compete in more than 80 judged events. For more information on the American Pie Council and its activities, go to www.piecouncil.org.

dish pie pan, center, and peel off the paper. Tuck the pastry into the pan, without stretching it, and sculpt the edge so it is even with the rim. Place in the freezer for 15 minutes, then partially prebake and let cool according to the instructions on page 16. Reduce the oven temperature to 350°F.

3. Combine all the filling ingredients in a large bowl and whisk briefly, until evenly mixed. Pour the filling into the cooled pie shell.

4. Place the pie on the center oven rack and bake until the filling is nicely browned and set, 35 to 40 minutes total. Rotate the pie 180 degrees, so that the part that faced the back of the oven now faces forward, 10 to 15 minutes before it is done. The middle should be jiggly but not soupy.

5. Transfer the pie to a wire rack and let cool thoroughly. Serve at room temperature, or, better yet, cover with loosely tented aluminum foil and refrigerate for at least 2 hours or overnight before serving.

Recipe for Success

▸ Use a light amber maple syrup for this pie, rather than a darker one. Since there are no other competing flavors, the pie has a more delicate, refined flavor when you use a better grade of syrup.

Ginger Custard Pie

When candied ginger is slowly baked in and sprinkled on top of a rich custard, the result is a deliciously smooth golden custard pie with a tropical profile. This one is so simple to make yet so delicious. I love it cold, served as is or with a drizzle of mocha sauce—just enough to have fun with the ginger flavor without being too chocolaty.

MAKES 8 TO 10 SERVINGS

1 recipe Basic Flaky Pie Pastry, Single Crust (page 31) or Extra-Flaky Pie Pastry, Single Crust (page 34), refrigerated

FILLING

1 cup heavy or whipping cream

1 cup light cream or half-and-half

2/3 cup sugar

1/4 cup plus 2 tablespoons minced candied (crystallized) ginger

1 large egg

4 large egg yolks

1 teaspoon vanilla extract

GARNISH

Warm Mocha Sauce (page 607; optional)

1. If you haven't already, prepare the pastry and refrigerate until firm enough to roll, about 1 hour.

2. On a sheet of lightly floured waxed paper, roll the pastry into a 13-inch circle with a floured rolling pin. Invert the pastry over a 9½-inch deep-dish pie pan, center, and peel off the paper. Tuck the pastry into the pan, without stretching it, and sculpt the edge so it is just slightly above the rim. Place in the freezer for 15 minutes, then partially prebake and let cool according to the instructions on page 16. Reduce the oven temperature to 350°F.

3. Combine the heavy cream, light cream, and sugar in a medium-size saucepan over low heat. Cook, stirring, until the sugar dissolves, 3 to 4 minutes. Remove from the heat and stir in ¼ cup of the ginger. Let cool for 5 minutes.

4. In a large bowl, whisk the egg and egg yolks until blended. Stir in the cream mixture ¼ cup at a time, adding all of the ginger that's in the saucepan. Stir in the vanilla. Slowly pour the filling into the cooled pie shell, again scraping out all of the ginger and scattering it over the filling.

5. Place the pie on the center oven rack and bake until set and no longer soupy in the center, 35 to 40 minutes. Rotate the pie 180 degrees halfway through the baking time, so that the part that faced the back of the oven now faces forward. Near the end of the baking, and as soon as the entire surface seems set enough to support the weight of the ginger without sinking, gently slide out the rack with the pie on it and sprinkle the remaining 2 tablespoons ginger over the top. Continue to bake until the pie is done.

6. Transfer the pie to a wire rack and let cool thoroughly. Cover with loosely tented aluminum foil and refrigerate for at least 2 hours or overnight before serving. Drizzle each slice with a spoonful of mocha sauce, if desired.

Recipe for Success

▸ For a less rich version, feel free to substitute whole milk for the light cream.

▸ Remember the golden rule for custard pies: low and slow. Never try to rush the baking of a custard pie by increasing the oven temperature. You'll damage the eggs and end up with a watery pie.

▸ Another nice garnish, in place of, or in addition to, the mocha sauce, is lightly sweetened whipped cream with a tablespoon or two of coconut rum added.

Talk About a Food Fight

It took 6 cement mixers, half a ton of custard powder, and 1,000 liters of water, but the record for custard pie throwing was set by 20 enthusiastic slingers at London's Millennium Dome in April 2000. In the space of 3 minutes, the rain slicker–clad volunteers heaved 3,312 gooey custard pies, besting the previous record (set in 1998) by 236 pies. Officials from the *Guinness Book of World Records* were on hand to verify the contest, organized to promote the UK launch of a Swedish entertainment Web site.

Rose Water Custard Pie with Sugared Peaches and Berries

During the summer, when fresh fruit is so good, I sometimes like to serve it as a pie garnish rather than in a pie. When I do, this rose water custard filling is the way to go. Distilled from rose petals, rose water makes a delicate flavoring that couldn't complement the fruit more perfectly. I first learned about it some years ago in several Shaker cookbooks. The Shakers used it in a number of dishes, including an apple pie baked with a rose water–flavored custard, which appears in my book *Apple Pie Perfect* (Harvard Common Press, 2002). The trick is to use the flavoring with a light hand, so there's just a whisper of it. As with perfume, a suggestion is often more enticing than a bold statement.

MAKES 8 TO 10 SERVINGS

1 recipe Basic Flaky Pie Pastry, Single Crust (page 31) or Extra-Flaky Pie Pastry, Single Crust (page 34), refrigerated

FILLING

2 large eggs

1 large egg yolk

3/4 cup light cream or half-and-half

3/4 cup heavy or whipping cream

1/2 cup sugar

2 1/2 teaspoons food-grade rose water (available at health food stores and gourmet shops)

1/2 teaspoon vanilla extract

1/2 teaspoon lemon extract

Pinch of salt

PEACHES AND BERRIES GARNISH

2 or 3 large ripe peaches, peeled, pitted, and thinly sliced

1 cup fresh raspberries

1 to 2 tablespoons sugar, to your taste

1 teaspoon fresh lemon juice

1. If you haven't already, prepare the pastry and refrigerate until firm enough to roll, about 1 hour.

2. On a sheet of lightly floured waxed paper, roll the pastry into a 12-inch circle with a floured rolling pin. Invert the pastry over a 9-inch standard pie pan, center, and peel off the paper. Tuck the pastry into the pan, without stretching it, and sculpt the edge so it is just slightly higher than the rim. Place in the freezer for 15 minutes, then partially prebake and let cool according to the instructions on page 16. Reduce the oven temperature to 350°F.

3. Whisk the eggs and egg yolk in a large bowl, then whisk in the light cream, heavy cream, and sugar. Add the rose water, vanilla, lemon extract, and salt; stir to blend. Carefully pour the filling into the cooled pie shell.

4. Place the pie on the center oven rack and bake for 30 minutes, then rotate the pie 180 degrees, so that the part that faced the back of the oven now faces forward. Continue to bake until the filling is set, 15 to 20 minutes. When done, the center of the pie should not be soupy; a little wobbly is fine. Give the pie a quick nudge to check. The filling should shake, not move in waves.

5. Transfer the pie to a wire rack and let cool to room temperature. Cover with loosely tented aluminum foil and refrigerate for several hours before serving.

6. When you're ready to serve the pie, prepare the garnish. Place the peaches, raspberries, sugar, and lemon juice in a medium-size bowl and stir gently to combine. Let sit for several minutes, then serve a spoonful alongside each slice of pie.

Recipe for Success

▸ **If you have rose water but it's been in your cabinet for some time, you may want to add an extra ½ teaspoon to the filling, in case it has lost some of its potency.**

▸ **For an afternoon tea or another such refined gathering, you might include a garnish of fresh, unsprayed rose petals on the plate.**

Butterscotch-Nut Custard Pie

This luscious custard pie separates into three layers: a thick layer of light golden custard on the bottom; a thin, dark gold butterscotch layer, where the dissolved butterscotch chips rise and settle; and a crunchy nut layer on the surface. As with all custard pies, I like this best served cold.

MAKES 8 TO 10 SERVINGS

1 recipe Basic Flaky Pie Pastry, Single Crust (page 31) or 1/2 recipe Nutty Pie Pastry (page 42), refrigerated

FILLING

1 cup pecan or walnut halves

3/4 cup butterscotch chips

1 cup heavy or whipping cream

3/4 cup light cream or half-and-half

3 large eggs

2 large egg yolks

1/2 cup granulated sugar

1/2 cup firmly packed light brown sugar

1 teaspoon vanilla extract

GARNISH

Fresh Whipped Cream (page 605; optional)

1. If you haven't already, prepare the pastry and refrigerate until firm enough to roll, about 1 hour.

2. Spread the nuts on a large baking sheet and place in a preheated 350°F oven until fragrant and lightly toasted, about 10 minutes (see Recipe for Success). Remove from the oven and immediately tilt the nuts onto a plate. Let cool thoroughly, then chop with a sharp chef's knife.

3. On a sheet of lightly floured waxed paper, roll the pastry into a 13 1/2-inch circle with a floured rolling pin. Invert the pastry over a 9 1/2- to 10-inch extra-deep-dish pie pan, center, and peel off the paper. Tuck the pastry into the pan, without stretching it, and sculpt the edge so it is just slightly higher than the rim. Place in the freezer for 15 minutes, then partially prebake and let cool according to the instructions on page 16. Reduce the oven temperature to 350°F.

4. Put the butterscotch chips in a large heat-resistant bowl. Set aside. Heat the heavy and light cream in a medium-size saucepan over medium heat until they come to a near boil, 3 to 5 minutes. Immediately pour over the butterscotch chips. Let stand for 5 minutes, then whisk to smooth and melt the chips. Set aside.

5. In another large bowl, beat the eggs, egg yolks, and sugars with an electric mixer. Whisk the melted chips, then add to the eggs and beat briefly. Blend in the vanilla, then stir in the chopped nuts. Ladle the filling into the cooled pie shell. Using a fork, gently rake the nuts to distribute them evenly.

6. Place the pie on the center oven rack and bake until the top is golden brown and the custard is set, 50 to 55 minutes. Rotate the pie 180 degrees halfway through the baking, so that the part that faced the back of the oven now faces forward. When done, the filling shouldn't move in waves, but rather jiggle slightly as a whole. To check, give the pie a little nudge.

7. Transfer the pie to a wire rack and let cool. Serve warm or at room temperature. Or cover with loosely tented aluminum foil, refrigerate, and serve cold. Garnish with whipped cream, if desired.

Recipe for Success

▶ I always use a timer when I'm toasting nuts, but if you're tuned in to their toasted fragrance, you often don't need it. Almost across the board, this simple rule applies: as soon as you can smell the nuts toasting, they're done. Generally speaking, that's somewhere between 8 and 12 minutes in a 350°F oven. When the nuts reach that point, get them out of the oven and onto a plate without delay. If you leave them on the baking sheet, the residual heat is liable to overtoast them.

Toasted Almond Custard Pie

This pie will remind you of a Good Humor Toasted Almond Bar—the kind I used to buy for about 15 cents when the Good Humor truck jingled through our neighborhood when I was a kid. Those bars have an all-around coating of perfectly toasted almonds; this pie has them on the surface. Beneath is a thick layer of cool almond custard and a great buttery crust. It's excellent just the way it is, but not bad either with a dollop of whipped cream.

MAKES 8 TO 10 SERVINGS

1 recipe Basic Flaky Pie Pastry, Single Crust (page 31) or 1/2 recipe Nutty Pie Pastry (page 42) made with almonds, refrigerated

FILLING
1 cup slivered almonds
1 1/4 cups sugar
3 large eggs

3 large egg yolks
1 cup heavy or whipping cream
3/4 cup light cream or half-and-half
1 teaspoon vanilla extract
1/2 teaspoon almond extract (see Recipe for Success)
Pinch of salt

1. If you haven't already, prepare the pastry and refrigerate until firm enough to roll, about 1 hour.

2. On a sheet of lightly floured waxed paper, roll the pastry into a 13 1/2-inch circle with a floured rolling pin. Invert the pastry over a 9 1/2- to 10-inch extra-deep-dish pie pan, center, and peel off the paper. Tuck the pastry into the pan, without stretching it, and sculpt the edge so it is just slightly higher than the rim. Place in the freezer for 15 minutes, then partially prebake and let cool according to the instructions on page 16. Reduce the oven temperature to 350°F.

3.   Heat a large, heavy skillet over medium heat. Add the almonds and toast, stirring very often, until light golden brown, 7 to 8 minutes. Don't overtoast them. Immediately turn the almonds onto a large plate. Let cool to room temperature, then refrigerate for 10 minutes.

4.   Place the chilled almonds and ¼ cup of the sugar in a food processor and pulse until the almonds are very finely chopped. Be careful not to chop them so finely that you make almond flour. Set aside.

5.   Combine the eggs and egg yolks in a large bowl and beat with an electric mixer, gradually adding the remaining 1 cup sugar. Add the heavy cream, light cream, extracts, and salt and beat briefly. Stir in the chopped almonds. Ladle the filling into the cooled pie shell.

6.   Place the pie on the center oven rack and bake until the top is golden brown and the custard is set, 50 to 55 minutes. Rotate the pie 180 degrees halfway through the baking time, so that the part that faced the back of the oven now faces forward. When done, the filling shouldn't move in waves, but rather jiggle as a whole. To check, give the pie a little nudge.

7.   Transfer the pie to a wire rack and let cool. Serve warm or at room temperature. Or, my preference, let cool thoroughly, cover with loosely tented aluminum foil, and refrigerate before serving cold.

Recipe for Success

▸ **As with vanilla extract, I feel that it pays to spend a little extra to buy pure almond extract rather than imitation. The imitation product has a harsher taste that I think is evident in a custard, whose flavor depends on so few ingredients. Incidentally, if you don't have any almond extract on hand but you do have amaretto, you can substitute 1 tablespoon of it instead.**

Coffee-Hazelnut Custard Pie

Here's a special pie for coffee and/or hazelnut lovers—one of the more unusual (but delicious) custard pies you're likely to run across. Built on a foundation of rich cream and eggs, this pie is flavored with instant coffee and hazelnut liqueur. Toasted hazelnuts are stirred into the custard, float to the top, and form a crunchy crust. It's an adult pie for those who like to serve sweets with a twist.

MAKES 8 TO 10 SERVINGS

1 recipe Basic Flaky Pie Pastry, Single Crust (page 31), refrigerated

FILLING

1¹/₂ cups light cream or half-and-half

1 cup sugar

1¹/₂ tablespoons instant espresso or coffee granules

1 cup heavy or whipping cream

3 large eggs

2 large egg yolks

1¹/₂ tablespoons hazelnut liqueur

1 teaspoon vanilla extract

Pinch of salt

1¹/₄ cups hazelnuts, toasted (see page 163) and finely chopped

GARNISH

Fresh Whipped Cream (page 605)

1. If you haven't already, prepare the pastry and refrigerate until firm enough to roll, about 1 hour.

2. On a sheet of lightly floured waxed paper, roll the pastry into a 13¹/₂-inch circle with a floured rolling pin. Invert the pastry over a 9¹/₂- to 10-inch extra-deep-dish pie pan, center, and peel off the paper. Tuck the pastry into the pan, without stretching it, and sculpt the edge so it is just slightly higher than the rim. Place in the freezer for 15 minutes, then partially prebake and let cool according to the instructions on page 16. Reduce the oven temperature to 350°F.

3. Heat the light cream, sugar, and coffee together in a medium-size saucepan over medium heat, whisking gently just until the mixture is warm and the coffee has dissolved, about 3 minutes. Remove from the heat and stir in the heavy cream. In a large bowl, whisk the eggs and egg yolks until blended, or beat briefly on low speed with an electric mixer. Blend in the cream mixture, liqueur, vanilla, and salt. Stir in the hazelnuts. Slowly pour the filling into the cooled pie shell. Using a fork, gently rake the nuts to distribute them evenly.

4. Place the pie on the center oven rack and bake for 25 minutes, then rotate the pie 180 degrees, so that the part that faced the back of the oven now faces forward. Continue to bake until the filling is set in the center, 20 to 25 minutes. To check, give it a little nudge. The filling shouldn't move in waves or be soupy in the center. A wobbly center is fine, however.

5. Transfer the pie to a wire rack and let cool thoroughly. Cover with loosely tented aluminum foil and refrigerate for at least 2 hours or overnight before serving. Garnish with whipped cream.

Recipe for Success

▶ **Other nuts may be used if you prefer. Pecans and walnuts are excellent and don't need to be skinned the way hazelnuts do.**

▶ **You also may substitute lightly toasted sweetened flaked coconut (see page 399) for the hazelnuts.**

▶ **If you don't have hazelnut liqueur on hand, you may use coffee liqueur instead.**

Sweet Summer Corn Pie

What to do with all that buttery fresh summer corn? Here's something out of the ordinary—a rich custard pie made with tender sweet corn. Some have described it as resembling a corn soufflé, although it's creamier and denser than a soufflé. If you're planning to make this pie, throw a couple of extra ears of corn into the pot when you're steaming it for dinner (see Recipe for Success). Can you make this with other kinds of corn? Yes, and it's still very good. Out of season, I've used thawed frozen corn as well as drained canned corn. I prefer the former, because the pie has a subtle flavor that can't quite mask the "canned" taste of canned corn.

MAKES 8 TO 10 SERVINGS

1 recipe Basic Flaky Pie Pastry, Single Crust (page 31) or Tender Cream Cheese Pastry, Single Crust (page 46), refrigerated

FILLING
1 1/2 cups corn kernels, frozen (thawed), cut from cooked fresh ears, or canned (drained)

2/3 cup light cream or half-and-half

3/4 cup sugar

1 cup heavy or whipping cream

1 teaspoon vanilla extract

Pinch of salt

Pinch of ground nutmeg

4 large egg yolks

2 large egg whites, at room temperature

1. If you haven't already, prepare the pastry and refrigerate until firm enough to roll, 1 to 1½ hours, depending on the pastry.

2. On a sheet of lightly floured waxed paper, roll the pastry into a 13-inch circle with a floured rolling pin. Invert the pastry over a 9½-inch deep-dish pie pan, center, and peel off the paper. Tuck the pastry into the pan, without stretching it, and sculpt the edge so it is just slightly higher than the rim. Place in the freezer for 15 minutes, then partially pre-bake and let cool according to the instructions on page 16. Reduce the oven temperature to 350°F.

3. Combine half of the corn, the light cream, and sugar in a blender and process briefly, until the corn is chopped up, but without turning it into a smooth puree. In a large bowl, whisk the heavy cream, vanilla, salt, nutmeg, and egg yolks together just until the mixture is evenly blended. Stir in the corn mixture and remaining whole kernels.

4. In a medium-size bowl, beat the egg whites with an electric mixer until they hold soft peaks. Add the whites to the filling and gently fold together until the mixture is smooth and uniform. Don't overfold or the egg whites will lose all of their volume. Slowly pour the filling into the cooled pie shell.

5. Place the pie on the center oven rack and bake until the top is a dark golden brown and the filling is set, 45 to 50 minutes. Rotate the pie 180 degrees, so that the part that faced the back of the oven now faces forward, about 15 minutes before it is done. To check for doneness, give the pie a quick little push. The filling should not move in waves.

6. Transfer the pie to a wire rack and let cool to room temperature. Cover with loosely tented aluminum foil and refrigerate for at least 3 hours or overnight before serving.

Recipe for Success

▶ **All custards, and by extension custard pies, are very heat sensitive. Baking them at too high a temperature may cause the custard to break, changing the texture from creamy to curdled and watery. With that in mind, when you bake a custard pie, always err on the low side if you suspect that your oven is little too hot, turning down the heat accordingly. You can't do any damage to a custard by cooking it longer and slower, but you can do plenty by cooking it too fast.**

▶ **If you're using very fresh, tender sweet corn, it isn't even necessary to cook it first. It will more or less cook right in the pie.**

Thick Coconut Custard Pie

Perhaps the best reason I can think of for owning a very deep pie pan is coconut custard pie, where thicker is always better. This one is rich and smooth, which is not surprising since it contains three whole eggs, two egg yolks, heavy cream, and light cream. The creaminess of the custard yields to a generous helping of sweetened coconut, which settles on top and gives the pie a gorgeous golden color. If you really want to dress it up, pipe freshly whipped cream over the top and dust it with toasted coconut—an exercise in gilding the lily, perhaps, but the perfect touch for a special occasion pie.

MAKES 8 TO 10 SERVINGS

1 recipe Basic Flaky Pie Pastry, Single Crust (page 31) or Basic Shortening Pie Pastry, Single Crust (page 30), refrigerated

FILLING

3 large eggs

2 large egg yolks

1 cup sugar

1 cup heavy or whipping cream

1 cup light cream or half-and-half

1 teaspoon vanilla extract

1 teaspoon coconut extract (optional but highly recommended)

Pinch of salt

1 cup sweetened flaked coconut

GARNISH

Fresh Whipped Cream (page 605; optional)

Sweetened flaked coconut, toasted (see box right; optional)

1. If you haven't already, prepare the pastry and refrigerate until firm enough to roll, about 1 hour.

2. On a sheet of lightly floured waxed paper, roll the pastry into a 13½-inch circle with a floured rolling pin. Invert the pastry over your deepest 9½- to 10-inch extra-deep-dish pie pan, center, and peel off the paper. Tuck the pastry into the pan, without stretching it, and sculpt the edge so it is just slightly higher than the rim. Place in the freezer for 15 minutes, then partially prebake and let cool according to the instructions on page 16. Reduce the oven temperature to 350°F.

3. Combine the eggs and egg yolks in a large bowl and beat with an electric mixer, gradually adding the sugar. Add the heavy cream, light cream, vanilla, coconut extract (if using), and salt and beat briefly. Stir in the coconut. Ladle the filling into the cooled pie shell.

4. Place the pie on the center oven rack and bake until the top is golden brown and the custard is set, 50 to 55 minutes. Rotate the pie 180 degrees halfway through the baking, so that the part that faced the back of the oven now faces forward. When done, the filling shouldn't move in waves, but rather jiggle as a whole. To check, give the pie a little nudge.

5. Transfer the pie to a wire rack and let cool. The pie can be served warm, which is the way my wife, Bev, likes it. I don't care for warm custards, so I always cover the thoroughly cooled pie with loosely tented aluminum foil and refrigerate it before eating. For a special presentation, refrigerate the pie for several hours. Make the whipped cream just before you need it, then pipe it over the pie using a pastry bag. Sprinkle the toasted coconut over the top. Slice and serve.

Recipe for Success

▶ Custard pies tend to give off a lot of moisture even when they're fully cooled. That's why I usually like to cover them with tented aluminum foil rather than plastic wrap. Plastic wrap traps moisture right next to the pie, making for an unappetizing puddle. Tented foil collects the moisture in the area away from the pie. Use caution, however, when you remove the foil. Don't knock it; just ease it off gently, or the moisture may fall onto the pie. Don't reuse the foil unless you wipe off the moisture with a paper towel.

Toasting Coconut

When a recipe instructs you to toast coconut, you have a couple of choices. The fastest method is to pan-toast it. Just put the coconut directly in a skillet over medium-low heat. Stir the coconut virtually nonstop until it develops a golden hue. It will take no more than 3 to 4 minutes. Don't try to rush the procedure by raising the heat, or you'll burn the oil-rich coconut. The second, and more common, method is to oven-toast the coconut. Just spread it on a large baking sheet (one with sides) and place the sheet in a preheated 325°F oven for about 10 minutes, stirring the coconut every few minutes. In both cases, immediately tilt the coconut onto a plate when it is done, or the residual heat in the pan can burn the coconut.

Tyler Pie

Tyler pie, sometimes called Tyler pudding pie, is said to be named for John Tyler, our 10th president. According to James Beard in his *American Cookery* (Little, Brown and Company, 1972), this sort of pie might have been called sugar pie in the South and maple sugar pie in the North, depending on the kind of sugar it was made with. In any event, it is basically a very sweet custard pie, typically—given the abundance of brown sugar and butter—with a caramel flavor. Like most early pies, there is nothing complicated about it: the ingredients are common, the mixing procedure simple and straightforward, and the results delicious.

MAKES 10 SERVINGS

1 recipe Basic Shortening Pie Pastry, Single Crust (page 30) or Basic Flaky Pie Pastry, Single Crust (page 31), refrigerated

FILLING

1/2 cup (1 stick) unsalted butter, cut into pieces

1 1/2 cups firmly packed light brown sugar

1 cup light cream or half-and-half, or 1/2 cup light cream plus 1/2 cup heavy or whipping cream

1/4 teaspoon salt

1 1/2 teaspoons vanilla extract

1 tablespoon granulated sugar

1 tablespoon all-purpose flour

1/4 teaspoon ground nutmeg or cinnamon

3 large eggs

1. If you haven't already, prepare the pastry and refrigerate until firm enough to roll, about 1 hour.

2. On a sheet of lightly floured waxed paper, roll the pastry into a 13-inch circle with a floured rolling pin. Invert the pastry over a 9 1/2-inch deep-dish pie pan, center, and peel off the paper. Tuck the pastry into the pan, without stretching it, and sculpt the edge into an upstanding ridge. Place in the freezer for 15 minutes, then partially prebake and let cool according to the instructions on page 16. Preheat the oven to 350°F.

3. In a medium-size, heavy saucepan over low heat, combine the butter, brown sugar, cream, and salt. Cook, stirring often, until the butter has melted. Remove from the heat and stir in the vanilla. Let cool for 5 to 10 minutes. In a small bowl, combine the sugar, flour, and nutmeg, then whisk the mixture into the brown sugar mixture.

4. In a large bowl, whisk the eggs until foamy, then slowly add the warm brown sugar mixture to them, stirring as you add. Position the cooled pie shell near the oven, then carefully pour the filling into the shell.

5. Place the pie on the center oven rack and bake until the filling has puffed around the edge and slightly less so in the middle, 30 to 35 minutes. Rotate the pie 180 degrees, so that the part that faced the back of the oven now faces forward, about 10 minutes before it is done. The entire filling will seem wobbly, but it should not be soupy in the center.

6. Transfer the pie to a wire rack and let cool thoroughly. Serve at room temperature, or cover with loosely tented aluminum foil and refrigerate for several hours before serving.

Recipe for Success

▶ This is just the sort of soupy filling that can leak under the crust if the fork holes in the prebaked pie shell haven't been plugged. Refer to page 18 for notes and recommendations.

▶ As with all custard pies, be careful not to overbake this pie or bake it at too high a temperature or the custard may "break" and turn watery. If you suspect that your oven might be baking a little hot, reduce the temperature by 25°F.

Shaker Boiled Cider Pie

This pie, in one variation or another, has appeared in many of the cookbooks I've written over the past 12 years. Frankly, I don't remember my original source for it. But I can tell you that one of the reasons it holds special meaning for me is that early in my cooking career, I had the good fortune to meet and interview two of the last Shakers—Eldress Bertha and Eldress Gertrude—not long before they passed away at their home in Canterbury, New Hampshire. As these gentle, humble women explained to me, the Shakers commonly used boiled cider and maple syrup to sweeten their baked goods and other dishes. Boiled cider is fresh apple cider boiled to one-seventh of its original volume, until it becomes a dark syrup. (One of the few producers of it today is Wood's Cider Mill, on the Web at www.woodscidermill.com.) As you might imagine, it has an intense apple flavor, and it's handy for pie makers who want to add a little extra kick to apple pies. Here we combine it with maple syrup to sweeten what is essentially a custard pie with a thin layer of meringue that rises to the top. I think this is best served chilled, with unsweetened whipped cream, as the pie itself is pretty sweet. If you'd rather make your own boiled cider, see Recipe for Success.

MAKES 8 TO 10 SERVINGS

1 recipe Basic Flaky Pie Pastry, Single Crust (page 31) or Basic Shortening Pie Pastry, Single Crust (page 30), refrigerated

FILLING

3/4 cup boiled cider

3/4 cup pure maple syrup

3 tablespoons unsalted butter, cut into pieces

Pinch of salt

4 large eggs, separated

GARNISH

Ground nutmeg

Fresh Whipped Cream (page 605; optional), unsweetened

1. If you haven't already, prepare the pastry and refrigerate until firm enough to roll, about 1 hour.

2. On a sheet of lightly floured waxed paper, roll the pastry into a 13-inch circle with a floured rolling pin. Invert the pastry over a 9½-inch deep-dish pie pan, center, and peel off the paper. Gently tuck the pastry down into the pan, without stretching it, and sculpt the edge so it is just slightly higher than the rim. Place in the freezer for 15 minutes. Preheat the oven to 350°F.

3. Gently warm the boiled cider, maple syrup, and butter together in a medium-size saucepan until the butter melts. Pour the mixture into a large heat-resistant bowl and add the salt. Let cool slightly. Put the egg yolks in a medium-size bowl and whisk a ladleful of the warm liquid into them. Repeat several times to temper the yolks, then stir the tempered mixture back into the warm syrup mixture.

4. Put the egg whites in a large bowl and beat with an electric mixer until they form soft, slightly drooping peaks. Add to the cider mixture. First fold, then whisk briefly to combine, but don't try to make a uniform mixture; much of the liquid is going to settle to the bottom. Pour the filling into the chilled pie shell.

5. Place the pie on the center oven rack and bake for 40 to 45 minutes, rotating the pie 180 degrees halfway through the baking, so that the part that faced the back of the oven now faces forward. To see if the pie is done, jiggle it slightly. The filling should not move in waves, just wobble a bit. The top should be dark brown.

6. Transfer the pie to a wire rack and let cool. Serve warm, or let cool thoroughly, cover with loosely tented aluminum foil—taking care that the foil doesn't touch the delicate top meringue—and refrigerate. When ready to serve, dust the top of the pie with nutmeg. Garnish with whipped cream, if desired.

Recipe for Success

❯ To make your own boiled cider, pour 7 cups fresh preservative-free apple cider into a large nonreactive saucepan or medium-large soup pot. Bring to a rapid boil and continue to boil until the cider is reduced to 1 cup. Keep a heatproof glass measuring cup nearby to check. Use any leftover boiled cider on pancakes or waffles.

❯ Sometimes I prebake the pastry for this pie, and sometimes I don't. The liquid filling makes a strong case for a partially prebaked crust (see page 16), but I'm fairly certain the Shakers didn't do so, which is the excuse I use when I'm feeling too lazy to bother.

B-Grade Creamy Yogurt Pie

The title is a joke, but not the pie. There's nothing second-rate about this satiny yogurt pie, except for the maple syrup that goes in it. The dark syrup gives the filling a pretty butterscotch hue and unmistakable maple flavor. Since you may be wondering, you can use lowfat (but not nonfat) yogurt in this pie, but I think you get a much better result with full-fat yogurt. As a former New Hampshire resident, I'm partial to the excellent Stonyfield Farm yogurt produced there and available pretty much nationwide. If you live in maple country, or even if you don't, you'll soon be circulating this recipe to all your maple-loving friends and neighbors.

MAKES 8 TO 10 SERVINGS

1 recipe Basic Flaky Pie Pastry, Single Crust (page 31) or 1/2 recipe Nutty Pie Pastry (page 42), refrigerated

FILLING

3 large eggs, at room temperature

1 large egg yolk, at room temperature

1/3 cup sugar

2¹/2 tablespoons all-purpose flour

1/2 cup pure maple syrup

3 tablespoons unsalted butter

1 teaspoon vanilla extract

Pinch of salt

2 cups plain yogurt (see headnote and Recipe for Success)

1. If you haven't already, prepare the pastry and refrigerate until firm enough to roll, 1 to 1¹/2 hours.

2. On a sheet of lightly floured waxed paper, roll the pastry into a 13-inch circle with a floured rolling pin. Invert the pastry over a 9¹/2-inch deep-dish pie pan, center, and peel off the paper. Tuck the pastry into the pan, without stretching it, and sculpt the edge so it is slightly higher than the rim. Place in the freezer for 15 minutes, then partially prebake and let cool according to the instructions on page 16. Reduce the oven temperature to 350°F.

3. In a large bowl, whisk the whole eggs and egg yolk together until frothy and evenly blended. Mix the sugar and flour together in a small bowl. Add to the eggs and whisk until smooth. Gently warm the maple syrup and butter together in a small saucepan. Let cool briefly, then gradually whisk into the eggs along with the vanilla and salt. Add the yogurt and blend until smooth. Ladle the filling into the cooled pie shell.

4. Place the pie on the center oven rack and bake for 25 minutes, then carefully rotate the pie 180 degrees, so that the part that was facing the back of the oven now faces forward. Continue to bake until the filling is set, 20 to 25 minutes. To check, give the pie a little nudge. The filling shouldn't move in waves, but rather jiggle as a whole. When done, the pie will have puffed slightly around the perimeter, but as with all custard pies, you want as little puffing as possible to prevent the custard from "breaking."

5. Transfer the pie to a wire rack and let cool. Serve warm or at room temperature. Or let cool thoroughly, cover with loosely tented aluminum foil, refrigerate, and serve cold.

Recipe for Success

▶ One of the reasons I like Stonyfield Farm yogurt is the rich layer of "yogurt cream" on top. Much as I love to spoon the stuff off and eat it as is, I refrain when I'm making this pie with a fresh container of yogurt. That added richness gives the pie extra body and an even smoother, creamier texture.

▶ If you find that your custard pies consistently rise dramatically along the edge, your oven is baking too hot. Reduce the oven temperature by 25°F and see whether that makes a difference. It should.

Cottage Cheese and Nutmeg Pie

I've long been an admirer of the cookbooks, and cooking style, of Deborah Madison, the highly regarded author of books such as *The Greens Cookbook* (Broadway Books, 2001) and *Vegetarian Cooking for Everyone* (Broadway Books, 1997). She has a very easy, confident writing style and knows her way around the kitchen. Deborah has a real knack for isolating and elevating flavors, so it didn't surprise me to find a recipe for a nutmeg pie in *Vegetarian Cooking for Everyone*. I was interested because, even though I like nutmeg, I've always used it with a light touch for fear that it would dominate a dish. What caught my eye was the fact that she uses a full teaspoon of it in her nutmeg pie. When I tried her recipe, I loved it. The nutmeg was just right, not at all overwhelming in the creamy filling. I liked the pie so much that I adapted her recipe to come up with my own version—a tad sweeter, a little less tart, and with a hint of lemon and vanilla. Deborah, however, gets most of the credit.

MAKES 8 TO 10 SERVINGS

1 recipe Basic Flaky Pie Pastry, Single Crust (page 31) or Tender Cream Cheese Pastry, Single Crust (page 46), refrigerated

FILLING
3 large eggs, at room temperature
1 large egg yolk, at room temperature
2/3 cup sugar

1/2 cup light or heavy cream
2 cups small-curd cottage cheese
1 teaspoon ground nutmeg
1/8 teaspoon salt
1/2 teaspoon grated lemon zest
1/2 teaspoon vanilla extract

1. If you haven't already, prepare the pastry and refrigerate until firm enough to roll, about 1 hour (or up to 1 1/2 hours for the cream cheese pastry).

2. On a sheet of lightly floured waxed paper, roll the pastry into a 13-inch circle with a floured rolling pin. Invert the pastry over a 9½-inch deep-dish pie pan, center, and peel off the paper. Tuck the pastry into the pan, without stretching it, and sculpt the edge into an upstanding ridge. Place in the freezer for 15 minutes, then partially prebake and let cool according to the instructions on page 16. Reduce the oven temperature to 350°F.

3. Whisk the eggs, egg yolk, and sugar together in a large bowl until well blended. Add the remaining ingredients, stirring until evenly mixed. Slowly pour the filling into the cooled pie shell.

4. Place the pie on the center oven rack and bake until the filling is set, 40 to 45 minutes. Rotate the pie 180 degrees halfway through the baking, so the part that faced the back of the oven now faces forward. When done, the perimeter of the pie may be slightly puffed. Because of the modest amount of sugar in the filling, the surface isn't likely to brown very much.

5. Transfer the pie to a wire rack and let cool to room temperature. Cover loosely with tented aluminum foil and refrigerate for at least 2 hours or overnight before serving.

Recipe for Success

▶ By coincidence, Deborah and I, in the course of our careers, have worked with the same fine food editor, Fran McCullough. When Fran was editing my books, she constantly chided me to use, and recommend, freshly grated nutmeg—something I always resisted on the grounds that most cooks simply won't go to the trouble to grate it themselves. That said, I think there's nothing quite as good as freshly grated nutmeg, and if you happen to own a nutmeg grater, by all means use it here, and the pie will be even better. You can find nutmeg graters in most well-stocked kitchen supply stores.

Sweet Cottage Cheese Pie with Plumped Raisins

I don't remember where I first found a recipe for cottage cheese pie. I do, however, remember thinking that it didn't sound all that appealing—a little like a diet food, more penance than pleasure. I was wrong, and now, some 15 years after I published a recipe for it in my first baking book, *Country Baking* (Galahad Books, 1999)—I'm still making it several times a year. This pie is all about texture: smooth, creamy, and cool. It will remind you of a very light, lemony cheesecake. The raisins, which are plumped ahead of time in orange juice, form a layer on the bottom. Do chill this for several hours before eating. Like cheesecake, it just isn't the same when it's warm.

MAKES 8 TO 10 SERVINGS

1 recipe Basic Flaky Pie Pastry, Single Crust (page 31), refrigerated

FILLING
3/4 cup dark raisins
Orange juice as needed
1 pound small- or large-curd cottage cheese
1/2 cup sugar
2 large eggs

1 large egg yolk
1/2 cup light cream or half-and-half
1 tablespoon fresh lemon juice
Grated zest of 1/2 lemon
1/2 teaspoon vanilla extract
1 tablespoon all-purpose flour
1/4 teaspoon ground nutmeg

1. If you haven't already, prepare the pastry and refrigerate until firm enough to roll, about 1 hour.

2. Put the raisins in a small bowl and add just enough orange juice to cover. Set aside for about 1 hour, while the pastry chills.

3. On a sheet of lightly floured waxed paper, roll the pastry into a 13-inch circle with a floured rolling pin. Invert the pastry over a 9½-inch deep-dish pie pan, center, and peel off the paper. Tuck the pastry into the pan, without stretching it, and sculpt the edge so it is even with the rim. Place in the freezer for 15 minutes, then partially prebake and let cool according to the instructions on page 16. Reduce the oven temperature to 350°F.

4. Combine the cottage cheese, sugar, eggs, egg yolk, cream, lemon juice, lemon zest, and vanilla in a food processor and process for 15 seconds. Sprinkle the flour and nutmeg over the filling and process again for about 15 seconds, until quite smooth. Set aside.

5. Drain the raisins (see Recipe for Success) and scatter them evenly over the cooled pie shell. Slowly pour the filling into the shell.

6. Place the pie on the center oven rack and bake for 40 to 45 minutes, rotating the pie 180 degrees halfway through the baking time, so that the part that faced the back of the oven now faces forward. When done, the perimeter will have puffed slightly, although it is better if it doesn't rise enough to develop deep cracks. The center of the pie may appear somewhat more jiggly than the rest of the pie, but it should not be soupy.

7. Transfer the pie to a wire rack and let cool to room temperature. Cover with loosely tented aluminum foil and refrigerate for at least 3 hours or overnight before serving.

Recipe for Success

▶ **You can add another layer of citrus flavor to the pie if you incorporate the orange juice used for plumping the raisins. Simply drain the raisins and reserve the juice, pouring it into a 1-cup glass measure. Add enough light cream to equal 1/2 cup of liquid, then add this to the processor instead of using all cream.**

Slipped Custard Pie

Before I actually started making this pie, I had always thought of slipped custard pie the way my kids seem to think, increasingly, of me: old-fashioned and quaint, perhaps, but with little practical value (other than when they need something with a price tag attached). I don't feel that way any longer. It *is* quaint, this notion of baking the filling and crust separately, then sliding the former into the latter. And it works as intended: when the pie is eaten right away, you get a perfectly crisp pie shell, since the moisture of the filling hasn't infiltrated the crust. If you're worried about the slipping part, don't. Even if you don't do it perfectly the first time, you get bonus points for trying. Before long, your neighbors will be stopping by on slipped custard pie day, just to watch a pro in action.

MAKES 8 TO 10 SERVINGS

1 recipe Extra-Flaky Pie Pastry, Single Crust (page 34), refrigerated

FILLING
2/3 cup sugar
2 1/2 cups whole milk, heated

4 large eggs, lightly beaten
1 1/2 teaspoons vanilla extract
Big pinch of salt

1.   If you haven't already, prepare the pastry and refrigerate until firm enough to roll, about 1 hour. Select two matching 9½-inch deep-dish pie pans. I prefer glass, since it won't tinge or color the custard in any way. Butter the one you'll bake the custard in.

2.   On a sheet of lightly floured waxed paper, roll the pastry into a 13-inch circle with a floured rolling pin. Invert the pastry over the ungreased pie pan, center, and peel off the paper. Tuck the pastry into the pan, without stretching it, and sculpt the edge so it is even with the rim. Place in the freezer for 15 minutes, then fully prebake and let cool according to the instructions on page 16. Reduce the oven temperature to 350°F.

3.   Put about ½ inch water in a large, shallow casserole (large enough to hold the pie pan easily) and place in the oven on the lowest rack.

4.   While the pan and water heat, make the filling. Put the sugar in a large bowl and whisk in the milk. Let cool for 5 minutes, then whisk in the eggs, vanilla, and salt. Pour the filling through a mesh sieve into the buttered pie pan to remove any lumps. If there is room for you to maneuver, reach into the oven and carefully place the pie pan in the casserole. Otherwise, slide the bottom rack out a little before putting the pie pan in the casserole, then gently slide the rack back in. Bake until set, 25 to 35 minutes. To check for doneness, give the custard a little nudge. It will be wobbly but not at all soupy.

5.   Transfer the custard to a wire rack and let cool to room temperature. Cover with loosely tented aluminum foil and refrigerate if you like your custard pie cold. When you're ready to serve the pie, gently slide a butter knife or flexible rubber spatula around the edge of the custard to loosen it. With the pie shell firmly on the counter, tilt one edge of the custard away from you, into the awaiting pastry. Tilt very gently at first, because once the custard starts to slip, it can do so unexpectedly fast. As the custard slides into the shell, back the custard pan away so that the custard can slide right in. Slice and serve right away.

Recipe for Success

▸ **The extra-flaky pastry is good for this pie because it is virtually shrink-proof. If the shell did shrink, it would take up space where the filling is supposed to be.**

▸ **Don't overcook the custard or let it brown on top. Overcooked custard will turn watery and make an inferior pie.**

▸ **Remember that we all love a little drama with our dinner. Don't be bashful about slipping out the custard. Do it gamely in front of your family or guests, and applaud the results, whatever they may be. If some of the custard winds up in a precarious position, just spoon it into the pie shell.**

Personal is a very appealing concept these days, isn't it? Those who are so inclined can now hire personal trainers, personal shoppers, even personal chefs. One pizza company has done quite well with personal pan pizza. The word "personal" conveys an aura of exclusivity, an individual claim not readily afforded to others. The same could be said of the pies in this section,

Personal Pies, Turnovers, and Other Little Pie Treats

although you don't have to be rich to make or enjoy one of them. • Personal pies are those, quite simply, that are meant to be served to one person, some-times two, especially when the two in question share a romantic link. A personal pie is special, made just for you. You control the entire destiny of your pie, knowing that if you choose to eat only half now, the rest will be waiting for you later. • They may be small, but personal pies have an impact on your family or guests that is well out of proportion to their size. For that reason, I often make little pies, such as Little Crème Brûlée Pies (page 420) or Charleston Pies (page 422), to serve at a party or other special occasion.

Although virtually any pie can be downsized, these are the ones I have a real soft spot for. Some are fruit pies, but there are cream pies, a molten chocolate pie, and turnovers as well. Turnovers are perhaps the best-known personal pies, and in the following pages you'll find recipes for several, both baked and fried—the latter a real treat if you've never tried one. Then again, I hope you'll agree that the same might be said for all these little pies.

Tips for Making Prizewinning Personal Pies

▶ Standard-size muffin cups and custard cups will do for many individual-size pies, but you'll want to have other pans on hand as well. I like small pottery pie pans, of about 1- to 1½-cup capacity, neither too deep nor too shallow. Often they come as a set of two or four. Don't spend too much on them, because you may ultimately find that the size isn't quite right for your purposes.

▶ Some individual-size pans are better suited to two servings than one. I have several like this. In addition to savory pot pies, I use them for dessert pies when we're having couples over for dinner. Women think there's something very romantic about eating dessert from the same dish as their partners, and so do men once they've been told so.

▶ When baking individual pies, it's usually best to place them on a baking sheet rather than baking them individually right on the oven rack. Individual pie pans are hard to handle and grasp with a potholder. The sheet allows you to move the pies all at once, rotating them as necessary for even baking.

▶ For quickie refrigerator pies and pies that aren't baked for any length of time, those mini store-bought graham cracker crusts are very convenient. If you give kids the basics—fresh berries, whipped cream, chocolate syrup, sprinkles, and the like—they can throw an impromptu make-your-own-pie party for their friends, with very little effort on your part.

Little No-Bake Butterfinger Pies

This is one of my favorite little pies, and if you have kids, I guarantee it will become a family favorite as well. The recipe is designed for those who want to go through the motions of making a pie, which kids love to do, but with as few steps as possible. There's no peeling or baking, just enough mixing, stirring, and assembly to make this a satisfying pie-making experience for young children and their parents (or older children, independent of their parents). As for the pie filling, it's a creamy peanut butter "mousse," with Butterfinger candy in the bottom and on top of the pie. Because these pies are made in small individual store-bought crusts, they chill faster and everyone can eat all the sooner.

MAKES 4 OR 5 SERVINGS

4 or 5 mini store-bought graham cracker crusts

FILLING

One 8-ounce package full-fat cream cheese, slightly softened

1 cup confectioners' sugar, sifted

2 tablespoons firmly packed light brown sugar

1/2 cup smooth peanut butter

1/2 teaspoon vanilla extract

3/4 cup cold heavy or whipping cream

One 2.1-ounce Butterfinger candy bar, finely chopped

1. Place the crusts on a baking sheet, prebaking them according to the package directions. Set aside on a wire rack to cool thoroughly, then refrigerate until ready to use.

2. In a large bowl, beat the cream cheese with an electric mixer until smooth and creamy. Add the confectioners' sugar and brown sugar and beat until smooth, scraping down the bowl once or twice. Add the peanut butter and vanilla and beat again until smooth. Wash and dry the beaters, then refrigerate for a few minutes.

3. In a chilled medium-size bowl, beat the cream with the mixer until stiff but not grainy. Reserve just enough whipped cream to garnish the top of each pie; refrigerate. Add the remaining whipped cream to the peanut butter mixture and blend briefly on low speed. Finish by folding the mixture by hand with a large rubber spatula until evenly combined.

4. Sprinkle some of the chopped Butterfinger in the bottom of each chilled pie shell. Spoon some of the filling into each shell, dividing it evenly among them. Sprinkle more of the Butterfinger over each pie. Put the pies on a small baking sheet and refrigerate for 1 to 2 hours, or longer if desired.

5. Right before serving, add a dollop of the reserved whipped cream to each pie and sprinkle with some of the remaining Butterfinger.

Recipe for Success

▶ For a really attractive presentation (kids love this), let the kids pipe the filling into the pie shells with a pastry bag. It's a good way to teach them manual dexterity.

▶ If you aren't piping and you want to add even more Butterfinger, you can fold it right into the filling.

▶ Give your kids a little lesson in mixer safety before starting. Even if they've heard it before, it never hurts to remind them to keep their hands away from the beaters and not to lift the beaters out of the bowl while the mixer is running.

Rice Krispies Marshmallow Mud Meringue Pies

Now there's a mouthful, and so is the pie. This is one of those fun pies that you'll want to put together with the kids. Or should I say, the kids will want to put it together, and may or may not allow you to help. It's certainly kid-friendly. Instead of a "real" crust, this one is made with melted chocolate and Rice Krispies pressed into individual pie pans. In goes a scoop of coffee ice cream and some chocolate syrup. After being chilled, the pies are topped with a marshmallow meringue that gets browned just before everyone digs in. It's a great project for kids to work on together, but you should supervise the browning of the meringue.

MAKES 6 SERVINGS

RICE KRISPIES CRUST

1/3 cup unsalted butter

3/4 cup semisweet chocolate chips

3 cups Rice Krispies cereal

1/3 cup sweetened flaked coconut

1/4 teaspoon ground cinnamon

ICE CREAM FILLING AND MARSHMALLOW MERINGUE

1 quart coffee ice cream

Thick chocolate syrup

3 large egg whites, at room temperature

3 tablespoons sugar

1 cup marshmallow crème (like Marshmallow Fluff)

1. Lightly butter 6 individual pie pans or custard cups of 1- to 1¼-cup capacity. Set aside.

2. To make the crust, gently melt the butter in a medium-size saucepan, preferably nonstick. When the butter is nearly melted, add the chocolate chips with the heat at the lowest possible setting. Leave the pan alone for 1 minute, then turn off the heat, swirling the pan so that the butter runs over the chips. Let sit undisturbed for 5 minutes, then whisk to smooth. Add the Rice Krispies, coconut, and cinnamon and stir until evenly mixed. Divide the crust mixture among the pans; you want enough in each pan to make a thick crust. Gently press the mixture into the bottom and up the side of each pan. If there's any left over, save it for garnish. Let the crusts cool to room temperature, then place them in the freezer until firm, about 15 minutes.

3. Take the ice cream out of the freezer to soften a bit. Put a large scoop of ice cream in each chilled pie shell, flattening it slightly. Cover with a little chocolate syrup, then freeze until firm but not rock solid, about 1 hour.

4. When you're ready to serve, preheat the broiler. Using an electric mixer, beat the egg whites in a medium-size bowl on medium-high speed until they hold soft peaks. Add the sugar 1 tablespoon at a time, beating well after each addition. When the whites are thick and glossy but not dry, add the marshmallow crème and blend on low speed. Don't worry if you can't blend the marshmallow in perfectly; finish folding it by hand with a rubber spatula. Smooth a thick layer of the meringue over each pie, down to and touching the edge of the pie shell or pan. Put the pies on 1 or 2 baking sheets and, one sheet at a time, run them under the broiler just until the meringue is golden brown. Don't leave the stove, because the pies will likely brown in under a minute.

5. Serve the pies right away. The pans may have heated up slightly in the oven, so do tell your guests or family members to be careful.

Recipe for Success

▶ To make a nutty crust, leave out the coconut and add ¹/₃ cup finely chopped pecans or walnuts instead.

▶ There are, of course, other flavor schemes that would work nicely with the same crust. You can use butter pecan ice cream and butterscotch sauce, or vanilla ice cream and a fruit sauce, with more fruit sauce on top for garnish.

▶ I think this tastes best with the contrasting warm meringue and cold center, but you can also brown these, then freeze them. Eat within several hours.

▶ Be aware that the salmonella bacteria is occasionally found in raw eggs. Although the risk of salmonella poisoning is extremely low, young children, the elderly, pregnant women, and those with compromised immune systems should exercise caution. You can minimize the risk by using very fresh eggs purchased from a reliable source and keeping them refrigerated.

Kids and Pie Making

Kids have a natural curiosity about pie making. I know; I have four of them, and they've all helped me make pies. I myself learned all about pie making by osmosis, watching my mom and dad bake apple pies together every fall. I still remember what alchemy it was: take a few common ingredients; chop, mix, and blend them together; then stick the concoction in the oven and out comes a gorgeous pie.

If you have kids, take the time to bake a pie with them. If you review almost any pie recipe ahead of time, you'll find age-appropriate tasks your kids can help with. They may be too young to use a paring knife, but with a little instruction, they can wield a peeler. They can turn on ovens, help you roll a pastry, crimp a crust, sprinkle sugar, measure ingredients, and crack eggs. Here are a few more pointers worth considering.

▶ *Don't sweat the mess.* Kids, by and large, are sloppy pie makers. But fretting over every spill will bring their pie-making interest to a quick halt. One mom I know had this novel solution: she spread a canvas tarp under her baking area when she baked with her kids, then took the whole thing out and hosed it off afterward.

▶ *Have fun with the numbers.* Grade school kids can get an early course in math by making a pie. They can learn to count by measuring cups of flour. They can even learn to add fractions by tallying up all those spices in a pumpkin pie. But don't get anal about it.

▶ *Make it safe.* Don't trust young kids with electric mixers, food processors, hot ovens, or sharp knives. Any potentially harmful kitchen tool should be used only with adult supervision.

▶ *Share it.* Giving a homemade pie to someone you love is one of those gestures that makes everyone feel good. Demonstrate this for your child, and you'll leave the world a better place.

Crème Anglaise Berry Pies

I love a formula like this, which I can use as the blueprint for all kinds of variations. These are darling little pies. All you do is make mini pie shells with a graham cracker crust and add your favorite fresh berries. Pour some thick crème anglaise (vanilla custard sauce) over the berries, then top with a dollop of whipped cream and more fresh berries. When you spoon into the pie, the sauce will ooze out into the pan and blend with cascading berries and whipped cream. Yum! Mixed berries? By all means! Sliced fresh peaches? Absolutely! See what I mean? With this one basic formula, you can make a dozen different desserts. And it will work with any size mini pie pans you have.

MAKES 6 TO 8 SERVINGS

1 recipe Graham Cracker Crumb Crust (page 51) or 6 to 8 mini store-bought graham cracker crusts

FILLING

1 pint fresh raspberries, blackberries, blueberries (picked over for stems), or other berries

1 recipe cold Crème Anglaise (page 606)

GARNISH

Fresh Whipped Cream (page 605)

Ground nutmeg

1. Preheat the oven to 350°F. Prepare the crust and press it into the bottoms and up the sides of 6 to 8 mini pie pans or custard cups. It's best if they have a capacity of about 1 cup, but not much less. (The store-bought crusts usually have considerably less than a 1-cup capacity. Your pies will just be smaller.) If you're using straight-sided custard cups, it may be difficult to get the crust more than about halfway up the sides. Don't worry about it. Refrigerate for 5 to 10 minutes. Put the pans on the center oven rack and bake for 7 minutes. Transfer to a wire rack and let cool. If you're using the store-bought crusts, prebake according to the package directions and let cool.

2. When you're ready to assemble the pies, which should be shortly before serving, arrange a layer of berries in each pie shell, reserving some of the berries for garnish. Pour enough crème anglaise over the berries to cover generously. Put a big dollop of whipped cream on top, then garnish with a few of the reserved berries and a pinch of nutmeg. Serve right away.

Recipe for Success

▶ If your pans are on the small side, they'll be easier to get in the oven if you place them on a large baking sheet. Bake them right on the sheet.

▶ Some of my nicest small pie pans are a little too big for one serving but perfect for a shared dessert. This is a fun way to serve this pie if you have couples coming for dinner. I strongly suggest that you not serve it this way to siblings.

▶ Peaches are great here, as are other juicy stone fruits, but you might want to let the sliced fruit sit in a colander for a few minutes to drain before putting it in the pie shells. Otherwise, you may get too much fruit juice in the shells, leaving less room for the crème anglaise.

▶ One other fruit filling that would work beautifully here is the cherry topping for Cherry Cheesecake Pie on page 589.

Black Forest Mini Angel Pies

If you like the angel pie on page 188, you might want to try these individual ones. It's the same idea, you just make smaller pie shells—either freeform, like the larger version, or by piping the meringue through a pastry bag with a wide tip. The super-simple filling consists of whipped cream, chocolate syrup, and cherries and is topped with a dollop of chocolate whipped cream.

MAKES 5 OR 6 SERVINGS

1 recipe Meringue Pie Crust (page 50), modified as instructed in step 2

FILLING

1 cup cold heavy or whipping cream

1/4 cup thick chocolate syrup

1/4 teaspoon almond extract

1 cup fresh sweet cherries, stemmed and pitted

1. Line a large baking sheet with a large piece of parchment paper. Grease the paper lightly and set aside. Preheat the oven to 250°F.

2. Prepare the crust, adding 1 extra egg white.

3. Since you'll want to end up with 5 or 6 pie shells, roughly divide the meringue into that many mounds and spoon them onto the baking sheet. Flatten the mounds somewhat, shaping each into a pie shell or bowl shape, flaring the side upward. The shells should be about 5 inches across. Don't make them too thin in the center; the meringue should be no less than about 3/4-inch thick at any point. Alternatively, you can spoon the meringue into a pastry bag and pipe it into rough pie shell shapes. (The pies look very attractive done this way.) Start with a thick bottom, then move your bag in circles to build up the side.

4. Put the baking sheet on the center oven rack and bake until the shells are light golden brown and crusty on the outside, 1 1/4 to 1 1/2 hours. Rotate the baking sheet 180 degrees, so that the side that faced the back of the oven now faces forward, after 1 hour of baking. Let cool in the oven for 1 hour, then carefully transfer to a wire rack.

5. When you're ready to assemble the pies, using a chilled medium-size bowl and chilled beaters, beat the cream with an electric mixer until it holds medium-firm peaks. Set aside just enough for a small dollop on each serving. Add the chocolate syrup to the larger portion and beat until thick and firm but not grainy. Beat in the almond extract, then

fold in the cherries. Divide the filling evenly among the shells. Garnish each with a dollop of plain whipped cream and serve right away.

Recipe for Success

▶ Keep an eye on the meringues and try not to overbake them. You want them to turn just a very light golden brown. Because they're small, they bake a little faster than a larger meringue pie shell would.

▶ Another way to do this is to use canned cherry pie filling instead of fresh cherries. Spoon some of it into each shell, then top with the chocolate whipped cream.

▶ I like to use Fox's U-Bet chocolate syrup.

Little Crème Brûlée Pies

For about the past 25 years, nearly the entire span of my food career, crème brûlée has had a run as one of America's favorite desserts. At first, I think in part because of its fancy name, you could find it only at better restaurants. Then, once everyone figured out it was simply rich custard with a good pedigree, it started popping up just about everywhere, in all flavors of the rainbow. As if it weren't rich enough, I've come up with a new spin on crème brûlée, baking it in individual pie shells. The buttery pastry adds another texture to the creamy custard and crunchy topping. You'll want to serve these for a special occasion, such as a small dinner party. Start them the day before, or early the same day, so that they have plenty of time to chill. The recipe can be doubled easily, if necessary. Either way, you're likely to have a little extra custard, which should be baked in custard cups along with the pies.

MAKES 4 SERVINGS

1 recipe Extra-Flaky Pie Pastry, Single Crust (page 34), divided as instructed in step 1 and refrigerated

FILLING
1 1/2 cups heavy or whipping cream
1/2 cup light cream or half-and-half

5 large egg yolks
1/2 cup granulated sugar
3/4 teaspoon vanilla extract

BRÛLÉE TOPPING
1/2 cup firmly packed light brown sugar

1. If you haven't already, prepare the pastry. Divide it into 4 equal-size balls. Flatten each into a 1/2-inch-thick disk and wrap in plastic. Refrigerate until firm enough to roll, about 1 hour. Lightly butter 4 individual pie pans of about 1-cup capacity.

2. Working with one piece of chilled dough at a time, roll it into a circle about 1 1/2 inches wider than the top of your pan on lightly floured waxed paper with a floured rolling pin. The pastry will be on the thin side. Invert the pastry onto your outstretched hand, peel off the paper, and gently tuck the pastry into the pan. Sculpt the edge of the pastry into a ridge that's even with or just slightly higher than the rim. Place in the freezer for 15 minutes. Repeat for the other pieces of pastry. Preheat the oven to 325°F.

3. Combine the heavy cream and light cream in a small, heavy pan over low heat. Heat the mixture until the top shimmers, about 5 minutes, then remove from the heat. Whisk gently to keep a skin from forming.

4. In a large bowl, beat the egg yolks and granulated sugar together until slightly thickened and pale yellow, about 2 minutes. Stir in a ladleful of the warm cream to temper the yolks, then continue to stir in the remaining cream a little at a time. Stir in the vanilla. Ladle the custard into the chilled pie shells, filling them nearly up to the rim of the pastry. (If you have any leftover custard, spoon it into custard cups.) Put the pies (and custard cups) directly on the center oven rack, evenly spaced, and bake until the custard is set, 25 to 35 minutes. To check for doneness, give one of the pans a little nudge. The filling shouldn't be soupy in the center. Don't let the custards get puffy or overbaked.

5. Transfer the pies to a wire rack and let cool thoroughly. Cover with loosely tented aluminum foil and refrigerate for at least 3 hours or overnight. When you're ready to serve them, preheat the broiler. Pushing the brown sugar through a mesh sieve, gently and evenly spread (without compacting it) about 2 tablespoons of it over each pie. Put the pies on a baking sheet and quickly run them under the broiler, moving the sheet as necessary so they brown more or less evenly. At the very first sign of scorching, remove the sheet from the oven. (Alternatively, fire up a propane torch and wave it over the brown sugar from about 2 inches away. The sugar will very quickly caramelize.) Serve at once, but warn your guests that the sugar and top of the pans are very hot.

Recipe for Success

▶ **By keeping the pastry thin, there's no need to partially prebake the pie shells. For small, thin pastry like this, you may find it easier to use a tapered, French-style rolling pin than a large round one.**

- Don't worry if the tops of the naked custards brown a little. Ordinarily, I don't let my custards brown, placing aluminum foil over them, if necessary. But because you're adding the brown sugar topping, a little browning doesn't matter.

- If you suspect that your oven bakes a little hot, reduce the temperature by 25°F. It's better to bake these longer and at a lower temperature than for the oven to be too hot and perhaps damage the custards.

Charleston Pies

My wife, Bev, who comes from Charleston, South Carolina, insists that these are Charleston *tarts*, of the sort the ladies there eat with afternoon tea. I, a Yankee who knows little of such things, insist that even if they are tarts, they're close enough to an open-faced pie for my purposes. Mostly, they're fun to make and just plain wonderful to eat. The original recipe is handwritten on one of Bev's tattered and spattered index cards, and its source has long since been forgotten. For my version, you start with a cream cheese pastry, cut into rounds and pressed into standard muffin cups. The pie shells are chilled, filled with raisins and chopped pecans, and then topped with a pecan pie–like mixture of egg, butter, sugar, and corn syrup. In just 25 minutes, they're baked to golden perfection—just-right single servings for any special occasion. These are meant to be eaten out of hand, but for a more formal presentation, they can be garnished with whipped cream and served with a fork.

MAKES 6 SERVINGS

1 recipe Tender Cream Cheese Pastry, Single Crust (page 46), divided as instructed in step 1 and refrigerated

FILLING

1 large egg

1/3 cup light corn syrup

1/3 cup sugar

3 tablespoons unsalted butter, melted

1/2 teaspoon vanilla extract

Pinch of salt

About 1/2 cup dark raisins

About 1/2 cup chopped pecans

1. If you haven't already, prepare the pastry and divide it in half. Refrigerate until firm enough to roll, 1 to 1½ hours. Lightly butter a muffin pan with 6 standard-size cups. You can use a 12-cup pan, if necessary.

2. On a sheet of lightly floured waxed paper, roll one half of the pastry about ⅛ inch thick (as thick as you'd roll any pastry) with a floured rolling pin. Slide the dough, on the paper, onto a baking sheet and refrigerate for 7 to 10 minutes. Using a 4½-inch-diameter cutter of some sort or a 4½-inch circle as a guide, cut out 3 pastry circles. Gently push each pastry into a muffin cup; the edge of the pastry will nearly reach the top edge of the cup. Repeat with the other half of the dough, lining a total of 6 cups. Place in the freezer for 15 minutes. Preheat the oven to 375°F.

3. Whisk the egg lightly in a medium-size bowl. Add the corn syrup and sugar and whisk again. Whisk in the butter, vanilla, and salt until evenly blended.

4. Divide the raisins and pecans evenly among the chilled muffin cups. Using a small scoop or measuring cup, spoon the filling over them, dividing it equally among the cups. Keep the filling just slightly lower than the upper edge of the pastry. Use a fork or knife to move the filling around gently, to make sure it flows around the raisins and pecans.

5. Put the pan on the center oven rack and bake until the tops are golden brown and puffed, about 25 minutes.

6. Transfer the pan to a wire rack and let cool for 5 minutes. Run a knife around the edge of each pie and continue to let cool in the pan for 1 hour. Slide a knife under each pie, lift it out of the pan, and finish cooling on the rack. Serve at room temperature.

Recipe for Success

▸ Refrigerating the dough after rolling it will make it easier to cut. If you're using a template, use a fluted pastry wheel to cut the pastry, if you own one.

▸ Instead of—or in addition to—the raisins, you can include 3 or 4 semisweet chocolate chips in each pie.

▸ To serve a crowd, the recipe can easily be doubled. Make the double-crust version of the pastry and simply double the filling ingredients. Refrigerated, these will keep well for 2 days, if you'd like to make them ahead. Just cover with loosely tented aluminum foil and bring up to room temperature before serving.

Little Cream Pies

These small pies are all about child's play. The dough is a simple press-in pastry, which, when made by the hand method, is easy enough for even young children to make, with a little help from an adult. The filling is pared down to the basics—flour, sugar, and light cream mainly— and it's mixed right in the little pie shells. A little too much of this or that isn't going to harm these pies, so get everything set up, then let the kids do their thing.

MAKES 4 SERVINGS

1 recipe Simple Press-In Pie Pastry (page 49), refrigerated

FILLING

About 6 tablespoons firmly packed light brown sugar

About 1/4 cup granulated sugar

About 1/4 cup all-purpose flour

Salt

About 1 1/4 cups light cream or half-and-half

About 1 1/2 tablespoons cold unsalted butter, cut into small pieces

Ground cinnamon

1. Preheat the oven to 350°F. If you haven't already, prepare the pastry. Butter 4 individual pie pans of about 1-cup capacity.

2. Divide the pastry crumbs evenly among the pans. Press the pastry into the bottom and slightly up the side of each pan. If there seems to be too much pastry for the pans, making it too thick, don't use all of the pastry. Place the pans on the center oven rack and bake for 15 minutes. Transfer to a wire rack and let cool. If you're letting children make these pies, let cool for at least 15 minutes before assembling.

3. Put about 1½ tablespoons of the brown sugar in each pie shell. Add 1 tablespoon of the granulated sugar, then 1 tablespoon of the flour. Add a pinch of salt. Using your fingertips, rub the dry ingredients together right in the pie shells until evenly mixed. Spoon about 5 tablespoons of the cream over the dry mixture in each pie shell, but do not stir it in. Dot the top of each with the butter and sprinkle with a pinch of cinnamon.

4. Place the pies on a large baking sheet and put the sheet on the center oven rack. Bake until the filling is golden brown and, most likely, crusted over, 30 to 35 minutes. If there is loose liquid visible, it may be bubbling.

5. Transfer the pies to a wire rack and let cool for at least 30 minutes before serving right in the pans.

Recipe for Success

▶ Don't let children dig into these pies until they have cooled for at least 30 minutes. The filling can stay hot for quite some time, and it has a way of sticking to the roof of your mouth, increasing the likelihood of a burn.

▶ These are delicious little pies, great for kids and their friends, but also a little homely and not really fancy enough for adult guests.

Little Banana-Coconut Cream Pies

These delicious little pies have a bottom crust of press-in pastry, topped with sliced banana, brown sugar, coconut, and heavy cream. There's nothing to mix or prebake, so they can be easily assembled for a weekend dessert for family or friends. Plan to eat these warm, 30 to 40 minutes after they come out of the oven.

MAKES 4 SERVINGS

1 recipe Simple Press-In Pie Pastry (page 49), refrigerated

FILLING

2 large ripe bananas

1/4 cup sweetened flaked coconut

1/2 cup firmly packed light brown sugar

Ground cinnamon

1 cup heavy or whipping cream

GARNISH

Crème Anglaise (page 606) or vanilla ice cream

1. Preheat the oven to 350°F. If you haven't already, prepare the pastry. Butter 4 individual pie pans.

2. Divide the pastry crumbs evenly among the pans. Press the pastry into the bottom and slightly up the side of each pan. (If there seems to be too much pastry, don't use it all.) Using about half a banana for each pie, slice the bananas, arranging the slices in 2 stacked layers in the pie shells. Sprinkle 1 tablespoon of the coconut, 2 tablespoons of the brown sugar, and a pinch of cinnamon evenly over each pie. Drizzle 1/4 cup of the heavy cream over each.

3. Put the pies on a large baking sheet, place on the center oven rack, and bake until bubbly and dark golden brown, about 35 minutes. Rotate the baking sheet 180 degrees,

so that the side that faced the back of the oven now faces forward, about 10 minutes before the pies are done.

4. Transfer the pies to a wire rack and let cool for at least 30 minutes. Serve with a dollop of cold crème anglaise or a scoop of ice cream.

Recipe for Success

▶ **For a spirited little kick, add 1¹/₂ to 2 tablespoons dark rum to the heavy cream and stir to combine. Then drizzle it over each pie as directed.**

Dahlia Bakery Butterscotch Pies

As far as the Seattle food scene goes, Tom Douglas is the man. He and his wife and business partner, Jackie Cross, not only own three of the best restaurants in town, including Etta's Seafood and the Palace Kitchen, but the guy also turns out wonderful cookbooks on a regular basis and has his own weekly radio show as well. One of Tom's enterprises, Dahlia Bakery, has a loyal following, and when you taste these little pies, which Tom serves as tarts, you'll understand why. First, he browns the butter to give it a toasty flavor. Then he adds lots of dark brown sugar. Milk, thickener, and egg yolks round out the filling, which goes into individual prebaked pie shells and is topped with whipped cream, banana slices, and a terrific pistachio brittle. This all takes time, so I think of this as a special occasion, wow 'em dessert. (It certainly wowed me.) Special thanks to Tom's co-author and quality control manager, Shelley Lance, for scaling the recipe down to home proportions.

MAKES 6 SERVINGS

1 recipe Extra-Flaky Pie Pastry, Single Crust (page 34), divided as instructed in step 1 and refrigerated

FILLING

11 tablespoons unsalted butter

1²/₃ cups firmly packed dark brown sugar

1¹/₃ cups hot water

¹/₄ cup cornstarch

2 tablespoons plus 2 teaspoons all-purpose flour

Scant ¹/₂ teaspoon salt

Scant 1 cup whole milk

4 large egg yolks

1 tablespoon vanilla extract

PISTACHIO BRITTLE

1 cup shelled natural (undyed) pistachios

3 tablespoons water

³/₄ cup sugar

ASSEMBLY AND GARNISH

2 or 3 medium-size ripe bananas, sliced

Fresh Whipped Cream (page 605)

The Dahlia Coconut Cream Pie

I asked Tom Douglas, whose fabulous butterscotch pie recipe is adapted opposite, to say a few words about the one pie his customers will simply not let him take off the menu—his pie of all pies. Here's what he had to say.

"When we opened the Dahlia Lounge, there were a few things I was determined to put on the menu: my favorite Delaware-style crab cakes; a grilled bread salad with fresh mozzarella; and a creamy, lush, old-fashioned coconut cream pie. All three were great sellers, but pie sales were phenomenal, with customers frequently requesting a whole pie to go.

"Why do people love the coconut cream pie? Picture a crisp, coconut-studded crust filled with soft, creamy pastry cream, topped with a cloud of whipped cream, and showered with toasted coconut and curls of white chocolate. It's a pie from your childhood memories—a pie the kid in you can't resist.

"Fifteen years and thousands of coconut cream pies later, we've added a large, well-staffed pastry kitchen and a retail bakery, the Dahlia Bakery, to keep up with the demand. We sell full-size coconut cream pies, 'baby pies' for two or three servings, pies by the slice, and even bite-size coconut pies you can just pop in your mouth. Our customers never seem to get enough."

1. If you haven't already, prepare the pastry. Divide it into 6 equal-size balls. Flatten each into a ½-inch-thick disk and wrap in plastic. Refrigerate until firm enough to roll, about 1 hour. Get out six 1-cup-capacity individual pie pans.

2. Working with one piece of chilled dough at a time, roll it into a circle large enough to line your pan on a sheet of lightly floured waxed paper with a floured rolling pin. Invert the pastry over the pan, center, and peel off the paper. Gently tuck the pastry into the pan, without stretching it, and sculpt the edge so it is slightly higher than the rim. Place in the freezer while you line the other pie pans, then fully prebake and let cool according the directions on page 16.

3. Melt the butter in a large, heavy saucepan over medium to medium-high heat, stirring a few times. Continue to heat until brown flecks begin to appear on the bottom of the pan. Add the brown sugar and continue to cook over fairly high heat, stirring constantly, for 2 minutes. Carefully stir the water into the saucepan; be prepared to step back away from the spattering. Remove from the heat.

4. Combine the cornstarch, flour, and salt in a medium-size bowl. Gradually whisk in the milk. Add the milk mixture to the brown sugar liquid and return to medium-high

heat, stirring or whisking constantly until it reaches a boil. Reduce the heat slightly and cook, whisking nonstop, for 3 minutes. The mixture will be very thick. Remove from the heat.

5. Whisk the egg yolks in a small bowl. Gradually whisk in 6 or 7 tablespoons of the hot brown sugar mixture to temper them. Add the tempered yolks to the brown sugar mixture. Return to the heat and continue to cook over medium heat, stirring constantly, for 2 minutes. Remove from the heat and pour into a bowl. Whisk in the vanilla. Press a piece of plastic wrap directly against the filling, without any gaps or air pockets, to keep a skin from forming. Put the bowl on a wire rack and let cool to room temperature. Refrigerate for at least 4 hours or overnight.

6. At least 1 hour before serving, make the pistachio brittle. Lightly oil a piece of aluminum foil and place it on a baking sheet. Arrange the pistachios close together in a single layer in the center of the sheet and set aside. Combine the water and sugar in a small, heavy saucepan over medium heat and stir constantly until the sugar dissolves, about 2 minutes. Turn the heat to high and *stop stirring altogether*. Heat, swirling the pan from time to time instead of stirring, until the mixture is light golden brown, 7 to 8 minutes. Slowly pour the mixture over the pistachios, taking care to cover all of them. Set the baking sheet aside and let cool thoroughly. Break the brittle into pieces, place in a food processor, and process into fine crumbs.

7. To assemble the pies, smooth the filling by stirring gently, then spoon some of it into each pie shell, leaving room around the outside for the banana slices. Tuck some banana slices here and there around the filling. Dollop generously with whipped cream, then sprinkle with the pistachio brittle. Serve at once.

Recipe for Success

> ▶ **You can, if you like, also make this in mini graham cracker crusts. Follow the directions on page 417.**

> ▶ **Be sure not to underbake the pastry. This sort of cream pie always tastes best with a crisp, golden brown crust.**

> ▶ **This filling tends to bubble more than some, so you might want to wear long sleeves when you're cooking it, to guard against spatters.**

> ▶ **Instead of the pistachios, use another kind of nut, if you like, for the brittle.**

Mini Cheesecake Pies for the Kids

Like the Butterfinger pie on page 413, this one is written around mini store-bought graham cracker crusts. Kids are very fond of the petite size and love nothing more than having the whole thing to themselves and adding a personal touch. Thus, rather than give you one topping with the recipe, I've given you several—none of which needs to be cooked. The filling itself is kid-friendly, too. With a little supervision, most children ages eight and up will likely be able to do most of this on their own. If your child mixes and bakes these pies in the morning, come afternoon, when his or her friends are over, they can have a little pie party. Just put all the garnishes out on the table and let them create their own pies.

MAKES 6 SERVINGS

6 mini store-bought graham cracker crusts

FILLING

Two 3-ounce packages full-fat cream cheese, softened

1/2 cup sugar

1 large egg, at room temperature

1/4 cup full-fat sour cream

1/2 teaspoon vanilla extract

1/4 teaspoon lemon extract or grated lemon zest

1. Because you'll be baking these for 20 minutes, it isn't necessary to prebake the crusts. However, remove them from the package and arrange them on a large baking sheet, leaving plenty of room between them. Preheat the oven to 325°F.

2. Using an electric mixer, in a medium-size bowl beat the cream cheese on medium speed, gradually adding the sugar. Add the egg and beat briefly. Add the sour cream, vanilla, and lemon extract, beating just until evenly blended.

3. Using a scoop or ladle, divide the filling evenly among the pie shells. You can fill each one very close to the top, but leave some room for the topping.

4. Place the baking sheet on the center oven rack and bake until the pies puff slightly and have a flat (not glossy) surface, about 20 minutes. Do not overbake.

5. Let the pies cool for 10 minutes on the baking sheet, then transfer them to a wire rack and let cool thoroughly. Cover loosely with aluminum foil and refrigerate for 2 to 3 hours. Garnish with one of the following toppings, or one of your own, before serving.

▶ **CARAMEL-NUT CHEESECAKE PIES** Spoon a little caramel sauce over the filling, then sprinkle with chopped nuts. Drizzle with chocolate syrup, if desired.

- **FRESH BERRY CHEESECAKE PIES** Arrange fresh blueberries (picked over for stems), raspberries (rounded side up), or hulled and sliced strawberries on top. Brush with raspberry or red currant jam, warmed and whisked to liquefy.

- **CHOCO-MALLOW CHEESECAKE PIES** Top with marshmallow crème (Marshmallow Fluff), chocolate syrup, and chopped nuts.

- **FRUIT GLAZE CHEESECAKE PIES** Buy prepared fruit glaze and spoon it over each pie.

- **CANDY FANTASY CHEESECAKE PIES** Pipe fresh or canned whipped cream over the filling. Sprinkle on jimmies ("sprinkles" to some of you), mini M&M's, or other favorite candy.

Recipe for Success

- Tell your child to handle the pie shells very carefully. They're so small that if you knock one against something, the side may break off.

- Remember to give your child an electric mixer safety lesson before beginning.

- This recipe is easily doubled or tripled for larger groups. Don't be embarrassed to use these pie shells for an adult party either. The aluminum pans aren't exactly classy, but if the party is casual, they'll be fine.

Chocolate Lava Pies

My stepson, Bryan, works at a great restaurant here in Annapolis, Maryland, where they make a chocolate lava cake that's baked to order. It's a fabulous dessert: the outside is like a soft brownie, while the inside is an oozing molten chocolate that I never get enough of. I've adapted that idea to these little pies, which have that same lava-like, flowing chocolate when eaten warm. By the time they're ready to be served, about 15 to 25 minutes out of the oven, the tops have formed a little crater that you can drop a dollop of whipped cream or coffee mascarpone into. Save these for a special occasion.

MAKES 6 SERVINGS

1 recipe Tender Cream Cheese Pastry, Single Crust (page 46), divided as instructed in step 1 and refrigerated

FILLING

1/2 cup light corn syrup

6 tablespoons (3/4 stick) unsalted butter, cut into pieces

2 ounces bittersweet chocolate, coarsely chopped

1/3 cup sugar

3 tablespoons cake flour, sifted

1/8 teaspoon salt

1/2 teaspoon vanilla extract

2 large egg yolks

GARNISH

Fresh Whipped Cream (page 605) or Coffee Mascarpone (page 607)

1.　If you haven't already, prepare the pastry and divide it in half. Refrigerate until firm enough to roll, 1 to 1 1/2 hours. Lightly butter a muffin pan with 6 standard-size cups. You can use a 12-cup pan, if necessary.

2.　On a sheet of lightly floured waxed paper, roll one half of the pastry about 1/8 inch thick (as thick as you'd roll any pastry) with a floured rolling pin. Slide the dough, on the paper, onto a baking sheet and refrigerate for 7 to 10 minutes. Using a 4 1/2-inch-diameter cutter of some sort or a 4 1/2-inch circle as a guide, cut out 3 pastry circles. Gently push each pastry into a muffin cup; the edge of the pastry will nearly reach the top edge of the cup. Repeat for the other half of the dough, lining a total of 6 cups. Place in the freezer for 15 minutes. Preheat the oven to 350°F.

3.　Combine the corn syrup and butter in a medium-size saucepan over medium heat and slowly melt the butter. Turn off the heat and add the chocolate, tilting the pan so that the hot liquid runs over it. Set aside for 5 minutes, then whisk until smooth and well combined. Pour the mixture into a medium-size bowl. Add the sugar, flour, and salt and whisk to blend. Add the vanilla and egg yolks and whisk until evenly combined. Using a small scoop or ladle, divide the filling evenly among the chilled muffin cups.

4. Put the pan on the center oven rack and bake until the chocolate rises up to the top of the cups and bubbles slightly, about 25 minutes.

5. Transfer the pan to a wire rack and let the pies cool in the pan for 15 to 25 minutes. When they've reached the proper serving temperature, the edges will be somewhat set, but the center will still be soft and concave. Serve on attractive dessert plates, with a dollop of whipped cream or coffee mascarpone in the center of each pie.

Recipe for Success

▶ The cup size is critical to the success of these little pies, so don't try to substitute individual pie pans or larger muffin cups.

▶ Take your time getting the pastry into each cup. It takes a little patience and finesse to do this well, but the end result is worth the trouble.

Little Fruit Crumb Pies

Here's another recipe for the kids—a great pie-baking project for those summer days when the fruit is ripe and plentiful and the kids are looking for something fun to do. Like Little Cream Pies (page 424), we begin with a simple press-in pastry. A thin layer of crumbs is pressed into each pan, fresh fruit is added, and then more of the pastry crumbs are scattered over the top. If you have several kinds of fruit available, kids will probably want to customize the filling. Encourage them to be creative and combine fruits they like. There's very little they can do to sabotage their efforts, so they might as well have fun.

MAKES 4 SERVINGS

1 recipe Simple Press-In Pie Pastry (page 49), refrigerated

FILLING
About 3 cups fresh mixed fruit (blueberries [picked over for stems], blackberries, pitted cherries, raspberries, and/or peeled, pitted, and diced peaches)

About 6 tablespoons sugar

About 4 teaspoons all-purpose flour

Ground nutmeg

About 2 teaspoons fresh lemon juice

1. Preheat the oven to 375°F. If you haven't already, prepare the pastry. Butter 4 individual pie pans.

2. Divide the pastry crumbs roughly in half, with one portion slightly larger than the other. Working with the larger portion, divide the pastry crumbs evenly among the pans. Press the pastry into the bottom and slightly up the side of each pan. Set aside along with the rest of the pastry crumbs.

3. If you have several children working together on these pies, they can measure out the ingredients for each pie, using one-quarter of the total amount. Otherwise, the filling can be mixed all at once. Assuming that you're making the pies individually, have each child put about ³/₄ cup of the fruit in his or her pie shell. In little cereal bowls, have each child mix together 1¹/₂ tablespoons of the sugar, 1 teaspoon of the flour, and a pinch of nutmeg. Have the children sprinkle the mixture over the fruit and mix it in gently, then spread the fruit evenly in the shells. Have each one sprinkle about ¹/₂ teaspoon of the lemon juice on top. Divide the remaining pastry crumbs among the pies and have the children gently press them into the fruit.

4. Put the pies on a large baking sheet and place the sheet on the center oven rack. Bake until the fruit is bubbly and the topping is golden brown, 35 to 40 minutes. Rotate the baking sheet 180 degrees, so that the side that faced the back of the oven now faces forward, about 10 minutes before the pies are done.

5. Transfer the pies to a wire rack and let cool for at least 30 minutes before serving.

Recipe for Success

▶ Since there isn't much filling and the fruit won't give off much juice as the pies bake, it isn't necessary to prebake the crusts.

▶ If your chosen pie pans can accommodate it, feel free to use more than ³/₄ cup fruit. That's about the least amount you need to make a respectable single-serving pie. As long as the top of the fruit sits a little below the rim of the pan, you're okay.

Junior Blueberry Crumb Pies

These pies are the perfect size for packing into lunches, and, of course, they also make a perfect single-serving dessert. Note that I make them with canned blueberries, rather than fresh, so you end up with a very compact layer of fruit; fresh blueberries take up too much space. For a fancy touch, put a puddle of crème anglaise on each plate, then place a pie right in the center. (My stepson, Bryan, after hearing me complain that I needed to come up with something more original than "little" to title all these small pies, suggested the "junior" moniker, which I obviously liked.)

MAKES 6 SERVINGS

1 recipe Tender Cream Cheese Pastry, Single Crust (page 46), divided as instructed in step 1 and refrigerated

FILLING

One 14-ounce can Wyman's wild blueberries in water, drained but juice reserved

1 tablespoon fresh lemon juice

1/4 cup sugar

1 tablespoon plus 1 teaspoon cornstarch

CRUMB TOPPING

1/3 cup sugar

1/4 cup all-purpose flour

1/8 teaspoon ground cinnamon

Big pinch of salt

2 tablespoons cold unsalted butter, cut into 1/4-inch pieces

GARNISH

Crème Anglaise (page 606)

1. If you haven't already, prepare the pastry and divide it in half. Refrigerate until firm enough to roll, 1 to 1½ hours. Lightly butter a muffin pan with 6 standard-size cups. You can use a 12-cup pan, if necessary.

2. On a sheet of lightly floured waxed paper, roll one half of the pastry about ⅛ inch thick (as thick as you'd roll any pastry) with a floured rolling pin. Slide the dough, on the paper, onto a baking sheet and refrigerate for 7 to 10 minutes. Using a 4½-inch-diameter cutter of some sort or a 4½-inch circle as a guide, cut out 3 pastry circles. Gently push each pastry into a muffin cup; the edge of the pastry will nearly reach the top edge of the cup. Repeat for the other half of the dough, lining a total of 6 cups. Place in the freezer for 15 minutes.

3. Combine the drained blueberries and ½ cup of their juice in a medium-size saucepan. Stir in the lemon juice. Mix the sugar and cornstarch in a small bowl, then stir the mixture into the fruit. Bring to a boil over medium heat, stirring, and cook at a low boil for about 1½ minutes. Scrape the fruit into a bowl and let cool. Preheat the oven to 375°F.

4. Meanwhile, make the crumb topping. Put the sugar, flour, cinnamon, and salt in a medium-size bowl and toss with your hands. Add the butter and rub it into the dry ingredients to make coarse crumbs that feel like damp sand.

5. Spoon the cooled filling into the chilled muffin cups, dividing it evenly among them. Sprinkle some of the crumb topping over each cup. Put the muffin pan on the center oven rack and bake until the fruit starts to bubble and the topping is golden brown, about 25 minutes.

6. Transfer the pan to a wire rack and let cool for 10 minutes. Run a knife around the edge of the cups to loosen the pies and continue to let cool in the cups for 10 to 20 minutes, then remove from the pan. Serve warm, garnished with crème anglaise. Or transfer the pies to the rack, let cool to room temperature, cover loosely with aluminum foil, and refrigerate until you're ready to serve. Rewarm for about 15 minutes in a 250°F oven before serving.

Recipe for Success

- There isn't much room in these cups for extras, but if you have some fresh raspberries on hand, adding 1 or 2 to each cup is a nice surprise.

- Speaking of other berries, for an attractive garnish, sprinkle a few assorted berries on each serving plate. Fresh berries taste delicious with the crème anglaise.

Little Preserves and Chocolate Finger Pies

These fun little finger pies are barely bigger than a cookie, and kids love making them. When my kids were younger, they used to make them all the time with pastry scraps, leftover dough from the fridge, or half of a double-crust pastry (if I needed only one crust). The basic idea is this: roll the pastry a little thinner than usual and cut with a $3^1/_2$-inch round cutter. Put a couple of teaspoons of fruit preserves and a few chocolate chips in the middle, then seal and bake. They're great for kids because they don't take too long to bake and you can eat them nearly right away—little patience is required.

MAKES 10 TO 14 SMALL PIES

1 recipe Tender Cream Cheese Pastry, Single Crust (page 46), Basic Flaky Pie Pastry, Single Crust (page 31), Basic Shortening Pie Pastry, Single Crust (page 30), or any other single-crust pie pastry, refrigerated

FILLING

Raspberry, strawberry, or other fruit preserves

Handful of semisweet chocolate chips

GARNISH

Confectioners' sugar

1. If you haven't already, prepare the pastry and refrigerate until firm enough to roll, about 1 hour. Grease a large baking sheet.

2. On a lightly floured sheet of waxed paper, roll the dough slightly less than $^1/_8$ inch thick with a floured rolling pin. Using a $3^1/_2$-inch round cutter or a $3^1/_2$-inch round template and a paring knife, cut the pastry into circles. Remove the scraps, leaving the rounds in place.

3. Spoon about 2 teaspoons of the preserves into the center of each circle. Scatter a few chocolate chips around the preserves. Moisten the entire edge of the pastry with a wet fingertip or pastry brush, then fold the circle in half and press the edges together to seal. Roll the edge up slightly, forming a sort of rope edge. As you work, transfer each pie to the prepared baking sheet, leaving a little room between them. Refrigerate for 10 minutes. Preheat the oven to 375°F.

4. Using a paring knife, poke 1 or 2 small steam vents in the top of each pie. Bake until golden brown, about 25 minutes.

5. Transfer the hot pies to a wire rack. As soon as they're cool enough to handle, put some confectioners' sugar in a small bowl. Roll each pie in the confectioners' sugar, coating it heavily, and return it to the rack. Serve warm or let cool to room temperature before serving.

Recipe for Success

▶ You can, of course, leave out the chocolate chips and add a bit more preserves. For that matter, you could leave out the preserves and just use chocolate chips.

▶ If you have only a 3-inch cutter, just roll the dough a little on the thick side, cut the 3-inch circles, and then roll each circle a little larger.

▶ Of course, if you're using pastry scraps rather than starting with a single batch of pastry, just use as much preserves and chocolate chips as needed.

Amish Half-Moon Pies

Given the amount of fruit the Amish preserve, it's no surprise that these pies include a direct reference to them. Here I start with dried apples, reconstituting them by simmering them in water and orange juice. When the apples are soft, I add some sugar—plenty by most standards, though not nearly as much as I've seen in similar Amish recipes—and some orange zest for added flavor. The apples are cooked a little longer, then cooled, and the filling is spooned onto rounds of cream cheese pastry. They're baked until golden brown, then served warm or at room temperature.

MAKES 4 SERVINGS

1 recipe Tender Cream Cheese Pastry, Single Crust (page 46), modified as instructed in step 1 and refrigerated

FILLING
1 1/2 cups coarsely chopped dried apple rings
1 cup water
1/2 cup orange juice
1/2 cup granulated sugar

1 tablespoon fresh lemon juice
Grated zest of 1 orange
4 teaspoons cold unsalted butter

GLAZE
Milk or light cream

GARNISH
Granulated sugar (optional)
Confectioners' sugar

1. If you haven't already, prepare the pastry. Divide it into 4 equal-size balls. Flatten each into a $1/2$-inch-thick disk and wrap in plastic wrap. Refrigerate until firm but not overly so, 1 to $1^{1}/2$ hours. If the dough is too firm, it will be difficult to roll. Lightly butter a large baking sheet.

2. Combine the apples, water, and orange juice in a medium-size saucepan over medium heat. Bring to a simmer, cover tightly, and let simmer until the apples are quite soft and have absorbed much of the water, about 10 minutes. Add the granulated sugar, lemon juice, and orange zest and continue to simmer, stirring often, until all the water has cooked off, leaving a fair amount of syrup. Transfer the filling to a plate and let cool to room temperature.

3. Working with one piece of chilled dough at a time, roll it into a $7^{1}/2$- to 8-inch circle on a sheet of lightly floured waxed paper with a floured rolling pin. Spoon about one-quarter of the cooled filling over half of the dough, leaving a $3/4$-inch border along the edge. Dot the top of the filling with 1 teaspoon of the butter. Moisten the edge of the pastry with a finger, then fold the empty half over the filling. Pinch the edges together, rolling them between your fingers into a sort of rope edge. Place on the prepared baking sheet. Refrigerate while you make the remaining pies, putting each on the sheet as it is assembled. Preheat the oven to 400°F.

4. Remove the sheet from the refrigerator and brush each pie with a little milk. Sprinkle with granulated sugar, then poke the surface 2 or 3 times with a fork to make steam vents. Place the sheet on the center oven rack and bake for 10 minutes. Reduce the oven temperature to 375°F and bake until golden brown, about 20 minutes. If the back ones are getting too dark, rotate the sheet 180 degrees, so that the side that faced the back of the oven now faces forward, about 10 minutes before the pies are done.

5. Transfer the pies to a wire rack and let cool slightly. While still warm, dust with a little confectioners' sugar, if you like.

Recipe for Success

▶ If you're feeding more people, you can make 6 smaller portions, dividing the dough into 6 pieces and making the rounds a little smaller. Or you can double the recipe for the filling and prepare a double-crust portion of pastry.

▶ When you fold the dough over the filling, lift and fold the waxed paper with the dough on it. It's easier than handling the dough itself.

These pies freeze nicely. As you assemble them, place them on a baking sheet and freeze for 1 hour. Wrap each in aluminum foil and return to the freezer. To bake, place the pies on a lightly buttered baking sheet and let stand at room temperature for 10 minutes. Bake as directed above, adding 5 to 8 minutes to the baking time.

Preaching Pies and Other Amish Treasures

"Some social chroniclers seem convinced that fruit pies as Americans now know them were invented by the Pennsylvania Dutch. Let's just admit that it's possible. Potters in the southeastern counties of the state were making pie plates early in the eighteenth century, and cooks had begun to envelop with crisp crusts every fruit that grew in the region. 'It may be . . .' [historian] Frederic Klees asserted, 'that during the Revolution men from other colonies came to know this dish in Pennsylvania and carried that knowledge back home to establish pie as the great American dessert. Why not?' Why else would there be no fewer than fifty kinds of dessert pies made today by various Pennsylvania Dutch cooks? Along with standard American apple, berry, butterscotch, chocolate, custard, lemon, mince, pumpkin, rhubarb, et al., the Pennsylvania Dutch certainly originated shoofly pie, really a molasses sponge cake baked in a crust. They also make *rosina*, which is a lemony raisin affair that is always baked when someone dies and therefore is called funeral pie. They also make Amish half-moon pies, whose other name is 'preaching pies,' because they are used to thwart the restlessness of children at long Sunday services."

—Evan Jones, *American Food* (Vintage Books, 1981)

Fresh Peach Half-Moon Pies

In the previous recipe, an Amish specialty, I use dried apples to make what the Amish call a half-moon pie. In this one, I use fresh peaches, cooked on the stovetop and thickened with cornstarch. The mixture is cooled, the pastry is rolled and covered with filling, and the pies are sealed and baked. See Recipe for Success for a berry variation.

MAKES 4 SERVINGS

1 recipe Tender Cream Cheese Pastry, Single Crust (page 46), divided as instructed in step 1 and refrigerated

FILLING

3 cups peeled and pitted ripe peaches cut into bite-size chunks

1/3 cup granulated sugar

2 tablespoons orange juice

1 tablespoon fresh lemon juice

2 tablespoons cornstarch

1/4 teaspoon vanilla extract

Big pinch of ground nutmeg

4 teaspoons cold unsalted butter

GLAZE

Milk or light cream

Granulated sugar

GARNISH

Confectioners' sugar (optional)

1. If you haven't already, prepare the pastry. Divide it into 4 equal-size balls. Flatten each into a 1/2-inch-thick disk and wrap in plastic. Refrigerate until firm but not overly so, 1 to 1 1/2 hours. If the dough is too firm, it will be difficult to roll. Lightly butter a large baking sheet.

2. Combine the peaches and granulated sugar in a medium-size saucepan over medium heat. Bring to a gentle boil, stirring occasionally. Reduce the heat a bit and let simmer gently for about 4 minutes.

3. As the filling heats, stir the orange juice, lemon juice, and cornstarch together in a small bowl. When the peaches have simmered for about 4 minutes, stir the cornstarch mixture into the peaches. Increase the heat and continue to cook, stirring, until thickened and clear, about 2 minutes. Remove from the heat and stir in the vanilla and nutmeg. Let cool.

4. Working with one piece of dough at a time, roll it into an 8-inch circle on a sheet of lightly floured waxed paper with a floured rolling pin. Spoon about one-quarter of the cooled filling over half of the dough, leaving a 3/4-inch border along the edge. Dot the top of the filling with 1 teaspoon of the butter. Moisten the edge of the pastry with a finger, then fold the empty half over the filling. Pinch the edges together, rolling them between your fingers into a sort of rope edge. Place on the prepared baking sheet. Refrigerate while you make the remaining pies, putting each on the sheet as it is assembled. Preheat the oven to 400°F.

5. Remove the sheet from the refrigerator and brush each pie with a little milk. Sprinkle with granulated sugar, then poke the surface 2 or 3 times with a fork to make steam vents. Place the sheet on the center oven rack and bake for 10 minutes. Reduce the oven temperature to 375°F and bake until golden brown, about 20 minutes. If necessary for even browning, rotate the sheet 180 degrees, so that the side that faced the back of the oven now faces forward, about 10 minutes before the pies are done.

6. Transfer the pies to a wire rack and let cool slightly. While still warm, dust with a little confectioners' sugar, if you like.

Recipe for Success

▶ For added color and flavor, place a small handful of fresh raspberries or blueberries on top of the peach filling before sealing the pastry.

▶ When you're assembling the pies, fold them in half by lifting up on the sheet of waxed paper. It's easier than handling the delicate dough when it is rolled thin.

▶ Even though these pies are portable, they're still delicate, so pack them carefully if you're taking them on a hike.

Fried Apple Pies

Whatever misgivings you might have when it comes to deep-fat frying, I suggest that you overcome or simply ignore them long enough to try this recipe and the next one. Fried pies are a special treat—a dessert you run across in pockets throughout the United States, particularly in the South. Frying does wonderful things to a pastry crust, not the least of which is accentuating the flaky layers. Fried pies emerge from the fat golden brown, crispy, and more tender than you can imagine. After a brief respite to let the crust cool enough to handle, the pies are dredged in confectioners' sugar, then served forthwith, while still quite warm. This version uses a dried apple and raisin filling, reconstituted on the stovetop in a mixture of water and orange juice. Dried fruit is often used in fried pies, since it packs a lot of flavor into a small space. I like to serve these at any time of year, but particularly in the fall, during apple season.

MAKES 5 SERVINGS

1/2 recipe Fried Pie Pastry (page 31), divided as instructed in step 1 and refrigerated

FILLING

11/2 cups coarsely chopped dried apple rings

1/2 cup dark raisins or sweetened dried cranberries (sold as Craisins)

1 cup water

1/2 cup orange juice

1/2 cup granulated sugar

1 tablespoon fresh lemon juice

1/2 teaspoon ground cinnamon

1/4 teaspoon ground nutmeg

FOR FRYING

Vegetable oil or corn oil

GARNISH

Confectioners' sugar

1. If you haven't already, prepare the pastry. Divide it into 5 equal-size balls. Flatten each into a 1/2-inch-thick disk and wrap in plastic. Refrigerate until firm enough to roll, about 1 hour.

2. Combine the apples, raisins, water, and orange juice in a medium-size saucepan over medium heat. Bring to a simmer, cover tightly, and let simmer until the apples are quite soft and have absorbed much of the water, about 10 minutes. Add the granulated sugar, lemon juice, cinnamon, and nutmeg. Continue to simmer, stirring often, until all the water has cooked off, leaving a syrupy fruit mixture, 5 to 8 minutes. Transfer the filling to a plate and let cool to room temperature.

3. Shortly before rolling and assembling the pies, heat about 4 inches of oil in a high-sided frying pan or chicken fryer over medium-high heat for 5 to 6 minutes. To judge whether the oil has reached the proper temperature, stick one corner of a pie into the fat. It should start to bubble and fry within 2 to 3 seconds. If you can set the temperature on an electric fryer, set it at 375°F.

4. Working with one piece of dough at a time, roll it into a 51/2-inch circle on a sheet of lightly floured waxed paper with a floured rolling pin. Put about 2 heaping tablespoons of the filling over half of the dough, leaving a generous margin. Moisten the edge of the pastry with a finger, then fold the uncovered half of the dough over the filling, pressing the edges together to seal. Roll the edge up slightly to make a sort of rope edge. Make another pie and set aside. You can assemble the others as the first two fry.

5. When the oil is hot, gently lower one of the pies into the fat. Fry until golden brown and crispy, 3½ to 4 minutes. Using a slotted utensil, transfer the pie to a paper towel–lined platter. Fry the remaining pies one at a time.

6. When the pies have cooled just enough to handle, dust them well with confectioners' sugar on both sides. Serve at once.

Recipe for Success

▸ Make sure you don't try to cram too much filling into the pies, or they won't seal well. Pinch together any holes in the pastry before you fry them.

▸ If you've made the filling ahead and refrigerated it, bring it to room temperature before filling the pies.

We Hear the Fried Pies Are Worth the Drive to . . .

▸ Fulton Fried Pies in Ardmore, Oklahoma. A trucker says these are the best he's had in several states.

▸ The Apple Barn Cider Bar in Sevierville, Tennessee. They sell as many as 1,500 fried apple pies a day.

▸ Flippens Hillbilly Barn and Fruit Farm near Hornbeak, Tennessee. A former cotton grower turned fruit grower has built a mini empire with his peach and apple fried pies.

Fried Cherry Pies

Unlike the Fried Apple Pies on page 441, which use only dried fruit, this version combines fresh and dried fruit. Fresh cherries are good for fried pies because they pack a lot of flavor for their size, especially when paired with dried ones. I use pitted fresh cherries at their peak in the summer, but the rest of the time I use frozen. Instead of the confectioners' sugar, you may want to dust the pies with a heavy coating of cinnamon sugar. Either way, they're wonderful.

MAKES 10 SERVINGS

1 recipe Fried Pie Pastry (page 31), divided as instructed in step 1 and refrigerated

FILLING

3 cups individually frozen pitted sweet cherries (not packed in syrup)

1/2 cup dried sweet or sour cherries

1/2 cup granulated sugar

2 tablespoons orange juice

1 tablespoon fresh lemon juice

1/4 cup water

1 1/2 tablespoons cornstarch

1/2 teaspoon vanilla extract

FOR FRYING

Vegetable oil or corn oil

GARNISH

Confectioners' sugar

1. If you haven't already, prepare the pastry. Divide it into 10 equal-size balls. Flatten each into a 1/2-inch-thick disk and wrap in plastic. Refrigerate until firm enough to roll, about 1 hour.

2. Combine the frozen and dried cherries in a medium-size, heavy saucepan and gradually bring to a simmer over medium heat. Add the granulated sugar, orange juice, and lemon juice. Cover and let simmer until the cherries are heated through and the mixture is quite juicy, 3 to 4 minutes.

3. Meanwhile, blend the water and cornstarch together in a small bowl. Stir the cornstarch slurry into the fruit. Heat the cherries at a low boil, stirring, until thickened and glossy, about 1 1/2 minutes. Remove from the heat and scrape the fruit onto a plate. Stir in the vanilla. Let cool to room temperature.

4. Shortly before rolling and assembling the pies, heat about 4 inches of oil in a high-sided frying pan or chicken fryer over medium-high heat for 5 to 6 minutes. To judge whether the oil has reached the proper temperature, stick one corner of a pie into the fat.

It should start to bubble and fry within 2 to 3 seconds. If you can set the temperature on an electric fryer, set it at 375°F.

5. Working with one piece of dough at a time, roll it into a 6½-inch circle on sheet of lightly floured waxed paper with a floured rolling pin. Put 3 to 4 tablespoons of the filling over half of the dough, leaving a generous margin. Moisten the edge of the pastry with a finger, then fold the uncovered half of the dough over the filling, pressing the edges together to seal. Roll the edge up slightly to make a sort of rope edge, or simply crimp with a fork. Make another pie or two and set aside. You can assemble the others as the first few fry.

6. When the oil is hot, gently lower one of the pies into the fat. Fry until golden brown and crispy, 3½ to 4 minutes. Using a slotted utensil, transfer the pie to a paper towel–lined platter. Fry the remaining pies one at a time.

7. When the pies have cooled just enough to handle, dust them well with confectioners' sugar on both sides. Serve at once.

Recipe for Success

‣ **These are slightly larger than the Fried Apple Pies, for no particular reason. If you need more servings, simply divide the dough into 12 pieces and use less filling per pie.**

‣ **If you'd rather not use the dried cherries, add an additional ³/₄ cup frozen cherries to the filling.**

‣ **Instead of dried cherries, you may use chopped dried peaches here.**

Fall Fruit Turnovers

I can think of so many occasions when a portable fruit pie like this one would be the perfect companion: tailgate parties, hikes, a trip to the beach, a romantic picnic for two, sack lunches, a long flight, a bike ride—I think you get the point. Turnovers somehow seem difficult to make, but I think they're actually easier than a whole pie, since there is less filling to prepare and they take only about half as long to bake. The filling for these is a combination of apple, pear, and dried cranberries, with a little bit of sugar and spice. The mixture is spooned into the flaky cream cheese pastry, dotted with butter, and baked to a bronze finish. I like to assemble these the night before, refrigerate, and then bake them for breakfast, but they also make a great dessert.

MAKES 4 SERVINGS

1 recipe Tender Cream Cheese Pastry for a single crust (page 46), divided as instructed in step 1 and refrigerated

FILLING

2 tablespoons orange juice

1 large Golden Delicious apple, peeled, cored, and cut into bite-size chunks

1 ripe pear, peeled, cored, and cut into bite-size chunks

1/2 cup sweetened dried cranberries (sold as Craisins)

3 tablespoons granulated sugar

1 1/2 teaspoons cornstarch

Big pinch of ground cinnamon

Big pinch of ground nutmeg

1/2 teaspoon grated lemon zest

1 1/2 tablespoons cold unsalted butter, cut into small pieces

GLAZE

Milk or light cream

Granulated sugar

GARNISH

Confectioners' sugar (optional)

1. If you haven't already, prepare the pastry. Divide it into 4 equal-size balls. Flatten each into a 1/2-inch-thick disk and wrap in plastic. Refrigerate until firm enough to roll, 1 to 1 1/2 hours. Lightly butter a large baking sheet.

2. Combine the orange juice, apple, pear, cranberries, and 2 tablespoons of the granulated sugar in a medium-size nonreactive saucepan. Bring to a boil over medium-high heat, cover, and cook for 3 minutes, stirring once or twice. Meanwhile, mix together the remaining 1 tablespoon granulated sugar, the cornstarch, and spices in a small bowl. Stir the mixture into the fruit and cook, stirring, for 1 minute. Remove from the heat and stir in the lemon zest. Spread the fruit on a plate and let cool to room temperature.

Tailgate Party Pies

Living here in Annapolis, Maryland—home of the U.S. Naval Academy—we love to attend tailgate parties whenever we can during football season. It's a great way to get outside during some of the nicest weather of the year and share good times, conversation, and, of course, great food with our friends.

Pies are always a welcome dessert at a tailgate party: Most of them travel well, and, other than refrigerated pies, they hold up well under a variety of outdoor temperatures. Win or lose, just about everyone loves a sweet slice of pie served with some good strong coffee and eaten in the great outdoors.

Here are a few pie suggestions for your next tailgate party.

- Apple Pie with Cheddar Cracker Topping (page 203)—especially for you Green Bay Packer fans.

- Streusel-Topped Pear Pie with Walnut Crust (page 253)—we're nuts about this one.

- Triple-Layer Pumpkin-Chocolate Pie (page 282)—for that big Thanksgiving Day rivalry.

- Funeral Pie (page 308)—you'll need it when you bury your rivals.

- Angus Barn Chocolate Chess Pie (page 364)—because we don't know anyone who doesn't like chocolate.

- Fall Fruit Turnovers (page 446)—the ultimate in portable pies.

3. When the mixture has cooled, working with one piece of dough at a time, roll it into an 8-inch circle on a sheet of lightly floured waxed paper with a floured rolling pin. Spoon about one-quarter of the filling over half of the dough, leaving a 3/4-inch border along the edge. Dot the top of the filling with some of the butter. Moisten the edge of the pastry with a finger, then fold the empty half of the dough over the filling. Pinch the edges together, rolling them between your fingers into a sort of rope edge. Place on the prepared baking sheet. Refrigerate while you make the remaining turnovers, putting each on the sheet as it is assembled. Preheat the oven to 400°F.

4. Remove the sheet from the refrigerator and brush each turnover with a little milk. Sprinkle with granulated sugar, then poke the surface 2 or 3 times with a fork to make steam vents. Place the sheet on the center oven rack and bake for 10 minutes. Reduce the oven temperature to 375°F and bake until golden brown, about 20 minutes. For more even browning, rotate the baking sheet 180 degrees, so that the side that faced the back of the oven now faces forward, near the end of the baking time.

5. Transfer the turnovers to a wire rack and let cool slightly. While still warm, dust with a little confectioners' sugar, if you like.

Recipe for Success

▶ The easiest way to dust these is to put the confectioners' sugar in a sieve and shake it right over the turnovers. For best coverage, sprinkle once while still quite warm, then again when they've reached room temperature.

▶ If you're planning to take these with you, cool thoroughly, then refrigerate for a couple of hours before wrapping rather snugly in aluminum foil. The cream cheese pastry makes these a tad delicate and chilling them first helps to stabilize them for handling and wrapping.

Pear and Brie Turnovers

I like these simple hand pies for a savory-sweet dessert. The texture of the pear is perfect for a turnover, because it's soft and requires no precooking. The raspberry preserves add just a hint of sweetness, a nice counterpoint to the rich, creamy Brie. For convenience's sake, these can be made up to several hours ahead, or even the night before, and baked shortly before serving.

MAKES 4 TURNOVERS

1 recipe Tender Cream Cheese Pastry for a single crust (page 46), divided as instructed in step 1 and refrigerated

FILLING

2 teaspoons all-purpose flour

2 teaspoons granulated sugar

4 teaspoons raspberry preserves

1 large ripe pear, peeled, cored, and thinly sliced

About 1/3 pound Brie, sliced

GLAZE

Milk or light cream

Granulated sugar

GARNISH

Confectioners' sugar (optional)

1. If you haven't already, prepare the pastry. Divide it into 4 equal-size balls. Flatten each into a 1/2-inch-thick disk and wrap in plastic. Refrigerate until firm enough to roll, 1 to 1 1/2 hours. Lightly butter a large baking sheet.

2. Mix the flour and granulated sugar together in a small bowl. Working with one piece of dough at a time, roll it into an 8-inch circle on a sheet of lightly floured waxed paper with a floured rolling pin. Dot with 1 teaspoon of the preserves, spreading it around the center of the circle. Sprinkle lightly with some of the sugar-flour mixture. Arrange a single row of overlapping pear slices over half of the dough. Leave a good $^3/_4$-inch border around the slices, more or less following the curve of the pastry. Sprinkle with a little more of the sugar-flour mixture. Lay 1 or 2 slices of Brie over the pears to cover. Moisten the edge of the pastry with a finger or pastry brush, then fold the empty half of the dough over the cheese. (It works best to fold the paper and dough together over the filling, then just peel back the paper.) Pinch the edges together, rolling them between your fingers into a sort of rope edge. Place on the prepared baking sheet. Refrigerate while you make the remaining turnovers, putting each on the sheet as it is assembled. Preheat the oven to 400°F.

3. Remove the sheet from the refrigerator and brush each turnover with a little milk. Sprinkle with granulated sugar, then poke the surface 2 or 3 times with a fork to make steam vents. Place the sheet on the center oven rack and bake for 10 minutes. Reduce the oven temperature to 375°F and bake until golden brown, about 20 minutes. For more even browning, rotate the baking sheet 180 degrees, so that the side that faced the back of the oven now faces forward, about 10 minutes before the turnovers are done. You may see steam coming from the vents.

4. Transfer the turnovers to a wire rack and let cool slightly. While still warm, dust with confectioners' sugar, if you like. These are best served 15 to 30 minutes out of the oven.

Recipe for Success

▶ **If you cut these turnovers into strips, once they've cooled for about 30 minutes, they make a nice appetizer. (If you cut them while they're too warm, the cheese will ooze out.)**

▶ **Another way to present them as an appetizer is to make 8 balls of dough instead of 4. Finely dice the pear, instead of slicing it, and proceed as if you were making the larger turnovers, scaling down the filling ingredients, proportionally, to fit into the small circles of dough.**

The icebox has pretty much gone the way of the horse and buggy, but icebox

pies are every bit as popular as they've always been, perhaps even more so,

in view of the fact that icebox pies often require very little hands-on cooking

time—a big bonus for so many time-pressed home cooks. • What, precisely,

is an icebox pie? Generally speaking, the term refers to nearly any pie that

A Plethora of Icebox Pies:
Cream Pies, Chiffon Pies, and So Much More

isn't baked. The crust, whether a pastry or crumb crust, likely will be pre-

baked, but the expectation of an icebox pie is that it will not require the same

sort of skills and diligence as, say, a baked fruit pie. • Which is not to say

that icebox pies never require any cooking whatsoever. That holds true for

some of the recipes—Banoffee Pie (page 526) and Millionaire Pie (page 527)

are two good examples of no-cook icebox pies—but by no means all of them.

Cream pies always start with a stovetop pastry cream. And chiffon pies often involve cooked mixtures as well. But no matter the route, all icebox pies are destined for the refrigerator for at least a couple of hours to make the filling palatably cool and the texture suitably firm.

Impressive as they can be, icebox pies are usually reserved for casual gatherings. They tend to be great family pies—everyday fare that kids not only love to eat but also don't mind helping to prepare. They have no season, per se, but it should come as no surprise that icebox pies are most common in the summer, when many a cook is reluctant to turn on the oven. I, for one, think a warm kitchen is a small price to pay for a fresh summer fruit pie. But there are far worse ideas than trying to beat the summer heat with a steady diet of icebox pies.

Tips for Making Icebox Pies

▶ Make sure your pastry crust is fully baked and crisp, since it will get no further cooking.

▶ In nearly all cases, icebox pies are best eaten within 24 to 48 hours. Many of them will keep longer, but after a certain amount of time, nearly all of them will show little signs of tiredness: weepy fruit, sagging pastry cream, soggy crust.

▶ When an icebox pie is topped with whipped cream, try to add it just before serving, rather than several hours before. That way, it will stay fresh and maintain its body.

▶ When making a cream pie, gently press a piece of plastic wrap over the filling to keep a skin from forming. Don't leave any gaps—for instance, where the crust meets the filling—or moisture will puddle there.

▶ Gelatin mixtures used to thicken chiffon pies should not be allowed to cool too much and become too firm or they'll be difficult to fold into other ingredients.

▶ Cover completely assembled icebox pies with loosely tented aluminum foil, not plastic wrap, which might cling to the surface. Bunch the foil up around the edges, letting it form a dome in the center—like those trays of popcorn you pop right over the burner.

Vanilla Cream Pie

This is the classic—quivering vanilla pastry cream slathered with whipped cream—beloved by all. A monument to solid, uncomplicated, middle-American cuisine, this pie should be in every cook's repertoire.

MAKES 8 TO 10 SERVINGS

1 recipe Graham Cracker Crumb Crust (page 51) or 1 large store-bought graham cracker crust

FILLING
1 cup sugar

1/4 cup cornstarch

1/8 teaspoon salt

2 1/4 cups whole milk

4 large egg yolks

2 tablespoons unsalted butter, cut into 1/2-inch pieces

1 1/2 teaspoons vanilla extract

TOPPING
Fresh Whipped Cream (page 605)

Ground nutmeg (optional)

1. Prepare the crust and press it into the bottom and up the side of a 9½-inch deep-dish pie pan. Refrigerate, prebake, and let cool as directed. Or simply use a store-bought crust, prebaking it according to the package directions and letting it cool.

2. Mix the sugar, cornstarch, and salt together in a medium-size, heavy saucepan, preferably nonstick. Whisk in the milk and egg yolks. Place over medium heat and cook, whisking virtually nonstop, until the mixture starts to thicken and comes to a low boil, 5 to 7 minutes. Continue to whisk and heat until quite thick, about 1½ minutes. Remove from the heat and whisk in the butter, one piece at a time, and the vanilla.

3. Immediately pour the filling into the cooled pie shell and set aside on a wire rack. Gently press a piece of plastic wrap directly against the filling, leaving no gaps or air pockets, to prevent a skin from forming. Let cool to room temperature, then refrigerate for at least 2 hours or overnight.

4. Shortly before serving, smooth the whipped cream generously over the pie. Dust with nutmeg, if desired, and serve.

Recipe for Success

▶ As frequently as you see recipes for this pie in a graham cracker crumb crust, you'll find it made in a fully prebaked pastry crust. It's your call. In addition to the plain graham cracker crust, the walnut and pecan versions (see page 53) are great choices here as well.

▶ You'll often find recipes for cream pies where the egg yolks are beaten separately and some of the hot liquid is added to them to prevent curdling. That's not necessary if you use this self-tempering method, adding them to the saucepan with the milk and gradually bringing the liquid to a low boil. The presence of the cornstarch and the constant whisking prevent the mixture from curdling.

▶ If you prefer a meringue topping instead of whipped cream, use the meringue for the coconut cream pie on page 469.

Classic Chocolate Cream Pie

I think you'll have a hard time improving on this. It isn't, frankly, all that different from other recipes for chocolate cream pie. It's simply tweaked to my liking, with just the right proportions of all the key ingredients. If you've never made one of these, I think you'll be pleased with how simple it is. I like to put this in a homemade Oreo crust, but if you prefer to use a small store-bought Oreo or graham cracker crust, that's fine. (You may have a little leftover filling, which you can pour into a single-serving cup for a snack, and there won't be much room left to garnish the pie with whipped cream, but it will taste just as wonderful.) Since it needs plenty of time to chill, try to make this early on the day you plan to serve it, or even the day before.

MAKES 8 TO 10 SERVINGS

1 recipe Oreo Crumb Crust (page 55) or 1 small store-bought Oreo or graham cracker crust (see headnote)

FILLING

3/4 cup plus 2 tablespoons granulated sugar

3 1/2 tablespoons cornstarch

1/8 teaspoon salt

2 1/2 cups whole milk

4 large egg yolks

2 tablespoons unsalted butter, cut into 1/2-inch pieces

2 teaspoons vanilla extract

3 ounces unsweetened chocolate, coarsely chopped

TOPPING

3/4 cup cold heavy or whipping cream

3 tablespoons confectioners' sugar

1. Prepare the crust and press it into the bottom and up the side of a 9-inch standard pie pan. Refrigerate, prebake, and let cool as directed. Or simply use a store-bought crust, prebaking it according to the package directions and letting it cool.

2. Combine the granulated sugar, cornstarch, and salt in a medium-size, heavy saucepan, preferably nonstick. Whisk to mix thoroughly or rub with your fingers to combine. Whisk in the milk and egg yolks. Place over medium heat and cook, whisking almost nonstop, until it starts to boil and thicken noticeably, 5 to 7 minutes. Cook for 1 minute more, whisking briskly to keep it from bubbling and spattering. Remove from the heat and whisk in the butter, one piece at a time, and the vanilla. Whisk in the chocolate, one-third at a time, until smooth and fully melted. Slowly pour the filling into the cooled pie shell and smooth the top with a spoon. Press a piece of plastic wrap directly over the filling, leaving no gaps or air pockets, to prevent a skin from forming. Transfer the pie to a wire rack and let cool thoroughly, then refrigerate for at least 4 hours or overnight.

3. Just before serving, make the topping. Using a chilled medium-size bowl and chilled beaters, beat the cream with an electric mixer until it holds soft peaks. Add the confectioners' sugar and continue to beat until stiff but not grainy. Smooth the whipped cream over the pie, pipe it on decoratively, or simply serve a good-size spoonful with each slice.

Recipe for Success

▶ When you chop unsweetened chocolate, use a large chef's knife and make your cuts close together so the chocolate comes off in flakes. This more or less guarantees that all of the chocolate will dissolve easily into the hot pastry cream. (You most definitely *don't* want to bite into a piece of undissolved unsweetened chocolate.)

▶ Remember that whipped cream will break down and start to weep if stored overnight. For that reason, if you're not serving all the pie at once, I recommend that you decorate or garnish only the part of the pie that you will be serving the same day. If you're serving guests, slice the pie in the wings, if you wish, so they don't see a partially garnished pie.

Hammett House Famous German Chocolate Pie

The Hammett House Restaurant has been serving up great food in Claremore, Oklahoma, since 1969. By the owners' own admission, their menu is neither extensive nor expensive, but they sure know how to do things right—including make pies. Take this German chocolate pie, for instance. It's one big dessert—in both proportions and flavor. You'll need either an extra-deep-dish pie pan or a large store-bought graham cracker crust. It is, essentially, a cream pie with coconut and pecans added to the filling. The whipped cream topping is flavored with chocolate syrup, coconut, and pecans and drizzled with more syrup.

MAKES 10 SERVINGS

1 recipe Graham Cracker Crumb Crust (page 51); enough pastry for a 9 1/2- to 10-inch extra-deep-dish pie shell, refrigerated; or 1 large store-bought graham cracker crust

FILLING

1 1/2 cups sugar

3/4 cup cornstarch

Big pinch of salt

4 cups whole milk

5 large egg yolks

6 tablespoons (3/4 stick) unsalted butter, melted

1 teaspoon vanilla extract

1/2 cup semisweet chocolate chips

1 cup sweetened flaked coconut

1 cup chopped pecans

TOPPING

2 cups cold heavy or whipping cream

1/3 cup thick chocolate syrup, plus more for garnish

1/3 cup chopped pecans

1/3 cup sweetened flaked coconut

1. Prepare the crust and press it into the bottom and up the side of a 9 1/2- to 10-inch extra-deep-dish pie pan. Refrigerate, prebake, and let cool as directed. Or prepare your choice of pastry, roll it into a 13 1/2-inch circle on a sheet of lightly floured waxed paper with a floured rolling pin. Invert the pastry over the pan, center, and peel off the paper. Gently tuck the pastry down into the pan, without stretching it, and sculpt the edge into an upstanding ridge. Place in the freezer for 15 minutes, then fully prebake and let cool as directed on page 16. Or simply use a store-bought crust, prebaking it according to the package directions and letting it cool.

2. Combine the sugar, cornstarch, and salt in a large, heavy saucepan, preferably nonstick. Whisk in the milk and egg yolks. Place over medium heat and cook, whisking virtually nonstop, until the mixture starts to thicken and comes to a low boil, 5 to 7 minutes. Continue to whisk and heat until quite thick, about 1 1/2 minutes. Remove from the heat and whisk in the butter, vanilla, and chocolate chips until the filling is uniform in color. Stir in the coconut and pecans. Pour the filling into the cooled pie shell. Gently press a piece of plastic wrap directly against the filling, leaving no gaps or air pockets, to prevent a skin from forming. Let cool to room temperature, then refrigerate for at least 3 hours or overnight.

3. Shortly before serving, make the topping. Using a chilled medium-size bowl and chilled beaters, beat the cream with an electric mixer until it holds soft peaks. Add the chocolate syrup and continue to beat until it is stiff but not grainy. Stir in the pecans and

Faux Chocolate Curls

Chocolate curls are a great way to garnish whipped cream–topped pies (and other pies), but they're not exactly a stroll in the park to prepare. First you have to melt chocolate, then spread it out on a baking sheet. When it reaches just the right temperature, you scrape it into delicate curls that may or may not hold their shape. I make real chocolate curls about as often as Halley's comet comes around.

There is an easier way to make them, though, and if they aren't exactly authentic, they score points for being fast and simple. Just position yourself and a sharp peeler above your pie. Take a large, flat bar of room-temperature bittersweet or dark chocolate and scrape down the long side with the peeler. You'll shave off delicate swirls of chocolate that drop onto your pie in a random, attractive pattern. Just be sure you don't accidentally use unsweetened chocolate for this purpose or your guests will be rather unpleasantly surprised.

coconut. Smooth the topping over the pie, mounding it in the center. Drizzle with additional chocolate syrup. Slice and serve generous pieces.

Recipe for Success

▶ A couple of thoughts about the pie shell: If you like, the nut versions of the graham cracker crust (see page 53) taste excellent with this pie. For a large pie like this, you may want to multiply the crust recipe by 1¹/₂ for a thicker crust. If you use a pastry crust, be sure it is fully prebaked and golden brown all over. Remember that you won't be baking the crust further and it needs to be crisp before the filling goes in.

▶ As for the chocolate syrup, I like to use slightly thicker "sundae syrup" here. (My favorite brand is Fox's U-Bet.) Since it has more body, it makes for a thicker, more stable whipped cream. Use it cold, rather than at room temperature, for best results.

Black Bottom Chiffon Pie

This version of black bottom pie is my rendition of the original, inspired in large part by an old James Beard recipe in his *American Cookery* (Little, Brown and Company, 1972). I won't try to tell you that this is a breeze, because it isn't. By the time you're done, you'll have dirty bowls, whisks, and beaters everywhere. The traditional recipe has a graham cracker crust, a layer of chocolate custard, and another layer of egg white–lightened vanilla rum custard. As if that weren't enough, the pie is topped with whipped cream.

Don't let my admonitions scare you, however. The key here is organization. Once you have your ingredients measured and your equipment out, and you've read through the recipe and understand the sequence of steps, you'll do fine. And you'll be the toast of your next party when you bring this to the table.

MAKES 8 TO 10 SERVINGS

1 recipe Nutty Graham Cracker Crust (page 53) made with walnuts

FILLING

2 tablespoons unsalted butter, cut into pieces

3/4 cup semisweet chocolate chips

1/4 cup cold water

1 1/2 teaspoons unflavored gelatin

3/4 cup granulated sugar

1 1/2 tablespoons cornstarch

Big pinch of salt

1 cup whole milk

1 cup light cream or half-and-half

4 large egg yolks

1 1/2 tablespoons light or dark rum (see Recipe for Success)

1 teaspoon vanilla extract

3 large egg whites, at room temperature

1/4 teaspoon cream of tartar

TOPPING

1 cup cold heavy or whipping cream

2 tablespoons confectioners' sugar, sifted

1 ounce semisweet chocolate

1. Prepare the crust and press it into the bottom and up the side of a 9 1/2-inch deep-dish pie pan. Refrigerate, prebake, and let cool as directed. Refrigerate until ready to use.

2. Put the butter in the top of a double boiler over, not in, barely simmering water. Add the chocolate chips and let melt over the heat for 5 minutes. Remove the pan from the heat, but let the chocolate and butter remain in the top of the double boiler. Do not whisk or stir.

3. Pour the water into a small bowl. Add the gelatin and set aside to soften.

4. Mix ½ cup of the granulated sugar, the cornstarch, and salt in a medium-size, heavy saucepan, preferably nonstick. Add the milk, light cream, and egg yolks. Place over medium heat and cook, whisking often, until the mixture starts to bubble and thicken, 5 to 7 minutes. Continue to cook, whisking virtually nonstop, for about 1½ minutes. Remove from the heat and pour half of the hot custard into the chocolate mixture. Whisk until evenly blended. Quickly pour the chocolate custard into the chilled pie shell and smooth to even the top. Stir the rum and vanilla into the custard left in the pan. Pour the rum custard into a large bowl and let cool for about 15 minutes.

5. Using an electric mixer, beat the 3 reserved egg whites and cream of tartar together in a medium-size bowl until they hold soft peaks. Start adding the remaining ¼ cup granulated sugar, 1 tablespoon at a time, beating the whites until they're stiff and glossy. Fold about one-third of the beaten whites into the cooled rum custard until evenly combined. Add the remaining whites and fold until evenly blended. Scrape the rum custard over the chocolate custard, smoothing the top with a spoon. Cover with loosely tented aluminum foil and refrigerate for at least 4 hours or overnight.

6. Shortly before serving, using a chilled medium-size bowl and chilled beaters, beat the heavy cream with an electric mixer until it holds soft peaks. Add the confectioners' sugar and continue to beat until stiff but not grainy. Smooth the whipped cream evenly over the pie, then grate the chocolate on top. Slice and serve.

Recipe for Success

▸ **This is meant to be a decidedly rich pie, so don't substitute lowfat milk for the whole milk. Indeed, many recipes call for all light cream for the custard.**

▸ **I've deliberately used a light hand with the rum, in the event you'll be serving this to children, who may not care for the flavor. If you like, it can be reduced to as little as a teaspoon or two or eliminated altogether. If kids aren't a concern, you can increase it to 2 tablespoons.**

An Indiana Pie Quest

When Marshall King's editor asked him if he'd like to embark on a quest to find the best pies in Elkhart County, Indiana, he didn't hesitate. A reporter for *The Truth* newspaper, King is a professed pie lover and this struck him as a dream assignment. Elkhart County is a bastion of fine pie makers. He'd find the best of them, and if he put on a few pounds in the process—well, all in the name of research.

Starting in early 2003, King traveled thousands of miles, chasing down pie leads from one corner of the county to the other. In the process, he sampled more than 150 pies, devising his own rating system, from "Five slices," meaning "practically perfect," to "One slice," meaning "well, it's pie." Indeed, not all of his finds were memorable, although none was bad enough to spit out. His quest, he says, has left him wary of certain pie shortcuts. Prepared whipped topping is one. And frozen pie shells, which, he claims, you can spot a mile away by the perfect crimping, are another.

When I first spoke to King, shortly before his quest was to end, he'd narrowed his search for the best pie down to four:

▶ **Coffee Toffee Pie at the Patchwork Quilt Country Inn in Middlebury.** "About 4 to 5 inches high. Just exquisite." (See recipe on page 538.)

▶ **Lemon Meringue Pie at the South Side Soda Shop in Goshen.** "Tart-sweet, good high meringue, really amazing."

▶ **Peach Cream Pie at the County Line Bakery, near Middlebury.** "They only make it when the peaches are fresh and in season. Very well done."

▶ **Dutch Apple Pie at the Strauss Bakery in Elkhart.** "They've nailed it."

In the end, King's favorite slice was the lemon meringue. He notes, "The filling is solid, both tart and sweet, and the meringue is light and sweet, but not weepy. The pie is sweet, but not overly so, and there's flavor from the lemon that rounds out the sweetness."

Black Bottom Pie

There are many types of black bottom pie, the first of them—according to James Beard, the "dean of American cooking"—appearing in cookbooks around the turn of the 20th century. Most of the recipes that are true to the original version are gelatin-based chiffon-type pies. This one borrows from the original but is a little different. The black bottom here is essentially chocolate ganache, a solidified sauce made from chocolate, butter, and cream. A whipped cream–lightened pastry cream goes over this, and, if you like, more whipped cream goes on top, although it's hardly necessary. This pie is a little more streamlined than the traditional version, but every bit as good. You must start this early in the day, so the top layer has enough time to firm up prior to serving it in the evening.

MAKES 8 TO 10 SERVINGS

1 recipe Nutty Graham Cracker Crust (page 53) made with pecans

BLACK BOTTOM LAYER

1/2 cup heavy or whipping cream

2 tablespoons unsalted butter, cut into pieces

3/4 cup semisweet chocolate chips

1/2 teaspoon vanilla extract

TOPPING

3/4 cup sugar

3 1/2 tablespoons cornstarch

1/8 teaspoon salt

2 cups whole milk

4 large egg yolks

2 tablespoons unsalted butter, cut into 1/2-inch pieces

1 1/2 teaspoons vanilla extract

1/2 cup cold heavy or whipping cream

GARNISH

Fresh Whipped Cream (page 605; optional)

1. Prepare the crust and press it into the bottom and most of the way up the side of a 9 1/2-inch deep-dish pie pan. Refrigerate, prebake, and let cool as directed.

2. Make the black bottom layer. In a small saucepan over low heat, combine the cream and butter, stirring constantly. When the butter melts, add the chocolate chips, and immediately turn off the heat. Swirl the pan so the warm liquid runs over the chocolate. Set the pan aside for 5 minutes to melt the chocolate, then stir in the vanilla. Whisk to smooth, then pour into the cooled pie shell, tilting to evenly coat the bottom with chocolate. Place on a wire rack and let cool to room temperature, then refrigerate.

3. Meanwhile, make the topping. Combine the sugar, cornstarch, and salt in a medium-size, heavy saucepan, preferably nonstick. Whisk in the milk and egg yolks. Place over medium heat and cook, whisking frequently, until the mixture starts to thicken and boil, 5 to 7 minutes. Continue to boil, whisking virtually nonstop, for 1½ to 2 minutes. Remove from the heat and scrape into a shallow bowl. Stir in the butter, one piece at a time, and the vanilla. Press a piece of plastic wrap directly over the pastry cream, leaving no gaps or air pockets, to prevent a skin from forming. Let cool to room temperature, then refrigerate until cold, at least 3 hours or overnight.

4. When the pastry cream is cold, using a chilled medium-size bowl and chilled beaters, beat the heavy cream with an electric mixer until stiff but not grainy. Fold into the pastry cream until evenly combined. Smooth the pastry cream into the pie shell. Cover with loosely tented aluminum foil and refrigerate for at least 3 hours, until firm.

5. Right before serving, garnish with whipped cream, if you like, piping it over the pie with a pastry bag. Slice and serve.

Recipe for Success

▶ **The beauty of a recipe such as this one is the way it can be broken down into easy steps. For instance, you can make the pie shell and pastry cream the day before, then finish and assemble the pie the following morning. Dividing a recipe into do-ahead segments is often the best strategy.**

▶ **To give this pie a bit of a mocha lilt, whisk 1 teaspoon instant espresso or coffee granules or 1 tablespoon Kahlúa into the hot cream mixture before adding the chocolate.**

Niel's Chocolate–Macadamia Nut Cream Pie

I had the pleasure of meeting and working with Niel Koep on a trip to Hawaii in November 2002. Niel is the head baker for the Lodge at Koele and the Manele Bay Hotel on the island of Lanai in Hawaii, where I had been invited to do several pie-baking demonstrations. In addition to being one of the most talented bakers I've ever known, he is one of the kindest and most generous, quick to share his time, his kitchen, and his recipes. Hawaii, of course, is known for its macadamia nuts, which Niel puts in this, one of the hotel's favorite pies. Some of the toasted nuts are scattered in an almond crust, then covered with a bittersweet chocolate cream filling and topped with whipped cream and more toasted nuts. It's a very classy chocolate cream pie that will make you want to head right to Lanai for more of Niel's baking.

MAKES 8 TO 10 SERVINGS

$^1/_2$ recipe Nutty Pie Pastry (page 42) made with almonds, refrigerated

FILLING

$1^1/_2$ cups macadamia nuts

$^1/_3$ cup plus 1 tablespoon granulated sugar

3 tablespoons cornstarch

$1^1/_2$ cups whole milk

$^1/_4$ cup sweetened condensed milk

5 large egg yolks

$1^1/_2$ tablespoons unsalted butter, cut into $^1/_2$-inch pieces

2 teaspoons vanilla extract

4 ounces bittersweet chocolate, coarsely chopped

TOPPING

$^3/_4$ cup cold heavy or whipping cream

3 tablespoons confectioners' sugar

1. If you haven't already, prepare the pastry and refrigerate until firm enough to roll, about 1 hour.

2. Meanwhile, toast the nuts. Preheat the oven to 350°F. Spread the macadamia nuts on a jellyroll pan or cookie sheet. Place on the center oven rack and toast until fragrant and very light golden brown, 8 to 9 minutes. Immediately tilt the nuts onto a plate or cutting board. Let cool, then coarsely chop. Set aside.

3. On a sheet of lightly floured waxed paper, roll the pastry into a 12-inch circle with a floured rolling pin. Invert the pastry over a 9-inch standard pie pan, center, and peel off the paper. Tuck the pastry into the pan, without stretching it, and sculpt the edge so it is just slightly higher than the rim. Place in the freezer for 15 minutes, then fully prebake and let cool according to the instructions on page 16.

4. Combine the granulated sugar and cornstarch in a medium-size, heavy saucepan, preferably nonstick. Stir in the whole milk, condensed milk, and egg yolks. Place over medium heat and cook, whisking virtually nonstop, until the mixture starts to boil, 5 to 7 minutes. Continue to cook, whisking nonstop to prevent it from spattering, for about 1 minute. Remove from the heat and whisk in the butter, one piece at a time, and the vanilla. Whisk in half of the chocolate, then the other half. Continue whisking until the mixture is smooth and the chocolate is completely melted.

5. Scatter about 1 cup of the chopped nuts in the bottom of the cooled pie shell and pour the chocolate filling over them, smoothing the top with a spoon. Press a piece of plastic wrap directly over the filling, leaving no gaps or air pockets, to prevent a skin from forming. Transfer the pie pan to a wire rack and let cool thoroughly, then cover with loosely tented aluminum foil and refrigerate for at least 4 hours or overnight.

6. Just before serving, make the topping. Using a chilled medium-size bowl and chilled beaters, beat the cream with an electric mixer until it holds soft peaks. Add the confectioners' sugar and continue to beat until stiff but not grainy. Smooth the topping evenly over the chilled pie, then sprinkle with the remaining nuts. Slice and serve.

Recipe for Success

▶ Niel simply spreads all the macadamia nuts in the bottom of the pie shell, for one crunchy-nutty layer. If you prefer, you can put 1/2 cup of the nuts in the pie shell and stir another 1/2 cup into the chocolate cream, to distribute them more evenly.

▶ It won't be quite like Niel's Hawaiian version, but you can substitute toasted pecans for the macadamia nuts, if you prefer.

Macadamias, in a Nutshell

▶ Macadamia nuts are not picked from the tree, but instead are harvested when they fall to the ground.

▶ The macadamia shell is the hardest to break of all nutshells, requiring 300 pounds of pressure per square inch.

▶ Virtually all of Hawaii's macadamia nuts come from the island of Hawaii.

Peanut Butter and Chocolate Cream Pie

With a few simple changes, your basic vanilla cream pie becomes a peanut butter and chocolate cream pie. It's simple: just mix half of the filling with chocolate chips, the other half with peanut butter chips. The two fillings are layered in a peanut graham cracker crust, topped with whipped cream, and garnished with good old chocolate syrup, if you like. Call it nursery food par excellence. Be sure to read the recipe through before beginning, because the timing is important here.

MAKES 8 TO 10 SERVINGS

1 recipe Nutty Graham Cracker Crust (page 53) made with peanuts

FILLING

3/4 cup granulated sugar

3 tablespoons cornstarch

1/8 teaspoon salt

2 1/4 cups whole milk

4 large egg yolks

2 teaspoons vanilla extract

1/2 cup semisweet chocolate chips

2 tablespoons unsalted butter, cut into 1/2-inch pieces

1/2 cup peanut butter chips

TOPPING

1 cup cold heavy or whipping cream

2 tablespoons confectioners' sugar, sifted

1/2 teaspoon vanilla extract

1 cup chopped salted dry-roasted peanuts

Thick chocolate syrup (optional)

1. Prepare the crust and press it into the bottom and up the side of a 9-inch standard pie pan. Refrigerate, prebake, and let cool as directed.

2. Combine the granulated sugar, cornstarch, and salt in a medium-size, heavy saucepan, preferably nonstick. Whisk in the milk and egg yolks. Place over medium heat and cook, whisking virtually nonstop, until the mixture starts to thicken and comes to a low boil, 5 to 7 minutes. Continue to whisk and heat until quite thick, about 1 1/2 minutes. Whisk in the vanilla and remove from the heat.

3. Immediately pour half of the mixture into a small bowl. Stir in the chocolate chips and half of the butter. Immediately turn your attention to the other half of the custard in the pan. Stir the peanut butter chips and the remaining butter into the pan. Using separate whisks, whisk both mixtures until evenly blended.

4. Scrape the chocolate custard into the cooled pie shell, smoothing the top with a spoon. Using a large spoon, gently spoon the peanut butter custard over the chocolate layer, smoothing to even it out without mixing them up. Gently press a piece of plastic wrap directly over the top of the pie, leaving no gaps or air pockets, to prevent a skin from forming. Place on a wire rack and let cool thoroughly, then refrigerate for at least 3 hours or overnight.

5. Shortly before serving, make the topping, Using a chilled medium-size bowl and chilled beaters, beat the cream with an electric mixer until it holds soft peaks. Add the confectioners' sugar and vanilla and continue to beat until stiff but not grainy. Smooth the topping over the pie, then sprinkle with the peanuts. Drizzle each slice with chocolate syrup, if desired.

Recipe for Success

▶ Just in case you store your chocolate chips and peanut butter chips in the refrigerator, bring them to room temperature 30 minutes before starting this recipe.

▶ Since you're relying on the heat of the milk mixture to melt the chocolate and peanut butter chips, it's important that you anticipate this step and act quickly while the mixture is very hot. Have your chips measured, a small bowl standing by, and 2 whisks in place—one for each flavor.

▶ As with all cream pies, press the plastic wrap snugly up against the filling without leaving any gaps, such as where the filling meets the pastry. Gaps will create a space where moisture can gather, leaving a puddle of water.

Coconut Cream Pie

It's a classic—uncomplicated, delicious, and simple to prepare.

1 recipe Basic Flaky Pie Pastry, Single Crust (page 31), refrigerated, or any 9-inch standard pie shell or graham cracker crust

FILLING

1/2 cup granulated sugar

31/2 tablespoons cornstarch

1/8 teaspoon salt

2 cups whole milk

3 large egg yolks

2 tablespoons unsalted butter, cut into 1/2-inch pieces

1 teaspoon vanilla extract

1/2 teaspoon coconut extract

1 cup sweetened flaked coconut

TOPPING

3/4 cup cold heavy or whipping cream

3 tablespoons confectioners' sugar

1/2 cup sweetened flaked coconut, toasted (see page 399)

1. If you haven't already, prepare the pastry and refrigerate until firm enough to roll, about 1 hour.

2. On a sheet of lightly floured waxed paper, roll the pastry into a 12-inch circle with a floured rolling pin. Invert the pastry over a 9-inch standard pie pan, center, and peel off the paper. Tuck the pastry into the pan, without stretching it, and sculpt the edge into an upstanding ridge. Place in the freezer for 15 minutes, then fully prebake and let cool according to the instructions on page 16.

3. Whisk the granulated sugar, cornstarch, and salt together in a medium-size, heavy saucepan, preferably nonstick. Whisk in the milk and egg yolks. Place over medium heat and cook, whisking virtually nonstop, until the mixture thickens and starts to boil, 5 to 7 minutes. Continue to cook, whisking nonstop, for about 1 minute. Remove from the heat and whisk in the butter, one piece at a time. Whisk in the vanilla, coconut extract, and flaked coconut. Immediately pour the filling into the cooled pie shell and smooth the top with a spoon. Press a piece of plastic wrap directly over the filling, leaving no gaps or air pockets, to prevent a skin from forming. Transfer the pie to a wire rack and let cool thoroughly, then refrigerate for at least 3 hours or overnight.

4. When you're almost ready to serve the pie, make the topping. Using a chilled medium-size bowl and beaters, beat the cream with an electric mixer until it holds soft peaks. Add the confectioners' sugar and beat until stiff but not grainy. Smooth over the chilled pie or pipe it on decoratively. Sprinkle with the coconut. Slice and serve.

Recipe for Success

▶ You can, if you like, also toast the coconut that goes into the filling, which I think brings out the flavor nicely. This is just a guess, but I think it's usually not done—at least on a commercial level—because you end up with toasted-brown flecks in the pie, which might look less than appealing to the buyer.

▶ Some pastry chefs recommend whipping cream with a balloon-style whisk after it starts to form soft peaks for maximum aeration and volume.

Coconut Cream Pie with Coconut Meringue Topping

This version of coconut cream pie incorporates several unique and delicious coconut twists. The first is the cream of coconut—the stuff you make piña coladas with—added to the filling. It not only bumps up the coconut flavor, but it also makes the filling even creamier, because of the high oil content. The other touch is the coconut folded into the meringue, adding both flavor and a bit of texture. These touches conspire to make this one of the most delicious coconut cream pies you've ever tried.

MAKES 8 TO 10 SERVINGS

1 recipe Basic Flaky Pie Pastry, Single Crust (page 31), refrigerated

FILLING

3/4 cup sugar

1/4 cup cornstarch

1/8 teaspoon salt

2 cups whole milk

4 large egg yolks

1/2 cup canned cream of coconut, well stirred

1 teaspoon coconut extract

1/2 teaspoon vanilla extract

COCONUT MERINGUE TOPPING

4 large egg whites, at room temperature

1/4 teaspoon cream of tartar

5 tablespoons sugar

Big pinch of salt

1/2 teaspoon vanilla extract

1/4 teaspoon coconut extract

1/2 cup sweetened flaked coconut

1. If you haven't already, prepare the pastry and refrigerate it until firm enough to roll, about 1 hour.

2. On a sheet of lightly floured waxed paper, roll the pastry into a 12-inch circle with a floured rolling pin. Invert the pastry over a 9-inch standard pie pan, center, and peel off the paper. Tuck the pastry into the pan, without stretching it, and sculpt the edge into an upstanding ridge. Place in the freezer for 15 minutes, then fully prebake and let cool according to the instructions on page 16.

3. Combine the sugar, cornstarch, and salt in a medium-size, heavy saucepan, preferably nonstick. Whisk in the milk, egg yolks, and cream of coconut. Place over medium heat and cook, whisking virtually nonstop, until the mixture starts to thicken and comes to a low boil, 5 to 7 minutes. Continue to whisk and heat until quite thick, about 1½ minutes. Remove from the heat and whisk in the extracts. Immediately pour the filling into the cooled pie shell and set aside on a wire rack. Preheat the broiler.

4. While the filling is still hot, make the meringue topping. Combine the egg whites and cream of tartar in a large bowl. Using an electric mixer on high speed, beat until the whites are firm and voluminous. Add the sugar 1 tablespoon at a time, pausing for about 10 seconds between additions. Beat in the salt and extracts. Continue to beat until the meringue is stiff and forms pointed peaks when the beaters are raised. Do not overbeat, or the meringue will become too stiff to be easily spread. Fold the coconut into the meringue. Spoon the meringue over the warm filling, spreading it to the edge and anchoring it to the pastry.

5. Set the pie on a baking sheet and very briefly run it under the broiler to brown the meringue. Don't leave the oven; this will take a very short time and you need to stand watch.

6. Transfer the pie to a wire rack and let cool. Serve slightly warm or at room temperature. Or cover with loosely tented aluminum foil and refrigerate up to 2 days.

Recipe for Success

▶ **If you prefer some sort of a crumb crust to a pastry crust, feel free to use a graham cracker crumb crust for this pie. The nut versions (see page 53) are very good with this filling.**

▶ **Cream of coconut is almost always separated when you buy it and needs a good, vigorous stirring to homogenize it, thus my admonition to stir it well.**

▶ **When I add a meringue topping, I like to use my pastry fork (see page 4) to make little pointed peaks in the meringue. I just slap the back of the tines into the meringue, then pull the fork up quickly—works great every time. It's also a** good way to tell if you've beaten the meringue properly. If the points want to fall over and collapse, you could have beaten it more. If the meringue doesn't want to pull up, you've probably beaten it too much.

Over-the-Top Banana Cream Pie

Nothing about a traditional banana cream pie should be understated. Indeed, it should be larger than life: lots of bananas, a thick layer of pastry cream, and way too much whipped cream topping. This one is all of that—a pie I like to make in my deepest ceramic pie pan. It starts with a graham cracker crust piled with pastry cream, chopped bananas are added, and then the entire thing is crowned with a thick layer of whipped cream. For fun, I coarsely chop a Butterfinger candy bar and sprinkle it over the top. I think it's best if you plan to eat the pie within an hour of adding the bananas and whipped cream; it just tastes fresher that way. If it is held for much more than a day, the bananas and whipped cream get a little tired, which is all the more reason to serve very big pieces the first time around.

MAKES 8 TO 10 SERVINGS

1 recipe Graham Cracker Crumb Crust (page 51)

FILLING

$3/4$ cup plus 2 tablespoons granulated sugar

$1/3$ cup cornstarch

$1/8$ teaspoon salt

3 cups whole milk or light cream

3 large egg yolks

3 tablespoons unsalted butter, cut into $1/2$-inch pieces

$1^1/2$ teaspoons vanilla extract

TOPPING

1 cup cold heavy or whipping cream

$1/4$ cup confectioners' sugar

3 medium-large ripe bananas

One 2.1-ounce Butterfinger candy bar, coarsely chopped

1. Prepare the crust and press it into the bottom and up the side of a $9^1/2$-inch deep-dish pie pan. Refrigerate, prebake, and let cool as directed. Refrigerate until ready to use.

2. Combine the granulated sugar, cornstarch, and salt in a medium-size, heavy saucepan, preferably nonstick. Whisk in the milk and egg yolks. Place over medium heat and cook, stirring more or less continuously, until the mixture thickens and bubbles, 5 to 7 minutes. Continue to cook, whisking continuously, for about 1 minute. Remove from the heat and whisk in the butter, one piece at a time, and the vanilla. Pour the filling into the

The Pie That Isn't: Boston Cream Pie

Precisely how Boston cream pie came to be called a pie and not a cake—which it, in fact, is—is open to speculation. The first near reference to it dates back to 1855, when a New York restaurant ran a recipe for a "pudding pie cake." The dual cake-pie reference may have had something to do with the fact that cake pans were once scarce in this country, so many cakes were baked in pie pans. The "pudding" was probably something akin to the vanilla custard filling we traditionally slather between the layers of sponge cake that make up a Boston cream pie.

When the Parker House restaurant opened in Boston the same year, on the menu there was a recipe for Boston Pie, modeled after the original New York recipe. A German pastry chef at the Parker House replaced the confectioners' sugar garnish with a layer of chocolate icing, and a legend was born.

So it's a cake, not a pie, which is why you won't find a recipe for it here. But we still tip our hat to the civics class of Norton High School, at whose urging Boston cream pie was adopted as the official dessert of Massachusetts, beating out other favorites such as Toll House cookies and Indian pudding.

chilled pie shell, smoothing the top. Gently press a piece of plastic wrap against the filling to help keep a skin from forming. Transfer the pie to a wire rack and let cool to room temperature, then refrigerate for at least 5 hours or overnight.

3. When you are ready to finish assembling the pie, make the topping. Using a chilled medium-size bowl and chilled beaters, beat the heavy cream with an electric mixer until it won't quite hold soft peaks. Add the confectioners' sugar and continue to beat until it is stiff but not grainy. Smear a thin layer of the topping over the filling, using no more than half of it. Cut the bananas into quarters lengthwise, then cut them crosswise into small chunks, letting them fall over the pie. Arrange the chunks in a more or less single layer, then mound the remaining topping over the top. You may also pipe on the topping using a pastry bag. Sprinkle with the chopped Butterfinger. Refrigerate until ready to serve, preferably not longer than an hour. There's no need to cover the pie for the first hour, but beyond that, cover with loosely tented aluminum foil.

Recipe for Success

▸ Take extra care when making pastry cream, especially if kids are helping. Once it has thickened, it will soon start to sputter and boil. The best way to contain this is to keep stirring it, rapidly. However, it's still a good idea to wear long sleeves and an oven mitt to avoid hot spatters. If kids are helping, be sure they keep their faces back from the pan.

Butterscotch Banana Cream Pie

Technically, this isn't true butterscotch, but the dark brown sugar used in the filling gives it that toasted butterscotch flavor most of us love. Here I start with a vanilla wafer crust and add some sliced bananas. I pour the thick butterscotch pastry cream over that, then slather whipped cream and a garnish of more wafer crumbs on top. It's an old-fashioned pie you'll adore—cool, creamy, rich, and particularly nostalgia-inducing for those of us who grew up in the '50s and '60s.

MAKES 8 TO 10 SERVINGS

1 recipe Vanilla Wafer Crumb Crust (page 52)

FILLING
3/4 cup firmly packed dark brown sugar

1/4 cup cornstarch

Big pinch of salt

2 3/4 cups light cream or whole milk

3 large egg yolks

2 tablespoons unsalted butter, cut into 1/2-inch pieces

1 teaspoon vanilla extract

GARNISH
3 large ripe bananas

Fresh Whipped Cream (page 605)

Handful of crumbled vanilla wafers

1.   Prepare the crust and press it into the bottom and up the side of a 9 1/2-inch deep-dish pie pan. Refrigerate, prebake, and let cool as directed.

2.   Combine the brown sugar, cornstarch, and salt in a medium-size saucepan, preferably nonstick, rubbing the mixture together with your fingers to break up any clumps of cornstarch. Add the light cream and egg yolks, whisking well over medium heat until the mixture starts to thicken, 4 to 6 minutes. Once the mixture is good and thick, turn down the heat slightly and continue to cook for 1 minute, whisking nearly nonstop to keep it smooth. Remove from the heat and whisk in the butter, one piece at a time, and the vanilla, whisking until smooth. Immediately pour the filling into the cooled pie shell and smooth the top with a spoon. Press a piece of plastic wrap over the filling, leaving no gaps or air pockets, to prevent a skin from forming. Transfer the pie to a wire rack and let cool thoroughly. Cover with tented aluminum foil and refrigerate for at least several hours or overnight before serving.

3.   Just before serving, garnish the pie. Cut the bananas into large dice and distribute them evenly over the filling. Spread a thick layer of whipped cream on top and sprinkle with the crumbled vanilla wafers. Slice and serve.

Recipe for Success

▶ For a milder butterscotch flavor, use light brown sugar instead of dark.

▶ After much experimentation, I have found that putting the bananas on top of the filling rather than underneath is the best way to make a banana cream pie. Otherwise, the bananas start to weep under the hot filling, leaving you with a weepy pie.

Buckhead Diner White Chocolate Banana Cream Pie

Atlanta's upscale Buckhead Diner is one of the area's most popular and acclaimed eateries, and this pie is one reason for that. An outright orgy of cream, bananas, and white chocolate in a buttery crust, it has won accolades from celebrities, as well as the James Beard Foundation, which voted it the best dessert in America in 1994. We hear that Elton John is a big fan, as is Elizabeth Taylor, who has been known to send one of her staff over to purchase a whole pie. The banana liqueur and crème de cacao help launch this pie over the top. It can barely contain itself, so expect it to ooze onto the plate as you serve it.

MAKES 8 TO 10 SERVINGS

1 recipe All-Butter Pie Pastry, Single Crust (page 28), modified as instructed in step 1 and refrigerated

FILLING

1 plump vanilla bean, slit lengthwise

1 cup whole milk

3 large egg yolks

1/3 cup granulated sugar

2 tablespoons cornstarch

1 tablespoon unsalted butter, cut into 1/2-inch pieces

3 ounces imported white chocolate, finely chopped

1 cup cold heavy or whipping cream

4 medium-size ripe bananas

1 tablespoon fresh lemon juice

1 1/2 tablespoons banana liqueur

1 1/2 tablespoons white crème de cacao

GARNISH

Unsweetened cocoa powder

1. Prepare the pastry according to the recipe, using a total of 3 tablespoons sugar. Refrigerate until firm enough to roll, about 1 hour.

2. On a sheet of lightly floured waxed paper, roll the pastry into a 13-inch circle with a floured rolling pin. Invert the pastry over a 9½-inch deep-dish pie pan, center, and peel off the paper. Tuck the pastry into the pan, without stretching it, and sculpt the edge into an upstanding ridge. Place in the freezer for 15 minutes, then fully prebake and let cool according to the directions on page 16.

3. Combine the vanilla bean and milk in a medium-size, heavy saucepan, preferably nonstick. Place over medium heat and bring to a near boil. Immediately remove from the heat and set aside.

4. Whisk the egg yolks and sugar together in a large bowl until pale and thick, about 2 minutes. Whisk in the cornstarch. Remove the vanilla bean from the hot milk, saving it for another use, and whisk the milk into the cornstarch mixture. Pour the mixture back into the saucepan. Place over medium heat and cook, whisking nonstop, until it comes to a boil, 5 to 7 minutes. Continue to boil, whisking nonstop, for about 1 minute, then remove from the heat. Whisk in the butter, one piece at a time, and the white chocolate, adding it in several stages. Scrape the filling back into the bowl and press a piece of plastic wrap on top, leaving no gaps or air pockets, to prevent a skin from forming. Transfer the pie to a wire rack and let cool thoroughly. Refrigerate for at least 3 hours or overnight.

5. Shortly before serving, using a chilled medium-size bowl and chilled beaters, beat the cream with an electric mixer until it is stiff but not grainy. Refrigerate.

6. Slice the bananas into a large bowl and sprinkle with the lemon juice. Fold the bananas, banana liqueur, and crème de cacao into the cold filling. Fold in the whipped cream. Spoon the filling into the cooled pie shell, then garnish with a dusting of unsweetened cocoa. Serve at once or refrigerate for up to 1 hour before serving. There's no need to cover the pie for the first hour, but beyond that, cover with loosely tented aluminum foil.

Recipe for Success

▶ There are a couple of ways to streamline this recipe. Instead of the vanilla bean, which you may not have on hand, you can simply whisk 1 teaspoon vanilla extract into the filling when it comes off the heat. You also can use a large store-bought graham cracker crust or a homemade graham cracker crust, if you like.

▶ The chef at the Buckhead Diner recommends that you serve this pie the same day it is made for the best results.

Maple Cream Pie

Southern and midwestern cooks are famous for their cream pies, but cooks in New England make a pretty mean one, too, and with $1/2$ cup of maple syrup in this one, there's no mistaking the flavor—or the pie's roots. Some of the filling is held back, then folded with the whipped cream that's slathered over the top. I have a set of miniature autumn cookie cutters, so when I serve this, I bake a couple of dozen maple leaf cutouts and make a garland to garnish the pie.

MAKES 8 TO 10 SERVINGS

1 recipe Basic Flaky Pie Pastry, Single Crust (page 31), refrigerated

FILLING

$1/2$ cup granulated sugar

$1/4$ cup cornstarch

$1/8$ teaspoon salt

$1\,1/4$ cups light cream or half-and-half

1 cup whole milk

$1/2$ cup pure maple syrup (see Recipe for Success)

4 large egg yolks

2 tablespoons unsalted butter, cut into $1/2$-inch pieces

$1/2$ teaspoon vanilla extract

TOPPING

1 cup cold heavy or whipping cream

2 tablespoons confectioners' sugar, sifted

1. If you haven't already, prepare the pastry and refrigerate it until firm enough to roll, about 1 hour.

2. On a sheet of lightly floured waxed paper, roll the pastry into a 12-inch circle with a floured rolling pin. Invert the pastry over a 9-inch standard pie pan, center, and peel off the paper. Tuck the pastry into the pan, without stretching it, and sculpt the edge into an upstanding ridge. (If you'll be adding a leaf garland, use a glass pan with a wide rim. Let the pastry drape over the edge and trim the pastry even with the outside edge of the pan.) Place in the freezer for 15 minutes, then fully prebake and let cool according to the directions on page 16.

3. Combine the granulated sugar, cornstarch, and salt in a medium-size, heavy saucepan, preferably nonstick. Whisk in the light cream, milk, maple syrup, and egg yolks. Place over medium heat and cook, whisking virtually nonstop, until the mixture starts to thicken and comes to a low boil, 5 to 7 minutes. Continue to whisk and heat until thick, about $1\,1/2$ minutes. Remove from the heat and whisk in the butter, one piece at a time, and the vanilla. Pour 1 cup of the filling into a small bowl. Immediately pour the remaining filling into the cooled pie shell. Gently press a piece of plastic wrap directly against the filling in the pie shell and the bowl, leaving no gaps or air pockets, to prevent a skin from forming. Transfer the pie to a wire rack and let both the pie and the filling in the bowl cool to room temperature. Refrigerate for at least 3 hours, preferably longer (up to overnight).

4. Shortly before serving, make the topping. Using a chilled medium-size bowl and chilled beaters, beat the heavy cream with an electric mixer until it holds soft peaks. Add the confectioners' sugar and beat until stiff but not grainy. Fold a little of the whipped cream into the reserved filling. Fold in the remaining whipped cream until evenly blended. Smooth over the pie and serve right away.

Recipe for Success

▶ In step 2, I tell you to let the pastry drape over the edge of the pan if you're going to make a decorative leaf garland. This will leave you with a relatively flat surface on which to mount the leaves.

▶ If you do make pastry cutouts to decorate the pie, read the box on page 19 first.

▶ Use a high-grade light amber maple syrup, if possible, so that you don't darken the filling too much. The flavor also will be smoother and subtler.

▶ To emphasize the maple flavor, sweeten the topping with 1¹/₂ tablespoons maple syrup instead of the confectioners' sugar.

Snickers Cream Pie

Charming as I can be when attempting to secure recipes from various sources, there are times when no amount of flattery or cajoling works. Case in point: I was jotting down Cindy Breitbach's recipe for raspberry pie (see page 149), when she casually let drop that the Snickers cream pie she makes for Breitbach's Country Dining, her family's restaurant in Balltown, Iowa, is something of a local legend. Hmm, might she be interested in sharing that recipe with my readers? Sorry, she told me, in a tone that was pure politeness, with just a dash of "don't push your luck, bub." I was down but not defeated, and sufficiently smitten with the idea of a Snickers pie that I fiddled around with the concept until I came up with something quite wonderful. I have no idea how it stacks up against Cindy's pie, but I'm very happy with this one.

MAKES 8 TO 10 SERVINGS

1 recipe Basic Flaky Pie Pastry, Single Crust (page 31), refrigerated

One 13-ounce bag mini Snickers bars, cut in half (about 2 cups)

FILLING

3/4 cup granulated sugar

3 1/2 tablespoons cornstarch

Big pinch of salt

2 cups whole milk

3 large egg yolks

1 tablespoon unsalted butter, cut into 1/2-inch pieces

3 tablespoons smooth peanut butter

1 teaspoon vanilla extract

TOPPING

1 cup cold heavy or whipping cream

2 tablespoons confectioners' sugar, sifted

3/4 cup chopped salted dry-roasted peanuts

1. If you haven't already, prepare the pastry and refrigerate until firm enough to roll, about 1 hour.

2. On a sheet of lightly floured waxed paper, roll the pastry into a 13-inch circle with a floured rolling pin. Invert the pastry over a 9 1/2-inch deep-dish pie pan, center, and peel off the paper. Tuck the pastry into the pan, without stretching it, and sculpt the edge into an upstanding ridge. Place in the freezer for 15 minutes, then fully prebake and let cool according to the directions on page 16. Scatter the Snickers pieces in the pie shell, using enough of them to make one crowded, but not solid, layer (see Recipe for Success). Set aside.

3. Whisk the granulated sugar, cornstarch, and salt together in a medium-size, heavy saucepan, preferably nonstick. Whisk in the milk and egg yolks. Place over medium-high heat and cook, whisking virtually nonstop, until the mixture starts to boil, 5 to 7 minutes. Continue to cook, whisking nonstop, for 1 to 1 1/2 minutes. Remove from the heat and whisk in the butter, one piece at a time, and the peanut butter, 1 tablespoon at a time. Whisk in the vanilla.

4. Scrape the filling into the pie shell, covering the Snickers pieces; shake the pan gently to settle the filling. Transfer the pie to a wire rack. Press a piece of plastic wrap directly over the filling, leaving no gaps or air pockets, to prevent a skin from forming. When the pie has cooled thoroughly, refrigerate for at least 3 hours or overnight.

5. When you're ready to serve the pie, make the topping. Using a chilled medium-size bowl and chilled beaters, beat the cream with an electric mixer until it holds soft peaks. Add the confectioners' sugar and continue to beat until stiff but not grainy. Spread or pipe the topping decoratively over the pie, then scatter the peanuts on top. Serve right away.

Recipe for Success

▶ In addition to the pastry crust, there are any number of crumb crusts that would work well here; in particular, try the Nutty Graham Cracker Crust (page 53) made with peanuts. For a timesaver, use a large store-bought graham cracker crust.

▶ About that Snickers layer: you want the peanut-butter pudding to be able to settle onto the crust here and there, which is why I don't recommend one solid layer of candy. Leave little gaps between the pieces so the filling can ooze through.

Indiana Butterscotch Pie with a Checkerboard Crust

By all appearances, Hoosiers love their butterscotch pies, often made with a meringue topping. This pie is typical of the genre, but to show off this pretty checkerboard border, I thought it best to forgo the meringue. Of course, if you're pressed for time, you don't have to do anything to the edge; just leave it plain. A little less sweet than some versions I've seen, this one is still sweet enough to serve with unsweetened whipped cream.

MAKES 8 TO 10 SERVINGS

1 recipe Basic Flaky Pie Pastry, Single Crust (page 31) or Basic Shortening Pie Pastry, Single Crust (page 30), refrigerated

FILLING

1 cup firmly packed light brown sugar

1/3 cup all-purpose flour

2 cups whole milk

3 large egg yolks

1/4 teaspoon salt

1 teaspoon vanilla extract

3 tablespoons unsalted butter, cut into 1/2-inch pieces

GARNISH

Fresh Whipped Cream (page 605), unsweetened

1. If you haven't already, prepare the pastry and refrigerate until firm enough to roll, about 1 hour.

2. On a sheet of lightly floured waxed paper, roll the pastry into a 12-inch circle with a floured rolling pin. Invert the pastry over a 9-inch standard pie pan, center, and peel off the paper. (I like to use a clear Pyrex pan here because it has a wide rim that does a good job of supporting the crust where the checkerboard design will be.) Tuck the pastry into the pan, without stretching it. Beef up the upper edge of the pastry somewhat by pushing any overhanging dough back toward the rim of the pan. Using the back of a paring knife, trim the pastry flush with the outer edge of the pan. Refrigerate for 20 minutes. Using a sharp paring knife or scissors, cut the edge of the pastry at $1/2$-inch intervals and about $1/2$ inch deep around the entire edge of the pie shell. Make sure the cuts are clean so that you can do the next step easily. Take every other cut section and gently push it toward the inside of the pie shell, creating a checkerboard appearance. Place in the freezer for 15 minutes, then fully prebake and let cool according to the directions on page 16, taking care not to cover the checkerboard part of the pastry with the aluminum foil and beans.

3. Combine the brown sugar, flour, milk, egg yolks, and salt in a medium-size, heavy saucepan, preferably nonstick. Place over medium heat and cook, whisking more or less nonstop, until the mixture thickens and starts to boil, 6 to 7 minutes. Continue to cook, whisking rapidly, for about 2 minutes. Remove from the heat and whisk in the vanilla and butter, one piece at a time. Pour the filling into the cooled pie shell.

4. Transfer the pie to a wire rack and let cool thoroughly. Cover with loosely tented aluminum foil and refrigerate for at least several hours or overnight. Serve garnished with unsweetened whipped cream.

Recipe for Success

▶ **You can substitute dark brown sugar for the light, if you like, but expect the pie to have a darker color and a stronger molasses flavor.**

▶ **Be careful when cooking this filling on top of the stove. Once it thickens, it tends to spatter, so watch your arms and hands, as well as the faces of inquisitive children.**

▶ **If you're watching calories, you can substitute lowfat milk and use half as much butter in the filling.**

Ivy House Indiana Sugar Cream Pie

Sugar cream pie is the unofficial Hoosier State pie, and as these things often go, there is not one recipe but many variations on the theme. The basic idea seems to be sugar-sweetened cream or milk thickened with cornstarch and enriched with butter, much like other cream pie fillings. The thing that apparently distinguishes this from other cream pies is the absence of eggs, which makes the filling a little less creamy but sturdier. This version, from innkeepers Jim and Linda Nolte of Fortville, Indiana's Ivy House Bed and Breakfast, is a great example. The filling is nearly pure white without the eggs and delicious.

MAKES 8 TO 10 SERVINGS

1 recipe Basic Flaky Pie Pastry, Single Crust (page 31) or Basic Shortening Pie Pastry, Single Crust (page 30), refrigerated

FILLING
1 cup sugar
1/4 cup plus 2 tablespoons cornstarch
21/4 cups whole milk

1/2 cup (1 stick) unsalted butter, cut into pieces
Big pinch of salt
1 teaspoon vanilla extract

GARNISH
Fresh Whipped Cream (page 605; optional), unsweetened

1. If you haven't already, prepare the pastry and refrigerate until firm enough to roll, about 1 hour.

2. On a sheet of lightly floured waxed paper, roll the pastry into a 12-inch circle with a floured rolling pin. Invert the pastry over a 9-inch standard pie pan, center, and peel off the paper. Tuck the pastry into the pan, without stretching it, and sculpt the edge into an upstanding ridge. Place in the freezer for 15 minutes, then fully prebake and let cool according to the instructions on page 16.

3. Combine the sugar, cornstarch, milk, butter, and salt in a medium-size, heavy saucepan, preferably nonstick. Place over medium heat and cook, stirring or whisking virtually nonstop, until the mixture starts to boil, 5 to 7 minutes. Reduce the heat slightly and continue to cook, whisking rapidly to prevent the filling from spattering, for about 2 minutes. Remove from the heat and stir in the vanilla. Pour the filling into the cooled pie shell, smoothing the top. Transfer the pie to a wire rack and let cool thoroughly, then refrigerate for at least a couple of hours or overnight. Serve by itself or with a dollop of whipped cream.

Recipe for Success

▶ This is a firm filling and quite delicious. I have tested the recipe with 5 table-spoons cornstarch instead of 6 and also have gotten excellent results—slightly less sturdy but still plenty firm enough to slice.

Classic Lemon Meringue Pie

Lemon meringue pie is an American diner standard and the measure of excellence among home bakers across the country. More dramatic to behold than it is difficult to prepare, our version has a perfectly balanced sweet-tart filling and a generous dome of golden, cloud-like meringue. I like this best while the meringue is still warm, but it will keep in the refrigerator for up to 24 hours, if necessary.

MAKES 8 TO 10 SERVINGS

1 recipe Basic Flaky Pie Pastry, Single Crust (page 31), refrigerated

FILLING

1 1/3 cups granulated sugar

1/4 cup plus 2 tablespoons cornstarch

1/8 teaspoon salt

2 cups water

1/2 cup fresh lemon juice

1 tablespoon grated lemon zest

4 large egg yolks

2 tablespoons unsalted butter, cut into 1/2-inch pieces

MERINGUE

4 large egg whites, at room temperature

1/4 teaspoon cream of tartar

Big pinch of salt

1/2 cup superfine sugar

1/2 teaspoon vanilla extract

1. If you haven't already, prepare the pastry and refrigerate it until firm enough to roll, about 1 hour.

2. On a sheet of lightly floured waxed paper, roll the pastry into a 13-inch circle with a floured rolling pin. Invert the pastry over a 9 1/2-inch deep-dish pie pan, center, and peel off the paper. Tuck the pastry into the pan, without stretching it, and sculpt the edge so it is just slightly higher than the rim. Place in the freezer for 15 minutes, then fully pre-bake and let cool according to the instructions on page 16.

3. Combine the granulated sugar, cornstarch, and salt in a medium-size saucepan, preferably nonstick, whisking to mix. Add the water, lemon juice, and lemon zest. Add the egg yolks, whisking the mixture well. Place over medium heat and cook, whisking virtually nonstop, until the mixture comes to a boil, 5 to 7 minutes. Reduce the heat slightly and continue to cook, whisking nonstop, for about 1½ minutes. Remove from the heat and stir in the butter, one piece at a time. Immediately pour the filling into the cooled pie shell, jiggling the pan to settle it. Press a piece of plastic wrap directly over the filling, taking care not to leave any gaps or air pockets, to prevent a skin from forming. Transfer the pie to a wire rack and let cool to room temperature. Refrigerate for up to 1 day if you're not adding the meringue right away.

4. Just before serving, preheat the broiler and make the meringue. In a large bowl, beat the egg whites with an electric mixer on medium-high speed until they hold soft peaks. Beat in the cream of tartar and salt. Gradually add the superfine sugar, 1 tablespoon at a time, beating until the whites are thick and glossy, though not dry. Add the vanilla and beat briefly. Mound the meringue over the filling, spreading it so it is domed in the center and touching the crust all around the edge.

5. Place the pie on the center oven rack and briefly brown the meringue under the broiler. It will just take a very short time, so don't walk away from the oven. Transfer the pie to a wire rack and serve right away. Or cover with loosely tented aluminum foil, making sure the meringue doesn't come in contact with the foil, and refrigerate until ready to serve.

Recipe for Success

▶ **If you use bottled lemon juice on every other occasion, do use fresh for this classic pie. With so much lemon juice in the pie, you want the authentic flavor of the real thing.**

▶ **Many recipes for lemon meringue pie instruct you to bake the meringue in a hot oven rather than browning it under the broiler. Not only is the broiling method faster, but you also avoid the sometimes rubbery skin that forms on baked meringues.**

Lemon Chiffon Pie

When most people think of chiffon pie, this is likely the one that comes to mind. Light as a cloud, with the sweet tang of lemon, this pie is best in a graham cracker crust, although it is just as frequently teamed up with a pastry crust (see Recipe for Success). It is the ideal summer pie, and its pale tones benefit from a garnish of fresh berries.

MAKES 8 TO 10 SERVINGS

1 recipe Graham Cracker Crumb Crust (page 51) or 1 large store-bought graham cracker crust

FILLING

$1/4$ cup cold water

1 envelope unflavored gelatin

$1/2$ cup lemonade or water

$1/2$ cup fresh lemon juice

1 cup sugar

4 large eggs, separated, whites brought to room temperature

1 teaspoon grated lemon zest

Big pinch of salt

$1/4$ teaspoon cream of tartar

$1/2$ teaspoon vanilla extract

GARNISH

Fresh Whipped Cream (page 605)

Fresh blueberries (picked over for stems), raspberries, or hulled strawberries

1. Prepare the crust and press it into the bottom and up the side of a $9^1/_2$-inch deep-dish pie pan. Refrigerate, prebake, and let cool as directed. Or simply use a store-bought crust, prebaking it according to the package directions and letting it cool. Refrigerate until ready to use.

2. Meanwhile, pour the water into a small bowl and sprinkle the gelatin over it. Set aside. In a medium-size, heavy saucepan, preferably nonstick, whisk together the lemonade, lemon juice, $1/2$ cup of the sugar, the egg yolks, lemon zest, and salt. Place over medium heat and cook, stirring nonstop, until the mixture thickens enough to coat the back of a spoon, 7 to 9 minutes. Do not let the mixture boil or it will curdle. Remove from the heat, stir in the softened gelatin, and immediately pour into a large bowl. Let cool for 10 minutes, then refrigerate just until the mixture turns lumpy, indicating that the gelatin is starting to thicken it, 50 to 60 minutes.

3. Immediately beat the 4 egg whites in a large bowl with an electric mixer until they hold soft peaks. Beat in the cream of tartar. Gradually add the remaining $1/2$ cup sugar, beating on high speed until the whites are thick and glossy. Beat in the vanilla. The whites should be firm but not dry. Gently fold about one-third of the whites into the lemon mixture. Add the remaining whites and continue to fold until the filling is evenly blended. Scrape the filling into the cooled pie shell and smooth the top with a spoon or rubber spatula. Cover with loosely tented aluminum foil and refrigerate for at least 3 hours or overnight. Serve garnished with a dollop of whipped cream and a scattering of berries.

Recipe for Success

▶ If you do use a pastry crust, Extra-Flaky Pie Pastry (page 34) and Basic Flaky Pie Pastry (page 31) would both be fine. Fully prebake the pastry according to the directions on page 16.

▶ It's a little tricky judging when the lemon mixture has thickened sufficiently and is ready to be removed from the heat. Pay close attention, noting the subtle changes in consistency. When thickened, the mixture will be like heavy cream.

▶ Be careful not to overbeat the egg whites or they'll turn dry and be difficult to fold into the lemon mixture.

Watermelon Chiffon Pie

This feather-light chiffon pie has the subtle but distinct flavor of watermelon, as well it should, since there are nearly three cups of watermelon juice in the filling. That juice is thickened with gelatin, then blended with whipped cream and beaten egg whites to give the filling that airy chiffon texture we all love. The pie makes a luscious summer dessert for any gathering of friends or family.

MAKES 10 SERVINGS

1 recipe Graham Cracker Crumb Crust (page 51) or 1 large store-bought graham cracker crust

FILLING
6 cups watermelon flesh (seeds are fine)
1/3 cup granulated sugar
2 envelopes unflavored gelatin
1 tablespoon fresh lime or lemon juice

2 large egg whites, at room temperature
1 cup cold heavy or whipping cream
1 cup confectioners' sugar, sifted

GARNISH
Confectioners' sugar
Fresh Whipped Cream (page 605; optional)

1. Prepare the crust and press it into the bottom and up the side of a 9½-inch deep-dish pie pan. Refrigerate, prebake, and let cool as directed. Or simply use a store-bought crust, prebaking it according to the package directions and letting it cool. Refrigerate until ready to use.

2. Combine the watermelon and granulated sugar in a very large bowl. Using a potato masher, mash until the mixture is quite liquid. Set aside for 15 minutes. Drain the mixture through a strainer, reserving almost 2¾ cups of the watermelon juice. Discard the pulp and seeds.

3. Put ¼ cup of the juice in a medium-size bowl and sprinkle the gelatin over it. Set aside for 3 to 4 minutes to dissolve. Meanwhile, heat ½ cup of the juice in a small sauce-pan over medium heat (or in the microwave) to a near boil. Whisk the hot juice into the dissolved gelatin. Pour the remaining 2 cups watermelon juice into a large bowl and stir in the gelatin–watermelon juice mixture. Stir in the lime juice. Place in the refrigerator.

4. Using an electric mixer, beat the egg whites in a medium-size bowl until stiff peaks form. Set aside. Clean and dry the beaters. Using a chilled medium-size bowl and chilled beaters, beat the heavy cream with the mixer until it holds soft peaks. Add the confectioners' sugar and beat until smooth and stiff but not grainy. Refrigerate.

5. When the watermelon juice mixture starts to firm up, add about one-quarter of the whipped cream and beat with the electric mixer until smooth. Add the beaten egg whites and remaining whipped cream and gently fold them in with a large rubber spatula. If necessary, use a whisk—very briefly—to smooth the mixture and break up any large globs of whites or whipped cream. Pour the filling into the cooled pie shell, shaking the pan gently to settle the filling. Cover with loosely tented aluminum foil and refrigerate for at least 4 hours, preferably overnight. To serve, garnish each slice with a dusting of confectioners' sugar, then add a dollop of whipped cream, if desired.

Recipe for Success

▶ **Wait until the height of watermelon season to make this pie, so you can count on a good, juicy melon.**

▶ **It looks sort of hip to serve this with a garnish of watermelon balls. Don't garnish until the last moment, however, to prevent a juice buildup on your serving plates.**

Strawberry Chiffon Pie

Frozen strawberries, available any time of year, are used here to make a sweet, blushing chiffon pie with little pieces of strawberry throughout. The filling looks quite attractive with the dark chocolate crust. If you make this in the summer to celebrate strawberry season—and what better time?—use the frozen strawberries in the pie and garnish the top with perfect, medium-size berries around the edge, with little piped swirls of whipped cream in between.

MAKES 10 TO 12 SERVINGS

1 recipe Chocolate Wafer Crumb Crust (page 54)

FILLING

2/3 cup cold lemonade

1 1/2 envelopes unflavored gelatin

One 1-pound bag individually frozen strawberries (not packed in syrup), partially thawed

1/2 cup plus 3 tablespoons sugar

Finely grated zest of 1 lemon

2 large egg whites, at room temperature

Pinch of salt

2/3 cup cold heavy or whipping cream

GARNISH

Fresh strawberries, hulled

Fresh Whipped Cream (page 605)

1. Prepare the crust and press it into the bottom and up the side of a 9 1/2-inch deep-dish pie pan. Refrigerate, prebake, and let cool as directed. Refrigerate until ready to use.

2. Pour the lemonade into a small bowl and sprinkle the gelatin over it. Set aside to soften.

3. Combine the strawberries, 1/2 cup of the sugar, and the lemon zest in a large non-reactive saucepan over medium heat. Gradually bring to a simmer, crushing the berries with a potato masher as they soften. Don't overmash them; leave some chunks. Simmer the berries gently for 2 to 3 minutes, then remove from the heat. Immediately add the softened gelatin, stirring well for 1 minute to blend. Pour the fruit into a bowl and let cool to room temperature. Refrigerate, stirring often, until the fruit is just starting to set. (To hasten the cooling, put the bowl in a second, larger bowl of ice water, stirring often.)

4. In a medium-size bowl, beat the egg whites and salt with an electric mixer on medium-high speed until they hold soft peaks. Gradually add the remaining 3 tablespoons sugar, 1 tablespoon at a time, until the whites are thick and glossy but not dry. Fold the whites into the strawberries until evenly blended.

5. Clean and dry the beaters. Using a chilled medium-size bowl and chilled beaters, beat the heavy cream with the mixer until stiff but not grainy. Fold the cream into the strawberry mixture until evenly combined. Pour the filling into the chilled pie shell, smoothing the top with the back of a spoon. Cover with loosely tented aluminum foil and refrigerate for at least 4 hours or overnight. Just before serving, arrange 10 or 12 whole strawberries around the edge of the pie, piping a little of the whipped cream between them. Serve at once.

Recipe for Success

▶ The reason I use frozen strawberries is that it makes more sense to use less expensive frozen berries when you're going to cook them anyway and texture isn't an issue.

▶ Remember that the more you fold ingredients, the more likely you are to deflate them. So when I make a chiffon pie, I like to add the whipped cream before the egg whites are fully incorporated to shorten the overall folding time required.

▶ It really does hasten the cooling to use an ice-water bath. I like to use my big stainless steel "everything bowl" for this purpose.

> "Chiffon pies are absolutely wonderful, rather like elegant Victorian ladies, often quivery or trembly, always delicate, but with a sound, well-bred constitution."
>
> —Marion Cunningham, *The Fannie Farmer Baking Book* (Knopf, 1984)

Manchester Highlands Inn Strawberry Margarita Pie

Any pie recipe that starts with two cups of ripe fresh strawberries has to be good, and this one certainly is. Like a real margarita, it has an icy texture and a bit of a kick. You can reduce the tequila by one or two tablespoons, if you like, for a mellower flavor. The recipe comes courtesy of Robert Eichorn, chef-owner of the lovely Manchester Highlands Inn in Manchester, Vermont.

MAKES 8 TO 10 SERVINGS

1 recipe Graham Cracker Crumb Crust (page 51) or 1 large store-bought graham cracker crust

FILLING
2 cups hulled and sliced fresh strawberries
1/4 cup sugar
3/4 cup sweetened condensed milk
6 tablespoons tequila

1/4 cup triple sec
1 tablespoon fresh lime juice
2 cups cold heavy or whipping cream

GARNISH
Fresh strawberries, hulled and sliced
Fresh mint leaves

1. Prepare the crust and press it into the bottom and up the side of a 9 1/2-inch deep-dish pie pan. Refrigerate, prebake, and let cool as directed. Or simply use a store-bought crust, prebaking it according to the package directions and letting it cool. Refrigerate until ready to use.

2. In a medium-size bowl, toss the strawberries with the sugar. In a food processor, combine the condensed milk, tequila, triple sec, lime juice, and sugared strawberries and process until smooth. Transfer to a large bowl and refrigerate.

3. Using a chilled large bowl and chilled beaters, beat the cream with an electric mixer until stiff but not grainy. Using a large rubber spatula, fold about one-third of the whipped cream into the refrigerated puree. Gently fold in the remaining whipped cream in 2 more additions until evenly combined. Pour the filling into the chilled pie shell and smooth the top. Cover with loosely tented aluminum foil and place in the freezer until the filling is semi-firm to firm, at least several hours or overnight. Garnish each slice with strawberries and mint leaves.

Recipe for Success

▶ Use only ripe fresh strawberries. The pie won't be half as good without that ripe strawberry flavor.

▶ The filling of this pie is looser than some when it goes into the pie shell and it doesn't mound in the center. If you have any extra, just pour it into custard cups and freeze.

▶ I consider this more of an adult pie, but if you're serving a mixed crowd, consider reducing the liquor to make it more kid-friendly.

Lime Margarita Pie

This and the preceding pie are dedicated to the free spirit of tropical islands, cheeseburgers in paradise, Jimmy Buffet concerts, and all that good stuff. And though some of those things can be elusive, these pies are accessible to anyone with an electric mixer and a hankering for a cool, refreshing dessert with a little bit of a kick. This pie is based on a cooked lime custard that's blended with tequila and triple sec, then combined with firmly whipped cream. It's poured into a graham cracker crust, then frozen for several hours. If you plan to serve it in the evening, be sure to get it into the freezer by noon. The pie is thick and creamy, with a frozen mousse-like texture you'll love. The sugared lime twists make an attractive garnish.

MAKES 8 TO 10 SERVINGS

1 recipe Graham Cracker Crumb Crust (page 51) or 1 large store-bought graham cracker crust

FILLING

1/4 cup tequila

3 tablespoons triple sec

1 1/2 teaspoons unflavored gelatin

4 large eggs

1 cup sugar

1/2 cup fresh lime juice

1 tablespoon fresh lemon juice

Finely grated zest of 1 lime

1 1/4 cups cold heavy or whipping cream

GARNISH

2 limes

Sugar

1. Prepare the crust and press it into the bottom and up the side of a 9 1/2-inch deep-dish pie pan. Refrigerate, prebake, and let cool as directed. Or simply use a store-bought crust, prebaking it according to the package directions and letting it cool. Refrigerate until ready to use.

2. Combine the tequila and triple sec in a small bowl. Sprinkle the gelatin over the top and set aside to soften.

3. Combine the eggs, sugar, lime juice, lemon juice, and lime zest in a small, heavy nonreactive saucepan. Place over medium heat and cook, whisking more or less nonstop, until the mixture thickens, 5 to 6 minutes. Remove from the heat and blend in the tequila mixture, whisking to dissolve the gelatin. Scrape into a large bowl, transfer to a wire rack, and let cool to room temperature. Refrigerate until the mixture is cool to the touch, stirring occasionally.

4. When the custard is cool, using a chilled medium-size bowl and chilled beaters, beat the cream with an electric mixer until it is stiff but not grainy. Fold about one-third of the whipped cream into the custard with a large rubber spatula. Add the remaining whipped cream and fold until the filling is evenly combined. Scrape the filling into the chilled pie shell and smooth the top. Cover with loosely tented aluminum foil and place in the freezer for at least 4 hours or overnight. If the pie gets very firm from an extended stay in the freezer, put it in the refrigerator for 30 minutes before slicing.

5. Shortly before serving, prepare the garnish. Slice the center portion of each lime into 4 or 5 thin, even slices. Place the slices on a paper towel and blot well. Dip the slices into a shallow bowl of sugar, coating both sides well. Set the slices aside on a plate for 5 minutes. Repeat twice more, waiting 5 minutes between each coating. Just before serving, cut each slice from the edge to the center. Twist the halves in opposite directions and garnish each slice of pie with a twist.

Recipe for Success

▶ **Custards like this one are often cooked in the top of a double boiler to prevent them from curdling. If you maintain a moderate temperature and keep whisking, however, your custard won't curdle.**

▶ **If you can find it, use genuine Key lime juice, available bottled in most upscale kitchenware shops. Fresh Key limes are also showing up increasingly in the produce section of many supermarkets.**

White Russian Pie

This feather-light chiffon pie with an adult theme is flavored with coffee, coffee liqueur, and bourbon. Mounded into a delicious pecan graham cracker crumb crust, it's the perfect ending—served with strong coffee—to an informal dinner party.

MAKES 8 TO 10 SERVINGS

1 recipe Nutty Graham Cracker Crust (page 53) made with pecans

FILLING

2/3 cup granulated sugar

5 large egg yolks

2 tablespoons bourbon

1/2 cup cold, strong brewed coffee

1 envelope unflavored gelatin

1 1/2 cups cold heavy or whipping cream

2 tablespoons Kahlúa or other coffee liqueur

1 teaspoon vanilla extract

1/3 cup confectioners' sugar

GARNISH

Chocolate-covered coffee beans (optional)

1. Prepare the crust and press it into the bottom and up the side of a 9-inch standard pie pan. Refrigerate, prebake, and let cool as directed. Refrigerate until ready to use.

2. Combine the granulated sugar and egg yolks in the top of a double boiler over, not in, barely simmering water. Heat the mixture, whisking nearly nonstop, until thick enough to coat the back of a spoon, 7 to 8 minutes. Remove from the heat and whisk in the bourbon. Remove the insert from the double boiler and set the custard aside to cool.

3. When the custard has cooled, pour the coffee into a small bowl and sprinkle the gelatin over it. Set aside for 5 minutes to soften. Transfer the coffee mixture to a small saucepan and gently heat, whisking, until the gelatin has dissolved, 1 to 2 minutes. Remove from the heat and gradually whisk into the custard mixture. Scrape the custard into a large bowl and refrigerate, whisking every few minutes.

4. As soon as you refrigerate the custard, using a chilled medium-size bowl and chilled beaters, beat the cream with an electric mixer until it holds soft peaks. Add the Kahlúa and vanilla and beat briefly. Add the confectioners' sugar and beat briefly again, until stiff but not grainy.

5. As soon as the refrigerated custard shows signs of thickening, remove it from the refrigerator and whisk in about 1/2 cup of the whipped cream until smooth. Add the remaining whipped cream in 2 parts, this time gently *folding* the mixtures together until evenly combined. Mound the filling in the chilled pie shell, smoothing the top. Cover with loosely tented aluminum foil and refrigerate for at least 4 hours or overnight.

6. Garnish with chocolate-covered coffee beans, if desired, before serving.

Recipe for Success

▶ When I specify "strong" coffee, I mean the stuff that's been left in the pot half the morning with the coffee maker still on. Lacking that, make half a cup of instant coffee, using the amount of instant coffee you'd use to make a full cup.

▶ It's important to catch the custard before it gets too firm. Otherwise, it will be difficult to fold in the whipped cream.

Chocolate S'mores Pie with Jubilee Cherry Sauce

A variation of Chocolate Mousse Chiffon Pie (page 495), this one features mini marshmallows, a coating of mini chocolate chips, and a special cherry sauce. Lest you be misled by the name, this cherry sauce—unlike traditional cherries jubilee—has no spirits added, in the likely event you'll be serving it to children. If not, feel free to stir in a tablespoon or two of brandy or kirsch when you remove the sauce from the heat. That will give it a traditional jubilee kick.

MAKES 10 SERVINGS

1 recipe Graham Cracker Crumb Crust (page 51) or 1 large store-bought graham cracker crust

FILLING

1 recipe filling for Chocolate Mousse Chiffon Pie (page 495)

3 cups cold mini marshmallows (see Recipe for Success)

3/4 cup mini semisweet chocolate chips

JUBILEE CHERRY SAUCE

3 cups individually frozen pitted sweet cherries (not packed in syrup)

1/2 cup orange juice

1/2 cup sugar

2 tablespoons fresh lemon juice

1/4 cup water

1 1/2 tablespoons cornstarch

1/4 teaspoon vanilla extract

1 tablespoon unsalted butter

GARNISH

Fresh Whipped Cream (page 605; optional)

1. Prepare the crust and press it into the bottom and up the side of a 9½-inch deep-dish pie pan. Refrigerate, prebake, and let cool as directed. Or simply use a store-bought crust, prebaking it according to the package directions and letting it cool. Refrigerate until ready to use.

2. Follow steps 2 through 5 for Chocolate Mousse Chiffon Pie. After folding the whipped cream into the chocolate mixture, fold in the marshmallows. Scrape the filling into the chilled pie shell, mounding it as much as possible near the center; smooth the top with a spoon. Sprinkle the chocolate chips over the surface. Cover with loosely tented aluminum foil and refrigerate for at least 6 hours or overnight.

3. At any time before you serve the pie, prepare the cherry sauce. Combine the cherries, orange juice, sugar, and lemon juice in a medium-size nonreactive saucepan over medium heat. Bring to a low boil, stirring often, about 5 minutes. Reduce the heat slightly and simmer, partially covered, for 2 minutes.

4. Meanwhile, blend the water and cornstarch in a small bowl. After 2 minutes, stir the mixture into the cherries. Bring the sauce to a boil, then boil gently, stirring, for about 1½ minutes. Remove from the heat and pour into a medium-size bowl. Stir in the vanilla and butter. Let cool to room temperature, then refrigerate until serving time.

5. To serve, slice the pie and transfer to serving plates. Spoon some of the sauce around each serving, drizzling a little over the top, if you wish. Garnish with a dollop of whipped cream, if you like.

Recipe for Success

▶ This is a festive-looking dessert, great for a celebration such as a birthday, shower, or anniversary.

▶ Notice that I specify cold marshmallows. The reason is simply to help chill the mousse filling that much quicker. All you have to do is put them on a plate in the freezer for 10 minutes.

▶ You'll love the cherry sauce and probably start looking for other uses for it. I use it on pancakes and as an ice cream topping.

Chocolate Mousse Chiffon Pie

I'm quite fond of a well-made chiffon pie, but I'm just plain ecstatic about this one. It is, as the name suggests, a gelatin-enhanced chocolate mousse in a graham cracker crust. And you know what that means: lots of chocolate, eggs, and whipped cream. Like all chiffon pies, it's nearly light enough to levitate over your plate. But unlike most, it has an extra measure of chocolate richness that puts the pie in a class of its own. For contrast, serve it with plain whipped cream. Make this pie in the morning to serve in the evening.

MAKES 10 SERVINGS

1 recipe Graham Cracker Crumb Crust (page 51) or 1 large store-bought graham cracker crust

FILLING

3/4 cup cold, strong brewed coffee

1/4 cup (1/2 stick) unsalted butter

8 ounces semisweet chocolate, coarsely chopped

3 large eggs, separated, whites brought to room temperature

1 teaspoon vanilla extract

1 1/2 teaspoons unflavored gelatin

1/4 teaspoon cream of tartar

Big pinch of salt

1/3 cup sugar

1/2 cup cold heavy or whipping cream

GARNISH

Fresh Whipped Cream (page 605; optional)

1. Prepare the crust and press it into the bottom and up the side of a 9 1/2-inch deep-dish pie pan. Refrigerate, prebake, and let cool as directed. Or simply use a store-bought crust, prebaking it according to the package directions and letting it cool. Refrigerate until ready to use.

2. Over very low heat, combine 1/2 cup of the coffee and 2 tablespoons of the butter in a medium-size, heavy saucepan, preferably nonstick. As the butter starts to melt, add the chocolate. Let the mixture stand on the heat for 3 to 4 minutes, stirring a few times. When the chocolate has melted, remove from the heat, whisking to smooth. Whisk the remaining 2 tablespoons butter into the mixture, adding about 1/2 tablespoon at a time. Transfer the pan to a wire rack and let cool, whisking occasionally. While the mixture is still warm, whisk in the egg yolks. Put the saucepan back over very low heat and heat the mixture, whisking virtually nonstop, for 3 to 4 minutes to cook the yolks. Remove from the heat and stir in the vanilla. Let cool to room temperature, then refrigerate, whisking occasionally.

3. Pour the remaining ¼ cup coffee into a small saucepan and sprinkle the gelatin over it. Set aside for 5 minutes to soften. Gently heat the mixture, whisking, until the gelatin is dissolved, 1 to 2 minutes. Whisk this into the chocolate mixture and return the mixture to the refrigerator, whisking occasionally, 30 to 60 minutes, until it has the consistency of a very thick fudge sauce.

4. Using an electric mixer, beat the egg whites in a medium-size bowl until they hold soft peaks. Beat in the cream of tartar and salt. Gradually add the sugar, beating on high speed until the whites are thick, glossy, and firm but not dry. Transfer the chocolate mixture to a large bowl and fold in one-third of the whites. Add the rest of the egg whites and continue to fold, until no white streaks remain. Wash and dry the beaters.

5. Using a chilled medium-size bowl and chilled beaters, beat the heavy cream with the mixer until stiff but not grainy. Fold the whipped cream into the chocolate mixture until evenly combined. Scrape the filling into the chilled pie shell, smoothing the top with a spoon. Cover with loosely tented aluminum foil and refrigerate for at least 4 hours, preferably 6. Serve garnished with whipped cream, if desired.

Recipe for Success

▶ **Be careful not to let the chocolate mixture boil once you've added the egg yolks or it might curdle. If you don't have a portable phone in the kitchen, get one. In the time it takes to answer the phone and become momentarily distracted, accidents such as this can happen.**

▶ **Especially with delicate pies like this, I don't like to cover them when they first go in the fridge, because the covering may stick to and blemish the surface. The only problem is that a rich pie like this may absorb refrigerator odors. One solution: save those plastic lids that store-bought graham cracker crusts come with and cover your pie with one of them. Use masking tape to hold it in place. Or use tented aluminum foil to cover the pie.**

Maple-Pecan-Pumpkin Chiffon Pie

Can't handle a heavy pumpkin pie after Thanksgiving dinner? Try this one. It has all that great pumpkin flavor, but without the heft. The amaretto gives the pie a subtle but distinct nutty flavor. Garnished with pecan halves and whipped cream and served with mocha sauce, it's a real treat.

MAKES 10 SERVINGS

1 recipe Nutty Graham Cracker Crust (page 53) made with pecans

FILLING

3 tablespoons amaretto

1 tablespoon water

1 envelope unflavored gelatin

1 cup whole milk

4 large egg yolks

1/2 cup firmly packed light brown sugar

1/4 cup pure maple syrup

1 cup pumpkin puree, canned or fresh (see page 286)

1/2 teaspoon ground cinnamon

1/2 teaspoon ground nutmeg

1/2 teaspoon ground ginger

1/4 teaspoon ground cloves

Scant 1/2 teaspoon salt

1 cup cold heavy or whipping cream

2 large egg whites, at room temperature

1 tablespoon granulated sugar

1/2 cup chopped pecans

GARNISH

Pecan halves

Fresh Whipped Cream (page 605)

Warm Mocha Sauce (page 607; optional)

1.   Prepare the crust and press it into the bottom and up the side of a 9 1/2-inch deep-dish pie pan. Refrigerate, prebake, and let cool as directed. Refrigerate until ready to use.

2.   Combine the amaretto and water in a small bowl. Sprinkle the gelatin over the liquid and set aside to soften.

3.   Combine the milk, egg yolks, brown sugar, maple syrup, pumpkin, spices, and salt in a medium-size, heavy saucepan, preferably nonstick. Place over medium to medium-low heat and cook, whisking virtually nonstop, until the mixture thickens somewhat (the change will be subtle), about 8 minutes. Do not let the mixture boil. Remove from the heat and immediately add the gelatin mixture, stirring well to blend. Place the bowl in a larger bowl of ice water and let the filling cool, stirring frequently, until cool to the touch. You may want to add more ice when the first cubes melt.

Perfect Chiffon Pies: Some Gelatin Tips

▶ Unprepared gelatin has an indefinite shelf life, so even if it's been in your cabinet for quite some time, it's probably still good.

▶ For best results, soften gelatin in cool or cold liquid before adding it to a heated mixture.

▶ Chiffon pies should be kept refrigerated until you're ready to serve them. This maintains the integrity of the gelatin.

▶ Don't oversweeten chiffon pies. Too much sugar will make for a softer filling.

▶ Never bring gelatin to a boil, or it may lose its thickening power.

4. Meanwhile, using a chilled medium-size bowl and chilled beaters, beat the heavy cream with an electric mixer until stiff but not grainy. Cover and refrigerate. Wash and dry the beaters.

5. Beat the egg whites in a medium-size bowl with the mixer until they hold soft peaks. Add the granulated sugar and continue to beat until stiff and glossy but not dry. Add the whites and about one-third of the whipped cream to the filling. Fold gently until evenly combined. Add the remaining whipped cream and fold again until evenly mixed. Fold in the chopped pecans. Scrape the filling into the chilled pie shell, smoothing the top with a spoon. Cover with loosely tented aluminum foil and refrigerate for at least 4 hours or overnight.

6. When ready to serve, garnish the top of the pie with pecan halves (see Recipe for Success). Serve with a dollop of whipped cream and a drizzle of mocha sauce, if desired.

Recipe for Success

▶ If you prefer not to use alcohol, just soften the gelatin in 1/4 cup water. Add 1 teaspoon vanilla extract to the pumpkin filling when it comes off the heat.

▶ Given the density of this filling, it takes a while to cool, which is why I recommend the ice-water bath. You could simply let this cool to room temperature, then refrigerate (stirring often), but my method is much faster and easier.

▶ For the pecan garnish, arrange a single row of them around the outside of the pie, if you like, or cover the entire top. If you do the latter, leave room between the nuts so you can cut the slices. Otherwise, when you try to cut the pie, the nuts will push down on the filling and make a mess of it.

Andrea's Maple-Pecan Chiffon Pie

Andrea is Andrea Chesman, a fine food writer and editor whom I had the pleasure of working with on one my earliest cookbooks, *Maple Syrup Cookbook* (Storey Books, 1989). She didn't tip me off to this recipe when she was editing my book, but she did recently when a variation of this appeared in one of her books, *Mom's Best Desserts* (Storey Books, 2002), one of the tastiest dessert collections you'll ever run across. I've tweaked her recipe a little, using a graham cracker crust instead of a pastry. And I've substituted pecans for her walnuts. But the inspiration for this light-as-a-cloud, subtly flavored chiffon pie—the best one I've ever tried—comes directly from Andrea.

MAKES 8 TO 10 SERVINGS

1 recipe Graham Cracker Crumb Crust (page 51)

FILLING

1/4 cup cold water

1 envelope unflavored gelatin

3 large eggs, separated, whites brought to room temperature

3/4 cup pure maple syrup, preferably light or medium amber, gently warmed

1/4 cup whole milk or light cream, heated

1 teaspoon vanilla extract

1/8 teaspoon cream of tartar

1/8 teaspoon salt

3/4 cup cold heavy or whipping cream

1/2 cup chopped pecans

1. Prepare the crust and press it into the bottom and up the side of a 9-inch standard pie pan. Refrigerate, prebake, and let cool as directed. Refrigerate until ready to use.

2. Pour the water into a small bowl and sprinkle the gelatin over it. Set aside to soften.

3. In the top of a double boiler, beat the egg yolks with a wire whisk until thick and lemon-colored. Gradually stir in the maple syrup and hot milk. Bring the water in the bottom of the double boiler to a simmer, stirring the maple syrup mixture constantly until it thickens just enough to coat the back of a spoon, perhaps 10 to 12 minutes. Add the softened gelatin and stir until it has dissolved. Stir in the vanilla.

4. Transfer the mixture to a heatproof bowl, then put the bowl in a shallow casserole filled no more than halfway with ice and cold water. Cool the mixture, whisking often, until it barely begins to firm up. Don't leave it in the cold water until it gets overly firm, or it won't blend evenly into the egg whites.

5. In a medium-size bowl, beat the egg whites with an electric mixer until foamy. Add the cream of tartar and salt and beat until stiff but not dry. They should hold their shape and look moist. Using a rubber spatula, gently fold the egg whites into the cooled maple syrup mixture.

6. Wash and dry the beaters. Using a chilled medium-size bowl and chilled beaters, beat the cream with the mixer until stiff but not grainy. Fold it into the filling until evenly blended, then fold in half of the pecans. Turn the filling into the chilled pie shell and smooth the top with a spoon. Cover with loosely tented aluminum foil and refrigerate for at least 3 hours or overnight. Serve garnished with the remaining pecans.

Recipe for Success

▶ **Just a reminder here that eggs should be separated cold, but the whites should be beaten at room temperature for the best results.**

▶ **If you don't own a rubber spatula whose business end is good and large— something you'd expect to see in a professional kitchen—buy one. Chefs know it's the perfect thing for efficiently folding together delicate fillings such as this one. To fold correctly, sweep down along the back of the bowl and up along the front of it, then push down into the center. Repeat.**

Eggnog Chiffon Pie

If you're looking for something a little different to serve at your next holiday party, here it is. Creamy, rich in egg yolks, and dusted with nutmeg, this pie is the real deal for eggnog lovers. Instead of serving the whipped cream garnish separately, you can spread it over the top of the pie.

MAKES 10 SERVINGS

1 recipe Nutty Graham Cracker Crust (page 53) made with pecans

FILLING

1/4 cup dark rum

2 tablespoons water

1 envelope plus 1 teaspoon unflavored gelatin

1 recipe Crème Anglaise (page 606; see step 3)

3/4 cup cold heavy or whipping cream

3 tablespoons confectioners' sugar, sifted

3 large egg whites, at room temperature

GARNISH

Ground nutmeg

Fresh Whipped Cream (page 605)

1. Prepare the crust and press it into the bottom and up the side of a 9½-inch deep-dish pie pan. Refrigerate, prebake, and let cool as directed. Refrigerate until ready to use.

2. Pour the rum and water into a small bowl. Sprinkle the gelatin over the mixture and set aside to soften.

3. Prepare the crème anglaise. As soon as you remove it from the heat, add the softened gelatin, whisking to smooth. Scrape the mixture into a bowl and set aside to cool, whisking occasionally. When it reaches room temperature, refrigerate.

4. Meanwhile, using a chilled medium-size bowl and chilled beaters, beat the cream with an electric mixer until it holds soft peaks. Add the confectioners' sugar and continue to beat until it is firm but not grainy. Refrigerate. Wash and dry the beaters.

5. When the crème anglaise is just starting to gel—not too long, likely, after it has been refrigerated—fold about half of the whipped cream into it. Add the remaining whipped cream and continue to fold until well combined.

6. In a medium-size bowl, beat the egg whites with the mixer on medium-high speed until they hold firm peaks. Add about ½ cup of the whipped cream mixture and blend on low speed. Add the egg white mixture back to the whipped cream mixture and fold until evenly blended. Scrape the filling into the chilled pie shell, smoothing the top with a spoon. Cover with loosely tented aluminum foil and refrigerate for at least 2 hours or overnight. Just before serving, dust the top of the pie with nutmeg. Slice and serve, with the bowl of whipped cream on the side.

Recipe for Success

▶ **One of the tricks to making this and other chiffon pies is to catch the gelatinized mixture just as it is starting to firm up. (I've seen this consistency compared to raw egg whites.) At that stage, it's easier to fold the mixture with your other ingredients. If it gets too firm, the filling will be a little lumpy. You can sometimes rescue an overly firm mixture by whisking vigorously to smooth.**

Chocolate Silk Pie

Recipes for chocolate silk pie, sometimes called *French* chocolate silk pie, abound. It seems there's no end to our taste for rich, chocolaty desserts, and this one is right up there with the richest of them. The ingredients and method vary very little. Some recipes call for unsweetened chocolate, some for bittersweet. Most use granulated sugar; others like confectioners' or superfine sugar. In nearly every case, the butter and sugar are well beaten, then the melted chocolate is added, followed by the eggs, each of which is given a thorough beating. In the end, you have a filling that's something like chocolate buttercream frosting, only this "frosting" gets piled into a pie shell and refrigerated, yielding a luxuriously smooth chocolate pie. If you have a stand mixer, I suggest using it here, given the lengthy beating involved. Use almost any crumb crust—a large or small store-bought one or a homemade one; the only difference will be the height of the filling.

MAKES 8 TO 10 SERVINGS

1 recipe Graham Cracker Crumb Crust (page 51) or 1 large or small store-bought graham cracker crust

FILLING

3 ounces unsweetened chocolate, coarsely chopped

3/4 cup (1 1/2 sticks) unsalted butter, softened

1 1/4 cups sugar

3 large eggs

2 teaspoons vanilla extract

GARNISH

Fresh Whipped Cream (page 605)

1. Prepare the crust and press it into the bottom and up the side of a 9-inch standard pie pan. Refrigerate, prebake, and let cool as directed. Or simply use a store-bought crust, prebaking it according to the package directions and letting it cool. Refrigerate until ready to use.

2. Put the chocolate in the top of a double boiler set over, not in, barely simmering water. Melt the chocolate, smoothing it with a whisk. Remove the insert and let the chocolate cool, stirring occasionally. Set aside.

3. Using an electric mixer, beat the butter in a large bowl until creamy. Gradually add the sugar and continue to beat, scraping down the bowl as needed, until the mixture is light-textured, about 5 minutes. Scrape the melted chocolate into the butter mixture. Beat for 30 seconds. Add the eggs, one at a time, beating on medium-high speed for 3 to

4 minutes after each addition. The filling should be very light and creamy. Add the vanilla and blend for 10 seconds to incorporate.

4. Scrape the filling into the chilled pie shell and smooth the top with a spoon. Cover with loosely tented aluminum foil and refrigerate for at least 3 hours or overnight. Serve with a dollop of whipped cream.

Recipe for Success

▶ Some fancier recipes use bittersweet chocolate for this pie. If that suits your taste, by all means do so, but reduce the sugar by about 1/3 cup.

▶ If you, like me, can't keep your fingers out of whatever you're mixing, you may notice some sugar grittiness in the filling as you taste it. Don't be too concerned; there should be none by the time the last egg has been beaten in, and any trace should have dissolved before the pie is served.

▶ If you prefer, spread or pipe the whipped cream over the entire pie.

Bittersweet Chocolate–Mascarpone Pie

This is one of the most luxurious cream pies you'll ever eat—a layer of whipped cream–lightened and chocolate-flavored mascarpone cheese under even more whipped cream topping. Given the cost and richness of mascarpone cheese—a smooth, soft cheese made from high-butterfat cow's milk—this is not your everyday pie. Save it for company or a special occasion. Besides the great taste, it takes just a few minutes to whip up, especially if you use a store-bought Oreo crust.

MAKES 8 TO 10 SERVINGS

1 recipe Chocolate Wafer Crumb Crust (page 54) or Oreo Crumb Crust (page 55), or 1 store-bought Oreo crust

FILLING

4 ounces bittersweet chocolate, coarsely chopped

2 teaspoons instant espresso or coffee granules

1 tablespoon boiling water

12 ounces (about 1 1/2 cups) mascarpone cheese

1 teaspoon vanilla extract

1 cup cold heavy or whipping cream

1/2 cup confectioners' sugar, sifted

1.   Prepare the crust and press it into the bottom and up the side of a 9-inch standard pie pan. Refrigerate, prebake, and let cool as directed. Or simply use a store-bought crust, prebaking it according to the package directions and letting it cool. Refrigerate until ready to use.

2.   Put the chocolate in the top of a double boiler set over, not in, barely simmering water and let it melt. Remove the insert and set the chocolate aside, whisking to smooth.

3.   Put the coffee in a small bowl and pour the boiling water over it. Stir to dissolve and set aside.

4.   Stir the mascarpone briefly in a medium-size bowl just to smooth. Add the chocolate, coffee mixture, and vanilla, stirring gently just until evenly blended. Do not overstir, or the filling maybe come grainy. Set aside at room temperature.

5.   Using a chilled medium-size bowl and chilled beaters, beat the cream with an electric mixer until it holds soft peaks. Add the confectioners' sugar and continue to beat until stiff but not grainy. Add about one-third of the whipped cream to the chocolate mixture and fold it in gently until evenly combined. Spoon the filling into the chilled pie shell, smoothing the top with a spoon. Smooth the remaining whipped cream over the filling. Cover with loosely tented aluminum foil and refrigerate for at least 1 hour or overnight before serving.

Recipe for Success

▶ **This is a classy pie, one that I think justifies the use of the relatively expensive bittersweet chocolate. If you prefer, however, you can use semisweet chocolate.**

▶ **If you really want to get carried away, garnish this with sliced strawberries and Warm Mocha Sauce (page 607).**

Bittersweet Chocolate Turtle Pie

This icebox pie, inspired by a favorite recipe of mine from an old Betty Crocker cookbook, is as delicious as it is fetching. Start with a graham cracker crust, add a layer of melted caramels and pecans (the turtle part), and then top with two more layers: sweetened cream cheese and chocolate whipped cream. If it sounds involved, it really isn't. It's simply one of those assembly jobs that requires a few bowls and a little puttering time when you're going to be in the kitchen anyway. Serve this kid-pleaser for a pajama party or after an athletic event to salute the winning team.

MAKES 8 TO 10 SERVINGS

1 recipe Graham Cracker Crumb Crust (page 51) or 1 large store-bought graham cracker crust

3/4 cup chopped pecans

FILLING

30 caramels

2 tablespoons unsalted butter, cut into pieces

2 tablespoons water

Two 3-ounce packages full-fat cream cheese, softened

1/3 cup confectioners' sugar

1/2 teaspoon vanilla extract

TOPPING

3 tablespoons water

4 ounces bittersweet chocolate, coarsely chopped

2 cups cold heavy or whipping cream

1/4 cup confectioners' sugar

1 teaspoon vanilla extract

1. Prepare the crust and press it into the bottom and up the side of a 9-inch standard pie pan. Refrigerate, prebake, and let cool as directed. Or simply use a store-bought crust, prebaking it according to the package directions and letting it cool. Sprinkle the chopped pecans over the cooled crust and set aside.

2. Combine the caramels, butter, and water in a medium-size, heavy saucepan over very low heat. Heat, stirring occasionally, until the caramels have melted. Whisk well to smooth, then pour over the nuts, covering the pie shell evenly. Refrigerate.

3. Using an electric mixer, beat the cream cheese in a medium-size bowl until smooth and creamy. Add the confectioners' sugar and vanilla and beat until smooth. Scrape this mixture over the chilled caramel, smoothing it with a spoon. Refrigerate for at least 30 minutes.

4. Make the topping. Combine the water and chocolate in a small, heavy saucepan

over very low heat, stirring frequently until the chocolate has melted and is smooth. Remove from the heat and let cool to room temperature.

5. Using a chilled medium-size bowl and chilled beaters, beat the heavy cream in a large bowl until it holds soft peaks. Add the confectioners' sugar and vanilla and continue to beat until stiff but not grainy. Transfer about one-third of the whipped cream to a small bowl. Cover and refrigerate.

6. Add the cooled chocolate to the remaining whipped cream and fold it in until evenly blended. Spread evenly over the pie. Cover with loosely tented aluminum foil and refrigerate for at least 2 hours or overnight. Shortly before serving, pipe the remaining whipped cream decoratively over the pie. Slice and serve.

Recipe for Success

▶ **If you don't mind the extra step, pan-toast the pecans before adding them to the pie shell for a nuttier flavor. Be careful not to scorch them.**

▶ **To make an even thicker layer of caramel, use 35 caramels instead of 30.**

▶ **If you have extra bittersweet or semisweet chocolate on hand, you can add an easy garnish by grating some chocolate over the top of the pie. Use the small holes of a box grater to do so.**

Chocolate Custard–Cream Cheese Pie

With a thick, creamy texture and flavor something like that of a rich Italian *gelato*, this pie is a favorite among the legions of chocolate fans I've served it to. It involves a few bowls but no baking—aside from the crust—so it's relatively fast to assemble. The hard part is waiting for it to chill. It tastes wonderful as is or with a dollop of Kahlúa-flavored whipped cream.

MAKES 10 SERVINGS

1 recipe Graham Cracker Crumb Crust (page 51) or 1 large store-bought graham cracker crust

FILLING

2/3 cup granulated sugar

4 large egg yolks

1 cup semisweet chocolate chips

1 1/2 cups cold heavy or whipping cream

1/2 cup confectioners' sugar, sifted

Four 3-ounce packages full-fat cream cheese, softened (see Recipe for Success)

1 1/2 teaspoons vanilla extract

1 to 2 tablespoons Kahlúa or other coffee liqueur, to your taste

1.   Prepare the crust and press it into the bottom and up the side of a 9½-inch deep-dish pie pan. Refrigerate, prebake, and let cool as directed. Or simply use a store-bought crust, prebaking it according to the package directions and letting it cool. Refrigerate until ready to use.

2.   Combine the granulated sugar and egg yolks in the top of a double boiler set over, not in, barely simmering water. Cook, whisking virtually nonstop, until the mixture is thick and creamy, 8 to 9 minutes. Scrape the custard into a medium-size bowl and let cool, stirring occasionally. Wash and dry the top of the double boiler.

3.   Meanwhile, melt the chocolate chips in the top of the double boiler set over, not in, barely simmering water. Remove the insert from the heat and set the chocolate aside to cool. Stir briefly to smooth.

4.   Using a chilled medium-size bowl and chilled beaters, beat the cream with an electric mixer until it holds soft peaks. Add the confectioners' sugar and beat briefly until stiff but not grainy. Refrigerate.

5.   In a large bowl, using the mixer, beat the cream cheese until light and creamy, about 1 minute. Add the vanilla and custard and beat on medium-high speed until the mixture is light and creamy, 1 to 2 minutes. Add the chocolate and blend on low speed until evenly mixed. Add about half of the whipped cream and fold it into the filling until the mixture is evenly combined.

6.   Pour the filling into the chilled pie shell, smoothing the top with a spoon. Cover with loosely tented aluminum foil and refrigerate until the filling is good and firm, at least 4 hours or overnight.

7.   Just before serving, beat the Kahlúa into the remaining whipped cream just to combine. Serve the pie garnished with a dollop of the whipped cream.

Recipe for Success

▸   **Don't substitute nonfat cream cheese here. Low fat cream cheese is acceptable, but be aware that the pie won't set up as firmly. You can remedy this at least partly by transferring the pie from the refrigerator to the freezer 1 hour before serving.**

▸   **Another way to present this is by smoothing the whipped cream over the pie shortly before serving, then garnishing it with chopped nuts.**

Chocolate–Peanut Butter Pie

If you like peanut butter and chocolate in the same bite, this is your pie. My wife, Bev, loves this. She calls it "dangerously good."

MAKES 10 SERVINGS

1 recipe Chocolate Wafer Crumb Crust (page 54) or Oreo Crumb Crust (page 55)

FILLING

1¼ cups smooth peanut butter

One 8-ounce package full-fat or reduced-fat (Neufchâtel) cream cheese, softened

1 cup confectioners' sugar, sifted

1 tablespoon vanilla extract

1¼ cups cold heavy or whipping cream

GLAZE

¾ to 1 cup Warm Mocha Sauce (page 607)

1. Prepare the crust and press it into the bottom and up the side of a 9-inch standard pie pan. Refrigerate, prebake, and let cool as directed. Refrigerate until ready to use.

2. Cream the peanut butter, cream cheese, and ½ cup of the confectioners' sugar together in a large bowl with an electric mixer. Blend in the vanilla. Wash and dry the beaters.

3. Using a chilled medium-size bowl and chilled beaters, beat the heavy cream with the mixer until it holds soft peaks. Add the remaining ½ cup confectioners' sugar and continue to beat until stiff but not grainy. Add about one-third of the whipped cream to the peanut butter mixture. Blend with the mixer until smooth and creamy. Fold in the remaining whipped cream until the filling is smooth and evenly mixed. Spoon the filling into the chilled pie shell and smooth the top with a spoon. Cover with loosely tented aluminum foil and refrigerate for at least 3 hours or overnight.

4. When the filling is good and firm, prepare the mocha sauce. When the sauce has cooled somewhat but is still pourable, pour it over the pie, tilting the pie to spread the sauce up to the edge. Set aside to cool. Re-cover with loosely tented aluminum foil and refrigerate until ready to serve.

Recipe for Success

▶ When you cream the cream cheese and peanut butter, the mixture will remain somewhat grainy. Don't be concerned. It won't become smooth until the whipped cream is added.

▶ Be sure the mocha sauce isn't too warm when you pour it on the pie, or the top of the filling will melt, resulting in uneven coverage.

Chocolate Malted Pie

When I was a boy, malted milk balls were my favorite candy. This infatuation has, I believe, worn thin only once in my life, in the seventh grade, when Sister Therese appointed me clerk in charge of candy sales for St. Mary's grammar school. This job afforded me ample opportunity to pilfer well beyond the recommended daily dosage of malt balls, a trespass that Sister Therese made perfectly clear would land me in purgatory for the equivalent of several millennia. It was with no small delight, then, that I learned—in the course of working on this book— that malted milk balls and malted milk powder play important roles in a small but tasty genre of American pies. Typically, as in this pie, malted milk powder is added to a chocolate filling. (You can find malted milk powder at most supermarkets. If your market doesn't carry it, ask the store manager to order it for you.) Often, crushed malted milk balls also are included—here in a chocolate whipped cream topping, with more used for garnish. If it all sounds like a childhood fantasy, well, it is, and a delicious one at that.

MAKES 8 TO 10 SERVINGS

1 recipe Oreo Crumb Crust (page 55) or 1 store-bought Oreo crust

FILLING
1 1/4 cups heavy or whipping cream
8 ounces semisweet chocolate, coarsely chopped

1/3 cup malted milk powder
1 teaspoon vanilla extract

TOPPING
3/4 cup cold heavy or whipping cream
1 1/2 cups malted milk balls

1. Prepare the crust and press it into the bottom and up the side of a 9-inch standard pie pan. Refrigerate, prebake, and let cool as directed. Or simply use a store-bought crust, prebaking it according to the package directions and letting it cool. Refrigerate until ready to use.

2. Heat the cream in a medium-size saucepan, preferably nonstick, over medium-high heat until it shimmers, 2 to 3 minutes. Remove from the heat and add the chocolate. Let the mixture stand for 5 minutes, tilting the pan from time to time so the hot cream runs over the chocolate. Add the malted milk powder and vanilla and whisk until smooth. Set aside to cool. When the mixture thickens slightly but is still pourable, pour about two-thirds of it into the chilled pie shell. Let cool thoroughly, then refrigerate for at least 2 hours, until fairly firm. Reserve the remaining chocolate at room temperature.

3. Meanwhile, make the topping. Using a chilled medium-size bowl and chilled beaters, beat the cream with an electric mixer until it holds soft peaks. Add the remaining chocolate and continue to beat until the mixture is firm and full-bodied. Cover and refrigerate until ready to use.

4. Coarsely crush about half of the malted milk balls and gently press them into the chilled filling. Spread the chocolate whipped cream over the filling and garnish with the remaining whole malted milk balls. Cover with loosely tented aluminum foil and refrigerate until ready to serve.

Recipe for Success

▶ **This pie can be made a couple of days ahead, in large part because adding the chocolate to the whipped cream helps keep the topping quite stable. This isn't usually the case with whipped cream–topped pies.**

▶ **Once you've added the chocolate to the whipped cream, it will quickly firm up. As soon as it becomes firm and full-bodied, stop beating, or it will lose its smoothness.**

Ultimate Rocky Road Pie

Everyone loves rocky road candy—chocolate chock-full of marshmallows and nuts. This combination works pretty darn well in a pie, too, especially when you add a topping of lightly broiled marshmallow crème. The chocolate base is a combination of coarsely chopped semisweet chocolate, chocolate chips, and vanilla stirred together with hot cream. As the mixture cools and thickens, mini marshmallows and walnuts are folded in, then the mixture is spread in a graham cracker crust. The pie is chilled, then shortly before serving spread with marshmallow crème and broiled. It sounds fancy, and it is impressive, but it's also a real cinch to pull together. It's a good keeper, too. You can make the pie two or three days ahead, if you like, but don't add the marshmallow crème until just before serving.

MAKES 10 TO 12 SERVINGS

1 recipe Graham Cracker Crumb Crust (page 51) or 1 large store-bought graham cracker crust

FILLING

2 cups heavy or whipping cream

8 ounces semisweet chocolate, coarsely chopped

1 cup semisweet chocolate chips

1¹/₂ teaspoons vanilla extract

1¹/₂ cups mini marshmallows

1¹/₄ cups coarsely chopped walnuts

TOPPING

One 7-ounce jar (2 cups) marshmallow crème

1. Prepare the crust and press it into the bottom and up the side of a 9¹/₂-inch deep-dish pie pan. Refrigerate, prebake, and let cool as directed. Or simply use a store-bought crust, prebaking it according to the package directions and letting it cool. Refrigerate until ready to use.

2. Heat the cream in a medium-size saucepan, preferably nonstick, over medium-high heat until very hot but not boiling, about 3 minutes. Remove from the heat and add the chopped chocolate and chocolate chips. Let stand for 5 minutes, then whisk until smooth. Scrape the mixture into a medium-size bowl and stir in the vanilla. Let stand, stirring occasionally, until it has cooled and become quite firm but still pourable, about 1 hour. (You can put the bowl in the refrigerator, if you like, to hasten the process.)

3. Stir in the marshmallows and walnuts until everything is well coated. Scrape the mixture into the chilled pie shell and smooth with a spoon. Cover with loosely tented aluminum foil and refrigerate for at least 6 hours or overnight.

4. About 30 minutes before serving, spoon the marshmallow crème over the top of the pie. Moisten your fingertips under running water, then spread the mixture with your fingers. Push it right up to the edge so none of the chocolate is exposed. Place the pie in the freezer for about 20 minutes.

5. Preheat the broiler. Slide the pie into a second pie pan to protect it from the heat of the oven. Very briefly run the pie under the broiler to brown the top. It will take only seconds, so don't take your eyes off it. Remove the pie from the outer pan and serve right away.

Recipe for Success

▸ Waiting for the chocolate mixture to thicken somewhat before it goes into the pie shell is an important step. If the mixture is thin, the solids will rise to the top.

▸ Don't walk away from the pie while it's under the broiler. It can get too dark in seconds. And don't try to broil it too close to the heat source. A little extra room usually yields a more evenly browned result.

Mocha Ricotta Mousse Pie with Warm Mocha Sauce

This is one of my favorite refrigerator pies—a chocolate-coffee ricotta cream lightened with whipped cream and flavored with vanilla and almond extracts. Not only is it simple to prepare, but even with the graham cracker crust, it's sophisticated enough to serve when you're entertaining.

MAKES 8 SERVINGS

1 recipe Graham Cracker Crumb Crust (page 51) or 1 small store-bought graham cracker crust

FILLING

1/2 cup sugar

1 tablespoon instant espresso or coffee granules

2 ounces bittersweet or semisweet chocolate (see Recipe for Success)

One 15- to 16-ounce container whole-milk or part-skim ricotta cheese

2 tablespoons milk

1 envelope unflavored gelatin

3 tablespoons cold water

3/4 cup cold heavy or whipping cream

1/2 teaspoon vanilla extract

1/4 teaspoon almond extract

GARNISH

Warm Mocha Sauce (page 607)

1. Prepare the crust and press it into the bottom and up the side of a 9-inch standard pie pan. Refrigerate, prebake, and let cool as directed. Or simply prebake the store-bought crust according to the package directions and let cool. Refrigerate until ready to use.

2. Put the sugar, coffee, and chocolate in a food processor. Pulse to chop the chocolate, then let the processor run continuously until the mixture is very finely ground, 30 to 45 seconds. Expect to see tiny flecks of chocolate throughout. Add the ricotta and milk. Process again, nonstop, until the mixture is very smooth, 30 to 45 seconds. Again, expect to see tiny flecks of chocolate.

3. Put the gelatin in a small bowl and pour the water over it. Let it soften for 5 minutes, then either heat it in the microwave for 20 seconds on high power or transfer it to a very small saucepan and warm over low heat, stirring. In either case, it should be liquefied. Let cool for 2 to 3 minutes, then add to the ricotta mixture. Puree for several seconds to combine.

4. Using a chilled medium-size bowl and chilled beaters, beat the cream with an electric mixer until firm but not grainy. Beat in the vanilla and almond extract. Add the ricotta mixture and beat on low speed, scraping down the bowl, until uniformly mixed. Spoon the filling into the chilled pie shell and smooth the top. Cover with loosely tented aluminum foil and refrigerate for at least 3 hours or overnight. Serve garnished with mocha sauce.

Recipe for Success

▶ Much as I prefer the superior flavor of bittersweet chocolate in this pie, it's not worth a special trip to the store if you have all the other ingredients on hand and only semisweet chocolate. To get the best results when you grind the chocolate, chop it coarsely, then put it in the refrigerator for 5 to 10 minutes before putting it in the food processor. The cold will make the chocolate more brittle, and thus it will chop more finely.

Pick-Your-Own Triple-Strawberry Cream Pie

When my four children were young, I often used to take them to a local pick-your-own farm, where I would gather boxes of ripe strawberries and they would manage to do everything but. What they didn't eat straight off the vine, they'd smoosh into their shirts, toss at their siblings, or simply squeeze between their fingers, because these things feel rather interesting when you're 20 months old. (The farm closed its operation to the public at some point, but I like to think we weren't the sole reason.) Those berries were unsurpassed for making strawberry shortcake, fresh strawberry ice cream, and a few other desserts—such as this pie—where only the best ripe berries will do. Here we have three distinct strawberry layers: a cooked, thickened strawberry sauce, a layer of fresh berries, and a topping of freshly whipped cream blended with some of the sauce. It's a little bit of work to assemble, though certainly easy enough to pull off. Most of the elements can be prepared ahead and the pie put together at the last minute. Think of this as a special treat for when you have friends over during the summer.

MAKES 8 TO 10 SERVINGS

1 recipe Graham Cracker Crumb Crust (page 51) or Chocolate Wafer Crumb Crust (page 54), or 1 large store-bought graham cracker crust

FILLING

1 1/2 quarts fresh strawberries, hulled

1/3 cup granulated sugar

1 teaspoon grated lemon zest

1 1/2 tablespoons cornstarch

1 1/2 cups cold heavy or whipping cream

1/4 cup confectioners' sugar

1. Prepare the crust and press it into the bottom and up the side of a 9 1/2-inch deep-dish pie pan. Refrigerate, prebake, and let cool as directed. Or simply use a store-bought crust, prebaking it according to the package directions and letting it cool. Refrigerate until ready to use.

2. Halve half of the strawberries and put them in a large bowl. Stir in 1 tablespoon of the granulated sugar and the lemon zest, then set aside for 10 minutes to juice.

3. Using a large fork or potato masher, crush the juiced berries just enough to make a coarse puree. Transfer to a medium-size nonreactive or nonstick saucepan. In a small bowl, mix the remaining granulated sugar with the cornstarch. Stir the mixture into the puree and gradually bring to a boil over medium heat. Cook, stirring nearly nonstop, until the mixture gently boils, thickens, and becomes translucent, about 1 minute after it starts to sputter. Scrape the sauce into a bowl and let cool thoroughly. Cover with plastic wrap and refrigerate until cold, at least 1 hour. (The sauce can be made up to 2 days ahead.)

4. Using a chilled medium-size bowl and chilled beaters, whip the cream with an electric mixer until it begins to thicken and hold soft peaks. Add the confectioners' sugar and continue to beat until stiff but not grainy. Fold in 1/2 cup of the strawberry sauce.

5. To assemble the pie, shortly before serving spread the remaining strawberry sauce over the bottom of the chilled pie shell. Halve the remaining strawberries—or quarter them if they're very large—and arrange the berry pieces in a tight layer on top of the sauce. If you run out of room, chop the remaining berries and strew them over the larger pieces. Spoon the strawberry whipped cream on top and smooth with the spoon. Serve immediately, or put the pie in the freezer for up to 10 minutes (no longer) and serve as soon as possible.

Recipe for Success

▶ Given that you'll be making this pie in the summer, likely during the hottest days of July or August, it's particularly important that you take the time to chill the bowl and beaters used for whipping the cream. Summer's heat can make whipping cream a relatively slow, sluggish process, and cream whipped under less than ideal circumstances is never quite as sturdy and stable as it could be.

▸ Don't slice the remaining berries until instructed, right before assembling the pie. Ripe summer berries can be very juicy, and you want the juice to stay in the berries as much as possible, not leak into the pie.

Creamy White Chocolate–Strawberry Pie

This is a great pie to make during strawberry season, when you can select beautifully ripe, same-size berries to garnish the top. Underneath is a layer of blended cream cheese, yogurt, and white chocolate, with a graham cracker crust. On top of the berries, a drizzle of white chocolate hints at what's to come. This is a relatively simple pie to pull off, even more so if you use a store-bought graham cracker crust.

MAKES 8 SERVINGS

1 recipe Graham Cracker Crumb Crust (page 51) or 1 small store-bought graham cracker crust

FILLING

3/4 cup white chocolate chips

One 8-ounce package full-fat or reduced-fat (Neufchâtel) cream cheese, softened

5 tablespoons sugar

1/3 cup plain or vanilla full-fat or lowfat yogurt

1 quart fresh strawberries, rinsed and patted dry

GARNISH

1/2 cup white chocolate chips

1. Prepare the crust and press it into the bottom and up the side of 9-inch standard pie pan. Refrigerate, prebake, and let cool as directed. Or simply prebake the store-bought crust according to the package directions and let cool. Refrigerate until ready to use.

2. Put the white chocolate chips in the top of a double boiler set over, not in, hot water. When the chips are shiny, 7 to 10 minutes, stir well until smooth. Remove the insert from the double boiler and set aside to cool.

3. Using an electric mixer, beat the cream cheese in a medium-size bowl on high speed until light and fluffy, about 4 minutes. Gradually add the sugar and continue to beat.

When the white chocolate has cooled to body temperature, add it to the cream cheese and blend until evenly mixed. Add the yogurt and blend until smooth.

4. Spoon the cream cheese mixture into the chilled pie shell and smooth it with a spoon. Cover with loosely tented aluminum foil and refrigerate for at least 2 hours or overnight.

5. Select as many perfect same-size berries as you can find. Hull them and take a very thin slice off the stem end. Arrange the berries in a single neat, compact layer on top of the filling, cut sides facing down. Refrigerate.

6. To make the garnish, melt the white chocolate chips as you did in step 2. Let cool, then spoon into a pastry bag fitted with a fine tip. Pipe a thin drizzle of white chocolate over the pie in any appealing pattern you choose—a jaunty zigzag or a spiral, perhaps. Slice the pie with a sharp serrated knife to cut cleanly through the berries and serve. Or cover with loosely tented aluminum foil and refrigerate until serving, preferably less than 1 hour.

Recipe for Success

▶ If you don't have a pastry bag, you can always spoon the melted white chocolate into a plastic sandwich bag and push the chocolate to one corner. With sharp scissors, snip a very small hole in the corner and, voilà!—instant pastry bag.

▶ If you'd rather apply an attractive glaze to the top of the strawberries instead of using the white chocolate, melt 3 tablespoons red currant jelly in a small saucepan, whisking to smooth. Let cool briefly, then brush the jelly over the berries with a small pastry brush.

Strawberry-Peach Icebox Pie

Cooked peaches folded with fresh strawberries make a great combination in this summer fruit pie. Like any icebox pie, it requires no baking (aside from the pastry) and just a few minutes of stovetop work to simmer and thicken the peaches. To lighten the load even more, you can use a store-bought graham cracker crust instead of a pastry. Plan on at least three hours to chill the pie. It's best eaten the same day it is made, because the longer the fresh strawberries sit, the more moisture they put off, resulting in a looser filling.

MAKES 8 SERVINGS

1 recipe Basic Shortening Pie Pastry, Single Crust (page 30), refrigerated, or 1 store-bought refrigerated pie pastry or graham cracker crust

FILLING

4 cups peeled and pitted ripe peaches, cut into bite-size chunks

1/2 cup granulated sugar

1 teaspoon grated lemon zest

1/2 cup lemonade

1/4 cup cornstarch

2 cups hulled and coarsely chopped fresh strawberries

TOPPING

1 1/4 cups cold heavy or whipping cream

3 tablespoons confectioners' sugar, sifted

1/2 teaspoon vanilla extract

Ground nutmeg

1. If you haven't already, prepare the pastry and refrigerate until firm enough to roll, about 1 hour.

2. On a sheet of lightly floured waxed paper, roll the pastry into a 12-inch circle with a floured rolling pin. Invert the pastry over a 9-inch standard pie pan, center, and peel off the paper. Tuck the pastry into the pan, without stretching it, and sculpt the edge into an upstanding ridge. Place in the freezer for 15 minutes, then fully prebake and let cool according to the instructions on page 16. If you're using the refrigerated pastry, simply line the pan, prebake according to the package instructions, and let cool.

3. Combine the peaches, granulated sugar, and lemon zest in a medium-size nonreactive saucepan, preferably nonstick. Cover, place over medium heat, and bring to a low boil, stirring often, about 5 minutes. Reduce the heat to medium-low and simmer until quite juicy, 3 to 4 minutes. Blend the lemonade and cornstarch in a small bowl and add to the peaches. Cook at a low boil, stirring, for 2 1/2 to 3 minutes. The mixture should be rather thick. Scrape into a shallow bowl and let cool to room temperature.

4. Fold the strawberries into the peach mixture. Scrape the filling into the cooled pie shell, smoothing the top with a spoon. Cover with plastic wrap and refrigerate for at least 3 hours.

5. Shortly before serving, make the topping. Using a chilled medium-size bowl and chilled beaters, beat the cream with an electric mixer until it holds soft peaks. Add the confectioners' sugar and vanilla and continue to beat until stiff but not grainy. Spread the cream on top of the fruit, then slice and serve, dusting each slice with nutmeg.

Recipe for Success

▶ Be sure not to underbake the crust. In a case such as this—where cooled filling sits on a baked pastry—the crust should be as crisp as possible to guard against sogginess.

▶ This method of making a pie—folding fresh fruit into cooked—allows the possibility of many variations. You could also fold in fresh blackberries, blueberries, or raspberries. If you use raspberries, fold very gently, as they're quite fragile.

Lemon-Raspberry Icebox Pie with an Oreo Crust

A center of fresh red raspberries, a dark chocolate crust, and a creamy filling and topping—this pie has some great contrasting colors and strikes a handsome profile. It takes just five minutes to blend the filling and get it into the crust. You have to wait a while for the filling to chill and firm up, then add a layer of fresh raspberries and top with whipped cream. Try this wonderful summer pie when the raspberries are fresh, local, and perfectly sweet-tart.

MAKES 8 SERVINGS

1 recipe Oreo Crumb Crust (page 55) or 1 store-bought Oreo crust

FILLING

Two 3-ounce packages full-fat cream cheese, softened

One 14-ounce can sweetened condensed milk

$^1/_3$ cup fresh lemon juice

1 teaspoon vanilla extract

RASPBERRIES AND TOPPING

1 pint fresh raspberries, plus more for garnish (optional)

1 cup cold heavy or whipping cream

2 tablespoons confectioners' sugar, sifted

1. Prepare the crust and press it into the bottom and up the side of a 9-inch standard pie pan. Refrigerate, prebake, and let cool as directed. Or simply use a store-bought crust, prebaking it according to the package directions and letting it cool. Refrigerate until needed.

2. In a large bowl, beat the cream cheese and condensed milk together with an electric mixer on medium-high speed until smooth and fluffy, about 2 minutes. Add the lemon juice and continue to beat for 1 minute more. Blend in the vanilla. Scrape the filling into the chilled pie shell and smooth the top with the back of a spoon. Cover with loosely tented aluminum foil and refrigerate for at least 2 hours, preferably longer (up to overnight).

3. Shortly before serving, scatter the raspberries evenly over the pie. Using a chilled medium-size bowl and chilled beaters, beat the cream until it holds soft peaks. Add the confectioners' sugar and continue to beat until stiff but not grainy. Spoon over the raspberries, smoothing it with a spoon. Slice and serve right away, garnishing each slice, if you like, with additional raspberries.

Recipe for Success

▶ I really like the Oreo crust here, for the contrasting flavor and color. But you also could use a small store-bought graham cracker crust.

▶ It's preferable that you don't rinse the raspberries before using them. Water is bound to end up in the cavities, and then on your pie. If you must rinse them, drain them, upside down, on paper towels.

▶ Blueberries, blackberries, or sliced strawberries also will work well here.

Berry Semifreddo Pie

One of my favorite books on Italian desserts is Michele Scicolone's delightful *La Dolce Vita* (William Morrow, 1993). She devotes an entire chapter to *semifreddi*, a word, she explains, that Italians use to describe many different types of cold or frozen desserts. I'm not sure whether a real Italian would consider this pie a true *semifreddo*, but it was certainly inspired by the genre. Basically, I blend together mascarpone cheese, whipped cream, and crème anglaise, then pour the mixture into a graham cracker crust. It is first refrigerated, until good and cold, then placed in the freezer until the mixture is firm enough not to ooze all over creation when the pie is cut. Just before serving, I scatter fresh berries over the top and dust with confectioners' sugar. It's very simple, but you need to do some advance work so you have the cold crème anglaise on hand before you begin.

MAKES 8 TO 10 SERVINGS

1 recipe Graham Cracker Crumb Crust (page 51) or 1 large store-bought graham cracker crust

FILLING

8 ounces (about 1 cup) mascarpone cheese, at room temperature

3/4 cup cold heavy or whipping cream

1/4 cup confectioners' sugar, sifted

1 cup cold Crème Anglaise (page 606)

1/2 teaspoon vanilla extract

BERRIES AND GARNISH

1 1/2 pints fresh raspberries, blackberries, blueberries (picked over for stems), or other berries, alone or in combination

Confectioners' sugar

1. Prepare the crust and press it into the bottom and up the side of a 9 1/2-inch deep-dish pie pan. Refrigerate, prebake, and let cool as directed. Or simply use a store-bought crust, prebaking it according to the package directions and letting it cool. Refrigerate until needed.

2. In a large bowl, stir the mascarpone to smooth. Set aside.

3. Using a chilled medium-size bowl and chilled beaters, beat the cream with an electric mixer until it holds soft peaks. Beat in the confectioners' sugar, 2 tablespoons at a time, until stiff but not grainy. Fold half of the whipped cream into the mascarpone, then fold in the other half. Fold half of the crème anglaise and the vanilla into the mascarpone mixture. Add the remaining crème anglaise and fold again, until evenly blended. If the mixture appears slightly curdled, gently whisk to smooth. Pour the filling into the chilled pie shell, smoothing the top with a spoon. Cover with loosely tented aluminum foil and refrigerate for at least 3 hours or overnight.

4. One and a half to 2 hours before serving, transfer the pie to the freezer and freeze until the filling it is still soft enough to ooze but portions of it are starting to freeze more solidly. To garnish, scatter the berries over the filling and dust with the confectioners' sugar. Serve right away.

Recipe for Success

▶ The key issue here is the timing. You want to serve this pie while the filling is still oozing, but not too much. To serve it successfully, you must be willing to fuss over it, checking it every 10 minutes or so when it is nearly time to serve.

▶ If the slices are a little ragged—which is bound to happen when you're cutting into fresh berries and a semisoft filling—don't worry. After your guests have taken one bite, all will be forgiven.

▶ Leftovers should be kept in the refrigerator. You won't be able to refreeze the pie, because of the berries, so expect the filling to be a little runny.

Opal's Banana-Blueberry Icebox Pie

Marian Clark's entertaining *Route 66 Cookbook* (Council Oaks Books, 2000) is an engaging armchair guide to the comfort food served up along America's historic and storied Route 66, the 2,400-mile artery stretching from Chicago to Santa Monica, California. Clark, who has traveled the route extensively with her husband, Ken, is a keen chronicler of its restaurants and the everyday hero-cooks who serve up unpretentious fare.

As you might imagine, one meets many fine pies and pie makers along Route 66. Opal Lyons, now retired, owned the Lyons Café in Bristow, Oklahoma. Opal's pie-making prowess, says Clark, was well-known throughout the area, and this pie was one of her specialties. It's a simple, tasty, straightforward pie, with layers of sliced bananas, thickened blueberries, and whipped cream—a homey sort of pie that a weary traveler would have loved to cozy up to at a stop along the road.

MAKES 8 TO 10 SERVINGS

1 recipe Basic Shortening Pie Pastry, Single Crust (page 30) or Basic Flaky Pie Pastry, Single Crust (page 31), refrigerated

FILLING

3/4 cup sugar

1/4 cup all-purpose flour

1/8 teaspoon salt

One 14-ounce can Wyman's blueberries in water, with their juice

2 teaspoons fresh lemon juice

3 large ripe bananas

TOPPING

1 1/2 cups cold heavy or whipping cream

5 tablespoons sugar

1.   If you haven't already, prepare the pastry and refrigerate until firm enough to roll, about 1 hour.

2.   On a sheet of lightly floured waxed paper, roll the pastry into a 13-inch circle with a floured rolling pin. Invert over a 9 1/2-inch deep-dish pie pan, center, and peel off the paper. Tuck the pastry into the pan, without stretching it, and sculpt the edge so it is even with the rim. Place in the freezer for 15 minutes, then partially prebake and let cool according to the instructions on page 16. Refrigerate until ready to use.

3.   Combine the sugar, flour, salt, and blueberries (with their juice) in a medium-size nonreactive saucepan. Place over medium heat and cook, stirring constantly, until the blueberries thicken considerably, 4 to 5 minutes. Remove from the heat and stir in the lemon juice. Set the pan aside on a wire rack and let cool, stirring occasionally.

4.   Slice the bananas over the chilled pie shell and arrange them in an even layer. Spoon the blueberries over the bananas, spreading them evenly. Cover with loosely tented aluminum foil and refrigerate for at least 15 minutes or up to several hours.

5.   Just before serving, make the topping. Using a chilled medium-size bowl and chilled beaters, beat the cream with an electric mixer until it holds soft peaks. Add the sugar and continue to beat until stiff but not grainy. Spread the topping over the pie. Slice and serve right away, or cover with loosely tented aluminum foil and refrigerate. This pie is best served within 3 to 4 hours.

Recipe for Success

▶   **Opal's original recipe is divided between two 8-inch pie pans. However, the same amount of filling fits beautifully into a 9 1/2-inch deep-dish pie pan, the way I've done it here. You can do it either way. If you're making 2 smaller pies, use 2 cups heavy cream for the topping instead of 1 1/2.**

- You can slice and serve the pie right after it is assembled—or soon after the blueberries and bananas go into the pie shell—but the blueberry filling will be a little firmer if you refrigerate the pie for a few hours first.

- This pie is best eaten the same day it is made, when the bananas have a freshly sliced texture.

Sweet-Tart Lemon Cloud Icebox Pie

This light-as-a-cloud pie gets its cloud-ness from whipped cream and its flavor from lemon curd, a thick, intense lemony spread that's much more common in Britain than here in the States. You can buy lemon curd, but for the texture and quantity needed for this pie, it's better to make it yourself—a process that will have you puttering over a burner for about 15 minutes, happily inhaling the lovely lemon fragrance rising up from the pan. So don't make this if you're in a hurry or feeling stressed. Once the lemon curd has cooled, then chilled, it's blended with the whipped cream and spooned into a prebaked cookie crust or other fully baked crust of your choice. This is a real lemon lover's pie, with a slight tartness that's tempered by a last-minute dusting of confectioners' sugar.

MAKES 8 TO 10 SERVINGS

1 recipe Vanilla Wafer Crumb Crust (page 52)

FILLING

1 large egg

5 large egg yolks

1 cup granulated sugar

$2/3$ cup fresh lemon juice

1 teaspoon finely grated lemon zest

$1/2$ cup (1 stick) unsalted butter, cut into $1/2$-inch pieces

1 cup cold heavy or whipping cream

$1/3$ cup confectioners' sugar, sifted

$1/4$ teaspoon vanilla extract

GARNISH

Confectioners' sugar

1. Prepare the crust and press into the bottom and up the side of a $9^{1}/_2$-inch deep-dish pie pan. Refrigerate, prebake, and let cool as directed. Refrigerate until ready to use.

2. Place enough water in the bottom of a double boiler to reach almost to the bottom of the insert; bring to an active simmer. Place the egg and egg yolks in the top of the double boiler and immediately start to whisk, gradually adding the granulated sugar, lemon juice, and lemon zest. With the water at an active simmer, continue to whisk until the mixture is

noticeably thicker, 12 to 14 minutes. It should be thick enough that when you stick a teaspoon in it and blow on the spoon for several seconds, the mixture pretty much stays on the spoon when you turn it upside down. Whisk in the butter, one piece at a time, adding each piece only after the previous one has melted. After the last piece of butter has melted, continue to whisk and cook for 1 minute. Scrape the curd into a medium-size bowl. Press a piece of plastic wrap directly over the surface so the curd doesn't form a skin. Let cool to room temperature, then refrigerate for at least 2 hours.

3.   At least 2 hours before serving, make the topping. Using a chilled medium-size bowl and chilled beaters, beat the cream with an electric mixer until it holds soft peaks. Add the confectioners' sugar and vanilla and continue to beat until stiff but not grainy. Do not overbeat. Spoon two-thirds of the lemon curd into the cream and beat on low speed just until uniformly mixed.

4.   Spread the remaining one-third lemon curd evenly in the chilled pie shell and slightly up the sides. Spoon the lemon whipped cream over the curd, spreading it evenly. Cover the pie with loosely tented aluminum foil and refrigerate for at least 2 hours. Dust the top of the pie generously with confectioners' sugar and serve.

Recipe for Success

▶ **Don't be concerned if the lemon curd forms a frothy head as you whisk it during the initial liquid phase. This is not the thickened texture you're hoping to achieve, and that froth will disappear as the curd thickens. The texture of the curd, after 12 to 14 minutes, will be more like that of heavy cream. If you're in doubt, leave it on the heat for another couple of minutes, but do continue to whisk the mixture nearly nonstop.**

10-Minute Lemon Meringue Icebox Pie

You can't make a lemon meringue pie from scratch in 10 minutes, but you can make an embarrassingly good facsimile. The price of admission? A jar of lemon curd and a store-bought graham cracker crust. While the crust prebakes, you start whipping up a fresh meringue topping. Run it all under the broiler, and you're good to go. For best dramatic effect, have the rest of the pie ready, then make the meringue at the last minute, offstage, where your ingredients and utensils await. (Everyone will wonder what heavenly creation those kitchen noises portend.) Then waltz back in, the very picture of composure, carrying a fresh-from-the-oven lemon meringue pie. Impressive stuff.

MAKES 8 SERVINGS

1 small store-bought graham cracker crust

FILLING

One 16-ounce jar (1 1/2 cups) lemon curd

MERINGUE

4 large egg whites, at room temperature

1/4 teaspoon cream of tartar

Pinch of salt

1/2 cup superfine sugar

1 teaspoon vanilla extract

1. Prebake the crust according to the package directions and set aside on a wire rack to let cool thoroughly.

2. Place the lemon curd in a small bowl and stir until smooth. Spread evenly in the cooled pie shell. Set aside.

3. When you're ready to make the meringue, preheat the broiler. Using a large bowl, beat the egg whites with an electric mixer on medium-high speed until they hold soft peaks. Beat in the cream of tartar and salt. Gradually add the sugar, beating on high speed until the meringue is thick, glossy, and voluminous. Beat in the vanilla. Stick a rubber spatula into the meringue to help judge the consistency. It should be soft but firm, though not dry.

4. Smooth the meringue evenly over the pie. Place the pie on a baking sheet and run it under the broiler just until golden brown. Slice and serve immediately.

Recipe for Success

▶ Usually, store-bought graham cracker crusts are considered "ready to eat," meaning that the choice to prebake the crust is up to the cook. In most cases, including here, I recommend doing so: you get a slightly more brittle crust that way—one that cuts cleaner, is less crumbly, and is easier to serve.

▶ This makes a smallish pie with 8 modest servings. If you want to bake a bigger version to serve 10 to 12, use the larger size store-bought crust and twice as much lemon curd. For the meringue, use 5 egg whites, increase the sugar to $9^{1}/_{2}$ tablespoons and the salt to 2 pinches, and add a drop or two more of vanilla.

Banoffee Pie

It's always a bit of a thrill to discover new pies. Sometimes you like a pie just because of the name, as I knew I would with this one. Banoffee is not a place: it's a combination of bananas and toffee, layered in a pastry crust with a whipped cream topping. I'd never heard of it until I picked up the recently published *King Arthur Flour Baker's Companion* (Countryman Press, 2003). Apparently, banoffee pie is a longtime favorite in England and a specialty of the Hungry Monk restaurant in Levington, East Sussex, where it originated. In place of the traditional boiled sweetened condensed milk, the King Arthur version uses prepared *dulce de leche*, a thick caramel sauce you can find in most grocery stores. I tried the recipe and found it not only simple to make but delicious, as I know you will, too. Here, with King Arthur's gracious permission, is the recipe.

MAKES 8 TO 10 SERVINGS

1 recipe Basic Flaky Pie Pastry, Single Crust (page 31), refrigerated

FILLING
$^{2}/_{3}$ to $1^{1}/_{3}$ cups prepared *dulce de leche*

3 medium-size ripe bananas

1 cup cold heavy or whipping cream

2 tablespoons sugar, preferably superfine

$^{1}/_{2}$ teaspoon instant espresso or coffee granules

1. If you haven't already, prepare the pastry and refrigerate until firm enough to roll, about 1 hour.

2. On a sheet of lightly floured waxed paper, roll the pastry into a 12-inch circle with a floured rolling pin. Invert over a 9-inch standard pie pan, center, and peel off the paper. Tuck the pastry into the pan, without stretching it, and sculpt the edge into an upstanding ridge. Place in the freezer for 15 minutes, then fully prebake and let cool according to the directions on page 16.

3. To assemble the pie, spread the *dulce de leche* over the bottom of the cooled crust. The greater amount will give you a very sweet dessert; the lesser amount, or something in between, may be more to your taste. Halve the bananas lengthwise. Lay them on top of the filling, starting in the center and working outward, cutting the bananas to fit as necessary. Don't worry if you can't get them to fit seamlessly; just do the best that you can.

4. Combine the cream, sugar, and coffee in a chilled large bowl. Using chilled beaters and an electric mixer, whip until stiff but not grainy. Spoon the whipped cream over the bananas. Serve immediately, or cover with loosely tented aluminum foil and refrigerate for up to 30 minutes before serving.

Recipe for Success

- Make sure you do a thorough job of prebaking the crust. You want it nice and crisp for good textural contrast with the soft filling.

- If for some reason you can't find *dulce de leche*, substitute a thick caramel sauce. It won't be as authentic, but it will still be quite excellent.

Millionaire Pie

I've not been able to discover the origin of millionaire pie, but from the little I can piece together, it is something of a classic of the no-bake pie genre, dating back to at least the 1950s. I've also seen several Texas references attached to the title, so perhaps it was fancied by some well-heeled Texas oilman. In any event, recipes for millionaire pie abound, most patterned after the basic recipe given here, leading me to believe that it may have been first introduced by a large food company and widely circulated. The filling is a creamy concoction of sweetened cream cheese, pineapple, pecans, and coconut, lightened with prepared whipped topping (such as Cool Whip). I rarely use whipped topping, since I much prefer fresh whipped cream, but I make an exception here, since the original intent of the pie clearly was speed of preparation. The pie tastes great, and if you have young children who want to "bake a pie," this is a good recipe to get them started.

MAKES 8 SERVINGS

1 small store-bought graham cracker crust

FILLING

One 8-ounce package full-fat cream cheese, softened

1/2 cup sugar

One 8-ounce can crushed pineapple, drained but juice reserved

1 cup sweetened flaked coconut

1 cup chopped pecans

One 12-ounce container whipped topping

1. Prebake the graham cracker crust according to the package directions and set aside on a wire rack to let cool thoroughly.

2. In a medium-size bowl, beat the cream cheese with an electric mixer on high speed for 3 minutes, gradually adding the sugar. Stir in the pineapple, 2 tablespoons of the reserved juice, the coconut, and pecans. Add about two-thirds of the whipped topping, folding it in until well combined. Spoon the filling into the cooled pie shell, smoothing the top with a spoon. Cover with loosely tented aluminum foil and refrigerate for at least 3 hours or overnight. Serve garnished with the remaining whipped topping, if desired.

Recipe for Success

▶ If this pie sounds good but you'd rather use fresh whipped cream, beat 1 cup cold heavy or whipping cream to soft peaks. Beat in 3 tablespoons confectioners' sugar and beat until stiff but not grainy. Fold into the filling in place of the whipped topping.

▶ If you wish, arrange pecan halves around the edge of the pie for garnish.

Sweet Avocado–Cream Cheese Pie

An avocado pie might sound like a bad joke perpetrated by avocado marketing types, but this is better than you might expect. The avocado flesh takes well to the rich cream cheese and sweetened condensed milk. A little lemon and lime juice gives the pie a citrusy lilt, and the pale green color will remind you of Key lime pie. It's made quickly, with a blender and an electric mixer, and there's no baking involved. A few hours in the fridge, and it's firm enough to serve. This pie was inspired by a prizewinning recipe from the 17th Annual California Avocado Festival in 2003.

MAKES 10 SERVINGS

1 recipe Graham Cracker Crumb Crust (page 51) or 1 large store-bought graham cracker crust

FILLING

1 large ripe avocado, halved and pitted

One 14-ounce can sweetened condensed milk

2 tablespoons fresh lemon juice

2 tablespoons fresh lime juice

Four 3-ounce packages full-fat cream cheese, softened

1/3 cup confectioners' sugar, sifted

GARNISH

Fresh Whipped Cream (page 605)

1. Prepare the crust and press it into the bottom and up the side of a 9½-inch deep-dish pie pan. Refrigerate, prebake, and let cool as directed. Or simply use a store-bought crust, prebaking it according to the package directions and letting it cool. Refrigerate until ready to use.

2. Spoon the avocado flesh into a blender. Add the condensed milk, lemon juice, and lime juice and process until smooth. Set aside.

3. In a large bowl, beat the cream cheese with an electric mixer until smooth and fluffy. Beat in the confectioners' sugar, then blend in the avocado mixture, adding it about one-third at a time. When the mixture is smooth, pour into the chilled pie shell, smoothing the top with a spoon. Cover with loosely tented aluminum foil and refrigerate until firm, about 6 hours or overnight. Serve garnished with whipped cream.

Recipe for Success

▶ This pie is, admittedly, best reserved for a group of adventurous and willing friends and associates. A tailgate party or islands bash would be the ideal venue; the monthly meeting of the Junior League, somewhat less so.

▶ The avocado needs to be nearly perfect to make this pie: good and ripe, without any dark spots and certainly not stringy.

I don't know anyone who doesn't like an ice cream pie. And if assembling one

entails few of the skills required for baking a fruit or other "real" pie, the

genre's near universal popularity is more than enough reason to include a

short chapter on the subject here. Short because these pies are so easy to

make that you barely need a recipe. And once you've seen how it's done,

Inviting Ice Cream
and Other Freezer Pies

you'll quickly be off and running, creating signature ice cream pies for all

sorts of occasions. • At its most basic, an ice cream pie is little more than a

crust—typically graham cracker—with softened ice cream smoothed in the

shell. The pie is put back in the freezer to allow the ice cream to harden, then

served. • In this chapter, you'll find only ice cream pies with a little some-

thing extra, such as an Oreo crust. The Oreo is one of America's favorite

cookies, and one of my favorite ways to use it is in a supporting role for a luscious coffee mud pie. If you love the new *dulce de leche* ice creams as much as I do, imagine using one in a frozen pie made with pieces of peanut butter cups. Yum! And what about meringue? Top an ice cream pie with a mountain of meringue, run it under the broiler, and you have a sensational baked Alaska pie. There are two in this chapter, and I can all but guarantee that you'll find them—and all the other pies on these pages—simply irresistible.

Tips for Making Irresistible Ice Cream Pies

▶ With few exceptions, a crumb crust makes the best pie shell for an ice cream pie. Pastry shells tend to get harder when frozen, and the flavor is more muted.

▶ Crumb crusts should always be prebaked when making ice cream pies, followed by a thorough cooling and chilling before adding the ice cream. Otherwise, residual heat from the pan can melt the ice cream.

▶ It's very important that the ice cream does not melt. If it does, it will have a gritty, crystallized texture—not at all creamy—after it refreezes.

▶ Ice cream must be softened before pressing it into the pie shell. The best way to do this is to place it in the refrigerator for about 15 minutes. When you scoop the ice cream out of the container, use the ice cream around the sides first—it will be softer—then the middle. Press the ice cream firmly into the pan, but take care to avoid breaking the crumb crust.

▶ Once filled, an ice cream pie will need to be frozen for up to three hours. If it gets too firm, transfer the pie to the refrigerator for a few minutes before serving to soften it a bit.

▶ When you're browning a meringue on top of a baked Alaska pie, slide the pie pan into another one to buffer the oven's heat, which might start to melt the ice cream.

▶ Like ice cream itself, ice cream pies taste great with a fruit or chocolate topping.

Frozen White Chocolate Pie with Raspberry Sauce

It's almost unfair that such a simple pie should taste so good. Made with a chocolate crumb crust or a store-bought Oreo crust, this is little more than melted white chocolate folded into whipped cream. It goes into the freezer for a few hours and that's all there is to it. The accompanying raspberry sauce can be made in less than 10 minutes and makes a pretty contrast with the pure white filling.

MAKES 8 TO 10 SERVINGS

1 recipe Chocolate Wafer Crumb Crust (page 54) or 1 store-bought Oreo crust

FILLING

$1/4$ cup plus 2 tablespoons whole milk

$1^1/3$ cups white chocolate chips

2 cups cold heavy or whipping cream

$1/2$ cup confectioners' sugar, sifted

1 teaspoon vanilla extract

GARNISH

Raspberry Sauce (page 608)

Handful of fresh raspberries

1. Prepare the crust and press it into the bottom and up the side of a 9-inch standard pie pan. Refrigerate, prebake, and let cool as directed. Or simply use a store-bought crust, prebaking it according to the package directions and letting it cool. Refrigerate until needed.

2. Combine the milk and white chocolate chips in the top of a double boiler set over, not in, barely simmering water. When melted, whisk to smooth. Remove the top insert of the double boiler and let the mixture cool to room temperature, stirring occasionally.

3. Using a chilled large bowl and chilled beaters, beat the cream with an electric mixer until it holds soft peaks. Add the confectioners' sugar and vanilla and continue to beat until firm but not grainy.

4. Fold the white chocolate mixture into the whipped cream until evenly combined. Spoon the filling into the chilled piecrust and smooth the top. Cover with loosely tented aluminum foil and freeze for at least 3 hours or overnight. (For a softer pie, refrigerate for 4 to 5 hours.)

5. If the pie has firmed considerably, let it stand a room temperature until softened somewhat before slicing. Drizzle raspberry sauce over and around each slice, garnish with a few fresh raspberries, and serve.

Recipe for Success

▶ **For a more formal presentation, suitable for guests, arrange a single, snug layer of fresh raspberries (stem ends down) over the top of the pie shortly before serving. Warm 2 tablespoons red currant jelly, whisking to smooth, and brush over the berries to make them glisten.**

Black Bottom Peanut Butter Cloud Pie

One bite of this pie, and you'll be on cloud nine! The cloud in the title is a reference to the light, almost mousse-like consistency of the peanut butter filling, which is aerated with both whipped cream and beaten egg whites. This is poured into a peanut graham cracker crust lined with melted chocolate—the black bottom—and frozen until the filling is nice and solid, which takes four to five hours. Kids love this pie because of the peanut butter, but it's fancy enough to serve for a dinner party.

MAKES 8 TO 10 SERVINGS

1 recipe Nutty Graham Cracker Crust (page 53) made with peanuts or 1 large store-bought graham cracker crust

1/2 cup semisweet chocolate chips

1/2 cup chopped salted dry-roasted peanuts

FILLING

1 cup heavy or whipping cream

Two 3-ounce packages full-fat cream cheese, softened

1 1/4 cups smooth peanut butter

3/4 cup granulated sugar

1/2 cup firmly packed light brown sugar

2 teaspoons vanilla extract

3 large egg whites, at room temperature

1/2 cup chopped salted dry-roasted peanuts

1. Prepare the crust and press it into the bottom and up the side of a 9 1/2-inch deep-dish pie pan. Refrigerate and prebake as directed. Or simply use a store-bought crust, prebaking it according to the package directions. In both cases, as soon as the crust comes out of the oven, scatter the chocolate chips evenly in the shell. Wait 5 minutes, until they melt, then spread the chocolate with a fork to cover the bottom. Sprinkle the nuts evenly over the chocolate. Transfer the pie shell to a wire rack and let cool thoroughly before filling.

2. Using a chilled medium-size bowl and chilled beaters, whip the cream with an electric mixer until stiff but not grainy. Do not overbeat. Cover and refrigerate.

3. In a large bowl cream the cream cheese and peanut butter with the mixer on medium speed until evenly blended. Gradually beat in the granulated sugar, then the brown sugar, until blended. The mixture may look lumpy, like cookie dough. That's the way it's supposed to be, so don't worry. Blend in the vanilla. Add the whipped cream, slowly blending with the mixer until smooth.

4. Clean and dry the beaters. Using a clean medium-size bowl, beat the egg whites until they hold stiff peaks. Fold them into the peanut butter mixture with a rubber spatula or gently beat them in with the mixer until evenly blended. Scrape the filling into the chilled pie shell and smooth with a spoon. Sprinkle the chopped nuts over the pie. Cover with loosely tented aluminum foil and freeze until firm enough to slice cleanly but not rock solid, at least 4 hours. Slice and serve.

Recipe for Success

▶ **If you're using a store-bought graham cracker crust, I suggest sprinkling the chocolate chips in the pie shell about 45 seconds before it comes out of the oven. The reason for this is that there may not be enough residual heat in the thin, disposable aluminum pan to warm the chips long enough to melt them completely.**

Frozen Peanut Butter Pie with Marshmallow Meringue

Here's a recipe that first appeared in *Gourmet* magazine some years ago, and I've been changing it a little here and there ever since. The filling is essentially a milk-based peanut butter sauce cooked on the stovetop, cooled, and then folded with whipped cream. The original topping was whipped cream, but I like the way it tastes even more with the marshmallow meringue. For garnish, I use roasted peanuts and the always decadent mocha sauce. Dessert doesn't get much better than this.

MAKES 8 TO 10 SERVINGS

1 recipe Chocolate Wafer Crumb Crust (page 54)

FILLING

1 cup whole milk

2/3 cup sugar

1 cup smooth peanut butter

1 teaspoon vanilla extract

1 cup cold heavy or whipping cream

MARSHMALLOW MERINGUE

3 large egg whites, at room temperature

3 tablespoons sugar

1 cup marshmallow crème

GARNISH

Warm Mocha Sauce (page 607)

1 cup chopped salted dry-roasted peanuts

1.   Prepare the crust and press it into the bottom and up the side of a $9\frac{1}{2}$-inch deep-dish pie pan. Refrigerate, prebake, and let cool as directed. Refrigerate until ready to use.

2.   Gently warm the milk and sugar in a medium-size saucepan over low heat, stirring until the sugar melts, about 5 minutes. Do not let it boil. Remove from the heat and add the peanut butter, whisking until smooth. Whisk in the vanilla. Pour the mixture into a large bowl, set aside on a wire rack, and let cool to room temperature, whisking occasionally. Refrigerate until it begins to thicken. (A faster way to do this is to put the bowl into a bowl of ice water.)

3.   Using a chilled medium-size bowl and chilled beaters, whip the cream with an electric mixer until stiff but not grainy. Fold about one-third of the whipped cream into the peanut butter mixture. Add the remaining whipped cream and fold until evenly combined. Scrape the filling into the chilled pie shell and smooth the top with a spoon. Cover with loosely tented aluminum foil and freeze until firm but not rock hard, 3 to 4 hours.

4.   When you're almost ready to serve the pie, make the marshmallow meringue. In a large bowl, beat the egg whites with an electric mixer on medium-high speed until they hold soft peaks. Gradually add the sugar, 1 tablespoon at a time, beating well after each addition. When the whites are thick and glossy but not dry, add the marshmallow crème and blend on low speed. Don't worry if you can't blend it perfectly; finish folding it in with a rubber spatula. Using damp fingers, spread the meringue evenly over the pie, mounding it slightly in the center. Place the pie in the freezer for about 5 minutes.

5.   Just before serving, preheat the broiler. Set the pie on a baking sheet and place under the broiler. Don't leave the oven; the meringue will take a very short time to brown. Serve at once, garnishing each slice with a drizzle of mocha sauce and a scattering of peanuts.

Recipe for Success

▶ **The relative firmness of the filling is a key consideration here. Like ice cream, the longer the pie is in the freezer, the firmer the filling will be. The texture is usually just right after 3 to 4 hours in the freezer. If it goes much beyond that, you'll probably want to put the pie in the refrigerator for up to 1 hour before adding the meringue.**

Patchwork Quilt Country Inn Frozen Coffee Toffee Pie

When I spoke with Marshall King about his Elkhart County, Indiana, pie quest (see page 461), the pie he was simply effusive about was this one, served at the Patchwork Quilt Country Inn in Middlebury. It has a nutty chocolate crust, a massive layer of ice cream–like chocolate filling, and a creamy coffee-flavored topping. King warned me that parts of the recipe were a little unorthodox— such as the Jiffy pie crust mix with all the add-ins—and that it used Rich's Whip Topping, which the inn's baker whips up and spreads on top of the pie. Still, he told me, you just have to get the recipe. So I spoke to the inn's dining room manager, who informed me that with all the travelers passing through, the pie has gained a reputation that extends well beyond Indiana. As for the shortcuts, she said you just can't argue with how well it works for this particular pie and how much it streamlines the preparation. In an ideal world, she said, whipped cream would be the way to go for the topping, but the Rich's product is more stable and allows them to keep the pie in the freezer for a few weeks.

Since I was unable to track down Rich's topping in my part of the country (Maryland), I used whipped cream instead. But if you can find Rich's topping, by all means try it. You'll need a KitchenAid or other large stand mixer to make this pie, and do read all the entries in Recipe for Success before starting. Warning: I doubt there's a richer recipe in this book.

MAKES 10 TO 12 SERVINGS

1 recipe Choco-Nut Press-In Pie Crust (page 57)

FILLING

2 cups (4 sticks) unsalted butter, at room temperature

2¹/₂ cups sugar

Two 1-ounce packages premelted unsweetened chocolate (see Recipe for Success)

1¹/₂ tablespoons instant espresso or coffee granules

7 large eggs, at room temperature but not warmed

2 tablespoons Kahlúa or other coffee liqueur

1 teaspoon vanilla extract

TOPPING

1¹/₂ cups cold heavy or whipping cream

¹/₄ cup sugar

1 tablespoon instant espresso or coffee granules, crushed in a small bowl

1. Prepare the pastry, pressing it into the bottom and up the side of a 9¹/₂- to 10-inch extra-deep-dish pie pan. Refrigerate, prebake, and let cool as directed. Place in the refrigerator for 10 minutes.

2. Cream the butter on medium-high speed with a stand mixer, gradually adding the sugar over a 4- to 5-minute period. Scrape down the bowl periodically. Add the chocolate and coffee and beat again until evenly mixed. With the mixer still on medium-high speed, add the eggs, one at a time, beating for $1\frac{1}{2}$ to 2 minutes after each addition. Continue to scrape down the bowl as necessary. When the filling is thoroughly combined and very light textured, blend in the Kahlúa and vanilla.

3. Scrape the filling into the pie shell, smoothing the top with a spoon and mounding it in the center. Place in the refrigerator, uncovered, for about 1 hour.

4. Make the topping: Using a chilled medium-size bowl and chilled beaters, beat the cream until it holds soft peaks. Add the sugar and coffee and continue to beat until firm but not grainy. Smooth the topping over the pie. Cover with loosely tented aluminum foil and freeze until firm but not too much so, 2 to 4 hours. If the pie gets too firm, let it sit at room temperature for 15 to 30 minutes before slicing and serving.

Recipe for Success

▶ The temperature of the butter and other ingredients is very important if the recipe is to work properly. The butter should be neither cool-firm nor squishy-soft. It should offer uniform, slight resistance. Don't try to achieve this by using the microwave. Rather, let the butter stand at room temperature until it has reached the proper consistency.

▶ The eggs should not be cold, or they may curdle the butter. Bring them to room temperature, but not by warming them (as I sometimes do) in a bowl of warm water. If an egg gets too warm, it could break down the butter.

▶ If you cannot find premelted chocolate, melt two 1-ounce bars unsweetened chocolate and cool to room temperature before using. Warm chocolate will melt the butter.

▶ If you are using Rich's Whip Topping, substitute it for the whipped cream and omit the sugar. The inn starts with 2 cups unbeaten topping for each pie. The Rich's Web site says that the topping beats up to 4 times its original volume, meaning that 2 cups unbeaten topping will result in about 8 cups beaten topping. That sounds like an extravagant amount, but I'm told the proportions are correct, so just pile it high!

▶ This pie is delicious but a bit sweet. You could easily reduce the sugar to 2 cups.

Coffee Mud Pie with an Oreo Crust

Here's a classic ice cream pie: layers of coffee ice cream, with a sandwich of Oreo cookies and chocolate sauce, all in an Oreo crust. Not to play favorites, but I'd have a hard time choosing another ice cream pie I like more. As with other ice cream pies, the key to doing this right is paying close attention to the texture of the ice cream. It needs to be softish and workable, but not starting to melt. (When melting ice cream refreezes, it has a texture that's more icy than creamy.) If you'd rather, you can use a graham cracker crumb crust, but the Oreo crust really makes this special. The kids will love to help with this one. Note that each time you pause to firm up the pie in the freezer, you should put the ice cream back in the freezer, too. Incidentally, this recipe was inspired by a similar one in Elinor Klivans's great book *Bake and Freeze Desserts* (William Morrow, 1994). Elinor is an excellent cook, and I suggest that you check out her book.

MAKES 10 SERVINGS

1 recipe Oreo Crumb Crust (page 55)

FILLING

1/2 gallon coffee ice cream

2 cups coarsely broken Oreo cookies (12 or 13 cookies)

1 recipe Warm Mocha Sauce (page 607), at room temperature but still pourable

1. Prepare the crust and press it into the bottom and up the side of a 9-inch standard pie pan. Refrigerate, prebake, and let cool as directed. Refrigerate until ready to use.

2. About 15 minutes before you plan to assemble the pie, put the ice cream in the refrigerator so it can start to soften.

3. To assemble the pie, spoon half of the ice cream into the chilled pie shell with an ice cream spade. With the back of the spade or a large fork, press the ice cream firmly into the shell. Place in the freezer for 10 minutes. Also return the ice cream to the freezer.

4. Remove from pie freezer and spread the broken Oreo cookies over the ice cream, gently pressing them in. Spoon about half of the mocha sauce over the cookies. Place in the freezer again for 10 minutes, along with the ice cream.

5. Mound the remaining ice cream over the cookies and sauce. Using the back of the ice cream spade, smooth the ice cream into a nicely rounded mound. (It helps to run your utensil under hot water briefly as you do this.) Drizzle as much of the remaining sauce over

the surface as you like. Cover with loosely tented aluminum foil and freeze for at least 1 hour or overnight before serving.

Recipe for Success

▶ **When you scoop out the ice cream, take the part around the edges first, where it is the softest.**

▶ **Do make sure that the mocha sauce isn't hot when you pour it over the ice cream, or the ice cream will melt.**

▶ **It may seem like extra work to refreeze the pie twice, but it will help prevent the ice cream underneath from squishing up and out the sides when you press on the top of the pie.**

The Ultimate Banana Split Pie

A half gallon of ice cream, gobs of whipped cream, sliced bananas, pecans, and two kinds of dessert sauce—tell me this isn't every kid's idea of creating the ultimate pie. You just prebake the store-bought crust, assemble the ingredients for the kids, and let them have at it. The only catch is that you'll have to eat this as soon as it's put together, because by that time the ice cream will be starting to get soft. See Recipe for Success for some more advice about timing.

MAKES 8 SERVINGS

1 large store-bought graham cracker crust

FILLING

1 cup cold heavy or whipping cream

3 tablespoons confectioners' sugar, sifted

Butterscotch or caramel sauce

Chocolate sauce or syrup

1/2 gallon ice cream (any flavor)

2 large ripe bananas

Handful of pecan halves or coarsely chopped pecans

M&M's or other candy

1. Prebake the crust according to the package directions. Set aside on a wire rack to cool thoroughly. Refrigerate until ready to use.

2. Using a chilled medium-size bowl and chilled beaters, beat the cream with an electric mixer until it holds soft peaks. Add the confectioners' sugar and continue to beat until firm but not grainy. Refrigerate.

One Food Editor's Thoughts on Kids and Pie Baking

Every writer should be as fortunate as I am, working with an editor like Cindy Littlefield. A senior editor at *FamilyFun* magazine, and the person I work most closely with in my capacity as writer for the magazine's monthly Cooking Class feature, Cindy is as passionate about good food as she is dedicated to making it accessible to families. Here's what she has to say about pies, one of her favorite food topics.

"I doubt there's a richer subject for family conversation and involvement than homemade pie. There's just so much happening at once when you make a pie. There's food science, history, gardening, and the building of family ties. The science alone is fascinating, and it presents parents and children with real-life opportunities for learning: How does cornstarch thicken a pie filling? Why should pie pastry be handled delicately, when yeast dough is handled roughly? A pie is full of curiosities.

"We live in such a fast-paced society today, and I think family pie making is a good antidote. Peeling apples together, picking wild berries, mixing and rolling pie pastry—those things help us rediscover something we've lost, which is one generation of cooks passing kitchen wisdom to the next. It takes a little time and patience to do that, and a few dollars for ingredients. But what you gain in the process is priceless."

3. If your butterscotch and chocolate sauces are firm-cold, loosen them in the microwave so that they're pourable. Without measuring, pour enough butterscotch sauce into the chilled pie shell to cover generously. Place the pie in the freezer for 10 minutes. Take the ice cream out of the freezer to soften a bit.

4. Using an ice cream scoop, mound scoops of ice cream in the pie shell on top of the sauce. Pile them on top of one another, if you like, using as much of the ice cream as possible. Slice the banana right over the top, letting the slices fall where they may. With a large spoon, dollop the whipped cream here and there over the ice cream. Garnish with the pecans. Drizzle more of the butterscotch sauce and the chocolate sauce over everything. Sprinkle the M&M's on top. Slice and serve at once.

Recipe for Success

- If you make this in a warm house, you may have to give the ice cream scoops an hour in the freezer to refirm once you've piled everything in the pie shell. Just monitor the progress, then make the decision.

- You realize, of course, that you don't have to use homemade whipped cream. You can use canned. Or use homemade and pipe it on with a pastry bag.

- In the summer, you can add a garnish of fresh berries to this pie, along with the banana. At other times of the year, I like to use canned pineapple chunks—drained, of course.

Chocolate-Cherry S'mores Ice Cream Pie

This rates an A-plus with the kids, in both the assembly and the eating departments. You begin with a graham cracker or Oreo crust. Then you pile in lots of cherry vanilla ice cream, a layer of chocolate-covered grahams and mini marshmallows, and more ice cream. The icing on the cake—rather, the pie—is marshmallow crème, which gets beautifully browned with a quick toast under the broiler. This is a great birthday party pie or rainy day pie project.

MAKES 8 TO 10 SERVINGS

1 recipe Graham Cracker Crumb Crust (page 51) or Oreo Crumb Crust (page 55), or 1 large store-bought graham cracker crust

FILLING

1/2 gallon favorite cherry vanilla ice cream

7 or 8 chocolate-covered graham crackers

Handful of mini marshmallows, frozen

TOPPING

One 7-ounce jar (2 cups) marshmallow crème

Warm Mocha Sauce (page 607; optional)

1.   Prepare the crust and press it into the bottom and up the side of a 9-inch standard pie pan. Refrigerate, prebake, and let cool as directed. Or simply use a store-bought crust, prebaking it according to the package directions and letting it cool. In both cases, refrigerate until needed.

2.   About 15 minutes before you plan to assemble the pie, place the ice cream in the refrigerator until it is spreadable but not too soft. Spoon half of the ice cream into the pie shell with an ice cream spade, smoothing it so it is more or less even. Put the ice cream back in the freezer, to keep it firm. Break the graham crackers into little shards and press them into the ice cream edgewise. Press 15 to 20 frozen mini marshmallows into the ice cream. Place the pie in the freezer for 20 minutes.

3.   Mound the remaining ice cream in the pie, smoothing it with an ice cream spade or spoon. Place the pie in the freezer for at least 1 1/2 hours.

4.   When ready to serve, preheat the broiler. Spoon the marshmallow crème over the ice cream, smoothing it out as evenly as possible with wet fingertips. Be sure to cover all the ice cream to protect it from the heat of the oven. Slide the pie into another pie pan to protect the ice cream from the heat. Quickly run the pie under the broiler, just until browned. Don't walk away; it should take only 30 seconds or so. Slice and serve right away, with or without the mocha sauce drizzled over the top.

Recipe for Success

▶ You can use chocolate or vanilla ice cream in place of the cherry vanilla. Chocolate brownie ice cream also tastes great.

▶ Instead of browning the marshmallow crème, just spread it on the ice cream and stick more chocolate grahams into it. Cut the graham crackers on the diagonal and stick them into the marshmallow crème edgewise, placing them like the spokes of a wheel, radiating out from the center. That way, when you go to cut the pie, you can cut between the crackers rather than through them.

Butter Pecan Ice Cream Pie with Bananas Foster

This sounds fancy and complicated, but it's really simple and delicious. It's less intimidating, too, than making traditional bananas Foster, since you don't have to flambé the bananas—you just pan-cook them with butter, brown sugar, and rum. When the bananas are soft and the juice syrupy, they're spooned right over slices of butter pecan ice cream pie, the hot and cold elements creating a flavor sensation.

MAKES 10 SERVINGS

1 recipe Nutty Graham Cracker Crust (page 53) made with pecans

FILLING

$1/2$ gallon butter pecan ice cream

10 pecan halves

BANANAS FOSTER

3 large, firm just-ripe bananas (see Recipe for Success)

3 tablespoons unsalted butter

$1/4$ cup firmly packed light brown sugar

Big pinch of ground cinnamon

$1/3$ cup dark rum

1. Prepare the crust and press it into the bottom and up the side of a 9½-inch deep-dish pie pan. Refrigerate, prebake, and let cool as directed. Refrigerate until needed.

2. About 15 minutes before you plan to assemble the pie, place the ice cream in the refrigerator to soften just until workable. Spoon it into the chilled pie shell with an ice cream spade or large metal spoon, pressing it in with the back of the spade and smoothing the top. Press the pecan halves around the edge of the pie to garnish each slice. Freeze until fairly firm, at least 2 hours.

3. Have someone slice and plate up the pie while you work on the bananas. When you're just about ready to serve the pie, cut each banana into 3 equal-size crosswise sections, then cut each section in half lengthwise. Melt the butter in a large nonstick skillet over medium heat. Add the bananas, cut side down, and fry for about 30 seconds. Flip over and fry for 30 seconds more. Shake the brown sugar evenly over the bananas, then pour on the rum. Bring to a boil, shaking the pan to "stir" the ingredients. Cook at a low boil until the liquid is good and syrupy, about 1 minute, then remove from the heat.

4. Spoon some of the bananas and syrup over and around each slice of pie. Serve immediately.

Recipe for Success

▶ **The key element here is the bananas. They can't be overly ripe, or they'll get too soft in the skillet. Buy them several days ahead, while they're still a little green, then use them when they're just ripe but still firm.**

▶ **This number of bananas makes enough garnish for about 6 slices of pie. If you're serving more than that, either prepare the bananas twice, back to back; cook them in 2 skillets; or double the recipe and use 1 very large skillet.**

Mascarpone Ice Cream Pie with Sugared Berries

When you blend mascarpone cheese with custard, then fold in whipped cream and freeze, you wind up with something akin to the richest, creamiest ice cream ever concocted. Served in a walnut graham cracker crust, it makes for a decadent dessert that is perfect for summer entertaining. The sugared berries add both color and flavor contrast to the rich filling. Spoon them over and around the slices right before serving. Texture is key here, so observe the timing for serving the pie to make sure it has the correct semifrozen texture.

MAKES 10 SERVINGS

1 recipe Nutty Graham Cracker Crust (page 53) made with walnuts

FILLING

5 large egg yolks

2/3 cup sugar

12 ounces (about 1 1/2 cups) mascarpone cheese

1 1/2 teaspoons vanilla extract

1/2 teaspoon lemon extract

3/4 cup cold heavy or whipping cream

SUGARED BERRIES

2 cups hulled and sliced fresh strawberries

1 cup fresh blueberries, picked over for stems

1 cup fresh raspberries or blackberries

3 tablespoons sugar

Big pinch of grated lemon zest

1. Prepare the crust and press it into the bottom and up the side of a 9-inch standard pie pan. Refrigerate, prebake, and let cool as directed. Refrigerate until ready to use.

2. Combine the egg yolks and sugar in the top of a double boiler set over, not in, barely simmering water. Whisk virtually nonstop until the mixture becomes thick and lemon-colored, about 7 minutes. Remove from the heat and scrape into a medium-size bowl. Set aside to cool for about 20 minutes, whisking occasionally.

3. Add the mascarpone to the partially cooled mixture. Using an electric mixer, beat the mixture until smooth, well blended, and airy, about 3 minutes. Add the vanilla and lemon extract and blend briefly.

4. Using a chilled medium-size bowl and chilled beaters, beat the cream with an electric mixer until stiff but not grainy. Fold about one-third of the whipped cream into the mascarpone mixture until evenly blended. Fold in the remaining whipped cream until no streaks remain, then carefully pour the filling into the chilled pie shell, smoothing the top with a spoon. Cover with loosely tented aluminum foil and freeze until semi-firm, 3 to 4 hours. It should have a thick, firm texture, a little like cold butter or cream cheese, but not be rock hard.

5. About 15 minutes before serving, gently toss the berries, sugar, and lemon zest together in a medium-size bowl. Slice and serve the pie, garnishing each plate and slice with the sugared berries.

Recipe for Success

> ❱ It's fine if you would like to make this the day before serving, but be aware that if the pie freezes for too long, the texture will be slightly grainy. If you need to prepare the pie ahead, cover it with loosely tented aluminum foil and refrigerate. Transfer to the freezer for 3 to 4 hours before serving.

Dulce de Leche and Peanut Butter Cup Pie

This pie was inspired by one of my favorite Breyers ice cream flavors, *dulce de leche*. If you haven't tried this caramel-flavored ice cream with caramel swirls, you're in for a treat. I think it tastes wonderful with peanut butter cups, which I've been known to eat, smeared with a spoonful of ice cream, in some of my weaker moments. The peanut butter cups are chopped and pressed into a bottom layer of ice cream, then the rest of the ice cream is spread on top. A layer of mocha sauce is the finishing touch.

MAKES 10 SERVINGS

1 recipe Graham Cracker Crumb Crust (page 51) or 1 large store-bought graham cracker crust

FILLING

1/2 gallon *dulce de leche* ice cream

12 regular-size (not mini) peanut butter cups, refrigerated

1 recipe Warm Mocha Sauce (page 607), slightly warm and spreadable

1. Prepare the crust and press it into the bottom and up the side of a 9½-inch deep-dish pie pan. Refrigerate, prebake, and let cool as directed. Or simply use a store-bought crust, prebaking it according to the package directions and letting it cool. Refrigerate for at least 10 minutes.

2. Let the ice cream soften to a spreadable consistency by transferring it from the freezer to the refrigerator for about 15 minutes.

3. Meanwhile, coarsely chop the cold peanut butter cups with a sharp chef's knife (see Recipe for Success). Put them on a plate and refrigerate for several minutes.

4. When the ice cream is spreadable but not overly soft, spoon half of it into the chilled pie shell with an ice cream spade. Press it into the shell with the back of the spade. Carefully dump the chopped peanut butter cups over the ice cream. Arrange the pieces in a more or less even layer, pressing down on them to embed them in the ice cream. Place in the freezer for 10 minutes. Put the remaining ice cream back in the freezer as well.

5. Spoon the rest of the ice cream over the peanut butter cups, pressing down lightly and smoothing it with the back of the ice cream spade. Place in the freeze for 30 minutes.

6. Spread the sauce over the top of the pie. Freeze briefly, about 5 minutes, then slice and serve.

Recipe for Success

▶ **Don't chop the peanut butter cups too large. Keep them in the small bite-size range. That way, when you're slicing the pie and your knife hits a chunk squarely, it will graze off the chunk and keep slicing.**

Creamsicle Ice Cream Pie

I've always loved Creamsicles, which I think are just about as good as it gets when it comes to ice cream on a stick. Here's a pie version of those flavors I adore: equal measures of vanilla ice cream and orange sherbet in a graham cracker crust, topped with orange-flavored whipped cream and a garnish of mandarin orange segments. This is a perfect patio dessert for those warm summer months.

MAKES 8 TO 10 SERVINGS

1 recipe Graham Cracker Crumb Crust (page 51) or 1 large store-bought graham cracker crust

FILLING

1 quart vanilla ice cream

1 quart orange sherbet

TOPPING

1 cup cold heavy or whipping cream

1 tablespoon frozen orange juice concentrate, thawed

1 teaspoon vanilla extract

1/3 cup confectioners' sugar, sifted

GARNISH

Canned mandarin orange segments, drained

1. Prepare the crust and press it into the bottom and up the side of a 9½-inch deep-dish pie pan. Refrigerate, prebake, and let cool as directed. Or simply use a store-bought crust, prebaking it according to the package directions and letting it cool. Refrigerate until needed.

2. Soften the ice cream and sherbet slightly by placing them in the refrigerator for about 15 minutes before assembling the pie. Using an ice cream spade or a large metal spoon, randomly spoon the ice cream and sherbet into the chilled pie shell in no particular pattern. Use the back of the spade or your fingers to pack it into the shell, being careful not to crack the crust. Smooth the top, mounding it slightly. Freeze until fairly firm, 1 to 2 hours.

3. Using a chilled medium-size bowl and chilled beaters, beat the cream with an electric mixer until it holds soft peaks. Blend in the orange juice concentrate and vanilla. Add the confectioners' sugar and continue to beat until stiff but not grainy. Spread the whipped cream over the pie, smoothing it with a spoon. Freeze for at least 30 minutes or overnight.

4. If the pie has become quite firm, let it stand at room temperature until it softens somewhat. Slice and serve, garnishing each piece with 1 or 2 mandarin orange segments.

Recipe for Success

▶ You don't need to use a fancy, high-end sorbet to make a wonderful-tasting pie. I actually prefer the flavor of regular old sherbet, from a plastic tub, because it gives the pie that good old-fashioned flavor I remember from my youth.

▶ You can make a smaller version of this pie in a small store-bought graham cracker crust. You'll need only about half as much ice cream and sherbet, but use the same amount of whipped cream.

▶ For a splash of color, add fresh mint leaves to the garnish.

Grasshopper Ice Cream Pie

All grasshopper pies have two things in common: crème de cacao and crème de menthe. Typically, these flavorings are blended with melted marshmallows and whipped cream, as they are here. But this one is a little different in that we start the pie with a base of vanilla ice cream, spreading it in a large graham cracker crust. The beauty of the ice cream layer is that it adds a firmer texture to the pie. Note that with the ingredients here, you don't get a green top layer; it's more of a mocha white. If you want the green, use green crème de menthe and white crème de cacao. A drop or two of green food coloring will brighten it up even more.

MAKES 8 TO 10 SERVINGS

1 recipe Graham Cracker Crumb Crust (page 51) or 1 large store-bought graham cracker crust

FILLING

About 1 quart vanilla ice cream

1/4 cup whole milk

5 cups mini marshmallows

3 tablespoons white crème de menthe

3 tablespoons crème de cacao

11/4 cups cold heavy or whipping cream

1/4 cup confectioners' sugar, sifted

GARNISH

Small chocolate-covered after-dinner mints

Fresh mint leaves

1. Prepare the crust and press it into the bottom and up the side of a 9 1/2-inch deep-dish pie pan. Refrigerate, prebake, and let cool as directed. Or simply use a store-bought crust, prebaking it according to the package directions and letting it cool. Refrigerate until needed.

2. Place the ice cream in the refrigerator for about 15 minutes to soften somewhat. Using an ice cream spade or a large metal spoon, spoon the ice cream into the chilled pie shell. Press it in evenly and smooth with the back of the spade, but take care not to crack the crust. Place in the freezer while you prepare the filling.

3. Combine the milk and marshmallows in a large saucepan, preferably nonstick, and melt over low heat, stirring often. Remove from the heat and let cool, stirring occasionally. When the mixture has cooled to room temperature, stir in the crème de menthe and crème de cacao. Set aside.

4. Using a chilled medium-size bowl and chilled beaters, beat the heavy cream with an electric mixer until it holds soft peaks. Add the confectioners' sugar and continue to beat until stiff but not grainy. Fold the melted marshmallow mixture into the whipped cream until evenly blended. Scrape this mixture over the ice cream, smoothing the top. Freeze for at least 3 hours. Once the surface of the pie has firmed up, cover loosely with aluminum foil. Ideally, the top layer should be firm but slightly yielding when the pie is served. To serve, garnish each slice with an after-dinner mint and 1 or 2 mint leaves.

Recipe for Success

> **Don't make a special trip to the liquor store if you don't have white crème de menthe and dark crème de cacao. Use what you have on hand and make the top layer green (see headnote).**

> **I prefer vanilla ice cream, but you can use mint or mint chip ice cream instead.**

Cranberry Ice Cream Pie

I don't know whether you can even buy cranberry ice cream, but you can make it easily enough, and this pie gives you a good reason to do so. This is the perfect pie to have on hand around the holidays, and it is a nice foil to the traditional pumpkin pie.

MAKES 8 TO 10 SERVINGS

1 recipe Nutty Graham Cracker Crust (page 53) made with walnuts

Grated zest of 1 orange

1 quart vanilla ice cream

FILLING

2 cups fresh cranberries, picked over for stems

$1/3$ cup granulated sugar

$1/2$ cup water

TOPPING

1 cup cold heavy or whipping cream

$1^1/2$ tablespoons orange liqueur

1 teaspoon vanilla extract

3 tablespoons confectioners' sugar, sifted

1. Prepare the crust and press it into the bottom and up the side of a $9^1/2$-inch deep-dish pie pan. Refrigerate, prebake, and let cool as directed. Refrigerate until needed.

2. Combine the cranberries, granulated sugar, water, and orange zest in a medium-size nonreactive saucepan over medium heat. Bring to a boil, then continue to boil until the mixture is syrupy, about 4 minutes. Remove from the heat and scrape the cranberries onto a plate to cool. Refrigerate to hasten the cooling.

3. When the cranberries are almost cold, put the ice cream in the refrigerator for about 15 minutes to soften and place a large bowl in the freezer to chill.

4. When the cranberries are cold, scoop the ice cream into the chilled bowl. Add the cranberries and using an ice cream spade or a large metal spoon, mix the fruit into the ice cream. Spoon the ice cream into the chilled pie shell, smoothing the top. Freeze until fairly firm, at least 2 hours.

5. Shortly before serving, make the topping. Using a chilled medium-size bowl and chilled beaters, beat the cream with an electric mixer until it holds soft peaks. Blend in the orange liqueur and vanilla, then add the confectioners' sugar and beat until stiff but not grainy. Smooth the topping over the pie, then put it back in the freezer for 15 minutes before slicing and serving.

Recipe for Success

▶ **Try not to cook off all the moisture when you cook the cranberries. A little bit of syrupy liquid will help flavor the ice cream.**

▶ **If you've ever been to one of those custom ice cream shops where "mix-ins" are prepared on a chilled marble slab, you'll know why I recommend chilling the bowl before adding the ice cream. A cold bowl will allow the ice cream to get soft without letting it melt. When melted ice cream is refrozen, it becomes grainy.**

Strawberry Baked Alaska Pie

I think you're going to like this pie very much, as there's so much drama and such good looks for a very small investment of time. All you do is smear strawberry ice cream in a store-bought pie shell, add a thick dome of meringue, and then brown it under the broiler. Even though there's only about 10 minutes of hands-on time, allow yourself 2 to 3 hours from start to finish so the ice cream has time to firm up in the pie shell.

MAKES 6 TO 8 SERVINGS

1 small store-bought graham cracker crust

FILLING

1 1/2 quarts strawberry ice cream

MERINGUE

4 large egg whites, at room temperature

1/4 teaspoon cream of tartar

Pinch of salt

1/2 cup superfine sugar

1 teaspoon vanilla extract

1. Prebake the crust according to the package directions. Set aside on a wire rack to cool thoroughly.

2. Place the ice cream in the refrigerator for about 15 minutes to soften just until workable. Using an ice cream spade or a large metal spoon, spoon the ice cream into the cooled pie shell, pressing it in firmly and mounding it toward the center. Cover with plastic wrap and freeze until the ice cream is firm but not rock hard, 2 to 3 hours.

3. About 10 minutes before serving, preheat the broiler and prepare the meringue. In a large bowl, beat the egg whites with an electric mixer on medium-high speed until they hold soft peaks. Beat in the cream of tartar and salt. Gradually add the sugar, beating on high speed until the meringue is thick, glossy, and voluminous. Beat in the vanilla. Stick a rubber spatula into the meringue to help judge the consistency. It should be soft but firm, though not dry. Smooth the meringue evenly over the pie.

4. Place the pie in a second pie pan to buffer the heat, then run the pie under the broiler just until golden brown. This will take a very short time, so don't leave the oven. Slice and serve immediately.

Recipe for Success

▶ If you want a quick-and-easy garnish for this pie, just hull and slice a pint or quart of fresh strawberries and add a tablespoon or two of sugar. Let sit for 5 minutes, then spoon over each slice.

▶ By far the best way to serve this pie is when the meringue is warm, soft, and crusty and the ice cream is firm but not rock solid. The contrasting textures and temperatures are a real treat. That said, if there's any way you can make and apply the meringue just before serving, by all means do so. It won't be a tragedy if you have to freeze the completed pie for later, but try not to.

Torch That Meringue

The only problem with browning your baked Alaska pies under the broiler is this: your broiler has a tendency to do an uneven job with dome-shaped meringues. Like a bald guy who's been in the sun too long, the top gets overdone, the sides less so. Although a little too much browning on top isn't a catastrophe, there are times—such as when company is coming—when you'd like to see a uniformly golden finish. The answer: a propane torch—the kind you keep in your workshop. Just fire it up, hold it a few inches away from the meringue, and wave it slowly back and forth over the entire surface. Sound odd? It's not. Professional pastry chefs do this all the time for meringue and crème brûlée. You can find smaller, pastry chef–type torches at better kitchen stores, such as Williams-Sonoma.

Mocha Turtle Baked Alaska Pie

Like the preceding strawberry pie, this one has ice cream in the center and a meringue topping, but with a few more bells and whistles. The first is a chewy layer of caramel and pecans slathered over the bottom crust. Then there's the mocha sauce that gets dolloped over the ice cream and drizzled over the meringue. Finally, chopped pecans are folded into the meringue itself, adding an unexpected surprise. Don't be put off by what looks like a long list of ingredients and a few too many steps. This is actually very easy; just take it one simple step at a time. If you know someone who likes these flavors, this would make a swell birthday pie.

MAKES 6 TO 8 SERVINGS

1 recipe Graham Cracker Crumb Crust (page 51) or 1 small store-bought graham cracker crust

CARAMEL LAYER

1 tablespoon water

1 tablespoon salted or unsalted butter

15 caramels

3/4 cup chopped pecans

ICE CREAM LAYER

1 1/2 quarts chocolate ice cream

1 recipe Warm Mocha Sauce (page 607)

MERINGUE

4 large egg whites, at room temperature

1/4 teaspoon cream of tartar

Pinch of salt

1/2 cup superfine sugar

1 teaspoon vanilla extract

1/2 cup chopped pecans

1. Prepare the crust and press it into the bottom and up the side of a 9-inch standard pie pan. Refrigerate, prebake, and let cool as directed. Or simply use a store-bought crust, prebaking it according to the package directions and letting it cool.

2. To make the caramel layer, combine the water, butter, and caramels in the top of a double boiler set over, not in, simmering water. When the caramels are soft, about 10 minutes, whisk into a smooth sauce. Remove from the heat and pour the caramel sauce into the cooled pie shell, spreading it over the bottom with a spoon. Sprinkle the pecans evenly over the caramel. Freeze until firm, 20 to 30 minutes.

3. To make the ice cream layer, place the ice cream in the refrigerator for about 15 minutes to soften just until workable. Spoon it into the pie shell with an ice cream spade or a large metal spoon, pressing it firmly into the crust and mounding it slightly in the center. Freeze until firm, 2 to 3 hours.

4. Pour half of the mocha sauce into a small bowl and leave the rest in the saucepan. Put the bowl in the refrigerator to help firm up the sauce. When it is semi-firm, spoon it over the frozen ice cream, dolloping it here and there.

5. When the ice cream is firm but not rock hard, preheat the broiler and make the meringue. In a large bowl, beat the egg whites with an electric mixer on medium-high speed until they hold soft peaks. Beat in the cream of tartar and salt. Gradually add the sugar, beating on high speed until the meringue is thick, glossy, and voluminous. Beat in the vanilla. Stick a rubber spatula into the meringue to help judge the consistency. It should be soft but firm, though not dry. Fold in the chopped pecans. Smooth the meringue evenly over the pie, mounding it quite high in the center.

6. Place the pie in a second pie pan to buffer the heat, then run the pie under the broiler just until golden brown. It will take a very short time, so don't leave the oven.

7. Rewarm the remaining mocha sauce over low heat and drizzle it over the pie. Or slice the pie first, then drizzle the sauce over individual slices. Serve immediately.

Recipe for Success

▶ You can facilitate the melting of the caramels if you gently press down on them as they start to melt.

▶ When you have a highly peaked meringue like this one (and the previous one), you have to expect that it's going to brown faster on top than on the sides. There's not a whole lot you can do about this, but if you keep moving the meringue from side to side and back and forth, you can probably facilitate a more even browning. Use your oven mitts when you do this. Or use a propane torch to brown the meringue instead (see page 554).

A book as large as this needs a cubbyhole, of sorts, to put those pies that don't

fit neatly into any of the categories already covered. This is that cubby. Here you

will find a pie made with Italian Arborio rice that will remind you of rice pudding,

as well as a polenta pie—thickened with fine cornmeal and having a texture and

flavor reminiscent of Indian pudding, a traditional New England dessert with which

you might be familiar. • Don't think for a moment that just because these recipes

are grouped here at the back of the book that they amount to a collective after-

thought. Nothing could be further from the truth. Each pie is deliciously unique and

worthy of your consideration, just hard to slot. Where else could one find a

comfortable home for the likes of the preserves-filled Linzer Pie (page 577)—my

adaptation of the famous Linzer torte—or the quirky Wheaten Breakfast Pie (page

600)? • So think of these as delicious misfits, if you will. But do think of them.

You're bound to find a few unexpected pie treasures just waiting for you to dis-

cover them here.

Bev's Brownie Pie

My wife, Bev, has a real weakness for rich brownies. In fact, her favorite cookie is a brownie recipe that I adapted to cookie form. (She's not the only fan. The cookie has become something of a holiday icon with many of the magazine editors with whom I work and who receive a tin of them annually. At least one has been known to call me in early December, just to make sure he's still on my list.) As for the pie, it has all the qualities of the cookie: soft, decadently rich, and with a deep chocolate flavor. The key is to bake the pie for 30 minutes, no longer, so it has the correct moist texture when it reaches room temperature, at which point it should be served with a large scoop of vanilla ice cream.

MAKES 10 SERVINGS

1 recipe Graham Cracker Crumb Crust (page 51) or a 1 large store-bought graham cracker crust

FILLING

5 tablespoons unsalted butter, cut into pieces

3 ounces unsweetened chocolate

1 cup granulated sugar

2 large eggs

2 large egg yolks

1 teaspoon vanilla extract

1/2 cup walnut halves or coarsely chopped walnuts

1 cup all-purpose flour

1 teaspoon baking powder

1/4 teaspoon salt

Confectioners' sugar

GARNISH

Vanilla ice cream

1. Prepare the crust and press it into the bottom and up the side of a 9-inch standard pie pan. Refrigerate, without prebaking. If you're using a store-bought pie shell, simply remove it from its packaging and refrigerate until needed. Preheat the oven to 325°F.

2. Put the butter, with the chocolate on top of it, in the top of a double boiler set over, not in, barely simmering water. When both are melted, remove the insert and set the chocolate aside to cool, whisking to smooth while the mixture is still warm.

3. Reserve 2 tablespoons of the granulated sugar and set aside. In a large bowl, beat the rest of the sugar, the eggs, and egg yolks with an electric mixer on medium-high speed until light and airy, about 4 minutes. Blend in the vanilla and chocolate mixture until evenly combined.

4.   Combine the remaining 2 tablespoons sugar and the walnuts in a food processor and pulse until finely chopped. Stir into the chocolate mixture. Sift together the flour, baking powder, and salt and stir into the chocolate mixture until evenly blended. Scrape the filling into the chilled pie shell. Dust the top lightly with confectioners' sugar.

5.   Place the pie on the center oven rack and bake for exactly 30 minutes—no more or less. Transfer the pie to a wire rack and let cool to room temperature. Slice and serve. Or cover loosely with aluminum foil and refrigerate for up to 2 days before serving (see Recipe for Success). Garnish with a scoop of ice cream.

Recipe for Success

▸   **Since the pie shell is going to be baked along with the pie and the filling is not wet enough to make the crust soggy, I don't bother to prebake the shell.**

▸   **If you have a stand mixer, use it to beat the eggs and sugar together so that you can be working on other parts of the recipe in the meantime.**

▸   **The pie can be made up to 2 days ahead and refrigerated. To serve, cut into slices while cold and put on individual plates. Heat each slice for several seconds in the microwave on the medium setting. You may have to heat a couple of slices to get the timing right, but start at 10 seconds and work from there.**

Kahlúa Fudge Brownie Pie

This pie is dangerous—way too rich and irresistible. Not that you'll much care once you've tried it. The secret is a double dose of chocolate—bittersweet and cocoa powder. When I want a chocolate pie to impress, this is the one I bake. Highly recommended for Valentine's Day, it's a surefire way to win that special someone's heart.

MAKES 8 TO 12 SERVINGS

1/2 recipe Nutty Pie Pastry (page 42) made with walnuts or 1 recipe Basic Flaky Pie Pastry, Single Crust (page 31), refrigerated

FILLING

3/4 cup (1 1/2 sticks) unsalted butter

4 ounces bittersweet chocolate

1/3 cup coarsely chopped walnuts

1 cup sugar

1/3 cup unsweetened cocoa powder

2 tablespoons all-purpose flour

Pinch of salt

4 large eggs, at room temperature

1 1/2 tablespoons Kahlúa or other coffee liqueur

1 teaspoon vanilla extract

GARNISH

Fresh Whipped Cream (page 605; optional), unsweetened

1. If you haven't already, prepare the pastry and refrigerate until firm enough to roll, about 1 hour.

2. On a sheet of lightly floured waxed paper, roll the pastry into a 13-inch circle with a floured rolling pin. Invert the pastry over a 9 1/2-inch deep-dish pie pan, center, and peel off the paper. Tuck the pastry into the pan, without stretching it, and sculpt the edge into an upstanding ridge. Place in the freezer for 15 minutes, then partially prebake and let cool according to the instructions on page 16. Reduce the oven temperature to 350°F.

3. Start melting the butter in a small, preferably nonstick saucepan over very low heat. Chop the chocolate and add it to the saucepan when the butter is almost melted. When the butter is completely melted, turn off the heat but leave the pan in place for another minute or so, tilting and swirling it once or twice so that the hot butter runs over the chocolate. Remove the pan from the heat. Wait 3 or 4 minutes, then whisk the chocolate until smooth. Set aside to cool. (If you prefer, you can melt the butter and chocolate in the top of a double boiler set over, not in, barely simmering water.)

4. Place the walnuts in a food processor with 1/4 cup of the sugar, the cocoa, flour, and salt. Pulse repeatedly until the nuts are very finely chopped. Set aside.

5. Using an electric mixer, beat the eggs and remaining 3/4 cup sugar in a large bowl until quite light and airy, about 4 minutes. Add the Kahlúa, vanilla, and nut mixture and beat again until smooth. Add the chocolate mixture and beat briefly until the filling is uniformly mixed. Pour the filling into the cooled pie shell.

6. Place the pie on the center oven rack and bake for 35 minutes. There's really no way to check the pie for doneness, visually or otherwise. Total baking time is all you have to go by. However, expect the pie to puff up, and don't be surprised if the top develops a crack or two. Also, expect the filling to seem relatively "loose" under the crusted top; this is as it should be.

7. Transfer the pie to a wire rack and let cool thoroughly. The pie can be sliced once it has cooled, but the texture will be better for slicing if you refrigerate it for at least 1 hour. Serve garnished with whipped cream, if desired.

Recipe for Success

▶ If you don't have any coffee liqueur but want the coffee flavor, add 1¹/₂ tablespoons instant espresso or coffee granules to the nuts when you process them.

▶ If you want nice neat slices, say for a dinner party, the best thing to do is to refrigerate the pie overnight, then put it in the freezer for 30 minutes. It will then be fairly solid and easy to slice. Do, however, leave the slices at room temperature for at least 30 minutes before serving.

Tar Heel Pie

Yet another recipe from my wife Bev's files, this one is from a postcard she picked up years ago on her travels through North Carolina. I've made a few minor changes, adding some coconut, a bit of salt, and chocolate chips, but it's not the sort of recipe that needs much altering. Since it is essentially a brownie in a crust, the key—as with any brownie—is to underbake it ever so slightly, so the center is soft. Vanilla ice cream is the only proper accompaniment.

MAKES 8 TO 10 SERVINGS

1 recipe Basic Shortening Pie Pastry, Single Crust (page 30) or Basic Flaky Pie Pastry, Single Crust (page 31), refrigerated

FILLING
¹/₂ cup (1 stick) unsalted butter
1¹/₂ cups semisweet chocolate chips
2 large eggs
¹/₂ cup granulated sugar

¹/₂ cup firmly packed light brown sugar
1¹/₂ teaspoons vanilla extract
¹/₂ cup all-purpose flour
¹/₈ teaspoon salt
³/₄ cup chopped pecans
¹/₃ cup sweetened flaked coconut

1. If you haven't already, prepare the pastry and refrigerate until firm enough to roll, about 1 hour.

2. On a sheet of lightly floured waxed paper, roll the pastry into a 12-inch circle with a floured rolling pin. Invert the pastry over a 9-inch standard pie pan, center, and peel off the paper. Tuck the pastry into the pan, without stretching it, and sculpt the edge into an upstanding ridge. Place in the freezer for 15 minutes.

3. Meanwhile, melt the butter in a medium-size saucepan over low heat. When it is melted, turn off the heat and immediately add 1 cup of the chocolate chips to the pan. Swirl the pan so the hot butter runs over the chips. Set aside for 5 minutes, then whisk to smooth. Scrape into a large bowl and let cool for 10 minutes.

4. In a separate large bowl, whisk the eggs, sugars, and vanilla until evenly mixed. Stir in the cooled chocolate mixture. Add the flour and salt and whisk just until evenly combined. Stir in the pecans, coconut, and remaining $1/2$ cup chocolate chips. Scrape the filling into the chilled pie shell.

5. Place the pie on the center oven rack and bake until the top has risen somewhat but the center still seems a little moist, 30 to 35 minutes. Check it with a toothpick, which should emerge with a bit of batter attached.

6. Transfer the pie to a wire rack and let cool. Serve just barely warm or at room temperature.

Recipe for Success

▸ **To save some time, feel free to use a store-bought refrigerated pie pastry. You could even use a frozen deep-dish pie shell—not my first choice for a crust, but it will do. Especially if you're using one of these convenience items, this is a simple recipe to double if you have a friend who loves chocolate. And who doesn't?**

▸ **If you're in doubt about whether the pie is done, you should probably err on the side of underbaking it. Another way to check for doneness is to press down gently on the center of the pie. It should be soft but not overly squishy.**

Snickers Brownie Pie

Take a thick layer of fudge brownie, add another of sliced Snickers bars, top it off with peanut butter cream, and you have one fine candy bar pie. It may sound like a child's dream, but don't be fooled; adults love this as much as kids. The pie needs several hours to chill, so make it in the early afternoon to serve at dinner.

MAKES 8 TO 10 SERVINGS

1 recipe Graham Cracker Crumb Crust (page 51) or 1 large store-bought graham cracker crust

BROWNIE LAYER

1/2 cup (1 stick) unsalted butter, cut into pieces

4 ounces semisweet chocolate, coarsely chopped

1 large egg

1 large egg yolk

1/2 cup granulated sugar

1 teaspoon vanilla extract

1/3 cup all-purpose flour

1/2 teaspoon baking powder

1/8 teaspoon salt

Two 3.7-ounce Snickers bars, sliced crosswise about 1/2 inch thick

PEANUT BUTTER CREAM

3/4 cup cold heavy or whipping cream

2/3 cup confectioners' sugar, sifted

1 teaspoon vanilla extract

2/3 cup smooth peanut butter

Two 3-ounce packages full-fat cream cheese, softened

GARNISH

Warm Mocha Sauce (page 607; optional)

1. Prepare the crust and press it into the bottom and up the side of a 9½-inch deep-dish pie pan. Refrigerate, without prebaking. If you're using a store-bought pie shell, simply remove it from its packaging and refrigerate until needed.

2. Prepare the brownie layer. Put the butter in the top of a double boiler set over, not in, barely simmering water. As the butter starts to melt, scatter the chocolate on top and leave for 5 minutes, then whisk to smooth. Remove the insert from the double boiler and set the chocolate aside to cool for 15 minutes. Preheat the oven to 350°F.

3. Meanwhile, in a large bowl, beat the egg, egg yolk, and granulated sugar together with an electric mixer on medium speed for 2 minutes. Add the chocolate mixture and vanilla and mix until evenly blended. Mix the flour, baking powder, and salt together in a small bowl. Add to the chocolate mixture and stir until evenly combined. Scrape the batter into the chilled pie shell, smoothing the top with a spoon.

4. Place the pie on the center oven rack and bake for exactly 18 minutes—no more or less. Transfer to a wire rack and let cool for 5 minutes. Arrange the sliced Snickers bars in a single layer over the brownie layer. Set aside to cool. Refrigerate, if desired, to accelerate the cooling.

5. When the brownie layer has cooled, make the peanut butter cream. Using a chilled medium-size bowl and chilled beaters, beat the heavy cream with the mixer until it holds soft peaks. Add the confectioners' sugar and continue to beat until stiff but not grainy. Blend in the vanilla. Set aside.

6. Combine the peanut butter and cream cheese in a large bowl. Using the mixer, beat until evenly combined. Add almost half of the whipped cream to the peanut butter mixture and blend on low speed. Add the remaining whipped cream and fold it in until evenly combined. Smooth the peanut butter cream evenly over the Snickers slices. Cover with loosely tented aluminum foil and refrigerate for at least 2 hours or overnight. Serve drizzled with mocha sauce, if desired.

Recipe for Success

▶ **Because the brownie batter is thick-textured and bakes for 18 minutes with the crust, it's not necessary to prebake the pie shell.**

▶ **Expect the brownie layer to rise dramatically in the pan, then settle back down to near its original volume. To keep the brownie good and fudgy, do not bake any longer than recommended.**

▶ **Use any kind of Snickers bar you like. In addition to the original, there is an almond version and some sort of crunchy one I haven't tried.**

▶ **If you don't have time to make the mocha sauce, you can use store-bought chocolate syrup instead.**

Amaretto-Amaretti Chocolate Fudge Pie

I lived in New Hampshire for quite a few years, so I've been through Waitsfield, Vermont, a number of times. I don't know what it is about the place, but for a tiny town, it has some great food. This chocolate pie from the Millbrook Inn is a good example. It has a delicious amaretti crust and a creamy, fudgy amaretto-flavored filling. The texture firms up as the pie cools, but this is as good warm as it is cold.

MAKES 8 TO 10 SERVINGS

1 recipe Amaretti Crumb Crust (page 56)

FILLING

1/2 cup (1 stick) unsalted butter, cut into pieces

3 ounces unsweetened chocolate

1 1/2 cups sugar

4 large eggs, at room temperature

1/4 teaspoon salt

3 tablespoons light corn syrup

1/4 cup heavy or whipping cream

2 tablespoons amaretto

1 teaspoon vanilla extract

GARNISH

Fresh Whipped Cream (page 605)

1. Prepare the crust and press it into the bottom and halfway up the side of a 9½- to 10-inch extra-deep-dish pie pan. Refrigerate, without prebaking.

2. Place the butter and chocolate in the top of a double boiler set over, not in, barely simmering water. Once they've melted, remove the insert and set aside to cool, whisking to smooth while the mixture is still warm. Preheat the oven to 350°F.

3. In a large bowl, beat the sugar, eggs, and salt with an electric mixer on medium-high speed until the mixture is thick, pale yellow, and foamy, about 4 minutes. Beat in the corn syrup, heavy cream, amaretto, vanilla, and chocolate mixture until evenly blended. Pour the filling into the chilled pie shell.

4. Place the pie on the center oven rack and bake until it has puffed considerably around the edge and slightly less in the center, about 50 minutes. Rotate the pie 180 degrees halfway through the baking, so that the part that faced the back of the oven now faces forward. When done, the filling will be wobbly but not soupy in the center. Give the pie a quick little nudge to check.

5. Transfer the pie to a wire rack and let cool. Serve barely warm or at room temperature. Or cover with loosely tented aluminum foil and refrigerate until slightly chilled before serving. Garnish with whipped cream.

Recipe for Success

▶ If you can't find amaretti or would simply rather not use this crust, use either Graham Cracker Crumb Crust (page 51) or Chocolate Wafer Crumb Crust (page 54) instead.

▶ The thorough beating of the eggs and sugar here results in a fair volume of filling, which rises more than a little in the pan. The filling itself should come no higher than two-thirds to three-quarters up the side of the pan. If you have extra filling, bake it in buttered custard cups.

Chocolate Cream Pie
with Cinnamon Meringue

This pie is wonderful even without the meringue, but it's really spectacular with it. The straight-forward filling and generous topping of golden meringue remind me of a pie you'd find in a great American diner. You can eat this warm, though the chocolate filling will still be soft. I think it's much better if the pie is refrigerated before serving.

MAKES 8 SERVINGS

1 recipe Basic Shortening Pie Pastry, Single Crust (page 30) or Basic Flaky Pie Pastry, Single Crust (page 31), refrigerated

FILLING

2¹/₄ cups whole milk

1¹/₄ cups sugar

¹/₃ cup cornstarch

2 ounces semisweet chocolate, coarsely chopped

3 large eggs, separated

¹/₄ teaspoon salt

1¹/₂ teaspoons vanilla extract

CINNAMON MERINGUE

3 large egg whites, at room temperature

¹/₄ teaspoon cream of tartar

¹/₄ cup sugar

¹/₂ teaspoon ground cinnamon

1. If you haven't already, prepare the pastry and refrigerate until firm enough to roll, about 1 hour.

2. On a sheet of lightly floured waxed paper, roll the pastry into a 12-inch circle with a floured rolling pin. Invert the pastry over a 9-inch standard pie pan, center, and peel off the paper. Tuck the pastry into the pan, without stretching it, and sculpt the edge into an upstanding ridge. Place in the freezer for 15 minutes, then fully prebake and let cool according to the instructions on page 16. Reduce the oven temperature to 350°F.

3. Combine the milk, sugar, cornstarch, chocolate, egg yolks, and salt in a large, heavy saucepan, preferably nonstick. Place over medium heat and cook, whisking virtually nonstop, until the mixture starts to boil, 5 to 7 minutes. Continue to cook, whisking rapidly to minimize any spattering, for about 2 minutes. Remove from the heat and stir in the vanilla. Carefully pour the filling into the cooled pie shell, smoothing the top with a spoon. Transfer to a wire rack.

4.   While the filling is still hot, make the meringue. Using an electric mixer, beat the egg whites in a medium-size bowl until they hold soft peaks. Beat in the cream of tartar. Mix the sugar and cinnamon together in a small bowl and add to the meringue 1 tablespoon at a time. Continue beating until the whites are thick and glossy but not dry. Carefully spread the meringue over the filling, anchoring it to the edge of the pastry all around.

5.   Place the pie on the center oven rack and bake until golden brown, 8 to 10 minutes. Transfer the pie to a wire rack and let cool. Serve barely warm or at room temperature. Or refrigerate, uncovered, and serve cold. This is best eaten within 24 hours.

Recipe for Success

▶   **Since the meringue topping isn't a great keeper, I prefer to make the pie in the morning and serve it later the same day.**

▶   **With practice, you'll learn when a meringue has been beaten long enough. It should not be underbeaten, lest it not achieve its full volume. Nor should it be overbeaten, or it will be a little too firm and difficult to spread.**

Chocolate Chip Cookie Pie

This and the following oatmeal–butterscotch chip pie are variations on the famous Toll House cookie pie—each essentially a big buttery cookie in a pie crust. America's signature pie may be apple, but something tells me that these pies are made more often. There's nothing to peel and no top crust, and they can be mixed up and in the oven in about five minutes. And are they ever good, like eating the fattest chocolate (or butterscotch) chip cookie you can imagine. I must have looked at a hundred variations of this pie, most of which were very similar. This one is a little different in that it uses three eggs instead of two; it contains some milk, for extra moistness; and it uses cake flour instead of all-purpose, for the most tender result imaginable. You could make a case for eating this at any temperature, but the extremes aren't recommended: too hot, and the texture is overly soft; too cold, and the flavors don't jump out at you. The best, I think, is slightly chilled—before the chocolate chips have rehardened, but not so cold that the flavor is dulled.

MAKES 8 TO 10 SERVINGS

1 recipe Basic Flaky Pie Pastry, Single Crust (page 31), refrigerated

FILLING

1/2 cup (1 stick) unsalted butter, softened

1 cup firmly packed light brown sugar

1/2 cup granulated sugar

3 large eggs, at room temperature

1 teaspoon vanilla extract

1/2 cup cake flour, sifted

1/4 teaspoon salt

1/4 cup whole milk or light cream

1 cup semisweet chocolate chips

1/2 cup coarsely chopped walnuts

1. If you haven't already, prepare the pastry and refrigerate until firm enough to roll, about 1 hour.

2. On a sheet of lightly floured waxed paper, roll the pastry into a 12-inch circle with a floured rolling pin. Invert the pastry over a 9-inch standard pie pan, center, and peel off the paper. Tuck the pastry into the pan, without stretching it, and sculpt the edge into an upstanding ridge. Place in the freezer for 15 minutes. Preheat the oven to 350°F.

3. Using an electric mixer, cream the butter on medium speed in a large bowl, gradually adding the sugars. Beat in the eggs, one at a time, beating well after each addition. Beat in the vanilla. Add the flour and salt and blend until evenly mixed. Blend in the milk. Don't be concerned if the filling looks a little curdled. Stir in the chocolate chips and walnuts. Pour the filling into the chilled pie shell, smoothing the top with a spoon.

4. Place the pie on the center oven rack and bake until the center is set, about 1 hour, rotating the pie 180 degrees halfway through the baking, so that the part that faced the back of the oven now faces forward. When done, the top of the pie will be a dark golden brown. That's fine; it doesn't mean that the pie is overbaked. Give the pie a slight nudge. The filling should not move in waves, even at the center.

5. Transfer the pie to a wire rack and let cool. Serve slightly warm or at room temperature. Or cover with loosely tented aluminum foil and refrigerate for 1 to 2 hours before serving.

Recipe for Success

▶ **This pie is excellent for shipping because it is sturdy and a good keeper. For shipping, you will want to use a pie shell in a disposable aluminum pan, either one of your own or store-bought. If you buy a frozen pie shell, make sure it is marked "deep-dish." Since the capacity of most disposable pie pans is less than many glass or ceramic pans, if you are making your own pie shell, sculpt** the edge so it is a little higher than usual, to hold as much filling as possible. Keep the filling about $1/4$ inch below the top of the pastry. When you ship the pie, it should be frozen or partially frozen. Wrap it well in plastic, then aluminum foil. Ship in a well-padded box.

▶ **This bears repeating: Don't be concerned if the top of the pie gets a little dark. That darkness is just a very thin crust and does not indicate that the filling is overcooked.**

Oatmeal–Butterscotch Chip Cookie Pie

This pie is like a thick cookie—an oatmeal cookie with butterscotch chips. The oats give the pie a little extra chewiness and the chips add that old-fashioned flavor kids love. A good keeper and easy to slice, this pie (and the previous one) is great for bake sales.

MAKES 8 TO 10 SERVINGS

1 recipe Basic Flaky Pie Pastry, Single Crust (page 31), refrigerated

FILLING

$1/2$ cup (1 stick) unsalted butter, softened

$11/2$ cups firmly packed light brown sugar

3 large eggs, at room temperature

1 teaspoon vanilla extract

$1/3$ cup old-fashioned rolled oats (not quick-cooking)

$1/3$ cup cake flour or all-purpose flour

$1/4$ teaspoon salt

$1/4$ cup whole milk or light cream

1 cup butterscotch chips, or $1/2$ cup butterscotch chips and $1/2$ cup semisweet chocolate chips

$1/2$ cup chopped pecans

1.　If you haven't already, prepare the pastry and refrigerate until firm enough to roll, about 1 hour.

2.　On a sheet of lightly floured waxed paper, roll the pastry into a 13-inch circle with a floured rolling pin. Invert the pastry over a $91/2$-inch deep-dish pie pan, center, and peel off the paper. Tuck the pastry into the pan, without stretching it, and sculpt the edge into an upstanding ridge. Place in the freezer for 15 minutes. Preheat the oven to 350°F.

3.　In a large bowl, cream the butter with an electric mixer on medium speed, gradually adding the brown sugar. Beat in the eggs, one at a time, beating well after each addition. Beat in the vanilla. Add the oats, flour, and salt and blend with the mixer until evenly combined. Blend in the milk. Don't be concerned if the filling looks a little curdled. Stir in the chips and pecans. Pour the filling into the chilled pie shell, smoothing the top with a spoon.

4. Place the pie on the center oven rack and bake until the center is set, about 1 hour, rotating the pie 180 degrees about halfway through the baking, so the part that faced the back of the oven now faces forward. When done, the top will be a dark golden brown. That's okay: the darkness is just a thin crust and doesn't mean the pie is overbaked. Give the pie a slight nudge. The filling should not move in waves, even at the center.

5. Transfer the pie to a wire rack and let cool. Serve slightly warm or at room temperature. Or cover with loosely tented aluminum foil and refrigerate for 1 to 2 hours before serving.

Recipe for Success

▶ If you plan to ship this pie or give it as a gift, consider using a disposable aluminum pie pan (see Recipe for Success on page 569). Since pies baked in these pans can be a little tricky to grasp and lift off the oven rack, here's a tip. Just lift the forward edge of it with a metal spatula. As you do, quickly slide one edge of a rimless cookie sheet under the pie, then lift the pie onto the sheet, remove it from the oven, and slide it onto a wire rack.

Hillbilly Pie

Down Arkansas way, you sometimes hear about, and even find on restaurant menus, something known as hillbilly pie. It's been described as the poor man's pecan pie because the filling is made with oats instead of the far more costly pecans. The most basic versions are little more than sugar, eggs, corn syrup, and oats. A reference to one such recipe suggests that the pie has been around for at least 40 or 50 years, perhaps longer—long enough, at least judging from some recipes, for modern cooks to start adding embellishments such as chocolate chunks, a shortbread crust, and even, yes, pecans to what began as a rather modest pie.

Oatmeal Butterscotch Pie

More than one source I consulted claims that oatmeal pies became popular during the Depression, when cooks devised all sorts of clever ways to stretch a dish at little cost. To what extent this is true, I'm not sure, although it certainly makes sense. What's more important is that all the oatmeal pies I've made taste wonderful. Here's one I find particularly delicious, and that's probably no accident when you consider the source: Quaker, the maker of Quaker Oats. I've taken a few liberties with the original recipe by adding butterscotch chips and a few nuts, which make it taste like a giant oatmeal cookie. The oats, for the most part, settle on top of the pie and form a cookie-like coating over the moist interior. This one is excellent with a glass of cold milk or a scoop of vanilla ice cream.

MAKES 8 TO 10 SERVINGS

1 recipe Basic Flaky Pie Pastry, Single Crust (page 31), refrigerated

FILLING

2 large eggs

3/4 cup sugar

3/4 cup dark corn syrup

1/4 cup (1/2 stick) unsalted butter, melted

3/4 cup rolled oats (old-fashioned or quick-cooking)

1/3 cup sweetened flaked coconut

2 tablespoons all-purpose flour

1/2 cup butterscotch chips

1/2 cup chopped walnuts or pecans

1/2 teaspoon vanilla extract

1.   If you haven't already, prepare the pastry and refrigerate until firm enough to roll, about 1 hour.

2.   On a sheet of lightly floured waxed paper, roll the pastry into a 12-inch circle with a floured rolling pin. Invert the pastry over a 9-inch standard pie pan, center, and peel off the paper. Tuck the pastry into the pan, without stretching it, and sculpt the edge into an upstanding ridge. Place in the freezer for 15 minutes. Preheat the oven to 375°F.

3.   Combine the eggs, sugar, corn syrup, and butter in a large bowl. Using an electric mixer, beat on medium speed until well blended, about 30 seconds. Stir in the oats, coconut, flour, butterscotch chips, nuts, and vanilla. Pour the filling into the chilled pie shell.

4.   Place the pie on the center oven rack and bake for 30 minutes. Reduce the oven temperature to 350°F and rotate the pie 180 degrees, so that the side that faced the back of the oven now faces forward. Bake until the center is set, 25 to 30 minutes. When done,

the top of the pie will be dark golden brown and crusty. Give the pie a sharp little nudge. The filling shouldn't move in waves.

5. Transfer the pie to a wire rack and let cool. Serve just barely warm or at room temperature.

Recipe for Success

▶ Not only is this pie a cinch to make, but it multiplies wonderfully if you're expecting a crowd or need a large quantity of something for a bake sale. Just double everything and divide the filling among 3 store-bought frozen pie shells, which in most ovens you'll be able to bake on one rack. (You'll need 3 pie shells because a frozen shell doesn't hold as much as crust in a 9-inch standard pie pan.) About halfway through the baking, change the position of the pans, from front to back, and rotate each 180 degrees.

Oatmeal Raisin Pie

This recipe is a favorite of my wife, Bev, and has been in her files for "at least a dozen years," making the trip from her former home in Charleston, South Carolina, to our current home in Annapolis, Maryland. She says the gooey texture of the pie reminds her of one of her favorite sweets, Charleston tarts, which are something like small pecan pies (and which served as the model for my Charleston Pies on page 422). Like that recipe, this one uses a cream cheese pastry, which has a slight tang and the perfect flaky texture. Always quick to find an excuse to eat pie for breakfast, Bev says that, as sweet as this pie is, the oatmeal makes it perfectly acceptable breakfast fare. I concur. If you're in a hurry, use a store-bought refrigerated pie pastry.

MAKES 8 TO 10 SERVINGS

1 recipe Tender Cream Cheese Pastry, Single Crust (page 46), refrigerated

FILLING
3 large eggs
1 cup light corn syrup
1/2 cup firmly packed light brown sugar
1/4 cup (1/2 stick) unsalted butter, melted
3/4 cup quick-cooking rolled oats

3/4 cup dark raisins
1 tablespoon all-purpose flour
1/2 teaspoon ground cinnamon
1/4 teaspoon salt

GARNISH
Vanilla ice cream or Fresh Whipped Cream (page 605)

1.   If you haven't already, prepare the pastry and refrigerate until firm enough to roll, about 1 hour.

2.   On a sheet of lightly floured waxed paper, roll the pastry into a 12-inch circle with a floured rolling pin. Invert the pastry over a 9-inch standard pie pan, center, and peel off the paper. Tuck the pastry into the pan, without stretching it, and sculpt the edge into an upstanding ridge. Place in the freezer for 15 minutes, then partially prebake and let cool according to the instructions on page 16. Reduce the oven temperature to 350°F.

3.   Whisk the eggs, corn syrup, and brown sugar together in a large bowl. Whisk in the melted butter. Add the oats, raisins, flour, cinnamon, and salt and stir well to combine. Pour the filling into the cooled pie shell. Using a fork, gently rake the filling to distribute the raisins evenly.

4.   Place the pie on the center oven rack and bake until the center is set, about 40 minutes. Rotate the pie 180 degrees halfway through the baking time, so that the part that faced the back of the oven now faces forward. When done, the top will form an oatmeal cookie–like crust and the center will be set, not soupy. To check, give the pie a quick little nudge.

5.   Transfer the pie to a wire rack and let cool. Serve barely warm or at room temperature, garnished with a scoop of vanilla ice cream or a dollop of whipped cream.

Recipe for Success

▶ **As with some pecan pies, it's a close call whether to prebake the crust for this pie. If you're pressed for time, you could skip that step and simply pour the filling into the unbaked pie shell and bake as is. The crust won't be as crisp as it could be, but it will still be good.**

▶ **This is a sturdy pie that travels well, even through the mail. Keep that in mind if you have kids away at college or in the armed forces. Bake it in an inexpensive aluminum pan, the kind you can buy at the supermarket for a couple of dollars. Wrap well in plastic, then aluminum foil. Freeze the pie overnight and ship using one of the faster forms of delivery so it arrives in 2 to 3 days.**

Norske Nook Raisin Pie

The Norske Nook restaurant in Osseo, Wisconsin, is a pie lover's heaven, and with pies like this on the menu, it's easy to understand why. The filling is what I think of as a classic dairy country sour cream custard, cooked on the stovetop and teeming with plump raisins. It's spread in a pastry crust, cooled, and then topped with delicate peaks of golden meringue.

MAKES 8 TO 10 SERVINGS

1 recipe Basic Shortening Pie Pastry, Single Crust (page 30) or Basic Flaky Pie Pastry, Single Crust (page 31), refrigerated

FILLING

2 cups full-fat sour cream

1³/₄ cups sugar

4 teaspoons all-purpose flour

4 large eggs yolks

1¹/₂ cups dark raisins

MERINGUE

4 large egg whites

¹/₂ cup sugar

¹/₄ teaspoon salt

1. If you haven't already, prepare the pastry and refrigerate until firm enough to roll, about 1 hour.

2. On a sheet of lightly floured waxed paper, roll the pastry into a 12-inch circle with a floured rolling pin. Invert the pastry over a 9-inch standard pie pan, center, and peel off the paper. Tuck the pastry into the pan, without stretching it, and sculpt the edge into an upstanding ridge. Place in the freezer for 15 minutes, then fully prebake and let cool according to the directions on page 16.

3. Combine the sour cream, sugar, flour, egg yolks, and raisins in a large, heavy saucepan, preferably nonstick. Cook the mixture over medium heat, stirring continuously, until it thickens and turns glossy, 8 to 10 minutes. Slowly pour the filling into the cooled pie shell. Let cool thoroughly on a wire rack, then refrigerate for at least 2 hours or overnight.

4. Just before serving, preheat the broiler and make the meringue. Put the egg whites in a large metal bowl over a pan of hot water. Stir in the sugar and salt. When the sugar has dissolved, use an electric mixer to beat the whites until they hold firm but not dry peaks. Spread the meringue thoroughly over the pie, so that it touches the entire edge of the crust, with no gaps. Briefly run the pie under the broiler until very lightly browned. Do not leave the oven, as this will take a very short time. Serve immediately.

Recipe for Success

▶ Be patient when you're stirring the sour cream custard. After 8 to 10 minutes, you should see a noticeable thickening and feel the increased friction against your spoon.

▶ I like to add about ¹/₂ teaspoon vanilla extract to the custard, although the original recipe doesn't call for it.

Peach Preserves and Applesauce Strudel Pie

Sometimes, when I don't want to mess with putting together a filling or rolling a couple of crusts, I make a pie like this. I take a cream cheese pastry, roll it into a long oblong, and cover half of it with preserves and applesauce—although you could leave out the latter if you don't have any on hand. Then I fold the dough over the filling, crimp the edge, and bake. It looks like a big flat calzone. I dust the warm strudel pie with confectioners' sugar, let cool briefly, and slice into thin wedges. If I'm expecting guests or family, I make the dough the night before and serve this as a welcoming breakfast pie.

MAKES 8 TO 10 SERVINGS

1 recipe Tender Cream Cheese Pastry, Single Crust (page 46), refrigerated

FILLING

1 cup good-quality peach preserves

¹/₂ cup sweetened applesauce

Confectioners' sugar

1. If you haven't already, prepare the pastry and refrigerate until firm enough to roll, about 1 hour. At the end of the hour, preheat the oven to 400°F. Get out a large baking sheet and line it with parchment paper.

2. On a sheet of lightly floured waxed paper, roll the pastry with a floured rolling pin into an oblong nearly as long as your baking sheet, perhaps 14 to 15 inches. Invert the pastry onto the baking sheet and peel off the paper. Smooth the preserves evenly over the lower half of the pastry, lengthwise. Spoon the applesauce over the preserves and smooth.

3. Moisten the entire edge of the dough with a pastry brush. Using the parchment paper to help you lift the pastry, fold the top half of the pastry over the filling and line up the edges. Press together, then roll them slightly, sealing the edge. Using a paring knife, poke 3 or 4 steam vents in the top of the pastry, entering the dough on an angle to help prevent you from poking through the bottom of the pastry.

4. Place the baking sheet on the center oven rack and bake for 10 minutes. Reduce the oven temperature to 375°F and bake until the top is a rich golden brown, about 25 minutes. Rotate the pie 180 degrees, so that the part that faced the back of the oven now faces forward, about 10 minutes before it is done. Transfer the baking sheet to a wire rack and let cool for 10 minutes. If the rack is long enough to support the entire pie, slide it, along with the parchment, onto the rack. If not, simply let it cool on the baking sheet.

5. While the pie is still quite warm, put a few tablespoons of confectioners' sugar in a sifter or sieve and dust the top of the pie. Let the pie cool for about 30 minutes before serving.

Recipe for Success

▶ **You can, of course, use other sorts of preserves. Blueberry is good, and you can scatter a few fresh blueberries right over the preserves. The same goes for raspberry preserves and fresh raspberries. Include the applesauce or not; you just don't want to go too heavy on the filling. Part of the beauty of this pie is its relative lightness, making it a good choice for breakfast.**

Linzer Pie

If you like pastries, you're no doubt familiar with the famous tart known as Linzer torte. Basically a rich almond or hazelnut pastry with a filling of raspberry jam, it's typically prepared in a tart or springform pan. My version is similar, although it should come as no surprise that I bake it in a pie pan, using a walnut pastry. This pastry is neither as rich nor as sweet as the traditional dough, but it's excellent nonetheless. As in the original, I lay thin strips of dough over the top in a crisscross lattice. The lattice lets the raspberry jam show through and makes for a very attractive pie indeed.

MAKES 10 TO 12 SERVINGS

1 recipe Nutty Pie Pastry (page 42) made with   1^1/$_4$ cups raspberry preserves
walnuts, refrigerated

1. If you haven't already, prepare the pastry and refrigerate until firm enough to roll, but not too firm, about 45 minutes. If the dough is too firm, it may be more difficult to handle.

2. On a sheet of lightly floured waxed paper, roll the larger half of the pastry into a 10^1/$_2$-inch circle with a lightly floured rolling pin. Invert the pastry over a 9^1/$_2$-inch deep-dish pie pan, center, and peel off the paper. Tuck the pastry into the pan without stretching it. The pastry will come only about halfway up the side of the pan. Spread the raspberry preserves evenly in the pie shell and refrigerate. Preheat the oven to 350°F.

3. On another sheet of floured waxed paper, roll the other half of the pastry into an 11-inch circle. Using a ruler and a fluted pastry wheel or pizza cutter, cut the dough into 14 strips about ^{1}/$_2$ inch wide. Lifting the strips slowly and gently, place 7 parallel strips over the filling in the chilled pie, leaving a little space between them. Pinch the strips to the edge of the pastry. Place the remaining strips across the others, laying them right over the top. Instead of running them at right angles to the other strips, lay them diagonally. Pinch to seal.

4. Place the pie on the center oven rack and bake until the strips are just turning golden brown and the raspberry jam has begun to bubble, about 40 minutes. Rotate the pie 180 degrees halfway through the baking time, so that the part that faced the back of the oven now faces forward.

5. Transfer the pie to a wire rack and let cool to room temperature. Cut into thin wedges and serve.

Recipe for Success

▶ **Flour the waxed paper well before rolling the pastry. This pastry tends to be a little tackier than some.**

▶ **If the pastry strips fall apart as you lift them off the waxed paper, don't be too concerned. Just piece them together on the pie, and they'll more or less fuse together as they bake.**

▶ **You can substitute up to ^{1}/$_3$ cup smooth sweetened applesauce for an equal measure of raspberry preserves, if you like. That will make the filling a little less sweet. Simply blend the two together before adding them to the pie.**

Double-Crust Marmalade Pie

So similar is this in flavor to Shaker Lemon Pie (page 582) that, had it not sounded borderline flippant, I might have called it Faker Shaker Pie. The big difference, and the reason I came up with this pie, is that it can be made very quickly, with a jar of lemon marmalade, whereas the authentic Shaker pie requires you to macerate thinly sliced lemons for several hours or overnight. As you might imagine, the marmalade pie is less textured, since you're biting into preserves, not lemon slices. Other than that, the flavors are pretty close, provided you use a marmalade that's made with at least some lemon. The brand I like best is James Keiller & Son's Dundee Three Fruits Marmalade, with lemons, oranges, and grapefruit.

MAKES 8 TO 10 SERVINGS

1 recipe Basic Flaky Pie Pastry, Double Crust (page 31), refrigerated, or 2 store-bought refrigerated pie pastries

FILLING

One 1-pound jar (1¹/₂ cups) part-lemon marmalade

3 tablespoons unsalted butter, melted

4 large eggs, lightly beaten

¹/₄ cup sugar

2 tablespoons all-purpose flour

Pinch of ground nutmeg

Pinch of salt

¹/₄ teaspoon vanilla extract

GLAZE

Milk or light cream

Sugar

GARNISH

Vanilla ice cream

1. If you haven't already, prepare the pastry and refrigerate until firm enough to roll, about 1 hour.

2. On a sheet of lightly floured waxed paper, roll the larger portion of the pastry into a 12-inch circle with a floured rolling pin. Invert the pastry over a 9-inch standard pie pan, center, and peel off the paper. Gently tuck the pastry into the pan, without stretching it, and let the overhang drape over the edge. Place in the refrigerator for 15 minutes. Preheat the oven to 400°F.

3. In a large bowl, combine the marmalade and butter, whisking until smooth. Whisk in the eggs. Stir the sugar, flour, nutmeg, salt, and vanilla into the filling.

4. On another sheet of floured waxed paper, roll the other half of the pastry into a 10-inch circle. Pour the filling into the chilled pie shell. Lightly moisten the rim of the pie shell. Invert the top pastry over the filling, center, and peel off the paper. Press the top and bottom pastries together along the dampened edge. Using scissors, cut the pastry, leaving an even ½-inch overhang all around, and sculpt the edge into an upstanding ridge. Poke several steam vents in the top of the pie with a fork or paring knife. To glaze the pie, lightly brush the pastry with milk and sprinkle with sugar.

5. Place the pie on the center oven rack and bake for 15 minutes. Reduce the oven temperature to 350°F and rotate the pie 180 degrees, so that the part that faced the back of the oven now faces forward. Continue to bake until the top is golden brown, 25 to 30 minutes. When done, the pie will be set in the center, not liquidy. Insert the tip of a paring knife into the center to check.

6. Transfer the pie to a wire rack and let cool. Serve barely warm or at room temperature, with a scoop of ice cream.

Recipe for Success

▶ **If you can't find a marmalade made with lemons, use what you can find and incorporate some lemon flavor into it. One-half teaspoon lemon extract should do the trick nicely.**

▶ **Do serve this pie with the ice cream, since marmalade can have a bit of a tart edge.**

Mango and Candied Ginger Pie

I use frozen mango chunks for this pie because they're fast and convenient: you don't have to cut or peel anything. Check your local supermarket or Trader Joe's, which is where I buy them. While you're there, pick up some candied (also called crystallized) ginger, which you'll also need for the pie. The combination of the two, plus the pineapple, gives this a Caribbean twist. The amount of ginger used results in a very pronounced flavor. I like it that way, but you can always cut it back by one-half, if you like.

MAKES 8 TO 10 SERVINGS

1 recipe Basic Flaky Pie Pastry, Double Crust (page 31), refrigerated

FILLING

5 cups frozen mango chunks, partially thawed

1 cup diced canned pineapple, drained but juice reserved

1/4 cup chopped candied (crystallized) ginger

1/2 cup plus 3 tablespoons sugar

2 tablespoons cornstarch

1 tablespoon fresh lemon juice

1/2 teaspoon grated lemon zest

1/2 teaspoon vanilla extract

GLAZE

Milk or light cream

Sugar

1. If you haven't already, prepare the pastry and refrigerate until firm enough to roll, about 1 hour.

2. On a sheet of lightly floured waxed paper, roll the larger portion of the pastry into a 13-inch circle with a floured rolling pin. Invert the pastry over a 9½-inch deep-dish pie pan, center, and peel off the paper. Gently tuck the pastry into the pan, without stretching it, and let the overhang drape over the edge. Place in the refrigerator for 15 minutes.

3. In a large bowl, combine the mango chunks, pineapple, ⅓ cup of the reserved pineapple juice, the ginger, and ½ cup of the sugar. Mix well, then set aside for 10 minutes. Preheat the oven to 400°F.

4. Mix the remaining 3 tablespoons sugar and the cornstarch together in a small bowl. Stir the mixture into the fruit along with the lemon juice, lemon zest, and vanilla. Set aside.

5. On another sheet of lightly floured waxed paper, roll the other half of the pastry into an 11-inch circle. Turn the filling into the chilled pie shell and smooth the fruit with a spoon. Lightly moisten the rim of the pie shell. Invert the top pastry over the filling, center, and peel off the paper. Press the top and bottom pastries together along the dampened edge. Trim the pastry with scissors or a paring knife, leaving an even ½-inch overhang all around, then sculpt the overhang into an upstanding ridge. Poke several steam vents in the top of the pie with a fork or paring knife. Put a couple of the vents near the edge of the crust so you can check the juices there later. To glaze the pie, lightly brush the pastry with milk and sprinkle with sugar.

6. Place the pie on the center oven rack and bake for 30 minutes. Reduce the oven temperature to 375°F and rotate the pie 180 degrees, so that the part that faced the back of the oven now faces forward. Just in case, slide a large aluminum foil–lined baking sheet onto the rack below to catch any drips. Bake until the juices bubble thickly at the steam vents and the top is golden brown, 35 to 45 minutes. If the top of the pie starts to get too dark, cover it with loosely tented aluminum foil during the last 10 to 15 minutes.

7. Transfer the pie to a wire rack and let cool for at least 2 hours before serving.

Recipe for Success

▶ Remember that it's important to partially thaw the fruit before it goes into the pie filling, or the pie will take longer to cook and the crust will likely become too brown. I just put the fruit in a bowl and stick it in the microwave on half power until the fruit is still cool and just shy of thawed. Sometimes my chunks are quite big, and I cut them in half.

▶ This pie is also good with a coconut crumb topping instead of a top crust. Check the index to find one that looks good.

Shaker Lemon Pie

I'm a big fan of the Shakers. When I lived in New Hampshire, I visited the restored Canterbury Shaker Village on a regular basis. The Shakers' thriftiness as cooks is well documented, although they were equally inventive and clever, always willing to try new ways to improve the foods they prepared. This delicious lemon pie is nearly always credited to the Shakers. Modern cooks find it fascinating, I think, because it includes the zest and white pith of the lemon, the latter being one of those things that food writers such as myself are always warning you to avoid because it is very bitter. Not so here, however, because the paper-thin lemon slices are first macerated with a full two cups of sugar, rendering the pith nicely palatable. Nearly all the recipes you see for Shaker lemon pie are identical, including this one. If you haven't tried this pie before, I think you'll be delighted by how delicious it is.

MAKES 8 TO 10 SERVINGS

2 lemons

2 cups sugar

Big pinch of salt

1 recipe Basic Flaky Pie Pastry, Double Crust (page 31), refrigerated

4 large eggs

2 tablespoons all-purpose flour

1 tablespoon sugar

2 tablespoons unsalted butter, melted

GLAZE

Milk or light cream

Sugar

1. At least 4 to 5 hours before you plan to make the pie, or the day before, grate the zest from the lemons and set it aside. Using a very sharp knife, slice the lemons paper-thin, removing the seeds as you encounter them. When the lemon gets too small to hold comfortably, put the flat (cut) surface down to stabilize it and continue to slice. Put the slices in a large glass or pottery bowl and add the sugar, salt, and grated zest, mixing well with your hands. Cover the bowl with plastic wrap and set aside at room temperature for at least 4 hours or overnight, stirring once or twice.

2. If you haven't already, prepare the pastry and refrigerate until firm enough to roll, about 1 hour.

3. On a sheet of lightly floured waxed paper, roll the larger portion of the pastry into a 12-inch circle with a floured rolling pin. Invert the pastry over a 9-inch standard pie pan, center, and peel off the paper. Gently tuck the pastry into the pan, without stretching it, and let the overhang drape over the edge. Place in the refrigerator for 15 minutes. Preheat the oven to 400°F.

4. Whisk the eggs in a medium-size bowl, blending well, then whisk in the flour and sugar. Add the egg mixture and butter to the lemon slices, stirring until evenly blended. Set aside.

5. On another sheet of floured waxed paper, roll the other half of the pastry into a 10-inch circle. Turn the filling into the chilled pie shell, smoothing the top with a spoon. Lightly moisten the rim of the pie shell. Invert the top pastry over the filling, center, and peel off the paper. Press the top and bottom pastries together along the dampened edge. Using scissors, cut the pastry, leaving an even ½-inch overhang all around. Sculpt the edge into an upstanding ridge. Poke several steam vents in the top of the pie with a fork or paring knife. To glaze the pie, lightly brush the pastry with milk and sprinkle with sugar.

6. Place the pie on the center oven rack and bake for 25 minutes. Reduce the oven temperature to 375°F and rotate the pie 180 degrees, so that the part that faced the back of the oven now faces forward. Continue to bake until the top is golden brown, about 25 minutes.

7. Transfer the pie to a wire rack and let cool. Serve just barely warm or at room temperature.

Recipe for Success

▶ When I say paper-thin slices, I mean paper-thin. Use your sharpest serrated knife, or sharpen your chef's knife before you begin cutting the lemon. I wouldn't even bother to try this without a good sharp knife. And if you're lucky enough to own a mandoline, now's the time to pull it out.

▶ Because you're using slices of lemon, you should serve pieces of this pie with a fork and knife, so that your guests can deal with any large pieces of lemon. Incidentally, I'm not religious about maintaining the integrity of the slices. In fact, on occasion I've coarsely chopped the lemon—giving them the once-over with my chef's knife—to keep the pieces to a manageable size.

Those Inventive Shakers

"Shaker men found time to develop a mechanical apple parer, a pea sheller, a water-powered butter churn, an automatic cheese press, a superior wood-burning stove, matches, and a revolving oven for baking dozens of pies at a time. The women charged with the community cooking did inventive things with all kinds of ingredients. Shakers perfected a way to produce dried corn—and thereby helped provide Americans generally with year-round supplies that would not spoil easily. . . . They created their own excellent architecture, designed furniture that is much coveted in the twentieth century, devised methods to increase productivity of soil and livestock, and became superior mechanics, responsible for inventions that helped improve the lives of many outsiders."

—Evan Jones, *American Food* (Vintage Books, 1981)

Colonnade Cafeteria's Lemon Meringue Pie

My pie connection in Louisville, Kentucky, Liz Reiter (see page 225), tells me that the gold standard for lemon meringue pie in her neck of the woods is the one served at the Colonnade Cafeteria, a local institution. Unlike what she calls "those firm-sided, perfect triangles" of lemon meringue pie, a slice of the Colonnade's has a gooey puddle of lemony filling that "seeps slowly from under its heavy meringue topping, forcing you to scoop, rather than slice, each bite." Sound good? It's delicious, and although I will freely admit that lemon meringue isn't my favorite pie, I find this one irresistible.

MAKES 8 SERVINGS

1 recipe Basic Shortening Pie Pastry, Single Crust (page 30) or Basic Flaky Pie Pastry, Single Crust (page 31), refrigerated

FILLING

1 1/4 cups warm water

1/2 cup plus 2 tablespoons sugar

Pinch of salt

2 tablespoons cornstarch

3 large egg yolks

3 tablespoons fresh lemon juice

1 teaspoon grated lemon zest

1 teaspoon cold salted or unsalted butter

MERINGUE

4 large egg whites, at room temperature

Pinch of salt

1/2 cup sugar

1. If you haven't already, prepare the pastry and refrigerate until firm enough to roll, about 1 hour.

2. On a sheet of lightly floured waxed paper, roll the pastry into a 12-inch circle with a floured rolling pin. Invert over a 9-inch standard pie pan, center, and peel off the paper. Tuck the pastry into the pan, without stretching it, and sculpt the edge so it is even with the rim. Place in the freezer for 15 minutes, then partially prebake and let cool according to the instructions on page 16. Reduce the oven temperature to 325°F.

3. Combine 1 cup of the water, the sugar, and salt in a medium-size, heavy saucepan. Cover and gradually bring to a boil over medium heat, stirring to dissolve the sugar. Combine the remaining 1/4 cup water and the cornstarch in a small bowl, mixing well to make a lump-free paste. When the sugar mixture comes to a boil, quickly whisk in the cornstarch paste; the liquid will immediately thicken. Remove from the heat and set aside.

4. In a medium-size bowl, beat the egg yolks, lemon juice, and lemon zest with an electric mixer until pale yellow and slightly thickened. Whisk about 2 tablespoons of the hot sugar mixture into the egg yolks. Continue adding the sugar mixture until you've used about ½ cup.

5. Place the butter on top of the remaining sugar mixture in the pan, but do not stir it in. Slowly pour the egg yolks into the sugar mixture in a long, continuous stream, whisking vigorously. (Taking the extra step to warm the egg yolks helps prevent curdling.) Set aside to cool slightly while you make the meringue.

6. Using the mixer, with clean, dry beaters, beat the egg whites in a large bowl until they start to foam. Gradually beat in the salt and sugar. Increase the speed to high and continue to beat until the whites are glossy and form peaks that don't bend at the tip when you lift the beaters.

7. To assemble and bake the pie, first adjust the oven rack to the lower-middle position. Pour the lemon filling into the cooled pie shell. Gently spoon the meringue over the top, pushing it right up to the crust, not leaving any gaps for the filling to bubble out. Bake for 40 minutes, rotating the pie 180 degrees halfway through the baking, so that the part that faced the back of the oven now faces forward. There are no visual cues for doneness; just take it out after the elapsed time.

8. Transfer the pie to a wire rack. The Colonnade likes to serve the pie hot or warm, but you may let the pie cool thoroughly before serving.

Recipe for Success

▶ Since the lemon filling is still rather liquid when the meringue topping goes on, it's important that you don't push down hard on the meringue. Gently spoon it over the filling, in small clouds, then push it from side to side to spread it up to the crust.

▶ Use a sharp serrated knife to cut the pie. This is the best way to slice through the meringue, which forms a bit of a skin in the oven.

Joe's Stone Crab Key Lime Pie

Many aficionados will tell you that the Key lime pie at Joe's Stone Crab Restaurant in Miami Beach is perhaps the best in Florida. Joe's certainly has enough practice, producing about 30,000 handmade pies a year. Joe's pie is prepared in a graham cracker crust and has a firm texture and taste that's slightly more tart than sweet, the way many Floridians prefer it. Instead of a meringue topping, this one is garnished with a dollop of whipped cream.

MAKES 8 TO 10 SERVINGS

1 recipe Graham Cracker Crumb Crust (page 51) or 1 small store-bought graham cracker crust

FILLING

3 large egg yolks, at room temperature

Grated zest of 2 limes

One 14-ounce can sweetened condensed milk

2/3 cup fresh lime juice, preferably Key lime

TOPPING

1 cup cold heavy or whipping cream

1 tablespoon confectioners' sugar

1. Prepare the crust and press it into the bottom and up the side of a 9-inch standard pie pan. Refrigerate, prebake, and let cool as directed. Or simply use a store-bought crust, prebaking it according to the package directions and letting it cool. Refrigerate until ready to use. Leave the oven set at 350°F.

2. In a medium-size bowl, beat the egg yolks and lime zest together with an electric mixer on high speed until somewhat fluffy and well aerated, about 5 minutes. (Set the timer; that's a lot of beating, and you might be tempted to cut it short.) Gradually add the condensed milk and continue to beat until the last of the condensed milk has been added and the mixture is rather thick and fluffy, about 4 minutes. Slowly add the lime juice, mixing it in on low speed just until evenly blended. Pour the filling into the chilled pie shell.

3. Place the pie on the center oven rack and bake just until the filling appears set, about 10 minutes (see Recipe for Success).

4. Transfer the pie to a wire rack and let cool thoroughly. Cover with loosely tented aluminum foil and refrigerate until very cold, at least 2 hours.

5. When you are almost ready to serve the pie, using a chilled large bowl and chilled beaters, beat the cream with the mixer until it barely holds soft peaks. Add the confectioners' sugar and continue to beat until stiff but not grainy. Do not overbeat. If you're serving all of the pie at once, slather the whipped cream over the pie, then slice and serve. If you're serving only a few slices, garnish each slice with cream.

Recipe for Success

- One of the best things about this pie is how simple it is—in spite of the fact that Key lime pie has a reputation for being beyond the understanding of everyday cooks. On the contrary, this is one of the easiest pies in this entire collection to make. I suggest that you keep a bottle of Key lime juice on hand so you can whip it up on short notice for a casual gathering.

- Even to an experienced pie maker, baking this pie is somewhat counterintuitive in that it takes only 10 minutes. That hardly seems like enough time for the filling to set, but in fact it is. Baking it longer is not recommended and may, in fact, ruin the filling.

Orange Pie with a Pistachio Crumb Crust

Very similar to Key lime pie, this recipe uses mostly reduced orange juice and only a little lime juice and calls for a pistachio graham cracker crust. It has a wonderful aroma and a sprightly citrus flavor that I love—and love to serve—in the summer. The pie is generously proportioned, baked in a deep-dish pan and ample enough to serve 10 people.

MAKES 10 SERVINGS

1 recipe Nutty Graham Cracker Crust (page 53) made with pistachios

FILLING

2 cups fresh orange juice (see Recipe for Success)

2 cups (about one and a half 14-ounce cans) sweetened condensed milk

5 large egg yolks

2 tablespoons fresh lime juice

$1/2$ teaspoon vanilla extract

2 teaspoons grated orange zest (optional)

GARNISH

Fresh Whipped Cream (page 605)

Threads of orange zest

1. Prepare the crust and press it into the bottom and about two-thirds of the way up the side of a $9^1/_2$-inch deep-dish pie pan. Refrigerate, prebake, and let cool as directed.

2. Bring the orange juice to a rapid boil in a medium-size nonreactive saucepan. Continue to boil until reduced to about ²/₃ cup; keep a heatproof measuring cup nearby to check. Pour into a shallow bowl and let cool briefly. Preheat the oven to 350°F.

3. Combine the condensed milk, egg yolks, lime juice, vanilla, and orange zest in a large bowl, whisking well to combine. Whisk in the reduced orange juice until evenly blended. Pour the filling into the cooled pie shell.

4. Place the pie on the center oven rack and bake for 20 minutes. Even if the filling does not appear solid, remove the pie from the oven; the filling will firm up as the pie cools. Transfer to a wire rack and let cool thoroughly. Cover with loosely tented aluminum foil and refrigerate for at least 4 hours, preferably longer (up to overnight). Pipe the whipped cream decoratively over the pie, or simply smooth it over the top. Decorate with the orange zest, if desired, using a lemon zester or sharp vegetable peeler to peel off long threads. Slice and serve.

Recipe for Success

‣ Note that this recipe is a little different from the previous one in that the ingredients are simply whisked together and not beaten. Don't be concerned. The Key lime pie may have a slightly lighter texture, but this one is delicious, too, creamy and dense.

‣ It's better to use fresh orange juice here if possible, but you can, in a pinch, use a good not-from-concentrate brand such as Tropicana.

Cherry Cheesecake Pie

I love cheesecake fruit pies, which are distinct from regular cheesecake in that the creamy layer is generally thinner and the fruit layer is a little thicker. They're easier to make than regular cheesecake, too, because there are no special pans to mess with. Here's one fine version—a smooth, sour cream–lemon filling beneath a sweet cherry topping made with frozen cherries. For convenience, you can use a large store-bought graham cracker crust. But if you have the time, the walnut crust is really great here. Start this well ahead so it has plenty of time to chill.

MAKES 8 TO 10 SERVINGS

1 recipe Nutty Graham Cracker Crust (page 53) made with walnuts or 1 large store-bought graham cracker crust

CHEESECAKE FILLING

Three 3-ounce packages full-fat cream cheese, softened

1/2 cup sugar

2 large eggs, at room temperature

1/2 cup full-fat sour cream

1/2 teaspoon vanilla extract

1/4 teaspoon almond extract

CHERRY TOPPING

3 cups individually frozen pitted sweet cherries (not packed in syrup)

1/2 cup sugar

2 tablespoons fresh lemon juice

2 tablespoons cornstarch

1/4 cup water

1/2 teaspoon vanilla extract

GARNISH

Fresh Whipped Cream (page 605; optional)

1. Prepare the crust and press it into the bottom and up the side of a 9^1/$_2$-inch deep-dish pie pan. Refrigerate, prebake, and let cool as directed. Or simply use a store-bought crust, prebaking it according to the package directions and letting it cool. Leave the oven set at 350°F.

2. In a large bowl, cream the cream cheese with an electric mixer, gradually beating in the sugar on medium speed. Add the eggs, one at a time, beating just until evenly blended. Add the sour cream, vanilla, and almond extract and blend. Carefully pour the filling into the cooled pie shell.

3. Place the pie on the center oven rack and bake until the center of the filling is set, 25 to 30 minutes. Transfer the pie to a wire rack and let cool to room temperature. Cover with loosely tented aluminum foil and refrigerate for at least 3 hours or overnight.

4. About an hour before serving, make the cherry topping. Combine the cherries, sugar, and lemon juice in a medium-size nonreactive saucepan. Cover and bring to a low boil over medium heat, stirring often. Reduce the heat to medium-low, partially uncover, and simmer for 2 to 3 minutes. While the cherries simmer, blend the cornstarch and water together in a small bowl, then stir the mixture into the cherries. Bring to a boil and continue to boil, stirring, for about 1^1/$_2$ minutes. Remove from the heat and stir in the vanilla. Let cool to room temperature.

5. Spoon the cooled cherries evenly over the chilled filling. Refrigerate for at least 30 minutes. If desired, pipe some of the whipped cream decoratively around the edge of the pie, using the rest for garnish. Slice and serve.

Recipe for Success

▶ Keep in mind that cheesecake is a custard and, like other custards, it will become watery and less tender than it should be if overbaked. That said, keep a close eye on the filling after about 20 minutes of baking. When you see the sides starting to rise slightly, the filling is getting close to being done.

▶ Much as I like the convenience of store-bought graham cracker crusts, it's sometimes a little tacky to pull out an otherwise special and attractive dessert like this one baked in a throwaway pie pan. So consider your options: One is to slip the entire pie pan into one of your own better-looking ones, which works well only if it's a good fit. The other is to slice and plate the pie in the privacy of your pantry or kitchen, where nobody will see the pan.

Black Bottom Ricotta Cheese Pie

Lighter than ricotta cheese cheesecake but with a similar texture, this pie is a fitting conclusion to a not-too-heavy Italian dinner—or almost any dinner, for that matter. Its rather plain appearance hides a razzle-dazzle of flavor: chocolate, lemon and orange zest, and almond play off one another like the notes of a jazzy song, coming at your taste buds from all directions. One of the few creamy pies I like warm, it is also great chilled.

MAKES 8 TO 10 SERVINGS

1 recipe Graham Cracker Crumb Crust (page 51) or 1 large store-bought graham cracker crust

BLACK BOTTOM COATING
2 tablespoons unsalted butter, cut into pieces

1 tablespoon light or dark corn syrup

3/4 cup semisweet chocolate chips

FILLING
1 1/2 cups whole-milk or part-skim ricotta cheese

2/3 cup sugar

3 large eggs

1/4 cup heavy or light cream

1 teaspoon grated lemon zest

1 teaspoon grated orange zest

1/2 teaspoon vanilla extract

1/2 teaspoon almond extract

1/8 teaspoon salt

1. Prepare the crust and press it into the bottom and up the side of a 9-inch standard pie pan. Or remove the store-bought crust from its wrapping. Refrigerate until ready to use.

2. To make the black bottom coating, combine the butter, corn syrup, and chocolate chips in the top of a double boiler set over, not in, barely simmering water. Let sit until the chocolate melts, 5 to 6 minutes, then whisk to smooth. Remove the insert and scrape the mixture into the chilled pie shell. Smooth it over the bottom and most of the way up the side of the shell. Refrigerate while you make the filling. Preheat the oven to 350°F.

3. Using an electric mixer, beat the ricotta, sugar, and eggs together in a large bowl until evenly mixed. Add the cream, zests, extracts, and salt and beat until evenly blended. Slowly pour the filling into the chocolate-lined pie shell.

4. Place the pie on the center oven rack and bake for 30 minutes, then rotate the pie 180 degrees, so that the part that faced the back of the oven now faces forward. Continue to bake until the center is set (no longer soupy), about 15 minutes. When done, the edge of the filling will be golden brown and will likely have risen slightly.

5. Transfer the pie to a wire rack and let cool. Serve barely warm or at room temperature. Or cover with loosely tented aluminum foil and refrigerate until ready to serve.

Recipe for Success

▸ **You can, if you like, skip the chocolate coating, but I don't recommend the idea with any enthusiasm. For one thing, the chocolate tastes wonderful with the filling. For another, it helps keep moisture from the filling away from the pie shell. I think it's worth the little extra time required to make it.**

▸ **The almond version of Nutty Graham Cracker Crust (page 53) also is excellent here.**

Ricotta Pie with Chocolate and Toasted Almonds

Some people pick up Italian cookbooks and immediately flip to the pasta dishes or vegetables. I go to the dessert section in search of great pies and tarts. Ricotta cheese turns up in many of them, sometimes made into an uncooked ricotta cream (see the coffee-flavored pie on page 512), other times used the way I have here, blended with eggs and flavorings such as vanilla or almonds and chocolate and then baked. Typically, these Italian pies and tarts are baked in a sweet, buttery pastry called *pasta frolla*. For this pie, however, I like a cream cheese pastry, because it has a softness and tang that I think are well matched to the ricotta filling. By all means, let this cool and then refrigerate before serving. It's not half as good warm.

MAKES 8 TO 10 SERVINGS

1 recipe Tender Cream Cheese Pastry, Single Crust (page 46), refrigerated

FILLING

1 cup whole almonds

One 15- to 16-ounce container whole-milk or part-skim ricotta cheese

3/4 cup sugar

4 large eggs, at room temperature

1 1/2 teaspoons vanilla extract

1/4 teaspoon almond extract

1 teaspoon grated lemon zest

1/4 teaspoon ground cinnamon

1 cup semisweet chocolate chips, regular or mini

1. If you haven't already, prepare the pastry and refrigerate until firm enough to roll, 1 to 1 1/2 hours.

2. On a sheet of lightly floured waxed paper, roll the pastry into a 13-inch circle with a floured rolling pin. Invert the pastry over a 9 1/2-inch deep-dish pie pan, center, and peel off the paper. Tuck the pastry into the pan, without stretching it, and sculpt the edge into an upstanding ridge. Place in the freezer for 15 minutes, then partially prebake and let cool according to the instructions on page 16. Reduce the oven temperature to 350°F.

3. Spread the almonds on a baking sheet and place them in the preheated oven. Toast until fragrant and darker by a shade, 8 to 10 minutes. Immediately tilt the nuts onto a plate and let cool to room temperature. Coarsely chop and set aside.

4. Combine the ricotta cheese and sugar in a large bowl. Using an electric mixer, beat in the eggs, one at a time, beating well after each addition. Add the extracts, lemon zest, and cinnamon and blend briefly. Stir in the chopped almonds and chocolate chips. Slowly pour the filling into the cooled pie shell, smoothing the top with a spoon. Using a fork, gently rake the nuts and chips to distribute them evenly.

5. Place the pie on the center oven rack and bake until the top is very light golden brown and the filling is set, about 40 minutes. Rotate the pie 180 degrees halfway through the baking, so that the part that faced the back of the oven now faces forward.

6. Transfer the pie to a wire rack and let cool to room temperature. Cover with loosely tented aluminum foil and refrigerate for at least 3 hours or overnight before serving.

Recipe for Success

▶ **Anytime you have a pie like this, comprising a liquid filling and solids such as nuts or chocolate chips, take a moment to redistribute the filling after you pour it into the pie shell. Simply take a large fork and rake it through the filling, moving the solids from the center of the pie—where they've likely piled up—toward the edge. It will make for a much more balanced slice.**

Richard's Rice and Ricotta Pie

My friend Richard Sax was one of the most beloved and widely respected food writers and cookbook authors of recent time. Not only was he a great cook and writer, but he also had a charming, engaging personality—and a generosity of spirit—that everyone who knew him found irresistible. This recipe is one I adapted from one of his early books, *Old-Fashioned Desserts* (Irena Chalmers Cookbooks, 1983). He, in turn, adapted it from one given to him by Mary Codola, a friend and native Rhode Islander of whom he spoke very highly. Anyway, I love the recipe—basically, rice pudding in a crust, only better. It's not as creamy as some rice puddings, perhaps, but it is utterly delicious. The recipe has some of those mysterious steps whose purpose I can't be sure of but that I do anyway, out of respect for tradition: the initial boiling and rinsing of the rice; the pressing of the ricotta through a sieve (probably to lighten the texture). A big dollop of whipped cream is perfect with this.

MAKES 8 TO 10 SERVINGS

1 recipe All-Butter Pie Pastry, Single Crust (page 28), refrigerated

FILLING

2 cups water

3/4 cup long-grain white rice

3/4 cup plus 2 tablespoons whole milk

1/4 cup plus 1/3 cup sugar

1/4 teaspoon salt

1 cup whole-milk or part-skim ricotta cheese, pressed through a sieve (see Recipe for Success)

1 large egg

2 large egg yolks

1 teaspoon vanilla extract

1/2 teaspoon grated lemon zest

1/2 cup cold heavy or whipping cream

Pinch of ground cinnamon

GARNISH

Fresh Whipped Cream (page 605)

1. If you haven't already, prepare the pastry and refrigerate until firm enough to roll, about 1 hour.

2. On a sheet of lightly floured waxed paper, roll the pastry into a 13-inch circle with a floured rolling pin. Invert the pastry over a 9½-inch deep-dish pie pan, center, and peel off the paper. Tuck the pastry into the pan, without stretching it, and sculpt the edge so it is just slightly higher than the rim. Place in the freezer for 15 minutes, then partially pre-bake and let cool according to the directions on page 16.

3. Bring the water to a boil in a small saucepan. Stir in the rice and boil, uncovered, for 5 minutes. Drain through a fine-mesh sieve, rinsing with cold water. Return the drained rice to the saucepan along with ¾ cup of the milk, ¼ cup of the sugar, and the salt. Place over medium heat and bring to a gentle boil, stirring occasionally. Partially cover, reduce the heat to medium-low, and simmer until the liquid is absorbed and the rice is tender, 15 to 20 minutes. Preheat the oven to 350°F.

4. Meanwhile, combine the remaining ⅓ cup sugar, the ricotta, egg, egg yolks, vanilla, lemon zest, and remaining 2 tablespoons milk in a large bowl, stirring to blend. Stir in the rice when it is done.

5. Using a chilled small bowl and chilled beaters, beat the cream with an electric mixer until it holds soft peaks. Fold it into the rice mixture until evenly blended. Pour the filling into the cooled pie shell. Sprinkle with the cinnamon.

6. Place the pie on the center oven rack and bake until the top is a rich golden brown and the filling is firmly set, about 50 minutes. Rotate the pie 180 degrees halfway through the baking, so that the part that faced the back of the oven now faces forward.

7. Transfer the pie to a wire rack and let cool. Serve barely warm or at room temperature. Or cover with loosely tented aluminum foil and refrigerate for several hours before serving. Garnish with a dollop of whipped cream.

Recipe for Success

▶ Richard paired this filling with a very buttery pastry in his book, so I thought my all-butter pastry would be a suitable match. Feel free to substitute another pastry, if you prefer.

▶ If you've never pressed ricotta cheese through a sieve before, you do just that: place it in a sieve, then just press and sweep with the back of a soup spoon to force the ricotta through. It doesn't require much force; the ricotta goes through quite easily.

▶ Keep an eye on this pie during the last 15 to 20 minutes of baking. Remove it from the oven as soon as it seems done; you don't want it to get overly dry. If you're in doubt, stick a butter knife into the center. If you see uncooked custard on the knife, continue to bake.

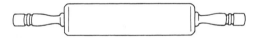

Arborio Rice Pie

Anyone who loves rice pudding will adore this pie. The idea of a rice pie first crossed my mind while I was leafing through Michele Scicolone's great little book on Italian desserts, *La Dolce Vita* (William Morrow, 1993). In it, she has a recipe for something called a *crostata di riso*, or rice tart, baked in a pastry-lined springform pan. I made the tart, found it simply delicious, and knew right away I would have to adapt the recipe to a pie. One of the key elements in this rice pie is the Italian Arborio rice, an extremely starchy rice that you can find at most specialty food stores. The starch is gradually released as the grain is cooked, prior to baking the pie, giving the filling a satiny, ultra-smooth texture I think you'll adore. My wife, Bev, who is always chiding me to keep my recipes as accessible as possible, pointedly asked me if one couldn't just use regular white rice. I thought about it for a minute, then gave her an unequivocal no: the texture just wouldn't be the same. For an unexpected finale, serve this after your favorite Italian dinner.

MAKES 8 TO 10 SERVINGS

1 recipe Basic Flaky Pie Pastry, Single Crust (page 31), refrigerated

FILLING

3 cups whole milk

1/3 cup Arborio or Vialone Nano rice

1/2 cup sugar

2 tablespoons unsalted butter

1/4 teaspoon salt

2 large eggs

1 large egg yolk

1/2 teaspoon finely grated lemon zest

1 teaspoon vanilla extract

1. If you haven't already, prepare the pastry and refrigerate until firm enough to roll, about 1 hour.

2. On a sheet of lightly floured waxed paper, roll the pastry into a 13-inch circle with a floured rolling pin. Invert the pastry over a 9½-inch deep-dish pie pan, center, and peel off the paper. Tuck the pastry into the pan, without stretching it, and sculpt the edge into an upstanding ridge. Place in the freezer for 15 minutes, then partially prebake and let cool according to the instructions on page 16.

3. Combine the milk, rice, sugar, butter, and salt in a medium-size, heavy-bottomed saucepan over medium heat. Bring to a simmer, then immediately turn the heat down very low. Watch the rice carefully, because when it first comes to a simmer—and for several minutes after that—the milk may rise quickly and boil over. At the first sign of such a problem, quickly remove the pan from the heat until the liquid settles down. Partially cover and very gently simmer, stirring occasionally, until the rice is tender and the liquid in the pan is starchy-thick, as long as 45 to 50 minutes. Remove from the heat, uncover, and let cool for 20 to 30 minutes. Preheat the oven to 350°F.

4. When the rice has cooled down, whisk the eggs and egg yolk together in a large bowl. Add a ladleful of the rice and whisk again. Add the remaining rice, lemon zest, and vanilla, stirring until evenly blended. Carefully pour the filling into the cooled pie shell.

5. Place the pie on the center oven rack and bake until the filling is set, about 45 minutes, rotating it 180 degrees halfway through the baking, so that the part that faced the back of the oven now faces forward. When done, the perimeter may puff slightly, but other than a few spots here and there, the top of the pie will likely not be too browned.

6. Transfer the pie to a wire rack and let cool. Serve at room temperature, or cover with loosely tented aluminum foil, refrigerate, and serve cold (the way I prefer it).

Recipe for Success

▶ For the pie to achieve the perfect texture, it's important to use the correct rice and to cook it thoroughly. The rice may actually become tender after 30 minutes of cooking, but don't be tempted to remove it from the heat at that point. Continue cooking until you can see and feel an unmistakable thickening of the liquid around the rice—a thickness somewhat like that of heavy cream. This is important, because that thickness is the textural quality that makes this pie so distinctive and memorable.

Smooth and Simple Polenta Pie

Polenta came of age in this country during the 1990s, and now almost everyone knows what it is. But if you're still uncertain, polenta is essentially what's called cornmeal mush in the good old US of A: a hearty dish of little more than cornmeal cooked in liquid. It can be served hot or cold, with a variety of sauces both savory and sweet. Since I love polenta, I set out to make a pie based on the same simple ingredients and method. This is it, and I'm very happy with the results. The filling is soft and creamy, not overly sweet, and with a hint of lemon. It's a little like Indian pudding, but without all the spices and heavy molasses flavor. Serve cool or cold for the best flavor, perhaps with a dab of Sweetened Mascarpone Cheese (page 606).

MAKES 8 TO 10 SERVINGS

1 recipe Basic Flaky Pie Pastry, Single Crust (page 31) or Tender Cream Cheese Pastry, Single Crust (page 46), refrigerated

FILLING

2 cups milk (any type)

1/4 cup plus 1 tablespoon fine yellow cornmeal (such as Quaker brand)

Scant 1/2 teaspoon salt

1/4 cup (1/2 stick) unsalted butter, cut into 1/2-inch pieces

1/2 cup sugar, or 1/3 cup sugar and 2 tablespoons pure maple syrup

1 tablespoon fresh lemon juice

1 teaspoon grated lemon zest

1/2 teaspoon vanilla extract

3 large eggs, at room temperature, lightly beaten

1. If you haven't already, prepare the pastry and refrigerate until firm enough to roll, about 1 hour.

2. On a sheet of lightly floured waxed paper, roll the pastry into a 12-inch circle with a floured rolling pin. Invert the pastry over a 9-inch standard pie pan, center, and peel off the paper. Tuck the pastry into the pan, without stretching it, and sculpt the edge into an upstanding ridge. Place in the freezer for 15 minutes, then partially prebake and let cool according to the instructions on page 16. Reduce the oven temperature to 350°F.

3. Combine the milk, cornmeal, and salt in a medium-size saucepan, preferably non-stick. Gradually bring the mixture to a simmer over medium heat and cook until thickened, about 5 minutes. It won't turn extra-thick, just full-bodied. Reduce the heat slightly and continue to cook for 5 minutes, whisking virtually nonstop to keep it from spattering. Remove from the heat and immediately whisk in the butter, one piece at a time, until melted. Whisk in the sugar, lemon juice, lemon zest, and vanilla. Let the mixture cool for 3 to 4 minutes, then whisk in the eggs. Slowly pour the filling into the cooled pie shell and smooth the top.

4. Place the pie on the center oven rack and bake until the filling is set, about 40 minutes, rotating the pie 180 degrees halfway through the baking, so that the part that faced the back of the oven now faces forward. When done, the filling will set firmly in the pan and won't have any tendency at all to wobble. The edge of the pie may puff very slightly, but not much.

5. Transfer the pie to a wire rack and let cool thoroughly. Cover with loosely tented aluminum foil and refrigerate for at least 2 hours or overnight before serving.

Recipe for Success

▶ I happen to love the subtle flavor of this pie, but you can flavor it more boldly, like the Indian pudding I mentioned. If that's your desire, add 1 teaspoon pumpkin pie spice and substitute light brown sugar for the granulated sugar. Serve it with Fresh Whipped Cream (page 605).

Wheaten Breakfast Pie

My friend Marion Cunningham, the estimable Fannie Farmer cook and baker, calls this type of pie, made with hot cereal grain, a breakfast pie. I like the name, and the pie, and I think you will, too. My version is made with Wheatena, the coarse hot cereal I've been eating since I was a boy. It's partially cooked with milk and brown sugar; blended with eggs, raisins, and nuts; and then baked in a partially prebaked pie shell. It contains just about everything you'd eat for breakfast in an easy-to-eat, portable package. The slices can be reheated in the microwave or eaten cold. Again, keep in mind that Wheatena gives this pie a coarse texture and the whole wheat crust contributes to a rather grainy package. If you like the idea, but would rather try something a little more refined and with a smoother consistency, consider Smooth and Simple Polenta Pie (page 598).

MAKES 10 SERVINGS

1 recipe Whole Wheat Pie Pastry, Single Crust (page 33), refrigerated

FILLING

2¼ cups whole or reduced-fat (2%) milk

⅓ cup Wheatena cereal

½ cup firmly packed light brown sugar

Scant ½ teaspoon salt

3 tablespoons unsalted butter, cut into ½-inch pieces

½ teaspoon vanilla extract

3 large eggs, lightly beaten

¾ cup dark raisins

½ cup chopped walnuts

¼ teaspoon ground cinnamon

1. If you haven't already, prepare the pastry and refrigerate until firm enough to roll, about 1 hour.

2. On a sheet of lightly floured waxed paper, roll the pastry into a 13-inch circle with a floured rolling pin. Invert the pastry over a 9½-inch deep-dish pie pan, center, and peel off the paper. Tuck the pastry into the pan, without stretching it, and sculpt the edge so it is even with the rim. Place in the freezer for 15 minutes, then partially prebake and let cool according to the instructions on page 16.

3. Combine the milk, Wheatena, brown sugar, and salt in a medium-size saucepan over medium heat. Bring to a gentle boil, then reduce the heat to medium-low and simmer until somewhat thickened, about 7 minutes. It won't become pasty-thick, just slurry-thick. Remove from the heat and stir in the butter, one piece at a time, and the vanilla. Let cool for 10 minutes. Preheat the oven to 350°F.

4. Whisk the eggs into the cooled Wheatena mixture. Stir in the raisins, walnuts, and cinnamon. Slowly pour the filling into the cooled pie shell.

5. Place the pie on the center oven rack and bake until the filling is set, about 40 minutes. Rotate the pie 180 degrees halfway through the baking time, so that the part that faced the back of the oven now faces forward. Overall, the filling will have a fairly firm texture when done.

6. Transfer the pie to a wire rack and let cool. Serve warm, or let cool thoroughly, cover loosely with aluminum foil, and refrigerate before serving.

Recipe for Success

▶ If you've never made whole wheat pastry before, be aware that the coarse flour makes it just a little trickier to handle than some other pastries. If you prefer, feel free to use another pastry here.

▶ Other nuts or dried fruits work beautifully in this pie, too. Consider pecans or almonds, as well as dried cherries or dried cranberries.

Pie for Breakfast

"I guess the one reason we eat pie for breakfast is because it's there from last night's supper. I can think of nothing more appealing than several warm, plump pies laid out for the morning meal—there is something old-fashioned and homey about it. If you have a hard time arousing breakfast appetites, pies are a sure-fire way to get everyone to clean their plates."

—Marion Cunningham, *The Breakfast Book* (Knopf, 1987)

We could live without garnishes, but sometimes a dab of this or a puddle of

that adds a little something extra to the pie experience. Ice cream is the gar-

nish everyone loves, and the more of it, the merrier. But whipped cream or the

occasional sauce—recipes for which appear on the following pages—makes

for a nice change from the expected. • As with the pie itself, the fresher the

The Final Touch

garnish, the better. Try to make these the same day you plan to use them, so

they taste as fresh as possible. If you're serving them on the side, use attrac-

tive serving containers, chilled if appropriate. Serve your pies with a tasty

flourish, and your family and guests will lavish you with appreciation.

Fresh Whipped Cream

Fresh whipped cream is so easy and quick to prepare that there's almost no reason to use canned. It can be made with either granulated sugar or confectioners' sugar. I prefer the latter, since the presence of cornstarch in confectioners' sugar makes the whipped cream more stable. This basic recipe can easily be scaled up if a greater quantity is required. To make unsweetened whipped cream, which is what you'd serve with a very sweet pie, simply omit the sugar.

MAKES ABOUT 2 CUPS

1 cup heavy or whipping cream

2 to 3 tablespoons confectioners' sugar, sifted, or granulated sugar, to your taste

A few drops vanilla extract

1.   About 15 minutes before you plan to prepare this topping, place a medium-size bowl and the beaters from your electric mixer in the refrigerator.

2.   When you're ready to proceed, pour the cream into the chilled bowl. Starting at medium speed, beat the cream until it starts to thicken. Increase the speed to medium-high and continue to beat until the cream holds soft peaks. Add the confectioners' sugar, stirring it in with the beaters so it doesn't fly up in your face when you restart the machine. Continue to beat the cream until it is stiff but not grainy. Cover with plastic wrap and refrigerate until needed, no more than several hours.

Recipe for Success

▶   Don't skip the part about chilling the bowl and beaters. It really speeds up the process, especially in the summer.

▶   To make a flavored whipped cream, beat in 1 to $1^{1}/_{2}$ tablespoons liqueur of your choice—amaretto, Kahlúa, Frangelico, Grand Marnier, crème de cacao, or other—at the very end.

▶   If the whipped cream sits for any amount of time in the refrigerator, it will separate slightly. Whisk it for 10 to 15 seconds before serving to reincorporate any liquid.

Crème Anglaise

This is a great sauce to accompany apple, berry, and many chocolate pies. It's not difficult to make, but you must be careful not to let it boil, or you'll end up with sweetened scrambled eggs. Do use light cream, not milk, for a full-bodied sauce.

MAKES ABOUT 2¹/₂ CUPS

6 large egg yolks

¹/₂ cup sugar

2 cups light cream or half-and-half

1 teaspoon vanilla extract

1.   Whisk the egg yolks and sugar together in a medium-size bowl.

2.   Bring the cream to a simmer in a medium-size saucepan over medium heat. Gradually whisk the hot cream into the yolks, adding about ¹/₃ cup at a time. Return the mixture to the saucepan. Stir the custard over medium-low heat for about 5 minutes, until it thickens enough to coat the back of a wooden spoon and a finger drawn across it leaves a path. *Do not boil.*

3.   Strain the sauce through a fine-mesh strainer into a small bowl and stir in the vanilla. Let cool to room temperature, then cover with plastic wrap and refrigerate until cold. This will keep in the refrigerator for 2 to 3 days. Whisk briefly before serving.

Sweetened Mascarpone Cheese

Mascarpone is a thick, soft, slightly tangy Italian cheese that's used in both savory and sweet dishes. Like ice cream and whipped cream, it goes great with pie—but only in small dollops, because it is so rich. Serve it unsweetened with very sweet pies. Otherwise, sweeten it just a bit, the way we do here.

MAKES ABOUT 1 CUP

8 ounces (about 1 cup) cold mascarpone cheese

1¹/₂ to 2 tablespoons sugar

Combine the cheese and sugar in a small bowl. Stir well with a wooden spoon until combined. Don't be concerned if you can still taste the grittiness of the sugar. As the cheese sits in the refrigerator prior to serving, the sugar will dissolve. Cover and refrigerate for 15 to 30 minutes or up to 2 days before serving.

COFFEE MASCARPONE Stir 1 tablespoon sugar and 1 tablespoon Kahlúa or other coffee liqueur into the mascarpone. For an even stronger coffee flavor, dissolve 2 teaspoons instant espresso or coffee granules into an equal amount of very hot water. Let cool thoroughly, then stir into the mascarpone with the other ingredients.

Warm Mocha Sauce

About the easiest chocolate-coffee sauce you're liable to find, this can be made in minutes. It tastes great on practically all ice cream pies, including the baked Alaska pies on pages 553 and 555. With a chocolate sauce this simple, there's hardly any excuse to buy prepared sauce. If you like, you can leave out the instant coffee, and you'll have a plain but delicious chocolate sauce.

MAKES ABOUT 1 CUP

1/2 cup heavy or whipping cream

1 tablespoon instant espresso or coffee granules

2 tablespoons unsalted butter, cut into 1/2-inch pieces

1 cup semisweet chocolate chips

1 tablespoon light corn syrup

1/2 teaspoon vanilla extract

1. Bring the cream, coffee, and butter to a simmer in a small, heavy saucepan over medium heat, whisking to dissolve the coffee. Remove from the heat and add the chocolate chips. Let the mixture stand for 2 minutes, then whisk to smooth. Whisk in the corn syrup and vanilla.

2. If you aren't using the sauce right away, transfer to a small bowl and let cool. The sauce will thicken as it cools. I like to use it while it is still slightly warm, once it has thickened a bit. If you're not using it right away, cover and refrigerate, then reheat in the microwave or in a saucepan over low heat.

Recipe for Success

▸ To make a spirited chocolate sauce, whisk in 1 to 2 tablespoons Kahlúa, crème de cacao, Frangelico, amaretto, or other liqueur.

▸ Tightly covered, this sauce will keep for at least 1 week in the refrigerator.

Raspberry Sauce

Fruit sauces such as this are simple to make, and they add a splash of color to a pie. Lean and slightly acidic, they're also a good contrast to rich, creamy pies, especially ice cream pies. This sauce can be made with either fresh or frozen fruit, and you'd be hard-pressed to tell the difference. If you are using fresh berries, pick them over carefully and discard any blemished or moldy specimens, lest they ruin the sauce. Blackberries are also excellent in place of the raspberries.

MAKES ABOUT 1 CUP

1 pint fresh raspberries or one 12-ounce bag individually frozen raspberries (not packed in syrup), thawed

3 tablespoons sugar

1 to 2 teaspoons fresh lemon juice, to your taste

1. Put the berries and sugar in a food processor and process to a smooth puree. Pour into a sieve placed over a bowl and strain the sauce, forcing it through the sieve with a rubber spatula. It will take several minutes to do a thorough job. Blend in the lemon juice.

2. Transfer the sauce to a small bowl. Cover with plastic wrap and refrigerate until ready to use. Stir well just before serving.

Recipe for Success

▶ To make a sauce with a little more body, whisk in a tablespoon or two of seedless raspberry preserves.

▶ Take a page out of the pastry chef's book and store this sauce in a squirt bottle. Squeeze it onto a dessert plate in a zigzag or other pattern, then put a slice of pie on top.

▶ Tightly covered, this sauce will keep for up to 2 days in the refrigerator.

The beauty of pie making is its simplicity. You probably already have, or can easily purchase, everything you need to make a great pie. That said, there are still a few places I like to visit, either in person or online, for certain equipment or ingredients you might have a hard time finding elsewhere. The following resources fall into those categories.

American Pie Council. This fine nonprofit organization, with close links to the baking industry, works very hard to promote pie—eating it, making it, buying or selling it. The council publishes a newsletter called *Pie Times* and organizes the Great American Pie Festival, an annual showcase and pie-baking contest for pies and pie makers from around the country. To learn more, visit the council's Web site, www.piecouncil.org.

Apple Journal. Mike Berst is one of the most knowledgeable guys in the country when it comes to apples and other fruit. He's taken his smarts—and knack for graphic design—and

turned them into a wonderful Web site, www.applejournal.com. If you want to know who is growing what; the best apples and berries for pies; sources for quality fresh and dried fruits, both mail-order and in your own state—virtually anything to do with the growing and use of fruit—I suggest you become a regular visitor to this literate, informative, and highly popular venue.

Friske Orchards. If I lived near Ellsworth, Michigan, I'd shop here in person. Friske Orchards has not only a swell selection of exemplary fresh fruit, but it's also the source for my beloved Balaton cherries (see page 75), which Friske can ship frozen right to your door. Before you call (231-599-2604), check out Friske's Web site (www.friske.com) to see what else sparks your pie interest.

Kermit's Key West Key Lime Shoppe. Head to Florida, and you'll find lots of places that sell authentic Key lime juice for making Key lime pie. If you aren't planning a trip anytime soon, this is a great mail-order source. Kermit's motto is "It doesn't get anymore [*sic*] authentic." Contact Kermit's at www.keylimeshop.com or (800) 376-0806.

King Arthur Flour Baker's Catalogue. You can get their paper catalogue or view it online, but for anyone who loves to bake, there's nothing quite like visiting King Arthur's brick-and-mortar store in Norwich, Vermont. People actually make pilgrimages there to shop at the store, buy from the bakery (and they do know how to bake), or attend baking classes (where, incidentally, I have been a guest instructor). You'll find all sorts of useful pie-baking products on the shelves, so come prepared to stock up. Contact King Arthur at www.kingarthurflour.com or (800) 827-6836.

King Orchards. Another fine Michigan fruit grower, King Orchards is well-known for its cherries, including sour pie cherries and Balaton cherries. You can learn all about its products at www.kingorchards.com or by calling (877) YES-KING.

Muirhead. Ed and Doris Simpson of Muirhead make the Pecan Pumpkin Butter I love so much and use in some of my favorite pumpkin pies. It's usually sold at Williams-Sonoma stores around the holidays, but you can order it any time of year online at www.muirhead-foods.com or by phone at (800) 782-7803.

Sunnyland Farms. I buy nuts locally, but occasionally I like to splurge and buy them right from the source, especially pecans for pies. A trusted grower is Sunnyland Farms of Albany, Georgia, which calls itself the largest shipper of pecans in the country. I like the fact that the people seem to be as picky about freshness as I am. When I order nuts from them, I know for certain that the nuts have been scrupulously handled and stored. They're nice people to deal with, too—so much southern sweetness and charm you can almost feel it oozing out of your phone. Contact them at www.sunnylandfarms.com.

Sur La Table. This high-end gourmet store chain carries an impressive assortment of pie pans, pie birds, and other pie-making essentials. Check it out at www.surlatable.com.

Twins Polish Pottery. This small mail-order company specializes in gorgeous, durable, direct-imported Polish pottery. If you aren't familiar with this product, I think you'll love the quality and patterns. The pie pans are among my favorites, and the prices are excellent. I've seen the same products sell for much more at other Web sites. Contact Twins at www.twinspolishpottery.com.

Williams-Sonoma. Williams-Sonoma stores are located in many malls across the country. They're known for carrying only the best products, and their selection of pie-making equipment, though not exhaustive, is impressive. Among other items, they carry the heavy ceramic Emile Henry baking dishes I like so much. If you can't find a store near you, you can shop online at www.williams-sonoma.com.

Wood's Cider Mill. I use boiled cider to make the Shaker Boiled Cider Pie on page 401. When I don't make the boiled cider myself, I buy it from Willis and Tina Wood, two of my favorite people. They're the antithesis of big business and slick marketing, one of the things I love most about them. They personally preside over the making of their products and have used the same bare-bones product labels for years. To them, quality counts, and their delicious boiled cider is proof of that fact. Learn more about them and their products at www.woodscidermill.com.

Wyman's. This Maine company, which I've mentioned elsewhere, is the big name in blueberries. Although I love fresh wild Maine blueberries, I never hesitate to use Wyman's canned berries (in water) in my pies, because the quality is so excellent. I buy them at my local Whole Foods Market. If you can't find them at your favorite store, contact Wyman's at www.wymans.com or (207) 546-2311.

Finally, my own Web site, www.applepieperfect.com, has information about all of my cookbooks, including *Apple Pie Perfect* (Harvard Common Press, 2002). If you'd like to send me a message or a favorite pie recipe or inquire about my pie-making demonstrations, which I give all across the country, you can contact me here.

Measurement Equivalents

Please note that all conversions are approximate.

Liquid Conversions

U.S.	METRIC
1 tsp	5 ml
1 tbs	15 ml
2 tbs	30 ml
3 tbs	45 ml
1/4 cup	60 ml
1/3 cup	75 ml
1/3 cup + 1 tbs	90 ml
1/3 cup + 2 tbs	100 ml
1/2 cup	120 ml
2/3 cup	150 ml
3/4 cup	180 ml
3/4 cup + 2 tbs	200 ml
1 cup	240 ml
1 cup + 2 tbs	275 ml
1 1/4 cups	300 ml
1 1/3 cups	325 ml
1 1/2 cups	350 ml
1 2/3 cups	375 ml
1 3/4 cups	400 ml
1 3/4 cups + 2 tbs	450 ml
2 cups (1 pint)	475 ml
2 1/2 cups	600 ml
3 cups	720 ml
4 cups (1 quart)	945 ml (1,000 ml is 1 liter)

Weight Conversions

U.S./U.K.	METRIC
1/2 oz	14 g
1 oz	28 g
1 1/2 oz	48 g
2 oz	57 g
2 1/2 oz	66 g
3 oz	85 g
3 1/2 oz	100 g
4 oz	113 g
5 oz	142 g
6 oz	170 g
7 oz	200 g
8 oz	227 g
9 oz	255 g
10 oz	284 g
11 oz	312 g
12 oz	340 g
13 oz	368 g
14 oz	400 g
15 oz	425 g
1 lb	454 g

Oven Temperature Conversions

°F	GAS MARK	°C
250	1/2	120
275	1	140
300	2	150
325	3	165
350	4	180
375	5	190
400	6	200
425	7	220
450	8	230
475	9	240
500	10	260
550	Broil	290

11-04

LAKE GENEVA PUBLIC LIBRARY